D1159085

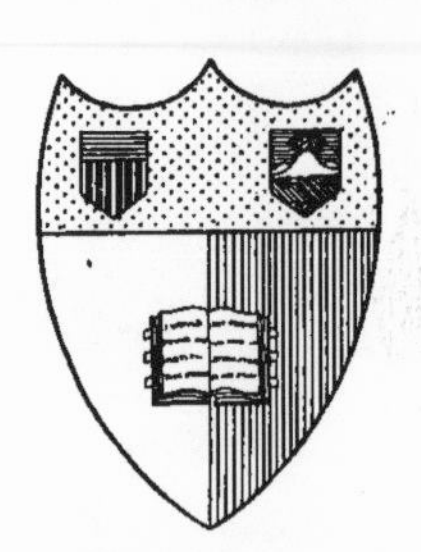

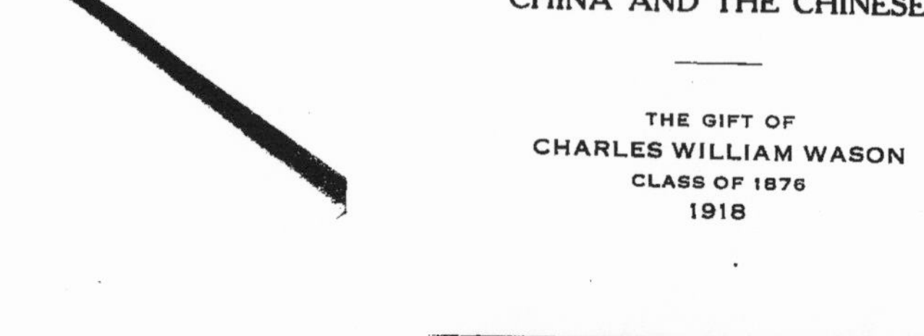

THE FLOWERY REPUBLIC

THE FLOWERY REPUBLIC

BY FREDERICK McCORMICK
SPECIAL CORRESPONDENT AT PEKING
AUTHOR OF "THE TRAGEDY OF RUSSIA IN PACIFIC ASIA" ETC.

WITH SPECIAL ILLUSTRATIONS BY THE AUTHOR
AND FROM
PHOTOGRAPHS AND THE CHINESE PRESS; MAPS, ETC.

LONDON:
JOHN MURRAY, ALBEMARLE STREET, W.
1913
G

PREFACE

At the outset of her Revolution China is at her zenith under a matchless though ancient and obsolete system. She has a full appreciation of her past and has received great gifts from the West. This is indeed, to her, the true Golden Age.

There is an idea in the world that China has grown old and that her civilization is in decay, whereas, under the system which she has developed in the past, China has reached the pinnacle of earthly glory so far as she has ever known earthly glory. After the Mongols extinguished the powers of conquest in Western Asia, leaving Europe disposed of, so to speak, China was free to absorb the so-called barbarian tribes remaining on her borders, and she steadily grew and progressed, until she is larger, greater, more prosperous than ever before, and exhibits a greater proportion, as well as a larger number of contented if not happy human beings than are to be found elsewhere on the globe. Civilization should treasure these facts as time brings its revolutionary crash, supercilious iconoclasm, and sacrilege.

Western civilization overtook China so speedily that she was unable to adjust herself to it. The ruling Manchu Dynasty, though old, degenerate, and decrepit, was not unaware of China's situation and had a truer knowledge of its own situation than had others. The last great warning of the approach of the West came with the Boxer War, and the task of the Throne to steer between the two hells of foreign intervention and internal rebellion became a hundredfold more precarious and dangerous. The Dynasty was obliged to take the course most likely to end in destruction. Everything it did led to its downfall, and at the last, added by so much to the momentum of its damnation. To save the country it proclaimed a complete modernization. Between 1904, when the revolutionary temper of the people had crystallized sufficiently to gauge it, and 1908, the time of their deaths, the rulers of China issued 36 edicts in promotion of the Constitution alone. The country could not assimilate such strong medicine as these reform ideas, which only increased the avidity of the revolutionaries and hurried on rebellion. Everything led down, down, down. With the knowledge of its impending fate, the Dynasty descended, open-eyed, under the ministry of its patriarchal high priest, Prince Ching, into perdition. We who love great events are fortunate to witness the passing of Pharaohs, of Cæsars, and of Moghuls in our time.

In the preparation of these pages on this theme I am indebted to my twelve years' observations and study in China, and my travels from the Argun to the Pearl during the disorders attending the rebellion against the Manchus. I am also indebted to the Chinese Press ; to the foreign newspapers in China, *The North China Herald* and its translators, and *The Central China Post*; as well as to *The London Times* for versions of certain events ; and to Hon. Edward T. Williams and Dr. Charles D. Tenney, Orientalists and sinologues, for several translations ; to all my thanks are expressed.

FREDERICK McCORMICK.

REVOLUTIONARY SCENARIO

1838–1911

1838

Protestant schools of Christian knowledge opened.

1842–60

Seventeen Treaty ports opened to foreigners.

1870

Chinese students arrive in numbers in America to study.

1898

Kang Yu-wei and Liang Chi-ch'ao, two reformers, arrive in Peking, and June 14–August 14 Emperor Kuang Hsu issues reform decrees, a period known as the "Hundred Days Reform." Old-style literary examinations abolished; troops ordered reorganized; colleges and high schools established; calligraphy as a test of merit abolished; newspapers ordered for all provinces; official classes exhorted to turn their attention to reforms; naval colleges and railway and mining bureaus ordered; obsolete offices and sinecures in Peking abolished; announcement that the Emperor would escort the Empress [Grand] Dowager to Tientsin to review the troops; officials of the Board of Rites all cashiered for suppressing a memorial to the Throne; modern roads and enrolment of militia ordered; and finally, all reform decrees ordered printed on Yellow Imperial Papers for general distribution. Empress [Grand] Dowager surprises and arrests Kuang Hsu in the Forbidden City, and resumes the Throne which she previously turned over to him. Kang Yu-wei flees; the Empress [Grand] Dowager executes six reformers without trial; and the Chinese Reform Party is established and begins a propaganda throughout the world.

1900

Trained bands, the "Boxers," appear in Shantung, encouraged by Yu Hsien, the Governor, and opposed by Jung Lu, Generalissimo at Peking; murder Christian converts, the Japanese Secretary of Legation Sugiyama, the German Minister Baron von Ketteler, and many other foreigners; destroy and burn; provoke foreign military occupation of North China; cause the Court to flee for safety, and cause an indemnity of Taels 450,000,000 to be imposed by the Allied Powers upon China. Rebellion in Kuangtung.

1901

Prince Chun goes to Germany to expiate the murder of Baron von Ketteler; an edict commands investigations for the improvement of government; Pu Chun, the evil Heir-Apparent, is deposed.

1902

The Court returns to Peking, and the Throne denounces foot-binding, neglect in establishing schools of modern learning, and recommends the adoption of modern laws. Thirty students are sent to Japan to study military education; Prince Tsai Chen goes to England as Envoy to King Edward's coronation; Chinese students at Tokio rise and assault the Chinese Legation. The Throne orders viceroys and governors to select suitable youths and send them to America and Europe to study; provincial armies are ordered to be reorganized; Kuang Hsu receives the Diplomatic Body; and the Government decides to establish a Ministry of Education. Newspapers take foothold in Peking and, 1903–1907, rapidly multiply. 1902-1910 Protestant missions unify in educational matters and extend colleges and universities. China sends students abroad, arranges to send fifty students annually to America for thirty years, and calls foreign teachers from Japan and the West. British and Germans establish higher schools of learning in Hongkong, Hankow, and Tsingtao. The Y.M.C.A. extends to all the principal cities. Rebellion in Kuanghsi.

1903

Jung Lu, protector of the Foreign Legations, dies at Peking, and Shen Chin the reformer is beaten to death by orders of the Empress [Grand] Dowager.

1904

Throne grants amnesty to all the 1898 reformers except Kang Yu-wei, Liang Chi-ch'ao, and Sun Yat-sen.

1905

Chinese boycott things American—the first Chinese boycott. Throne creates special Mission to study governmental methods abroad; abolishes the old-style literary examinations. Three high officials of the special Mission are wounded by a revolutionary bomb on leaving Peking, one attaché is killed and three underlings are wounded. Modern review of the Imperial Grand Army is held; the Peking-Hankow Railway and Shanghai-Nanking Railway (first section) are opened.

1906

Throne creates the Bureau of Governmental Methods, urges higher officials to promote education and prepare the people for constitutional government, and proscribes opium. The World's Chinese Student Federation is organized and establishes a Federation newspaper.

1907

Throne orders poppy culture for 1908 reduced one-half, and closes opium dens in Shanghai, Canton, Wuhu and elsewhere, and prohibits opium smoking and planting. The Board of War decides to open a Naval Academy and naval schools. En Ming, Governor of Anhuei, is assassinated by revolutionaries, and the principal of the Tatung School, Kashing, Chekiang, the lady Chiu Chin, is executed for complicity in the assassination. The Throne orders administrative reforms, asks for recommendations from officials, establishes the Bureau of Governmental Methods to prepare for the Constitution; receives plans from Prince Ching and Sun Chia-nai for reorganization of provincial governments; sends three commissioners to study the governments of England, Germany, and Japan; orders preparations for Provincial Assemblies and the National Assembly and the diffusion of knowledge of representative government; protests through its representatives at The Hague Conference to being rated as a third-class Power, and decides to send nobles to Europe and America to study, but not to Japan. Ministry of War decides to reorganize the navy and make a naval base at San Men Bay. *Ching Pao*—Chinese newspaper at Peking—suppressed. Rebellion in Kuangtung and Kuanghsi.

1908

The Ministry of War decides on establishing three arsenals. Shansi redeems vast mining concessions from the British for Taels 2,700,000. Chinese in America petition Empress [Grand] Dowager to restore the throne to Kuang Hsu. Throne takes effective measures to reduce opium culture, promulgates new mining laws, appoints Sir Walter Hillier Adviser to the Government, sanctions the general principles of a Constitution, and dispatches Tang Shao-yi to foreign countries to negotiate financial matters and obtain a loan. Deputations of reformers reach Peking to demand Parliament immediately; the Emperor Kuang Hsu dies and is succeeded by

Pu Yi as the Hsuan Tung Emperor; the Empress [Grand] Dowager dies. The Imperial Army opens manœuvres at Tai-hu in Anhuei; 1000 soldiers mutiny at the Capital, Anking. Concerted opposition to foreign loans for railways and industrial development in China is established. Rebellion in Kuanghsi.

1909

Yuan Shih-k'ai is dismissed; the Emperor and the Empress [Grand] Dowager are ceremonially buried; the Peking-Kalgan Railway is opened. Chang Chih-tung dies; Tuan Fang is dismissed; the Provincial Assemblies are opened, and work by Chinese begins on the Szechuan Railway. Continuous opposition in Hunan and Hupeh to foreign loans for railways and industrial development.

1910

The Throne abolishes slavery; the National Assembly opens at Peking, and secures a promise from the Throne to rule through a Cabinet and to summon the National Parliament in 1914 instead of 1917.

1911

Queue-cutting is formally inaugurated at Shanghai; the Throne commands reform, and retrenchment in expenditures; and abrogates torture in the Courts. Li Lien-ying, chief eunuch for forty years and leading corruptionist in Peking, dies; Central Government embarks on its policy of industrial development, contracting loans aggregating $87,500,000 gold. Emperor becomes supreme commander of the army and navy; Fu Chi, Tartar General at Canton, is assassinated; revolutionaries attack Viceroy's yamen at Canton; Throne proclaims its policy of nationalization of railways; Tuan Fang recalled to office as Director-General of Railways; reformers and revolutionaries, fearing substitution of graft on Imperial scale and deprivation of incomes of the provinces by railway nationalization, threaten rebellion, causing outbreaks in Hunan. The National Assembly opens at Peking amid demands from the people for control, itself clamouring for legislative powers and government of the Empire by Parliament.

CONTENTS

LIST OF ILLUSTRATIONS

THE FLOWERY REPUBLIC

CHAPTER I

FLEEING WITH THE AMBAN OF MONGOLIA

I WAS skirting China's northern frontier, passing Lake Baikal, which almost touches Mongolia, and which was so long the barrier to the Trans-Siberian Railway. It was the beginning of winter 1911. The Mongolian "Independency" had just been declared at Urga, over the Mongolian border and directly south. It embraced those territories of China known as Outer Mongolia, which were the last to fall away from the Manchu Throne. This straw of Mongolian secession came but a little while before the breaking of the Manchu camel's back.

The Manchu Imperial Resident at Urga, San Ta, was in full flight from Mongolia's religious and political Capital, driven out by the lama rulers. He was approaching the Siberian frontier. Duly warned of impending events at Urga, he had begged protection of the Russian Governor-General of Trans-Baikalia at Irkutsk. The telegraph line which crosses Mongolia's heart—the Desert of Gobi—and reaches to Kiachta, was busy clicking off distress signals from San Ta dispatched in both directions to Peking. Over the same wires went Russian political dispatches, inquiries of the Board of Colonies at Peking, and messages of the Mongol conspirators at all points. A train of two hundred camels weighted with Berdan rifles discarded from Russian arsenals, was leaving Kiachta for Urga to equip the new army of the "Independency."

The Russian Governor-General reading dispatches from the Director of Russian Railways at Harbin, discounted San Ta's apparent danger, and sent him a reassuring telegram. In Russia there was no danger, he would require no protection that all did not have—this was the gist of the Governor-General's message to San

Ta, which concluded with an offer of the hospitality of the Trans-Siberian Railway, to enable the fleeing Resident and his suite to return to China.

Dispatches forwarded by agents of the Russian Government to St. Petersburg in explanation of these movements had been handed to me. Aboard the Siberian express, with these dispatches in my hand, with the knowledge that the distressed Resident with his face turned to the Russian frontier was straining the energies of his whole party to reach this Imperial military-protected railway, this and the vision of an awakened Mongolia meant more to me possibly than it meant to any other person in the train. To a war correspondent like myself, who had followed the armies of twelve years in these regions, these present events seemed more important in the lives of the Mongols than anything that had happened at Urga since Temudjin confederated the Tartar tribes into the Buriat State in the Middle Ages and became Genghis Khan. I had seen the Russian Frontier Guards cross the barrier of the Great Wall in 1900. I had seen the Russian Army flow around the Baikal and over the Great Kinghan in 1904. I had visited the capitals of forgotten Tartar kingdoms, made pilgrimages to boundaries whose monuments no man can read, and pictured in valleys visible from the car windows and now deep in Siberian snows, seas of Mongols mount oceans of horses and ride away to the Altai, the Caucasus, and the Carpathians.

The atmosphere of the train resembled that of the time of the Boxer War—charged with the current of prevailing, world-encircling revolution, of which the Chinese " Republic " was in all the circle the most amazing manifestation. Present conditions in Eastern Asia were forcibly illustrated by the mixture of types on the train. Japanese officials recalled from Europe and America were being sent by their Governments to Southern Manchuria. Two Chinese student-revolutionists were hurrying to join the army of the " Republic " at Wuchang on the Yangtse. Sales agents of European ordnance and ammunition factories on the Thames, the Elbe, and elsewhere, as well as battleship agents, armourers, and military engineers, were *en route* to Peking the Imperialist, and Nanking the Republican, capital. Anxious foreign merchants returning in haste from Europe were making their way to Shanghai, and connoisseurs and curio dealers from the Seven Seas, in anticipation of a second Boxer harvest, were hurrying to Peking to be in time for the loot. The figure of a wild-eyed French correspondent, with an imagination inflamed by grotesque ideas of Eastern Asia and intolerant of everybody, completed, but was not necessary to complete, this remarkable company. It was with these companions and in these circumstances that I was moving to a point of juncture with the Manchu refugee from Urga and his disconsolate company.

The Imperial representative at Lhassa in Tibet, as well as the one at Urga in Mongolia, besides being " Resident " is also called " Amban." I knew that ambans' flights are few and far between, and it was worth while knowing their cause, and especially the cause of the flight of San Ta the Amban, from Urga.

The drama of disorder in the Buddhist world of Central Asia as I had watched it from Peking was like this : The Russians and Japanese went to war in the spring of 1904, arousing Eastern Mongolia, Manchuria, and China. Great Britain sent a military column into the forbidden land of Tibet, arousing China and Central Asia's Buddhist world, sending the Talai Lama—spiritual head of Tibet and Mongolia—fleeing from Lhassa, his capital, to Urga and arousing all Mongolia. Japan successfully invaded Manchuria in 1905–6, in turn arousing Russia and Mongolia. China escorted the Talai Lama back to Lhassa, but later dispatched a military column there which sent him fleeing in haste to India, where he remained an exile. Because of their Buddhistic interests at stake, China's act alarmed Great Britain, Russia, and Japan. The Chinese reformers and revolutionaries, led by students educated abroad, brought about rebellion and republicanism, arousing Tibet and Mongolia, and severing their allegiance to the declining Manchu Dynasty.

These events consolidated the ideas of both Russians and Mongols respecting Mongolia. Mongolia no longer had a bulwark in the Manchus. Russia no longer had in the Manchus even a weak barrier against the Japanese. Mongolia, fearing everybody but conscious that she had never been defeated or made subservient, had to take an independent course, though she could not flee.

The princes of Northern Mongolia stated that, although they would accept the rule of their Manchu kinsmen, they would never recognize a new Chinese Government or submit to its sway. Russia was powerless to arrest Japanese expansion Westward along her frontier, and was obliged, by her reasoning and policy, to devise a new buffer state of Outer Mongolia in order to complete a chain of buffer states continuous from the Caspian to the Amur. As time went on the effect of these ideas at Urga aroused San Ta, who came into conflict with the lamas a year before the time of which I am writing. The allegiance of the lamas was tested by San Ta, in the matter of tribute, in an unusual manner. He demanded of the lamas that his Residency should be supplied with horses from the herd on the sacred hill, a demand outrageous to the ecclesiastics. The Mongols may be said to live on horseback. The horses are the most precious of all their animals. The best gift which a Mongol can make to the Church and to his pontiff is a noble horse. These gifts, most of them from the princes of Mongolia, are sacerdotal in character, and at least supposedly remain secluded in the hallowed precincts connected with the pontifical temples.

The Amban's demand resulted in an attack by the lamas upon the Amban's followers, who were badly beaten. The Amban, perceiving his mistake, arranged in Peking a suspension of the punishment for the lamas decreed by the Throne, and secured their formal forgiveness for them. The lamas, however, nursed their anger through a series of smaller antagonisms until the declaration of the inde-dependence or autonomy of all Outer Mongolia. This was the accumulated anger from which San Ta fled, and against which he begged the protection of Russia.

Disturbed international relations on the Mongolian-Siberian frontier, and complications with Russia and Japan, preceded the Rebellion in China. Disputed boundary lines were among those questions which led to the declaration of the independence of Outer Mongolia, the fringe of khanates or principalities touching Manchuria and Siberia. The Japanese were the first to cross China's border and raise China's boundary questions in an acute form. They selected to cross at Chien-tao, a region north of the Tumen River, in Eastern Manchuria, abreast of Korea. The Manchurian Viceroyal Administration at Mukden then immediately took up the whole question of boundaries in Manchuria and inaugurated surveys. It bought at one purchase eighty-five thousand taels (about $60,000.00) worth of surveying instruments, though it had no qualified surveyors to use them.

Japan's aggression in Chien-tao was settled by an

agreement by which Japan remained in Chien-tao, and then the boundary questions with Russia on the Manchurian-Siberian frontier were taken up. The Imperial Government at Peking, not only took up the boundaries on the Japanese-Russian frontiers, but those of the whole Empire, and ordered the viceroys and governors of the provinces to conduct surveys and establish lines of demarcation on its frontiers, and monuments to mark them. The contentions over these questions appeared interminable, and the disputes affected regions extending from Tongking on the south-east, through Burmah, India, Turkestan, and Siberia, to Korea, along a line perhaps eight thousand miles in length.

In 1910 Russia threatened to move troops into Ili, in Western Mongolia, to protect what she called her frontier rights. There was a boundary question on the west, in Northern Ili. There was another where the Trans-Siberian Railway joins the Chinese Eastern Railway entering Manchuria, and here Russia claimed the Manchurian town of Manchuli. A gradual development of the regions along the Russian-Chinese and Japanese-Chinese frontiers, due to the expansion of Western civilization among Asiatic peoples, was going on, so that these questions arose as a matter of course. But there are several race movements that account for these questions. Among them is the rise and regeneration of the Buriat Mongols, whose ancient Capital is at Selinginsk, on the Selenga, in Siberia, below Lake Baikal. A national movement assumed form and dimensions here a decade or more ago, and this branch of the Mongols established a newspaper and a printing plant for making books. The influence of the Buriat Mongols extended not only to the members of their race in Siberia but in Mongolia. Buriat Mongols, as officers in the Russian Navy and in the land forces, distinguished themselves in the Russo-Japanese War. In civil positions the Buriats were found in the Russian service throughout Eastern Asia. Buriat women had married well among Siberians, and Buriat men everywhere found equality in Siberia.

The relation between Russians and Mongols has been one of fraternity, which is nearly the opposite of the relationship which has existed between Chinese and Mongols from time immemorial. In Urga thirty to fifty years ago, according to Gilmour, the life of the Chinese engaged in trade there was one of self-imposed exile, wherein they were prevented by Chinese law from bringing their wives and families with them, and were unable to visit their native homes oftener than once in every five or ten years. At that time Mongolia was to China a kind of neutral zone, or what in Western parlance is called a buffer state. China wished to keep her own people attached to their homes, and pursued a policy of encouraging celibacy and ecclesiasticism in Mongolia, in order to guard against military regeneration among her ancient Tartar enemies and persecutors, keeping them enervated by religious pursuits. China's judgment was not ample. She made the mistake of miscalculating the state of the outside world, and failed to apprehend the importance of Russia and her future influence upon Eastern Asia—Mongolia in particular. China's policy, while it weakened the Mongolian or Tartar danger, gradually prepared Mongolia for Russian influence and invasion, and the probable absorption of Mongolia by Russia.

The Manchus and the whole intellectual aristocracy of China regarded the Mongols as a bulwark of China and of the Manchu Throne. The Russians courted the Mongols so that they might ultimately become a bulwark against the Japanese, and a bulwark of the Manchu Dynasty. The organization of the Mongols into a military force on horseback with a large part of their ancient military efficiency was a dream of both the Russians and the Japanese. At least one hundred and fifty thousand Mongol horsemen await this endeavour. Each of these nations shrinks from being suspected of it by the other. The knowledge of this possibility and of Russian and Japanese aims aroused the Chinese military with hopes of anticipating these two arch-enemies of China and consummating this magnificent plan as a patriotic Chinese achievement, thus converting Mongolia's weakness into a wall of strength essential to China's safety.

All this country was a theatre of political and religious strife, wonderful with that machinery known as modern progress which regenerates races and has aroused the Mongols after eight centuries of somnolence. Through this region robed in snow and rigid with cold, San Ta the Manchu, having failed to retrieve Mongolian allegiance for his Emperor, and thrown upon the mercy of his Russian opponents, was making his way, himself a phenomenon of these changes marking the advance of Western civilization. Convoyed by Russian couriers and Frontier Guards over the Kiachta Post Road, thirty persons, men, women, and children, bundled in felt and fur, drawn in sledges down the frosty Selenga and through the frozen forests on its banks, reached the railway station at Verkneudinsk. A moment later, the dark and the cold changed to the light, warmth, and luxurious fittings of the Trans-Siberian train. Here was at his disposal the railway carriage of the Governor-General of Trans-Baikalia, and of the Russian Chinese Eastern Railway, and into it he slipped, with the remnants of his domestic and ambassadorial belongings.

Lights burned in the station windows. The samovar steamed in the buffet, giving out an endless chain of glasses of tea—this great drink of Russians. Cauldrons of hot soup—*borsch* and *tschi*—filled the buffet with appetizing vapours. Travellers passed backwards and forwards from the train, itself emitting clouds of steam, suffused in their ascent with reflected light. San Ta, the defeated and humiliated Amban, heeded little of this as, solaced only by his family, he shrank into the luxurious seclusion of his salon, a mere creature of fate.

CHAPTER II

FLEEING WITH THE AMBAN OF MONGOLIA—*concluded*

IF ambans' flights are rare, rarer still are the opportunities of a war correspondent to witness one. Such adventures belong to the dead centuries. I found it hard to realize that this was happening in the present, that we ourselves were not messengers or envoys of a forgotten era. In my mind, San Ta, the unsuccessful envoy of the baby Emperor and representative of the decrepit Manchu Dynasty, linked his name with all the political agents in history, from those of Genghis Khan, the Magician of Empire, to those of Japan's Mutsuhito, the Napoleon of Asia.

Even as I got off the train at the Manchurian frontier station, Manchuli, where I was confronted by China's modern Customs examination, I had not readjusted myself into my role of a modern war correspondent. I looked about for some Chinese with whom to talk, and found one in the newsdealer in the buffet.

" How's business ? " I asked.

Recovering his astonishment at hearing his own language from a traveller who had just crossed the frontier, he replied :

" Passable." He then politely inquired :

" What nationality are you ? "

" He's not Russian," said a Chinese waiter in the buffet, who, with equal interest, had stopped to hear the sound of his native tongue.

" Certainly not," replied the first, and then asked : " Are you English ? "

" Guess again," said I.

" American ? "

" Pshaw, don't you know a native when you see him ? "

He laughed. " You're not a Chinese," said he in disgust ; " you have no queue."

" No, I have no queue, but we don't all have queues nowadays."

" You have no beard."

" I'm not old enough; besides, fashions are not the same now."

" What is your honourable age ? "

" You say."

" Fifty years."

" Too much. You don't know a Chinese well enough to recognize him or tell his age ! You must be a Russian."

He gave a disgusted laugh and said :

" You're too tall for a Chinese."

" I'm no taller than a Manchurian."

" Your colour is different."

" I'll tell you," said I. " If I'm not true Chinese, I've lived in the Capital—Peking—twelve years, and I'm an American, and we Americans and Chinese are nearly the same, isn't that so ? "

" America is a good country and a friend of China."

" Everybody says so, and I hear now China wishes a Government like ours. Have you heard any news ? "

" In the South there is trouble."

" Have you any war here ? "

" No, all is peaceful."

" Are there any soldiers ? "

" Yes, there are some Manchu soldiers, and at the first station to the east there are more. They watch the people and the officials and keep them in order."

I also learned of him that the news of the rise of the Mongols at Urga had not reached Manchuli. However, Mongol dignitaries were making frequent journeys to the " great Russian official " at Harbin.

Many Mongol agents and envoys pass Manchuli *en route* to Harbin as well as to Mukden and Peking. Unless they come from Urga or farther west, they always take train at Oloviannaya or Borzia, in Trans-Baikalia, a short distance from the frontier. They supply a fine colour note of orange, purple, and red to the drab of Russia and the cold indigo of the Chinese dress. Though uncouth, they are not slovenly, like the Siberians. There is no denying it, the Siberians are certainly frowsy, and in the matter of customs, manners, and dress are at a disadvantage with their neighbours the Chinese. After seeing from Siberian trains poorly dressed, unkempt, and slouchy Siberians, the Chinese of Manchuria seem like cultured gentlefolk. The Chinese peasant has an attitude, a gait and an air, with his own standardized, sealed, and stamped manners and intelligence, which gives Chinese society the character of real civilization.

Siberia to the Western mind spells gloom in the syllables snow, night, and exile. It stands for the mediæval mosaic comprehended in the word Russia. But in Manchuria winter is brilliant with sunlight. The snow-clouds have to do their work quickly and move on. The snow disappears, absorbed by the dry air. All is light, vigour, and promise, expressive of the modern, republican, revolutionary China.

The bizarre gathering of races, allegiances, and personalities represented in this Russian train coming through Siberia, received added emphasis by entering Chinese territory. The "Five Continents" passed into China. An inner curtain lifted, showing China the real stage of the drama. Revolutionary complications began. Trains left going Eastward, carrying rebels *en route* to Harbin to beg munitions of war from the Russian authorities in the Railway Administration. The Mongol princes know that the segregation of Mongolia is the dearest wish of Russia's political agents at Harbin and in St. Petersburg, who regard the independence or inviolability of Mongolia as a political necessity to Russia. It would constitute a barrier against Japan, and also against the demoralizing frontier influences and dangers of a too-progressive China. The Mongols were followed by other Mongols loyal to the Manchu Throne and hopeful of preserving the Chinese union. The Russian officials in Manchuria and the local Chinese officials were kept busy with the essential formalities of this exciting traffic. A Chinese official took a train leaving in advance of the Amban's party, but whether or not to escape the awkwardness of meeting a Manchu dignitary, and the responsibilities and embarrassments of aiding his enemy, could only be suspected. His gendarme escort at the door of his closed coupé was loath to talk.

There was yet no revolution in Northern Manchuria, where the Manchu soldiers, according to the station agent at Manchuli, had "kept the Chinese conspirators straight." These soldiers watched for evidences of rebellion, so as to prevent on this railway line of Russia's, what was most feared by China—further complications with Russia, which would also mean the same with Japan.

The Amban, on reaching Manchuria, appeared deserted and left to the mercies of these Manchu troops. In the light of day his suite was seen with its servants and baggage crowded into its coupés. The principal members of the party got out at Manchuli to take the air, to have a look at their native soil, and, like myself, to see what was going on. Among them was a young man believed to be a brother of the Manchu Prince Kung. I wondered if the Throne at Peking had been using the younger members of the Manchu Imperial Clan among the Mongolian khanates to win them back after the furore of the Dalai Lama's visit. The members of the Amban's suite, in groups here and there, kept their own counsel, talked in low tones among themselves, and were naturally loath to talk with others of experiences which represented their official shortcomings and failures, and of a voyage of humiliation. Fellow-passengers refrained from venturing any overtures in this direction.

The Russian train at this moment represented an immemorial division of the Chinese Empire, North and South, now Empire and Republic. It was Republican at the fore, Imperialist at the rear. Another situation developed when the train entered Manchuria. The Empire, represented by San Ta, was on its own ground; the Republic, represented by the two young revolutionists, was in hostile territory.

The young men became quite nervous, moving about the fore part of the train and finally isolating themselves in the company of foreigners, where they felt more secure and discussed in their native tongue what was of greatest concern to them, the plunge they were taking into their disturbed country. No one in the train, except San Ta, knew what had been happening in China since this train had left Moscow. There was no precise knowledge of the condition of Manchuria.

Penetrating farther and farther into this region, still outwardly loyal to the Manchus, and in company with representatives of the Throne, the nervousness of the young revolutionists increased. The revolutionary party known as "Young China," to which they belonged, though small, had for ten years been preparing for a revolt which was to overthrow the ancient Imperial Government and establish the rule of the people. They now understood how this had come about in their absence, and talked of the achievements of their fellow-students in the remote province of Szechuan, in September 1911. These latter had overthrown the Provincial Government, defeated and beheaded the brother of the now Viceroy of Manchuria, a man who had been one of the most tyrannical, most bloody, and most feared of China's generals.

The great event, however, had been the establishing of the Republic of China at Wuchang, November 9, 1911, by Li Yuan-hung, to whom one of the young men said he was secretary. This fact he afterward repeated with caution. The knowledge among the passengers in the train that they had with them the Secretary of the Chinese President and War Minister, swayed their vacillating interest heavily in favour of the Republic. This calabash Government of three months' growth now claimed fourteen of the eighteen provinces of China proper, with three rival leaders from whom it was impossible to pick the winner.

The boys were very loyal to their leader Li Yuan-hung, were against Sun Yat-sen, whom their chief, Li, had disowned as a force in the revolt at Wuchang; and as for the other leader, Yuan Shih-k'ai, they looked upon him as a dangerous man.

Simultaneous with the rising interest and excitement, there was in the minds of the passengers a recollection of the events of 1911 that formed this calabash Government. There was the successful revolt in the province of Szechuan, September 14; the Throne's appeal to Yuan Shih-k'ai, October 14, to reunite the country; the assassination of Feng Shan, one of the two foremost Manchu generals, October 24; the rebellion at Hankow and Wuchang, October 25–29; the revolt in Shensi, October 25, and the battle and bloody destruction of Hankow following; the secession of Shanghai, November 3; the secession of Kuangtung, and the declaration of the Republic of China at Wuchang, November 9; the nearly simultaneous secession of Shantung, November 14, and Central Manchuria; the evacuation of Nanking by the Imperialists, December 1; the abdication of Prince Chun, the Regent of the Empire, December 6; the recognition of the Rebellion by the Throne and its overtures for terms of compromise, December 18; the recognition of the revolutionary party by France, Germany, Great Britain, Japan, Russia, and the United States, December 20.

The boys, too, were well acquainted with these events, which they had followed in the European papers. They were well acquainted with the fact that the Republic sustained a set-back. General Li Yuan-hung had been defeated at the battle of Hankow, which was to pass into history as the only battle of the Rebellion. He had been unable to maintain discipline among his troops or to defend the city of Hankow, which had been destroyed in a festival of carnage. The province of Shantung, partly on account of the reverses Li Yuan-hung had sustained and partly because it had foreign questions with Germany, had reconsidered its hasty secession and apologetically rejoined the Empire. Manchuria, whose administration and affairs might be taken over by Japan in twenty-four hours, and instantly invaded by Russia, was unable to make good its hasty scheme of independence, and fell back into a position of *statu quo*, resuming connections with the Peking Government. Li Yuan-hung, who had not yet been succeeded by Sun Yat-sen as Provisional President, with the Capital at Nanking, was the arch-rebel of China. He was the Chieftain of these two boys, which was the crux of the situation for them. All China, with its internal and external complications, and which had been called " The Sick Man of Asia " for a quarter of a century, was like twenty Turkeys rolled into one. We, for the time being, were in the middle of this confusion.

" Japan is helping the Manchus," said the Secretary of the Chinese President and War Minister ; " didn't you hear the foreign Customs agent at Manchuli say that Viceroy Chao had cut off the heads of sixty of our men at Mukden in the last two weeks ? "

" That's like his brother in Szechuan, who is hated by everybody because he is so bloody," said the other.

" One wouldn't think that old Father Chao could be such a traitor to his own people."

" No, but that is not the worst. If he is working against the Republic, it will be the same as turning the Three Eastern Provinces [Manchuria] over to the Japanese. Japan is very treacherous. She can never be relied on. Twenty thousand of our students have studied in Japan, and the Japanese pretend to be our friends. They use both sides. They are worse than all the other foreigners together."

" We cannot go into Feng-tien " [the Japanese sphere of Manchuria].

" No, it's no place for us, if the Japanese are arresting our people and turning them over to Viceroy Chao. If we wish to keep our heads on our shoulders," said one, talking rapidly, " we had better stay in this train and go to Vladivostok, where we will be safe on Russian soil and can go by foreign steamer to Shanghai at the first opportunity. The Russians are better than the Japanese—at least they don't interfere between the Chinese and Manchus."

The conversation of the young revolutionists showed that they had not been less active in inquiring for news at the frontier and along the line than had I. Manchuria was the land of the Manchus, with a considerable Manchu population and a soil sacred as the burial-place of the ancestors of the Dynasty. Dominated by Russia and Japan, complicated in all its affairs by their interference and participation, it was very debatable ground for the young revolutionists.

As the train approached Harbin they were seen standing in the vestibule still discussing their plans, but they had decided to abandon the Japanese route south through Manchuria, fearing possible arrest, and to go by Vladivostok to Shanghai. We separated at Harbin. Later, when their train had recrossed the Manchurian-Russian frontier into the Ussuri Province, and I knew they were safe, I sent a Press telegram announcing their escape.

CHAPTER III

THE MONGOL REBELS

I ARRIVED in Harbin, Russia's big, bedraggled, war-maimed Manchurian city stretched on the bottom lands and bluffs of the Sungari, and flaunting its coarse and tawdry splendours in the winter sun. After the Russo-Japanese War it received the Russian political mantle that rested on Port Arthur when the latter was Russian, vying with Peking, where the Imperial Russian Legation complained of its pretensions in international politics.

The whole Japanese, Russian, and Chinese frontiers in Eastern Asia were in a state of widespread intrigue, not only involving Russia and Japan, but their allies and all other interested nations, with China. Harbin was again a Russian centre, as it had been before the Russo-Japanese War, and Manchuria was again demonstrating its vitality as China's and the Eastern World's great, unsolvable political problem. Whereas before it was a closed Russian capital, the centre of Russia's railway and industrial interests in Manchuria, it had since—with all the Chinese regions to the north of it—been invaded by the Japanese, who brought with them the representatives of all the Great Powers to watch its entangling and disentangling processes.

Russia's course in Mongolia had been watched by Japan as its processes unfolded in the cities and provinces from Kashgar to Kuldja, Tarbagatai and Kobdo, from Ulliassutai to Urga and Kerulon, and from To-nan-fu to the Tumen River. She had sent a civil official to visit the regions between the Baikal and Urga when Russia had sent a new consul—a military officer—to the latter. Japan had taken special interest in the fact that Russia had sent an experienced consul, trained at Harbin in the ramifications of Manchurian politics, to Ulliassutai. The state of political suspicion existing between Japan and Russia was shown by the detention and expulsion from the Russian province Ussurri of a high Japanese officer who had crossed that frontier to the north of Lake Hanka.

The Japanese General Staff sent an officer of rank in uniform openly to explore the Mongolian-Russian frontier. He left Peking in July 1911, taking the road across the Gobi Desert to Urga and turning westward to Ulliassutai and continuing westward through Kobdo to the Altai Mountains, which he reached October 4th. Leaving Mongolia (Ili) at Tarbagatai, he returned by the river Irtish and the Trans-Siberian Railway, completing his observations of the frontier from the Siberian side. Japan's access to the Russian frontier from Mongolia is one which Russia would like to deny, but her officials receive Japan's travellers with at least outward hospitality. Every servant of Russia is a uniformed officer, in Imperial quarters, equipped with office, soldiers, and all the machinery of state, which in such events turns all its wheels.

The Japanese wonder what on such occasions may be behind this hospitality.

"I do not know," said one of these Japanese travellers who had crossed Mongolia, "what is in their minds and hearts when they receive me with such cordiality. Their hospitality is intimate and faultless. I was taken aback by being asked why I had not been there before."

The motive behind the Japanese General Staff in Tokio, acting with the knowledge and consent of the Japanese Government in thus sending an official party into the Russian sphere, can confidently be stated to be that of moral effect upon Russia's Mongolian politics, coupled with the intention to miss no opportunity of discovering what is new in those intentions. Japan's agents and officials on the Continent were aroused by the reports of Russia's doings along the frontier to a pitch of unusual alertness and considerable excitement. They were afraid that Japan's expansion Westward was already blocked by this new "Independency" of Outer Mongolia, which appeared to destroy Japan's hope of crossing the Kinghan Mountains. They alleged that the lamas in their revolt at Urga had not acted without suggestion from Russia, and intimated that Russia wished these regions for her own.

This was Japan's side of the question. The Russians were equally alert, enterprising, excited, and frank. Many agents of the Czar whom I had known in the earlier stages of the Manchurian drama, and in fact whose personal fortunes I had shared in the time of its greatest tragedies, were still upon the scene at Harbin, still struggling with this question, on the one side with Japan, and on the other with China and the Powers. We had been comrades off and on for the past twelve years, studying the same problems. We admitted our awe at the possibilities of the Present.

With the Russians, Mongolia was the prime question of the moment. The headquarters of the Czar's agents was a busy one, somewhat like the scene here during the Russo-Japanese War. The interpreters and translators of Mongolian were most in evidence as I entered. Long dispatches from Mongol princes reciting the aspirations of Mongolians to escape from complications with the Manchus and the Chinese Republic were being translated. The Mongol rebels who preceded us from Manchuli, when they arrived here, asked the Russians to supply them at once with arms sufficient for one hundred thousand infantry and fifty thousand cavalry. General X—— diplomatically told them he had no arms not required by the railway guards (Frontier Guards) and that Russia could not send arms out of the railway zone.

"Not much is known of Mongolia," said General X——, handing me a Russian cigarette, and laying down before me a long dispatch from Eastern Mongolia, written in the curious and beautiful characters of the Mongolian language. "It has a religious government, with many princely divisions. Our people have studied it perhaps more than others, but very imperfectly. The people are nomads and like to be left alone, and have consequently been somewhat disturbed at seeing the Chinese increasing in Mongolia and at the prospect now of having a new Government over them. Russia takes a greater interest than other nations in Mongolian affairs, perhaps because of Russia's special rights by a treaty with China. Russia has had a long intercourse with Mongolia through trade."

"Personally, as you know," said I, "I appreciate these facts very fully. But I would like to ask you about the charges so often made by your rivals regarding the political intentions of Russia in Mongolia."

"I know what you want," said he, "and I will tell you. Russia does not want Mongolia. She is accused of wanting to take Mongolia, but Russia wants Mongolia to be a buffer state, like Afghanistan, to remain between Russia and China."

"How can Mongolia become a buffer state? I understand that it is only the ecclesiastics at Urga who have declared their autonomy."

"Yes," said he, "but that is important, for the reason that the Talai Lama whom China has exiled and the Talama at Urga who is the third highest in the world, have the power to unite the Mongol princes in support of Mongolian independence."

As we talked I had in mind two interesting Russian dispatches emanating from these regions which in their official form as they appeared in St. Petersburg in the Russian Government organ, one closely following the other, were in substance as follows :

"*A Mongol deputation has indicated in Government circles Mongolia's desire to live under Russian protection. The Government must not hesitate to recognize the Independence of Mongolia.*"

The second dispatch was dated Harbin and ran thus :

"*The Mongol princes of North Mongolia have informed General Horvat that although they submit to the activity of China* [respecting Mongolia] *and recognize the Manchu Dynasty, yet they will never recognize a new Chinese Government* [*i.e.* non-Manchu], *or submit to its rule. The only obstacle to shaking off the yoke of China is lack of rifles. They have money in plenty. Among many capable Mongols in the army there are 120 of the rank of Commanders. Many Mongols serve in the Manchu Imperial Guard and are ready to desert. If the Mongols cannot alone oppose the new Government in China, then Mongolia is ready to accept Russia's sceptre.*"

I was startled with the first realization of the primary political issue between Russia and China thus exposed in this interview. It is the question between these two great countries as to whether Mongolia is an integral state of the Chinese Empire or an independent political Federation with its supreme ecclesiastical Government under China's suzerainty. If the latter could be established by Russia, and Mongolia could make good her claims of autonomy, Russian rights in Mongolia and Russian authority would be equal to those of China. The question in my mind was whether this was not *de facto* the case at the moment and whether Russia had not already succeeded in eliminating all other Powers from Mongolia. The first thing which Japan did in her process of annexing Korea was to set up the principle that Korea was not a conquered nation, that it had never been subjugated by China, and that it was an independent state. As I left the great building which from the Sungari bluff overlooks the vast western prairies, reaching out to Mongolia, and looked up at the familiar architecture, it seemed again to rock with the fate of kingdoms as in the days of Russia's Eastern Empire and her conquest of Manchuria and Korea.

Just before my arrival here Russia had halted her time-expired Frontier Guards *en route* home, a little west of Manchuli, and returned them to their stations. Regulars who had reached Harbin on their way home to Russia were sent back to their quarters in Nickolsk, in the Ussuri Province. Russia's new military strategy, devised after the war with Japan, provided for mobilization directly against both Austria and Eastern Asia. France protested against her ally Russia leaving the Russian-German border open and thus throwing the burden of menacing Germany upon her. Russia thereupon did not actually move large bodies of men to the Far East, although her plan set aside an army of 200,000 men to be ultimately stationed there, east of Lake Baikal. Russia, however, made all preparations for an even larger force than this in Eastern Asia. Foreign military agents, judging by the visible preparations, reckoned this would number 400,000 men. With respect to the Chinese disorder and revolution which awed the world, the first Eastern emergency since this strategy was devised, Russia now had an expeditionary organization ready, with plans to instantly grasp this political and military situation in Mongolia and Manchuria, and had placed her railway in a state of preparation to mobilize in Manchuria. Military headquarters had been prepared at Harbin.

Travellers from the east arrived here, augmenting the motley crowd going south, and I joined them. The country seemed full of foreign military agents, the Europeans and Americans in mufti—civilian dress—as the English say. The Japanese military uniform was the only one in evidence save the Russian. Openly dressed, or in disguise, these military agents, who in war are called spies, were everywhere. The Russians and the Japanese were so busy with each other that they had no time for the English, the Germans, and the Americans. Although it was a matter which concerned their country and they were the only other nationality to be considered by us, it was a game in which the Chinese were completely lost. Their officials occupied themselves with the Amban, who stopped over at

Harbin. His suite, broken up at that point, straggled southward.

I was the only foreigner in the railway carriage filled with San Ta's refugees from Urga. The train was made up of such elements as could be assembled only in times of war and revolution—Mongols, Manchus, and Chinese, each suspicious of the other, yet willing fellow-passengers. They were hedged about by at least a dozen other nationalities. Picturesque was a Cossack horsewoman who had ridden across Central Asia; romantic was a Polish girl from the Sorbonne at Paris, seeking her Chinese husband in the South. In my carriage were the ladies of the Amban's suite, with their serving-women packed in separate coupés and children in the corridors, shy and fearful of me, but willing to be friends when they heard their own tongue. The children and servants mixed with the train-boys and amused themselves watching the steaming samovars and the serving of tea to the passengers.

Attached was a dining-car, far more crowded than before. Baggage was stacked under the tables. Fur-lined orange and purple silks showed that the Urga lamas and princes were there. Their attendants filled up the aisles and vestibules. The buffet was overtaxed, but there was a table d'hôte dinner. The courses followed each other irregularly, served by the Chinese.

Among others around me was a revolutionary Chinese—a school-teacher at Mukden. My table-mate was a Chinese ex-naval officer, secretary and agent of perhaps the only Chinese in China that could be called a "prince of industry." This latter was involved against his intentions in the Republican revolt. His high position and the reforms with which he was connected caused him to be charged with precipitating by his official acts the outbreak of revolution.

The Mongols kept apart and conversed discreetly among themselves. It was not easy to engage any one of them. It was not until after the meal that I had an opportunity to speak with them. I offered a cigarette to a lama of magnificent physique, big, of striking colour, and dressed in a silk, orange-coloured coat, belted in, and with a carmine cap with gold braid. He accepted the cigarette, likewise a match.

"You manage what honourable affairs?" said he, with perfect self-possession, but surprised at my addressing him.

"I am an American and a journalist. I have been

in these regions twelve years. I passed along with the Amban's party and heard that you have had important affairs in your Capital. Is that not so?"

As I approached this subject I could see the lama hedging. Had he been a Frenchman, he would have shrugged his shoulders at this inquiry. Being a Mongol, he gave a quizzical duck of the head and showed that he was waiting for the next question. The lama's companions got up and left, and we were alone. I continued:

"The Russian official newspaper in St. Petersburg has said that Mongolia wanted to have its own Government. Americans do not think this any affair of their own, but are interested and like to hear of Mongolia's welfare. I have heard that the lamas and princes at Urga have made a new Government of their own. Many new things are happening nowdays in China and I hear it said that Russia wants Mongolia."

"Russia wants Mongolia." Here I put my finger on the pulse of Genghis Khan, the Mongol's pride of independency, of which General X—— had told me. I was surprised at the suddenness with which the unconquered Mongol in him leaped to its defence. He said in the shortest, quickest words:

"Mongolia will not be Russian." He shook his head. Again he looked up at me.

"The Japanese and many others say that Russia has had a hand in this affair at Urga," said I. "Russia has been a very good friend of Mongols."

He continued to hedge along this line of talk, but admitted that Mongolia had good relations with Russia and a very friendly trade.

"But you have Russian soldiers at Urga, isn't that so?"

"Russia has been friendly. The soldiers are not many, not more than one hundred and fifty."

"But I hear they have a regiment on the frontier and that they can take Maimaichen and then march to Urga."

"They have no soldiers at Maimaichen."

"Well, they don't need them," said I. "Mongolia has no soldiers, and if Russia used soldiers she would only make enemies of your people. Russia is a great country, with many interests in Mongolia. It is important to her to have Mongolia independent. She would do whatever she could to help you in this."

He listened intently to this reasoning, and without committing himself in words, acquiesced in actions. He bowed in the affirmative, and waited for the next.

Due to the fact that he was on a mission to Peking, it was not expected that he would be communicative, as is plainly shown by the style of our conversation. But he took care to impress upon me these facts : the Ta Lama's success in promulgating his declaration of autonomy for Mongolia ; the non-interference of the Russian soldiers at Urga ; the unimpeded departure of the Amban ; the orderly state of Urga and the quietude of the country. More important than all was the fact that from the lama's standpoint, representing the Government of Mongolia and linked with their kin the Manchus, they of the North as conquerors—the ancient conquerors of all China and parts of Burmah—could not recognize the advance of the Chinese against the North. Rather than do so, they would break with their kinsmen the Manchus.

It was extremely interesting to me, facing this magnificent Mongol, to see the exhibition of fine caution which the Mongols were obliged to exercise before the Russians, Manchus, and Chinese. It showed the acuteness of the revolutionary situation in the North. I considered that Mongolia at this moment was in a position nearly parallel to that in which Shantung was at the time of its secession, and in which Manchuria was after declaring its independence. Mongolia had perhaps not yet realized that it was at the mercy of foreign antagonists, that by cutting itself off from China it was in fact exposed to three sets of claws : on the South to those of the Chinese Dragon ; on the East those of the Japanese Tiger ; and on the North and West those of the Russian Bear. It appeared to have but one expectation : in order to obtain security from China—from which it had just parted—and Japan, it must make a questionable bargain with Russia, in which its independence must, sooner or later, disappear.

Manchuria, through which we were now passing, never had more than a nominal independency through its Act of Secession, November 14, 1911. The staid and loyal old Viceroy, Chao Er-hsun, adroitly turned the Administration into a Committee of Safety (Society of Order), of which he took the Presidency, a device that satisfied all but the most clamorous reformers. He then informed the Throne at Peking that the people through the Provincial Assembly at Mukden had forced him into this position, which it was impossible to avoid. A mutiny among the troops at Liao-yang occurred, which he successfully suppressed, secretly executing the ringleaders and suspects, estimated at sixty in number. Notwithstanding the cleverness and adroitness with which the experienced old Viceroy met emergencies, a state of disorder resulted, and for a time there was a hurried flight of progressives into the Japanese railway zone, especially at Mukden, where they paid dearly for Japanese protection under the name of rents and hotel fees. Doubtful of the army, the astute Viceroy called in the two principal chiefs of Manchuria's ancient and picturesqe robbers, known all over the world as the "Red Beards" (Hung-hu-tzu), sat them down at his table, made them his chiefs of police, and in conformity with their dignity as "generals" sanctioned the enlistment of a military body of their followers. In a speech to the Committee of Safety, members of the Provincial Assembly, and the people, he stated Manchuria's position, warning them to remember in whatever they proposed to do, Japan could take possession of the Government within twenty-four hours. The result was that Manchuria was now ruled by the Viceroy through the Committee of Safety, was politically unchanged, and impossible of changing without danger of being crushed by the millstones Russia and Japan, between which it was placed. The Throne at Peking was curiously silent respecting these secessions of Shantung, Manchuria, and Mongolia. To Shantung the Prime Minister, Yuan Shih-k'ai, sent this terse warning: "Watch the Germans." Not even this was needed for Manchuria. The tempestuous, international ocean in which it rocked, righted its staggering ship of state.

The Chinese as rulers of the Empire had already performed the best work in Manchuria and Mongolia of which they had thus far been capable. They have not been soldiers in these later generations, and, as a race, conquerors only in the absorption of the Manchus and the conquest of their governing institutions and processes. Their efforts at reform and industrial development in Manchuria have been costly failures, which with respect to Manchuria have brought them to provincial bankruptcy. All efforts of the State to promote the welfare of its Northern territories and defend their frontiers have been pitifully futile. It is China's own race and people, with their inherent virtues, working their way through these regions in successful colonization, that constitute the only bulwark in these vital times which China possesses there. I consider that in this influence, obtained almost in spite of herself, China has been given a provision for this Northern situation: this bulwark of the Chinese Pioneer.

The lama and his companions, their curious and motley train-fellows, their servants, their smoking samovars, passed through the Great Wall that divides China proper from Manchuria, and disappeared in the direction of Peking.

CHAPTER IV

WITHOUT THE GREAT WALL

THESE representatives of the awakened Mongols had passed the barrier which Old China had erected as the limit of Mongolia. The question of the delimitation of China—quiescent through centuries—which to Mongols was fixed by this same Great Wall, was now a living issue. China, who built this barrier to keep others outside it, had for a score of years been labouring herself to get outside. After centuries of content within its limitations, the Chinese race turned Northward to find its Wall a barrier to expansion. In seeking air beyond the stifling plains of Chihli and Shantung the moving race of Chinese has already abolished that boundary. The rulers at Peking who built at the outer slope of the mountain barrier fifty miles and more away, this mural defence that held the Mongol Tartars at bay, have now blown up the Great Wall and tunnelled the mountains on which it is built, in order to get out.

The Great Wall of China is left high and dry by the flood of emigration.

At the time of my arrival here, in the Revolution and for a time preceding, there was an exodus greater than that of the innumerable workmen with their families and cattle who had come in past ages and builded this aerial monster, suspended like a dragon on the mountain peaks. The depleted, impoverished descendants of the workers at the Wall, having long ago exhausted all forests and vegetation, have been fed through unnumbered years by their little terraced fields, and now from the rocky crannies of the sun-baked mountains where they dwell, they see their long-forgotten kinsmen following them.

As I contemplate these emigrants from the Southern plain pour through the passages and tunnels and pass on, disappearing in the North not to return, I realize the break with the Past which China has made. Heirs of that age whose spirit, sinews, and substance surged into these mountain recesses and receded, see only the crumbling monument upon whose summit and in whose towers and recesses shepherds graze their flocks.

The mills of the gods are unceasingly grinding on China's frontiers. Her boundaries are carved and fashioned by the powers with which she is beleaguered. The erosive earth-hunger of Western nations carries away whole mountain ranges, valleys, and seas, drawing closer and closer to the inner, fertile vale of this ancient civilization. As if this were not enough, there is within, the grinding of the confines of her Chinese civilization against those of her barbarian colonies.

This region was an intimate one to me—the field of my journalistic labours for years. On my present journey I had passed three thousand miles of borders stirred by political and racial contentions, yet I was only retracing familiar paths. I had watched the pioneer movement when the pioneers were relatively few. Now their rapidly increasing numbers made Chinese immigration the vitals of the Chinese-Mongolian problem.

During nearly two years in the saddle I had visited between the Great Wall and the Amur River all kinds of inhabited and uninhabited places, from the ancient and populous "Kingdom of Liao" to the unsettled forests of the Madan and the Ussuri, from the placer mines and lumber camps of the Upper Sungari to the tunnels and the quarries of Nankou and Kalgan, and from the Yalu to the sand dunes of the Liao. I had followed the Palisades, the historical frontier between the Manchus—the ruling house of China—and the Mongols, a barrier which begins at the Great Wall and extends north-eastward to the Amur. Its relics, still found in the vicinity of Kai-yuan, prove no more than that it was a row of willow trees topping a trench. It was parallel to this barrier that the first lines of emigration traced themselves. Traversing the Gulf of Chihli, the emigrants went up the Liao, and later, when the railways came, passed through the Great Wall, northward along between the Palisades and the sea. They took three roads: to Inner Mongolia, Eastern Mongolia, and Central Manchuria.

In my travels here I left the Great Wall by the middle road to Eastern Mongolia. It was summer. To the north I crossed the Palisades and found myself in Mongolia. Above Kulon, which long marked the frontier trading-place of the Chinese with the Mongols, I passed the last outpost of houses, and entered the wild, nomadic lands. Lying straight ahead of me, across one hundred and fifty miles of disputed ground, was To-nan-fu, the pioneer centre of Eastern Mongolia and the goal of the middle highway. I recrossed the Mongolian border where the Liao River enters Manchuria and turned in the direction of the first pioneer region opened by the Manchus—the Imperial Forest Hunting Park, in Central Manchuria. I passed through sand dunes along the west bank, soon coming out into the valley itself. Here an occasional low promontory stood out boldly, topped by a grove of stunted chestnuts or pine, marking the grave of some forgotten dignitary and the unforgotten frontier.

I followed the road through rich fields which the moving sand dunes had not yet conquered, very close to the Liao, until opposite Ku-yu-shu, where I forded the river and spent some time afterward getting free of the thick brown mud which the water left upon me and my two horses. After passing through swamps to slightly undulating lands, I found the country rich in grain, with great roads of trade and commerce, protected all the way back to the Liao by fortified villages and hamlets. The fine condition of the walls of the farmsteads beginning at the Liao, showed me that this was the fighting line where law struggled against disorder—the frontier home of the pioneer and the " border ruffian "—the early Nebraska or Wyoming of China.

The land was steaming hot in the sun after a soaking rain. Passing the Manchurian Railway, I entered the hills leading to the Imperial Forest Hunting Park. This park or reserve, consisting of uplands, forms a watershed between the Liao and Sungari. On the west slope of this watershed I repassed the line of the Palisade barrier and stopped for the night at Ho-er-shu, a market town consisting of one long street.

I put up with a merchant. His premises must have been the dirtiest in all Manchuria, though they did not excel his hospitality. I mention one thing—flies. They alone were past description. Of all places on earth, Manchuria is the paradise of these household pests. The place where I picketed my mare was such an insult to her, that for days thereafter I was ashamed to climb into the saddle.

The men of the establishment visited me at supper-time, curious about my food. The women did not come out.

I opened some canned stores with which I had supplied myself on passing the railway. The merchant's own cook furnished me with drinking-bowls, which he wiped out in my presence with a dirty pair of old Chinese overalls picked out of the flies and dirt on the " kang " (brick bed with flues beneath), the same pair with which I had already wiped the mud from my boots. Into one of these bowls I poured a fine French wine. I was perhaps the first foreign guest they had ever had. My Chinese ostler was busy in the corral giving his master a gorgeous reputation, so that I sat amid the various generations of the family like a feudal lord. As usual, all the articles of my equipment and personal adornment passed under critical inspection, audible and inaudible, and I was kept answering questions as to the quality, price, and use of everything of mine that was visible. They were Shantung Chinese.

There is little that is private in China. My supper was a meal of state. While I ate I noticed that one of the elder members of the family was more inquisitive than the rest. His attention was centred on a can of extract of beef, condensed so as to be equal in nourishment—according to the makers—to several pounds of fresh beef. As its contents disappeared during the night, I concluded that the inquisitive elder had found its temptations irresistible, and devoured it in the darkness. Only the empty can remained, lying suspiciously on its side. In my journal I wrote it down as the " Rape of the half-bullock."

Passing over the divide, I set out the next morning on a long, lonely, upland trail, sixty miles in length. For some distance there was a well-defined road and little pioneer hamlets. I kept crossing small streams fed by springs and the warm rains, and occasionally traversed profound bogs which seemed to have no bottom and out of which it was problematical if I would ever emerge. China proper is a woodless land overrun with human beings, and it does not seem possible that it could still possess a virgin spot like this. I passed occasional farmhouses entirely surrounded by wood stockades, above which only the thatched peaks of roofs were visible. I saw no one on the embryo highway, but a few natives at these stockades regarded me with awe, the children sometimes taking fright and disappearing inside, or remaining with their elders, abstractedly filling themselves with small, yellowish-white melons. This obviously appetizing fruit gleamed in the miniature green and brown fields like stars in the sky.

It was a beautiful land for pioneering, full of flowers and game birds, especially golden pheasants. Farther on I passed woodmen felling trees. The slopes on each side of the way were being cleared and glimpses of primeval forest appeared between in the distances. I was approaching the new " City " of Ta-ka-ta. The trail led over a pass from which a high valley stretched away to a hilltop overlooking the town. I arrived at sundown and found quarters in a large, new, clean compound, in sweet-smelling buildings of newly cut wood. A servant of the place drew out of a cool well a jar of sweet, cold water. At evening the western sky was festooned with fleecy clouds, and all was as restful and inviting as a countryside at home.

Few travellers, war correspondents or otherwise, ever have the opportunity of seeing a Chinese " city " or " ch'eng " in the making. It comes into existence by devious ways and methods. A " ch'eng " is a walled town or city. The wall is the emblem of its rank and authority, and does not refer to its size. It is the dignity and respectability as well as the sign of community position, and rank, in the Middle Kingdom. The Chinese have a saying that a city without a wall is like a woman without a skirt, making of the wall one of the essential proprieties. Ta-ka-ta was little more than a market, of something like the importance of an American " cross-roads."

Before evening I went out on a tour of inspection. There were still a few faggot-sellers in the market. The place was beautiful, located on the flat ground sheltered by the hills. High grass grew among the outlying buildings. Houses were going up, and the settlers' wives were busy about their new homes, employing pioneer makeshifts strange to conventional ideas of the fixedness of Chinese society. They were cooking in the open, dyeing cotton cloth with indigo, hanging out washing, and performing other tasks only carried on behind compound-walls in settled portions of China.

When the settlement had been given its rank as a prefectural City, the prefect, with due consideration of the good and evil influences presiding over the abodes of all things Chinese, called in the geomancers, who discovered natural lines for the City's walls. It happened that these lines did not enclose all of the settlement, but took arbitrary courses, leaving out parts of it. A curious thing I noticed was that the gates were built first, beginning with the most important. As the direction of the road communicating with the outside world was east and west, the East and West Gates were already constructed. There were no North or South Gates, and only a small moat dug to indicate where the walls ultimately were to be.

Leaving Ta-ka-ta, the road splashed through a mountain stream, dived into more upland bogs, and through hill-passes and occasional settlements of prosperous and hospitable natives. At noon I stopped at the home of a poor farmer. The place was a humble little patch of thatched huts, where we fed our horses and rested. But the people were surprisingly intelligent and asked many questions. The region was not unlike the valleys I have seen in the foothills of the Ozarks. Secluding our horses in his stockade, I crawled in under the thatch of his roof-tree to get out of the hot sun. While I was resting and taking a cup of tea, the place was surrounded by a gang of mounted and armed Chinese, of whom I was warned by a shout of summons from them. Going outside, I saw a half-dozen dashing, picturesque, war-hued but quite peaceable-looking Chinese soldiers. I hailed them in a friendly manner, and found that they were a patrol, belonging to the Magistrate of Tung-ping-hsien, to which I was going. They said that they kept the road free from robbers. After the customary exchange of courtesies, they warned me to beware of the "Red Beards," and mounting their timid native horses, disappeared in a flash down the road by which I had come.

"What is the name of this place?" said I to the settler.

"Lao-hu," he replied.

Translated, the word means "Tiger." It suggested great wildness.

"Are there any tigers here?" I asked.

"Not just here, but farther back," said he, pointing to the hills.

"What is this about the 'Red Beards'? Have you got 'Red Beards' here?"

Several persons replied that there were "Red Beards," but that the real robbers were the soldiers. This was a characteristic remark, such as is heard all over China.

Patches of trees on all the hilltops, and streams choked with tree-trunks and brake, were lingering evidences of the Imperial Hunting Park, in which the chieftain ancestors of the present Manchu Dynasty held their annual hunts.

Three beautiful pheasants, including a golden-tailed male, watched me from a fallen tree. From time to time I rode through fields of millet, maize, beans, hemp, cucumbers, and melons. Just as the sun hovered on the western rim of a wide depression in which the town lay, I rode into Tung-ping-hsien, a pioneer City of even more recent date than Ta-ka-ta. The geomancers had applied their art to the determination of where the real " City " was actually to be, but there was as yet not even a gate, and the inhabitants were unable to say, in every case, whether they lived inside the " City," or outside it, not knowing, as they say, the " ch'eng-wai " (outside) from the " ch'eng-li " (inside). Nevertheless, when I asked for certain places, they spoke of them as being " outside the City," or " inside the City." But looking, I saw no dividing line.

Tung-ping-hsien translated, means " City of Eastern Peace." Already a " ch'eng " in the making, by and by it will vie with Ta-ka-ta. Here was the Oriental bud of the same kind of civic pride that made St. Louis and Chicago, Melbourne and Sydney, vie with each other. The prairie grass, as at Ta-ka-ta, was still waving in the market-place, and on the site of the coming walls that in the minds of the Chinese are to outlast all time. Here, also, the Chinese Peggies, Charities, Pollies, and Patiences, under the names of " Purest Gold," " Precious Jewel," and so on, were hanging out their washing and dyed cotton in the open. The men were hewing timbers or fixing boundary stones in virgin sod, preparatory to building walls about their homes. Traders speaking the Shantung dialect were offering foreign trinkets brought in by the railway for sale in the new shops.

The hostelry where I stayed was also a factory and shop. It was an establishment similar to what one sees in the newer regions of America and Australia, where often a water-mill, a forge, a general store, etc., are combined. Here already was a corral, a mill for extracting bean oil and making bean cakes (fertilizer), inn quarters, and a general store. The greasy smell from the bean-mill pervaded my sleeping-room, but did not interfere with my enjoyment of the cleanliness of the place. Here there were other travellers, including an official from Chihli and a commercial traveller from the same province. We met in the merchant's company in the general stores, following the cleaning-up processes necessary after the day's travel in the sun and dust.

CHAPTER V

WITH THE CHINESE PIONEERS

In travelling in China, the first thing the foreigner does after his arrival at evening is to arrange for a bath, generally enjoyed in an open court, with the water poured over him by a Chinese servant, and appreciated as much by spectators as by the traveller himself. To the Chinese perhaps the most astonishing detail of my toilet has been the self-performed shave, made all the more interesting by the use of soap and lather. This operation, performed in the morning light, attracts everybody within view, and they in turn send for the neighbours. The servants from the cook-house, the shop-boys, the merchant himself, and even his son, who was something of a scholar and literary man, came to look on.

With my face well lathered and my curious foreign razor in hand, I was conscious of being the centre of an amazed but admiring crowd who took in every detail of my appearance and waited for the beginning of the operation, some of the workmen and boys in gaping suspense. No longer a stranger in a strange land, I did not object to being the centre of a smiling, good-natured crowd, ready to burst into laughter on any pretence. Alone among the Chinese, the sympathetic traveller able to fraternize with them finds that the world immediately doubles in size.

Most men who are their own barbers dislike to have their shaving tools handled, especially if this attention by the rustic spectators occurs when one is occupied with getting over some ticklish locality on the face, like the upper lip or the Adam's apple. One doesn't wish the soap or shaving-brush handled by miscellaneous fingers, however much these curious objects are admired and coveted, apart from the danger of it. I was so impressed by the disadvantages of shaving myself that when it came time to shave again, I called in a Chinese barber and had a shave in the native pioneer way. I thought it would attract less attention, and this was the case, because the very moment curiosity began to arise, the Chinese "ti-to-ty," or barber, impressed by his own importance at being called in to serve a foreign dignitary (everyone who travels as foreigners travel is regarded by the Chinese as a person of official rank and position), laid down the law of the human relations and the politeness due to strangers with the authority of Confucius, and with such effect that the inquisitive idlers fell back. I almost forgot what, in the meantime, was happening to me.

Perched on a stool, holding my breath during the operation, I found my face slowly becoming fixed in a grin such as I had so often seen on the faces of Chinese in the same circumstances and which I had always supposed to be due to an irritating razor. My pioneer artist had a three-cornered, thin piece of rusty steel sharpened on one edge and mounted at the corner in a little bamboo handle, which he called a "knife." He bathed my face, using something which I at first thought was the old pair of overalls with which, several days before, I had cleaned my boots, and which almost exactly matched the rags of his clothing. He shaved me in more different directions than I had hitherto believed to exist on the human face, even when younger than I am now. He shaved my face in more different places than it had ever been shaved, for a Chinese barber is not satisfied with the way Nature has shaped and placed the eyebrows and the borders of the hair, both of which he trims discreetly. I cannot say that I appreciated all these little touches, but they were obviously necessary, as one could see by the dexterity with which they were performed, especially that with which he flipped the gleanings from the razor's edge with his fingernail, and demonstrated the utter superfluousness and uselessness of shaving-soap.

Parting from my genial merchant host and his two guests from Chihli, who bowed me out of the door, I rode off through the grass in search of the trail to Hai-lung-cheng. The Imperial Forest Hunting Park was now behind me. I had crossed the heart of it. After leaving Hai-lung-cheng, I looked to the south-east over range after range leading to the Long White Mountains—the cradle of the Manchu Dynasty; then I turned down the Huifa River for a short distance in the direction of the Sungari, and circled round and crossed the northern and wilder portions of the newly opened Hunting Forest reserve. I say *new*, because though thrown open fifteen years before, it is new for China. I had to swim swollen streams, and in some places traversed great mud ponds in the round-top hills, such as I had never seen before, but finally striking a charming mountain-trail, rode for two days through upland meadows, fields, and woods.

Springs burst from the mountain-sides, growing into babbling brooks, so familiar and natural as to make the children of the pioneers seem to speak English and to take me back to America. Chipmunks scampered along the fallen trees. The settlers were using hollow tree-trunks for flues. Masses of flowers grew in their little garden clearings, and for long stretches at a time the mountain-road was lined with fragrant, overhanging bloom like lilacs and wild honeysuckle. Little fields of white buckwheat glistened sometimes high up on the mountain-sides.

At nightfall I stopped at a Chinese house in a ravine and was taken to a beautiful pool of clear water in the bed of a brook hung with red lilies, and there, at sundown, I had a cool, refreshing plunge alone. The delight of the bath was almost erased by the experiences of the night. Vermin are not the pests in China they are in Western lands, but here I had such an experience with them as I had never had more than once before. I found that Central Manchuria had not been settled by man alone. A night's warfare with cockroaches is a lingering and gruesome memory of the red lily ravine.

The last memory picture I have of this matchless ride across this pioneer region is an immense bed of blue iris in full bloom, which I came upon suddenly where the road left the hills for the plains of the Sungari. It surprised me at a point where I turned sharply round a low ridge of luminous red clay. I came out where were continuous fields of several varieties of millet, and also maize, tobacco, hemp, and indigo—the latter strikingly like smartweed in appearance. The indigo was gathered into the huge tanks dug in the earth, where it is rotted with lime and water and afterwards evaporated and made into commercial form. Indigo raising in Central Manchuria is one of the established industries taken up by the pioneers, who are rapidly becoming a part of the older Manchu communities about them.

The general appearance of the Manchus is better than that of the incoming Chinese. This may be due in part to the appearance of the Manchu women, with their natural feet and stately head-dress. Generally speaking, the inhabitants of Central and Western Manchuria have a stalwartness, a prosperity, and an air of leisure not to be seen in South-eastern Manchuria and south of the Great Wall. In the unfrequented regions the women are very superstitious. I found the "evil eye" superstition—so often mentioned by writers on China—observed when mothers cover the eyes of their children before strangers, especially foreigners. But I believe this is done as often to allay the fears of children as because of superstition.

Manchu women are more natural and sensible than Chinese. The latter are modest, but often only apparently so. I was disgusted when passing through a street to see a Chinese woman, nicely dressed, plunge through a filthy pool of mud rather than pass near me. It was done only for show. In some such things the Chinese are still grotesque. I found the children generally unafraid and easily won. The women, while not afraid, always retired, especially from before the camera. Chinese men I have always observed to be easily approachable, reasonable, and friendly.

I was now nearing a point abreast of the rich grassland regions of Eastern Mongolia, against which the greatest Chinese emigrant aggression presses. I crossed the Imperial highway (Yu-lu) at I-tung-chou, and reached Kuan-cheng-tzu.

From this point my course was eastward in the direction of Kirin. To spare my horses, which had become tired out by weeks of travel in the most trying seasons, I decided to make this journey of eighty miles in a native or "Peking" cart. Kuan-cheng-tzu is a very big agricultural city, the mart and metropolis of the vast emigration region of North-eastern China, close to the Mongolian frontier. It has intimate connections with Mongolia and pays rent-tribute to Mongol chiefs. It has something of the conservatism of China proper and of a metropolis, some of its denizens being in marked contrast with the rough-and-ready settlers I had just left, as is shown by the following experience which I had on leaving.

Accustomed to unceremonious departures and to pushing on, I wasted no time, and when I had reached a decision, gave rather peremptory orders for the preparation of food and an early start the following day. The order was that we should be ready to start at five o'clock in the morning. I had accepted the services of a "comprador," or Chinese manager, to send me the Peking cart, which was to be ready at the hour fixed. A "comprador" may be described as a native who learns the weaknesses and incapabilities of a foreigner and then often makes him more helpless than he naturally is, in order to supply his needs at a fair price. In consideration of the same, however, he keeps his bargain, and in this case the cart and carter were duly on hand.

My own servant, or "pai-t'ai"—picked up for this part of the journey—had received the most careful instructions as to the start. He was to cook a chicken and stock the provision-box. He wasted some time in getting a cart which he had not been instructed to get, and in the morning was not at hand. At half-past seven o'clock I nearly gave up on seeing he had arranged a formal parting from his venerable mother. She came bringing his best travelling-clothes and to take part in his departure, which was obviously an event.

The Chinese are not travellers, the middle classes seldom leaving a home once fixed. Besides, this one was going to be gone a whole week. By their conversation I noticed they had canvassed over and over the whole catalogue of his possible needs. More care was being taken for his comfort than for mine, showing how soon the Chinese emigrant forgets his migration. He had to take his gown, which may be called the Chinese full dress, and his mother in her solicitude had loaded him with little bundles of food, linen, and toilet articles, as though she were bidding him good-bye for ever. As I stood in my rough field-clothes, fully expecting and prepared to wash my linen at nightfall by the river-sides, eat the simplest food of the land, and sleep on the brick-paved beds of the inns, my hands involuntarily went up in the air. Then I sat down to wait, thinking how foolish it had been to fret and hurry, even on the hustling frontier.

We did not get off so late but that we met the country-people coming to market in carts loaded with coops of chickens and ducks. The simple servant-boy sitting on the cart shaft with the carter was one of the few true rustics I have known. He alternately sang or dozed all the way, once begging a variegated plant of luminous gold and wine colour from a passing workman, probably thinking of his mother, treasuring it *en route*, and was much cast down at evening to find that it had withered away.

The road was an established trade route, well travelled,

with spacious inns at intervals of a half-day's march. As the weather warms, and especially in the hot days of September, the traveller is roasted by the sun at midday and by the heated "kangs" or beds in the inns at night. Winter and summer these "kangs" are heated by flues from the cooking furnaces, there being no provision for shutting off the heat. I have been so tortured in this way in China that I have made it a practice when entering an inn in summer, solemnly to take down the inn doors—generally two single boards—on arrival and place them on the "kang," with considerable air space beneath them, and place my bedding there, to show that I intend to make use of them till morning. As the Chinese are invariably good-natured, and this on the face of it is so whimsical and absurd, we unite in a laugh and are placed on a good footing at once.

It was delightful weather, resembling the American Indian summer. I passed emigrant labourers with their packs on their backs making their way farther inland. Some, having stopped by the wayside to earn road money, were working as harvest hands cutting millet, a grain that is in all North China the staff of life to the humbler Chinese. In one place there was a millet-cutting competition going on good-naturedly, the whim of the moment. The harvesters shouted out boasts and taunts as they slashed away at the grain stalks rustling about their ears. Those whom I met in the roadway were always delighted when I spoke to them in their own language, and smiled pleasantly as they trudged on.

It took two days to reach Lao-yeh-ling, a pass famous in Manchuria, admitting the traveller to the Sungari, on which the city of Kirin in the province of the same name is situated. From a temple here the Sungari looked like a flake of silver lying low in the nest of blue hills to the east. I stopped at the foot of the pass until morning, and then walked seven miles along a shady roadway to the City, one of the finest in China, the head of navigation on the Sungari and the centre of the Sungari lumber trade and gold industry. About 120,000 people dwell here on a long bluff twenty to sixty feet high, to reach which, the Sungari coming out of the hills makes a courtly bend. Many great rafts of pine logs, with bark-built huts erected upon them, lie in the river. The Great Street runs along the bluff, lined with shops and restaurants, some of which overlook the water.

Kirin is a strategical centre which was first recognized by the Chinese settler, became a Russian outpost in Russia's conquest of Manchuria, and was now the objective of two Japanese railways, one from Kuan-cheng-tzu, the other from Northern Korea—the Japanese-Russian frontier. Hence the emigrant could continue on the Imperial Road to Ninguta, where he had three lines to the Japanese and Russian frontiers. He could go by the Imperial Road to the Tumen. He could take the Russian Railway to the Ussuri boundary, or he could go down the Madan River to the Sungari and Amur. From Kirin he had the alternative of going down the Sungari direct to Mongolia, where he could strike inland, or of going up the Nonni.

Every year by the line of coasting steamers running between Chefoo and Newchwang and over the railway between Tientsin and the cities in Manchuria goes a tide of labourers, or "coolies," estimated at not less than 100,000. Most of them go North in the spring, and return to their native places at the beginning of winter, but many remain in Manchuria and Eastern Mongolia to become permanent settlers. The per cent. of those who remain becomes greater year by year. They make their way on foot hundreds of miles in order to save railroad fare, reaching Harbin and the remotest places on the railway visited by their more fortunate fellows who are able to travel by rail. They even go farther on along the Amur Railway east of Stretensk. At this point the Russians employ them in limited numbers to work on the extension of the Amur Railway. In the distant north-east, Chinese emigrants settle in Ussuri, where they become an economic problem to the Russian Administration in the Ussuri Province, since they find Russian settlements more prosperous than their own, or at least more prodigal.

Words are ineffective to describe the great inspiration of this centre of Manchuria—a reward for all the fatigue of the journey. I felt it was well to have visited it so early in the period of Manchuria's development, largely promoted by Japan, the marvel of whose enterprises in Eastern Asia is that she does not appear to be afraid of the incalculable forces which they are raising up, and does not hesitate. I felt that here with her railways facing the Mongols and the Russians she would be a bulwark to China's settlers and they would be a bulwark to her.

From Kirin I returned westward, glad to get back

to my horses, glad to walk and escape the treacherous tactics and murderous character of the Peking cart. It resembles a bell in which the occupant is imprisoned like an inverted clapper, with no choice but to clap his head as he is flung from one side of the dome to the other, against the open ribs.

So far as the necessities of this subject of China's populating of her frontiers after the policy of Russia and Japan are concerned, my travels here end at the big bend of the Sungari. I was on the eastern end of the Chinese emigrant frontier, fifteen hundred miles in length, where the advance of the settlers moves Northward for at least one thousand miles of this distance at the rate of about four miles a year. Progress is more swift in the East, where a new life began after the Russo-Japanese War, due to Japanese and Russian development, and a consequent Chinese Government activity aimed at off-setting Japanese and Russian influence. Emigration was accelerated by the demand for labourers, the Chinese in 1910 shipping large numbers of famine refugees from the crowded districts in the valley of the Yangtse River to Northern Manchuria.

It may be said that all of this emigrant, political, and industrial movement has made To-nan-fu the most important centre of the problems of China's expansion into Mongolia. Grown up without the cognizance of the outside world, not yet marked on any map, jealously watched in its development by the Russian Government, surreptitiously spied on by Japan, marvelled at and feared by the Mongols, denied and concealed by China as a bird or hunted thing conceals its nest, it sprang, 1908–1909, into the arena of Manchurian affairs. It later attracted international attention on account of being one of the objectives of a new trunk-line railway which China laid out to run from the Great Wall on the Gulf of Chihli to Aigun, on the Siberian frontier, opposite Blagovetschensk, and for which American financiers and British contractors signed a loan and building contract for funds and materials.

But at the time of which I speak, To-nan-fu may be said to have been known only to China, Russia, and Japan. It lies in a belt of grass-lands and mountain valleys, skirting the whole western border of Manchuria, and is just west of the great bend of the Sungari River. As it grew the Russian traders from Harbin and Tsitsihar on the Russian Railway established themselves there as commercial agents. China was alarmed, and requested them to leave, and in 1909 they removed, under protest, outside the City walls on instructions from their Government. Russia took up the question in Peking and claimed the privilege of residence and trade rights on the same basis of her exclusive rights by treaty which she possessed on the rest of the Mongolian-Russian frontier. By these she had similar commercial colonies at Kashgar, Kuldja, Urumtschi, Kobdo, Ulliassutai, and Urga. China's answer to this was that To-nan-fu was not in Mongolia. The reply was a thunder-bolt from the blue. She had moved the frontier, as it were, in a night, something like 200 miles.

The situation was this :—By the commercial treaty with Japan, made after the Russo-Japanese War, Manchuria was opened to the trade of all nations, with right of foreign residence and trade at stated centres. By this arrangement Russia lost her special rights—by an old treaty—in the trade zone along the Manchurian-Siberian frontier, but not in Mongolia. She reacted after this loss, with the plan to push into the To-nan-fu district, so as, if possible, to hold back the Japanese. But she was not quick enough, and I have no doubt the Japanese played an interesting rôle in connection with China's action. Russia was astonished by China handing her an edict that some time before had incorporated the To-nan-fu region under the administration of Manchuria. Its audacity and absurdity was so colossal that the Russians made appreciable concessions in their claims.

The struggle for pre-eminence, however, continued. Fearing her hold to be but temporary in a district pressed upon from opposite directions by Japan and Russia, China devised the Kinchow-Aigun Railway scheme already mentioned, with the object of separating and harmonizing her antagonists, strengthening her settlements, shortening with a railway the emigrant route along this middle highway of the emigrants, and making fast her hold upon her invaded Northern regions. Like all other of China's devices to save Manchuria, this failed in a most humiliating way. It threw her antagonists together and they joined to defeat it. As I stand on the Sungari, abreast of To-nan-fu, with Outer Mongolia now in its accomplished secession beyond, I see the drama of the frontiers, and of China's external menace, involving itself with that of internal revolution.

Many who know China well believe that her settlers

will still in this contest win a realm for the Chinese. The belt along the Mongolian frontier outside the Great Wall to which the Chinese settlers are going extends through other towns and cities not yet mapped, but which occupy the regions to the north of Chao-yang and westward to Lama Miao, the northern great bend of the Yellow River, and beyond. In the inviting pastoral regions east of the Yellow River, where the line of Chinese emigration moves Northward with such regularity, access from the South is gained through three passes in the mountains, spanned by the Great Wall.

Settlers first went into the country about Hada, above Chao-yang, 1885 to 1890, by the opening between the mountains and the sea at Shan-hai-kuan. The road is from Kin-chou to Chao-yang.

One hundred miles in a straight line farther west is the ancient road to Jehol through the pass Ku-pei-kou, the second access. Through this pass the Government followed the emigrants with the telegraph line to Chao-yang and the whole emigrant border which I have just described, to Hun-chun on the Japanese-Russian frontier, and to Aigun on the Amur.

The third access is by the famous Nan-kou Pass and the immemorial trade route across the Gobi Desert. It is through this pass that China has built her first self-constructed railway, now moving westward from Kalgan and carrying her settlers far out on the yet more ancient trade route of Central Asia leading to the Koko Nor and the New Dominion (Hsin Kiang).

The Mongols, who are a peaceful people, surrender their lands to the Chinese purchasers with little persuasion. The insinuating industry, patience, and superior intelligence of the Chinese is accepted good-naturedly among the Mongols, who fall back before this pacific invasion, mollified by the benfits of larger markets for the cattle, sheep and horses, and, in their simplicity, pleased by the patronage which they receive. On the Yellow River Chinese and Mongol camps are seen side by side, the Mongol people here completely subject, as though already passing from a nomadic to an agricultural life. They have even welcomed the "iron road" and "vapour car," as they call the railway and locomotive, and travellers looking from the car windows see them playfully race their ponies through the Chinese fields with the train. Here are repeated the same processes that converted the western plains of

America from an empty expanse of grass supporting a few nomads to populous farms and towns yielding livelihood to thousands of settlers. The whole order of life is changing, and this ancient realm of the Tartars is being civilized by skilful Chinese husbandry, the introduction of implements, and the establishment of manual trades.

China's agents and officials, who have dwelt so many ages remote and alone, find themselves being surrounded by their own people, with the territorial administration of the Board of Colonies at Peking disappearing, and new counties springing into existence just like those in China proper—in time to be formed into provinces. In addition to extending railways and telegraphs, the Peking Government encourages the emigration movement by giving settlers land at nominal prices, and the inherent power of colonization in the Chinese is well rewarded by the fertile valleys, and in some places by the extensive forests, and elsewhere by the undeveloped mines.

A large part of Mongolia has thus already become an integral part of China proper. Whether the division of China actually takes place or not, this change marks one of the world's important race migrations. The vast territory available for settlement and development is calculated to be 1,200,000 square miles in area, with a population of not quite two to the square mile. The Mongol inhabitants maintain their primitive tribal organizations and are governed by their own chiefs. It has been pointed out by Mr. E. T. Williams, the Orientalist, that, as indicated by their pastoral life, the culture of the Mongols is on the whole of a higher type than the barbarian American Indians. They offer no resistance to civilization, and the progressive tendencies manifested by several of the Mongol princes have been a decided encouragement to the Chinese to promote Mongolia's industrial development. Although China's enterprises in Manchuria and Mongolia have been said to be merely political by her neighbours Russia and Japan, it will be seen that economic considerations and the welfare of her crowded population in other parts might outweigh even these. Respecting criticism levelled at China for her unsuccessful railway projects in these regions which her settlers are struggling to conquer, it is certain that those settlers will ensure the commercial success of such railways.

In the course of time the Gobi and Ordos deserts will be reclaimed and populated somewhat after the manner of the irrigated districts in the great American desert. They will undergo a modification in climate and rainfall, from cultivation of the soil and re-forestation, and will become productive like China proper. The present insignificant production of Mongolia is almost wholly from flocks and herds. Eastern Mongolia has estimated exports per annum of 25,000 horses, 10,000 head of horned cattle, 250,000 sheep, 300,000 hides, and a large quantity of furs for which there are no figures. For North-western Mongolia the exports are given at 70,000 horses, 30,000 camels, and 1,500,000 to 2,000,000 sheep. This represents the scanty surplus of the sparse nomadic population, but it enables one to estimate what Mongolia may be under the Chinese with their intensive industry. While the region is higher than China proper and the soil on the whole not so uniform, yet it is fertile and its possibilities are very great. It is rich in minerals, timber, and game. Rivers fed by warm springs sustain waterfowl, especially in the southern valleys. There are also great flocks of bustard and other game birds, while in the hills are antelope and goat, with numerous fur-bearing animals. To hunt these, the Mongol natives and even the Chinese have only antiquated flintlocks, and an occasional matchlock shotgun is seen. Falconry is still a royal sport in Mongolia.

China has met with failure outside and north of the Great Wall, save for the individual efforts of her settlers and some smaller achievements by not more than two viceroys. In the west the Viceroy at Lan-chou built a new steel bridge over the Yellow River to let the settlers over the border to the Tsaidam and Hsin-kiang, and established land reclamation to promote immigration and conquer the regions west and north of him. It was Hsi Liang, the last Manchu Viceroy of Manchuria, who moved the boundary line of Manchuria westward in 1909, and in 1910, among his last important official acts, sent to the Throne at Peking a memorial solemnly warning his country of the Russian and Japanese aggressions on Manchuria and Mongolia.

It is evident that if the increase of China's millions continues at the present rate, they will seek a domicile, not only here but in other and even alien regions that are now barred to them. China's actual need of Mongolia and Manchuria—not to mention Tibet—for surplus population, makes it vitally necessary from her standpoint that these regions should be preserved to her for this purpose. Preposterous indeed are the claims of other countries, such as Japan, to these regions, claims based on the same principle of the necessities of crowded population at home, or of Russia.

Altogether Mongolia's situation, surrounded as she was by those who would devour her, was enough after seven hundred years to arouse her sleeping leaders to the defence of their country. While the civilized wolves were yet at her throat, I followed my lamas and Mongol princes through the Great Wall into the ancient "Middle Kingdom," China proper, the region that was the centre of the revolutionary Rebellion.

CHAPTER VI

WITHIN THE GREAT WALL

AT Shan-hai-kuan, over the City gate, guarding the road to the Middle Kingdom, is the inscription: "First Gate of the World."

This is the spot where the Manchus entered China. This is the scene where Dorgon, the Manchu Regent, and the Chinese rebels enacted the drama by which the Manchus were seated on their now tottering throne, 200 miles to the West. I paused to look at the Great Wall, which seems to rock upon the mountain-top and come tumbling down the spurs and ridges that here approach the coast—that approach it to tumble this hoary "old man of the sea" from its leagues upon leagues of back, down into the ocean waters; for here, like Johnson's cataract that "fell from precipice to precipice," the Wall is seen no more. Here, where its wave-cloven masonry disappears in the ocean, I stood for some moments awed anew by the magnificence and wonder of its physical construction, illustrative of the matchless civilization of China, her family development, morality, art, industry, her vast social and governmental structure and immeasurable resources. Fifty miles of watch-towers and fortresses, multiplying as they advance, lead to this spot where castles, bastions, and battle-grounds indicate the tangled history and the complicated problems of the theatre within.

As for the mountains and the plains alone, I might have been travelling in any country in the same latitude. All mountains and plains are the same, but the towns and the people are different. It is they, the people, who have indelibly stamped their heritage "China." I entered a Chinese-print environment at the town of Chang-li, with its name like a rippling lute, with its airy towers, walls firm as the rock behind, its gentle people in full garments—in summer a pastoral place of tent-like hats, fans, carrying poles and baskets of plenteous fruits. It is such a thing to look upon as in old pictures has given the world the notion it at present possesses of what China is. This is the beaten track—the line of travel that I, hurrying to Peking, cannot avoid. It is the railway along the sea to China's Capital taken by the eleven Powers of the West in 1900 for their communication with Peking. It bars China from her ancient ocean; but beyond it, behind Chang-li, at Yung ping-fu, is the Manchu military outpost guarding the "First Gate of the World" and the highway to Peking. From here its own troops, November 26, 1911, sent the ultimatum that forced the Throne to swear allegiance to a new and revolutionary Constitution of nineteen articles that had been formulated by the Imperial Assembly.

This railroad is already garrisoned by foreign troops—English for the moment because it is security for English loans, but later to be guarded by troops of all the Great Powers so as to ensure foreign access to Peking, in spite of all emergencies of Chinese revolution. By the Protocol with the Powers settling the Boxer War, China's troops may not come within short artillery range, and are nowhere seen except as ordinary passengers and in small numbers.

Under the Protocol, this railway zone and the trains have become an asylum where there are more elements of revolution than can be seen in the country through which I have travelled. But all is peaceful. All meet on this line of communication for safety. They travel here because all is secure.

As our train rolls into Tientsin we are on foreign soil. Here are the great settlements governed by Britain, France, Germany, Japan, and Austria, in which the higher Chinese and Manchu families of Peking and the surrounding country have taken refuge. Because of high foreign prices or limited native means they have in many places packed themselves into foreign rooms as closely as in the coupés in our train. A quiet English street, *Victoria Terrace*, holds families of smaller officials of the Board of Communications at Peking. Places that surprise the onlooker because of the use to which they are put, hold the families of secretaries and ministers of the Board of War, the Board of Finance, the Board of Education, and the Board of Foreign Affairs. Barons, marquises, dukes, and even princes, have sequestered their women and children in quaint Nuremburg houses in the German Concession. The old abandoned Y.M.C.A. building is the refuge of the family of the Premier, Yuan Shih-k'ai.

Tientsin is also the refuge for Oriental anarchists,

revolutionary assassins, and secret societies ; for revolutionary generals who have precipitated premature revolts, and Republican editors who have anticipated the Republican millennium—all living for the most part in the discomfort of foreign expense and luxury, wishing for their own homes, fearful of the tidal wave of revolution, and waiting for it to pass. Everywhere about them are the visible signs of order and foreign power. Here is the base from which the Powers operate to handle the situation as it affects their interests.

Those natives who have taken refuge in Tientsin represent only a small per cent. of the privileged element. All China lies without and beyond these confines, and it is this interior China that centres in itself all interests. The pioneers have passed the barrier, the privileged classes have fled to the foreign settlements and to Japan, but the stay-at-home Chinese within the Great Wall face me in unnumbered millions as I turn inland.

A marvellous condition prevails. There is no *Government.* The Republic on the Yangtse has no Government, only a military and civil Junta. The North has no Government, only a Premier, powerless and marked for assassination. In the North the country is quiet and there is only seen here and there a skulking robber. Below the Yellow River in the East is famine, brigandage, and the disheartening levies of the troops of two opposing armies upon that region's beggarly resources. The Yangtse Valley is seething with plans for a new nation.

In the South-east the Cantonese are preparing to march upon Peking, and their leaders are defying authority and order. In the South-west the feudal ages have been restored. In the West the great province of Szechuan is working from a state of chaos to one of competent self-government. In the North-west, along the Yellow and Wei Rivers, the age of Genghis Khan is reproduced, and the bodies and members of men, women, and children are dragged in the streets by dogs.

What is the matter with the people within the Great Wall ? All know that they have been moving socially since they began to take to heart the lessons of their contact with Western countries. Is it the many or the few ? Is it the reform of a nation, or is it a conspiracy ? Is it the rebellion of the race or of the individual ? And what is it about ?

The answer comes from the few. The comparative

condition of the people is the greatest answer of all, but there is no use to turn to the masses for a concrete answer—they are incapable of enlightened thought. The statement of the case comes from the thinking few whose intelligence and education have enabled them to compare China with the West. Having discovered the Magna Carta and tasted of individual rights, these few set up reform clubs, secret societies, schools, and newspapers, to cry to the world that answer. To them, their Mandarinate, the immemorial Chinese officialdom, is at the bar. Hear the indictment of it : " Officials can burn the houses of the people, but the people are not allowed even to light their lamps [of knowledge]. An official cares for his family only and nothing for the Country. The official is like a tortoise, able to protect himself from harm by withdrawing into his hard exterior. They are multi-faced and have masks for every occasion. They are ' side-steppers ' and shifters like crabs. There is nothing they will not do for money. Even before the oncoming bomb of the revolutionary assassin, the official is not deterred from his nefarious work of heaping up money. It is his ceaseless occupation. If he only gets his money he stops his ears and blinds his eyes even to the theft of the Nation's railways. He sucks the lifeblood of the people and fattens while they grow lean. Not satisfied with ' squeezing ' them to the extremity, he devises new taxes.

" His eyes are without pupils and his ears are plugged up. Make a surgical operation upon him and no heart can be found among his vital organs [literally, ' in the stomach ']. He sits in his garden beside the wine-jar, or in his conservatory among flower-pots. His occupation is to enjoy himself, but to do nothing for the Country. He has a sharp head for pushing himself in and all sorts of instruments to open his own career. The long hat [emblem of the self-seeking official] is always admired by him. He butts into office, but what does he do there ?

" The Foreign Office is merely sleeping—it is not doing anything. China cooks ready coffee for others, Chinese stand with difficulty upon this globe. The Nation's strength is wasted upon diplomatic dealings—foreign diplomacy lives upon China. In her terror of the thief within, China has forgotten the lion outside. The Chinese Government is at bay before wolves and tigers ; but the Chinese Official grovels before the confident Foreigner, he is patronizing and fearful. He takes the Foreigner in

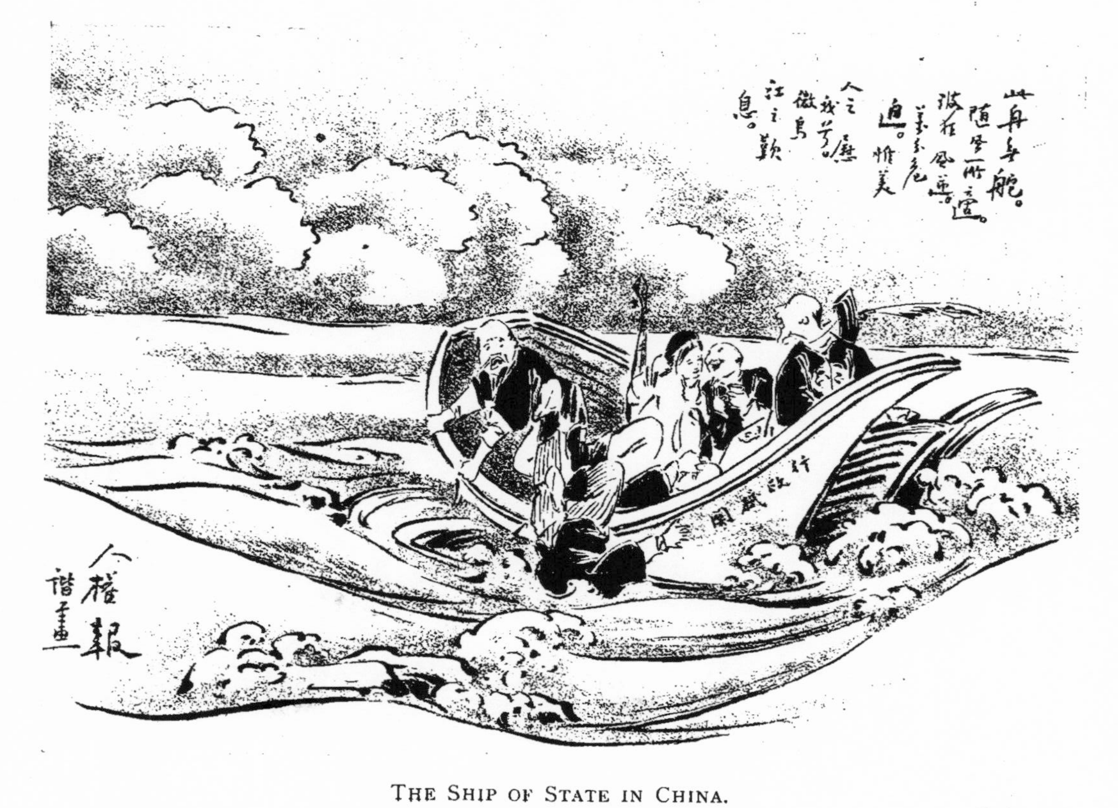

THE SHIP OF STATE IN CHINA.

To face p. 48.

his arms, but his own people he stamps upon. He falls into the net of the Foreigner, and once in, he can never get out.

" Even at The Hague Conference [1909] China was a captive led by the neck by the Powers. She is something hunted by them like a deer. Their greedy hands are breaking the Chinese bowl. They are plundering her mines while Chinese officials only weep. The third of the old Grand Councillors [Yuan Shih-k'ai] is sent away, and two are dead [Chang Chih-tung and T'ai Hung-tze], why not bury the other two? The ore in the mine cries to them, 'You two old men must protect us.' China is asleep with the tiger. The Government is a ship without a rudder. Let it go any old way. The waves are getting larger, the wind stronger, danger nearer, and within is beauty and dissipation alone to cheer you."

So begin the lamentations of the several years preceding the Rebellion. And they go on, eventually swelling into the reform battle-cry. Confucius, just before he died, went to his doorstep and, taking a last view, wept for the condition of the world. His act is like that of the reformers on the eve of the Rebellion. To them the last state of the Mandarin was one of complete degeneracy. No man was so hideous or debased that he could not become an official, and having got office, lived a life of duplicity and went down to the perdition of the habitual opium-smoker, parting from everything, even his official rank, rather than surrender his pipe.

The reform leaders of the people were vigorous and not without hope for the densely ignorant masses. To them the world was a scene of nations, each trying to oust the other from its position. Though China held with difficulty her mundane footing, " she," said they, " can stick to the globe, if her people have worthy minds." " China is now getting a small ray of light, but the people are in a debased state. China can wash her clothes, but if she would be clean, she must wash her body. She is burdened with debt, her foreign loans are like the stories of a tall pagoda resting upon her shoulders, or like a heavy stone crushing her vitals. Men honour the rich—the very dogs bite the poor. If China cannot get on, she will become a beggar and the nation will be dead. When a country dies its people become beasts of burden. Chinese are already slaves to slaves [a reference to India's dictation in the affairs of Tibet]. . . . The future human beings will be fearful to look upon, harsh outside, lean inside, with a face like a wolf, and armed to make trouble for everyone. . . . Chinese are now strayed and lost in a winter's snow. They have heavy responsibilities and few privileges. In spite of her burden of debt China must get to the top of the mountain, yet her people only weep under their taxes, they know little more than to eat, drink, and sleep."

In this condition the people persist in their "blindness, vices, and ignorance. Dazzled by the sight of money, they are frantic in pursuing it. The bait of official rank and its attendant prospects of profit will tempt the Chinese to any danger. They are under the pressure of money and will do anything to get it.

"China's only special kind of shop not found in other countries is that which sells official rank; Chinese are the only people who have shops selling letters of recommendation. The fortune-tellers are the leaders and guides of the people, who leave everything to fate. They promote superstition and burn incense in the temples to imaginary deities, with the consequence that they have fear without reason. They flee in fright before their own officials. As for the foreigner, his voice to the Chinese is like that of the demon of thunder; China is indeed like a sick man and needs strong medicine. Her people will not give so much as a hair to help their country. Those who have advantages abroad return to be no longer Chinese, yet neither are they foreign. Alas, that it is often necessary to ask, 'To what nationality do you belong?' The students spend their money for foreign luxuries, and their holidays they spend with singing girls. The people are looking into a perished country's mirror—perished because of the unworthiness of its people."

Following this lament of the decline of the faith, patriotism, individuality, and hope of the Chinese, comes the indictment against the Government. Borrowing from the phrase so often used in his edicts by the Emperor and referring to the state of the Yueh and Wu kingdoms, the Chinese reformer, speaking of China's condition, says she should "sleep on tinder and taste the bitter sausage," so as not for a moment to forget the critical state of the Empire. "The cart is before the horse," says he, and asks with respect to China's shorn condition, outside dangers and the only weapon at her command, "What is the use of a fan in winter?"

"I can only speak," says the student returned from

abroad, " but can do nothing. I cannot even get a post in the schools." China was without leaders, but nevertheless could not accept leadership from those whom she sent abroad and educated for that purpose. " China," wrote a reformer, " is like a sorrowful man standing on the deck of a vessel, anchored, with no one to work the sails."

" The Chinese people are shut out by the officials from the Government as birds are shut out from the mountains by the clouds. The Throne has granted the right of a Constitution, but the Government is hindering it. The people are warming up constitutional affairs while the officials are trying to cool them. The office for carrying out the Constitution is doing nothing; it is out of business, like a deserted temple. The people are trying with little strength to drive home the reform programme, but the officials who have the power to aid them do nothing. Parliament is like a boat far from the land and beyond reach. The hopes of the people for self-government are like bubbles, gone in a moment. While the people mend the Treasury, the Government embezzles from it. The Courts are choked with delayed law cases. Everything is stifled by the Conservative Government. To attempt to teach the Conservatives is like making music for cattle. Alas! the day is ending and the goal is distant."

Of all her troubles, it remained for famine, the pressure of her poverty and the fear of enslavement to the foreign money-lender, to force China to revolt. " Every nationality is free to do anything in China," said one. " China is imprisoned beneath a network of foreign railways," said another. " We must not allow the foreign foot to stand upon our railways," said a third. The external danger was recognized to be the cupidity and greed of foreign peoples, who look upon China as fair game. China is seen beset by them and asking: " With whom shall I go?" They are likened to woodmen cutting off the trunk and all the branches of the Chinese tree. China is the last ten-pin in the game of bowls played by the stronger Powers: India, Egypt, Turkey, Persia, Korea, and others have fallen—her turn comes next. The menace of Japan and Russia in the foreign danger is second only to that of the money power. " Though the younger," says a writer, "Japan has struck China, knocked her down and enslaved her." In the presence of Russia and Japan, who dominate Northern China principally through their railways there, Old China is made to remark to Young China, "I am dying, you can well deal with such people."

The newspaper Press of the Chinese reformers furnishes in its cartoons of the three years preceding the Revolution a comprehensive picture of what is the matter within the Great Wall and what is in the hearts and minds of many of the people that now transforms them. Out of three hundred of these cartoons, eighty-one complain of the vices of the officials or Mandarins. Thirty-seven picture the evils for which Mandarins are responsible. The most frequent grievance in this category is the obstruction of the plans for a Parliament.

Seventy cartoons depict with heartfelt emphasis foreign oppression of China through loans, indemnities, and abuse of power. An equal number with equal acuteness and equal bitterness follow to show China's shortcomings. Twelve out of these latter point out the vanities and vices of females, one cartoon representing wives of the day to be luxuries. The ignorance of the people and their indifference to their condition get nine cartoons. China's helplessness in general due to vice follows with eight, and next in order come, the profligacy of Chinese youths, religious darkness, opium, gambling, the money evil in other forms, worship of office and power, disloyalty, and national shame from conduct toward foreigners. Cigarettes come last.

Twenty-six cartoons show the burdens of the people and their sick and broken condition under them. Taxation heads this list, closely followed by persecution of the Press. The Chinese mind is singularly balanced, and so in this general pictorial gloom there appears such hope as can be injected into nine cartoons picturing China's triumphs over her evils and dangers. Five of these nine refer to the educational and moral awakening of women and the importance of their awakened influence. The small remainder of the three hundred devoted to other topics are of such miscellaneous nature as more than anything else perhaps to emphasize the importance, in the minds of the reformers, of rebellion and revolution.

By this campaign of education carried on by newspapers, books, secret societies, lecture courses and schools, the people of China, who individually had always distrusted the officials and Government, *found out* that they *all* distrusted the officials and the Government. This was the greatest

1.　　　　　　2.

1. Fat Officials and Lean People.

2. The Mandarin and the Foreigner—"The Rare Bird."

To face p. 52.

force in the Rebellion, which to the minds of the masses was relief from taxes and the putting down of the Manchus. To the students and reformers it was the dawn of enlightenment, the putting of the government into clean hands, and social and industrial regeneration. To the literati who constitute the Mandarinate against which the voice of the reformers was raised—along with the Manchus—it meant the destruction of the Confucian system and exposing a defenceless people to the rapacity of hungry foreign Powers.

There was a greater thinking than China had ever had. The voices of the people were heard. Their thoughts were seen and read, and at last with all the agitation, and the publicity by the Press, the so-called inscrutable Chinese mind was exposed and laid bare. Above the cries of all the people was heard more clear and strong than anything else, that of faith lost in the Government, the friendlessness of the Manchu rulers, and the determination to set up a new Government before the corrupt and worn-out Mandarin government of the Manchus could mortgage the country and its resources to foreign money-lenders, and by filching the proceeds, obtain additional power to obstruct the people in their realization of self-government. The great infirmities of the people, especially ignorance, have always left them the prey of the Mandarinate when it was the only thinking class.

In parallel column with the thinking, rising minority—the Chinese mind—is placed the great unleavened, unthinking mass. The only inscrutable mind in China is that of this mass which cannot think—in our meaning of the word—because it has not the tools with which to think. But the true answer to the question, "What is the matter within the Great Wall?" is contained in the dumb reply of this mass, whose condition speaks for itself.

CHAPTER VII

WITHIN THE WALLS OF PEKING

As I approached Peking, the old familiar landmarks were unchanged. It was a warmer day in a warmer latitude than that of my recent travels. The only change was in the walls of the cantonments built up along the route of British Admiral Seymour's relief march in 1900 (Boxer War), where the bricks laid in the loopholes had been punched out. There were a few Sikh soldiers outside the cantonments, just as in 1900 and after. The sun streamed through the dust that always hangs in suspension over the Peking plain. The winter wind cut up the sand in the sand dunes in little flurries as I passed the Hunting Park and entered the familiar region of the flower nurseries around the villages of Feng-t'ai and Ma-chia-p'u. This is abreast the walls of the Chinese City of Peking, through which the train goes.

All was unchanged. A formerly discredited, humiliated, and discarded statesman was in charge and was camping in the empty halls of the modern Foreign Office building (Wai-wu-pu), hitherto shunned by the Throne and Government because built under the supervision of the fallen statesman and his protégé, one of the Cantonese party. There was no Government, it had disappeared. It was almost as in 1900. "Is Government superfluous to these people? Are they completely Government-proof?" thought I. Only a police guard of Chinese appeared at the outer wall when the train passed, later to arrive at the Ch'ien Men, the front gate of the Forbidden City and palaces of the Manchu sovereigns. There it was a curiosity to the American Legation Guards on the parapet above, as Peking now was to me.

Here are the foundations of six cities that have succeeded one another. This was the Capital of China when China became known to Europe through Marco Polo. This is the third time that it has been without a Government in 267 years, or since the Manchus entered China. The first time was when the Court fled before the British and French allies in 1860. The second was when the Court fled before the enraged allies of a dozen countries in 1900. It has now slunk away before the immense figure of its own enraged people, and has relinquished its authority and delegated, somehow, somewhat of its enigmatical powers to a "Premier," who can neither rule nor test the measure of his power.

The representatives of the Powers wonder from dawn till nightfall what will happen, and from nightfall to dawn why it has not happened. There is nothing unusual in the general appearance of the Chinese streets. A few more troops have been gathered around the Capital, but they are not noticeable. The only evidences of China's great internal upheaval to be seen in her Capital are the crowding of foreign troops in the Legation Quarter, the barricades in the streets, and the German and American defences on the adjoining City wall.

It is strikingly like 1900 in the Legation Quarter. But here the parallel ends. There is no besieging enemy. On the contrary, the enemy of 1900 is now the grateful refugee within the Legation walls. Everywhere without the foreigner is received with open arms, in great contrast to the days of the siege, when no foreigner's life was safe and those who went to parley left their heads on the gates of the City. He is now a surety and safeguard. Without the dominating Court, without the overshadowing Palace, without the anti-foreign menace, with an overaweing Republic in the South, Cathay is indeed dead. Peking is her death-mask. The Throne is passing, leaving the lifeless image of the Empire stretched upon its Northern bier. It has surrendered its authority and annulled the ancient Manchu seal. Its "sacred edicts" have already become *mandates* of the Chinese Premier, Yuan Shih-k'ai, and members of the Cabinet. Its attentions to Government are confined to audiences with the Premier upon what terms of abdication the Republic will grant to it and what security it can wring from the Republic. There is no Regent, and the eight-year-old Emperor and the Lung Yu Empress Dowager hold meetings with the princes of the Mongols, their Northern kinsmen, respecting a Manchu-Mongol state as an asylum, in the last extremity, from the aroused Chinese. Outer Mongolia has already fallen away. Inner Mongolia remains, but is already under conquest of the Chinese pioneer; while in Manchuria upon the Manchu hearthstone there sits the Chinese pioneer and the Japanese and Russian invaders.

Even had they not abandoned it for the glories of the Jade Sceptre, the Dragon Throne, and the fleshpots within the Wall, and had not the Chinese pioneers inched them from their birthright, the Manchus could not now call their home their own. The courts of their ancestral altars are crowded with strangers, and they could not retire from within the Wall without begging crumbs of mercy from Japan and Russia. Retribution for fifty years of Imperial error lies heavy upon the widow of the martyr Emperor Kuang Hsu—the Lung Yu Empress Dowager—and the little Emperor orphan Pu Yi. They hold audiences with the Manchu princes, with the Mongol princes. The Manchu and Mongol princes confer with each other, and together they convene with the Cabinet. The question is: Will the Lung Yu Empress Dowager and the Emperor retire to Mukden under the protection of Japan, to Mongolia under protection of Russia, take refuge in the foreign Legations, or accept the questionable guarantees of the irresponsible leaders of the Republic? The most trusted Manchu Viceroy, Hsi Liang, has been placed in charge of the old summer capital, Jehol, outside the Great Wall, in the mountains of Old Mongolia, to keep open the way to the North. Here is the road 150 miles long that has made of Mongolia a retreat and has been the route of flight in times past. Long cart-trains are leaving Peking by this road with materials to refurbish and store the palace at Jehol.

It is the last days—December 1911–January 1912—of the Imperial Assembly, a dignified body created by the late Empress Grand Dowager according to the rules for the adoption of a Constitution. Its sittings excited the admiration of foreign visitors, but in its last days it is passing into the eclipse of opera bouffe. The ranks of its members are thinned by the withdrawal of converts to the Republican cause, by terrorism from the Republican assassin and fear of Manchu reprisal. It dwindles below the level of a quorum, holds a few irresolute meetings, and disappears. Before its demise it receives a telegram from mutineers of the Manchu military outposts at Yung-ping-fu saying that the army there has unanimously elected to support the Republic, and asking the Assembly to send at once deputies to tell it what to do. On the occasion of its last communication with the Yung-ping-fu army, the Imperial Assembly responded with forcing a provisional Constitution for parliamentary government upon the Throne. A month later it had practically disappeared. Two battalions of the Yung-ping-fu troops mutinied and awed the whole region of Lan-chou, threatened destruction of the railway there guarded by foreign troops, and were not suppressed for several days. Mails and telegrams were interrupted and Peking seemed now to be cut off on three sides by the Republicans, but there was no response from Peking.

I had seen the preparations for its birth, and I was now in at the death of the Imperial Assembly. Something of the poise and sovereign dignity of the Chinese race seemed to disappear with it. To me Peking had all the appearances that accompany the breaking up of a social system. I stopped in the street to see old General Chiang Kuei-ti go by. A Mohammedan Chinese, a warrior, but a dignitary of the old school, a big man with round shoulders, a thin white beard, a ruddy face and a ready smile, he rode along in his under-sized, native-made, rickety old four-wheeler with raggedy out-riders, to give confidence to all. Though the Imperial Government with all its departments and their army of officials have disappeared, General Chiang remains a link with the Past. He was the late Empress Grand Dowager's trusty helper. It was he who covered the rear of the Court's flight from Peking in 1900, after which he was rewarded with command of the forces that are the Court's protection and bodyguard. He has perhaps 7000 soldiers with which to keep Peking quiet. They are known among foreigners as a mob of rapscallions who cannot be trusted out of his sight, who at the first sign of disorder would overrun the region, plundering and burning far and wide, and before whom not even foreigners would escape.

There is no conflict of opinion on this score. At the height of alarm, with disorder from Kalgan to the Yellow River on the West, mutiny and plunder on the South reaching to the sea, and with mutiny and broken communications on the East, he says, when asked of possible trouble in Peking, "Yu wa" ("You have me"). He might be likened to the popular comedian whose appearances are a relief from the harrowing tension of a too-serious drama. Though trained in Central Asia, he had attuned himself to the cosmopolitan life of Peking in his old age, with gentle adaptations and with little concessions to foreign customs. But he never changed old customs for new any more than old maxims for new. When he held a review of his riff-raff troops on the Peking plain, for some distinguished foreign general, and entertained the military attachés of all Europe, America, and Japan at luncheon, he stood like a soldier by his temperate habits. He raised his wineglass to his guests but never drank. Now the foreigners in the Legation quarters could laugh with, but not at an old man who so confidently and good-naturedly trusted himself to thugs and blacklegs. As a matter of fact there was no Treasury and no Government behind him, and it was doubtful how long the Imperial Clan or the Lung Yu Empress Dowager would pay his troops, to say nothing of how long these troops would obey discipline. His sturdy confidence made the denizens of the Legation Quarter laugh.

General Chiang rode on through the Legation Quarter and out at the barricade of sand-bags and *chevaux de frise* erected by foreign soldiers defending the Legations. The Foreign Legation Quarter looked more like it did in the days of the siege (1900) than at any time since. Once since then, sand-bags were gathered on the wall when the American Guard (1907) took alarm at the Chinese firing rockets at night and reported that their pickets were being shot at on the wall beside the great gate Ch'ien Men. But nothing happened until the Legation garrison of ten nations was called to arms by the unfurling of the Republican flag. Soldiers whose fortunes for ten years had been those of bridge whist, were called from their card-tables in drawing-rooms and clubs to string barbed wire on the *glacis*, turn gunny sacks and Peking dust into "sand-bags," knock out the brick veneer covering the portholes of its enclosures, and mount machine-guns and artillery in the streets, and on the City walls along the South.

The City wall bounding the Legation Quarter on the South is divided among the Americans, Dutch, and Germans. The latter garrisoned their block-house on the wall and cut off by wire entanglement the great gate Hata-Men. On the East the Legation wall is divided among the Germans, French, and Austrians. The French mounted machine-guns in a fort in the centre of the East wall. On the North are the Austrians, Japanese, Italians, and British, with underground listening-galleries, gun platforms and guns, and their position, together with that of the British, Russians, and Americans on the West, faces the Forbidden City. The latter is overlooked by the American block-house on the City wall facing the great gate Ch'ien Men.

The American Guard has taken possession of the Ch'ien Men. The place has associations, for it was the scene of a struggle at the time of the relief of the Legations when Captain Riley was killed. Here still lie some of the old cannon that for ages were the defence of the Tartar City, rolled down the incline on which stands the gate-tower and left under the parapet of the semi-lune. The American recruit muses with one foot upon a cannon and the other upon the immemorial pavement over which, as it is written, three or four teams of horses may drive abreast. He sees the Forbidden City, which with its red walls and yellow roofs looks to him like a great agricultural fair. The multi-coloured flags of all nations flying, each over its own Legation in the Legation Quarter, are the only visible life and strength of this scene behind the curtain of whose walls is a rare tragedy in the drama of a vanishing Asia.

The American Guard's companions off duty lounge in the great gate-tower whose outward beauty conceals its sterner uses as an armoury. Standing on blocks of white marble set in the brick paving, its rectangular walls of grey paving-brick and red plaster rise to the first roof, which is supported by a row of lacquered columns on the outside and rows of similar columns on the inside. Three roofs of green and yellow tiles cap the superstructure, supported by multi-coloured, intricate, iridescent rafters—the whole a pillar of fire, light, and beauty. This is the watch-tower of the fortress of the Legations. Looking South toward the Republic there is the great South Gate two miles away, and to the left the famous Altar of Heaven. To the right the Temple of Agriculture stands. Looking toward the cold Northern regions that offer the Manchus their only apparent refuge, there is on the left the now abandoned Imperial Assembly hall and the new law buildings and courts. The Palace of the Lung Yu Empress Dowager and Emperor with the pagodas of the Western Park come next. There are the Drum and Bell towers and the famous Coal Hill, and then the Board of War, the Anting Gate, and beyond, in the ancient city of the Mongol khans, the Altar of Earth and the Yellow Temple, thereafter the Lama Temple, and the Confucian Temple with its great monuments in earth and stone reaching back nearly 3000 years; and last, on the right, is the new Foreign Office building that is the asylum of the Premier, Yuan Shih-k'ai. Within them all, and under this eye of the civilized world looking from the Ch'ien Men, is the Forbidden City with its invisible tragedy, or comedy, of the passing of the Manchus, the demise of a Dynasty, the death of an Empire

The barbed wire stretched, the *chevaux de frise* set up, the sand-bags and the guns hauled out, the reinforcements brought up from the sea off Taku, by barge and train, and new guards posted, the bridge-tables are again brought out, the cross-country paper race and the club bowling tournament entries are posted, invitations for the New Year's skating carnival are sent out, and the Legations stolidly recommence their accustomed diversions.

The swan-cry in the Palace of the Manchus is accompanied by the clatter of hockey in the rinks at the Peking Club and the American Guard compound. The Imperial Clan listening to the voice of doom, also hears the heavy roll of foreign cannon, wheel, and hoof, gently thundering through the streets. And equally welcome to them, the sound of the feet of foreign soldiers drilling on the parade-ground; for when worst comes to worst, these soldiers will be a defence against primeval savagery in Peking.

Peace negotiations have begun and the Revolution lags. Events do not move fast enough for the Occidental watchers at the bedside of this Sick Man of Asia—China—and they increase the pace of their diversions, mixing them with rumours and speculations from the bottomless pit which results from a mixture of European and Asiatic thought. The receptions, dinner-parties, conferences, card-tables, are interrupted by messages from the Mission stations in the outlying streets bringing information from the country or asking for guards for the Missions. The dispatches from the chancellories of the Great Powers in Europe and America begin to come in to Peking at the dinner-hour and after. The day's rumours are sifted at the K.T.K.—cocktail club. The secretaries slip from the glittering dinner-tables shortly after nine, and relight the lamps in the Legation chanceries. Nightly they burn midnight oil over cipher despatches to their home Governments. Press correspondents come and go, here and there challenged by sentries, and when the chanceries are dark, file their Press dispatches to the great capitals of America, Europe, and Japan.

Without are darkness and silence. The stolid Chinese lie down in peace at night. The night is reserved for the Emperor. It is his immemorial hour of toil. At midnight the great Ch'ien Men is thrown open, and from the Chinese

City on the South come Court ministers and officials called to audience, joining the little stream that nightly trickles in from the East, the North, and West through the East Gate of Peace and the Flowery Eastern Gate of the Forbidden City, after their audiences or attendance at the Throne Hall to return home at dawn.

But now closed is the great Ch'ien Men. The boy-Emperor sleeps and nocturnal vigils are resumed by the Manchu Clan. The Bureau of Constitutional Affairs, the Bureau for Opium Suppression, the Ministry of Education, the Board of Interior, the Board of Posts and Communications are empty. Their ministers and secretaries, if not fled from the City, remain at home. The Ministry of Finance and the Foreign Office are suspended. People inquire where the ministers are and do not care sufficiently to wait for a reply. From the Board of War nine-tenths of the staff have departed. Abandoned by the State, the City is reverting to the condition of the provinces. Always more liberal than the provinces, its Administration has left it to its own devices. With the increase of danger the Manchus more and more give rein to the reformers, and confine themselves to increasing the efficiency of their Capital police, gendarmes, and military bodyguard. The guilds and merchants have banded together and formed their own defences, arming their watchmen like soldiers. There is toleration for the newspapers advocating even abdication. While newspaper offices are being closed in Manchuria and Shantung and newspaper premises mobbed and destroyed at Shanghai in the Republic, the Press and people of Peking are left unrestrained. At dawn they awaken and see the secretaries, the last to cling to the Manchus and the Premier, leaving for Tientsin. A shudder shakes the City, and a little mob possessing some rumour originating in the Press district of the Chinese City filters through the traffic of the Ch'ien Men, grows as it moves between the Forbidden City and the Legation Quarter, surges along past the Palace gates, and when strength is dissipated vanishes near the great Anting Gate. In the tea-houses are heard stories of the coming of the princes from the North, of the Mohammedan rebels from the West, of the mutineers from the East, and the Republicans from the South. At the close of another day the Premier's secretary dispatches valuables to Tientsin, while many receiving some warning flee by train to safety at Tientsin, Dalny, Tsing-tao, or even Japan. Incoming trains bring gentry from the country, who knowing no other place flee to Peking.

At the very gates of the Palace the shops vend lurid pictures of the fall of Nanking, and the battles of Hankow and Hanyang, with Japanese portraits of the rebel leaders and conspirators. Beside the old portraits of Kuang Hsu and the late Empress Grand Dowager, the boy-Emperor and the new Lung Yu Empress Dowager, are exhibited the likenesses of the Republican leaders Li Yuan-hung, Sun Yat-sen, and Hwang Hsing,—as it were, flaunting the Republic in the face of the Empire. Doomed to remain, the poor booth-keepers under the shadow of the executioner's knife are compelled by their condition to turn disloyalty and loyalty alike into pennies, thus "parching their millet on the floor of hell."

At afternoon tea members of the Legations receive requests from their Chinese friends for permission to store art works and other articles of value in the Legation houses. In the atmosphere of old Ming paintings, Sung porcelains, T'ang jades, Han potteries, and Shang bronzes, the French class at the —— Legation reads Cyrano de Bergerac. In purple gowns of Chinese silk, the "Purple Cows," from legation, bank, barracks and press, meet under the Milky Way to read essays on modern thought and life and to discuss the French Revolution and the spectacles in Asia. Events or the lack of events had brought up a comparison among watchers by the Manchu bier of the French and Chinese revolutions.

Such sights as heads dragged through the streets by their queues, midnight assassinations, not to mention wholesale massacres of Manchus in the West and South, suggested some such fate for China's autocracy of privilege as had overtaken the autocracy of title, wealth, and privilege in France. Was the foreign debt, the Manchu-Chinese incubus at Peking, and the new army, merely the Church, the Throne, and the Army of French Revolutionary history? Was the demand for the return of foreign Concessions, the throttling of the Stamp Tax and railway construction levies, the Gallic cry for "bread and speech with the King"? Were the Amazons of Shanghai *en route* to Nanking the fishwives marching on Versailles? Were the "Bomb Pioneer Auxiliary" the Mesdemoiselles Theroignes of China? Was the Imperial Assembly usurping powers of actual legislation and imposing a Constitution, merely the National Assembly of Mayor

Bailly? Were the rabble soldiery and highwaymen of Hsian-fu in their ruthless massacre of 7000 helpless Manchus—leaving their bodies to the dogs—other "Sans Culottes" carrying the heads of the late aristocrats on pikes? Were the decadent Manchu Clan and Government a second French Court? Was Chang Hsun of Nanking, now "the last chance of guiding and controlling this revolution"—Chang Hsun, the dissolute voluptuary, briber of Prince Ching, swashbuckler and leading Imperialist General with the character and morals of Mirabeau, a rebel or a loyalist? Was Li Yuan-hung or Sun Yat-sen the Robespierre of China? And who were the Marats, Dantons, and the Desmoulins? As for the Allies—we were the Allies. Was the "lai lo" (It has come)—the fall of the Manchus—only the "ça ira" of the French street mobs, or was this a Revolution the like of which had never been? Was the ubiquitous headsman of China merely La Guillotine?—These are the themes of the cosmopolitan raconteur of the "Purple Cow."

From these diversions the Legation students, philosophers, and critics turned and took photographs of all the sights and scenes, and exchanged their portraits in commemoration of the historic times in which they were living. Was this the birth-chamber of the Mongol Napoleon whose rise Europe has dreaded since the Mongols swept Western Europe, greater than Mutsuhito, the king-destroyer of Japan? Impressed by the august manner of his return to power after his dismissal in 1908, the world has selected Yuan Shih-k'ai as the Napoleon of Asia. But to many Legation critics he was a turncoat and a betrayer comparable with the greatest traitors of Chinese history. He was numbered with the arch-conspirators of the Han Dynasty, Wang, Tung and Ts'ao, and many believed that like Wang he was plotting to usurp the throne for himself.

I can recall no situation in Chinese history that seemed to me exactly to resemble the conditions in the Capital. After the resignation in September of Prince Ching as Premier and his recommendation of Yuan Shih-k'ai as the ablest man available to be his successor, no voice was raised in Peking in defence of the Throne or against it. The immemorial institutions of the Grand Secretariat, the Grand Council, the Board of Censors, and the Hanlin College were silent. The head of the Manchu Clan had handed over the Government to the betrayer of the Emperor. In times past men of the Censors memorialized the Emperor in protest against the evils of the times and killed themselves in evidence of their convictions. Now not only was there no voice raised, but, so far as the Government at Peking was concerned, it was not possible to state if any life of its mandarins or scholars was at stake. It would have been more in keeping with the social disorder of China to have had a carnival of assassinations. I had just made this observation to a fellow-journalist in a room in the Legation Quarter where we were sitting when a reporter burst through the door.

" Did you hear the bomb ? " said he.

" No ; what bomb ? "

" A bomb has just been thrown at Yuan Shih-k'ai while he was passing from the Palace to his residence. The chief of his bodyguard has been killed, with several horses, and altogether about thirty people wounded."

My sensations were somewhat like those of another occasion when the war opened between Japan and Russia and the first shells of the Japanese fleet fell in Port Arthur. The attempts upon the life of Yuan Shih-k'ai seemed to be the announcement that the Republic had come to Peking. I thought it all over slowly, took a field camera and went out to look over the scene. The police had rapidly cleared the streets for about a mile abreast the East Gate of the Imperial City and were searching the adjacent houses. A few foreigners were permitted to pass the spot where the bomb had exploded, and there was a wrecked hydrant and a dead horse. The Premier's carriage had instantly changed its route and passed on, arriving home before another horse fell dead. It escaped other assassins believed to have been posted at two or three places. Arrests of the assassins in a tea-shop opposite where the bomb fell followed in a few moments. The street was patrolled by an increased guard for twenty-four hours. An arm of the Republican bomb-throwers operating from Tientsin was said to have furnished the men for this deed—which men disappeared after the announcement that they had been tried and found guilty.

The fire struck at Cheng-tu in Szechuan on the borders of Tibet in September, and which blazed up at Wuchang in October and at Shanghai and Canton in November, had now flashed out in Peking.

MEETING OF YUAN SHIH-K'AI'S CABINET.

THE BOMB EXPLOSION.

To face p. 64.

CHAPTER VIII

WHEN SZECHUAN REVOLTED

THE bomb of the assassin seemed to shift the comparison from the soil of France to that of Russia. The causes of revolution, however, remain the same, regardless of the weapons employed. Comparison with France in the Revolution still holds good. It is hunger that always precedes revolt, and from the famine zone on the sea to the mountains of Tibet, China was hungry. And she was rebellious in all her hunger zone.

All that had happened in Peking was but a reflection of what had happened in Central China. The great events of the "Republic" had begun four months before. Their causes go back years. Just after the year 986 A.D. rebellion broke out in Szechuan, "due to the extreme poverty and misery of the people, aggravated by the unscrupulous rapacity of the local magistrates." It is not necessary to go back of the ninth century, nor even so far as the ninth century, to explain how the torch of twentieth-century rebellion was lighted for China in Szechuan.

In 1905, the Chinese believing that American capitalists had illegally transferred a concession for a great trunk-line railway from Canton to Hankow to the Belgians, caused its restoration to themselves, though at a costly money sacrifice, in the form of indemnity to the American concessionaires. They began what was called the "rights recovery" movement, by which China forced foreign concessionaires to return to her vast coal, iron, and oil lands in Shansi, rich copper mines in Anhuei, railway rights in Chekiang, and tin mines in Yunnan. The people thus put an end to the granting of railway and all other concessions to foreigners by their Central Government.

In 1909 the people discovered that foreign capital and enterprise were securing the same advantages through loans to the Central Government for the development of provincial resources, and that the National Government had evolved an enormous scheme for nationalizing railways whereby the profits of railways were lost to the people. The foreign money-lenders had banded together, and now the Central Government at Peking by a four-Power loan from British, French, German, and American financial syndicates, of £6,000,000 (to be increased to £10,000,000), in 1910 was to build railways in three directions out of Hankow. For nearly two years the people prevented the ratification of these plans. Then, January 1911, the Throne brought a distinguished Chinese "prince of industry," Sheng Hsuan-huai, from Shanghai to Peking, as Minister of Posts and Communications, to consummate its plans and policy. The £6,000,000 loan was concluded, and another of £10,000,000 to reform the currency, as well as two smaller loans.

One of these railways out of Hankow was to penetrate Szechuan. But Szechuan had already organized the Szechuan Railway Company to build this railway with Chinese capital. By 1911 the funds from the sale of shares by the Szechuan Railway Company had been embezzled. Left without either money or railway and threatened with being dispossessed by the National Government, the people reached a state of acute exasperation and formed an Anti-Foreign-Loan Society, called the "Tung Chi Huei" (Patriots' Society), to combat the Government.

The spread of the cause was shown in the latter part of August, when a strike of the schools throughout the province occurred. At Cheng-tu, the provincial Capital, where the movement was centred, a large meeting was called by this Society, and it became so lively that the members threw their teacups at the four taot'ais present representing the Provincial Government. The meeting passed a resolution to stop all public business as well as all payments of taxes until the dispute with the National Government was settled. The Cheng-tu shopmen began putting up the shutters of their shops, encouraged where there was any hesitation by entreaties from the crowds. It was at the time of the Moon festival, and any delinquent shopkeeper was first showered with moon-cakes, and if he resisted was subject to a battery of mud, then stones, and assaults upon his wares.

Soldiers were called out, and patrolled the City with fixed bayonets. Food rose in price, and the Anti-Foreign-Loan Society made collections to feed the poor, "so no excuse could exist for lawlessness." Only the rice-shops were allowed to open. By September 28 all the towns in

Central Szechuan had closed their shops in sympathy with the movement to boycott the railway loan.

A proclamation from the Viceroy Chao Er-feng at once forced the shops to open, but it also ended the passive resistance of the people. The Anti-Foreign-Loan Society was incensed by the appointment of the distinguished ex-Viceroy and scholar Tuan Fang, as Director-General of Railways, to take charge of railway matters. Seeing their popular rights being gradually overthrown, it began active resistance to the Provincial and National Governments.

A slip of paper was posted up over the City before which the people began burning candles and incense. It had three inscriptions. That on the right read : " The different policies are to be decided by public opinion." That on the left : " The Szechuan Railway is hereby permitted to be constructed by the people privately." The central inscription read : " The tablet for the spirit of His [late] Majesty, Kuang Hsu, the Virtuous Ancestor and Emperor of the great Ching Dynasty."

The people here and there in the country began smashing the tax offices (salt and likin), and the Viceroy, who was prepared for the disorder, executed nineteen looters in one place and a similar number in another.

" This speaks for itself," wrote an observer from that distant realm of 45,000,000 restless, rising people. " It proves what I wrote you before : that there is more in it than an organized resistance to the Peking Railway policy ; there is a deep-seated hatred of the scandalous ways the officials have been squeezing the people of late years.'

" The cartoons issued in the City I find are becoming slanderous," he continued ; " one or two depict the horrors of the Indians in India under the reign of the British. A bad one is out this morning—hawkers are selling it through the streets."

When the Anti-Foreign-Loan Society at Cheng-tu got ready to present its demands to the Viceroy and take possession of the Provincial Government, it distributed placards saying that the resident foreigners were in no way connected with the agitation. It sent speakers into the streets who took up prominent positions and repeated to the people : " Don't touch the foreigner or his property, or our cause is doomed."

Secret societies circulated the report that the Viceroy Chao Er-feng could not depend on his troops, as many of them were secretly members of the new movement ; that he was afraid to act. His sobriquet among the people was " The Executioner." He was something of a despot. Both sides knew that it was a game of heads.

In the forenoon of September 6, 1911, " The Executioner " got documentary evidence of the secret plans of the Anti-Foreign-Loan Society through a student who visited his yamen (official headquarters) in the guise of a seer, and secured audience with the Viceroy under the plea that in a dream he had witnessed the destruction of the provincial Capital, which would occur on the sixteenth of the moon—September 8. When presented he exhibited some antics in imitation of familiar Chinese demoniac performances, during which he handed the Viceroy a copy of the Book of Preparation showing the ultimate plans and ends of the Anti-Foreign-Loan Society. It was a scene suggesting Rome under the Cæsars and the soothsayer's " Beware the Ides of March," or of the Egypt of the Pharaohs.

The Viceroy, through the senior Consul-General, the British, sent word at once to all foreigners to collect without delay at the Canadian Mission Hospital in Tzu-shen-tzu Street. The first foreigners to assemble arrived at 5 o'clock in the afternoon, and at 11 o'clock all but two or three families had been gathered in. The Ko-lao-huei, or Elder Brother Society, an ancient secret organization, spread the rumour that " The Executioner " was going to attack the Anti-Foreign-Loan Society at midnight. But he did not act until the forenoon of September 7. Then he telephoned to the leaders that he had just received an important communication from Peking about which he wished to consult them privately, and he invited them to his yamen.

Pu Tien-chun, Lo Lun, Teng Hsiao-k'o, Chang Lan, and Wang Min-hsin, the leaders, responded. The Viceroy received them in person and served them with tea. A meeting of the Directors of the Railway Bureau and the Anti-Foreign-Loan Society, in fact a revolutionary council, was cordonned with soldiers. Two of the important leaders of the anti-Government movement, Yen Chia and Hu Yung, who had refused the Viceroy's invitation, were seized in their houses. Under pretext of fire in the City, " kindled by ' The Executioner's ' orders " said a secret society member, troops closed the City gates and took possession of the streets. For weeks past three or four vernacular newspapers had been fomenting the agitation, and their editors were now seized at their newspaper office doors, and the doors shut and sealed.

" Why have you compelled the merchants to close their shops, and persuaded the people to refuse to pay their taxes ? " said " The Executioner " to his guests. " I have always treated you kindly, why are you so unkind to me and to your country ? I have reported your conduct to our Emperor. Do you understand the position you have placed yourselves in ? To-day I have prepared dinner for you——"

At this " The Executioner " called out to his retainers : " Sung K'eh " (Escort the guests). Soldiers guarding the audience hall stepped in, seized the leaders before they could resist and bound them. They were searched. Documents and papers were brought from the Railway Bureau offices and from the Anti-Foreign-Loan Society (Patriotic Society) headquarters. Ten agitators and leaders were arrested and imprisoned.

While this action was going on the Viceroy's agents posted a proclamation in the streets announcing Lo Lun's arrest and ordering the tablets and staging erected by the Anti-Foreign-Loan Society to be taken down. Cavalry galloped through the streets, taking the people by surprise and stampeding them. The soldiers pulled down and destroyed the brightly ornamented platform erected in the market-place in the centre of the City and threw down the shrines that had been set up for the worship of the martyr Emperor Kuang Hsu, with whose name and wrongs was associated the title of the people to the building of their railways.

When it became known that the leaders of the Anti-Foreign-Loan Society were imprisoned in the yamen, a crowd of students rushed to demand their release. Men, women, and children appeared from every quarter, bearing lighted incense in one hand, and the desecrated yellow paper spirit tablets of the Emperor from their broken shrines in the other, and pressed toward the yamen. Sympathizers arrived from outside the City, and joining the throng in Great East Street — the main artery of the City—turned into the side streets, and in a mob of several thousand strong surged clamorously about the Viceroy's gate. As they swayed hither and thither they cried :

" Give us back our Lo Lun—give us back our Lo Lun ! " meaning their leader.

The soldiers exhorted the people to disperse.

The people answered demanding their leader.

"K'ai p'ao" (Open fire)—a volley went into the air. Screams—howls— Men fell or fled in all directions, or were trampled down. Thirteen persons were instantly killed and more than that number wounded. Men were wounded throughout the City, and at dark crowds still surged in the streets.

Rain commenced at nightfall and continued throughout the 8th. The secret societies who controlled the militia joined their fraternity members of the surrounding region and concentrated outside the East and South Gates, where they engaged the Viceroy's troops.

On Sept. 9 military law began, when the City was closed to all except those having passes. The public granaries were thrown open, so that the people might have rice. On Sept. 10 most of the merchants opened their shops.

166 foreigners, exclusive of Japanese—the ever present "Allies"—were shut up in Cheng-tu. 124 of these were in refuge at the Canadian Methodist Mission. Hear the words of one of these writing on September 10:

"Reports of the coming of the militia threw the City into a panic. Children screamed in the streets, and older voices cried: 'They are coming, they are coming!' During church services someone shouted through the window, 'Get the women and children out the back way. If they go into the street they will be shot.' Houses were suddenly closed and all gates bolted. Then the soldiers passed the word that it was a false alarm. But it was a 'Sunday closing.'

"Three of our colony who went out of the City just before the gates closed to collect their belongings from their houses on the University site caused uneasiness by their failure to return. On account of engagements between the militia and the yamen troops in the vicinity of their houses, they were prevented from returning until 9 o'clock on the night of the 9th, when they were escorted back by soldiers. Others had come in at 2 o'clock in the morning under escort. The Viceroy has requested foreigners not to leave the City but remain under his protection and refrain from going into the streets as much as possible. There is fighting all around Cheng-tu, the roads are blocked for days, and the wires are all cut.

"The troops are trying to reopen the road to Chung-

REVOLUTIONIST VOLUNTEERS.

ARTILLERY LEAVING HSIAO-CHIA CHIANG.

To face p. 70.

king. They report communications possible between Cheng-tu and Tze-chow. 200 rebels and four soldiers are reported killed at one place ; 100 rebels killed and two soldiers wounded at another. Seventeen soldiers have been massacred at a feast through trickery, only three of their party escaping."

The British Consul-General writes to his colleague at Chungking :

" Can you get messages up to Cheng-tu, in particular the telegrams which must have accumulated at Tze-chow? The fu-t'ou [driver] of a baggage train might be one way—a single messenger would be stopped by insurgents and searched. Perhaps a fairly large box addressed to me in English and Chinese might get through, just as these cases to-day have got through, where a single letter would be seized. Pack the telegrams in an empty tin surrounded by unopened tins of any kind of stores, groceries, etc., for which, of course, I will pay."

To the Viceroy Chao Er-feng he wrote asking that in view of the now apparently peaceful state of the City some of the foreign residents might return to their homes about the Capital, and the Viceroy replied :

" In all directions just now there are large bands of marauders, some thousands strong, whose object is to rush the City. Precautions cannot be laid aside, and gates have been closed. Inside the City, moreover, tranquillity is not yet restored, and it is impossible not to exercise more than ordinary care.

" The return to their old abodes of the gentlemen of your honourable country and of all other foreigners should be postponed for a time. When all is settled inside the City and out, I will again write, and action can be taken."

Shadow and sunlight in Cheng-tu is mingled in the voice of the missionary refugee at this repulse :

" September 15. Raining steadily all day," he writes. " We had a concert to-night to keep up the good spirits of the colony." And again : " The Viceroy seems to be getting matters pretty well in hand. Everything points to an early settlement of the trouble."

So closes the account of the bystander in the Capital of Szechuan. Exit the bystander : Chao Er-feng, the Viceroy, is talking with the Throne.

CHAPTER IX

WHEN SZECHUAN FELL

CHAO ER-FENG, the Viceroy, has already announced to the Throne the conspiracy, and recapitulated all the events of the railway dispute and uprising of the Anti-Foreign-Loan Society, and he says :

" After the attack perpetrated by the rebellious people upon the Viceregal yamen, September 7, several thousand volunteers of the people of Ta-mien-pu and Niu-shi-kao concentrated just outside the City on the same evening. On subsequent days there arrived from each of the ten and more districts around Cheng-tu several divisions of the people's volunteers, every division numbering from a few thousand to ten thousand men. They pillaged, burnt, and committed all kinds of atrocities along their routes, causing the people near by to flee. The army and the guardsmen of the defence force were at once ordered to meet and punish them. But these volunteer corps, relying upon their numerical strength, surrounded the City on all sides and opened fire with their guns, wounding and killing some soldiers. When they were fired on in return, they dared to hold out in defiance until death. It was not until they were utterly unable to make resistance that they retreated.

" Later there was a great mass meeting of several thousand rebellious volunteers on the crest of the Lung-chuan Hill, about fifty li [sixteen odd miles] in distance from the capital City, where the strategical points were all guarded and guns were put up in position, declaring that they would march on and attack the capital City.

" When Government troops proceeded there to punish them, the rebels fired upon them. The soldiers resolutely assaulted their positions under cover of night, and occupied the hilltops, capturing several tens of big guns, innumerable small firearms, cartridges, swords and other weapons. The rebels escaped down the hill in disorder. At the same time, the rebels in the West direction, in Si-pu, Chung-ho, and other places, had also been repulsed by the troops.

" A branch party of the rebels then surrounded and bombarded the City of the Shuang-liu district, burnt its barriers, streets and temples, and the siege was only raised after confronting them a whole day and night with the troops. They flocked to Si-pu and Chung-ho, and then to Tang-chia-tzu, at each of which places the rebels were successively defeated and beat a retreat.

" From September 8 continuous battles raged for seven days, in which a great number of rebels were captured or killed, and over two thousand swords, lances, standards, and banners secured. The telegraph lines had been cut in all directions ; dispatch of documents by couriers had been prevented, and in some cases the bearers were searched and killed. At present alarming reports from different places are still pouring in. It is intended that as soon as the repairs to the City shall have been concluded, punitive expeditions are to be sent after the rebels. Those ignorant people who have been forced to join the rebellion, when captured and brought in now and then, have been enlightened as to their foolishness and liberated."

The Viceroy's account accepted by the Throne seemed to agree with the observation of the bystander as to an early settlement of the trouble.

Herewith the Throne :

" The procedure of the Viceroy and his forces has been tolerably well suited to the occasion. Judging from the previous distribution by the rebels of their military orders by means of wooden sticks, their rebellious conspiracy is amply proved to have been concocted not in a day. When their treacherous plot was discovered, their rising was echoed and supported in all four quarters. In a word, the peace of the populace was destroyed. Truly they must have been deliberately intentional in causing this revolution. Such disloyal and treasonable manifestations have been apparent to all eyes. Their depredations should not be permitted at all, but speedy means for their extirpation should be adopted.

" As the Hupeh Army has already reached Szechuan, and reinforcements from Kueichou Province have started on their march, Chao Er-feng is hereby again commanded strictly to direct all the forces to punish or disperse the rebels in their several directions, permitting no growth of the rebel strength day by day. He shall still exercise a discrimination between the good and the bad, and administer punishment or consolation accordingly. All those foolish people, compelled by the rebels to join them, are hereby pardoned. Let him issue a proclamation throughout his province and devise proper means for the future welfare of the people, keeping it in view to spare as many as possible, so as to dissipate suspicions and alarms.

" He shall still continue to report to Us by telegraph what he has done from time to time.

In our Chinese Versailles, the Manchus, who had for a long time been looking for worse things than had until now happened in Szechuan or elsewhere in the Empire, were already started on that course of belated measures that to our critics placed them parallel to the house of Bourbon. The *Wisdom Opener* of Cheng-tu, the leading revolutionary newspaper there, among its rebellious articles preceding the outbreak, published successive cartoons showing Sheng Hsuan-huai dragged forth to execution from his burning house. The Anti-Foreign-Loan Society and the Railway Bureau sent such cogent telegrams to their fellow-provincials in Peking that a grand meeting was called of Szechuanese at the Peking Szechuan Guild. As a result a joint petition by Szechuan officials denouncing Sheng and demanding his dismissal was handed to the Board of Censors, and the authors of the petition threatened to resign their positions *en bloc* if it was not acted upon. The Censors petitioned the Throne to have the case of the railway agitation by the Szechuanese thoroughly investigated in order " to maintain the normal position and to suppress the disturbing element." September 14, the Throne appointed Tsen Chun-hsuan, a former popular Viceroy of Szechuan, to return there and take charge of all military matters, and an even more celebrated man, Tuan Fang, to proceed at once to Szechuan to arrange all railway difficulties. Both were instructed to use the utmost clemency in dealing with the people. Chao Er-feng was to continue the administration of civil and general affairs. The two civil dignitaries looked for the first means to ingratiate themselves with the people as measures of safety for themselves in the desperate region to which they were going.

Tsen began his work with a memorial to the Throne asking that, as the State ownership of railways was unalterable, the losses of the people through the Railway Bureau and the embezzlement of the proceeds of the Szechuan Railway Company's shares should be paid by the Board of Posts and Communications. He requested also that Viceroy Chao Er-feng should be ordered to release the people's leaders.

Tuan Fang began his work by issuing a proclamation to the people of Szechuan, saying: "I have been appointed to come to Szechuan solely to make known the benevolent intentions of the Throne. The troops I am bringing with me are simply for the purpose of suppressing brigands. The object of the Throne in taking over the railways is that of their great importance to the State, and it is taking over the railway in Szechuan because that railway is especially difficult to construct. It costs from 15,000 to 16,000 taels a li [say £2000 to £2600—gold value—per mile] and will take from ten to twenty years to finish. The construction of this road is a burden greater than the Szechuan people can bear and is likely to reduce them to poverty before they can get through with it. As a special favour the Government takes over this burden from the Szechuan people and puts a stop to enforced subscriptions, proposing to provide all the necessary funds itself. The people of Szechuan ought to have been delighted and grateful for this favour, but instead of that busybodies have been declaring that the Government is robbing them, and that in connection with the loans they will lose their independence. They do not know that the Imperial Railways of North China and the Peking-Hankow Railway were built with foreign money and that they have been extremely lucrative enterprises to the country without its losing a grain of its independence. Further, the new loan agreements are much more favourable to China than those under which the previous railways were built. These things they did not inquire into, but proceeded to raise disturbances, shutting the schools, closing down the markets, refusing to pay taxes, and in every way acting like rebels. They did not think that the real rebels would use this opportunity given them to plunder the people, to kill your sons and daughters, to burn and destroy till you all had tasted the miseries of insurrection. For brigands of that sort the Throne has no mercy, and it has sent me to deal with them alone. Now the books [of Preparations] containing the names of those who formed societies are to be burned. Although the railway belongs to the State, it will still be the people's railway. New shares will be given by the Government for the old. Let there be no more trouble, so that the railway can be built, the Throne gratified, myself gratified, and all the people of Szechuan will reap the benefit."

These telegrams between the Throne and its High Commissioners to Szechuan, and the Viceroy there, show some of the methods of the revolutionists, but especially the most accomplished methods of procedure of the so-called astute and wily "Chinese" officials as well as the naïveté and gaucherie of the Government at Peking. But in this case these methods were only leading to a terrible tragedy.

Tuan Fang continued up the Yangtse River into Szechuan, from where he sent to the Throne the last words it ever received from him:

"The market strikers and school strikers in Szechuan neither killed officials nor officers, nor robbed the barns nor treasuries. They were emphatically not rebels bent upon creating disturbances.

"The fire [in Cheng-tu] September 7 broke out accidentally from a private house in South Gold-Beating Street. Owing to the arrest of Pu Tien-chun, Lo Lun, and others, the people went to the yamen to request their release. Commander Tien Cheng-kuei shot the people down, unordered, killing several tens of merchants in the street. The people in the neighbourhood heard this, and presented themselves before the City with heads covered with white cloth to pray for mercy for their fellow-people. Several tens of them were also shot dead. Now their feelings were quite aroused.

"As to the distribution of their book named 'Self-Preservation of Merchants' Rights,' no characters meaning *independence* appear therein, and neither the chops [seals] of the Tung Chi Huei [Patriots' Society] nor those representing the scholars' meeting are attached thereto. On the contrary, sentences such as 'Millions of generations for the Imperial Throne' are included in its contents. But this book was not penned by Pu Tien-chun, Lo Lun, or by others of the gentry. The spiritual tablet and the blood-written letters which have been stopped were not the work of the Szechuan scholars, but were forged by rebels.

"Chou Shan-pei, Wang Tan, Jao Feng-tsao, and other officials, owing the gentry a grudge on account of the Provincial Assembly's having impeached them, had purposely made out a hideous case to harm them.

"The question of not paying taxes and dues was proposed by a united meeting of the officials and the gentry, but it was only a proposal to defer these payments, and to discharge the land taxes by the interest due [on the railway capital]. The shareholders were not in reality to collect or receive taxes and dues of the Government."

Next the Throne's last reply to Tuan Fang :

" Since the present incident in Szechuan resulting in expensive devastation has been investigated and found by Tuan Fang to have originated in differences between the officials and the people, the territorial officials who mismanaged their duties should certainly be punished in proportion to their deserts. Wang Jen-yen, formerly officiating as Viceroy of Szechuan, and Chao Er-feng, the present Acting Viceroy of Szechuan, cannot be exonerated from blame; for, holding the government of a province, they have failed effectively to control the situation at the outset and afterwards to suppress the trouble. Wang Jen-sen and Chao Er-feng are both handed to the Cabinet for the consideration of a penalty. Tien Cheng-kuei, Acting Commander of the Sung-pan Military Circuit, Director of the General Staff, and an expectant Taot'ai, having acted most recklessly in greedy hope of achieving success, and having killed common people without authority, is hereby cashiered instantly, and ordered to be deported to the hinterland of Tibet and to render some signal service in expiation of his crime. Chou Shan-pei, industrial Taot'ai acting as Commissioner of Justice, has been frivolous and fond of creating trouble, inconsistent in method and treacherous in intent ; Wang Tan and Wang Tze, expectant taot'ais, engendered ill-feeling among the gentry and merchants, and made their names notoriously odious : these three are hereby cashiered instantly. Jao Feng-tsao, expectant Taot'ai, young and inexperienced, has been adversely criticized by the public; he is hereby degraded to the rank of Sub-Prefect, to give him a warning."

Thus reversing the action of the Viceroy Chao Er-feng, the Throne therein released Lo Lun, Pu Tien-chung, and the seven other leaders, and these were taken under the care of the Tartar General at Cheng-tu to prevent their being killed by Viceroy Chao, " The Executioner," in a fit of bloodthirstiness.

Tuan Fang deserves well of foreigners. He had saved many from massacre in Shensi Province in the Boxer year. He was an enlightened progressive man who had contributed to the future provisional Republican capital, Nanking, all that had been done to make it modern and progressive. He had suffered undeserved ill at the hands of the young men, Prince Chun and his brothers in charge of the Throne, and for this Throne he was about to lay down his life.

The 31st and 32nd Regiments of the Hupeh Army were assigned to him at Wuchang. On Sept. 20, 1911, he was at Shashi in Hupeh with a bodyguard of 250 men of the 32nd Regiment—Manchus. On Oct. 5 he reached Wanhsien, Szechuan, and on Oct. 9 he requested more soldiers, telegraphing to Wuchang to have the Szechuan relief force (of reinforcements) march speedily. His request was rejected by the Cabinet in Peking. He reached Chungking October 18, and getting no reply from Wuchang he proceeded with his two regiments by the Cheng-tu highway, along the telegraph line, where he might expect to keep in communication with Cheng-tu. Tsen Chun-hsuan had remained at Wuchang, where great events had taken place. Wuchang had revolted, and Tuan Fang was cut off from telegraphic communication with Peking.

Tuan Fang's soldiers were revolutionary, like their comrades at Wuchang. They were in contact with the Anti-Foreign-Loan Society—the Tung Chi Huei—by the time they had reached Chungking. Here they began to desert to those whom Tuan Fang had called "busybodies" and to emulate those whom he had called the "real rebels," "the brigands," who used the present opportunity to plunder, kill, burn and destroy," and "spread the miseries of insurrection."

As he proceeded the soldiers learned that Wuchang had fallen and that Hankow had been burned, and his force was still further diminished. He stopped at Yungchuan on the Cheng-tu road nearly two weeks before moving on to Tze-chow, his last stop. Those of his men who had remained took umbrage at having been kept in ignorance of the revolt at Wuchang, their home. In the meantime the Viceroy of Szechuan accepted terms from the people's movement, and Cheng-tu fell.

On Nov. 26 the soldiers heard of this, and Tuan Fang was now thoroughly intimidated. He was surrounded. He sought to make terms with his men, and preliminary to this gave them a feast, killing oxen, sheep and pigs, and inviting some of the local gentry. His younger brother, who had accompanied him, explained to the soldiers that their mission was ended, over half of China had revolted against the Manchu rule and that it was impossible for them to go any farther. Tuan Fang wished to return and pay his respects to the Emperor, and if they would give him a safe escort to Sianfu in Shensi he would pay them 40,000 taels (gold value £5600).

The men of the two regiments quarrelled over the offer. Those of the 32nd considered themselves as particularly the bodyguard of Tuan Fang and thought the money belonged to them. They tried to get Tuan Fang to go back the way they had come, as that would take them home, but he refused because the cities on the Yangtse had gone over to the revolutionists.

The men of the 32nd declined to give up their claim to Tuan Fang's money. Those of the 31st demanded that the whole amount should be paid down, and threatened to shoot the commander of the men of the 32nd if he did not force Tuan Fang to pay all before starting. Tuan Fang had to tell them that he had but 20,000 taels with him, but would pay the balance at Sianfu. The soldiers refused to parley, and dispersed. That night they plotted to murder Tuan Fang.

By morning all his officers and men had withdrawn from about him except four of his old bodyguard. The Manchus had fled. He implored a foreign-educated medical student who had followed him from Chungking, and who brought back the story, to think of some plan whereby he might escape from the region. The man advised him to go quietly on a boat down the river, but Tuan Fang thought the only way lay to the North, and asked the medical student to exchange chairs with him, so that he might go Northward in disguise.

The medical student consented, and November 27, at 2 o'clock in the afternoon, Tuan Fang in the medical student's chair, with his brother, accompanied by the four faithful bodyguards, started off. The party was apprehended by the soldiers of the 31st Regiment, who compelled it to return. They plundered the Envoy's baggage. He himself was taken out of his chair and compelled to walk between two soldiers to a temple near by. On entering the temple court, one of his ears was struck off by a sword-blow from behind. He turned and asked his assailants :

" Do you want to kill me ? "

" Kill, kill ! " they yelled, and ordered him to kneel. He refused to do so, and his two captors with several blows decapitated him standing.

As Tuan Fang was being led to the temple his brother appealed to the commander of the 32nd Regiment to save Tuan Fang's life. The commander pushed the brother away, and left him to be decapitated in the outer court.

The head of Tuan Fang was packed in a tin, covered with lime, by the Hupeh soldiers, who then started back to Wuchang with it.

In December Tuan Fang's personal effects, after the soldiers who looted them had passed on, were for sale in Chungking. They included his foreign decorations. "Photographs of his head with his two executioners standing beside it could be purchased in the street." The remaining soldiers of the 31st and 32nd Hupeh Regiments, about 1500 men in all, reached Ichang, December 28, and passed into their own province, where they soon after delivered the head of Tuan Fang to President Li Yuan-hung at Wuchang.

After making terms with the rebels, Chao Er-feng sent a number of letters to Tibet, where he had been Warden of the Tibetan Marches, to call out his old soldiers of the Lhassa campaign of 1908. On December 21 a messenger was caught bearing one of these letters, according to which fires were to be started at the North, East, and West Gates of Cheng-tu, and during the excitement Chao Er-feng and his soldiers, who were virtual prisoners in Cheng-tu under control of the Revolutionary Government, were to "kill" their way out of the City by the south and escape to Hsuang-liu-hsien, thirty miles away. "From here, should the place be untenable, they were to retreat to Tibet and there set up a self-government." The letter fell into the hands of the Military Government of Szechuan, which at daylight on December 22 sent a battalion of soldiers to surround the Viceroy's yamen. A captain of the old-style provincial troops arrested Chao Er-feng. One of the ex-Viceroy's female servants fired a revolver at the captain, missing him. The captain replied with deadly effect.

The soldiers took "the grim old Warden of the Marches" to the military headquarters, where they tried him before Lo Lun, his first enemy, and the soldiers. When asked to explain the Tibetan letters, he denied them. The soldiers were asked for their verdict, and they unanimously condemned him to death. He was executed and his head carried through the streets at the front of a procession led by the Military Governor Yuin. From an upper story five men fired at the Governor, killing his horse, but leaving him unharmed to proceed. Chao Er-feng's head was then put up on a pole with this inscription: "In life you loved to look down on men; even in death you have your desire.'"

Nine days later, Chao Er-feng's captain of the yamen guard, Tien Cheng-kuei, who had given the order to fire on the people who demanded the release of their leaders in September, met a similar fate in Chungking, where his head was carried through the streets on a pole. "He was an elderly man over sixty," writes a correspondent, "his hair and eyebrows being shot with grey. Foreigners should give him but scanty sympathy, as he assisted Yu Hsien, Governor of Shansi, in the massacre of missionaries in 1900."

The missionary observation from Cheng-tu that "the Viceroy seems to be getting matters pretty well in hand" was as good a guess as any heard elsewhere. The Throne made no better: Szechuan had seceded, and the Chinese Versailles—the Forbidden City—beheld the Rebellion.

CHAPTER X

WHEN WUCHANG SECEDED

PEKING, like Versailles, heard the cry of the people from afar, but did not know that it was the oncoming Rebellion.

News of fighting in Szechuan died down because the telegraph wires were cut. Then in the revolutionary stillness of the afternoon of October 9, 1911, a bomb exploded prematurely in a Chinese house outside a German butchery in the Russian Concession at Hankow. The Russian authorities were notified, and gave orders to watch the place and arrest suspicious persons. After a while, a man appeared and came out to ask what had happened. He was arrested. Later another, who could no longer withstand the gnaw of anxiety, came out and did the same. He also was arrested. The place was then searched. A revolutionary centre was discovered, the hands of the revolutionists forced, and the Republican Rebellion began.

There were two men in the house. They made an effort to destroy it by pouring kerosene oil on the floor and setting this on fire, but failed. The place contained a dynamite plant, flags, revolutionary badges, numbered in accordance with the revolutionary organization, a map showing the plan of attack on Wuchang, some false queues, and the Seal of the Republic.

The Concession police, through the Chinese deputy of the Mixed Court in the Foreign Concessions, handed them over to the Viceroy Jui Cheng, across the river at Wuchang. There were six imprints of the Seal of the Republic in the building that had been the workshop of the revolutionists. Handing these imprints, which were all on one sheet, to a foreign friend, the Mixed Court Deputy said : " Be careful what you do with this, put it in a safe place and let no one see it."

He then fled.

The evening was spent by the Viceroy Jui Cheng at Wuchang, in consultation with the police and his Manchu

Military Adviser and head of the Hupeh Army, General Chang Piao. After the closing of the City gates, in the night, he brought a sergeant of the 13th Regiment suspected of being a revolutionist to his yamen and raided the rendezvous of the students and reformers, arresting twenty-eight conspirators, soldiers and civilians. There was an attempt to assault the Viceroy's yamen. Three of the arrested conspirators were beheaded outside the yamen at daylight. The City gates under strong guard were reopened only at 9.30 a.m., when all passes were examined.

An examination of the remaining revolutionist captives took place. One of those from the Hankow Concession was a member of a regiment of gendarmes. He was asked why he had joined the revolutionaries :

" Because the Manchus have usurped the rights of the Han people, and practised extortion on them."

" What do you expect to do ? "

" Assassinate Tieh Chung, the Adviser of the Hupeh Provincial Division, and Viceroy Jui Cheng."

Further questions he refused to answer, saying indignantly that the Manchu Government was unfit to ask questions of him. His decapitation followed instantly, followed by that of his companion—followed by four other decapitations . . . decapitations too numerous to mention.

Eight soldiers caught in the act of stealing a field-gun from artillery park, shot. All leads up to the memorable night of October 10. The Torch, the first weapon of the conspirator, revolutionist, and the downtrodden masses when they can bear no more, was brought forth. Night calls for flames. 7.45 p.m., three fires start in the ancient provincial Capital in the vicinity of the Eastern Camp. Three hundred Hupeh troops from the suburbs have broken down the gates and have started out to take the City. They have got into touch with the gunboat *Kien Wei* in the river. Rifle firing. The 8th Regiment mutinies and fights with the loyalist remainder. It wins, and is joined by the 15th Regiment. They attack the magazines and win. 8.50, fire in the artillery barracks. The ammunition has exploded and starts a conflagration. Great explosion of firecrackers mixed with crack of cartridges.

9 p.m., soldiers appear on all the Wuchang ramparts, passing backward and forward against a background of flame, and foreign inquisitors from the Hankow Concessions seeking the Wuchang shore behold the scene and gaze

11 p.m. there is another conflagration. General Chang Piao is at the head of his Imperial troops resisting the conquest of the City. He cannot protect the Viceroy's yamen, and the Viceroy has fled with his family. The Viceroy's yamen is burnt, together with that of the Provincial Treasurer. These Imperialist officials warn the foreigners in the Hankow Concessions of revolt in a note to the British Consul-General, and say that any attack upon them must be met by themselves, as the Government can give no help. Viceroy Jui Cheng—he has received Tuan Fang's telegraphic request to send the Szechuan relief force speedily—is in consultation with General Li Yuan-hung, late Colonel of the 21st Regiment, his Chinese Military Adviser, but does not know he is a General. He tells him :

"I have been elected Generalissimo," said General Li, "in spite of my own protests. I advise you to choose either of two courses, death or escape. Should you elect to die, you had better be quick, if you wish to avoid ignominious treatment. Should you wish to live, I will personally escort you to a place of safety."

At nightfall, in consideration of their official associations and acquaintance, the Viceroy Jui Cheng was escorted by General Li to a launch at the water's edge, where with the old Yangtse fleet of nine war-junks he crossed to the Russian Concession, Hankow.

With careful arrangement, General Li Yuan-hung's regiment or division seems to have been distributed with reference to an outbreak. Even the nucleus of the division at his own headquarters was away when he arrived back from his mission of saving his superior Viceroy Jui Cheng as in duty bound, because of "jen hsin"—human feelings—"Confucian ethics," or some good and ancient reason of military ethics, by escorting him to the river and seeing him well on his way to safety. "When the revolutionary army had driven Jui Cheng out of the City," said General Li Yuan-hung, "they came to my camp, surrounded it and made a search. I having dressed myself in civilian clothes, hid myself in a rear room, where I was discovered and captured and reprimanded for want of patriotism. All around me were pistols and guns, my head and body would certainly have parted company upon the least attempt at resistance on my part ; therefore I had to consent to their demands [to be their leader] as a means of policy."

One must know the Chinese to imagine the revolutionary scene the night of October 10, the men of the 21st Regiment working out their destiny with their under-officers and setting about their work of uprising, taking discipline in their own hands, leaving their quarters, bent on their work, oblivious of their leader, who, alike oblivious of them, was intently set on threading the maze of streets to get to the Viceroy's yamen or his place of hiding, working out a secret exit through tangled passages, and, as it were, making his way toward the river with his exalted charge. Neither Jui Cheng nor Li Yuan-hung broke the silence as to what were their words of parting, but Li Yuan-hung has left upon the tablets of history his statement of their last interview. I can see him as, after warning his superior to flee, he watches the Manchus in the person of their Viceroy Jui Cheng, and Old China, typified by the war-junk fleet—its Ship of State—slip away into Oblivion. It is as if one stood on the shores of Palestine, this October night 1911, and saw proud Tyre and Sidon slip into the sea.

As he turns away he faces the New China and the Republic. The Old has put off on the tide. Returning to his quarters, he divests himself of the uniform of the Empire, of loyalty to the Manchus, and puts on the clothes of a *citizen*. All the proprieties have been observed. Now he is searched for—it is all as in a theatre. Who can doubt that it has been so staged? He is neither on the one side nor the other. He can no longer be accused of being an Imperialist. He is a citizen—he has no superiors, no inferiors. He can give no orders, and having no inferiors, his late subordinates "reprimand" him for want of "patriotism." He is a helpless and unworthy Son of Han, surrounded by pistols and determination. They command him to put on the uniform of their leadership. He pleads his unworthiness, his humble origin, his lack of all talent, his meanness, wretchedness, inferiority wholesale and utter. But in the end he must "consent to their demand as a means of policy." It is a fine game. There is no Orient. It is more French than France.

General Li Yuan-hung to the People, before escorting Jui Cheng to safety:

"Eighth moon, 4609th year of the Wuchang Dynasty: I, the Hupeh General of the People's Army, am to overthrow the Manchu Government, and am here to revive the rights of the Han people. Let all remain orderly and obedient to military law.

"Those who conceal any Government officials will be beheaded.

"Those who inflict injuries on foreigners will be beheaded.

"Those who treat merchants unfairly will be beheaded.

"Those who interfere with commerce will be beheaded.

"Those who indulge in wanton slaughter, burning, or adultery will be beheaded.

"Those who fight against the volunteers will be beheaded.

"Those who attempt to close the shops will be beheaded.

REWARDS

"Those who supply the troops with foodstuffs will be rewarded.

"Those who afford protection to the Foreign Concessions will be highly rewarded.

"Those who guard the churches will be highly rewarded.

"Those who lead the people to submission are to be highly rewarded.

"Those who encourage the country-people to join the revolution will be rewarded.

"Those who give information as to the movements of the enemy will be rewarded.

"Those who maintain the prosperity of commerce will be rewarded."

It is the night of the 10th. While the fighting goes on from the north-west across to the south-east of the City, the north is quiet except for a few shots. Three soldiers with white bands of revolution on their arms appear and tell foreigners to leave the City, as "the revolutionists are after the Viceroy." "Kang Yu-wei is on the river," they said. "There is no danger for foreigners, but it would be better to go. We mean you no harm and will protect you, but if you are wounded by a stray bullet do not blame us."

"Shai li"—*union is strength*—comes from a side street. It is the password. The soldiers move on. From the direction which they have taken come three successive rifle-shots. At dawn a dead man lay close to where the foreigners had stood in the night—with three other dead men farther away.

It is the morning of the 11th: the writers of Republican proclamations in the name of the leader of the rebellion have done their work. American student Chinese and other student reformers have done their work, and now they see it stamped with the new Seal and spread upon the walls of Wuchang, selected to be their Capital. It is admirable work. It shines in the daylight and starts on its conquest of the languages and the newspapers and books of the world—as the spark struck out by the hoof of Paul Revere's horse started its conquest of the hearts of downtrodden nations.

The gates are reported closed, and men are lowering people over the wall by a rope at 4000 cash each (20 cents). The mob in seeking descent is fired on by the guns on Serpent Hill. The revolutionists are shooting at sight all soldiers not wearing the white brassard on the arm. Their passwords are "Kung chi" or "Chi ho"—*attack* and *co-operation*. Three fingers held up is a sign of the revolutionists, and means *foreigners*, *merchants*, and *common people* are not to be injured. Jui Cheng has gone from launch to gunboat and is on the *Tsao Kiang*, with his family housed on a launch made fast alongside. He is hailed by a foreign acquaintance, who asks what expectation there is of crushing the revolt, and gets the reply, None—it is hopeless. He is not in disguise, but his movements are secret.

The war-junks lie under the bund at Hankow; they take to the wind at times, but render no aid to the Imperialists, who are running the gauntlet of the revolutionaries to get out to the river and aboard sampans. Three or four hundred reach the foreshore near the Hanyang Gate of Wuchang, and commandeer launches found there, firing over their heads to intimidate the boatmen. The revolutionists on the top of the City wall watch them with amazement, and forget to fire upon them, until all are off but a single sampan, when they pour a hail of bullets upon the waters around.

An officer of rank, begrimed and weary, gets away on a launch and reaches the Hanyang shore, only to be overhauled before landing by a foreign reporter who asks:

"Speak English?"

Answer: "Speak German?"

" No."

" Parlez-vous Français? Do you speak Chinese?" he fired, as though he were working a machine-gun—greatly puzzling the reporter. But with a working use of several languages he chose Chinese and said he had been fighting a whole day and night and was driven out by the revolutionists, who now had possession of Wuchang. Not more than one-fourth of the troops had proved loyal.

General Chang Piao falls back before the revolutionists and withdraws to Hankow. The Chinese cruiser *Ch'u-yu* and two torpedo-boats fire upon Wuchang to cover his retreat, while his troops fight their way back with their small-arms. They do not know where to go—they go to Hanyang and Hankow because these are sister-cities.

The revolutionist artillery at Wuchang replies. Crossing under shells now falling in the river, Nelson T. Johnson, the American Vice-Consul, attempts to visit the missionaries in Wuchang, but fails. A council of war takes place on the *Ch'u-yu* with Viceroy Jui Cheng, General Chang Piao, the Hupeh Provincial Treasurer and Hupeh Provincial Judge, and the Senior Chinese Naval Commander in the river, present. Lu Yuan-tung, whoever he may be, is the reported leader of the revolution. Wuchang is lost. Fires continue, and there is a great exodus to the country, disorder and looting. The revolutionary troops are slaughtering the Manchus left in Wuchang. Human report numbers those for the shambles at 800—men, women, and children.

There are rumours of the death of the Viceroy—self-poisoned by taking opium or gold-leaf, or he has been murdered. They are a wall-loving people; every man's mediæval house his own fortress. They take refuge behind bolted doors and barricades, where they are out of sight, and where they cower at the sounds that reach them over the walls and roofs of their houses. They are a rabbit-footed people shod in cotton, scampering noiselessly to cover in a whiff of bullets. A Manchu soldier in khaki plunges into the street from a side alley as though discharged from a catapult. Startled onlookers take alarm and bolt into their houses or any hiding-place. Two revolutionaries with unslung rifles pursue and take the wrong turning. Several shots are heard.

Then come reassurances of the revolutionary soldiers, and men stand awed by the passing of mounted officers or official chairs. There come dreadful silences. Women with sanguinary shudders drag their children into another court. They do not prepare, but know they will jump into wells, and their children, if old enough, will hang themselves. " Ta p'ao "—great guns. Shells from the warships howl across the sky. The last of the fear-ridden people begin to pack a few belongings, and furtive and nervous secrete a few valuables or a little treasure under flagstones. The riff-raff take advantage of the turmoil to loot, pay off old scores, and levy blackmail. They gorge at food-stalls, are bought off from terrorizing the helpless, and with their ill-gotten gains join the revolutionists or decamp.

General Chang Piao's men have escaped, and General Li Yuan-hung starts after them. Viceroy Jui Cheng, with his Provincial Treasurer and his Provincial Judge, decide upon escape while there is time, and they disappear down the Yangtse on their gunboat. October 12, at 2 o'clock in the afternoon, General Li Yuan-hung's revolutionist soldiers having crossed the Yangtse, are in possession of the Hanyang Arsenal and Hanyang Iron Works, together with 140 three-inch guns, 5000 rounds of gun ammunition with powder for manufacturing 2,000,000 additional rounds, and 32,000,000 rounds of small-arms ammunition. At 3 o'clock the loyal Chinese cruiser and gunboats are firing on Hanyang. Hankow is in disorder, with the people looting.

By Oct. 13 General Li Yuan-hung has Wuchang in a state of order, has taken Hankow to which he sends money to relieve panic, and is in possession of the north shore of the Yangtse down to Seven Mile Creek and " Kilometre 10," where Chang Piao faces him. Upon the outside of the Tartar General's yamen at Hankow is this proclamation by General Li Yuan-hung, posted where that of the Imperialist Manchu Commander otherwise might be :

" I have the honour of the Military Government, my dear countrymen, to let you know that ours is a righteous cause. Don't be suspicious of our army, as wherever its soldiers march they go with a true reason. I raise up the National Army against the Manchus, not for the good or merit of myself but for us as a whole, to rescue you out from the hot fires and the deep waters ; to deliver you from the sufferings coming from the Manchus, just as to heal your ulcers and sores.

" Why have the Manchus put you under such suffering ?

Because they are of a different tribe and naturally cast you away as a bit of straw.

"Unto this day you must have known that the Manchus are not the Sons of Han. Although you have been so loyal and righteous to them, yet they pay nothing for your service. Now I can bear it no longer, therefore we are suddenly gathering ourselves together under the righteous flag; the foremost thing we want to do is to demolish what is harmful or injurious to you, and to gladly exert whatever effort we can only for your welfare. We will not permit those who are traitors to the Sons of Han and those of our countrymen who are thieves among us [referring to Sheng and other Chinese agents of the Throne in its railway policy] to breathe any longer. Formerly they ate our flesh, and now we shall eat them.

"Those who are in favour of the righteous movement are requested to enrol their names. Come and consult with us about the object, how to recover our kingdom, China. Now is the time for us to re-establish our country and faithfully work out our duty as the countrymen of China should do.

"We wish you, my dear brothers, not to misunderstand each other. You—scholars, farmers, workers, and merchants—should try with one accord to drive out the savages. Lastly, I wish all of you to treat each other as justly as possible. I wish you all, my dear brothers, to listen to my words.

"By order, Huang Dynasty 4609, eighth moon, 19th day."

To this proclamation was appended the following:

"Oath of Enlistment of the Revolutionary Army.

"I, a native of —— Hsien, prefecture of ——, in the province of Hupeh, through the introduction of ——, am able to understand that the aim of the People's Army Government is to drive out the Manchus, to recover the losses of the Sons of Han, to establish a Government for the people, and to foster liberty and equality, am now self-willing to be listed as a member of the Central Association of Hupeh. Hereafter I will for ever obey all its constitutions and by-laws. In case of any violation, I am prepared to receive due punishment. I respectfully beg the Adviser-General Sung Chiu-chen to submit this confession to the General Secretary Liu to be sanctioned. And through the special officer Hsiung Chen-sung, I hope this will be made known to the President of the People's Army

Government, Hsiung Chung-shan (sometimes known as Sung Wen).

The name of the Introducer (Signed).
The name of the Admitted Member (Signed).
Huang Dynasty 4609, eighth moon."

Recruiting for the "Republic of China" began on the 13th, and continued until in a short while the "Republic" claimed 26,000 men centred at Wuchang. Order had not yet been restored outside the walls, where fires on the 14th continued into the night. But within, the Republic had a Commander-in-Chief of the Republican Military Organization—Li Yuan-hung, a military Capitol in the Hupeh Provincial Assembly building, officers of state, a People's Army drilling for the Revolution, a Seal of the "Republic," and a Republican newspaper in the *Ta Han Pao*.

General Li Yuan-hung informed the foreign consuls on the opposite side of the river that he had been elected Commander-in-Chief by representatives of the Military Governments (Republican) of the provinces of Anhuei, Chekiang, Fukien, Hunan, Hupeh, Kiangsu, Kuangsi, Shantung, Kiangsi, Kuangtung, and Kueichou.

The wreck of the Imperial Government on the Yangtse was epitomized in the ruins of Viceroy Jui Cheng's yamen, outside which the first Republican martyrs had been beheaded. About half its vast mass of buildings remained, but the front entrance and the private quarters at the back had been burned. Among a maze of passages and rooms, "impossible," said a visitor, "to describe," there was a universal debris—books, writing materials, documents, plans, utensils, letters, maps, broken porcelain and trinkets, together with the insignia and the paraphernalia of authority, littered the floors and were strewn in the courts. Pilferers were turning over the sorry remains, gathering metal, discarded clothing, soiled pictures, electric wire, books, lumber, even pulling down doors and taking out windows. The guest-rooms had not been burned, and contained the wreckage of an elegant suite of European furniture. The mantel-top was torn off and broken on the floor. Its nest of drawers had been wrenched from a fine writing-desk.

On the opposite side of the street from the Viceroy's yamen, covering a large area, were the dwelling-houses in which had lived the families of the yamen guard. They were hardly more than an ash-heap.

The appearance of the morning star, Venus, still shining brilliantly after sunrise, was heralded by many Chinese as portending a new Dynasty, and a new China taking its place among nations.

"We are like your Napoleon," said a revolutionary, when foreigners came from Hankow to look after their missionary countrymen and visit the Republic. "We war against rulers, not against nations."

The revolutionary soldiers were dressed in black. They had thrown away all ornaments, and all wore simply the white rag brassard tied on the arm. In one place sixteen soldiers wearing the khaki uniforms were shot, and it was death to enter the City in that guise. Khaki clothing, the uniform of the Imperialist soldiers, was seen lying in the streets, no one daring to carry it off.

Crowds of soldiers trampled under foot the bright ornaments and facings and other paraphernalia of the Imperialists. "They resemble in their demeanour the Swiss soldiers," remarked a foreigner. Recruits marched past, their ranks filled with coolie labourers, old servants, and country youths. The parade-ground opposite the improvized Capitol was thronged with horse and foot. Within, a Military Court was sitting for the purpose of executing remaining Manchus and Imperialists, or otherwise punishing them by due process of law.

Having once secured the Commander-in-Chief's pass to the City, neither soldier nor civilian required further permissions. The Capitol was filled with men who came and went without hindrance. Visitors entered unopposed. Secretaries were preparing military passes and proclamations for Hanyang and Hankow, together with dispatches, and for the revolutionist provinces. Officers' swords clanked in the passages, and soldiers were hurriedly eating. Flags were displayed at the entrance and in the headquarters building with the inscription, "The New Han [Dynasty or Power]. Exterminate the Manchus." (Hsin Han Mieh Wan.) The first Republican headquarters' emblem was that of exaltation of the Hans.

Behind the secretaries, the soldiers and officers in their uniforms, was Li Yuan-hung, wearing his plain Chinese silk gown.

"I couldn't help it," he exclaimed to Roger S. Greene, the American Consul, as the latter entered his reception-room after the revolt.

CHAPTER XI

WHEN WUCHANG SECEDED—*concluded*

CHINA now had two Capitals—Republican and Imperialist. Wuchang was the Republic—it was Paris. Peking, the Forbidden City, was only Versailles. With the smell of the powder of Wuchang in its nostrils, Peking was a different thing from what it was when merely crossed by the shadow of the Szechuan revolt like a distant cloud on the mountain peak.

Peking under the last Court of the Manchus has an absorbing interest. It grips the imagination. The Prince Regent had appointed Viceroy Tsen Chun-hsuan and the Minister Tuan Fang to co-operate with Chao Er-feng to pacify Szechuan and arrange the railway difficulties there. September 15, 1911, he conferred upon his brother Prince Tsai T'ao and upon Tsai Fu, the son of the head of the Imperial Clan, Prince Ching, the ancient and famous Order of the Yellow Jacket, in recognition of their services in training the Imperial Guard. September 16, he reviewed the Imperial Guard in person at Peking and presented it with his own colours, an almost unprecedented glorification in China of the military. Manœuvres on a scale never before attempted were arranged to take place at the ancient outpost inside Shan-hai-kuan, in the region of K'ai-ping. These arrangements then collapsed in the face of the revolutionary situation. Shih Hsu, one of the aged and decrepit Grand Councillors whom the reform Press had proposed to bury as an actually deceased individual months before, tried to resign. Prince Ching, who had many times attempted to lay down his responsibilities as head of the Imperial Clan, seeing as with a premonition the deluge, begged leave of the Throne to resign. The Throne's Viceroy in Szechuan was then besieged in Cheng-tu, his capital, and Prince Ching was refused by Imperial edict, September 29, in the following words :

" Though over seventy years of age, he [I Kuang, Prince of Ching] is still strong and healthy. At the present difficult time, when many affairs have to be managed and the establishment of a constitutional regime is in progress, it is most essential to rely on the assistance of an aged, experienced, and venerable person in carrying out measures of reform. As the said Prince has hitherto been renowned for his honesty and loyalty he can never lay aside the existing condition of affairs. We hereby command that his request to be relieved of his duties as Cabinet Minister and Officer in Charge of the Affairs of the Wai-wu-pu [Foreign Office] need not be considered."

The Throne feels the first earth-tremors and its own dissolution. Tuan Fang has started, but is still far from Cheng-tu; Tsen Chun-hsuan has not yet started. The Szechuan revolt is unmanageable, and the Throne seems to be getting ready for the tidal wave, to ride it safely. Its old machinery of Empire—the vastest in the world in bulk—oiled by its misfortunes, begins to work with a marvellous action. It fears to permit its lieutenants in Peking to desert the colours. The aged and decrepit ministers who have held on to their posts know they are not equal to the times, but the Prince Regent cannot persuade himself to trade horses in mid-stream. Prince Ching's further supplications are therefore denied.

A Chinese adage always remembered by Chinese rulers is, "The water that bears up the ship can also capsize it." On Oct. 4, 1911, as if to turn the clash of arms to its own account and to pour oil on the troubled waters, it issues an edict for the adoption of patriotic airs. Its sacred words are:

"The art of music has close relation with the administration of government. Owing to the lack of a special poem as our national anthem and of a standard form of national music, we some time ago ordered the Board of Ceremonies and the various yamens satisfactorily and judiciously to compile a book on this subject. Now the Board of Ceremonies and the said other yamens have submitted jointly their composition of a special poem with standard forms of music enclosed for our perusal. We find the wording sonorous and the strains tolerably martial and beautiful, and its rhyming and musical part very well phrased and melodious. We hereby command that the book be universally adopted as the standard of national music."

The national anthem was as follows :

"May the golden bowl be preserved!
May heaven shelter us!
Let the people and all living things
rejoice as ducks, among
the pond lilies!
We are happy to wear the
same clothing.
In this time of the Ching
Dynasty we are fortunate
to see real splendour and
glory :
May the heavens protect the Imperial Family!
Very high are the heavens,
Carelessly roll the waves of
the sea."

The reformers had come to hold the Throne's edicts in contempt. Each additional edict emphasized the hollow mockery of the Throne itself.

On Oct. 10, before they had received Viceroy Jui Cheng's report of his *coup* of the revolutionaries and the nipping of their plot in the bud on the night of the 9th, the Throne issued another edict bearing on the railway situation that had brought on the rebellion. It explains the whole position of the Government in its nearly three years' struggle with the people on this question. Tuan Fang and others had reported the nationalization of the portions within the Hupeh Province adjoining Szechuan on the East of the Canton-Hankow Railway and the cancellation of the private companies of the same, in accordance with an Imperial Order, and submitting their decision as to the plan of taking over the railway capital. It runs as follows :

" Owing to the nationalization of the railways, arrived at some time ago, orders have been issued to the Director-General of the Canton-Hankow and the Szechuan-Hankow Railways to act in conjunction with the viceroys and governor of the said provinces as to the disposal of the funds that have been collected in different ways [by the provincials for the building of the railways themselves as well as by the National Government], in accordance with the decree of June 17, 1911.

" Now, according to their memorial, the capital of the Hupeh Railway may be divided into four classes. Private capital of both the Canton-Hankow and the Szechuan-

Hankow Railways has all been fully paid. It shall, in obedience to the decree, be covered by the issue of Government Railway Bonds without distinction, or if shareholders are unwilling to take up the bonds, it shall be redeemed by cash. With regard to the capital derived from lottery tickets of the Szechuan-Hankow Railway, as these are different in nature from common lottery tickets, as they have been long superseded by share certificates issued to their holders, and as interest has been paid on them at regular intervals, the memorialists suggest that they be treated in a way similar to the other shares, by giving their holders bonds bearing interest, and participation in dividends.

"Coming to the private capital raised by private persons, this item is mostly composed of small sums, and the shareholders live in scattered parts, so that it is impossible to learn the opinion of all of them. They suggest that the gentry who are members of the Railway Association of the said province be entrusted with the task of disposing of this class of capital by refunding it all. Should there be persons who wish to subscribe, they can pay money for the bonds, separately, so as to arrive at a clear settlement.

"Besides the above, there is another class representing famine and rice-sale contributions. They suggest that this may be regarded as the public property of the localities concerned, as was done in the case of Hunan Province."

The edict goes on to say that, having reached an "unanimous conclusion between the officials and gentry," the taking over of the railways of Hupeh by the National Government was completed on September 29, 1911.

Viceroy Jui Cheng was without doubt in office at Wuchang because of his support of the policy of nationalizing the railways. In 1908, in a memorial to the Throne, he had recommended the borrowing of immense sums of money abroad and the building of trunk-line railways in all directions as the only means of saving the Empire—that is, the only means of self-delivery from its foreign enemies, the only means of saving it for the Manchu Dynasty, the only means of saving the Manchu Dynasty. The first step in nationalization was completed, and the satisfaction of the Throne regarding the policy which had been so strongly championed by Jui Cheng was expressed in the closing paragraph of the edict :

" The said high officials have managed the transfer of railway matters in a manner tolerably satisfactory and just. Jui Cheng, Viceroy of Hukuang, is clear-sighted and rapid in the execution of duty. He has exerted himself to a still greater extent, in devising means carefully and laboriously for the disposal of railway affairs, disappointing not Our Trust. The scholars and gentry of the said province really understand their duty very well, in defining the benevolent idea of the Throne by being the foremost in obeying Our Plan. Let an Imperial message of eulogy be transmitted to them. The said high officials are hereby commanded to execute speedily, in conjunction with the Ministry of Finance and Ministry of Posts and Communications, the different plans as suggested, for the settlement of the different questions, and for an early construction of the lines, to emphasize the importance of the communication."

The Regent, as custodian of the Imperial Seal, had hardly sealed this edict, and the Cabinet presidents and vice-presidents had hardly signed it, before Jui Cheng's telegraphic report of the revolutionary plot at Wuchang arrived. Herewith Jui Cheng on China's " battle of Lexington " :

" Information was received of the secret assembly of the revolutionaries in Wuchang, where they decided to effect a rising during the night of October 10. Your memorialist was just giving orders for precaution and for their capture when a telegram from Ch'i Yao-san reported the capture of one important rebel named Liu Yao-chao at Hankow, with seizure of a number of sham seals, sham proclamations, sham documents, etc. Thereupon your memorialist and General Chang Piao and others directed the officers and soldiers to arrest in succession thirty-two rebels, either leaders or members of the revolutionary party, within or without the capital City, as well as to discover and seize a large quantity of arms, ammunition, and bombs. Of the captives, Liu Ju-k'uei opened fire in resisting capture, Yang Wen-shen secreted arms and weapons, and Pun T'su-fan raved most madly and violently in his speech. These three prisoners were executed after a trial."

The Viceroy Jui Cheng concludes with an account of the action of his officers participating in the capture and asks for instructions.

The Throne and Cabinet took up their pens upon which

the ink of praise for Viceroy Jui Cheng was still wet, and in another edict in the name of the Emperor said :

"These revolutionaries aimed at a great rising by beginning their rebellious activity in Hupeh : they had no regard for law. The said Viceroy crushed the first budding of the danger and suppressed the rebellion in a moment. His action has been expeditiously executed. The civilian and military officials are also commendable for their bravery. . . . The remainder of the captives are hereby ordered to be severely tried and punished with the utmost rigour of the law. At the same time, the Viceroy shall direct the territorial officials, both civil and military, to search for and arrest strictly and secretly all the rebels that are fleeing ; whilst proclamations are to be issued, permitting those who have been coerced into joining the rebels to repent and turn over a new leaf. As to the constabulary force and the civil and military officials, who have failed in foresight, they are hereby all granted exemption from the consideration of a penalty, in view of their having rendered assistance in effecting the capture."

Now they dipped their pens in gall. Hear the result :

"Peking, October 12. Jui Cheng reports by telegraph that he was disposing by trial of the rebels captured during the night of the 9th, when their comrades conspired with the engineer and transport regiments and suddenly burst out in support of each other on the night of the 10th. The engineer regiments ferociously assaulted the arsenal of Ch'u-wan-ti, while the transport regiments set fire to their own camps and forced an entrance by destroying the gate of the City. Jui Cheng, in company with Chang Piao, Tieh Chung, and Wang Li-k'ang, directed the army and police and conducted in person the gendarme corps to resist this attack. But owing to the rebel assault being made simultaneously from several points and their number being very large, Jui Cheng had to retreat on board the cruiser *Ch'u-yu*, which moved to Hankow. Having already telegraphed for reinforcements by the transfer of the defence corps from Hunan and Honan to Hupeh, he requests that high officials may be sent to Hupeh with as many units of efficient force as is possible, to punish and suppress the rebellion, etc. Upon perusal of this memorial We are very much surprised. The conspiracy between soldiers and rebels must have been planned long ago ; yet Jui Cheng had neither taken any precautions nor made any preparations in advance to meet the sudden outburst of the evil plot, culminating in the loss of the capital City. He is really unpardonable for his ungrateful and negligent behaviour. Jui Cheng, Viceroy of Hukuang, is hereby cashiered instantly, but permitted to expiate his crime by some signal service. He is therefore to continue Acting Viceroy of Hukuang, in order to have a chance of future achievements. The said Viceroy is hereby held responsible for the recovery of the capital City. Should he fail to accomplish anything, the said Acting Viceroy shall certainly be punished severely."

The Throne then took up General Chang Piao :

" Chang Piao has been training the Hupeh Army now for a number of years ; that such a conspiracy between soldiers and rebels, resulting in the loss of the capital City could have happened, clearly proves that he has been training it without method; moreover, he had neither taken precautionary measures in advance, nor had he the discipline to control them at the time of emergency, which shows that he has not obtained the sympathy of his army. He even dared to escape from his camp and abandon his trust. He has really committed a very grave offence and is unpardonable. Chang Piao, Commander-in-Chief of the new Army and Provincial Commander, is hereby cashiered instantly, and Jui Cheng is commanded to order him speedily to punish the rebels very severely and to recover the capital City."

Alas! the disappearing Viceroy never received these edicts. He was *en route* to Shanghai. Seeking first a refuge at Nanking, he disappeared in the foreign settlements at Shanghai, from where he escaped to Japan. He was honoured by a cartoon in the reform Press in which he was shown begging protection of the British Consul-General at Shanghai. He was a man of slight stature, alert, and possessing considerable ability, but showed no special qualities. Surrounded by enemies, many of whom were assassins, his course in taking flight was highly practical. He was a victim of the new times in China.

Tsen Chun-hsuan appointed to pacify Szechuan had arrived at Wuchang to await his old guard of Yunnan troops which he had ordered up from Canton. He asked the Throne for funds. The Ministry of Finance granted him 20,000 taels to defray the travelling costs of his journey, but it rejected his proposal to pay his old Yunnan soldiers out of funds to be granted by the Ministry, whose resources were " unable to meet the costs." The Cabinet, at the instigation of Sheng Hsuen-huai, instructed him to travel double stages daily, and to think out his plans in advance for the pacification or punishment of the people when he arrived. Tsen Chun-hsuan brought from his experiences as Viceroy at turbulent Canton an intimate knowledge of revolt and the new reform movement, and he at once discovered himself to be again upon hostile ground.

At Wuchang the officials had lost confidence in the troops, and for a week preceding the outbreak officers were required to report at three regular intervals during the night hours, to show they were not preparing for a mutiny. The men were forbidden to see outsiders and their letters were censored. Following the outbreak in Szechuan, 300 men had deserted, and although a few were captured they were not punished for fear of inflaming the rest of the troops. In the face of this situation, with the Szechuan revolt growing, Tsen Chun-hsuan brought forth the universal Mandarin excuse—illness. As he was an old official, his disease, whatever it was, had become standardized and chronic in the Dynastic archives. He had used it many times before in the buffetings which he and the Empire had received in all the evil days of the past fifty years. It was a convenient resource when the revolt on October 10 occurred. He repeated his prayer to the Throne to be permitted to resign, but the Throne only granted him respite to regain his health at Wuchang before proceeding. He straightway sent away his staff and directed his private employees to return to Shanghai. His whereabouts from that moment were unknown until he telegraphed to the Cabinet at Peking to the effect that the rising in Hupeh was so sudden that, being a man to whom the revolutionaries had paid special attention, he had been obliged to leave the City alone. Now he was afflicted with his old complaint and was being doctored at Shanghai. The decree appointing him Viceroy of Szechuan filled him with perturbation and alarm to the highest degree. He said that he was so aged and decrepit that he could not possibly be equal to such responsible duties, and begged the rescinding of the order and the appointment of a competent official for the welfare of the Government.

All those agents in whom it had placed its reliance were aged, decrepit, or by other disqualifications incompetent. The Throne's props had fallen, and it was throwing its searchlight about its Empire, looking for a saviour.

CHAPTER XII

OCTOBER IN PEKING

As I went about Peking the events of October were fresh in the mind. It was a month of days, like France's October Fifth in the year 1789, "from which is commonly dated the French Revolution," "a phenomenon henceforth absorbing all others for mankind."

It was a month overburdened with events, under pressure of which the machinery of the Throne collapsed. There was a rain of edicts—not ordinary edicts, of which the Throne in ordinary times furnishes perhaps a dozen a month, but history-making edicts, such as the Throne issues only in times of great national danger. There were about two a day. Their issue commenced in fact in September, and gained such momentum as to continue on into November.

It is in October that the Throne by appointments and reappointments is still attempting to swing great Szechuan back into line. It is "much astounded" at events. It orders cities to be recaptured "at a prescribed time without delay," exalting some officials and degrading others, while aiming at recovering the confidence of the people and inciting rivalry among its officials.

On October 11, when General Li Yuan-hung begins to mobilize at Hankow, to attack the Imperial forces under his late colleague General Chang Piao, there is a special Cabinet meeting at Peking to consider the situation there, and the Throne revises the military distribution in the Empire. It orders two divisions to concentrate before Hankow, to which it joins the fleet under Admiral Sah Chen-ping, to assist in putting down the rebellion. It clings to Tsen Chun-hsuan and will not allow him to resign, but places him in command of all the military forces of Szechuan, together with the reinforcements from Kueichou on the South and those marching in the direction of Szechuan from the North.

For twenty years historians have talked of the decline of the Manchu Dynasty. The remark oftenest made of the Manchus during that time has been that the Dynasty had no visible leader. In its frantic efforts at collecting munitions, assembling armies and ships, at recalling officials, at dispatching officers and trying to recover cities and provinces, the Throne looked for a leader among the Chinese. It knew where to turn its searchlight, but for complicated reasons of *amour propre*, Court intrigue, and so on, almost too intricate to follow, it left until the eleventh hour the humiliating task of appealing to a man whom it had discarded. Yuan Shih-k'ai, the late Empress Grand Dowager's reliance in military and foreign affairs, was this man. His name was in everyone's mouth. Vengefully and perfidiously cast off in January 1909, the Throne, on Oct. 14, 1911, summoned him from his country place in Honan Province to save the Empire. It appointed him Viceroy of Hukuang, to succeed Jui Cheng.

On the occasion of his dismissal the edict ordered him to vacate all his offices and return to his home on account of "rheumatism of the leg," adding ominously, "thus our clemency toward him is manifested." Up to that time any diseases which Yuan might have had, had not got into the archives. But his fellow grand councillors who conferred this ailment upon him by signing the decree placed before them by the Prince Regent were wise, not so much in the symptoms of the Mandarin as in diagnosing the symptoms of the Court. Yuan now had an official disease. He disappeared into official eclipse, which in China is total.

Yuan Shih-k'ai was officially entombed until thus now resurrected. After nearly three years, hearing the Gabriel blast of an edict from Peking, he looks about him. It is a new world. The things he feared and prophesied have come to pass. He knows that he is being appealed to to bear the burdens of the Government's mistakes, but he cannot refuse in such a time for patriotic reasons and except at the risk of his life. He is a patriot and he gratefully accepts the honour imposed upon him; at the same time, having done so, he pens one of those exquisite Chinese pages of political irony that testify to the profound depths of Chinese humour, and, engrossed upon the archives, are the amazement of foreigners. He says he has not yet recovered from "rheumatism of the leg," and prays to be given a little while longer in which to doctor himself.

When Yuan Shih-k'ai was dismissed and the Emperor Kuang Hsu was on his bier, at which his Empress, now the

Lung Yu Empress Dowager, daily came to wail, she and the late Emperor's brother Chun, now the Prince Regent, had not yet parted political company, and they carried out with one accord what was known to be the wish of the late Emperor. This was the punishment of Yuan Shih-k'ai for his failure to support the reform programme of the Kang Yu-wei party in 1898. Yuan Shih-k'ai out of the way, the waters of factional strife flowed under the bridge. The Lung Yu Empress Dowager and the Prince Regent became the heads of opposing Court parties—the so-called Yehonala Clan, that to which the late Empress Grand Dowager belonged and known as the Red Girdle party, supporting the Lung Yu Empress Dowager, and the so-called Aisin Gioros or Yellow Girdle party supporting the Prince Regent.

The division between these two parties was marked by the dividing line of power between the Lung Yu Empress Dowager and the Emperor. The late Empress Grand Dowager had conferred her mantle upon her successor, the emblem of power of the Yehonala Clan. The Prince Regent's power aside from that of his office lay in his being the father of the Emperor and through the mother of the Emperor, Princess Chun, who aspired to be a rival to the Lung Yu Empress Dowager.

By October 1911 the factional fights have ceased. The whole Imperial Clan is awed. It is a crisis not only for the reign but one holding the fate of the Dynasty. Fateful is October in the household of the Emperor. Pu Yi, five and one-half years old, in his third Dynastic year is splashing through the autumn mud puddles in the courts of the Forbidden City, ruining his new velvet boots and flabbergasting eunuch Chang and his fellows, who must plunge through unhesitatingly with the yellow umbrella.

The Imperial schoolroom in the Su-ch'ing Palace awaits His Majesty's arrival when he has reached his sixth year, when the Imperial learning will commence. In his playroom are toys from most of the crowned heads of Europe. The Czar of All the Russias has sent him gifts of value fabulous in Toyland. The Kaiser has sent him a toy aeroplane, a gilded metal chair, a hook-and-ladder wagon. Everything has in it a musical box. A mechanical dog emits bow-wows, whereupon from his interior come tunes. When the little Emperor sits down in his chair, music begins to play. The attendants are more pleased even than the little Emperor. The latter has inherited similar things from the previous Emperor—such playthings as were not looted by the foreign troops in 1900.

While Pu Yi is playing with his toys and waiting for his Imperial education to begin, the Lung Yu Empress Dowager, who is his adopted mother, is establishing the rule of what is known as the " Lowered Curtain," by which women of the Imperial Family wield the sceptre for the male occupant of the Throne, who alone has the right to govern. Her star, that of the Yehonalas, is rising. The administration of the Regent has failed, and his princes and his partisans shrink into the background. The Lung Yu Empress Dowager is coming into the fierce light that now beats upon the Manchu throne.

Two hundred and fifty thousand Chinese and Manchus, more than one-third its population, flee from Peking. They go by foot, by animal, and by railway. Extra trains cannot carry enough of them away to Tientsin. They crowd into railway trucks, and even on the tops of vans and coaches. If there is room for the individual there is none for his luggage, and from his precarious position on the steps or couplings he reluctantly watches it disappear on the railway platform, left behind.

There is no *need* of flight—it is panic that sets this pace. There is no need for everyone to flee—a few can find refuge in the Legation Quarter. Officials who have condemned foreign Powers for keeping foreign troops in China do not hesitate to accept the protection which their presence and the Legation Quarter fortifications offer. Officials are hard to find. They are like foreign money now to the Lung Yu Empress Dowager, who for the time being has neither Yuan Shih-k'ai nor a foreign loan to lean upon. Peking and its Versailles were near to their Paris. The Palace treasure guarded by the American General Chaffee in the Forbidden City in 1900 and 1901, she hoards. Some say it is £40,000,000, some say £50,000,000. The foreign bankers refuse China a small loan of $3,000,000.

On Oct. 15 24,000 Imperialist troops are under way to go to the battlefield before Hankow. Yin Chang, the Minister of War, has gone to the South, and on the 17th is in conference with Yuan Shih-k'ai at Chang-teh-fu, in Honan.

On Oct. 15 the foreign correspondents are refused right to accompany the troops. This is the day that marks the uprising of the National Assembly, which is not to meet until the 22nd. Nevertheless, sixty out of its 196 representatives, who are present in Peking, meet and pass a resolution demanding the right of the Szechuan Assembly to meet at once; also that its President (Pu Tien-chun) shall be released from prison to preside over it, and that Sheng Hsuan-huai, the Imperial Commissioner for negotiating foreign loans in Peking, shall be dismissed as soon as possible. These it submits on Oct. 16 by committee in person to the Cabinet.

Runs have begun on the banks, and the Board of Finance hands over $125,000 to meet demands of the small depositors of the Government Deposit Bank. The Powers view the Rebellion with grave concern. The Chinese Press at Peking comments upon the suspicious presence of the Japanese Admiral Kawashima and Colonel Saito at Hankow when the outbreak occurs, and the charge is raised of Japanese complicity in the Rebellion. It was Colonel Saito who raised the Chien-tao Question, by which Japan acquired special rights in Eastern Manchuria. As a matter of fact Colonel Saito is on his way from Peking to Szechuan to report on the outbreak there. Ijuin, the Japanese Minister at Peking, in view of the excitement, sees fit to deny officially the charges.

On Oct. 16 refugees from the regions of the Rebellion reach the coast after journeys extending to 700 and 1000 miles and seek asylum at Shanghai. Troop trains leave Peking and Paoting-fu with precision and order surprising to the foreign military agents. Peking officials estimate that not less than 6000 trained soldiers are taking part in the Rebellion, but do not know yet the names of the leaders who have organized it. October 18, Japanese officials of Tokio regard the situation as likely to develop phases alarming to outside nations. The Imperialist Admiral Sah Chen-ping has arrived in the river at Hankow with the flagship and a fleet of eight gunboats.

On Oct. 18 and 19 General Li Yuan-hung fights the "battle of Kilometre 10," outside Hankow. Both sides claim victory. On Oct. 19 the Throne begs for aid in rewards and punishments, which it offers to stop the "Rebellion in Szechuan, Hunan, and Hupeh." "We hereby order that those who have been compelled to become accessaries and who will personally capitulate at an early date will be allowed to repent without being punished for past errors, no matter whether they are soldiers or common people. Any person who shall achieve merit by killing the rebels or arresting and tying them up for presentation to Us shall be specially rewarded. If the roll-call lists of revolutionists be found, they should be destroyed at once, so that no one shall be involved in the trouble." The Throne commands the Minister of War, General Yin Chang, " Viceroy " Yuan Shih-k'ai, Marshal Tsen Chun-hsuan, and Commissioner and Director Tuan Fang to carry out these rewards and punishments. They are a kind of Imperial Commission to pacify all Central China.

To replace the modern troops sent to Hankow, the Throne brings in a division of its old-style troops to protect Peking. It is ready to move troops from Mukden to the South. A division starts, leaving Chingwantao for Hankow by steamer. Twenty thousand men altogether have been dispatched Southward on the 20th.

There are eighteen foreign warships at Hankow, and land communications are cut. Peking and the outside world are receiving their news by foreign wireless. General Yin Chang has reached the front and proclaimed pardon for all who desert the rebels in accordance with the Throne's edict. The representatives of the Powers in Peking assume that all Southern China is about to secede.

It is a gloomy hour in Peking. The Middle Kingdom already trembles with the footsteps of the rebels, and now, October 22, General Li Yuan-hung in his capital at Wuchang doffs his queue. It is reported that the Emperor has fled, that with the Lung Yu Empress Dowager he has gone to Jehol, or taken refuge in the Foreign Legations.

There is not any real fighting at Hankow, only trumped-up " battles." It is in this situation that Yuan Shih-k'ai's acknowledgment of his appointment and his prayer for time in which to recover from his leg and other ills reaches the Throne. It is in such a critical moment that he adds with exasperating indifference that as soon as he thinks it is in any way possible for him to work, he will try and do so. It comes coincident with the opening of the yet more trying National Assembly. Only 117 of the 196 members are present, and at the last moment a substitute, Prince Shih To, arrives to act for the Prince Regent in opening the Assembly.

" Since Our accession to the Throne," says the Emperor, " We have been diligently and tremblingly striving to attain an ideal Government day and night. Now, upon the occasion of opening the second session of the National Assembly, you members should respectfully listen to Our exhortations. The present civilization of the world demands that Constitutional Government should take the foremost precedence of all important affairs." Continuing, Prince Shih To read the three closing fourths of the Regent's and Cabinet's words put into Pu Yi's mouth, consisting of the best specimens of that worthless drivel from the Throne which the reformers and revolutionaries utterly despise.

The cities of Ichang and Changsha go over to the rebels. The revolutionary spirit has broken out in the North, the native Press is defying the censorship. Foreign banks have suspended all loan negotiations with China, and on Oct. 24 the foreign diplomatic corps has taken up the question of garrisoning with foreign troops the line of communications to Peking. Foreign women and children in the interior have been ordered by their Legations to concentrate at the Treaty ports and in the capitals, where they can be protected.

Yuan Shih-k'ai is still confined to his residence by "indisposition," an ailment that gives more pain to the Court than to Yuan, for in a state of desperation it has made all arrangements to flee to Jehol.

Now comes October 25. There are almost too many events for the calendar. Hsian-fu, the capital of Shensi, refuge of the Court in 1900, revolts and sets up an independent Government. China's financial condition is desperate. She formally requests the Powers to allow her to postpone the payment of monthly instalments of the Boxer indemnity during nine months, so that she may have ready money for the war. She is now seeking a loan of 12,000,000 taels. All South-eastern China is in a state of unrest. Admiral Sah Chen-ping's gunboats are missing from Hankow, and are unable to find any friendly port. The capital of Honan, Kai-feng-fu, is at the mercy of revolted soldiers. General Yin Chang is reported unwilling to move against the rebels, who have 400 guns, unless his troops are paid, and now the National Assembly impeaches Sheng Hsuan-huai and demands his dismissal and punishment. He has received anonymous letters threatening him with all kinds of atrocities, and has intimated to the Prince Regent his desire to resign, but is not permitted to do so. General Feng Shan, a Manchu, second only to Yin Chang the Minister of War, in the Manchu military lists, is assassinated at Canton by a bomb. The Imperial fleet is escaping to Shanghai. The Manchu officials are deserting the Yangtse River cities for Shanghai. The National Assembly passes its impeachment with shouts of

"Decapitate Sheng!" The city of Foochow falls. Canton is ready to pass into the hands of the rebels. The capital of Shantung, Tsinan-fu, is with the revolutionists. Szechuan is now completely controlled by the rebels. The condition of the Court can be described as that of a panic. The minds of the Court personnel cannot be described. The Manchu Court members are seeking leave of absence, and foreign protection.

On Oct. 26 the Throne surrenders to the National Assembly and dismisses the Commissioner for the negotiation of the foreign loans, Sheng Hsuan-huai.

Nothing but its financial desperation and desire not to offend the foreign bankers and their Governments has persuaded it to hold out so long against the known wishes of its revolutionaries, but now it seizes the opportunity offered it by the National Assembly and makes of the Imperial Commissioner a scapegoat. It endorses the charges of the National Assembly that "the source of the rebellion is all to be explained as having been caused by Sheng Hsuan-huai, Minister of Posts and Communications, who has cheated and deceived the Throne, violated the law, and added to the hatred of the people. He obstructed the exchange of views between the people and the Government, depriving the National Assembly and the Cabinet of the right of consideration and decision. The causes of revolt in Szechuan may be mainly attributed to his decision, and he is truly the chief culprit and has jeopardized the State. The nationalization of railways is intended by the Throne for the good of the merchants and people, yet Sheng Hsuan-huai has been incapable of divining Our virtuous idea. He has received high favours from the State, but is truly ungrateful. He is hereby cashiered instantly, never again to be employed."

Tang Shao-yi, a Cantonese progressive and reformer and chief lieutenant of Yuan Shih-k'ai, is appointed Minister of Posts and Communications in his stead, but this does not stay the revolutionary deluge.

The National Assembly circulates a petition demanding Sheng's decapitation, whereupon the French, German, and British ministers and the American chargé d'affaires visit Prince Ching, head of the Foreign Office, and lodge an objection against any such possible decree. Sheng Hsuan-huai takes refuge in the Legation Quarter, and an international guard of the four Powers, France, Germany, Great Britain, and the United States, under command of the American military attaché, Captain Reeves, escorts him to the foreign settlement at Tientsin. At the railway station in Tientsin, in the early hours of October 28, he is met by two closed carriages under the care of the American Vice-Consul, and before anyone is aware is taken by his escort of foreign soldiers marching on each side and placed safely aboard an outgoing steamer lying in the river.

It is still the 27th, and October is under full headway. General Li Yuan-hung, proclaimed " President of the Republic of China," is heard above the wrath of the people, and the venom of the Throne hurled at Sheng Hsuan-huai. The Throne appropriates 1,000,000 taels for military expenses in Hupeh, so that General Yin Chang can pay his troops and attack the revolutionists. As " men's heads rock upon their shoulders," the Throne totters. As it totters, it strikes at men's heads. The Imperial Clan decrees death for the renegade Viceroy Jui Cheng. This is the day of a very storm of edicts. Eighteen appear in the *Official Gazette*, fifteen of which refer to the political and military situation. No one knows how many rescripts, edicts, and orders have been thrown off secretly.

The wave of the Throne's courage broke when the Throne turned upon Sheng Hsuan-huai. Its edict was greeted by onlookers as the signal for a culmination of disasters. Now, amid the anathemas hurled at Sheng's head, the distrust levelled at Viceroy Jui Cheng, the hope in Director and Envoy Tuan Fang, the pain of the assassination at Canton of General Feng Shan, is heard again the appeal to Yuan Shih-k'ai, now " Viceroy " of Hukuang. To-day an edict appoints him Imperial Commissioner with plenary powers over all the Yangtse land and naval forces. Authority for suppression and pacification of the rebels is placed in his hands. " . . . Yuan Shih-k'ai is to act at his own discretion with expedition, as military aspects may develop a thousand changes in a moment," says the edict. " The Military Council and the Minister of War shall not interfere, in order to concentrate authority [in Yuan Shih-k'ai] for the speedy achievement of success."

It is two weeks since the Throne first appealed to Yuan Shih-k'ai to save the country and he has not moved from his place of retirement. Now the Throne's second appeal is balm warranted to cure " rheumatism of the leg." To a man who has been waiting to see the full dimensions of a Rebellion which the errors of the Throne have hurried on and to see the full penitence of the Throne, it is sufficient, and he telegraphs the Throne that he will go and fixes the date of his departure. Yuan Shih-k'ai is something of a heroic figure as he buckles on his armour in his country home near Changteh-fu, and in accordance with the Throne's edict "devises and takes proper measures so as to accelerate his movements towards the front." The Throne recalls General Yin Chang, the Manchu Minister of War, to Peking, and appoints the Chinese Generals Feng Kuo-chang and Tuan Chi-jui to assist and not hamper Yuan Shih-k'ai.

On Oct. 28 the Throne is still struggling with the question of Szechuan and the problem of getting its appointees Tsen Chun-hsuan and Tuan Fang to the front. The revolutionists attack General Yin Chang before Hankow, which prevents him returning to Peking. The massacre of Manchus in various parts of the Empire has inflamed the imagination of Manchus and Chinese in Peking, where a counter massacre of revenge by Manchus under the leadership of Prince Tsai T'ao is feared. The Lung Yu Empress Dowager turns over 4,000,000 taels from her privy purse, and a panic begins. Six thousand men of the 20th Division—part of the force intended to carry out the army manœuvres at Kaiping—refuse to entrain at Lanchou to go to Hankow, but instead send a memorial to Peking requiring the immediate granting of a Constitution. The Provincial Assembly at Tientsin and a large number of the populace there declare for the revolutionists. T'ai-yuan, capital of Shansi, adjoining Chihli, Province, goes over to the revolutionists, who massacre the Governor and many Manchus. On Oct. 29 an edict orders the capture and trial of the renegade Viceroy Jui Cheng. Another commands General Yin Chang to await the arrival of Yuan Shih-k'ai, and commands him and Admiral Sah Chen-ping to encourage their officers and men to recapture Wuchang and Hankow. The Government is prepared to cut the Peking-Hankow Railway to prevent the revolutionist advance on Peking.

The revolutionists lose Hankow to General Yin Chang, whose Imperialist soldiers begin its destruction by fire. Their excesses of looting and debauchery are awful, and red war is now loose in the land. On Oct. 30 Hankow begins to burn.

The Government prepares to resign. All the princes and high ministers write their resignations. The Throne then issues a penitential edict confessing its shortcomings, and follows with proclaiming the resignations of its ministers. Shih Hsu, the old Grand Councillor, resigns from the presidency of the National Assembly. Prince Ching, the Premier, resigns along with Na Tung and Hsu Shih-chang, associate premiers and ministers of the Foreign Office; Duke Tsai Tse, Minister of Finance; Chou Chia-lai, Minister of State; and Prince Tsai T'ao of the Military Council.

But wait, they have arranged something else. Under these senior ministers have been condemned all the reformers of the past and present now alive against whom sentences are lodged in the Board of Punishments. Some are banished, some have prices on their heads. The star of these is rising. Those ministers whose star is now setting, and who have "charged with punishment the scroll," want no Banquos at their tables, no assassins with bombs at their doors. General Feng Shan's fate and the threats against Sheng Hsuan-huai remind them of this. In the name of the Emperor and under the signatures of the Prince Regent and themselves, they issue a decree of amnesty and pardon for political offenders, and walk out.

Bishop Bashford at Shanghai, quoting De Tocqueville, commenting on China's condition, said: "The weakest hour for any Government follows its admission of the necessity of reform." The truth of this axiom was demonstrated in the Empire and in Peking by lack of all confidence in the Goverment. On the 31st, the events of October culminate and the Throne is already seen to be falling. There is no Cabinet because it has resigned. The National Assembly has a lengthy conference with Prince Ching, now merely a privy councillor. Replying to the National Assembly, the Throne has granted an immediate Constitution and Parliament.

The revolutionary arm of the troops has become known as the Army League, which now controls the troops of Shantung and Chihli. "The Regent is unnerved and weeps bitterly." Without leave, officials are deserting the Capital for Tientsin. The Chinese number possibly 600,000 in Peking, with Manchus in and around Peking numbered at 100,000. Each fears an attack from the other—the Chinese fearing massacre from the Throne's Manchu troops. "Peking is a powder magazine." High mandarins are "deluging the Legations with appeals for protection." The Legation Quarter though in no danger is preparing for emergencies. The gates of the City and of the palaces are placed under stronger guards. Foreign troops are arriving, and in Tientsin they parade the native city to overawe malcontents.

By all these signs and tokens, the machinery of the Throne is collapsed. There is no Throne except to the Imperial Clan. There is absolutely no Government. Yuan Shih-k'ai is temporizing. He has not yet done anything. Edicts continue to be issued, but they are without force except where they are backed up by money disgorged from the Imperial purse. The capitulation of the Throne, its agents and ministers, is complete. Told in the penitential edict published on Oct. 30 in pursuance of the plan of capitulation, the ministers named put into the mouth of the child-Emperor Pu Yi these words :

"I have reigned for three years and have always acted conscientiously, in the interests of the people. But I have not employed men properly, not having political skill. I have employed too many nobles in political positions, an act which has contravened constitutionalism. On railway matters someone whom I trusted fooled me. Thus public opinion was opposed to this policy.

"When I urge reform, officials and gentry seize the opportunity to embezzle. When old laws are abolished, high officials serve their own ends. Much of the people's money has been taken, but nothing to benefit the people has been achieved. On several occasions edicts have promulgated laws, but none have been obeyed. The people are grumbling, yet I do not know of it. Disasters loom ahead, but I do not see them.

"In Szechuan trouble first occurred, the Wuchang Rebellion followed; now alarming reports come from Shensi and Honan. In Canton and Kiangsi riots appear. The whole Empire is seething, the minds of the people are perturbed, and the spirits of our nine late Emperors are not able to enjoy properly the sacrifices made to them, while it is feared that the people will suffer grievously.

"All these things are my own fault. Hereby I announce to the world that I swear to reform and with Our soldiers and people to carry out the Constitution faithfully, modifying legislation, developing the interests of the people and abolishing their hardships, all in accordance with the wishes and interests of the people.

"Old laws that are unsuitable will be abolished. The union of Manchus and Chinese mentioned by the late Emperor, I shall carry out.

"As regards Hupeh and Hunan, for their grievances,

though precipitated by the soldiers and caused by Jui Cheng, I only blame Myself, because I had mistakenly appointed him. The soldiers and people are innocent. If they will return to their allegiance, I will excuse the past.

" Being a very small person standing at the head of My subjects, I see that My heritage is nearly falling to the ground. I regret my fault and repent greatly. I can only trust that My subjects will support the soldiers in order to support Me, to comfort the millions of My people, to hold firmly to the eternity of the Dynasty, and to convert danger into tranquillity. The patriotism of the Empire's subjects will be appreciated and trusted for ever.

" Now finances and diplomacy have reached bed-rock. Even if all unite, there is still fear of falling. But if the Empire's subjects will not regard nor honour the State, and are easily misled by outlaws, then the future of China is unthinkable. I am most anxious by day and night, I only hope my subjects will understand."

CHAPTER XIII

HANKOW—A BATTLE

Part I

CONFUSING all the plans of the Government in Peking and bringing it to a state of collapse and ruin, is the Revolution centred at Wuchang, and the Republic headed by General Li Yuan-hung.

Whereas October is the month of the downfall of the Throne, it is the month of the rise of the Republic. October days are as fateful in Wuchang as in Peking. The Imperialist Government struggles to hold merely what it has, the revolutionists have to create. They have hardly more than a division—not more than 8000 really trained troops —to start the "People's Army." There are at least twelve foreign-trained divisions in the Empire, of which four are south of the Yangtse River. These latter, together with one division in Manchuria, are claimed by the revolutionaries as being on their side. A revolutionary Rebellion has been planned by Sun Yat-sen, but its headquarters are to be at Canton. The revolutionary movement has grown so rapidly in these last days of the Empire that there are many leaders, and now that circumstances have forced an outbreak at Wuchang, the conspirator and revolutionary Sun Yat-sen's plans are dislocated. It is necessary for General Li Yuan-hung to reform all and to bring all revolutionary elements into harmony at Wuchang.

After issuing his first proclamation for the guidance of the people, threatening punishments and promising rewards, General Li Yuan-hung addresses a letter to Admiral Sah, asking him to join the revolt. According to the revolutionist newspaper, *Ta Han Pao*, the first soldiers organized at Wuchang are the gendarmes, to preserve order in the streets of the three cities, Wuchang, Hankow, and Hanyang. To restore order and discipline after the promiscuous fighting in the streets of Wuchang, General Li Yuan-hung commands officers and men, and especially recruits, not to ramble about the streets, nor leave their camps without orders. He forbids ransacking of houses without instructions, orders camp guards to be organized to maintain military order, and the men to be instructed by speakers who are to address them respecting the revolution.

Wuchang originates the "Dare to Die" soldier's oath, that afterwards achieves so much newspaper fame. Money presents are given to the soldiers of a regiment of artillery who adopt a determination to sacrifice their lives for the Republican cause. Scouts are next organized, and rewards are offered for the capture of renegades and enemies. Any band of soldiers that can capture a gunboat will receive £50 per man. Anyone capturing Viceroy Jui Cheng or the Hupeh Commander-in-Chief, General Chang Piao, will receive £100. £100 will be paid to the family of any soldier killed in battle.

Under the inspiration of these announcements the Republican Army more than trebles in size and grows until the Commander-in-Chief announces that he has all the soldiers he needs. The *Ta Han Pao* says that he has given the veteran soldiers all double pay so they can send money home. The Amazon idea has taken hold in its ancient Chinese form, and a Wuchang student-Theroigne proposes to start a regiment of Amazons. Madam Li, wife of General Li Yuan-hung, is the centre of the woman's Republican movement and is preparing for Red Cross work. She is to visit the Red Cross stations at Hankow and Hanyang. General Li Yuan-hung makes a personal inspection of the Republican Army to examine into the discipline and to re-establish the military courts. The soldiers are busy organizing their commissariat, are making flags, and have opened the old powder-mills and are making powder. Provisions have gone up. No meat is to be had, eggs are more than four times the ordinary market price, with fish and chicken in proportion, to say nothing of turnips. This greatly concerns General Li Yuan-hung, who relies upon the normal progress of industry and business for success in financing the revolution. He has been a commissariat officer himself, and as the purchaser for the Wuchang Army in the past is known as the "Man who won't take bribes." The Press prints the following story about him :

"You do not seem to be acquainted with the customs of the place," said a merchant with whom he had dealings. "It is customary," he continues, "to give army purchasers some sort of commission."

" I do not want any bribe," said Li, " and the reason why I have come to this particular shop is because others persist in offering me ' squeezes.' "

The new Government in its organization has recognized the Press. One editor first becomes chief of the Republican headquarters in Hankow and is then advanced to be Taot'ai, or highest civil official, there. The newspaper men have secured General Li's approval of cutting the queue. They inaugurate the fashion in the three cities, and at the same time put on foreign dress. Queue-cutting is then ostentatiously taken up by the soldiers, and it is a notable day, October 22, when, in the quiet of his home, the household barber cuts off the queue of the Commander-in-Chief and leader. Queue-cutting in the Republic is thus officially sanctioned.

The appearance of Venus in the early morning just after the revolt had greatly impressed the common people as an omen of New China. Another omen was a moon-bow seen on the night of the revolt. Now, with the fall of their leader's queue, came an eclipse of the sun. The mysterious and supernatural exercises greater power in convincing the people of the importance of the revolutionary movement than does the famine, death, and destruction of warfare, which is actually but an exaggeration of their daily life, meaning little more than that the " evil influences " have for the time being gained the upper hand of the " benevolent influences."

The people having grown a taste for blood-letting and looting, are engaged in Manchu hunting. They did not wait for the Manchus to vacate their houses but hunted them out like wild animals. The abandoned homes, some of them very large, running up to 200 or 300 rooms, are being occupied by the Military Department and the recruits as they are enlisted. In one house, in an otherwise empty room, eight corpses are found, three of men and five of women, all hanging by the neck from the beams. They committed suicide rather than fall into the hands of the revolutionists. Those Manchus who escaped the first massacre are waiting favourable opportunities to steal away. Hsi Kang, a Manchu attached to the Prefect's yamen, tries to escape from Wuchang disguised as a water-carrier, while his wife follows in a common sedan-chair. The revolutionist newspapers say that they are discovered just outside the City by the patrols and immediately executed. A man named Chung Shan connected with the Department of Public Granaries escapes, and the baffled, indignant people execrate him for sharp dealing with the farmers and revengefully behead his son, who is left behind.

" Manchu boys in the mission schools are in some cases the only members of their families left alive," says the *China Post* at Hankow. " Two Manchus were killed on the Sin-seng Road yesterday within view of the windows of our office. They were living in hotels in Wuchang from which they escaped, but being identified here were promptly dispatched, and the head of one was stuck up on a lamp-post." The Manchu soldiers who failed to get across the Yangtse after the fall of Wuchang took to the country, where the villagers gather in thousands and pursue them. Fleeing for their lives, the soldiers soon exhaust their ammunition and are beaten to death or escape in disguise. The magistrate of a district outside Wuchang first sends away his family and then disguises himself as a countryman, shaving his moustache and changing his clothes. He is caught by the militia and forwarded to Wuchang.

The queue-cutting spirit gives an impetus to these barbarities, whereupon General Li Yuan-hung is obliged to issue a proclamation stating that the extermination of the Manchus is not a part of the revolutionary programme. The revolutionists simply want to make the Manchus powerless in order to establish the Republic. A supposed Manchu is killed on a charge of poisoning wells. According to a Chinese reporter, his body is quartered and exposed in the streets. When two Chinese are captured trying to poison the wells, revolutionists find that the Manchus are not their only enemies. The suspects are charged with having packages of poison and are beheaded. Criers are sent into the streets beating gongs and warning the people not to drink from the wells.

The people are hungry, and General Li Yuan-hung has two problems, that of money and that of rice. He has confiscated all public treasure, has restarted the Mint, and is issuing Republican script. He legalizes the National Government's banknotes as well as the notes of banks. The banks in the three cities have been closed by runs, and from his captured bullion he makes loans to permit them to reopen and to revive business. But on account of the stagnation of business and the increase in recruits he cannot get enough rice, and is sending agents to the rice districts to persuade the people to send cargoes to Wuchang as formerly. Representatives arrive bringing the submissions of outlying cities, and the army sends back deputies with them to get rice for its men. Stories of the landing of rice cargoes on the water front are circulated all over the City. The revolutionaries are led into searching craft on the river in hope of finding contraband rice which they can confiscate. At least, they find contraband accessaries, as the following from the Press shows : " The steam launches belonging to the traitor Feng Sao-chou and his property in the street have been confiscated. Since the outbreak he has several times made use of his launches to transport rice and coal for the Manchus."

Under the security of the guns of Serpent Hill, which hold the Imperial fleet at a distance, the revolutionists continue the organization of the Government. General Li Yuan-hung issues a proclamation abolishing likin, one of the most vexatious of China's taxes both to native and foreign traders. All but salt, tobacco, wine, and opium are exempted. The land tax for six months is remitted. He warns the people against fabrications of rumours that " damp the ardour of the soldiers," such as that large forces are arriving from the North. His proclamation notifies the people that half of the Northern men are highly patriotic and in favour of the revolution, and are not to be feared. They may be depended upon to declare in favour of the Republican cause and join in suppressing the Manchus and reviving the authority of the Han people. Anyone caught circulating rumours will be promptly dealt with according to military law. He hears that both officers and soldiers have been seen in pleasure-houses, whereas they should sleep on brushwood and drink gall, so as not to forget China's condition. At such time as this, indulgence means ruin for the revolution, and all officers are required to take warning and rigorously suppress these practices.

In their security and preoccupation the revolutionists do not forget their antagonists, of whom they hear various reports. " General Chang Piao has been wounded in the left shoulder by a bullet, and is so sick of vexation that he is likely to die from it, and takes no food." " Admiral Sah has been pondering deeply over General Li's letters to him, and it is expected that he will openly declare for the revolution ere long." The Hanyang Iron Works have closed, and the Press hears that it is " because they are the property of Sheng Hsuan-huai, who ought to be cut into ten thousand pieces." They have heard that when the

Hupeh troops with Tuan Fang heard the news of Wuchang, they proclaimed the independence of Szechuan, killed Tuan Fang, are taking cities on their way back, and are expected at an early date. They do not mention Tuan Fang's head, which his bodyguard is bringing.

Sun Yat-sen is mentioned early in events at Wuchang, where his brother Sun Yu has been made President of the Provincial Assembly to succeed Tang Hua-lung, who has been elected Governor of Hupeh. Sun Yat-sen's first appearance upon the ground where he seems to have stationed his brother on an important outpost is that of the bright angel of revolution. In the imaginations of the poverty-stricken Republicans he is bringing £400,000 sterling and 17 war-vessels, and will arrive at Wuchang shortly. But the real situation is that, having organized the civil governments for Wuchang, Hankow, and Hanyang, the revolutionists are beginning to be anxious about what the Imperialists are doing.

General Chang Piao, after being cashiered by the Throne and ordered speedily to punish the revolutionaries severely, set obediently about his task. He claimed to have got away from Wuchang with about 2000 men. He made his camp at Seven Mile Creek, just below Hankow, in company with the gunboats and the Chinese cruiser *Ch'u-yu*. The revolutionists, with their artillery on Serpent Hill, Wuchang, commanded the upper reaches of the river and its communications with Hanyang and Hankow. The Imperialist war-vessels could not go above Hankow, but could support General Chang Piao and the Northern Imperialist troops from below. The revolutionists asked to be allowed to send 1500 men through the Foreign Concessions, on account of the paved roads there, but were refused by the foreign consuls, and instead marched along the railway embankment toward Seven Mile Creek.

On Oct. 15 General Chang Piao announces that he has 4500 troops at Kilometre 10, to which place he has moved his men to meet the revolutionists. On Oct. 16 Admiral Sah Chen-ping with his flagship arrives to command the cruisers and gunboats that are to assist in the recovery of the three cities. The river contains four British, two American, two German, and one Japanese war-vessels anchored opposite the Foreign Concessions of Hankow. On Oct. 17 two additional British and one additional German ships arrive. There are present the Japanese and British admirals, Kawashima and Winsloe.

General Li Yuan-hung sends a notification to the foreign consuls in Hankow that he intends to attack the Imperialists, which he does under cover of early morning on Oct. 18. A masked battery on the Wuchang side first opens fire on Admiral Sah's fleet to cover the advance of the infantry toward Kilometre 10. The infantry is assisted by five field-guns. The gunboats reply to the masked battery, which ceases after the land battle begins.

The "battle of Kilometre 10" begins. 9.30 a.m. there are 100 killed and wounded, and the battle rests until 2.30 p.m., when the revolutionists advance 1000 infantry from their reinforcements arrived from Wuchang, among which are nine additional field-guns. General Yin Chang, Imperialist Minister of War, arrives at Hsiao-kan, 40 miles up the railway, and sends five train-loads of troops to Kilometre 10, and at 5 p.m. the revolutionists are retiring toward Race Course Road that leads into the Hankow Concessions. They carry with them 150 wounded and leave 50 dead. Buildings set on fire by shells along the railway to Hankow burn until 8.30 p.m. General Li Yuan-hung issues a bulletin claiming a great "victory." On the strength of this victory he raises his reward on the head of his late colleague and present antagonist, General Chang Piao, to 5000 taels. Resting quietly aboard his launch in Seven Mile Creek, General Chang Piao says he has no intention of renewing the fighting until reinforcements arrive from Peking.

On Oct. 19 the revolutionists, reinforced with 3000 additional men from Wuchang, return to the attack on Kilometre 10. Toward evening the Imperialists give way, retreating up the railway, strewing the embankment with cartridges and accoutrements. 6 p.m. the victorious revolutionists, led by their General and accompanied by the Wuchang viceregal band, return to Hankow, their troops in possession of the battlefield.

All that was seen of this two days' fighting from a foreign window in the Concessions is described by an absorbed onlooker. He sees the troops move past, then 25 wounded men brought to the London Mission Hospital, a mob of rebel coolies destroy Culvert Bridge, a train loaded with Imperialists coming down to the Bridge, where officers descend from the engine, make an inspection and retire, after which the mob of coolies resume.

There are large numbers of the Imperialists, and toward three o'clock the onlooker sees the rebels advance and the

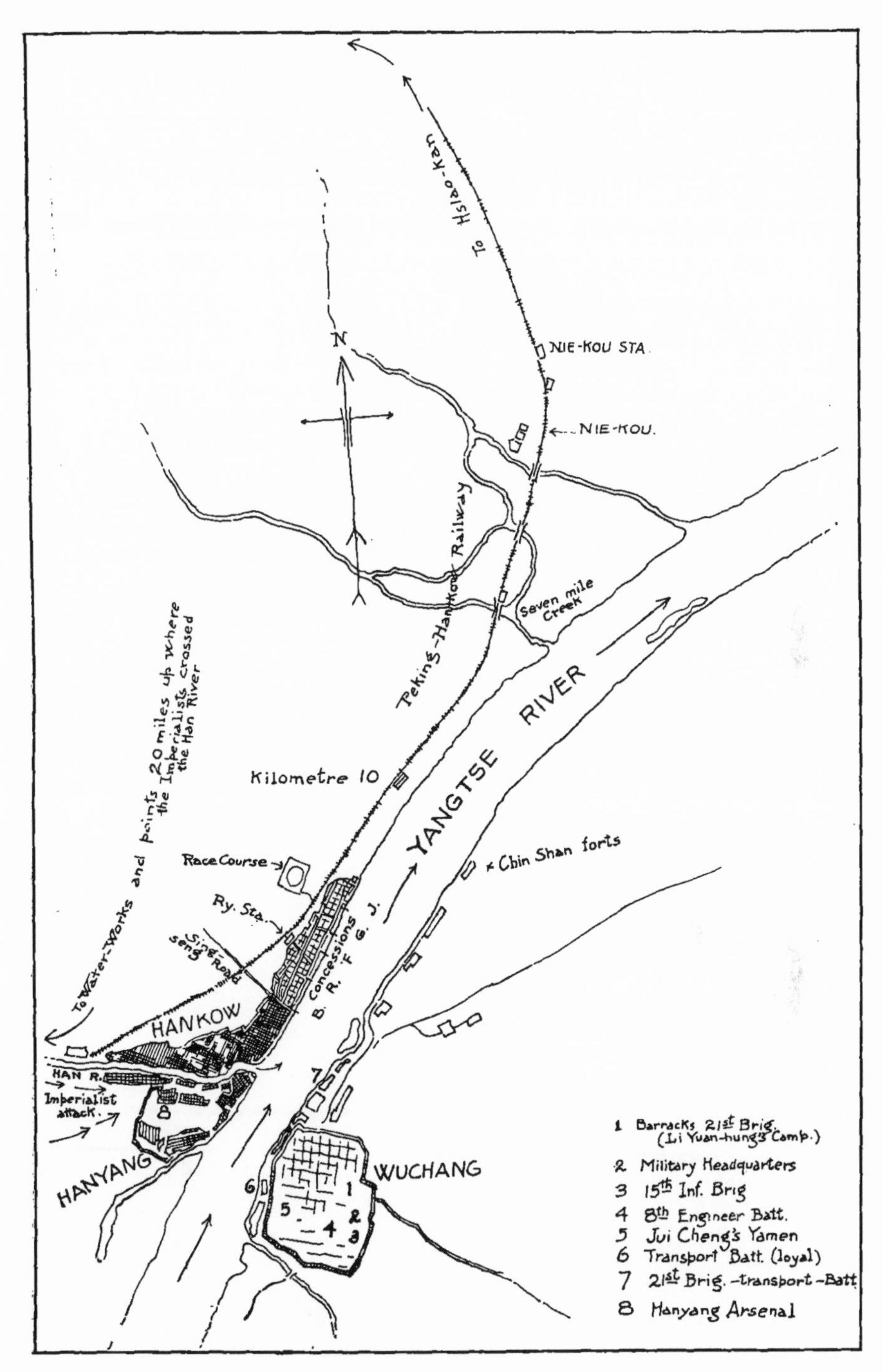

WUCHANG, HANKOW, HANYANG, AND SURROUNDINGS.

To face p. 120

Imperialists in the train move back behind Kilometre 10. The cheering of the revolutionists is louder than the firing, and only a dozen shots can be heard. These shots are sent after the train, and great numbers of revolutionists advance along the railway embankment. They fire into the south side of Chinese Town ahead of them, where three shells from the Chinese cruisers drive them away. They desert their little field-gun which stands on the embankment for a time and then disappears, either being destroyed or recaptured. A shell from one of the Chinese cruisers drops near the pigeon-shooting tower in the Race Club grounds, and revolutionist officers directing operations from it come down *chop chop*. Only two shots graze the framework. By 5 p.m. the revolutionist troops seeming thoroughly frightened by the fire from the cruisers are retreating as fast as they can. One horse is riderless. They retreat as far as Race Course Road, after which they are hidden from the writer's view. The Imperialists on land do not fire at any time.

On Oct. 19 the onlooker sees a handful of Imperialists just this side of Kilometre 10 Station. Several revolutionist officers are up in the Race Club pigeon-shooting tower. The rebels are making a detour by the north at double quick. No firing except a few shots from Imperialists' outposts. At 1.10 p.m. the cruisers are manœuvring in the river. The revolutionist troops are followed by large numbers of coolies. A mule drawing a field-gun appears on the railway embankment. The cruisers go down to Seven Mile Creek. After twenty minutes' silence, the revolutionists fire three shells into the Imperialists' position and a company of revolutionist soldiers advances along the railway. About thirty of the Imperialists' khaki tents are seen. The cruisers are still farther down the river. The revolutionists at two o'clock send coolies to Kilometre 10 Station to investigate, and finding no one, the troops advance and carry away the Imperialists' tents, and return in great numbers to Hankow.

This is the "battle of Kilometre 10." It is like America; it is like Russia, and even more like China. Another foreign spectator said one of the shells fired by the Imperialists and accidentally landing in the German Concession was made of wood, and the revolutionist newspapers report that the "bullets and cartridges captured from the Imperialists at Liu-kia-miao are of wood." "This precisely recalls the story of the Chinese-Japanese

War," observes the Press ; " some great official has evidently found a contractor who is willing to supply wooden shells at the price of steel, and divide the difference." Behold the Chinese version of the wooden nutmeg of Connecticut.

It is a busy time in the Foreign Concessions and on the river. On Oct. 18 a German torpedo-boat came bearing the German Vice-Admiral von Krosig, and additional German and British war-vessels arrived. One British vessel, the *Britomart*, dropped down the river to act as relay for wireless telegrams that are the only source of information for the outside world respecting what is going on in the heart and centre of China's industrial life and revolution. Another has gone up the river to Ichang, which has been taken possession of by the revolutionists.

After raising the price on his antagonist's head, Li Yuan-hung contents himself for two days with securing the removal of the Chinese Imperial flag from the foreign merchant-vessels on the river—their captains agreeing not to fly the Imperialist flag while at Hankow.

Firing does not begin again until October 22, but continues throughout the day, both the naval and land forces participating. This is characterized by observers in the Foreign Concessions as " no startling development." Events are not moving fast enough for the foreign spectators, who ridicule the type of warfare with which they are being entertained. " I have been down to Kilometre 10 Station this afternoon," says a sight-seer, " and found the rebels fortifying its northern side. They are there in large numbers, bringing over quantities of ammunition from Wuchang. If the Northerners are willing to fight, we think the rebels will be thoroughly beaten back. They are a motley crew."

The Imperialist land troops are now directed by General Yin Chang from Hsiao-kan, October 27. They are preparing to take Hankow, and the only battle of the rebellion has commenced.

The onlooker who on Oct. 19 poked fun at the " battle of Kilometre 10," hears that the casualties for two days are estimated at 2000. But it is no doubt an exaggeration.

General Li Yuan-hung has issued an order placing his soldiers under stricter discipline on account of their unorganized fighting at the battle of Kilometre 10, and now its effects may be seen even from the Foreign Concessions. The spectator standing in the window of the foreign Hospital sees the coolie recruits of the revolutionist army working up the railway line fighting the Imperialist machine-guns. Their efforts are futile but resolute. One man steps behind a tree to put a cartridge clip into his rifle, and having done so marches on, kneels, fires with deliberate aim, and advances. All do the same, repeating these tactics until bowled over. All, sooner or later, go down before the machine-guns, but this has not deterred those behind. The revolutionists are making a determined attack on the Imperialists' position.

To the Imperialist officers it was like a massacre. It gave the Northern Army a terrible taste of blood. "In the morning before dawn," said an Imperialist colonel, "the revolutionists were reported advancing. As it became light we could make them out through the glasses coming forward in straggling lines, which I estimated at about 1500 men. I had only about 800 men, but beside our rifles we had machine-guns. The enemy continued in his straggling line formation, and when his colour-bearer came into rifle range, I ordered up a dozen of our sharpshooters. When the lines arrived within good firing distance, I ordered the sharpshooters to pick off the standard-bearer, plainly visible under a broad banner of white foreign sheeting with the characters of the Republican Army written upon it. The man fell, and the standard was picked up by another. He also fell, and this was repeated until eight men had been killed under the standard. The rebel line was drawing in, and I brought forward the machine-guns. By this time the rebels were getting too near, and there was nothing to do but mow them down. Their force was obliterated."

The attack of the revolutionists was assisted by the Wuchang forts, which bombarded the gunboats. The fighting was so near to the Concessions that the families of foreigners were all removed to safety down the river. The Imperialists captured and lost the railway station before the reckless advance of the revolutionists in close formation cheering and firing wildly in face of the machine-guns. The revolutionists in the afternoon of October 28 lose the railway station to the Imperialists, which October 29 the Imperialists still hold.

Having advanced ten kilometres, General Feng Kuo-chang, in command of the Imperialist left, has turned the revolutionists' right flank and is preparing to enter Hankow. He has lost 40 killed and 150 wounded, but has captured all of the revolutionist camp equipage and stores, as well as arms, at Kilometre 10.

The Imperialists claim to have captured 30 guns and to have inflicted losses of 400 upon the revolutionists the first day. The revolutionist loss is given at 500 men killed, 1500 wounded, together with prisoners and 15 field-guns.

The Imperialists enter Hankow. The revolutionists attack for half an hour, keeping up a brave defence at the same time from the housetops. The fighting is one-sided, and the rabble revolutionist troops are driven to bay by the Imperialist trained army. Fires have been started either by explosions of shells or by incendiaries and the burning of Hankow begins.

The battle is waged with uncertain effect all throughout October 30. The revolutionists make a strong attack from their base across the Han River at Hanyang, but lose three field-guns. Losing, they offer a determined resistance. Their losses on Oct. 31 are no less than 1000 killed and 3000 wounded. What the Imperialist losses are no observer can find out. Exasperated by the revolutionists shooting their men down from cover, among the crowded houses, and the last stinging blows they receive as they invade Hankow, they begin to burn. Fires spring up everywhere, and as the last day of October closes, the climax of conflagration is reached—two-thirds of the City are reduced to ashes. For three days street fighting and massacre rages with the flames. It is a wild scene of burning, looting, and killing, by the Chinese themselves, carried on by the worst elements which a state of war can let loose to prey upon men, and by the soldiers of two contending armies. The soldiers of both sides kill prisoners and wounded and commit all the barbarities of savage warfare.

"The end of the British Concession presents at present a strange sight," writes a British observer. "Soldiers and people are looting the doomed City, the latter making their way on to the Concession with their booty. There, in accordance with our declared neutrality, looters have to give up their spoil unless they can prove their right to the things in their possession. Bluejackets as police and missionaries as interpreters have charge of the proceedings, and the accumulated piles of loot carted from time to time to the police station till further orders, bear witness to their industry." "This burning of the City is the work of devils, not men. . . . The people, at least thousands, had stayed believing it would be all right."

" Loot is being taken out of the City by gangs," says another. " Cash-shops and pawn-shops are those most raided. . . . All night through the City has been one red glare. The light has lighted up Wuchang so that houses could all clearly be seen. It is a terrible sight, but oh ! the poor people. The well-to-do merchants and their families fleeing from the burning City and nowhere to flee. They sit down in the road and just burst out crying. It is all too horrible for words. ' Where can we go ? ' they ask, and we have nowhere to suggest."

Part II

After the " battle of Kilometre 10 " the roll of dead and wounded showed that no real fighting took place. The Imperialists had only been trying to draw the revolutionists away from the Foreign Concessions and on to ground where the warships could shell them. On the other hand, the revolutionists had been staying under shelter of the Foreign Concessions and of their own guns in Hanyang. Perhaps they felt their military weakness and were discouraged by their first attempts. In any case, they appealed to strategy. After seeing the attempts of General Chang Piao and Admiral Sah to draw them into ambush, they tried to win over Admiral Sah. The student revolutionaries of the three cities addressed a letter to him which concluded with the appeal : " Therefore, Admiral, we appeal to your generous sympathy and wisdom, and plead for the safety and welfare of 400,000,000 souls and for the free growth and development of the Chinese, who, if allowed to be free, are bound to make a wonderful contribution that will go to enrich the civilization of the whole world. If you would disarm your gunboats and cruisers and steam up to Hankow, all the people in these three cities will be enraptured to welcome you with wild enthusiasm and intense honour."

The cause of the rebellion was to be successful through persuasion. It made its own way, led by the persuasion of its leader, General Li Yuan-hung. He had already addressed one letter to the Imperialist Admiral Sah, and on the eve of the battle of Hankow he sent him another, in which he said :

" MY DEAR MASTER,—My last letter must have reached

Your Excellency. But having received no order from you, my mind is much perturbed and ill at ease. The reason why I come out this time as leader of the men is owing to *force majeure* ; and I would respectfully beg to explain it more fully to you. At the time when the Wuchang rising broke out, all the troops under my command were away, leaving me in an empty camp absolutely without means of defence. When the revolutionary army had driven Jui Cheng out of the City, it came to my camp, surrounded it and made a search. I, having dressed myself in civilian clothes, hid myself in a back room, in which I was discovered and captured, and reprimanded for want of patriotism. All around me were pistols and guns, my head and body would certainly have parted company upon the least attempt at resistance on my part ; therefore I had to consent to their demand as a means of policy. You, my Master, must know all along that I am always very careful, and must have wondered greatly that I could have behaved thus in an emergency. Although attending business for several days, I dared not lightly move, because I did not know the true sentiments, the strength of unison, and the chances of success of my compatriots. Should I lightly make a rash move, it might entail disastrous results which would throw us into a state of chaos, and not only would we be unable to redeem the humiliation of the Han Clans, but would augment their peril and danger. Now, having commanded the army for eight days, I find that all of us are one-minded, imbued with the same enmity and hatred towards our common foe.

" In old times Wu Wang said : ' Ch'ou has millions of servants, but they possess millions of minds ; I have 3000 servants, but of one mind.' Now of one mind, we have more than thirty thousand ; and still, scholars from all the provinces, mostly having studied in special schools in Japan and Western countries, members of the gentry of the purest blood for generations, with useful knowledge and rich experiences, as well as officials, the gentry and others of this province, are joining us continually.

" Therefore when we opened diplomatic relations for the first time the Powers have admitted us as one of the belligerents, and declared their neutrality. The revolutionary army has, on the other hand, been careful not to injure the foreigners or the effects and property of any private individual. This is not only new in Chinese history, but also seldom attained in civilization by revolutionaries of any Power.

" We may conclude that the fortunes of the Ching nation must be on the wane, and she must be incapable of employing the worthy and the brave, to cause such an influx to our standard of clever, accomplished, and wise men from all four quarters. Could this possibly be attributed to my influence alone? Take the battle of yesterday, for instance: the soldiers fought individually and rushed forward bravely even without urging; our brother Chinese who helped us to fight bare-handed, and to destroy rails, were innumerable; and even women and children came upon the scene with bread and tea as presents. Such pathetic scenes will incite heroism by a mere recounting of them. Who have no liver and gall? [*i.e.* Who are without courage?] Who have no warm earnestness? Who are not the offspring of Huang Ti [Yellow Emperor]? Could they be willing to remain slaves of the Manchus and to injure their brothers? I, being aware of all this and confident in the great possibility of future prospects, have sworn and declared with our army to recover the Han [Chinese] territory, to abrogate the oligarchic form of government, to establish a Chinese Republic, and to maintain the peace of the world.

" Therefore, in these few days, we have explicitly notified all the Powers and extensively informed our brothers, in all the provinces, each of which we advise to declare independence by itself, in preparation for an ultimate amalgamation, and for the holding of a public election of a President to govern us at a place to be then fixed. The glad voice of our brothers in welcoming this declaration has been so hearty and strong as to vibrate the heaven and the earth. So, in a single battle, several hundreds of our enemies were slain. Now, since the resuscitation of Han or the destruction of Man has long been foreshadowed, it can be understood by everyone, not by the wise alone. It is due solely to the teachings of you, my dear Master, that I myself can divine the delicate feelings of patriots.

" The rising of Wuchang this time, as I have ascertained and can assure you, is a genuine outburst and not comparable to any other revolutionary movement. Within a few hours' time, we were fortunate enough to regain possession of the three towns of Wu-Han [Wuchang, Hanyang, and Hankow], in which there are arsenals and armouries, iron-works, cotton weaving and spinning mills, linen factories and silk filatures. They are the centre of the whole nation, commercially and politically; and as this is an epoch of communication, the Capital of a nation should be established here, in order to be able to vie with either London, Berlin, Paris, St. Petersburg, or Washington.

" It is reported that in the Autumn Manœuvres the Man and the Han soldiers have quarrelled and fought with each other. If this be true, then Heaven has ordained it so; how could human contrivance avail anything? Yuan-hung [himself] has received instructions from Your Excellency, but is deficient in learning and knowledge, and cannot bear such heavy responsibility; he has already informed his compatriots that he is going to invite his Master to take up the duties which they demand from him; he will even come on board his Master's cruiser to beg of him to accept.

" The ancient people once spoke of Hsia An thus: ' If that man did not come forth, how would human lives fare? ' Now the brothers exclaim in myriads of voices but in one breath, my Teacher does not come forth, [therefore] how will the lives of our 400,000,000 brothers fare?

" Judging by the present aspect of affairs, if my Teacher will only consent to come forth and save the 400,000,000 of our brothers, hills and dales will at once change colour at the approach of our patriotic flag. With 400,000,000 to contend with several thousands of Manchu Clans; with the citizens of a Republic just budding forth to confront with the Ching Dynasty nearing the end of its course; I say, though Washington spent eight years in waging bloody battles to renovate America, my Master, if he will only come forth, can contemplate in barely eight months the flying of the Chinese republican flag on the map of Asia.

" The master best knows his disciple, so the disciple best knows his master. Though Yuan-hung is unworthy, he will not be the slave of the bannerman; but that does not prevent him from being the disciple of a great mind.

" Tang and Wu [two feudal lords or princes who flourished during the reigns of King Chih and King Ch'ou respectively] having saved the people, both became themselves their Kings. My Master will certainly not let Washington monopolize the good name alone for saving his people. I am not praying my Teacher with selfish motives for the salvation of the lives of our 400,000,000 brothers. The living or dying of either Man or Han depends upon the single body of my Teacher alone. Prince

Chi's example may be well worth emulating, as I have thought of it again and again. Otherwise, all our brothers would regard you as a person opposing their sentiments, and would treat you as a Manchu slave, then even Yuan-hung will not be able to forbid them striking the blow.

"Should you not think me in the wrong, I hope you will issue instructions which I shall obey by leading the brothers of our Han Clans to the outskirts of the City to welcome the coming of our Hero."

Admiral Sah thereupon had nothing to say respecting General Li's letter except that he was under the orders of Yuan Shih-k'ai. Yuan Shih-k'ai was Viceroy of Hunan and Hupeh (the Hukuang provinces) and had command of all military in that region. Li Yuan-hung's "motley" soldiers were again attacking between Seven Mile Creek and Kilometre 10, and on Oct. 27 Admiral Sah again turned his guns on the revolutionist advance from Hankow. Admiral Sah then had a personal reply for General Li, which he spoke of to the foreign consuls. He notified them that on the following day at 3 p.m. (October 28) he would bombard Wuchang, the rebel commander's capital and headquarters. He kept the appointment, shelling Wuchang for fifty-eight minutes. Thus the "master" to his "pupil."

General Li had ready a counter reply to his "teacher" Admiral Sah. When Admiral Sah notified the Allies, represented by the foreign consuls at Hankow, that he would shell the revolutionists' capital, General Li notified them that he had been proclaimed "President of the Republic of China." He had received reports from other provinces showing that the cause was moving on without help of military conquest—it was fighting its way on moral lines. "The Anhuei provincial troops are mutinous and proceeding to join him." "The Imperialist gunboat crews are mutinous and are turning to the Republican side; representatives are sent from Wuchang to explain the present movement to the crews." "All the gunboats are short of coal and the sailors are deserting. The rest are threatening death to their officers if they do not get their pay."

Hunan Province adjoining on the south "declared its independence" at Changsha, the Governor joining in, and the Military Administration there telegraphed Li Yuan-hung "it is one with him in raising the Hans and exterminating the Manchus." It asks for rifles, ammunition, some money, but will send rice and charcoal in return. The new order has given assurance to the people in Hankow, where foreigners are impressed with the Republican idea, especially its scrupulous regard for foreigners and for the common soldier. " An officer from Wuchang comes to the hospitals [foreign] in Hankow each day to inquire about the welfare of the men wounded in the recent fighting." " Consideration for ordinary soldiers is a kind of new thing among the Chinese," says the foreign Press.

The proclamation of a President in China awakened curiosity as to this Wuchang and its gathering of conspirators. Out of the revolutionary recruits, delegates, soldiers of fortune, conspirators, flocking to it, was constructed a Council or " Senate," whose members stood for ten other provinces beside Hupeh, the mother province of revolution. Fukien, Shensi, and Kiangsi provinces revolted, General Feng Shan was assassinated at Canton, and Canton revolutionists asserted Canton's readiness to join the cause. The Republic was something that could be grasped in the hand. Claiming credentials from the " Military Governments " of eleven provinces, the " Senate " of Wuchang, October 28, 1911, " elected " Li Yuan-hung President.

CHAPTER XIV

FOREIGN CONCESSIONS UNDER FIRE

"THEY are all coming on to the Foreign Concessions, also a great swarm of bad characters. A shell burst on the warehouse-roof alongside our kitchen—the noise was terrific."

Hankow is the only place in China where foreigners have been caught between the lines of contending Chinese armies. The children and most of the women have been sent away to Shanghai, but the men remain and have formed a volunteer corps to guard property.

On Oct. 11, when the Viceroy Jui Cheng warned them he could give no protection in case of attack, they were on patrol at six o'clock in the evening, and thenceforth co-operated with the defence forces of marines landed from the foreign warships anchored in the river.

The foreigners are confined to five Concessions, British, Russian, French, German, and Japanese, extending along the Yangtse River from the east end of Hankow native city. The Concessions are neutral ground, which only refugees and wounded may enter, and to which foreign missionaries, teachers, and others from outlying stations in Wuchang, Hanyang, Hankow, and elsewhere have repaired. From the first, when the bomb exploded in the Russian Concession, ushering in the Republic, the colony has played a spectacular part in the drama of the "Republic." With the river on one side patrolled by war-vessels and the railway from Peking forming a highway for the military on the other parallel with its west wall, with Hankow at its south end possessed by the revolutionists, and the camp of the Imperialists on the north, it has been completely surrounded by the military of the two contending sides.

On Oct. 11 foreign warships in the Yangtse River are starting for the scene. The Japanese Admiral Kawashima, in the flagship *Tsushima*, is among the first to arrive, and being the senior officer, the foreign consuls and naval and volunteer commanders join in requesting him to take command. He gives orders to place the Concessions in a state of defence, and asks the Chinese war-vessels in the river to confine their fire to waters away from the Concessions—a request which they comply with by retiring farther down stream.

On Oct. 13, four British, two American, two German, and one Japanese war-vessels are at the Hankow Concessions, and the merchant-steamer *Han-ping* has started with the foreign women and children for Shanghai. An additional American gunboat arrives on Oct. 14. On Oct. 16 the last foreigners from Wuchang retire to the Concessions. Two German and one British war-vessels arrive on Oct. 17, and a German torpedo-boat on Oct. 18. On Oct. 20, one German and one British war-vessels arrive, and the foreign colony has altogether 22 warships for its protection. They are trying to keep commerce open.

The consuls and foreign refugees note that from time to time the *hongs* (business houses) are doing some "merchandizing." At the end of October the surgeon of the British gunboat *Nightingale* is treating the wounded of Admiral Sah, the Imperialist naval commander, who has been bombarding Wuchang, while receiving some well-directed rebel shells on his decks. The surgeons and physicians ashore have been keeping open the foreign Hospital at Hankow, where bullets have been flying since October 18.

The bluejackets, or marines, are guarding the boundaries of the Concessions, especially at the back, where the land fighting is going on, and have stopped an inundation by the belligerents. A Red Cross Department has been organized under the American Dr. Wylie and is running a Red Cross Refuge at the Wesleyan Mission in Hankow, where on Nov. 1 it has 150 wounded under its care. There is also a British Hospital, a German Hospital, and at St. Paul's Cathedral a Roman Catholic Hospital.

The foreign doctor in charge of the Hospital at the Wesleyan Mission is spending his nights in the Concession and his days in the Hospital. When Hankow is fired he is in the Concession with others, but at dawn a relief party of a dozen or more doctors, volunteers, and missionaries board a Red Cross launch on the bank of the Yangtse and try to reach the Hospital by water. Entering the Han River, they find the Hanyang side swarming with revolutionists. Their boat is soon stopped and refused permission to proceed. Bullets are whistling, and the relief party can hear a rapid-fire gun in action in the neighbourhood, which is enveloped in smoke. The Hospital, as well as a school of blind boys under missionary care, lying almost in the direction of fire, are cut off.

The revolutionists are vacating Hankow for Hanyang, and the foreigners are waiting to see if the north and south ends of the City are to be burnt, as the centre has been.

On Nov. 3, the now invested foreign community having witnessed the horrors of sacking and destruction in Hankow, takes a thoroughly serious view of the situation. Someone suggests that the belligerents should remove themselves and fight out their quarrel from a safe distance. Acrimonious criticism is made of those foreigners who are charged with excessive sympathy with the revolutionaries, which is believed by some to be dangerous to the future situation of foreigners. Now come the phenomena that is the obvious result of miscellaneous foreigners of incompatible ideas and temperaments assembled in close quarters under abnormal conditions, recalling the clashing of temperaments during the siege of the Peking Legations in 1900. They are the clash of individual idiosyncrasies, national prejudices, the civilian protest against the conditions to which they are subjected by the military, and the old antipathy between the missionary and lay elements.

The community is now cut off from telegraphic communication and knows next to nothing of the outside world. Its Red Cross flag has been fired on both by the Imperialists and the revolutionists. These incidents have an interesting effect in pointing out that the Red Cross flag is the Concessions' flag, the flag of all nationalities, and inspires in the otherwise incompatible elements composing the community the spirit of loyalty to each other.

"The fighting throughout has been of the most terrible character," one of the besieged writes. "No prisoners are taken on either side, the wounded are often killed where they lie, and suspicious persons are arrested and on failing to give account of themselves are immediately beheaded." The Red Cross volunteers working in the doomed native city bring out reports of looting and rape and say that it does not look safe for foreigners now. One of the Chinese Red Cross workers is seriously wounded by a rifle bullet. Missiles are entering the Concessions. A shell lands in the Roman Catholic compound, British Concession, pierces a tree and explodes with a terrific report bespattering the wall of the house with fragments. A large piece of the shell enters a bedroom shutter, crosses under the bed of one of the Roman Catholic fathers who is sleeping, strikes the farther wall and rebounds into the middle of the room. A Chinaman is wounded in front of the *hong* of Jardine, Matheson, & Company. The *godown* of the Nippon Kisen Kaisha is burned at a loss of half a million taels. An idea of the events taking place on the confines of the Concessions is afforded by the stories brought in by scouting parties from the Concessions.

The energy displayed by the Chinese coming out of the native city with loot contradicts any imputation of laziness. Coolies otherwise thin from starvation arrive wearing silks and looking as robust from the multiplication of fine garments on their backs as though they have always been wealthy compradors. "Beggars parade the streets in silk gowns while forgetting to change their tattered shoes," says a reporter for the *Central China Post*.

At the pawn-shops guarded by Imperialist soldiers the looters hustle each other to gain an entrance, or busy themselves with purloining from those who are coming out. "Here comes the officer!" shouts a boy, and the soldiers fire a volley into the roof of the building opposite. Up comes an officer, compliments the soldiers on the manner in which they are keeping back the looters, and passes on. The place again swarms with them.

At the entrances to the Concessions the piles of loot commandeered by the Concessions' police steadily grow. Cottons, silks, furs, lie "in a glorious heap," continues the *Post*, "with colours so dazzling as to render Joseph's coat a garb of sombre hue." There is every article of dress, from the blue cotton of the peasant to the embroidered theatrical costume of silk and cloth of gold

One looter using a plausible story to the effect that he is the owner of a shop is allowed to make away with three cart-loads of its goods. Half an hour later he repasses the spot with four empty carts *en route* into the City. This time when he returns he has become the owner of five shops and deals in "everything from tobacco to tiger-skins," and the police think it time to gather him in and confiscate his levies. One looter appears at the Concessions with two cases of hog bristles—a common article of export in China—for an outgoing steamer Examined, they are found to contain silks and other plundered valuables. Looters appear with their clothes stuffed with valuables, and the Concessions' police amuse themselves by shaking bolts of silk, rolls of velvet, carvings, or fine clocks out of their captives.

Outside the Concessions the Chinese are not always so considerate of looters as the Concession police. Three looters caught by the Imperial soldiers at the railway station are made to put on clothes they have stolen and are then shot. Others captured in the evening are tied to telegraph-poles to await the arrival of the executioner. A supposed spy captured in the Imperial camp is hung up for the soldiers to dig their bayonets into, and then stoned to death.

General Feng Kuo-chang is the Imperialist Commander directing his force from Kilometre 10. General Huang Hsing (a noted conspirator and revolutionist who arrived at Wuchang on Nov. 5) is made Chief Commander under President General Li Yuan-hung, later to become famous in the Republic. His soldiers with their outposts in Hankow are virtually defending the river bank of the Han. The artillery fight is between Tortoise Hill in Hanyang and the Race Course behind the Concessions.

The whole life of the foreigners in the Concessions has now become one of activities for relief of native distress surrounding them. They have called for outside aid, and their appeals have been answered by appropriations of money from Shanghai. The most interesting event of the 6th is the striking of the post office by a shell which penetrates two thick walls and lodges in a third but does not explode. The native postal staff, however, is not deterred by this from returning to its work of sorting 2,000,000 native letters that have accumulated during the panic.

The volunteers of the British Concession have found their work "no sinecure"; they bear the brunt of the pressure of the Chinese refugees on account of their Concession joining the native city. They are relieved from time to time by the German and French volunteers. "They have been doing splendidly," paternally remarks the appreciative editor of the *Central China Post*.

On Nov. 7 the event of the day is the visit of the wife of President General Li Yuan-hung to the Red Cross hospitals, where she presents the wounded, revolutionist and Imperialist alike, each with flowers, two oranges, and two dollars in money (silver), and speaks a few kind words. "One Northern soldier protested that he could not receive the gift, as he had fought for the other side. He was reminded that all were brethren, and he accepted the presents, saying, 'This kindness makes my heart feel very uncomfortable.'"

While President General Li Yuan-hung remains steadfastly in Wuchang awaiting the arrival of Huang Hsing, to make him a General, and to confer upon him the military chieftainship highest under the President, his soldiers in Hankow and Hanyang have been fighting without qualified leaders. He has still before him the problem of provisioning his army, but supplies of all kinds are coming in. At last there is corn in Egypt, and President General Li Yuan-hung is able to send rice to the extent of 1600 piculs and $10,000 (silver) to the Red Cross Society for use in the hospitals of Hankow, and to sell to the foreign community. He is not in danger of being starved out of his capital, but the defeat before Hankow, accompanied by the loss of 30 guns, has weakened his defences.

Boatloads of reinforcements from Hunan are arriving. They come from Changsha in steam launches and junks. For a mile and a half down the river from the Foreign Concessions at Hankow the Imperialists have placed batteries at short intervals, to command the river. President General Li Yuan-hung is erecting batteries at Wuchang, in which he is mounting antiquated smooth-bore, muzzle-loading cannon. Some of his cannon that have been firing into Hankow and occasionally dropping a shell into the Concessions are using black powder which his reopened powder-mills have been turning out since the middle of October.

In his letter to Admiral Sah, General Li Yuan-hung said that the Republic advised the provinces each to declare independence by itself. Amalgamation was to be arrived at in the future. According to this, the object aimed at was not so much the defeat of the military forces of the Throne as the cutting off of its resources. When, therefore, upon the fall of Hankow the Imperialist soldiers appeared at the water's edge opposite him, he invited them to surrender to the Republican side in a proclamation from "the General of the Hupeh Army to the Northern soldiers":

"(1) First several boats are moored in the river at the place of reception.

"(2) Brothers in the Northern Army who sympathize with our sentiments are requested to come to the bank of the river and raise their hands by way of signal, whereupon small craft will immediately appear to welcome them.

" (3) Whoever wishes to surrender must throw away his arms.

" (4) Brothers of the Northern Army who have surrendered will be accommodated in specially engaged buildings, with their meals supplied ; and when matters are settled they will be employed according to their respective merits.

" (5) If anyone wishes to return home, his passage expenses will be paid to him.

" Emperor Huang, 4609th year, ninth moon, 16th day (Nov. 6, 1911)."

In this proclamation no mention is made of the advanced pay of $50 (silver) hitherto offered deserters, indicating that Imperialist troops are deserting for causes which make it unnecessary to offer special inducements. In the Tungting Road in the Foreign Concessions at Hankow a deserting Imperialist soldier fleeing for his life has found sanctuary and is throwing off his regimental clothes. Imperialist officers come to the Concessions in search of red cloth for bands to wear as a sign that they would not fight the revolutionaries, obviously intended to be used as a sign of surrender and to enable them to pass over to the revolutionist lines at a convenient opportunity.

President General Li Yuan-hung prepares an inn and other houses at Wuchang in which to welcome deserters. An engine-driver from the Peking-Hankow Railway escaped from Hsaio-kan and arrived there says the Northern soldiers are very ignorant about trains, insisting on travelling when they have neither coal nor water and not allowing trainmen to replenish. They tied him on to the engine, from which he managed to make his escape. " They are always telegraphing to the North asking for more money or more food," said he.

Forty officials offering their services at the reception building provided by the President are given offices. Several hundred " Dare to Die " men have come forward, and " in all over 2000 men have offered their services."

Troops are so numerous as to elicit the observation from foreign spectators that the killing of a Republican immediately raises up more to take his place. The idea has been embodied in a cartoon elsewhere in the Republic showing the death of the revolutionary to be the immortality of the Revolution. The troops all appear queueless, and the Republican newspapers say that President General Li Yuan-hung has issued orders that all who enter or leave the City must have their queues cut and that there is a band of students in the City who go about with sharp knives cutting off queues whether the possessors of the queues are willing or not. Once shaven, the queueless head quickly finds its way to a foreign hat or cap.

The troops sent from Hunan on launches and junks are numerous and conspicuous because of the turbans they wear and their training and discipline. They have been divided between the Capital and the sister-city of Hanyang. Huang Hsing, Chief of Military under President General Li Yuan-hung, on the day of his arrival is seen riding through Wuchang at the head of an escort of twenty soldiers. " His outward appearance," writes a spectator, " is not particularly attractive. He was in uniform, riding on an old-fashioned wooden saddle, with coloured glasses over his eyes, and a big cigar in his mouth." His arrival has already heartened the troops.

On the nights of November 5 and November 7 detachments of revolutionaries from Hanyang went through the almost ruined city of Hankow in search of Imperialists whom they might find looting or hiding there. The first night they captured more than a hundred, who were brought to Wuchang and deprived of their arms. They left numbers killed in the streets and lanes. On Nov. 6 they beheaded many looters, tying the heads to poles upon which was also hung the loot of the victim.

Outside the walls of the Republican capital there is no evidence of the unusual except the constant drilling of recruits outside the North Gate. The farmers are at work in their fields. Inside there is some suspicion, but no fear except from spies and poisoners of wells. All but food- and water-carriers must have passes to enter the City gates. On account of the comparative quiet of Wuchang some of the missionaries have returned to their stations there, but are regarded in about the same revolutionary light as the Chinese and are subject to the same scrutiny and even suspicion. Every aid is given to commerce. All markets are open, and quantities of fresh supplies are coming in, including rice, salt, fish, fruit, and vegetables. The name of President General Li Yuan-hung is in everyone's mouth. The pervading testimony respecting him is: " He is good [worthy], he loves the people." His influence upon the people must be considerable, inasmuch as it shows itself in their lives. " Everyone," says our foreign observer, " from general to common soldier, lives on 250 cash per day or less, and is cultivating the simple life."

CHAPTER XV

THE PEN OF LI YUAN-HUNG

By November 10 between 800 and 900 deserters from the Imperialist forces have reached Wuchang. In the face of the disasters across the river there come from surrounding provinces these encouraging telegrams to General Li Yuan-hung :

" Tsai Ao-han, Military Administrator of Yunnan, to Generalissimo Li :

" From a distance we have seen your patriotic banner and offer our congratulations. On Nov. 9 we raised our own, and the whole province has joined with us—the garrisons at Linan-fu and Tali-fu—although there are many places in our provinces from which news comes slowly. We desire you to inform us regarding the progress of the movement in other provinces and how matters are progressing in Hupeh."

All the surrounding regions are appealing to President General Li Yuan-hung for advice and instructions as to how to co-operate with him. The province of Kueichou expects to advance against the North. Its Military Administrator, Yang Han, telegraphs that Kueichou declared its independence and has already dispatched Deputy Yuan to represent it at Wuchang with a view to advancing to the North.

Szechuan asks for news of how the war is progressing in the neighbourhood of Wuchang.

It is not progressing as satisfactorily as in Szechuan. President General Li Yuan-hung is on the defensive, and is merely holding his own. The Imperialists are trying to cross the Han River in order to turn his left flank and drive his men out of Hanyang. This they are unable to do within the range of the revolutionists' cannon on Tortoise Hill, but will ultimately accomplish to the north of the Black Mountain (Hei Shan). The revolutionists are running the arsenal day and night and claim to have more than 500 guns there with which to equip their defences.

How to beat the Rebels, how to beat the Imperialists, are the questions of November.

Following his proclamations inviting the Imperialist soldiers to join the Revolution, President General Li Yuan-hung again appeals to Admiral Sah Chen-ping to join. This time Admiral Sah consents to reply, and the substance of what he says is given out at the Republican headquarters. According to this, he objects to the Republican form of government because it is one thus far adopted only by a few nations. It would be better, he thinks, to convert the monarchy into a completely Constitutional government. He is credited with saying that he considers there has been enough of fighting.

General Li Yuan-hung's reply to this is given in full. He says :

"In reply to your kind letter, I have great pleasure in expressing our gratitude for your advice in reference to the kind of government we should adopt. This advice shows that you are full of desire to relieve the people and reform the government.

"The Revolution in Hupeh is but a token of the feeling against the poisonous monarchy. Since we declared only a month ago that the government would be made Republican, over ten provinces have joined our cause. People young and old are sick of the Manchu Government and delighted to welcome the Republican troops. Those who lead the people and the troops could not but take advantage of this opportunity. We have already deeply considered the subject you discussed. The problem of what kind of government we should adopt will be solved in the grand conference of the representatives of the various provinces when China proper is made independent. It is generally believed that your idea will be adopted, but anyhow the Manchu Government should be got rid of. You may be assured that the present monarchy will perish. I shall marvel if you do not join us. The various provinces will without doubt welcome you with all their hearts. You will play a great part in the conference that will be held.

"In your letter you say that we have shown our military power in these few days of fighting, but we assure you we could not help fighting against the Northern troops, as otherwise they would have seized us. It is with regret we inform you that the Northern troops have burned down the city of Hankow. This has caused me great unhappiness. But the merchants know it was not we that did this mischief.—Hoping for your favourable reply, etc.,

"LI YUAN-HUNG."

On Nov. 7 the Chinese fleet lying at Yang-lo below Seven Mile Creek consists of three cruisers, three gunboats, and three torpedo-boats. Admiral Sah is awaiting the arrival of his chief, Yuan Shih-k'ai. For some reason unintelligible to landsmen, but probably to attempt to blow up the railway bridge, one of the gunboats enters the mouth of Seven Mile Creek while a cruiser waits outside. They retire later, and nothing more is noted respecting them until the three cruisers are reported far down stream flying the revolutionist colours, and on Nov. 12 all remaining war-vessels heave anchor and follow them.

Admiral Sah has not seen the glories again pointed out to him by General Li Yuan-hung, but he alone of all the fleet has remained loyal. What became of Admiral Sah was a question for a month. Rumour said that he took leave of the fleet in these words : "I cannot turn to the revolutionists' side myself, the movement is too big for me. You, however, must do something for your country." He then went ashore at some point down the river and proceeded by merchant-steamer to Shanghai. This was the only answer to Li Yuan-hung's letter.

Since his recall from retirement Yuan Shih-k'ai has tried to get into direct touch with Li Yuan-hung. After he is appointed to the command of all the military and naval forces of Central China he writes to him, but gets no reply. He writes again when he is appointed Premier, and after he has started for Hankow, which is now in possession of his troops. He proposes amnesty and pardon for the revolutionists, the establishment of constitutional government for the country, and exclusion of members of the Imperial Family from high office, as a basis of peace. Li Yuan-hung hears that a delegate is coming from Yuan Shih-k'ai, and on Nov. 8, in counsel with General Huang Hsing, head of the Republican Ministry of War, and the generals commanding the revolutionary forces, it is unanimously decided to ask Yuan Shih-k'ai to be the President of China.

Yuan Shih-k'ai's letter, sent by hand to Li Yuan-hung, is as follows :

"Your Excellency, I have already written you twice, but

having received no answer, I am not aware whether or not the letters have reached you. In accordance with Imperial instructions I have now to state that an edict has been issued offering, first, full pardon for all past offences; second, the establishment of constitutional government; third, amnesty to all political offenders; fourth, that members of the Imperial Clan will not be employed in high office.

"These points being granted, in my opinion the government of our country can be renovated and prosperity brought back. I hasten to communicate this to you and desire that a method may be devised by which the present difficulties may be peacefully settled.

"The sooner the war is stopped the sooner peace will be enjoyed by the people and the country. If fighting goes on, regardless of who is the victor or the vanquished, not only will the people perish but the resources of the country will be wasted until, should that condition continue unduly, affairs will get into such a state that the country itself will be ruined. Furthermore, the soldiers of both sides are Chinese, and those who suffer are all Chinese. Whether the one side or the other succeed, it is the Chinese that must foot the bill.

"Personally I have been a long time dissatisfied with the Government, and therefore went into retirement, never intending to accept office again. In leaving my retirement now my only object was to be instrumental in composing the present differences. Furthermore, the Government is now repentant as it never was before. I admit that but for your valorous actions, the present proposals would never have been made. The merit of them belongs to you, and in my humble opinion nothing could be better than to take advantage of this opportunity, and, by concluding peace, secure the realization of the Throne's proposals. We can at least see how the Throne will act, and, if it is honest, then we will unitedly use our utmost efforts to promote the reforms. If it is not honest, we can still in consultation devise other plans, and, as far as I can see, there can be no failure to secure the full measure of our hopes. This is my view, and I will ask you to send me an answer in agreement with this, so that I may be able to report the matter to the Throne and carry out the necessary arrangements.

"As regards your associates,—all men of great ability, —not only will no fault be found with them, but I can guarantee they will be appointed to high positions to assist in carrying out the reforms.

" The Throne trusts me as one whose word can be relied on, and you also, I hope, believe that I would on no account break faith with respect to you and your associates. I understand that the Throne is issuing another edict, which will reach you within a few days. I, because of the many important affairs which I cannot venture to neglect, would urge you to send me an early answer by the hand of the bearer of this letter.

" My respectful prayers. Wishing you peace and prosperity, YUAN SHIH-K'AI."

Li Yuan-hung replied. It was like the " answer to the Sultan." All the terms offered were refused, but instead Yuan Shih-k'ai was urged to join the revolutionist camp, which action would immediately end all strife. Expressing the sentiments of the generals of the revolutionist army, Li Yuan-hung closed with the observation that Yuan Shih-k'ai's previous history was such that no camp would suit him better, and if he would come over, he would be made Provisional President of the United States of China.

Li Hou-chuan, Yuan Shih-k'ai's delegate in these communications, returned through Hankow to his superior at Nie-kou on the railway on Nov. 8, and on the next day Yuan Shih-k'ai left for Peking. Before leaving the battle area, he delegated Liu Chung-en and Tsai Ting-kan to proceed to Wuchang to ask Li Yuan-hung and the Revolutionary Government to appoint a peace conference. He had not given up. His next effort is described by the Republican newspaper *Ta Han Pao* :

The delegates arrive November 11 at Wuchang and enter by the Tsao Hu Gate. " They were asked by General Li," says the *Ta Han Pao*, " the reason of their coming over. Liu stated his opinions as follows : ' At present independence has been declared by most of the provinces, and the main power is now being entirely held in the hands of the Hans, which renders the Manchu Government totally incapable. But as Yuan Shih-k'ai has served the Manchu Dynasty during three generations it seems impossible for him to look at its annihilation without lending a helping hand.

" ' The Manchu Government has already pledged itself to establish a solid Constitution, demolish all sorts of unreasonable taxation, and give the different provinces freedom in arranging their financial affairs. In view of these promises, Yuan Shih-k'ai desires that the different provinces shall not open war again in order by not doing so to save the people from further suffering.

"'Regarding the Manchu Government, it is at present simply like an idol worshipped by monks—a master in appearance only. Moreover, we recently have been warned that Japan and Russia have both dispatched an admiral to China, with what intentions we are at a loss to anticipate, but should like Your Excellency to have a thorough consideration of the matter before too late, so as to prevent the calamity of the partition of China.'

"'Oh, how absurd you are!' interrupted General Li. 'In what manner can the word "partition" intimidate the revolutionists of Hupeh? Regardless of whether international law is strictly observed by all the Powers, they should not have made any improper movement. But in case they should do so, a suitable settlement may finally be arranged with them. Among the millions of our Hupeh brothers there is not one but is enthusiastic and courageous and who will decidedly not allow the Manchus to continue their usurpation of our hereditary right to the country. On the other hand, if our Chinese brethren encourage no revolution, is there any possibility by which the Manchus could guarantee that the Powers would not "carve the melon"?

"'In reference to the purpose of Yuan Shih-k'ai in sending you here, we have now already had the honour to be informed. According to our calculations we venture to guess that he is now contriving to inveigle the generals of different provinces not to declare war or draw their swords against him, temporarily, so that he may have time for employing counter-stratagems deliberately among them to raise unnatural frictions for his own advantage. Yuan Shih-k'ai then shall be able to take possession and to wield an influence in military and civil affairs which shall enable him to drive out the Manchus and proclaim himself Emperor of China. Alas! it is a wise scheme, but rather difficult to perform. It would be better for him to capture the provinces of Chihli and Honan with his detachments immediately for the revolution, then a General's position shall certainly be open to him for his merits. After this grand achievement a public election will take place, and being a person of high reputation he may probably hope to be voted as the President of New

China. Otherwise nothing more should now be said except to appoint a time for decisive battle.

"'As for his having served the Manchus during three generations and received heavy benevolences from them, does he still remember that at the time when Pu Yi [the Hsuan Tung Emperor] was to be enthroned his head was rocking on his shoulders? At present, the general order in China has been overturned, and we apprehend that there will be no more days for Yuan Shih-k'ai to serve the Manchus again. Besides, the land of China is originally the lawful property of our Hans, and it may be compared with a home illegally occupied by banditti who have seized the family possessions, enslaved the husbands, wives, and children, and used them again as stewards. I should think that even the most cold-blooded creature would not acknowledge these bandits as his benefactors. You two gentlemen are both the descendants of Han, what do you think of my words?'

"On hearing the above," continues the *Ta Han Pao*, "Tsai deeply blushed without saying anything, while Li replied: 'The sayings of Your Excellency are all precious words which will awaken us as a sleeping lion from his dreams, and we shall surely report the same on our return.'

"At this juncture everyone present except the two delegates rose and severely reproved the low grade of Yuan's personage as well as the worthlessness of the delegates' mission. The latter only listened silently with crimson cheeks. Finally, General Li invited the delegates to a feast, and asked them to remain as his guests for a whole night, with a promise to send them over the river with due ceremonies in the morning. At the feast were all the principals of the different departments of the Government. The delegates were lodged for the night in the Municipal Hall, and took their leave the next morning."

It was also the day when the fleet below Wuchang took its leave of the Empire and turned over to the Republic.

The delegates carried with them Li Yuan-hung's letter to Yuan Shih-k'ai. Rehearsing his views on the terms offered the Manchus for peace, in similar words to those contained in his reply to Admiral Sah, Li Yuan-hung in this letter calls attention to how the Manchu Government has tried various tricks to gain a hold on the people's hearts, and how the foundations of the Empire remain still in the grasp of childish, ignorant Manchus.

Man to man, he then goes on : " Surely you cannot bear with composure to see the property and lives of 400,000,000 Chinese wasted by a mere handful of Manchus? Are you not the most famous and most able man among the Chinese? Have you forgotten that, after you had been relieved of your command of the Northern troops and your political influence had been weakened, you narrowly escaped being murdered as well as cashiered? All this is evidence of the Manchus' jealousy of the Chinese.

" Since Hupeh was made independent many other provinces have joined the cause with heart and soul. The Manchu Government has fallen into a swoon and can no longer stand by its own strength. So it is trying the scheme by which it quelled the T'aiping Rebellion—using Chinese to kill Chinese. If you are willing to be reinstated on such a commission, then you have super-human patience.

" In your dispatch you state emphatically that the government must be constitutional. In reply I wish to explain that in this age, whether a government be monarchical or republican, it must ultimately be founded on constitutionalism, and there is little difference between a republic and a constitutional monarchy. The form of the new government will be settled in the conference of delegates from the various provinces. Whatever form it takes, it will not violate constitutionalism.

" If we had agreed to your terms, had you any means of compelling the Manchu Government to fulfil its promises?

" For you to live in retirement for your own enjoyment as you have done is of no benefit to China.

" The success of the present movement has come by the strength not of men but of God. What man could convert Szechuan, Kiangsi, Anhuei, Kiangsu, Kuangtung, Kwangsi, Yunnan, Kueichou, Shansi, and Shensi to republicanism? Besides, all the gunboats and torpedo-destroyers have turned revolutionist.

" There is no Manchu force to hinder us from marching on Peking, with the exception of your little army.

" The renaissance of the Chinese and the maintenance of China's sovereignty depends on you. If you are really in sympathy with the Chinese, you should take your opportunity to turn Republican with your troops and attack Peking. If you are hankering after the dignities and honours that the Manchu Government may confer, then you should pray that the revolutionary army may hasten its march to the Yellow River. For, when the Manchus see that they cannot withstand the revolutionary advance, they will give you all the higher honours to induce you to fight for them. If we should yield now, it is to be feared that the honours bestowed on you would vanish in a few days. Remember the proverb: 'When the rabbits are caught the hounds are cooked.' Your merit would be so great that you would not avoid jealousy, and your power would make you liable to constant suspicion. It would be impossible for you to retire again to Changteh-fu. I would remind you that the Empress Dowager [Lung Yu Empress Dowager] is still living and that she will never forgive the slaughter of the reformers. Consider if there is any affection between yourself and the Manchus. All of us working together can complete the emancipation of the Chinese, and none of us are willing to continue under the rule of the Manchus.

"As to your suggestions that foreign Powers may seize this opportunity of bringing about the partition of China, we have read many articles from foreign papers and we feel sure that none of them will do us any harm during our civil war.

"We have learned from a wireless telegram to a certain gentleman that Peking is in great agitation and that the young Emperor has fled. Should this be true, the ruling race has already lost its dignity and has no right to present our territory to any foreign Power.

"It is reported that the Manchu Government has recalled you. If that is so, I offer two suggestions for your consideration. First: It may be that the Government suspects your loyalty and intends by recalling you to deprive you of your military authority; in that case, you may disobey the summons by virtue of military rule, that a general need not obey an Imperial edict when he is on service abroad.

"Second: If Peking is actually in a critical condition—I must tell you a story. During the Boxer rising, when the International Force entered Peking, it summoned Li Hung-chang. That was an opportunity for Li to become Emperor. But he was stubborn and lost the chance. You may learn from his experience.

"Mencius said that a man with complete education will protect the people. I am but a military man and do not know much. I have learned largely from Mencius, so that I have no desire except to protect the people. It is believed that your experience and ability are much higher than mine. Yet I am sorry for you that you have to consider things so very long before you can make up your mind. Remember that we should never hesitate or delay in doing what is benevolent or righteous. We should do the right thing at once.

"All the brethren of this land are waiting for you. Do not face me any longer with a mask.

"Your delegates will inform you further in regard to my sentiments. LI YUAN-HUNG."

CHAPTER XVI

HANYANG—A BATTLE

Yuan Shih-k'ai left Nie-kou to the sounds of the battle by which his " little army " was to take the second of the three sister-cities of the Republic.

The fighting was for the possession of the city of Hanyang, covered a period of three weeks, and was prolonged by the necessity of building bridges across the Han far up and moving troops to flank the revolutionists' left. On Nov. 7 Hankow observed that the Imperialists were advancing from Kilometre 10, and heard they had moved twenty-four 15-centimetre guns into a semicircular position in the plain threatening Hanyang. They were being shelled from Wuchang, the shells striking in Hankow and even falling in the Concessions.

This was the day of Li Yuan-hung's refusal of Yuan Shih-k'ai's proposal on behalf of the Throne. Yuan Shih-k'ai's reply to this may be said to have been expressed by his General Feng Kuo-chang, who on Nov. 8 issued a proclamation announcing satisfaction at the behaviour of his troops—which may be mistaken for an attempt to justify their past barbarities, and stating that the capture of Hanyang and Wuchang may be expected momentarily. Those who have offended or done harm to the Government will be severely punished. The merchants of Hankow are exhorted to carry on business, as the Imperialists have no intention of creating damage in the City and no more burning will be countenanced. The battle to bring Li Yuan-hung to terms begins.

General Chang Piao visits Hankow to see what the immediate condition is. The condition is expressed by a miserable-looking native in the Hanyang end of Hankow to a missionary who consents to listen :

" Master, may I say a word ? " said he. " Which is the best way to flee ? "

On Nov. 9 the artillery engagement begins—the conventional battle order—between Imperialist batteries at Kilometre 10 and the Wuchang batteries (Chin Shan). It is for half an hour. The Imperialists lose several railway trucks, hit and fired. There is fighting along the Han, in Hanyang, with rifles all day, but during Nov. 10 and 11 there is a cessation by the Imperialists to await the outcome of two days of demonstration and the mission of Yuan Shih-k'ai's delegates, Liu and Tsai.

On Nov. 12, when the delegates have departed for the North, and shortly after 5 p.m., the heaviest bombardment of the attack takes place, and lasts 45 minutes. Imperialist soldiers are intermittently occupying the China Merchants' Steam Navigation Company's cargo hulk *Volga* and sniping at passing sampans near the Concessions, when on Nov. 13 it is sunk by revolutionist shells. The shore batteries at Wuchang are trying to sink a second hulk close by, and a shell enters the dining-room of the Manager of Jardine, Matheson, & Company's house, while three other concerns in the Concessions receive shells in their buildings.

If the revolutionists can drive the Imperialists out of that part of Hankow between the Concessions and the Han River, they can send troops across the Yangtse and up the Han.

The Imperialists are moving by rear waterways in the direction of the Han and shipping sampans by rail, for pontoons, to a point twenty miles west of Hankow.

The war-invested foreigners in the Concessions are again anxious. On Nov. 13 the British Admiral Winsloe and the German Vice-Admiral von Krosig departed for Nanking, while on Nov. 14, Colonel Willoughby, British military attaché from Peking, and Commander Lynes, with G. P. Byrne as interpreter, proceed to Wuchang and protest against the bombardment of the British Concession. This Concession is in the most exposed position, adjoining the section of Hankow occupied by the Imperialists. The Japanese Concession is at the other extreme of the Concession Quarter and farthest from present danger, but the Japanese flag-captain afloat, protests against the firing by the Wuchang guns on a Japanese gunboat the previous day.

The revolutionists reconnoitre Hankow to see what damage has been done by their artillery fire. The middle part is already destroyed by past fires. " From the river," says a spectator, " it reminds one of nothing so much as Messina after the earthquake." The fighting has already started an exodus from that eastern sixth of Hankow next to the British Concession, which is not wholly destroyed and which is crowded with refugees. "Chinese have been making their way out of Hankow with bedding and what baggage they can carry. Not one seems to expect ever to see his house again." The French telegraph their Government respecting the inadequate protection it is giving them. During Nov. 16 the revolutionists in force—stated at more than 2000—crossed the Han at Tu-lu-kou and attacked the Imperialist right flank in the rear, and retired after being repulsed.

On Nov. 17 the big battle begins. The buildings of the China Merchants' Steam Navigation Company go up in flames set by Wuchang shells. The Imperialists lose 300 killed in pushing back the revolutionists on their base on the Sin-seng Road. There are wounded and dead coming into the Concessions all afternoon. The contract price for burial is fifty cents with coffin, and twenty-five cents without. The municipal coolies, in the Concessions, have become undertakers and visit the Red Cross hospitals regularly. About 5 p.m., under cover of their bombardment, revolutionist reinforcements from Wuchang enter the Han on lighters in spite of the Imperialist fire. A Red Cross worker behind the guns of a Wuchang battery sees steam tugs, each drawing six or seven empty ferry barges, cross under a withering fire in an attempt to enter the Han and deliver their barges to make pontoons between Hanyang and Hankow. The first attempt fails, but the second succeeds. The revolutionists are now prepared to drive the Imperialists out of the burned City. The revolutionary General of the 3rd Division is killed, but General Li Yuan-hung seems confident of victory. He has intimated through the Red Cross Society that in the event of revolutionist victory all Imperialist troops who surrender will be treated as non-combatants, and that if the foreign authorities are willing to allow such to seek refuge in the Concessions and feed them, he will pay the cost.

The revolutionists cross the Yangtse and attack the Imperialist rear in the region of Nie-kou. The Imperialists are coming down the Han from Hsiao-kan. The fighting continues through the night. The British gunboat *Woodcock*, under Commander Lynes, is struck for the second time during the present battle, and British residents appeal to their Government for more efficient protection. The Germans take similar action.

A good and creditable artillery duel between Kilometre 10, that began the battle, and the Wuchang Golden Hill forts distinguishes the day of November 18. November 19 sees the reappearance of the Chinese fleet, which having put ashore their Imperialist Admiral Sah returns under the revolutionist flag. While manœuvring opposite Seven Mile Creek it bombards the Imperialists 45 minutes in the morning and for a time after 2 p.m.

Word passes from man to man in Wuchang that "the gunboats have arrived." The people seem filled with fresh confidence. "A noticeable feature nowadays is the absence of the half-dressed, half-trained recruit of a fortnight or so ago." "The presence of the turbaned, well-trained Hunanese gives the impression that the City is no longer in the hands of coolies." "Huang Hsing has thoroughly reorganized the army."

Three-fourths of Hankow are destroyed.

During Nov. 20 and 21 the antagonists prepare for the last week of fighting. On Nov. 21 Li Yuan-hung holds a memorial service for the dead. The Government headquarters are hung with red flags, and other decorations and offerings are set on tables. Representatives of all bureaus are present. On Nov. 22 fighting begins at six in the morning by the revolutionists sinking the remaining cargo hulk of the China Merchants' Steam Navigation Company. The Imperialists join in at 11 a.m., and begin bringing up supplies and massing soldiers near Nie-kou. The Red Cross workers bring in 51 wounded revolutionists in one line from Hanyang, and on Nov. 23 more than 100 from the revolutionists' lines. The Imperialist losses increase in the same ratio. They continue to reinforce.

The Imperialists have bridged the Han in three places, at Chiao-kou, Tu-lu-kou, and Tsai-tien, above Black Mountain, and are moving in force (in the excitement estimated at 10,000 to 20,000) against Hanyang, the revolutionist left. A ninety-six hours' battle has commenced.

On Nov. 24 the fleet enters the fight, and the fighting line from the fleet to Hsiao-kan is nearly thirty miles long. Firing ceases for only two hours. The revolutionists are making their main action in the neighbourhood of Hankow and declare that the Imperialists will never reach Hanyang. The Imperialists are firing the unburnt area of Hankow adjoining the British Concession. When the fighting first began over the ruins of two-thirds of Hankow it was a hot place for people who say, in peace, that the big eat the small, the small eat the little, and the little eat mud. Now, when men, who have asked in vain for some place to flee to, burrow in mud and ashes, the cats of Hankow and Hanyang take to the waters of the Han. Additional shells fall in the Concessions on Nov. 24 and 25. The Shensi guild-house, the most costly and famous building in Hankow and one of the architectural monuments of China, vanishes in the flames. On Nov. 26 the Russian gunboat *Mandjour* is struck by a shell. There are five fires, and 13,000 gallons of burning American kerosene is giving out a black pall of smoke that extends ten miles along the line of battle from Kilometre 10 to Hanyang.

Fires are seen in the direction of the Imperialist advance down the Han, toward Hanyang.

Wuchang remains relatively peaceful. The Golden Hill (Chin Shan) forts abreast Kilometre 10 have forty wounded from shrapnel fired from Kilometre 10. Shrapnel also falls near General Huang Hsing's headquarters at Serpent Hill. The revolutionist fleet is down the bend supporting the landing party of Kiangsi troops working against the railway.

On Nov. 27 Hanyang is lost. The Hunan troops, those that came up from Changsha on launches and junks and gave the Republican capital such a martial appearance; those whom the *Ta Han Pao* has said are to be distinguished by their turbans and straw sandals, and in accordance with Li Yuan-hung's orders are to be shown special kindness; those who, according to the foreign correspondents, inspired Wuchang with confidence that the Republic was no longer in the hands of coolie recruits, have given way. They have first been held in reserve awaiting the time of the Imperialist onslaught, when the revolutionary mixed regiments will need to be reinforced by regulars. Now through the revolutionist lines and camps goes the rumour that the Hunan troops have deserted the battle-line. The Hunanese accuse the Hupeh troops of throwing the burden of the fight upon them, and they quit the field in retaliation. Black Mountain is lost. Bright Hill and Tortoise Hill are lost. Hanyang is lost. The revolutionists are beaten out of their strongholds. They give up another city, the iron-works, and the arsenal, with guns and ammunition.

On the morning of November 27 the Imperialist flanking force on the Han is driving the revolutionists before it out of Hanyang. As the revolutionists retire they seek a crossing to Wuchang, farther up the river, or retreat into the country. But a fraction of them seeks boats on the Yangtse water front of Hanyang, or on the Han, and trusts itself to the water. Caught in the current and unacquainted with the boats, these are carried past the eastern end of the burnt Hankow native city, which has never been taken from the Imperialists. An awful carnage ensues. In addition to the Imperialist rifle and machine-gun fire from the shore, the artillery of Wuchang and that of the Imperialists back of Hankow are playing upon the spot. About midday more than a score of sampans and larger boats pass helplessly abreast the Imperialist rifles and machine-guns on shore and are riddled by shot, some of them converted into mere hulks of half-sunken lumber.

The water is strewn with crimson corpses.

As the helpless drifting wreckage of boats and bodies passes beyond the Hankow shore occupied by the Imperialist marksmen, it encounters the foreign war-vessels, which lower men in launches and pinnaces to receive the living and dead. The Red Cross launch puts out from the Concessions, and foreign merchants send their launches.

Corpses float by, slowly sinking beneath the yellow waters of the Yangtse.

Clinging to one sampan freighted with an equal number of dead are three or four revolutionary soldiers, on the far side, away from the fire. They are hauled out and landed safely at the Concession bund. Some of the boats contain fleeing families of which only one living member remains. A number of boats come down empty, their occupants having taken to the water, from where numbers are picked up.

Carlowitz & Company's launch tows ashore the hulk of a great war-junk that started with a hundred people from Hanyang. It is packed with the bodies of twenty-seven dead, twenty-six badly wounded, and twenty-two who have escaped injury. As the hulk moves inshore, another, who is hauled along in the water, loses his hold on the hulk and drowns, as it were, in the arms of safety.

"We were fighting at Mei-niang Mountain," said a survivor, a sergeant of the revolutionist 7th Regiment, "and had been on duty four days and nights without undressing or sleeping. All our officers were wounded or killed, and only about two camps of the Regiment remained. We were driven back to the banks of the Yangtse, fighting all the time, and when we got there we found this war-junk tied up to the bank for repairs. We went aboard to get shelter, and were joined by others. Finally, being pressed, we pushed the junk off, and the current took charge. By this time the Imperialists had occupied Hanyang Hill and the temple at its foot beside the Han, so they opened on us with machine-guns and rifles. Our own batteries at Wuchang also fired at us, and we were shot at all the way to the Concessions."

" Some thought our batteries at Wuchang were trying to cover our retreat," said a soldier of the 8th Regiment who had retreated from the Hanyang Iron Works. " Others aboard believed our batteries were firing at us thinking we were deserters. Anyway, we got it from both sides."

The soldiers rescued from the bloody war-junk did not know they were defeated. They wanted to get back to the front, and on second thought wanted to eat and to sleep. " One said he would fight as long as he was alive, and would not admit defeat until he was dead." None knew how the Bright Hill and Tortoise Hill had been lost. " All they knew was that a red flag went up and they were shot at." When told that Hanyang Hill was taken, " they denied it, and said Huang Hsing was still driving back the enemy."

The Chinese police in the Foreign Concessions and the house " boys " would tell passers-by : " They say Hanyang is fallen. It is false, do not believe it." Sometimes a Chinese would stop the same person several times and tell him this.

On Nov. 28 the following bulletin was issued by the revolutionist paper the *Ta Han Pao* : " Yesterday the spies of the Northern Army fabricated and circulated a bulletin to the effect that the Bright Hill and Tortoise Hill of Hanyang had been seized by the Northern troops. This is all empty words. No such thing has ever happened, for I have but this morning returned from Hanyang to Hankow and know that it is false. On the contrary, it is a scheme to lead the Northern troops into ambush, when their whole army will be annihilated."

The Republican Government at Wuchang recognized the situation thus created for it by the following proclamation put out by the Assembly :

" The Manchu Government is in an extreme financial panic and is collecting funds from the Imperial Family for military purposes. What it has in hand is only 2,000,000 taels. All foreign nations have declared a strict neutrality, so that the Manchu Government cannot raise any loan from any foreign nation. The fall of Hanyang will not involve the whole situation of the Republicans. It is sincerely hoped that the Republican Army in this province will do its utmost to keep possession of Wuchang. All the other provinces will do what is in their power to drive the Manchu Government out of this region."

General Li Yuan-hung put out a bulletin for the information of the people, giving the substance of a great hoax devised by a man named Chu Fei-huang, who came to see him and claimed to have been sent by Yuan Shih-k'ai for the purpose of arranging for peace negotiations. Chu Fei-huang said Yuan Shih-k'ai, joined by General Chiang Kuei-ti, had led the Chinese soldiers in Peking against the Throne and was recognized as the sole authority by the foreign Powers in Peking; that he had not recalled the troops from Hankow and Hanyang because he was not sure his authority would be recognized here. General Li Yuan-hung says in the bulletin that he is willing to defer to Yuan Shih-k'ai but that the whole thing may be a trick, and he exhorts the officers and soldiers to continue their vigilance and remain on their guard.

At the end of November 1911 the revolutionist Press admitted the fall of Hanyang, but placed the blame on Chinese traitors who, it said, had gone to the Imperialist General Feng Kuo-chang and asked for a reward.

"It is reported that the reward he gave was to take off their heads," adds one paper.

CHAPTER XVII

NOVEMBER IN PEKING

It is now November in Peking. The flames of Hankow fire new fuses to the mine underlying the Capital. Hankow, the great capital of industrial China, in the first days of November is burning—a lurid attraction for the eyes of the world; but Peking is the centre of centres. It is against Peking that all these forces springing up in the Empire operate. They operate to complete its discomfiture and demoralization.

Events supply the Throne with ample material for edicts, which flow on unchecked. It descends from precipice to precipice. In its progress of disintegration it goes on vacating offices, surrendering its powers, retracting, abjuring, renouncing. It says that "Prince Ching and others have memorialized Us that having fulfilled their offices unworthily, they request to be instantly dismissed"; that Tsai Tse (Minister of Finance) and others "have memorialized Us" that as the State affairs are "important" they request the appointment of other "competent officials"; Minister of State Chou Chia-lai and others have also memorialized, praying leave to resign, all in order to conform with constitutionalism, "to facilitate the administration," "adjust national principles," and "rectify the popular belief" (disabuse the minds of the people). "*They have memorialized quite rightly*," says the Throne; "*their requests are all hereby granted*."

To stay the flood of these "resignations" and dismissals, the Throne has but one safety valve—"the Strong Man of China," Yuan Shih-k'ai, so on Nov. 1, 1911, the Throne appoints him President of the Cabinet, or Premier. On Nov. 2 it orders him to come to Peking immediately from Hupeh, where he has gone to take command of the Imperial forces facing President General Li Yuan-hung. He is to form a complete Cabinet and "take measures to improve the political administration quickly." The penitential "danger of falling" becomes an act of reality. The Throne is rushing to the "unthinkable future." It has received a memorial by telegraph from the insubordinate General Chang Shao-tseng of the 20th Division at Lanchou, saying that his army is "weeping in gratitude" at the action of the Throne in granting on Oct. 30 an immediate Constitution and Parliament in response to the demands through the National Assembly. Speaking of these acts of compulsion on the part of the military, the Throne says that they are made "with the object of supporting the Imperial Family" and "pacifying the source of disturbance." "Their loyal love for their country [that of the General and his troops] is apparent," it continues, and adds, "We appreciate them deeply, indeed."

General Chang Shao-tseng's telegram to the Throne was immediately followed by two memorials from the National Assembly, one of which requested the Cabinet to assume the responsibility of government and to see that persons of Imperial blood should not be made ministers, the second compelling the issuance of a decree transferring the authority for drawing up the Constitution to the National Assembly. Following this the Throne now immediately hands over all constitutional matters and the task of framing the Constitution, from the Imperial Prince Pu Lun and other nobles, to the National Assembly. The reason for this action given in the edict is to "show the Throne's desire in sympathizing with the inclinations and disinclinations of the people," and "in maintaining the strictest justice without selfishness."

While these edicts are being issued the cities of Nanchang and Hankow have passed over to the revolutionists. The troops in Shansi have mutinied in the last days of October and taken possession of the pass through which runs the railway communicating with the capital, Tai-yuan-fu. General Wu Lu-cheng, Commander of the 6th Division, has left Paoting-fu, with 3000 men, to recover the pass and protect the Peking-Hankow Railway from the Shansi rebels.

On Nov. 1 the excitement in Peking is very great. Natung, late Grand Councillor, Vice-Premier, and President of the Foreign Office, has taken refuge in the Grand Hotel des Wagon-Lits in the Legation Quarter, and Li Ching-fang, son of the famous Li Hung-chang, late Vice-Minister of Communications, has removed to the Banque de l'Indo-Chine. Other notables have gone to Tientsin, Tsingtao, Dalny, and Japan.

On Nov. 2 the Governor of Shansi, his wife and two sons are killed at the provincial capital, Tai-yuan-fu, and his yamen is looted and burned. The revolutionists set the Manchu Quarter of the City on fire, but allow most of the people to escape. It is utterly destroyed, and a score of Manchus are killed. The troops then loot and fire all the shops of the City, turning the main streets into ruins and rubbish. This news now reaches the Court.

The National Assembly has become a revolutionary body in concert with the revolutionary assemblies of the revolted provinces. It has cowed the Throne and reduced Imperial authority to a mere shadow. It has received the Throne's edicts conferring upon it the authority to draft a Constitution, with applause and shouts of "Long live the country and the Emperor!" It has telegraphed to Republican President General Li Yuan-hung to suspend hostilities while it endeavours to secure all necessary reforms. It is working for a monarchy. Hankow is burning.

The National Assembly has now submitted 19 fundamental principles of the new Constitution to the Throne. The act is an ultimatum, and the Throne capitulates and at once issues an edict of acceptance of the articles. "We shall arrange a day," says the Throne, "to swear before Our ancestors in the temple, and to issue the Constitution to the whole Empire on yellow [Imperial] papers." It is a historical edict. It has the force of an abdication. It is a relinquishment of Imperial powers. All that the Constitution of the Manchu Dynasty hitherto held sacred and inviolable in its authority is given up. It submits itself to parliamentary domination and control.

The 19 articles guarantee the security of the Dynasty and hold the person of the Emperor to be sacrosanct. His power is to be limited by the Constitution, and the whole questions of the Succession, the Constitution, and the Parliament are placed in the hands of the people. Instead of the "barbaric despotism, guided by a capricious weakling under the pernicious influence of Palace women and degraded eunuchs," there is to be a "constitutional monarchy, a parliamentary government, a responsible cabinet appointed by the Prime Minister, and a parliamentary control of the budget, including allowances to the Imperial household." The regulations governing the Imperial Family and for the administration of the Court are to be drawn up in conformity with the Constitution.

The National Assembly, holding its sessions in a foreign-style building in the western part of the City, now reaches the zenith of its fame. In a day it frames and passes the demands from General Chang Shao-tseng, and it secures the adherence of the Throne to them. It springs to the pinnacle of grandeur and at the same time fulfils its destiny. The world rings with its acclaim, and its members who frame the 19 articles are compared with the statesmen of Rome or of the American Revolution because they have thrown off a masterpiece.

The Assembly's magnificence, importance, and power arouse the apprehension and jealousy of the revolted Republican provinces, and President General Li Yuan-hung telegraphs that it had better leave the question of the future of China to those who are doing the fighting. It is already reduced in numbers from 196 to 117—from desertions through fear or through secession. Hardly more than sixty members are active, and these include a part of the 100 appointees of the Throne. All of the Throne's appointees are barred from debate. The Chamber has become a mere *Committee of State* dominated by forty or fifty radicals. They will not allow even the moderates to oppose them, and they draft and pass the 19 articles in a single sitting. Objections are cried down.

On account of the Assembly's obedience to General Chang Shao-tseng, foreign observers apprehend that it is intimidated by, and is under, the army. They hope that the "Army League" may be able to establish a Dictator in Peking to save the Empire. "The country has gone mad," says one, "and only a strong Dictator will save it." But it is the Republic, and not the monarchy, that is now in the ascendant. The National Assembly never recovers from the blight of Li Yuan-hung's warning.

The sparks of Hankow seem falling over the country, bursting into flame in many places. A state of chaos is rapidly approaching. At the direction of the National Assembly—or the revolutionary group that calls itself the National Assembly—the Prince Regent puts out another edict in which the Throne recognizes the revolutionists as "political parties," thus abrogating the Imperial law against political parties, if not against rebels. The reason given is in order "to cultivate the accomplished faculty to be employed for the benefit of the Government." The situation is so bad that the Throne apologizes for the military measures taken to which it has been compelled to resort. It says they were originally intended for the protection and preservation of the public peace. It calls upon the generals in all places commanding Imperial troops to "divine Its idea by enforcing strict discipline and prohibiting disorder and rapine." They and the troops "should not injure even a hair," it says of military whose only business is to kill, in defence, if for nothing else.

Yuan Shih-k'ai is demurring to his new appointment as Premier, granted by a power and authority that now has no visible existence. On Nov. 3 Shanghai passes over to the revolutionists and forms a Republican Government. Eight other cities follow its example, together with the whole of Yunnan Province. Continuous fighting proceeds at Hankow, night and day. On Nov. 4 the National Assembly telegraphs to Yuan Shih-k'ai to accept the Premiership immediately. Two Chinese torpedo-boat destroyers on the Yangtse hoist the Republican flag, and the revolutionists are in possession of the mouth of the Yangtse.

But on Nov. 5 Yuan Shih-k'ai still declines to accept the Premiership, and there is no tangible head of government visible. It is represented solely by the lately resigned ministers. Chaos is appreciably near. General Wu Lu-cheng has been appointed Governor of Shansi by the Throne and ordered to proceed to his post at once. He is suspected of conspiracy with General Chang Shao-tseng to turn over the province of Shansi to the revolutionists and march on Peking. The National Assembly is panic-stricken and is considering the advisability of dissolving. The Imperialist Army becomes paralysed just at a time when it could take Wuchang. Kiangsu, Chekiang, and Fukien declare independence.

On Nov. 6 the Throne is seeking emergency loans from the four financial syndicates of Great Britain, France, Germany, and America, or other sources. The Boxer indemnity instalment for November has not been paid. The national treasury and the war-chest are depleted, and the National Assembly declines to approve the Regent's plan for loans. Amoy falls. In its despair the Throne issues an edict applauding the virtues of General Chang Shao-tseng, the revolutionary who forced the Throne to its knees. Appreciably successful with Yuan Shih-k'ai, it looks for heroes in other directions. Having belauded General Chang, it appoints him a Commissioner to mollify the revolutionaries in the South by conveying the Throne's "benign intentions" and restoring the revolutionaries to loyalty.

The Throne has now reached the conviction that the revolution cannot be suppressed by force, and the Court is paralysed with fear. Chingkiang City falls. Shaohsing City falls. The Throne instructs the Viceroy of Nanking, Chang Jen-chun, not to oppose the reformers and revolutionaries. On Nov. 7 the foreign Powers, who have been landing troops at Tientsin, Canton, and Shanghai on occasion, now take effective measures for the protection of their citizens and subjects in China. They hold large bodies of troops along the seaboard ready to send to Peking and other inland places. The Legations consider the end of the Dynasty imminent, with no hope of saving even a nominal Throne. The National Assembly now facing a crisis owing to the protests of various provincial assemblies against its measures and action, receives word that General Wu Lu-cheng has been assassinated and adjourns, never to meet again as a body with any appreciable authority. Its power is broken.

General Wu Lu-cheng reached the mud village of Shih-chia-chuang in the flat plain of South-western Chihli and was asleep in his tent when forty soldiers rushed in past the guards, shot and beheaded him. "On hearing the firing," said the Commander of the 6th Division, "I called the other officers and accompanied by a crowd of my men ran to the scene. We captured thirty Manchus belonging to the 3rd Battalion of the 1st Division who had committed the outrage."

On account of the commanding position of General Chang Shao-tseng, "the man on horseback," this assassination thrilled Peking and the onlookers at this drama. "The 3rd Battalion looks like fighting," says the Commander of the 6th Division; "we are making preparations."

General Chang Shao-tseng declines the appointment to go to the Yangtse provinces to conciliate the people. On Nov. 8 the Court in Peking is preparing for flight. It is passing into one throe after another. The Manchu troops responsible for the murder of General Wu Lu-cheng are *en route* returning to the Capital. The Legations are being put on a defence footing. Fighting has commenced at Nanking and an uprising around Canton. The largest exodus from Peking since the beginning has started. The Manchus, including members of the Imperial Family as well as numerous Chinese, are sending sealed boxes of treasure into the Legation Quarter. Throughout the day bullion and fine objects come to the banks and the houses of foreign residents. Compradors of foreign firms are making small fortunes out of storage charges. All day long special trains are run to Tientsin.

The revolution in its most spectacular aspects has reached Peking. November is the month of the high tide of flight of dignitaries. They leave their houses in panic, carrying only a few belongings, and take refuge in some foreign house in the Legation Quarter until the trains leave, when they disappear in the direction of Tientsin. Only servants are left behind, or some member of the family, to forward valuables and watch over abandoned hearthstones. Orientals more than Occidentals seem animal-like in their panic and bolt for no visible reason. They fly from instinctive fear or delusion. Perhaps it is because of the imperfection of communications and lack of knowledge. Foreigners witness their flights with wonder and amazement, and conclude that the dangers to the natives are something a foreigner cannot fathom.

Those who cannot or will not flee disguise themselves or prepare some defence of their houses. Manchu women wearing the showy head-dress which since the Manchu conquest has been a picturesque feature of Peking life, change their fashion of hair-dressing. However, as they are further distinguished by their natural feet, some of them seek to disguise their identity by shoes peculiarly constructed, so as to give their feet the appearance of being bound like the feet of the Chinese.

A few vacant rooms and houses in the Legation Quarter not hitherto occupied by native refugees are now filled with the wives and children of officials. Some of the women are putting on foreign dress.

There are 27,500 soldiers and police to protect the Capital, of which at least 20,000 are Manchus. By night these parade through the City. The best-drilled body of troops, they make a fine appearance in their light grey uniforms and give confidence. The people stand outside their shops, gaze upon the soldiers, and wonder about everything. Out of their blank minds come fears. They start rumours after they return home or go back into their shops. Each day they say there will be an outbreak in twenty-four hours.

Although the people are friendly to foreigners, the latter are coming into the Legation Quarter for security. The Foreign Office, which seems to be endowed with immortality and is held in place by the presence of the foreign

Powers and cannot escape, is annoyed at rumours respecting the flight of the Court, the suicides of princes and kidnapping of the little Emperor, and asks the Press to deny these stories. The Lung Yu Empress Dowager and the Emperor are in the Winter Palace as usual, and Prince Chun the Regent, and father of the Emperor, is either there or staying quietly in his house, between the Drum Tower and the Teh Shang Gate.

The revolutionists at Wuchang are chuckling over Peking's discomfiture and are advertising it to the world in their Republican papers. " We know that the troops stationed in Peking to protect the Manchus are few and feeble," say the Republican editors. " Chang Kuei-ti is in the Imperial City, but half of his men are of no use, and Prince Ching has summoned him there for the mere purpose of protecting his own retreat with his family to Mongolia. Since the beginning of revolt the Imperial bodyguard has been deserting, so that not more than half of the Manchu soldiers remain, while from these Heaven has taken their senses, and they have no intention of resisting."

" The Manchus learned that we have slaughtered a great many of that tribe, and they have planned to drive out all the Chinese from the Imperial City with sword and rifle. Therefore the Chinese officials great and small are fleeing. Some 50,000 or 60,000 Chinese have already fled, and the hotels at Tientsin and Shanghai are overcrowded with them. Great ministers and members of the Privy Council have disappeared from the Capital and no one knows where they have gone."

" The Manchu usurper in Peking seeing the spread of revolt through every province and that he has lost the people's heart, is unable to do anything but issue edicts about constitutions, cabinets, sovereignties, and regulations. He wants all fighting to be stopped and matters to be discussed, but it is a mere pretence. What we have got to do is to stick to our resolution and steadily advance. There is not much likelihood that anyone will be deceived by the Imperial claptrap."

The Press throughout the country no longer calls the decrees " edicts " or " sacred edicts," but *Cabinet decrees* or *Manchu decrees*, and does not use the reign date of Hsuan Tung, 3rd year, but uses the cycle date, not unlike the French revolutionaries, entirely ignoring the little Emperor. The revolutionaries have become so bold that they approach the foreign superintendent of the Imperial Bureau of Engraving and Printing, controlled by the Minister of Finance, and ask him to design the flag of the Republic. The superintendent refers them to the Board of Finance. A revolutionary member of the National Assembly from Shansi seeks advice on the *Republic* in the Legation Quarter, where an American tells him: " Here, now, I can agree with you about reforms, but not with respect to a Republic for China. I cannot see what you want to go so far for: China is not ready for a Republic. It would be better to aim first at a monarchy."

" Well, you don't understand," says the Assemblyman. " We don't so much care what the form of government is, but the Manchus must go. We want a Republic because it gets rid of the Manchus. We will get rid of the Manchus."

The Forbidden City is being prepared for a state of siege, and those members of the Imperial Clan, the eight " iron-capped " princes and their families, or what is left of them after the exodus, who are entitled to refuge therein, are making preparations to take advantage of their privileges. Prince Ching states that Peking will not be defended against the invasion of Chinese troops. The exodus from the City reaches 150,000, according to foreign estimates, in a single day.

The Throne has seen nothing of Yuan Shih-k'ai, who has gone farther and farther away, until he is at Hsiao-kan, only twenty-five miles from Hankow, and even Nie-kou, twelve and one-half kilometres away, and is in touch with the revolutionists. On hearing of his arrival to open peace negotiations, President General Li Yuan-hung makes the announcement that his five generals commanding the revolutionary forces have unanimously agreed to ask Yuan Shih-k'ai to become President of the first Republic of China.

The Throne tries to depend upon General Chang Shao-tseng, whom it is trying to win over by cajolery. Secretly and anonymously, certain influences in the Imperial Clan are threatening him with assassination. Under these circumstances and further to complicate matters and bring about chaos in the expectations of Chinese and foreigners alike, General Chang Chao-tseng on Nov. 8 tries to resign from the army. He is not permitted to resign, but is given " sick leave," so on Nov. 13 he goes to Tientsin, arriving with a guard of thirty men. These men clear the station platform and form an alley through which he hurries from the train to a carriage, and goes thus guarded and takes refuge in the Japanese Concession. He refuses to go to Peking to renew his allegiance, and the last heard of him is that he is reported shot at in an abortive attempt at assassination, on Nov. 15, presumably for deserting his post.

There is no Chinese general in the North upon whom the Throne can rely. With Generals Chang Shao-tseng and Wu Lu-cheng gone, there are but three other names anywhere heard, those of General Feng Kuo-chang who has taken Hankow and is fighting for Hanyang, General Tuan Chi-jui his associate, and that of General Chang Hsun at Nanking. But they are 600 miles away. All agree that China's destiny is in the hands of Yuan Shih-k'ai, who has not yet accepted the Premiership of the Empire and has been offered the Presidency of the Republic.

On Nov. 9 the city of Foochow falls, and the province of Kuangtung declares a Republic at Canton. Anking City passes over to the revolutionists, followed by Swatow, Chefoo, and the province of Kueichou. For its satisfaction the Throne has the capture of Hankow, standing out as a horrible but convincing victory in an Empire of revolt. Six hundred miles away on the line of communications, the Peking-Hankow Railway, that may be broken at any moment, is its victorious and blood-stained army of less than 20,000 men (not more than 4000 or 5000 are in line of battle), with their Field Marshal, Premier Yuan Shih-k'ai, surrounded by no one knows how many millions of indifferent or hostile Chinese.

Yuan Shih-k'ai being met merely with arguments from President General Li Yuan-hung, to persuade him to join the Republic, leaves Hsiao-kan, or Nie-kou, in the vicinity of Hankow, on Nov. 9, for Peking. Before leaving he telegraphs to Prince Ching: "The outlook is decidedly gloomy. I do not expect to be able to effect the desired pacification. Moreover, my health is so feeble that I am unable to come to Peking and assume the post of Premier."

"It seemed as if the last prop of the Throne had given way," said an observer in Peking. The best that could be hoped from the negotiations at this moment was that the country might be divided at the Yangtse River into a Republic on the South, with a monarchy on the North.

CHAPTER XVIII

THE REPUBLIC AT THE GATES OF PEKING

THE whole Empire seems to have rested on Nov. 10 to permit of a little panic on the Peking-Kalgan Railway, where the members of the Staff abandoned their posts. This is the foremost event chronicled for that day.

About the only hope discernible in Peking in the first days of November is that expressed by a few optimistic officials on Nov. 11 to the effect that the Wuchang Army will be won over, leaving the irreconcilable partisans of Sun Yat-sen the only enemies, as before the outbreak. This day also the Throne is assailed by an appeal from Wu Ting-fang, carrying the full force of the Shanghai Republic behind it, to abdicate. It reminds the Throne of the atrocities and inhumanities in which the Imperialist Army indulged upon capturing Hankow.

The details from Hankow have now reached all Peking, and these great events transpiring in the heart of China, have shaken from the declining National Assembly one of the last echoes of its power and authority, for on Nov. 12 it is heard to demand capital punishment for those Imperialists responsible for the Hankow massacres. It appears for the moment to have revived, but its star is rapidly dimming. On the same day the province of Shantung declares its independence, and its highest officials take oath of allegiance to the Shantung Independency.

Again, "thousands and thousands" are in flight from Peking. The Republic is now but 150 miles distant. It has conquered the most populous of all China's provinces, Shantung on the South, the sacred soil from which Confucius sprung and which holds his holy ashes,—Confucius, the apostle of Imperialism, whose moral system with an almost supernatural authority conquered the Chinese race and rendered it subservient to its superiors, and made the Emperor the "Son of Heaven." The people have lifted the disciple Mencius above his teacher, Confucius,

The revolutionaries and Republicans have taken Mencius the disciple for their lawgiver, because Mencius taught the divinity of the people and their supremacy to the Emperor.

The Republic is in Shansi on the West, and in twenty-four hours it will reach the Great Wall on the East, but 200 miles away, following the very line of march taken by the Manchu conquerors of the seventeenth century themselves.

What November will bring forth is the uppermost thought. It is not yet half over, but all signs and sounds indicate the end. There are already six republics and independencies in China: the Szechuan Independency, the Republic of China at Wuchang, the Republic of Kuang-tung at Canton, the Republic of China at Shanghai, the Independency of Yunnan and Kueichou, and the Independency of Shantung. The Republic at Shanghai has issued a manifesto dated November 11, exhorting the provinces to unite and consummate the Republic. It now sends out telegraphic invitations to all the seceding provinces to send delegates for a National Assembly at Shanghai. All the Chinese war-vessels at Hankow withdraw their support from the Imperialist Army and start down the river. Three cruisers are already flying the white flag of the Republic.

November 13 sees the arrival of Yuan Shih-k'ai at Peking, where he is greeted with President General Li Yuan-hung's rejection on the part of the Republic of China of the offer which he has made to them on behalf of the Throne, of amnesty, constitutional government, and a share of the offices. Over against this the Throne greets him with one of its best edicts, appointing him to the command of all troops in the vicinity of the Capital. It is a forlorn hope of the Throne that it can thus rally about itself the Northern armies, of which Yuan Shih-k'ai was once the leader and idol. Manchuria furnishes the answer to this move by the Throne declaring its autonomy and independence of the struggle within the Great Wall. Revolution has reached the Great Wall.

With all his "enfeebled health," his "rheumatism of the leg," his failure to reconcile Li Yuan-hung and the estranged provinces on the Yangtse, almost smothered in appointments, and loaded with honours, responsibilities, and the acclaim of Europe and America, pursued by the jeers of the Cantonese, the threats of the Shanghai Republic, and the warnings from Wuchang, this single strong man appearing above 275,000,000 of Mongolian heads, some say 400,000,000, has reached Peking. He is associated in the minds of men of Europe and America with five other men, the theatres of whose achievements form a circle around the globe: the American Washington, the French Napoleon, the Greek Alexander, the Mongol Genghis, and the Japanese Mutsuhito.

He comes with 2000 troops. The public is only impressed by the physical spectacle, and from the shops and intersecting streets to which it is pushed back by the Manchu soldiers, in packed, silent crowds, it stands in awe more of this great man's escort and the spectacle of his procession to the temple where he is to stay, than of the man himself. The foreign ministers are under the impression that his arrival has given a steadying effect. It is a sensation which they themselves feel. The only possible effect which it can have upon the people must be exerted through the soldiers, which is the only influence that Yuan Shih-k'ai has ever possessed over the people. His maintenance of order in the metropolitan province of Chihli in the past, as in Shantung, has corresponded to the number of heads he has cut off and the decision and rapidity with which they fell. It is the custom of the Empire.

On Nov. 14, the day following his arrival in Peking, Yuan Shih-k'ai confers with the Lung Yu Empress Dowager, the Prince Regent, and Prince Ching respecting his status in the Empire. He has been appointed Premier by the Throne, elected Premier by the National Assembly, and on Nov. 9 confirmed by the Throne " in accordance with the 8th clause of the Statute of the Constitution." He goes to the Palace in the Forbidden City in response to a summons which he has been expecting, but he gives no definite reply as to whether he will accept—he must fully consult the Assembly and leaders. It is in the early morning hours. The Lung Yu Empress Dowager shows signs of weeping. The Regent is white with fear, his moroseness and intolerance are gone. He is uneasy before Yuan Shih-k'ai; he has *kuai*-ed (taken offence at) Yuan in Cabinet councils in the past, and Yuan Shih-k'ai in exile has said of the young man, " What can you do with one like that? " It is the Regent's hour of humiliation. The Lung Yu Empress Dowager, and therefore Yuan Shih-k'ai, ignore him in this meeting under the shadow of the Imperial ruin which he has largely made.

While Yuan Shih-k'ai is hesitating, the Throne puts out two decrees with his sanction. The first meets the action of the Republic of China at Wuchang and that of the Republic at Shanghai, in calling for delegates to form Governments. The Throne calls for representatives to meet in Peking, " to decide the nation's policy and to tranquillize the people's minds." It seeks to forestall the Republics in their conventions. It is not a long edict but an urgent one, in which the viceroys and governors are commanded to instruct scholars and gentry quickly to nominate three to five persons from each province, " well known and respected, conversant in politics and rich in experience," to come at once to Peking for a public conference. The situation has become so critical, according to this edict, since the rising of Wuchang, that it involves the life or death of the nation, and the little five-and-one-half-years-old Emperor is made to say that the Throne " being of fatherly inclination does not hold fixed views. Therefore it is expedient to obtain at once opinions from the subjects in order to decide means to avoid a collapse." It seeks to make the most of having secured Yuan Shih-k'ai's presence in Peking. It seeks to regrasp at least the semblance of its ancient exalted state by putting *Yuan Shih-k'ai* forward as a Government, against the Republican pretenders.

In its second edict of November 14 the Throne does not wait for the representatives whom it called for in its first edict, but appoints *Condolence Commissioners* for the twelve provinces that have revolted. They are to proceed with dispatch to their different districts " to pardon, condole, persuade, and lead the people," and to make known the Throne's principles of carrying out political reform. The Throne in this edict fears that the people of all classes are not able to know the facts. It has " repeatedly promulgated its political administrations, conciliating all in order to save the nation." But it considers it expedient at this moment of disturbance to send " well-known and honoured officials," " to proclaim the virtue of the Exalted [the Emperor], and to ventilate the desires of the lowly [the people]."

As the Throne closes its struggle against anarchy on Nov. 14, its tear-stained eyes are turned to Jehol the old summer Capital and its chosen refuge in case of flight. The journalists who gather in Peking to watch the decay of China have called this the climax. Anxious for the security of Jehol, it appoints Hsi Liang, the Manchu ex-Viceroy of Manchuria, to take charge there.

Alongside this decree published in the *Official Gazette* is an expression of thanks from Yuan Shih-k'ai for his appointment as Premier. Following his conferences of the early morning of November 14, he has accepted this appointment. In reply to his anxiety as to its nature and the scope of his powers, the Lung Yu Empress Dowager says she had relied upon the Prince Regent, who has been unable to direct affairs, and instead has muddled everything. There is now no longer any hope of the Prince Regent being able to restore order, and she wishes to place everything in Yuan Shih-k'ai's hands. She has no reservations to make, she says, but will do whatever he advises.

The effect of this is to determine Yuan Shih-k'ai. Such an appeal cannot be resisted : these are the convictions of Yuan Shih-k'ai himself. The views of Prince Ching and the Lung Yu Empress Dowager are that the country has reached such a state of disorder as would require months for the people to settle down, and that at least during this period the Throne will have to give way entirely. The course to be pursued under the Premiership is that of conciliation. This is disclosed in the two edicts of November 14. Yuan Shih-k'ai confirms it by an official statement on Nov. 15, to the effect that he will form a Cabinet immediately and endeavour to carry on the Government with the support of as many provinces as he can unite together, allowing the remainder their own course for the time being, while trying to win back their allegiance gradually.

This policy is now begun by Yuan Shih-k'ai and the Throne by consenting to Governor Sun Pao-chi allowing himself to be elected President of Shantung, when the famous telegram is sent : " Watch the Germans." But the policy is doomed in its inception. Before the close of November 15, the Premiership and the Throne receive a Memorial from the Chihli Provincial Assembly at Tientsin calling for a Republic. The Provincial Assembly is acting under the direct influence of Shanghai. The Tientsin members leave Peking, and the National Assembly now virtually dissolves.

Nanking has become a battle-ground threatening to eclipse Hankow, which the foreign Press describes as an " Inferno." On Nov. 16 Yuan Shih-k'ai names a Cabinet representative of the country in revolution. He appoints reformers both republicans and monarchists, a Minister of Foreign Affairs and a Minister of Army from Kuangtung

Province, a Minister of Finance from Chihli, a Minister of Communications from Anhuei, a Minister of Navy from Fukien, a Minister of Justice from Chekiang, a Minister of Agriculture from Kiangsu, a Minister of Interior from Honan, and a Minister of Education from Kuangsi. Kuangtung, the Canton province, is represented by five appointments in this Cabinet, Chihli has two and Chekiang two, Hupeh has none.

The great reformer, Liang Chi-chiao of Kuangtung, is appointed to the Board of Justice as Vice-Minister. The curious appointments do not give confidence. Their announcement seems to be a signal for flight among those appointees who are in Peking. The newly named Minister of Foreign Affairs, Liang Tun-yen, is in Europe. Liang Chi-chiao has made his first visit to China since 1898. Having been pardoned by the general law of amnesty, he has journeyed to Mukden in Manchuria, which he reaches on Nov. 14, but returns to Dalny. He cannot believe that he has been really appointed to the Ministry of Justice and says that he would not think of accepting it. "Whether true or rumour, I will never accept the appointment," he says. Chang Chien appointed Minister of Agriculture signed with Wu Ting-fang the demand for the Throne's abdication. But he has only just been appointed *Condolence Commissioner* for the province of Kiangsu, at Shanghai, and is kept busy telegraphing his refusals to Peking. It gives him ample opportunity to express his views, which he takes advantage of, recapitulating past events, blaming the Government for scoffing at public opinion in the past, and reminding it that it has rejected his advice hitherto. He calls attention to the atrocities of the Imperialists at Hankow following upon the heels of the penitential decree, as well as atrocities committed at Nanking when there was no state of war. With respect to his appointment as *Condolence Commissioner*, he states that all, both Chinese and foreigners, find the inhuman acts committed under General Yin Chang at Hankow hateful without exception. "What condolence can I offer to the masses? What virtue can I ascribe to the Throne?" he asks, and then advises the reigning house of the Manchus to admit the necessities of the times by acknowledging the Republic. It could thus give him some footing to go upon in its favour. "If the recognition is withheld longer I cannot tell what will be the ultimate fate of the Dynasty's ancestral temple." "I decline the

Ministership of Agriculture, Industry, and Commerce, also," says he, " because the people have no shelter even with which to cover their heads, much less any capacity to pursue industry."

While Yuan Shih-k'ai's cabinet is breaking down, President General Li Yuan-hung informs the consuls of the foreign Powers at Hankow that the Republican states have elected their representatives to the Capital at Wuchang and asks international recognition of the Republican Federation. Wu Ting-fang claiming to be Director of Foreign Affairs in the Republic is also demanding recognition for the Republic, but it is not clear whom he means.

Twenty-four hours were all that were needed to tarnish the hope of Yuan Shih-k'ai's ability to administer government under a Cabinet from Peking. His expressed views were that it was better for China to retain the Throne under a limited monarchy, but the revolutionists were determined upon making no compromise. In a belated reply to General Chang Shao-tseng at Lanchou, which General Chang never received, President General Li Yuan-hung answers proposals for an armistice and the consideration of establishing a monarchical system with these words : " The overthrow of the Government is the only conclusion." Yuan Shih-k'ai's alternative, in fact, is that the question of China's future government is too vital to be determined by a single man, but is in the hands of the many, and whether it is to be republican or monarchical should be decided by the delegates from the provinces who have been summoned to Peking.

Yuan Shih-k'ai has reached a complete understanding with the Manchu Clan through Prince Ching to abandon all destructive activities and to pursue constructive activities on the basis of the 19 articles of the new Constitution. There is to be no more fighting by Imperialists except in defence. Yuan Shih-k'ai is to recover the allegiance of the army and to persuade the provinces. He is the only man in North China with aplomb. With his Cabinet resigning and the opponents of the Dynasty still bent on destructive activities and the determination to overthrow and not build up in Peking, while successfully constructing Republican cabinets and assemblies, he proceeds to the business of the most difficult problems of government under revolution.

He must borrow money. Including the Lung Yu Empress Dowager's gifts from her private hoard, there is less than 4,000,000 taels in the Imperial treasury. The sums required are those necessary to pay the army. The first thing is to regain the army's confidence, and money alone can accomplish that.

General Chang Shao-tseng's successor, General Lan Tien-wei, is not a monarchist like his predecessor, but a republican, and Yuan Shih-k'ai is glad to get rid of him at Lanchou, when he, like General Chang Shao-tseng, flees. He takes refuge in Dalny, where he prepares to lead the revolt in Manchuria. It is meet for the Throne to swear quickly before the tablets of its ancestors to the 19 articles imposed upon it by General Chang Shao-tseng through the National Assembly, and on Nov. 19 it announces by edict that it will do this on Nov. 26. The ancestors are presumed to know nothing yet as to what has happened in the world. Only an accident and a calamity, a succession, or a diminution of the Dynastic heritage, or some great achievement, ever causes the Throne thus to disturb the august dead.

The officials of all the yamens are commanded by edict dated Nov. 21 to attend the ceremonies with reference to administering the oath to the Throne at the ancestral temple. The solemn performance is preceded by rumblings in the Empire as of the dragon turning over. Yuan Shih-k'ai is threatened by assassins. Immediately following the assertion of his absolute mastery over the army, one of the Imperial cruisers at Seven Mile Creek bombards the Imperialist soldiers 45 minutes in the morning and returns to the attack at 2 p.m., accompanied by other war-vessels manœuvring in the neighbourhood and watching the proceedings. The navy is entirely lost to the Throne, the army is disintegrating, and Yuan Shih-k'ai continues unsuccessful in the effort to obtain loans. Only on the bounty from the Court are the guards in the Capital kept loyal, while it is upon the plunder at Hankow that the army there pays itself and is inspired to fight for the city of Hanyang.

Unable to dislodge the troops at Lanchou by persuasion or orders, Yuan Shih-k'ai tests the loyalty of the division in Manchuria claimed by the Republicans, and finding that its regiments respond to the Throne's orders, he redistributes them between Mukden and Lanchou.

The tremendous burdens under which Yuan Shih-k'ai labours seem further lightened by the return of Shantung to the Imperial fold, which he can accept as the direct answer to his injunction that Shantung "watch the Germans." His lieutenant, Tang Shao-yi, is disheartened with his master's support of the Dynasty, and fears that Yuan Shih-k'ai is going too far in the interests of the monarchical idea to effect again the unity of the country.

Yuan Shih-k'ai is awaiting the restoration of quiet at Hankow and Hanyang. The foreign Press has raised a great hue and cry of impending warfare at Nanking that has greatly impressed the world. Foreigners in the interior of China have asked for greater protection by their Governments, which have for the most part ordered their subjects and citizens to leave for the seaboard. The danger of China's situation to the Christian element in Eastern Asia is expressed in the action of a Committee of the Foreign Missions in New York City who on Nov. 25 call on the Churches of Canada and the United States for prayers for China. On Nov. 26, when the Prince Regent swears on behalf of the Throne and the Dynasty to uphold the constitutional 19 articles, the so-called Nanking battle begins, and the representatives of the foreign Powers in Peking make representations to Yuan Shih-k'ai of the necessity of avoiding disorder at Peking. On Nov. 27 the revolutionists are winning at Nanking, Tibet revolts, and Canton is getting ready to send 10,000 troops against Peking.

Yuan Shih-k'ai is overburdened with work and with going each day to audience with the Lung Yu Empress Dowager. To ease his labours the Lung Yu Empress Dowager excuses him for little intervals of two or three days from reporting in person to her. The Throne tries to stay the complete dissolution of the Cabinet by gently refusing resignations here and there. There is no Cabinet in truth, and the National Assembly is only a name and stands for nothing.

The full magnitude and horror of the massacre of 8000 Manchus at Hsianfu (October 22) and its terror for the ruling race is having full effect in Peking. Yuan Shih-k'ai, to extricate himself from the last ditch and save even a footing for the Premier Government, is promoting the investment of Hanyang. The movement is successful, and Hanyang falls on the night of November 27, and is occupied by the Imperialists on November 28.

Troops that take cities can pay themselves, and the army before Hankow has now had two cities. But Yuan Shih-k'ai must have money for those troops who do not take cities and for many other purposes of a Premiership Government. On Nov. 29 Yuan Shih-k'ai telegraphs to Hankow granting a three days' truce, and proceeds to the question of an armistice, which General Feng Kuo-chang has learned from President General Li Yuan-hung would be acceptable to the Republic.

Two of the three sister-cities of the Yangtse have been recovered by the Imperialists, thereby placing the Premier in a position where he can be magnanimous toward the Republic of China.

Yuan Shih-k'ai has become an object of quizzical wonder to foreign officials and others for his endurance, discretion, and silence. On account of his statesmanship at Hanyang, by which he has sacrificed his announced principle of non-destructive action and non-aggression, to gain the essential footing necessary to bring President General Li Yuan-hung to negotiate the question of unity and further hostilities, he is accused of working to obtain the Throne. His resolves are rather magnificent. On the strength of his success at Hanyang he optimistically affirms that eight days will find the crisis over. If he can only get a few thousand taels per month, he tells the bankers, he can tire out the revolutionists and force a reaction. The foreign bankers report only 2,000,000 taels in the Inperial Treasury, Yuan Shih-k'ai is hopeful of loans from the French and later from others. "Members of the Legations" "believe he will succeed," "if he can retake one or two provinces."

Since reaching Peking Yuan Shih-k'ai has ignored the National Assembly, because it has merely persecuted the Government and is doing nothing constructive under the treatment meted out to it by the Republic at Wuchang and the assemblies of the revolted provinces. It has become a mere remnant which Yuan Shih-k'ai himself ignores. But it has more elements of life than the Cabinet and is more useful. Besides, there is no possibility of a foreign loan without a sanction of some representative body of the people. It is the first thing the Premier has to ask of the National Assembly, and it is the Assembly's expiring breath when on Nov. 30 it meets secretly at Yuan Shih-k'ai's request to consider the question of negotiating a big loan. The footing which the Premiership acquired by the military success at Hanyang and in arranging an armistice does not give it sufficient power to revitalize the National Assembly. When the wand of the

Premier, Yuan Shih-k'ai, passes over it, it seems only to sink into a deeper and longer sleep.

In the last days of November division of the Empire seemed imminent. The Government at Peking was dead. The Empire from the Throne's point of view was a mass of Dynastic wreckage. In four weeks the rebellion had swept away the Throne's government, its ministers and Cabinet, and those ministers disappeared from view. The Throne was brought to its knees by a general commanding 5000 troops. It capitulated to the National Assembly, which in turn was cowed by President Li Yuan-hung and dispersed by the power of the revolted provinces The rebels had become patriots, and two additional republics and three independencies had arisen. Doubtful of its success in recalling Yuan Shih-k'ai, it looked for other converts and failed to find them. Even monarchists like General Chang Shao-tseng and the reformers of 1898 fled from it. It committed everything to one man without reserve. All its measures were fruitless. The Imperial Army that should have taken Wuchang seemed paralysed. The Capital was intermittently in the throes of panic. The navy had gone bodily over to the revolutionists. The metropolitan province itself asked for a Republic. Hankow was an " Inferno," and Nanking arose as another battle-ground. The one man called to save the Empire was unable to form a Cabinet, and the Throne represented by the Prince Regent foreswore its heritage before the manes of its ancestors.

Nanking is falling. The Imperialist General Chang Hsun, the swashbuckler who has sworn " to die in the last ditch before surrendering Nanking," in the last hours of November is giving up the City without a struggle. As Nanking falls, a note of pathos in the Premier's position is struck by the words circulated in the Legation Quarter that his friends are arranging for his protection at the Legations. His victorious army at Hanyang is about to be withdrawn, in accordance with an armistice which he has sanctioned. " They have started to talk," says a common Chinese on the street in Hankow, " so there will be no more fighting. They will talk until they agree, and then they will make a bargain. That is Chinese."

CHAPTER XIX

DECEMBER IN PEKING

PEKING in December 1911 was slowly going out of business as a Capital. To the Republican Press at Wuchang it was a kind of *morgue*. "Prince Ching has drunk poison and is dead," said one of its papers. "Yin Chang is certainly dead, but the high ministers are keeping the matter secret." "Yuan Shih-k'ai is killed." They have even killed General Feng Kuo-chang commanding the Imperialist Army. "It is a thousand pities that Feng the thief has been poisoned," they go on to say; "since he burned Hankow and plundered and killed several thousands of people, it is but right that he should die, but he ought to have been caught alive and had his head chopped off."

None of these things is true. Peking is quiet in its decline, so far there is nothing bloody about it.

The very last thing as November closed, the Throne issued an edict commanding that henceforth all ministers of state "are to ride on horseback within the precincts of the Imperial Palace." This has been an honour conferred in the past only on princes and grand councillors and other specially favoured dignitaries. The edict does not increase the traffic in the deserted courts and avenues of the Imperial premises. Nanking, the seat of the Chinese Ming Emperors, which arose as a battle-ground is again ascending, now as a Capital. On Dec. 1 the Imperial troops lose their last position on Purple Hill—the purple, as it were, seems to fall from the shoulders of the Manchus with this loss, and when the revolutionists occupy Nanking on Dec. 2, not a single province has yet responded to the Throne's call for representatives to a national conference at Peking. There is no Treasury in Peking, the most important branch of government. The Minister of Finance appointed by Yuan Shih-k'ai refused to serve. The Vice-Minister disappeared, fleeing in a darkened railway coupé to Tientsin, and then going to Shanghai. They joined the flight while the running was good.

The situation in China is one of lively inspiration to European and American caricaturists, who have long loved "Hop Lee," with his goggles, flirtatious fan, and swishing queue, as a subject. Threatening letters received by Peking officials are to them the last call to decamp. If this keeps up, the Emperor of China will not have even the outer shell of a government, nor yet a Court.

The Regent, Prince Chun, resigns in an attempt to save the situation for his son the Emperor, and is dismissed by the Lung Yu Empress Dowager. The eye of the initiate sees the late Empress Grand Dowager rising from her tomb in the Eastern Hunting Park. With the mantle of the Empress Grand Dowager's power, the Lung Yu Empress Dowager takes over the State, or what is left of it. Down goes Prince Chun, and the Lung Yu Empress Dowager triumphs over her factional rivals.

The exit of the Prince Regent is the simplest possible. The edict attributes to him a formal resignation, but shows him to be summarily removed. It says the Regent has verbally memorialized the Lung Yu Empress Dowager that he has held the Regency for three years but that the Regency has been unpopular; the constitutional government has not been established, owing to which complications have arisen, the people's hearts have been broken, and the country thrown into turmoil. "The Regent regrets that his repentance came too late, and feels that if he continues in power his commands will soon be disregarded. He wept and prayed to resign the Regency, at the same time expressing his earnest intention to abstain from politics. I, the Empress Dowager, living in the Palace, am ignorant of the state of affairs, but I know that rebellion exists and fighting continues, causing disaster everywhere, while the commerce of friendly nations suffers. The Regent is honest though ambitious. Being misled, he has harmed the people. Therefore his resignation is accepted. The Regent's seal is cancelled. Let the Regent receive 50,000 taels annually from the Imperial household allowances. Hereafter the Premier and Cabinet shall control appointments and the administration. Edicts shall be sealed with the Emperor's seal."

In closing this edict of dismissal the Lung Yu Empress Dowager said something so much in the style of the Empress Grand Dowager that it startled even the Imperialist reformers. "I will lead the Emperor to conduct audiences,' said she. This cost her something to explain, because it appeared to be a taking over of the Throne for herself. The concluding paragraphs of the edict are drawn so as not to invalidate this interpretation while at the same time admitting of an opposite interpretation. The latter was in fact seized upon by the Republican Government. The closing paragraphs are :—

" The guardianship of the holy person of the Emperor, who is of tender age, shall be a special responsibility. Hsu Shih-chang and Hsih Hsu are appointed therefore Grand Guardians of the Emperor.

" As the time is critical, princes and nobles must observe this. The Imperial Family, rulers, and ministers, who have undertaken great responsibility, must be loyal and help the country and people, who now must realize that the Court does not object to surrender the power vested in the Throne. Let the people observe order and continue business, and thus prevent the country's disruption and restore prosperity."

Prince Chun's political career was brief. Nothing more could have been expected of him, since he was a young man and in the modern political sense without education or training. The Legations sympathized with and pitied him as one who was unselfish, and who without the essential capabilities nevertheless sought the welfare of the Throne, and did it in the midst of surroundings in which success was hopeless.

Yuan Shih-k'ai is rid of the exasperating young man who had "*kuai*-ed" (taken offence at) and hectored him in times past. The whole State is now on Yuan Shih-k'ai's shoulders, as before, and he has an equally incapable and helpless woman and child-Emperor on his hands as before. In substance the Throne has really abdicated, for it is clinging only to mere Imperial forms, with a diminishing hope of ever retrieving their substance.

The National Assembly's memorial on the queue reaches the Throne, and it issues an edict (December 7) as follows : " All Our servants and subjects are hereby permitted to cut their hair at their own free will." Appended to this brief statute like a tail comes the large Imperial seal, and the long signatures of the Premier and ten other ministers of state with their titles. There are only three ministers in Peking and these are the least important ones. Six of the signatures are of " acting " ministers. The signature of the Minister of Justice in his " absence " is signed by another.

Hsu Shih-chang, an able-bodied recipient of many favours from the Throne in the past, is trying to evade his responsibilities. " I am in receipt of an edict from Her Majesty the Lung Yu Empress Dowager," says the little Emperor, " wherein Hsu Shih-chang prays for the rescission of a former order [appointing him Grand Guardian of the Emperor]. Her Majesty decrees that as the protection of my sacred person is a most weighty responsibility, and in view of the trustworthiness of the said Grand Secretary, who is honest and large-minded and a veteran in experience, he has, in consequence, been appointed Grand Guardian. He should, at this moment, exert his loyalty and devotion, sparing neither fatigue nor pain. His request that I rescind the former order need not be entertained."

So much had the acts of the Throne resembled abdication to the revolutionists that they ascribed to Yuan Shih-k'ai the credit of accomplishing without disorder in Peking the removal of the Dynasty and the transition to a Republic or to a Chinese monarchy. The Throne had dismissed the Prince Regent. It had finally abandoned the wearing of the queue as a sign of loyalty, and now, simultaneously, it sanctioned the substitution of the calendar of the solar system for the Dynastic one.

These epoch-making edicts gave the impression of dissolution of the Throne's power. But one high official, Governor Chen Chao-chang, at Kirin in Manchuria, who could not conceive such self-denial and mistook it for strategy, memorialized the Cabinet, representing the Lung Yu Empress Dowager as endeavouring to obtain private power in her own interest, and called attention to the gravity of the Government's situation. His memorial startled the Lung Yu Empress Dowager, who issued an edict reprimanding Chen Chao-chang and others for their extraordinary ignorance of present affairs and inability to comprehend their duty. " The said Governor and others having indulged in rash surmises," said the Lung Yu Empress Dowager, " by hastily giving utterance to such words as ' indiscriminate and chaotic changes have thus far taken place in the Imperial Government,' and ' disunion in political authority and dissension in the Palace. They are really not aware of the Throne's earnest desire in introducing new methods suitable to the moment, and of its high sense of justice precluding selfish motives."

In this edict the Lung Yu Empress Dowager then

explains the situation of the Court and of the Emperor: "This time Prince Chun's prayer to resign his Prince-Regentship has been accepted by me, and the responsible duties in connection with official appointment, political administration, etc., have been entrusted to the Premier of the Cabinet and Ministers of State, in strict accordance with the constitutional form of government, the only provision being made that the Decrees for promulgation shall be stamped with the Imperial Seal, and that I shall lead and accompany the Emperor to attend the holdings of ceremonial audiences. The latter procedure is entirely different from the lowered curtain politic duties in the former reign; it is truly the actual reform of political foundation, so as to show no monopolizing of Our Sovereign Power in beginning a new life with Our subjects."

This edict, bearing the Emperor's seal and signed by Yuan Shih-k'ai and others representing all the Ministries, closed with these words:

"At present the general position is very critical, as if it would not last a day. The popular mind is easily agitated, and rumours are rampant on all sides. The said Governor and others should unite in mind as well as in strength, to endure it with calmness, to preserve peace and order, and to prevent perturbation." On Dec. 20 the Lung Yu Empress Dowager, further confounding the opinions of Governor Chen, issued an edict that all memorials must be submitted to the Cabinet, and not to the Throne as in the past, thus driving home her protest that "the Court does not object to surrendering the power vested in the Throne."

Well may the Throne adjure the living leaders to be calm and unperturbed at a time when it is paying homage to its loyal dead. "Feng Ju-kuei, Governor of Kiangsi," says an edict on Dec. 5, "has devoted many years to Our service, and he was assiduous in performing his duties. Owing to the fall of the capital City of Kiangsi [Nanchang], he committed suicide with composure, demonstrating the inviolability of his great honour, which action calls forth Our deep compassion. . . . He is to be appointed to highest honours and favours which are customarily granted to a Viceroy who has died in battle. All his demerits on record during his official career are hereby cancelled."

His two sons are promoted "as an encouragement of the dutiful honour of an official and to soothe the loyal soul of the deceased."

On Dec. 9 the Throne pays similar posthumous

honours to Sung Shou, Viceroy of Fukien and Chekiang. An official " ripe in experience and loyal in sentiment," who also " committed suicide with composure, owing to the fall of the capital City of Fukien " [Foochow].

On Dec. 24 the Throne paid its respects to the spirit of a former officer of guards in the Palace, General Chao Kuo-tsien, who committed suicide at his post in Kuangtung, owing to the fall of the City. " His loyalty and self-sacrifice are really worthy of the best tradition," says the Throne.

The Throne has little else to do than mourn over and pay rites to its loyal dead. It is like a bird fluttering about the old nest, touching here and there preparatory to its last departure.

So satisfied in their minds are the revolutionists and Yuan Shih-k'ai himself of the passing of the Dynasty, that they agree to indefinite armistices, which now reach to December 21. President Li Yuan-hung and the Republic at Wuchang have recovered confidence since the loss of Hanyang and its evacuation by the Imperialists and are unwilling for anything but a Republic. Delegates of five provinces at Shanghai will submit to nothing less than abdication. Both republics are willing to concede full power to Yuan Shih-k'ai if he will eliminate the Manchus from the Central Government. Only Canton opposes him.

The Peking Government is willing to agree to a compromise with the revolutionists on any terms, and Yuan Shih-k'ai secures the aid of his old lieutenant, Tang Shao-yi, as envoy, to make overtures of peace to the revolutionists. As has been the case steadily from the beginning, each succeeding overture has only advanced the revolt and hurried on the final capitulation.

Now that Nanking has fallen to the revolutionists, the balance of Republican power is on the side of the coast provinces. After the fall of Hanyang, Shanghai is able to dictate to Wuchang. Led by Wu Ting-fang, it repudiates the equivocal announcement of Li Yuan-hung made on the fall of Hanyang to the effect that he would defer to Yuan Shih-k'ai and is willing to compromise on a constitutional monarchy, and Wuchang stands firm with Shanghai and Canton for a Republic.

On Dec. 7 Tang Shao-yi is ready to proceed to Wuchang, where Yuan Shih-k'ai is most hopeful of reasonable terms on account of the able conservatism of Li Yuan-hung. On Dec. 8, however, Li Yuan-hung gives out a draft Constitution for the Republic one day before Yuan

Shih-k'ai's envoy carrying plenipotentiary power leaves Peking to negotiate with him. Wu Ting-fang takes occasion to announce that no negotiations conducted at Wuchang can be regarded as official. Shanghai has become the Republican centre and is the meeting-point of the refugee members from the National Assembly at Peking, the exiles and revolutionaries from Japan, the students and reformers from America, the conspirators and reformers from Hongkong, the Straits Settlements and Europe, and the Republicans from Canton and the Yangtse Valley.

On Dec. 11 Li Yuan-hung and his delegates at Wuchang reply to Wu Ting-fang by choosing him as negotiator in the peace conference and inviting him to Wuchang. Supported by the delegates at Shanghai, who claim to represent nearly all China, he declines to go to Wuchang on account of its not being a fit place for peace negotiations, being the scene of recent defeats of the revolutionist troops.

From this moment Yuan Shih-k'ai has for his antagonist Wu Ting-fang, who first assails him on the loans he is endeavouring to consummate. Yuan Shih-k'ai, as Hanyang fell, got together the remnant of the National Assembly, consisting mostly of the members that were the Throne's appointees, and on the last day of November secured their approval of a Belgian loan proposal for 30,000,000 taels and another for 14,000,000 taels, money ostensibly for administrative and industrial purposes.

The National Assembly thereby attracted more bitter criticism than ever before. Many of its Southern members—those who were not at Wuchang or Canton—were at Shanghai. They denounced Yuan Shih-k'ai's trumped-up Assembly, and Wu Ting-fang on Dec. 12 notified the consuls and foreign banks in Shanghai and cabled to the financiers in America and Europe not to lend money to Yuan Shih-k'ai on the plea that it was intended for peaceable objects, because its real destination was the Imperialist war-chest.

When Tang Shao-yi gets to Wuchang he finds a constitutional Republican Government that has nothing to say to him except that he should go on to Shanghai. While he is journeying, out of touch with events and helpless, down the Yangtse River, the revolutionists at Shanghai organize the "Republic of China," so as to be ready for his arrival. On Dec. 14 they announce the establishment of a Republican Government of all China, with Sun Yat-sen as

Provisional President of the ten revolutionist provinces, with General Huang Hsing to act for him until his arrival. He is *en route* to China from America.

The delegates of these ten provinces meeting as a national convention adopt peace terms—an ultimatum to Yuan Shih-k'ai and the Throne—to hand to Tang Shao-yi. The next day, when Tang arrives, they hand him their programme for the abolition of the Dynasty, the establishment of the Republic, with Yuan Shih-k'ai as President, and Sun Yat-sen Vice-President, under a Cabinet to be selected by the revolutionists. They then have nothing to negotiate except the terms of the Court's seclusion. That is the peace conference.

Having nothing else to do, or believing he has nothing else to do, Yuan Shih-k'ai's envoy successively gives way in the questions arising at the peace conference, until on Dec. 20 he is " convinced that only the abdication of the Emperor and the establishment of a Republic will satisfy the people and prevent further shedding of blood." Friends in Peking of Tang Shao-yi, the envoy, receive telegrams from him requesting them to persuade Yuan Shih-k'ai to agree with him.

Yuan Shih-k'ai fears that a Republic means China's dissolution. Tang Shao-yi then proposes to Yuan Shih-k'ai that the question of the future form of government for China be submitted to a national convention to be called at Nanking especially for this purpose. Everything imaginable is suggested in Peking to avoid a Republic, including the retirement of the Lung Yu Empress Dowager and the creation of a Chinese regency.

The power of the Republic has annihilated all loan prospects until this question is settled. All other questions vanish before that of the future form of government, and on Dec. 26 an historical conference takes place at which Yuan Shih-k'ai presents the proposal submitted by Tang Shao-yi and the Republicans, to the Lung Yu Empress Dowager and the princes and nobles of the Imperial Clan. Members of the Court realize that there is no hope for the Throne in the support of only a few provinces or districts of questionable loyalty. Yuan Shih-k'ai telegraphs to Tang Shao-yi the acceptance of the principle of his proposal, and in doing so he loosens his last frail grasp of the Throne.

On Dec. 28 there is another conference to arrange the edict of acceptance. The Republic was already set up in the old Capital of the Mings, Nanking. Fearing they will be forced to accept worse terms, they grasp with eagerness the principle of the proposed referendum, and disclose their willingness to agree under certain conditions to abdication itself.

The scenes in the audience-chamber and the passages surrounding it during this momentous conclave of the last representatives of the Manchu conquerors were described by the vernacular Press as impressive and awful: the Lung Yu Empress Dowager swooning in the arms of her attendants and ladies-in-waiting, while the dissenting princes, Yu Lang, Tsai T'ao, and others, prefer death to dishonour amid lamentations that fill the audience-hall and the courts outside.

The Lung Yu Empress Dowager's account, issued in the name of the little Emperor, is quite different. In an edict accepting the proposal and authorizing the special conference to determine the future form of government, she says: "In response to a request of the ministers of state, I have summoned an assembly of the princes and dukes nearly related to the Imperial Family for a conference, and have questioned them in person, but no dissentient words have been spoken."

"We granted the request of the National Assembly [hitherto] and promulgated a constitutional statute of 19 articles," continues the Lung Yu Empress Dowager, "taking an oath of adherence in Our Ancestral Temple expecting an early cessation of hostilities. . . . However, owing to incredulity in Our good faith, political strife has repeatedly arisen. In my opinion the question of which of the two forms, monarchical constitution or republican constitution, would better suit Our country to-day . . . is not one which a single section of the people may monopolize, nor can it be decided by the Throne alone." Proceeding, the Emperor is then made to command the Cabinet to frame proper rules of election to be later adopted, in order to summon the Parliament within the shortest time.

Throughout the several recommendations and orders of the Emperor, the Lung Yu Empress Dowager goes right on talking, in an almost pitiful way, expressing her opinions, hopes, and wishes. "I am of opinion," she says, "that Heaven will give new birth to the people, and then elect a Monarch for them, to shepherd [guide] them." She then makes a plea for the Throne in these words: "It is intended that one man should feed the world [the nation], and not that the world should support one man. The Emperor has ascended and inherited the Throne at a tender age; and as for me, I am certainly not hard-hearted enough to sacrifice human lives and injure the whole nation. My only hope is that the Parliament will discuss and decide what is beneficial to the nation and helpful to the people. Heaven sees what the people see, and Heaven hears what the people hear. I wish my patriotic and loving soldiers and people, each imbued with the highest sense of justice, to join in their deliberations as to the adoption of the best policy, for which I entertain the sincerest hope."

The Throne and Yuan Shih-k'ai have been completely abandoned by Tang Shao-yi. Tang Shao-yi carried but one requirement with him to the South, expressed in three parts: first, the retention of the Emperor and Throne with authority in the hands of the President of the Council; second, the election of the President of the Council by the people to possess the same prerogatives as the President of a Republic; third, the autonomy of the provinces under these conditions. Possessing full plenipotentiary powers and with no obligations whatever to the Court—perhaps the widest latitude ever enjoyed by a Chinese envoy—he abandoned the Premier and Court under the circumstances. Yuan Shih-k'ai felt himself defeated. Supported in his conservative views on the necessity of a monarchy by all his friendly advisers in the Foreign Legations, he felt the country had gone mad, and was for borrowing what money he could, defending the country north of the Yangtse, and leaving the Republican provinces on the South to take their own course.

The Throne's edict was unwelcome to the revolutionists. They would accept nothing that did not permit of the carrying out of the Republic without delay and that did not at least recognize the Provisional Republican Government. They had never hesitated in the assumption that the *Republic* was the Government, and not the *Throne*.

When Yuan Shih-k'ai realized that the revolutionists expected, and intended, to authorize and carry out the conference for determining the future form of government themselves, he felt himself betrayed by his envoy. He bitterly resented what he called the bad faith of his antagonist, Wu Ting-fang, and the Republican party, in insisting upon a trumped-up conference and not a representative one. He asked of the Throne three days' sick leave so as to be exempt from attendance at Court. His objections to the agreement entered into by his envoy at Shanghai with the revolutionists received their answer on Dec. 29, when Sun Yat-sen was elected Provisional President at Nanking. The revolutionists would not wait for a national conference, and did not intend that the Throne should ever have an opportunity to repudiate its action on the question of China's future form of government, which action it regarded as a virtual abdication. They already treated the Throne as a thing of the past, " because eighteen provinces have already voted for a Republic, and the Throne's edict says it will accept the decision of such a convention of voters."

Yuan Shih-k'ai telegraphed to Tang Shao-yi to ignore the Throne's edict, hoping to secure delay in the appointment of members of the conference. " I want a true referendum on the question of the Republic," said he.

The remnant of the National Assembly which ten days before tried to retire on account of the peace conference and was not permitted to do so by Yuan Shih-k'ai, is now heard in a faint cry declaring against the Republic. Yuan Shih-k'ai says Tang Shao-yi may be President, but he himself will never serve the Republic. He repudiates Tang Shao-yi's actions, and approves only the armistice to which his envoy has agreed. Tang Shao-yi, however, goes on discussing at Shanghai the details of the abdication, and as one of the conditions of the sequestration of the little Emperor Pu Yi suggests ex-territoriality at the Summer Palace or at Jehol. The revolutionists magnanimously offer him treatment equal to that of any deposed foreign potentate.

Yuan Shih-k'ai was deeply engrossed with the details of Imperialism and was appointing men to vacancies in the National Assembly, and to his Cabinet which was a kind of Chinese fireworks-machine firing off men rapidly as it revolved. The speed with which events were moving at Shanghai was something to which Yuan Shih-k'ai could not consent, he could not bring himself to catch up with those events. When Tang Shao-yi had apparently committed him to entrusting the question of future government to a national conference, Yuan had telegraphed in protest to Li Yuan-hung that " he was sympathetically inclined toward the Republicans ; but the three questions of the disposal of the infant Emperor, the Royal Family, and of the Manchus in general, are difficulties not easy to be surmounted."

The whole fate of his wards has now been prearranged

and decided. On Dec. 30 he receives the foreign correspondents, to whom he confesses all his perplexity. The Throne has no question before it but that of disgorging its riches or abdicating. The Imperialists are no longer able to fight and defeat the revolutionists because of the impecuniosity of the Government. " He [Yuan Shih-k'ai] is placing entire responsibility on the Manchus," says a critic, " and is making a last effort to 'save face.' "

Yuan Shih-k'ai maintained his contention for a proper election of delegates at the national conference and that its gathering-place should be Peking, and his envoy sought a compromise on Chefoo, or even Hankow, but the revolutionists insisted upon Nanking or Shanghai. The fact was the whole suggestion was dead and there never was to be any conference at all. Tang Shao-yi's mission was ended. It was ridiculous except as a complete surrender on behalf of the Manchu Dynasty, and having accomplished this surrender he resigned.

Sun Yat-sen had arrived in Shanghai and was now ready to proceed to Nanking for his inauguration, which took place on the first day of the new year. In his oath of office he swore to overthrow the Manchu Dynasty. In Peking the Court was actually making its plans with a view to abdication, and many believed it had already made secret arrangements by which the Lung Yu Empress Dowager and little Emperor might take refuge in the Legations.

The state of things in the Palace is suggested in the semi-official announcement that the little Emperor has " ceased his studies." The Imperial tutor has been dismissed.

This was my Peking. I had thought the Dynasty was immortal, it had lived so long. It was uprooted. Abdication was now a matter of mere formality. It was impossible that a Republic could give it such a shock. Even in 1900, after the Court had fled Peking, the Throne pervaded the land—now there was nothing. I had seen the Court on parade in all its ancient and barbaric grandeur—remembered its return to Peking and its last Imperial funerals. When it went out it was a sin to look upon it, people were hustled off the streets, spectators were likely to be shot dead by the bowmen with arrows. Tradition says that in the history of persons living this has been done. All this pomp and panoply is now vanished. Nothing remains but the sorrowful spectacle of a woman and a little boy seeking a place of safety.

CHAPTER XX

JANUARY AND ABDICATION

I do not know from what kind of founts of imagination those edicts of November and December were pumped up in such a drowning flow. I confess to a sense of bewilderment at all those edicts and events when I arrived in Peking in December—the last day. It was New Year's Eve when I arrived at the house of Mr. Williams, the First Secretary of the American Legation. It was from his home, strange coincidence, that on New Year's Eve 1903 I left Peking for the last war in China. At that time it was a question which would be the most lively and interesting, Manchuria or Peking—the war in Manchuria or the revolution in Peking. But it had taken eight years for the crash to come. The stuffed Legation Quarter, bulging with art works and treasure and headquarters of refugees, testified to this.

It was eleven years since war had visited Peking. A few days after my arrival I was reminded of 1900—and the distress of Peking and its sovereigns. I saw from the City wall a procession of prisoners in carts going to the execution grounds. They always go the same way from the Board of Punishments, out the Shun-chih Gate. Dr. Ferguson, who lived by the roadside, thoughtfully diverted the attention of his family, so that they might not think of the pitiful spectacle.

So, too, we pitied the present Throne. This Manchu woman and little boy, led by the Chinese Yuan Shih-k'ai, are watched by the world. The living Son of Heaven, and the Lung Yu Empress Dowager, widow of the last adult Emperor, have put their trust in, and left their fate in the hands of, " China's only statesman." Is he friend or traitor? Whither will he guide them?

At the beginning of January 1912 Peking awakens to a *coup d'état* which if recognized by the Manchu Court and permitted to stand puts an end to civil war as it has been carried on since September 1911, and opens the way for uniting the two opposite sections of the country. The

Republicans are determined to hold the Government at Peking to the terms of Tang Shao-yi's agreement, which in effect provides for abdication and popular government. But Yuan Shih-k'ai cannot but be aggrieved at the revolutionists for thus leaving him without a basis for negotiations by which to provide for the security of the future. This to him means determination of the form of government by the conservative element of the Chinese after mature deliberation under peaceful circumstances, as well as a safe and honourable provision for his helpless wards.

Circumstances impel Yuan Shih-k'ai to offer his own resignation to the Lung Yu Empress Dowager. She cannot accept it, and this being the case the Throne and Court are obliged to proceed with the work of abdicating or of reconsidering and revising their policy of drifting.

The heads of the loyal army around Peking demand the opening of the Imperial purse-strings and the carrying on of the war. This and the restlessness of a section of the Manchu Clan lead the Lung Yu Empress Dowager to decide to do so.

On Jan. 1 a section of the army at Lanchou (Yung-ping-fu) mutinies and threatens to march on Peking. It has telegraphed to the ministers of foreign Powers at Peking to this effect and to the senior consul (Japanese) at Tientsin. Yuan Shih-k'ai insists that unless the Imperial Clan responds to the demand for funds his resignation must be accepted.

On Jan. 2, in a long audience at the Palace, Yuan Shih-k'ai explains the entire situation, repudiates Tang Shao-yi's agreement with Wu Ting-fang as unwarranted, and charges Tang with treachery.

The Imperial Clan and the Court suspect that they have been led into a trap. Realizing their loss, some felt themselves already betrayed. Yuan Shih-k'ai and his makeshift Cabinet accept Tang Shao-yi's resignation.

The Lung Yu Empress Dowager gives up 80,000 ounces of gold and promises to compel contributions by the Clan members. Yuan Shih-k'ai comes into possession of a large sum of money, informs the Legations that he will fight for a monarchy, and believes he can hold the North and that the South will disintegrate.

The Republicans are determined that Yuan Shih-k'ai shall not recover his ground lost through Tang Shao-yi. Yuan Shih-k'ai receives a telegram from Sun Yat-sen offering to surrender the Presidency to him, and Wu

Ting-fang of the Republican Government announces the Republic's readiness to resume war now that Yuan Shih-k'ai has repudiated Tang Shao-yi's action. The American Minister cables to Washington for troops. All other Powers have troops at command, and the Allies unite in garrisoning the railway from the sea to Peking.

The armistice expired, the revolutionist troops attack the Imperialists north of Hankow, where on Jan. 4 there are several hundred casualties and the Imperialists are reinforced. Yuan Shih-k'ai thanks Sun Yat-sen for his offer of the Presidency, at the same time receives from him through Wu Ting-fang an invitation to come to Shanghai to negotiate, as correspondence is impracticable. Yuan Shih-k'ai retorts that as Wu Ting-fang has nothing to do, he had better come to Peking.

Wu Ting-fang is surprised at Yuan Shih-k'ai's "delay" in agreeing "to submit the question of a future Government to a convention" and telegraphs to the Legations in Peking blaming Yuan Shih-k'ai for the deadlock in the peace negotiations. On Jan. 5 Yuan Shih-k'ai submits all the correspondence with the Republican peace commissioner to the Foreign Legations, and the foreign diplomats take his view. He telegraphs at length to Wu Ting-fang in reconsideration of the matter of the conference, but the Republicans refuse to go back and take up that question. Wu Ting-fang declines Yuan Shih-k'ai's invitation to come to Peking, and also his proposals as to a method of electing members to a conference on government which would take six months to carry out.

There has been no armistice since 8 a.m. December 31, and on account of the deadlock with Wu Ting-fang, Yuan Shih-k'ai is arranging directly with Sun Yat-sen for a continuation of the armistice.

The Republicans are trying to hold Yuan Shih-k'ai to an agreement which they have signed with his envoy to submit the question of what form of government China shall have, to a conference of all the people. But immediately after signing it they have made the Government a Republic without the least hesitation, and "elected" a President who has taken oath to overthrow the Dynasty which Yuan Shih-k'ai represents, and their object is the confirmation of this Government by every means. The great Powers encourage Yuan Shih-k'ai, who in the midst of the deadlock telegraphs to Wu Ting-fang protesting that it is inconsistent to establish a Republican

Government the President of which has taken oath to overthrow the Manchu Government, inquires what is the object of establishing the Republican Government, and wants to know whether the President will be removed from office if a monarchy is decided on. This is the *retort cordiale*.

Yuan Shih-k'ai's situation is desperate. He is unable to regain his ground by arguing the principle that his envoy had plenary powers only to discuss, and not to sign, agreements. The Republic is going right ahead, overthrowing the Manchus. Yuan Shih-k'ai's last defence is uttered on Jan. 10, when he says: "I appointed a Peace Commission because I recognized that force would never solve the differences between Northern and Southern China, which can only be fused by a compromise. I obtained what is unprecedented, Imperial sanction to a convention empowered if it so chooses to vote away the Dynasty and legally establish a Republic. But instead of accepting this remarkable offer, the revolutionary leaders believed that they could trick me into accepting a packed revolutionist convention, which I never will do."

Yuan Shih-k'ai thus disposed for ever of the question of a conference on the lines contemplated by the Republicans to determine the future government of China. He did not abandon his principle. At the same time that he was awaiting the dissolution of the republican South or abdication in the North to solve the problem in China, he went right on negotiating the Manchu Dynasty and Court out of existence, while hoping for an eventual monarchy that would be more in accord with the ideas and traditions of China's millions.

The confusion in Peking was measurably increased by the expectation of abdication. The foreign correspondents in long anti-climaxes, promised it to the world from day to day. The Foreign Legations have given up all efforts at summarizing the situation and are trying merely to report to their Governments daily events.

What impresses me most in making my rounds of observation is the indifference of the people, stolid amid an immense quietness due to the lull in the machinery of State. Gone are the green chairs of the officials, the red carts of the princely families, and the yellow Imperial chairs with their paraphernalia and retinues, and except for the traffic to and from Yuan Shih-k'ai's headquarters and residence in the Foreign Office building, official carriages. In their places are additional police, and at the princes' palaces, where bright cavalcades and processions otherwise come and go, are silent soldiers in grey groups. To the ubiquitous amateur photographer craving Oriental picturesqueness for his films, these latter in their semi-foreign uniforms are a tame substitute. There remains only the background of Imperial buildings and the blue-gowned people, upon all of which falls the idle sunshine.

All the palaces are silent. Ninety per cent. of the officials of the War Department have vanished, and a few remaining members of the General Staff meet and drink tea, but do nothing else, having no funds and no authority. The Cantonese have threatened all Canton officials on duty in Peking with all kinds of atrocities unless they abandon the Peking Government. The pressure upon Southern officials in Peking, by their families, is great, and in addition the Republic is offering opportunities which attract them and they go. The various yamens or Government buildings are in the hands of the gate-keepers, messengers, and janitors.

The Imperial Clan alone is the paramount institution of affairs in Peking. Most of its members have received threats from the revolutionists, and there is a new excitement arising from the fear of bombs. Together with the pressure from the Lung Yu Empress Dowager to force contributions to the war-chest, some of the princes under this apprehension prepare to flee. The Lung Yu Empress Dowager orders that none of them are to leave Peking.

Peking already has many republican and revolutionary agents, and is becoming a centre of low conspirators and assassins. The alarmed princes resolve to advise the Throne to retire at once to Jehol.

The Court now receives from the Republic at Nanking an offer of terms for its abdication. The Emperor will be treated with dignity such as a sovereign of a foreign nation would receive in China; the Court will be allowed to reside at the Summer Palace; the Emperor will receive a liberal allowance; the ancestral mausoleums and temples will be secured to the Court families; the Imperial Family will be fully protected in person, property, and wealth; Manchus, Mohammedans, Turkestanese, and Tibetans will be on the same footing as Chinese; the Manchu pensioners will continue to draw their stipends until further means can be devised enabling them to earn their livelihood; restrictions between pensioners and others will be removed; and finally, the Imperial princes will retain their property and titles.

This awakens new discussions. The division among the princes continues. The Mongol princes demur to the proposal of abdication and are said to have formed a party with the Manchu princes Yu Lang, Kung, and Tsai T'ao. But the head of the Clan, Prince Ching, leads a stronger opposing party that has already considered all the circumstances of abdication. On Jan. 13 Prince Chun, the ex-Regent, on behalf of the Lung Yu Empress Dowager and the venerable leader Prince Ching, goes in person to consult Yuan Shih-k'ai about the Republic's proposal.

Yuan Shih-k'ai impresses upon the ex-Regent the hopelessness of the situation by again regretting his inability to suppress the revolt, and dwells on the paramount importance of uniting the country. The ex-Regent shows that the leading princes and members of the Imperial Clan favour abdication. On Jan. 15 Prince Ching and Prince Chun meet at a conference in the Palace with Yuan Shih-k'ai, and they conclude a tentative plan by which abdication can be carried out and Yuan Shih-k'ai will be enabled to unite the country. The Throne is to take back the State to its own control, formally accepting the resignations of Yuan Shih-k'ai and his Cabinet, and in a final edict is to appoint Yuan Shih-k'ai peacemaker and abdicate, whereupon Yuan Shih-k'ai is to formulate at the port of Tientsin a Provisional Government.

Seeing the edict of abdication—which necessarily represents the failure of his efforts at pacification—actually in the process of being drawn up, Yuan Shih-k'ai hastens again to resign. Not so, says the Court. The Throne is not ready to issue the edict.

As Yuan Shih-k'ai leaves the Council Hall he is between two fires. The assassins have arrived in Peking and he is marked by those of both sides, by those Manchus who believe he has been a traitor to the Dynasty, and by those revolutionists who believe he stands in the way of the Republic. It is at this moment, when he is returning in his carriage to his place at the Foreign Office accompanied by his chief body-servant and guard, that the bomb to which I have alluded is thrown at him.

To the Republicans the Court's plan of abdication meant a delegation of the powers of the Throne to Yuan Shih-k'ai, and therefore represented the opposite of what the Republicans wanted. They would not agree to the delegation of power by the Manchus to anybody. In reply to Yuan Shih-k'ai respecting the Court's plan of abdication, the Republic imposed four conditions, to the effect that the Emperor must abdicate and surrender all sovereign power; that no Manchu could participate in the impending Provisional Government of China; that the Provisional Capital could not be at Peking; and that Yuan Shih-k'ai could not participate in the Republican Provisional Government until the foreign Powers had recognized the Republican Provisional Government as the successor to the Manchu rule of the country, and until the country had been reconstructed and peace and harmony established.

The Republicans gave notice that unless these demands were agreed to, fighting would begin 8 a.m. January 29, when the armistice expired. Yuan Shih-k'ai communicated the Court's whole plan to the Foreign Legations, who telegraphed it to their Governments and proceeded with arrangements for communicating from Peking with the new seat of government for the North, when it should be established at Tientsin. They thought all this would come about.

The effect of the Republican ultimatum, and of the bomb explosion—the first since 1905 and only the second in the whole history of Peking—was to upset the work of the Clan councils and again to demoralize what little order had been arrived at temporarily. The chronic condition of stampede being restored, Prince Ching and Prince Chun notify the Premier and the Cabinet that the Lung Yu Empress Dowager's approval of the abdication edict is obtained. Nevertheless, the Lung Yu Empress Dowager and the Imperial Clan confer with as much indecision and confusion as ever.

Following the bomb explosion, Yuan Shih-k'ai claims sick leave of three days and attends memorial services for the dead of his bodyguard, especially the commander of his escort. But before his leave is up, he is commanded to return to the conferences.

The situation is so complex that no elucidation is possible. Distrust of Yuan Shih-k'ai in Peking culminates in resistance to the abdication by some of the troops. The Manchu soldiers distribute placards calling upon the people to resist abdication to the death. A general uprising around Peking is feared. The Court receives appeals to devise measures that will satisfy the bulk of the people and restore peace. It would gladly do so, but its despair of its ability in that direction and its belief in the deluge after its own passing is shown by the fact that it offers for sale the treasures of its Mukden palace. Its councils at the Palace are persistently reported "stormy." By Jan. 19 the foreign Legations have all informed their Governments that abdication is decided, but the Clan councils continue to dissolve without reaching a decision.

The various councils and conferences are almost too numerous to follow. They are so numerous and futile as to border on hysterics, and the wise old leader Prince Ching calls off his partisans to allow the excitement to subside in the Council Hall. Profiting by the lessons of the attempt upon his life, Yuan Shih-k'ai employs the interval in taking precautions, and makes arrangements by which in case of necessity he can escape through the Legations and by railway to Tientsin.

The ex-Regent Prince Chun, as father of the Emperor, is obliged to attend the almost daily Clan councils at the Palace. But Prince Ching, Prince Pu Lun, and Prince Hsun absent themselves for five days, leaving the burden of decision upon the reactionaries. The ultimatum of the Republic has abrogated the whole plan of the national convention to decide upon the future form of government. Yuan Shih-k'ai, who has not left his house since the bomb attack upon him, advises the Imperial Clan members to sink their differences, co-operate to raise a war fund, and resist attack. The Lung Yu Empress Dowager accepts the advice of the reactionaries, and now refuses to abdicate. Her position is that the Manchus are acting for the welfare of China, which in the state of disorder and disunion existing would be left without a Government in case the Throne abdicated in accordance with the demands of the Republicans. It could not abdicate except on behalf of a united country. For the Emperor to throw down the government as the Republicans demanded would be to act the poltroon.

It is interesting to note what the Emperor is doing during these momentous days. He has "ceased his studies," and his Imperial tutor, the only one empowered to reprimand him, is gone. His Majesty is domineering over his constant companion, eunuch Chang, or, in a royal dudgeon over his food, throwing dishes at the serving-men. In two years he has forgotten his alley playmates, and from chatting with child-scavengers in front of his father's house, he has turned to frightening the Palace birds, or chasing the terrorized dogs of the Imperial kennels with his new whip, just like any other boy.

The Imperial Army and the emasculated Board of War are ordered to prepare to resist. Manchu reservists called to the colours in the camps outside the City are drilling. Yuan Shih-k'ai, who has been slowly augmenting his own defence guard of 3500 men, begins to bring in larger numbers from the ranks of his old army. He then makes a statement on the subject of his position. He is now proceeding from a desire to serve the best interests of the whole people of China, and not of one party or the other. He is not following a personal ambition, and only hopes to continue in office as Premier for the purpose of securing a proper election of representatives to the national conference, or by other means ascertaining the actual views of the majority of the people as to the Government of the future. In view of the attitude of the Republican leaders rendering a proper general election difficult of realization, he desires to bring about peace and some form of substantial government as quickly as possible. To this end he would be willing to resign and turn over control to any capable leader who would effect a solution of the situation in the best interests of China.

" I am not fighting to maintain the Manchus," says he, " but to maintain law and order. For the present my military plans are purely defensive. I shall not attack the Republicans, but if hostilities are resumed the generals at the front can act with great latitude given them."

The Court fails to produce the war fund which it repeatedly promised, and the dissenting or reactionary princes suggest appealing to a friendly Power for aid. Unable to induce any of the four capitalistic Powers, France, Great Britain, Germany, or the United States, to lend the Imperial Government money, they recommend that Japan should be approached on the subject. The Lung Yu Empress Dowager consents to the princes approaching Japan with reference to finding out what can be done. This touches upon the most sensitive affairs in the politics of all Asia, and at once arouses the Premier and Cabinet. Persisted in, it would have alienated Yuan Shih-k'ai and could not be supported by the Lung Yu Empress Dowager. It would have been a larger bomb in Peking than any assassin might explode.

On Jan. 25 Prince Chun excites open-eyed wonder in the streets of Peking by a visit to Yuan Shih-k'ai under escort of an immense number of military and police. The lull which followed this visit and the calm of speculation was broken on Jan. 26, when to his surprise Yuan Shih-k'ai was created a Marquis by Imperial edict.

The title of Marquis in modern China is always associated with the name of Tseng Kuo-fang, who " put down the T'aiping Rebellion " and was created Marquis in consequence as a reward. Yuan Shih-k'ai recoiled from the proffered honour. The correspondence between the Premier and the Throne resulting from this action of the Lung Yu Empress Dowager is highly interesting. " I am personally," says the little Emperor, " in receipt of an edict from Lung Yu Empress Dowager, stating that Yuan Shih-k'ai, President of the Cabinet, public-spirited and loyal to the nation [Throne], has achieved conspicuous service assiduously. Since his entry into the office [of Premier], his meritorious services in planning and laying out the national policy and in sustaining the situation is still more grand. He is hereby granted the Marquisate of the First Class as a mark of exemplary reward, and he is not permitted to decline it."

The Premier composed his reply to the sound of a bomb in a neighbouring street. General Liang Pi, recently appointed Commander of a Banner Corps and a fighting General advocating war, had paid a visit to Prince Su, a genial Manchu who had become in a sense mediator between the Premier and the reactionaries. As General Liang Pi reached home, a man having the appearance of a soldier of the Imperial bodyguard approached in a rickshaw and sent in his name at the General's door. The General turned back to see him, and when they met the caller exploded a bomb, by which he himself was killed and the General was wounded so severely in his legs as to require an amputation of one of them and to cause his death two days later.

As though cut short by the explosion, Yuan Shih-k'ai's reply was brief. He said that his opinions (abilities) were humble and he therefore requested the rescission of the Throne's honour. He twice declined it, the second time recapitulating events of the past and showing his failures. According to the replies by the Lung Yu Empress Dowager in each case, these protests only proved his " modesty and worthiness." Notwithstanding the reasons given by Yuan Shih-k'ai, " the said Minister," said the Lung Yu Empress Dowager, " has single-handed sustained the strain and saved and preserved intact a great deal indeed, in spite of intense difficulties. The present revolution is an extraordinary one, having no parallel in former times, the said Minister in preserving the Government's position is beset also with greater difficulties. During the last several months all kinds of distressing circumstances have been endured [by him], therefore he is more entitled to be the recipient of such an extraordinary reward." To reinforce her argument, the little Emperor is made to say that the words and emotion of Yuan Shih-k'ai praying for Our rescission of Our former decree, "are very earnest, emanating from his inmost heart in good faith. However, the exemplary reward has been bestowed after weighing the question and regarding it as a most suitable reward by the Throne. Let him respectfully obey the respective decree and not again pray to refuse it."

In the meantime much else is happening. Yuan Shih-k'ai has telegraphed to Wu Ting-fang asking him to consider a compromise of views as to the location and composition of the national conference to consider the future of the country. In addition Sun Yat-sen, powerfully impressed by Yuan Shih-k'ai's dangers and responsibilities, affirms his conviction of the sincerity and *bona fides* of Yuan Shih-k'ai, leaving the way open for the negotiations to go on.

On Jan. 27, in fulfilment of the promises of Republican agents for a bomb campaign in Peking and Chihli Province, an attempt is made to assassinate the loyal General Chang Huai-chih at Tientsin, a bomb exploding near him at the railway station there. He is uninjured, but the would-be assassin is wounded and captured.

There is plot and counterplot. The Imperialist General Tuan Chi-jui from his headquarters in Honan, where he is opposing the mixed revolutionary soldiers and brigands from Shansi, arranges a wholesale refusal of the generals and commanders of the Throne's troops to oppose the advance of the revolutionary soldiers, and the Cabinet receives a signed ultimatum from forty-six of them memorializing it to this effect.

It is the greatest bomb of all. With one accord the adherents of both sides exclaim, " This is the end." Yuan Shih-k'ai's friends give out that he is to be President and that the whole Cabinet is agreed upon on the lines of equal representation for North and South. Yuan Shih-k'ai brings up eight train-loads of troops from Tientsin in anticipation of disorders.

On Jan. 29 bomb outrages are renewed and bomb-throwers are discovered near Tungchou, twelve miles east of the Capital.

There is now no armistice, but none is needed, for the Republic has conquered the generals and commanders of its antagonists. The Manchus are helpless. While the various members of the Imperial Clan renew their interminable discussions, the Lung Yu Empress Dowager, Prince Ching, and Prince Chun determine finally upon abdication in accordance with the conditions laid down by the Republican Government at Nanking. Yuan Shih-k'ai gives out another statement to the effect that he is ready to accept any solution which will guarantee peace. He has no fear for the country's future if the settlement is the fruit of reason, truth, and justice. He has no ambition to become President of the new Republic, and only desires the establishment of a stable Government. Bombs are thrown at the Imperialist headquarters at Hsiao-kan, destroying a railway carriage that is transporting Imperialist soldiers—an obvious protest against opposing the revolutionists. The Lung Yu Empress Dowager issues a summons to the Cabinet to meet in the Palace to-morrow and arrange the details of abdication.

On Jan. 31 the Throne makes its last reply to Yuan Shih-k'ai respecting the Marquisate. It merely acknowledges the receipt of his prayer of "leave to defer the acceptance of the same [the honour of the Marquisate] until the present situation shall have somewhat improved [subsided]." At the meeting with the Cabinet the Lung Yu Empress Dowager announces that the Throne has decided on a solution of the situation which will ensure peace, and instructs the ministers assembled to arrange accordingly.

CHAPTER XXI

ACROSS CHIHLI AND SHANTUNG WITH POLICE AND SPIES

ON January 28, 1912, I left Peking to cross Chihli and Shantung, to see what the " Flowery Republic " was like.

Before leaving I had tiffin with Mr. and Mrs. Mayers, English friends, who told me of their morning ride and the almost instantaneous clearing of the streets from the Drum Tower to Morrison Street (Wang-fu-ching Ta chieh) to make way for one of the princes, probably Prince Ching or Prince Chun. A police whistle blew and the people of the streets were gone. The distance cleared was about a mile and a half, showing the efficiency of the police of Peking, which Mr. Mayers, who is one of the authorities on Chinese affairs, calls " the best in the Empire."

The same thing had already impressed itself upon me. In a horseback ride around Peking I had found police and gendarme patrols as well as military in black, grey, and blue in every street and at important buildings.

I met Dr. John Ferguson, my travelling companion, at the station just over the wall that forms the southern boundary of the Legation Quarter, and we boarded one of those strikingly made-up and strikingly peopled trains that were running so frequently between Peking and Tientsin. But before we had an opportunity to explore the crowd in the coupés and saloon compartments, an awesome accident occurred. As everyone knows who has travelled by rail out of Peking to Tientsin, the line follows closely the south wall of the Tartar City until it reaches the eastern wall, when it turns in a sharp curve to the cardinal south. Here the train suddenly stopped : a peasant had been struck by the locomotive. It was a short winter day, there was no sun, and a cold wind was blowing. At this point, still within the walls of Peking (the Chinese City), there are fields with groups of houses here and there like hamlets. We were immediately opposite one of these. Before I could get out of the carriage a police whistle was blown from the carriage platform, and immediately a uniformed police captain appeared from this outlying hamlet. Every one of these hamlets seemed garrisoned. A score of peasants who had gathered had their eyes all turned to the carriage platform, from which a small southern Chinese in civilian dress descended and consulted with the uniformed police captain. In the meantime, Dr. Ferguson and myself examined the injured peasant, who was lying, still breathing, a short distance behind the locomotive. Dr. Ferguson gave his card, as Director of the Chinese Red Cross, to the mysterious Chinese who had descended from the train, recommending that the injured peasant should be taken to a foreign hospital. The card was handed in turn to the uniformed police captain, and we re-entered the train and moved on. As we left the Chinese City by the breach in the south wall we saw through the window the police guard drawn up to mark our departure.

"This is Captain Chang," said Dr. Ferguson, turning to me, and the mysterious little man doffed his cap in the Occidental fashion and modestly shook hands. "Captain Chang is an old student of mine from Nanyang University," continued Dr. Ferguson. We asked him to stay in our carriage, which he did, and later explained to us the working of the police system, now a modern organization. It had in fact been developed by the aid of German police masters, and the Japanese detective system brought by Japanese experts to Peking. This latter system was marked by its infinity of detail. Captain Chang travelled on the railway between Peking and Mukden. He had just been over the line to Mukden, and was now starting on another trip.

While we were talking we had opposite us a Chinese of evasive personality, the only other passenger in our coupé. He sat leisurely sipping tea from a cup, now and then filled by the train attendant, from a teapot resting on the portable table between us. Captain Chang was interested in him and introduced himself. The stranger proved to be a police captain from Tientsin.

"We should feel well protected," said Dr. Ferguson to me in English while the two Chinese were talking. "How much slyness the stranger's face shows,—what cunning the man must be capable of!" he continued. They were going into detail as to their identity, and were exchanging notes. We ordered more tea and the cakes and confections which the Chinese are so fond of, and toy with at their leisure. As we sat munching melon seeds the stranger told the interesting story of how the bomb was thrown at General Chang at the Tientsin railway station, where it exploded without injuring the General, but on the contrary wounded the would-be assassin. He thought the bomb campaign in Chihli Province amateurish. Its futility seemed to be his main thought. His opinion, valuable as that of a detective, was supported by the Tientsin Chinese newspapers, one of which printed an editorial strongly urging the bomb-assassins to abandon their campaign on the ground that it was more fatal to them than to their intended victims. In each case the weapon had proved a boomerang. Five bomb-operators, it said, had lost their lives in the attempt on Yuan Shih-k'ai, the would-be assassin of General Liang Pi had been killed instantly without even the least realization that he had injured his victim, while the only injury inflicted by the would-be assassin of General Chang was upon himself.

The train was crowded with officials and secretaries going to Tientsin for the week-end, to their families in exile. Baron Liang, a well-known Peking mandarin, was aboard, and in the saloon compartment there was a large gathering of official agents and Chinese newspaper men from both Peking and Tientsin. Captain Chang moved in quietly and sat down among them to listen to their talk. Here was a scene that sharply pictured the upheaval that had come about in Chinese society—the breaking with the Asiatic social system of the past. The Chinese newspaper men were playing with a woman, of Suchow, one of the two cities in China which a Chinese proverb says, on account of its beautiful women, reconciles man to this world until heaven is reached. They were a bright-looking lot of men and well dressed. Wreaths of cigarette smoke filled the upper part of the saloon so that the heads of those standing up were in a cloud.

The woman was rather fine-looking, was the centre of conversation, and her replies in the cross fire of wit from the men were instantaneous. It was something that rarely occurs in China, where there is no indiscriminate intercourse of the sexes. It was even a violence to foreign ideas of propriety—perhaps the idea of Young China respecting the West and the thing modern.

Near the end of the journey one of the party who had held aloof from the frivolities of his companions, and was more serious than they, came and sat in our coupé. His preoccupation impressed Dr. Ferguson, who remarked that here was a man who must have cause to be nervous and anxious about the times. I noticed that the most interested of the merrymakers, who in fact held the attention of the woman, was a powerful man dressed in fur garments with a fur cap and a complexion full of colour, who looked as though he had come from Mongolia. His reverberating voice, the thunder of the train, and his antics, as he tried to keep his balance in the centre of the saloon, seemed to turn the scene into a Mongol carousal of the Middle Ages. Anything which resembled the social life of Mongolia would to the Chinese suggest a reversion to barbarism. The barbaric licence of the scene jarred upon the sensibilities of at least one, he who sought refuge in our coupé.

The unknown police captain left the train at the native city of Tientsin, and Captain Chang journeyed northward toward Manchuria. It was night when we reached Tientsin settlement and drove through the dimly lighted streets for more than a mile after leaving the railway station, to the Astor House.

At no time since the Boxer War, 1900, when it resounded with the clatter of swords and spurs and the clink of glasses, had this hotel presented such an appearance as now. There were a dozen American officers of a battalion of the 15th Infantry from the Philippines gathered in the foyer, and a number of distinguished Chinese refugees in the halls and brilliantly lighted dining-room. From our table we could see the ex-Governor of Shantung, Sun Pao-chi, toward whose late Capital our steps were directed, dressed in foreign costume and presenting a distinguished appearance at a large table, where he was surrounded by men of his family and suite.

He had a rather heavy beard for a Chinese, of alternate black and white streaks, high forehead, with thin hair left somewhat in pompadour fashion by the cutting of his queue. He was a man of distinction, and there was an expression of sympathy that showed itself in a kind of awed silence in the dining-room. When he got up I saw he was dressed in a long frock-coat like a typical American statesman or a London business man of the last decade. He was tall, with a firm vertebra. He impressed me with the realization that here was the first time I had really seen the anatomy of the human clothes-rack which the Chinese mandarin actually is,—whose movements are exactly those of a scarecrow. I do not believe that anyone unacquainted with the " side " and swagger affected by mandarins would ever have noticed this.

I could not but be continually struck by the circumstance of so many flights among the officials, begun in the case of the Amban of Mongolia—the first thing to impress me on entering revolutionary China.

Sun Pao-chi from the moment Shantung Province began to wobble and proclaimed independence was " riding the tiger," as the Chinese say of the mandarin sitting on the people's back, where he must keep his place successfully or if he falls be devoured. He had followed the people until they had repudiated their secession and independence, and until the seaport of Chefoo turned revolutionist and the Republic forced the Throne to negotiate for peace, when his position became too complicated for safety. In this sheltered spot at Tientsin, in the heart of the Foreign Concessions and surrounded by foreign police and soldiers, he was sitting, safe in the cyclone cellar, waiting for the storm to blow over. The brain-storm in Cathay was something which even the astute and experienced Sun could not safely weather. It was one to which the immemorial Chinese umbrella was no protection, and in which only the foreign roof was rain-proof, and the brilliant hotel lights rainbow-like drew a magic circle of safety.

It was still night and very cold as we drove several miles in an open carriage from the hotel to the railway station at the native city of Tientsin to take the train to Shantung. As we entered the station area the first rays of dawn lighted up the spot where the bomb had been thrown at General Chang. On the train we were joined by Dr. Tenney, an envoy of the United States Government detached from the Legation at Peking for the purpose of proceeding to Nanking to investigate the Republican Government and the revolutionary situation. The Government in Washington gave out prematurely this announcement before their agent had reached Shanghai, somewhat to his embarrassment.

The train was warm, and soon after we turned southward parallel to the Grand Canal the sun came up, flooding the carriage with light. We were the only foreign passengers. This was the German railway and one of those interests of the Germans whose influence induced Yuan Shih-k'ai to send the message of warning to Governor Sun Pao-chi at the time of Shantung's secession. It furnishes one of the most comfortable railway journeys in China. The Chinese newsboys had come into the train at Tientsin before we started and our party was supplied with native newspapers.

Early in the morning these newspapers were explored by us to see what the Chinese paragrapher and cartoonist were doing. An article on the bomb campaign was accompanied by a cartoon suggestive of the terror being endured by officials. " News from 'the four corners and the eight sides '" reads the headline in one paper. The reference is to the table universally used in China, commonly seating four and capable of accommodating eight—in Chinese "*Si mien pah pien*"—four surfaces and eight sides. It means " Everybody's say," or, " Reports from all quarters,"—very appropriate with respect to Chinese news, which depends more on rumour perhaps than does the news of countries having better news communications.

A paragrapher produces a satire with respect to the conferring of the title of Marquis upon Yuan Shih-k'ai by the repetition of the phrase " Yuan has been made a Marquis " in words of dual meaning. The effect is fully appreciated only by the Chinese, owing to the subtle power of Chinese character writing. Another paragraph is more plain and will be universally understood because of its provincialism. The writer is a native of Honan Province, to which Yuan Shih-k'ai belongs. He observes that he is struck with the fact that it requires a Honan man to take the helm in Chihli Province, but that it is not apparent that the courage of any Chihli man had been sufficient to enable him to make his way to Honan, or that such is needed at the helm there.

At Tehchou, in Shantung, we passed the big Imperial Arsenal which was transferred from Tientsin after 1900 in order to get it away from foreign garrisons and the foreign-controlled line of communications between the sea and Peking. It was now between the Imperialist territory of Chihli Province and the revolutionist troops and bases at Chefoo and Tengchou, with fighting going on at Huang-hsien on the road to the capital Tsinan-fu. About two weeks previous, the Japanese secret service in Manchuria observed at Feng-huang-cheng in the interior but on the Japanese railway, as well as at Antung on the Yalu, Chinese strangers in numbers, and reported the fact to their headquarters in Port Arthur, from where it was forwarded to Tokio, Mukden, and Peking. A week later about 200 Chinese dressed as coolie labourers went aboard a small Japanese steamer at Dalny belonging to what the Japanese call their "mosquito fleet" plying between ports on the Gulf of Chihli. The next thing heard of them came from Chefoo, where the Japanese skipper reported to his Consul-General, and the Foreign Commissioner of the Chinese Maritime Customs took steps to confiscate his vessel for having entered a port (Tengchou) not open to foreign trade. The Japanese skipper told this story: He embarked 200 Chinese coolies at Dalny bound for Chefoo. When some hours out of Chefoo the coolies discarded outer coats with which they had concealed their revolutionist uniforms and ordered him to put into Tengchou. When they arrived in the harbour of Tengchou the ship was surrounded by sampans and the revolutionists disembarked, taking French leave, so that he was left without even their passage-money.

Tengchou welcomed the band of revolutionists, rose in revolt, and became the revolutionist base for the march on the provincial capital at Tsinan-fu.

At evening we arrive at Tsinan-fu and are in the heart of a province that has revolutionist armies on both sides of it. General Liang Tien-wei is reported in command on the North, while on the South is a force from Nanking sent up by the Republican Minister of War, General Huang Hsing. It is opposed by the Imperialist General Chang Hsun, who some weeks before gave up Nanking almost without a struggle. Travellers have brought favourable impressions of Chang Hsun from his headquarters at Hsu-chou. He is said to be a fighter of the old Manchu type, one of the "catch-'em-alive-and-eat-'em" kind, but a real fighter, who has said that if the Throne abdicates he will gather 100,000 men around him and go on alone. He "will never take orders from those half-baked fellows at Nanking."

Considering that it was said that the most pronounced swashbuckler libertines of France were his prototypes, his language must have been much richer and more picturesque than this and altogether too lively for publication. On the eve of our arrival we received a report that General Chang Hsun had abandoned his army and started for Japan. It was agreed that, if true, this fact would refute the favourable impressions of travellers. Those who had looked up Chang Hsun's record found that in Peking he had been a profligate, never trusted with any important office, and had been always in the military service in connection with the old-style troops and knew not the moderns. He had frequented the lowest quarters and had cultivated and corrupted his superiors with the most sordid offerings, such as singing-girls and the like. It was observed that there could not be much expected of such a man, who doubtless had nothing else in him, and he was certainly not to be relied upon. Then Mirabeau was instanced as a combination of profligate and man of ability, to refute this argument.

The successor of Governor Sun Pao-chi was trying to keep down assassins in the Capital and to maintain quiet in the province. He had an Imperialist army on one side and revolutionist army on the other. It was no easy matter for him to perform the conventional mandarin feat of sitting on the fence. He had placed a censorship on the press, promulgated curfew laws, and was harrying amateur revolutionary suspects. At the same time that he was forwarding munitions and men to the Imperialist army under General Chang Hsun he dispatched an emissary to spy upon the revolutionists in the northern part of his province to gauge the strength of their movements, so that he might know at what moment to make overtures to them. We found this emissary on our train when we left Tsinan-fu the following morning. He was to go to Tsing-tao and thence by sea to Chefoo the revolutionist base, from where he was to go or send agents to Tengchou and to Huang-hsien, where the fighting was going on.

We followed in the rear of a detachment of troops going to oppose the Huang-hsien movement. Beside our party there were but two other passengers in the first-class carriage. One was a German commercial traveller, and the other the Governor's emissary. The latter's name was Ho Ying-p'ei, formerly Magistrate at Lai-yang in Shantung Province. It did not take long to discover his identity and what his mission was. He completely lacked such information as we were able to give him respecting the condition of China. He had implicit faith in foreign dispatches. When told of the action of the forty-six " generals," including Chang Hsun, in sending their ultimatum to Peking, he was flabbergasted. He had not heard of it. A little later the text of the ultimatum of the " generals " as it appeared in one of our Tientsin papers was shown to him, and he collapsed.

The question of moving the national Capital recurred with the Republican rebellion as it had recurred in every other outbreak in China for several thousand years and for at least a score of times enumerated in history. The Republicans now insisted that it must be at Nanking, because Nanking was centrally located and was the ancient seat of learning detached from material surroundings and corrupt traditions. In discussing this Dr. Tenney said that it was traditional also in China that the Capital must be near the border—that is, the Northern border—and pointed out that the region of danger still lay on the North, just as when the proverb "As the chou [Capital] moves eastward the Tschins move in," was crystallized.

In the minds of the Northern men the removal of the Capital southward would be followed by the moving in of the enemy who had replaced the Tschins on the North, namely, Russia and Japan. I felt that we were in the atmosphere of old times in all these discussions, and looking out of the car window I perceived that we were passing ruined cities on the hilltops. And aptly enough, while we were speculating upon the parallels in present and past China, and while the mandarin spy lay in his coupé, in comfortable safety under German protection, reading over and trying to fathom the ultimatum of the forty-six "generals" to the Capital at Peking, a dweller in the land pointed out that we were passing the tombs of the rulers of the "Three Kingdoms."

The tombs consisted of earthen pyramids terraced on all sides with little fields and dating from 420–750 A.D. We were passing through one of the oldest parts of China and one that had experienced many vicissitudes of politics and government. This was pre-eminently China, the home of Confucius and Mencius. Here Mencius's famous mother plied her loom in her native town, and because of the town's undeserving state "cut the threads of her loom and moved to a worthier neighbourhood." Here Confucius only a few hours before his death stood in his doorway and mourned for the political state of the world.

The emissary Ho was a charming type of the Confucian school, a very large man with an inverted egg-shaped head and a sparse queue that disappeared where it looked over the apex at the spectator. He was about forty years of age and had enormous jowls, with a double chin. He had a large but refined mouth draped with a meagre bronze Oriental moustache. His eyes were like jet swimming in amber, making his red and iron-rust brocaded silk coat

FIGHTING AT TENG-CHOW.

EXPEDITION TO GULF OF CHIHLI.

To face p. 210.

appear in perfect taste. When he took off the coat it left him in a brilliant blue gown. He was the most impersonal, detached Chinese gentleman I think I ever met, utterly mild and anything but the revolutionary spy.

I was detailed to invite him to share our tiffin. We had a steak brought in from the buffet by the Chinese combined caterer, cook, and waiter; and pieced out the table with a suit-case so as to make room. I found the "Spy" in his coupé reclining. "*Wa men ch'ing ta jen chih fan,*" said I: that is, "We invite you to eat with us." The "Spy" looked confused, and I repeated. He gently protested, rising to a sitting attitude. I insisted. He would put me away. "Please come," I reiterated, and took the gentle official by the arm, leading him, still protesting, down the corridor of the carriage to where my companions were sitting.

To get the "Spy" to eat was an equally ceremonious and equally difficult matter. He never did really eat, though he sampled in a dainty manner such as only an immense being like himself can do, our foreign delicacies of coffee, and preserves, and light bread which Dr. Ferguson carried made up into sandwiches. He allowed himself to be occasionally aroused from the state of preoccupation into which our news had thrown him—it must have been a shock to him, what we had to tell him—and he replied very agreeably but absent-mindedly. He was a joy to look at, and to listen to when he consented to speak. He allowed himself to be persuaded to taste a rather hard and juiceless Shantung pear, with which he concluded his meal, and resumed his Confucian detachment and reserve.

The "Spy" had finished reading the text of the memorial of the forty-six "generals" in the Tientsin paper. He said that this action was final, that there was nothing more for the Throne to do but abdicate. As for himself, he said his family was safely quartered in Tsing-tao, where he had moved them for safety, and he would stay there with them. Later in the afternoon we met and passed the Tsing-tao train that was *en route* to Tsinan-fu. It had an empty private car attached to it, a fact significant to Ho, who said it was for the escape of the Governor, his chief, and he collapsed again.

I wondered how much of the apparent story was true. As it worked itself out in Ho's mind it was something like this:

General Chang Hsun had not fled to Japan, but had only joined in the ultimatum to Peking. The Governor receiving an intimation from General Chang Hsun of the ultimatum to the Throne, and knowing that he would have to make overtures to the revolutionists or flee, had sent his emissary, Ho himself, to establish communications with them. Having arranged this and seeing Ho off, he was now bringing up a private carriage to be held in readiness, so that, in case he could not swap his Imperialist horse for a revolutionist horse safely, he could flee to Tsing-tao, the German colony.

As we neared Tsing-tao we received word that Tsi-mou, one of the towns in the neutral territory of the German colony, had revolted and gone over to the revolutionists and that the Governor of Kiao-chou had sent troops there. Two hundred German mounted infantrymen had been already sent. "Spy" Ho remained quietly in his coupé during the rest of the journey, and when we bade him good-bye at the station in Tsing-tao I believe he had firmly fixed in his mind that his chief, the Governor, would follow by the next train to take refuge there. Shantung had in fact gone over permanently to the Republic.

We had just time to hurry across the vacant ground with Consul McNally to the dock and catch the Shanghai steamer, and by starlight in Kiao-chou Bay we left Shantung for the Yangtse.

CHAPTER XXII

SHANGHAI JUNTA AND WU TING-FANG

We went up the river Huang-pu leading to Shanghai, in a cold fog. The first thing I looked for was the new revolutionist or "rainbow" flag, of red, yellow, blue, white, and black parallel bars, which I supposed would be everywhere displayed, but it was not noticeable. It was not until I reached my room that I could see the colours flying here and there from the housetops, in the Shanghai foreign city. In another direction, when the fog lifted, I could see the river with all its shipping, with the Chinese war-vessels that had mutinied at Hankow, cruisers and torpedo-boats, passing up and down at intervals. Up the river lay the foreign warships, German, British, American, French, Italian, and others, abreast the long bund or quay, and beyond was the Chinese arsenal where occurred the "fight" that gave birth to the Shanghai Republic or Independency.

Szechuan may be called the September Republic, Wuchang the October Republic, and Shanghai the November Republic. Shanghai had only to sketch the "brilliant success" of its September and October predecessors in a note to the consular representatives of the foreign Powers at Shanghai, to explain comprehendingly its acts of secession, and to secure foreign co-operation. "Citizen soldiery," fifty quasi-belligerent loyalist soldiers, with a Krupp cannon, some rifles, two machine guns, and a 3-pounder, together with an orderly unnumbered mob of the floating population, inaugurated the City's independence. In an upper room of the American Consulate-General, where we overlooked the landmarks of Shanghai's republican drama, those who had seen and heard these things told them to me.

On Nov. 3, 1911, foreign correspondents and others went out from the foreign settlements to look, and found a band of men said to be seeking the Director of the Kiangnan Dockyard adjoining the Arsenal. This was the first incident out of the ordinary. It was in the afternoon.

As if all had been prearranged, the two most prominent officials of the Dockyard and Arsenal, Admiral Wu and Mr. Kuang Kwo-hua, had vanished. But outside the Director's house at the Arsenal was a bodyguard which rushed into the Dockyard to meet the searching party, a mere crowd of roughs, which it fired on from behind a hedge, and dispersed it.

It was after 4.30 p.m. and the place began to be filled with people. The casualties from the firing were like a small accident at a country fair. The people began distributing and tying white bands and white handkerchiefs around each others' arms, as though volunteering for the Red Cross. But no, this was the emblem of the Republic. The soldiers of the Dockyard Guard and the people of the crowd mingled in the cordial fraternity created by this white brassard, after which the crowd and spectators left and the Dockyard was locked. The local newspaper said that all Shanghai "changed its allegiance without a murmur except for self-gratulations of the enthusiasts."

Yet there was still the affair of the "fifty." On Nov. 4, 1911, the "citizen soldiery" of the revolutionists came to take possession of the Arsenal and Dockyard, which had already been morally surrendered, and advanced from the foreshore side with the Krupp gun. The fifty of the Arsenal and Dockyard Guard received the "citizen soldiery," firing upon them as they approached from the Dockyard side. Although their aim was poor, they brought down a revolutionist leader who was waving a long-handled sword and cheering on his men, but were unable to arrest the "citizen" advance. They broke, and with an equal number of their half-hearted companions either fled to the Huang-pu or into the country, leaving a few killed and wounded. They were men of a company of Imperialists sent from Wusung, at the mouth of the Huang-pu, to defend the Arsenal and Dockyard. A few hundreds of the old quiescent soldier-guard inside joined the "citizen soldiery," and then the mob flowed in through the now bullet-splashed gates and made free with the contents of the premises. Only one official was found, the "Ammunition" Taot'ai, but he was not molested. One after another the Arsenal stores were opened by the crowds, who satiated their looting propensities by carrying off hundreds if not thousands of the Mauser model rifles which they contained.

In the meantime the fifty who had executed the demonstration of resistance on behalf of the Imperialist military, perhaps to save the honour of the army, in part reached the Huang-pu, where about twenty of them escaped by two junks to two torpedo-boats lying in midstream. These torpedo-boats after receiving the refugees struck their Imperial colours of a blue dragon and red sun on a yellow ground, and hoisted the white ensign as prearranged. During the day two batteries on the river, and the forts and powder-mill at Lung-hua—place of the famous pagoda of that name—together with the forts at Wusung 4 p.m., turned over to the revolutionists. Everything needed was in the hands of the revolutionists when four war-vessels of Admiral Sah's late squadron from Hankow arrived in the Huang-pu, to which they were driven by hostility along the Yangtse and the shortage of coal and ammunition. The only available ammunition for them was in the Kiangnan Arsenal, and they were promptly counted in among the assets of the Shanghai Republic. They did not all fly the Republican colours until November 13, but it was a coincidence to go with the fact that already it was decided how independent government was to be formed and what men were to carry on its departments.

More citizen soldiers were being recruited. Patriots were imitating the revolutionists of Wuchang creating a white badge for a regiment of martyrs. The name " Dare to Die " was borrowed, while the foreign Press of Shanghai appropriated the style " Death or Glory boys " of the Hankow foreign newspapers with which to designate them

" We are very happy," said one of the " Dare to Die " soldiers proudly wearing the badge of martyrdom. Some who do not enlist, send subscriptions to a war-chest fund that is started, one Chinese lady sending $250 (gold) with a note saying, " It is the only service I am able to render."

The foreigners in the Shanghai settlements cannot make out what the revolutionary organization is, but are trying to make it out from the various letters, handbills, and proclamations appearing. The British unnecessarily send a military guard to the Shanghai-Nanking Railway station on Chinese soil, to protect it. But on Nov. 6 comes a proclamation by General Li Ping-shu as "Civil Governor of the Republic of China." He speaks for the two provinces of Kiangsu and Chekiang respecting their grievances, and in a sentence abolishes all their petty taxes, together with those of the sister-provinces of Anhuei and Fukien. He calls for subscriptions to the war-chest and warns the people to strengthen their position, lest they suffer the fate of the merchants and people at Hankow murderously slaughtered by the Manchus. In response to a circular issued simultaneously, the Chinese people hang out white flags as a signal of their allegiance.

The Military Government of General Li Ping-shu claimed the recovery of Shanghai for the Hans without soiling revolutionist weapons. Feeling the responsibilities of government upon them, refugee revolutionists, National Assemblymen from Peking, and others hold meetings to draw up a " declaration of independence " and a plan of defence. One meeting adopts resolutions abolishing the National Assembly at Peking and annulling all its past acts.

Shanghai is full of prominent reformers and distinguished refugees. Many like Jui Cheng have come and gone, but the refugee officials from Peking, and others, are here; Chen Chin-tao, Vice-Minister of Finance; Mr. Sze of Cornell University, appointed Minister to the United States to placate the reformers; and, most distinguished of all Chinese in Shanghai, Wu Ting-fang, who long before saw the approach of the cataclysm to the Manchus and became a permanent refugee in Shanghai. Chen Chin-tao is living in the Astor House, consulting quietly with other reformers. Mr. Sze has begged leave of the Throne to delay his departure for Washington, and with his family is immured safely in the house of a foreign friend in Kiangsu Road. Wen Tsung-yao, hitherto also a candidate for the post at Washington and an able reformer, is here.

Wu Ting-fang is settled in his own mansion in the rural outskirts of the foreign settlement, where, protected by the Indian police of the British Municipality, he receives many visitors, foreign as well as native. With General Li Ping-shu head of the Military Government, these chief reformers set up a department of Foreign Affairs that as a matter of course falls to the senior diplomat, Wu Ting-fang. The fact grows, nobody knows how, until from an appointment by local Republicans it is announced that he is Secretary for Foreign Affairs under the whole revolutionary regime.

I am told that in answer to a question as to whether this was true he asked, " Who has appointed me? " He questioned his own appointment, and was seeking a clue to what was going to come out of the rapidly spreading revolutionary movement. He was in fact one of those whom the times produced as its leaders. I have regarded Wu Ting-fang as a pure opportunist in the Rebellion whose talents made it incumbent upon him to seize upon whatever kicking leg he could, in the scrimmage. He did this, and having found that it brought to him the portfolio of Foreign Affairs, with the genius of a practised revolutionist he expanded it to its widest dimensions.

In an expression of his views published on Nov. 8 he is mentally rummaging among revolutionary possibilities. He says that " if the present movement succeeds, it will have to be decided whether there is to be a constitutional monarchy or whether the country will become a Republic. If a Republic, it will be modelled upon the lines partly of the United States and partly on those of the German Federation."[1]

At this time, less than a week after the Shanghai revolt, he opposes any definite announcement until all the provinces can co-operate in a decision. The movement, however, had already gone so far that " many who disliked it at first were won over, and few were against it." He was evidently in doubt as to its final success, beyond the certainty that in any case it was for the good of the country. This was evidently the timidity of one who had been in retirement, as well as of one who was doubtful of his credentials. Before another week Wu Ting-fang stated that he was prepared to represent all Republican provinces in all matters relating to foreign affairs, and disclaimed the obvious fact that his appointment was merely a provincial one, and asserted that it was national. With a grand revolutionary flourish such as he became more and more skilful in making, he delivered himself of the magnificent assertion that the provinces from Kuangtung to Chihli and Shantung to Szechuan had confirmed his selection as head of Foreign Affairs—a figure which in view of Wu Ting-fang's long American experience suggests the Americanism, " Maine to California—the Great Lakes to the Gulf." He claimed all of China proper, and said that within a few days representatives from all the belligerent provinces would convene in Shanghai and form a Provisional Government. " China," he proclaimed, " is thoroughly united."

A " boy wonder " is often as nothing to a clever young

[1] *N.C. Daily News.*

man of seventy odd like Wu Ting-fang, who has promised to visit Washington D.C. in the flesh in 1959. He was making for himself a permanent place in the Chinese Revolution. Historians will say that the credit which he deserves is considerable. He was one of those mandarins who knew the dangers surrounding the leaders, freely confessed his fear, and without possessing the actual backing which he so positively claimed, worked steadily ahead. He "rushed in where angels feared to tread," but knew he was a—Russian. In this he seemed to the outsider to be like the late enemies of Japan, who had to rush out again. But this was not the case with Wu Ting-fang. From his vantage in Shanghai, where he was 600 miles from President Li Yuan-hung and out of reach of Sun Yat-sen, who at the first opportunity, when he reached Hongkong in December, disclaimed Wu's activity as having no authoritative sanction from the Revolution, he pushed forward undaunted. Shaping his course by the obvious requirements of the Republic, his ideas were actually admitted to be in accordance with what the Li Yuan-hung revolutionists and the Sun Yat-sen republicans wanted, and the leaders of these parties saw no reason for stopping them. He put the dragon through its paces. He executed some remarkable acts, creating amazement at the time, but which largely command the approval of scoffers and historians alike.

With those associated with him he indicted the Manchus, he challenged them to abdicate, and he clamorously demanded recognition by the Powers. On Nov. 11 he published an appeal to the Prince Regent to abdicate, wilily turning the Prince Regent's own weapons against the latter. "Your Highness," he begins, "since the risings in Szechuan and Hupeh, the issuance of the self-accusation [penitential] decree was immediately followed by excesses in the form of an atrocious murder of human beings culminating in the secession without a struggle of more than ten provinces within ten days." He tells the Prince Regent that apart from "republicanism" there is no way to avoid the sacrifice of human lives, a circumstance in which neither the public nor foreigners disagree, therefore the monarchical form of government cannot possibly meet with toleration in the future of China. "In the interest of the Emperor and Your Highness," continues the wily diplomat, "you should just now regard yourself as Yao or Shun [Emperors of the past who abdicated]. . . .

If you will but wake up and change your attitude, and co-operate in ' republicanizing China,' treating the citizens with justice and with consideration, as the civilization of the world demands, the citizens doubtless will be able to show you every courtesy in return, with due regard to your living in wealth and honour as becomes the Imperial Household, the peace and safety of the Manchu Clans being not excluded from our aims."

Having made his most powerful appeal to the cupidity of the already terrorized and helpless Prince Regent, he hammers it down with this threat : " Otherwise the curse of war will be prolonged and extended, and the hatred accumulated and intensified. Since the atrocity [massacre at Hankow] indulged in by the Northern Army has been so inhuman, how can it be possible for the Great Seat to exist alone ? " The conclusion is a supplication : " We, Ting-fang and others, cannot sit by and view our affairs in ease, therefore we presume to tender you this our final faithful advice. Our voice is hoarse, and our tears exhausted, and no more can be said."

Taken out of their time and environment and thus analysed apart from the circumstances in which they were devised, these acts of Wu Ting-fang nevertheless stand the test of criticism. " Ting-fang," as he humbly calls himself, was the first to recommend abdication to the Regent, which events proved was sound advice. It was three months before his advice was acted on. No one can deny that courage and wisdom came to him early. Being to the foreign Powers the outstanding figure in the Republic and claiming the authority of nearly all China as Minister of Foreign Affairs, he constituted a material threat to the Prince Regent and the Imperial Government. He made almost frenzied use of this position, first attacking the Prince Regent and the Manchu Dynasty and then scolding the Powers, the first because they would not abdicate and " republicanize " the Empire, the latter because they would not recognize " the Republic." He first claimed eleven provinces and then fourteen, and exclaimed, " Why don't you recognize us ? "

" Whom do you mean by ' us ' ? " asked the listener, one of the foreign correspondents.

Hesitating only a moment, he said : " Why, why Me, recognize Me."

Wu Ting-fang is a philosopher, and disputant. Being a good disputant, he knows that Me and Us in politics mean one and the same thing. He was perfectly honest in wanting himself recognized. If he could get himself recognized by the foreign Powers, it would give him perhaps his *first* real credentials. Even yet he is not able to prove that he has any credentials from the provinces which he claims belong to the "Republic." He is perfectly honest in cajoling them while he attacks the foreign Powers and the Manchu Government. If he can only accomplish something he will be satisfied, and his position in history will be secure.

He has associated with him three countrymen, including Wen Tsung-yao, an American university graduate. On Nov. 14 with the latter he frames a letter of explanation and appeal to foreigners in which he tells the Manchus what he thinks of them as frankly as he had expressed himself to the Prince Regent. "The Manchu Government," he says, "has in the course of its dominance of China demonstrated its incapacity to rule its people or conduct the affairs of the nation in a manner compatible with the forward movement signalizing the modern history and development of the civilized world. The Manchu Dynasty has by its benighted conceptions and barbaric leanings brought China to a position of degradation. The Nation is scorned," continues his joint declaration, "and its institutions and general retrogressive policy are the subjects of contempt. . . .

"The Manchu Dynasty has triumphantly carried on its reactionary policy despite the strongest pressure exerted from within and without, until the oppressed people could endure the disgrace and the contumely of it no longer. . . .

"The Manchu Dynasty has been tried by a patient and peaceful people for centuries, and has been found more than wanting. It has sacrificed the reverence, forfeited the regard, and lost the confidence freely reposed in it by all Chinese.

"Its promises in the past have proved delusions and snares. Its promises for the future can carry no weight, deserve no consideration, and merit no trust.

". . . The shameless destruction of life and property that has signalized the latter days of the Manchus' attempt to resist the termination of their reign is but their characteristic valedictory message to the world.

"To the Manchus is the blame for a continuance of hostilities and the perpetration of outrages. They have received from a majority of the provinces an unmistakable pronunciamento of the popular wish; they know that their race is run and that the China of To-morrow can never be as the China of Yesterday.

Wu Ting-fang's place in history will be largely that of one who has added much to the gaiety of nations. True to his training as a diplomat and to diplomatic precept, he pursues this characteristic, so fixed in the minds of foreigners, with irrepressible diligence. The last two-thirds of this document to which he has joined the name of Wen Tsung-yao, who has done the work of writing it, show its real aim. He now attempts to belabour the Dynasty with the mock weapon of the foreign Powers. Eleven paragraphs beginning with the pronoun "We" tell what the "Republic" has done and is doing, and are an appeal on its behalf to outside nations, and then follows the appeal for foreign aid to influence the Manchus to abdicate.

After showing why the "Republic" is entitled to recognition for its efforts, Wu Ting-fang says: "We ask our foreign well-wishers to unite with us in our appeal to the Prince Regent to abdicate and so end the strife that is now shaking the land. For our part, our conduct is open to the full view of the world. We are fighting for what Britons fought in the days of old; we are fighting for what the Americans fought; we are fighting for what every nation that is now worthy of the name has fought in its day. We are fighting to be men in the world; we are fighting to cast off an oppressive, vicious, and tyrannous rule that has beggared and disgraced China, obstructed and defied the foreign nations, and set back the hands of the clock of the world.

"We must not be judged by the past; we are trying to bring China into her own; to elevate her to the standard that the people of the Occident have ever been urging her to attain, and the stumbling-block to-day, as it has been through the past centuries, is the Manchu Dynasty.

"Our foreign friends must from a sheer sense of fairness concede that we have the right to win the laurels of freedom by a fair fight in the field, and to avoid the rest we again appeal to them to use their influence to secure in the Manchu mind recognition of the utter hopelessness of the continuance of the Dynasty."

It was like a game of bowls where the player was struggling strenuously to knock down a few pins that would count most. In this document he lays hold of the ball marked by him " Foreign Powers " with which to bowl over the Manchu Dynasty. The indefatigable Wu Ting-fang is doing a yeoman's service. Pending the arrival of Sun Yat-sen he is the chief luminary to the public. He is anxious for success and is firing at every target a Foreign Office commands. The wily old diplomat sitting in his mansion and peering between the foreign police pacing the roadway in front, is somewhat exasperated that the targets do not fire back. He is his own and the Republic's best Press agent, and he hectors the foreign Press correspondents on the subject of recognition.

The effect of these fulminations is, to express more elaborately and more subtly the real and imaginary grievances of reformers and revolutionists, to carry farther the interpretations of the Revolution begun by the proclamation of Li Yuan-hung, and to not only give the reasons for the Shanghai " Republic " but to be an expression of what the China of the future is to be. They are both preceded and followed by exhaustive and bitter denunciations and indictments of the Manchus made with intense conviction and with apparently all but perfect sincerity. The expression of this was certainly untempered by any lingering doubt in the minds of those who framed these indictments and might be expected to know China's history best. Perhaps the fact that they were a war-cry and a political instrument for the attainment of an all-important end accounts for the moiety of justice.

The loading of the responsibility for all the evils of China upon the Manchus was a thing which struck me at the very first as the prime incongruity and error of the Rebellion, for which the Republic might in future have to pay very dearly. The Chinese will appreciate our position as foreigners and our detached and disinterested view in this, that we cannot accept their wholesale denunciation of the Manchus and of a Dynasty certainly one of the greatest China ever had. The reasons are very simple. The Manchus have been reckoned by foreigners as numbering not more than 7,000,000, and perhaps not less than 3,000,000. A proclamation issued on Nov. 9 by the " Military Government of the Republic of China," in a complaint against having to support them, gave their numbers at 5,000,000, and the revolutionaries no doubt have not minimized under the circumstances. It is obvious that 5,000,000 of Manchus have not appreciably clogged the Chinese wheels of progress which bear those

" 400,000,000 of the descendants of Holy Han," named in the same proclamation.

But these and other reasons are not so convincing to the Shanghai leaders as to us. Their denunciation of the Manchus is coincident with Yuan Shih-k'ai's arrival in Peking to undertake the preservation of the Throne. His efforts to raise a foreign loan and to preserve the North, with still the nucleus of a powerful army apparently loyal to him, are circumstances which still cause the wily old diplomat at Shanghai to lie uneasily in his sleep.

Afterward, when the passion and resentment had subsided and the time came for Wu Ting-fang to take a dispassionate view of the Manchus in the atmosphere of conditions in which all the responsibilities ever placed upon the Manchus, and more, were upon the leaders of the Republic, he had changed his expressed opinions more in accordance with the facts.

As he had been in retirement, away from the battleground of reform at Peking, it was some years since I had seen him,—not since 1908, when he was seeking leave of absence from the Board of Justice with a view to retirement. The story of those days he now told me more intimately, unchecked by the restraint of official fealty to the Manchus.

My experiences with Wu Ting-fang have always been in his native country, where he has been subject to the customs of China and subservient to the Court. The Regent has now abdicated, the Government of the reformers had been organized and was assured, and I found a somewhat different " Wu," as he has been familiarly called. He was still the crusader, known to his wide though intimate circle of foreign acquaintances as the champion of vegetarianism, a doctrine which he once carried so far as to persuade the late Empress Grand Dowager to adopt in her pursuit of longevity, with the result that his enterprise received the Imperial rebuke. After an absence during a term as Minister to Washington, she startled him with a tale of her disastrous experiment with vegetarianism, which had resulted in a severe illness.

He had good reason to be generous with the Manchus, to whom he had owed in his appointments the best he had gained out of life, and who, he had to confess, had tried some of his prescriptions only with disastrous results, notwithstanding which he had increased the dose to a point where it meant the extermination of the Dynasty.

I found him, notwithstanding the restrictions of his foreign house, surrounded by Chinese objects and dressed in the substantial native style. His chief characteristic to me is a vigilant outlook for the latest circumstances that are to govern the framing of his next remark. More than anywhere, the politician in China — the oldest political environment—has been forced to operate along the lines of the opportunist and the sail-trimmer, which have been the only visible means to accomplish the little that could be hoped for.

" Are the Manchus as bad as you thought ? " I asked of him.

Wu Ting-fang tilted back his head, a characteristic mannerism expressive of the Chinese scholar's expectation of receiving the benevolent influences from Heaven. He replied :

" They are the stumbling-block."

His answer blocked any criticism of the joint indictment published by him with his own and Wen Tsung-yao's signatures. He grasped at perhaps the only invulnerable point made therein.

" How would you explain the obstruction by the Manchus and your contention that Peking the seat of the Court is not a proper place for the Capital ? "

" It has its advantages," said he, and continued in an elaboration of his own experiences when we had known each other in Peking. " The foreign Powers must be considered. They have their Legations there and their treaties. Also, Peking has the palaces. But it has its disadvantages. The atmosphere is bad. Atmosphere has a powerful influence ; we are all affected by atmosphere—we are unconscious of it and yet we cannot resist it. You know I was in Peking—I was appointed to office there, as Vice-Minister of the Board of Foreign Affairs. Well, I went there. I looked over what they were doing, and I went to see all the officials. I formed my ideas : ' Here,' I said, ' this won't do—we must change this.' I even had my recommendations read by the Throne. Nobody disputed me, I had no direct hostility—they listened to me and even agreed with me. But they said the time had not come.

" I wanted to reform finances. All seemed to agree with my recommendations. These were referred to the Board of Finance and were pigeon-holed. I was discouraged : I couldn't do anything, and I wanted to resign. They wouldn't let me. I sent word that I was sick—you know that is a Chinese custom. At last they let me off, and I came here.

"I got off on leave, and I thought I was free. But one day there came a recall—I was surprised. They commanded me to come back. I thought it over, and I said to myself, 'They want me up there; I must go back. But I must change my tactics.' So I went back.

"I wasn't there very long, but it was just the same, and in a little while I found I was becoming just as they were. It was the atmosphere. I was soon of their opinion that 'The time hadn't come'—of just the same opinion as were they. Then I saw the danger and I became alarmed. It was time for me to get away from the place. I had become a Conservative without knowing it. That is the stumbling-block of Manchuism. I quitted Peking for good."

I left the splendid old diplomat who had in his old age—youth, as he calls it—risen so magnificently to the occasion, with a keen conviction of the essential difference between his standpoint and mine. "Will the Republic find at Peking and everywhere in China a vague, indefinable, but irresistible atmosphere, an atmosphere of unchangeableness," thought I, "when the Manchus are gone?"

Wu Ting-fang has been called by his countrymen more of a foreigner than a Chinese from the fact that he is foreign-trained and foreign-educated and has made his career entirely in channels of foreign influence and affairs. Necessarily his point of view when in the Capital and elsewhere is essentially one coloured by foreign ideas. And the point of view of nearly all the reform and revolutionary leaders must be the same. To the Republicans, and the revolutionaries before them, there was nothing good in Peking. It was the Gibraltar of the spirit of the past with which China was afflicted. As it represented the whole obstacle of the reformation in China, it deserved both the fear and the hatred of the reformers. Li Yuan-hung and Wu Ting-fang as well as Sun Yat-sen were right in believing it to be the fortress of the enemy because it was a picture of the condition of China, and a priceless object-lesson such as it was recognized to be by Wu Ting-fang. But my belief has been that the value of this object-lesson lies in the fact that an understanding of Peking furnished a complete education to the revolutionaries which could not be despised, because Peking was China herself. History must show that the atmosphere called Manchu by Wu Ting-fang was, in fact, Chinese.

CHAPTER XXIII

CANTON THE GIPSY QUEEN AND MOTHER OF REVOLUTION

THE best way to enter a city like Canton is to wake up as the machinery of the boat stops and look out of the cabin window. Thus I looked out shoreward 7 a.m on a sky of boat-hooks and rain. Crossing our steamer amidships, I looked on a little Pearl River instead of the very big one my mind had pictured, but on both sides an immense city wherein the river seemed to be perishing —perishing from life and boats crowding upon it.

Many peoples have been in the boat business, in Asia and out, from the time of Noah, but there is no place, certainly, where the big boats, and the little boats, multiply on the face of the waters as at Canton. Here, at the largest city of China and of Eastern Asia, the boat-hive has swarmed.

I ate my breakfast aboard, catching glimpses of the British, American and French war-vessels in the river, and thinking over the strange history of Canton, a place that saw the beginning of China's foreign relations and stamped them with the sanguinary character they have always retained. Here was the beginning of foreign influence upon China, but it is hard to say from the appearance of the City that there is any evidence of foreign influence. Even the Rebellion that has produced the "Canton Republic" is only the immortal Canton piracy, and rebellion against the rest of China.

The chief characteristics of Cantonese to foreigners are a fiery, untamable spirit, brigandage, and piracy. Their authorities have always declared themselves powerless before the Canton populace, which they dared not coerce. This is a reply that has often been given to the foreign Powers.

The Cantonese have never stood for anything but themselves. They are the only Chinese who do not call themselves the "Sons of Han." All other Chinese have claimed this lineage since 206–194 B.C., the period of the

FIGHT AT THE T'AIPING GATE, BATTLE OF NANKING.

To face p. 226.

Han Dynasty. The Cantonese seem always to have had an indomitable rebelliousness, and Canton is a city of plots and conspiracies carried out with utmost desperation. The Cantonese delight in the superlative and the extreme. When they rebelled under the style of " Republicanism," which closely followed the revolt of Shanghai, they formed a " Dare to Die " corps. They were not satisfied to adopt the term from their Northern brothers, but called themselves the " Determined to Die." The first were merely willing martyrs, but the Cantonese were desperate for death. A foreign wag in Shameen, the foreign settlement of Canton, dubbed them the " Much wanchee dies."

China's ancient seat of rebellion was glorified by the success of revolution and republicanism. Canton in the extreme South is the centre for rebellion within the Great Wall. Though it has never been able to change *itself*, it is nevertheless the Mother of Revolution. The whole subject of revolution is brought up by mention of it. Nearly all revolts in China from the " stink-pot " and cutlass days of a century ago in the Canton delta, have emanated from Canton, and when she joined the ranks of the republics she came with her old, bloody skirts, and scarred with murder and piracy. She came with the aid of the outlaw in the good old-fashioned way. On April 8, 1911, she assassinated her Manchu Tartar General Fu Chi. He was shot dead in the street by a man claiming to be a follower of Huang Hsing, associate of Sun Yat-sen and later Minister of War. On April 27 her people attacked the Viceroy's yamen, from which the Viceroy escaped and fled to Hongkong. On Aug. 13 they attempted to assassinate Li Chun, the Admiral of the Southern Fleet, by a bomb thrown from a housetop. On Oct. 25 an assassin killed the new Manchu Tartar General Feng Shan with a bomb in the streets immediately after his arrival to succeed Fu Chi. A mass meeting took place ostensibly for the protection of life and property, but was turned into a permanent Committee of Peace, and passed resolutions of independence.

Canton was in fact the second working republic in China, Shanghai having only carried out a revolt and formed a nucleus for a government of all China. At the same time, reviewing the events of Canton's revolt in my mind, it did not appear that she had done anything essentially different from her uprisings in the past.

I was the last to leave the boat. I went ashore in a

slight drizzle of rain. I had never been here before. This is the home of Canton China, Canton crêpe, ginger, and the American laundryman. Reverend Frank Li, a product of Chinatown, New York City, the respected pastor of a Christian Church in Canton, is Assistant Secretary of State. Though his mother was German, he identifies himself with his own race. General Homer Lea, who knew intimately the principal revolutionary conspirator Sun Yat-sen and saw the workings of Chinese patriotism in foreign countries, told me that no Chinese abroad deserved more credit for the revolution in China than the 80,000 or so Chinese in the United States, because of their unstinted contributions of money. If this is a Cantonese-made rebellion and revolution, as some claim it is, then it is a monument to the laundrymen, truck-growers, section-hands, miners, servants, and shopkeepers of the United States, as well as to the Cantonese merchants, manufacturers, and shippers of the East Indies and Oceania. John Chinaman—the card-shark of Poverty Flat, the cook of the Union Pacific section-hands gang, the laundryman of Omaha, the stoker of Callao, the Havana contractor, and the plantation coolie of Samoa—on a pedestal; the hero of the battle which Wu Ting-fang says is the same as that by which the Briton won his supremacy, the American his independence,—what a comment on the worship of the nations around the Dynastic fetish at Peking!

The little picturesque stretch of Canton between the boat-landing and Shameen had no appearances of revolution, not even in the display of the Republican flag. What the revolt had been, and still appeared to be in the eyes of some, was concretely illustrated by the island of Shameen divided by a small canal from the vast hive of human voices and portentous sounds called Canton. The eastern end of the island is occupied by the French. Passing over the little canal bridge into this quarter, I noticed nothing unusual—no guards or fortifications—an obvious expression of sympathy and confidence on the part of the European Republic. I was told this was in accordance with the desires and opinions of the French Government. But in the larger British quarter, occupying the rest of the island, conditions were quite the opposite. When I came to pass from the French to the British quarter the streets were barricaded. Wire entanglements supported by breastworks of sandbags extended the whole length of its mainland side. Indian infantry were camped in the fortifications, and behind them on the river front were two pieces of artillery. Machine-guns were mounted in redoubts at all avenues of approach. The Quarter was under martial law.

Shameen offered a sharp contrast of the republican and monarchical conception of the fitness of things at Canton. The French were of course joined in their sympathies by the Americans. The conservative, hard-headed British considered that the Cantonese had really learned little in the seventy or eighty years of their foreign relations and were treating them as in the thirties and forties of the last century. Shameen was a place where the war-teeth were set and grinning, and where Great Britain was observing to the letter the injunction implied in " Lest we forget." At the expense of being laughed at by the French and Americans, the British chose the safe course of preparation for those attacks which had continued in magnitude at intervals up to 1900, when Kipling's " Lest We Forget " was inscribed on the embattled walls of their Legation at Peking.

Great Britain wonders if these Canton brigands are ever going to be civilized and the ancient feud with foreigners ended. She is guarding millions of Chinese treasure both in British and American banks here. Behind these island breastworks are the yet more formidable engines of war, the foreign gunboats and cruisers, anchored in the Pearl. The whole air of the place, notwithstanding the nonchalance of the French, is of some impending surprise from the resourceful Canton populace.

The visitor naturally wonders what is the meaning of all the ominous noises and hum of voices that reaches him from across the canal at Shameen, as he sits in his hotel balcony or walks in the little parks and boulevards. It seems impenetrable because of the little streets whose entrances are obscured by the street-life. Mr. Burkwall, an old resident acquainted with the construction and life of this thing called the City, became my guide to explore the region of these sights and sounds. We parted from barricades and guards at the outer end of the British Concession bridge and plunged into the City. It was like a dive into a stream filled with fish and vegetable wreckage, where we were borne along in the arterial currents by Chinese mermen. The stone-paved passages were exuding moisture, chairs were creaking, and chair-coolies, water-coolies, and other carriers were perspiring. No place seems so much the tangled arteries of life as does Canton. This was only the suburb, and but at two places did we stop, once to greet a fine old man by the alley-side, but little of whose Cantonese dialect I could understand, and who surprised me by saying in English, "And how long have you been in China?"

"Twelve years."

"I was in San Francisco fifteen years," said he. He was the best kind of a revolutionist.

"What do you think will be the outcome?" he asked.

"It will be all right if you all hold together," said I, "but you must join with the North and go slowly."

"Yes, but there is no money. That is the difficulty. We cannot keep order without money."

"That is true in Canton. Foreigners tell me you are all in the hands of the pirates. But Canton can do anything—Canton must begin all over again."

He sighed deeply and smiled brightly, and we passed on through the narrow, lofty aisles of the famous "Eighteenth Street" into the narrower newspaper street where we went in to look over the revolutionist and republican newspapers. The predominating theme was Yuan Shih-k'ai, for whom the Cantonese seemed to have no conceivable use. They were lampooning him in these revolutionist newspapers as a monkey and a tortoise, the Chinese names of which are alike *yuan*.

The Canton Republic in fact is preparing to march on Peking. At this time of my visit in February the country is virtually united, and it has for some time been decided that Yuan Shih-k'ai is to be President and that the country is fortunate in possessing such a man, upon whom the various sections of the late Empire can unite. Military operations have ceased. The Cantonese ignore all this. They picture Yuan Shih-k'ai carrying the Throne on his back, willing either to re-establish the Manchus or take the Throne for himself, and meanwhile crying "Peace" in order to deceive the people.

Through even narrower lanes we quit the suburb and enter the West Gate, and mounting the walls from the inside rise like deep-sea divers to the open sky. What variety of structure and colour in wall, pagoda, pawn-shop, yamen, hill, garden, moat, gatehouse, and all the buildings.

Under a sky of Canton blue and fleecy clouds we can see all the noted landmarks, the Five Tower Gate House, the Round Pagoda, the Flowery Pagoda, and other structures that in old engravings made Canton famous in the days of the clipper-ship and before. We look over a kingdom that has fallen into the hands of pirates. The piratical army that assembled to establish independence and that has never done more than scare the Viceroy out of his palace, claiming 35,000 strong, has fastened itself upon the merchants and gentry and refuses to be dislodged. It is under the command of Liu Yung-fu, famous as the "Black Flag Chieftain," who fought the French in Tonking, and later the Japanese in Formosa, and whose name spells terror wherever he is known in South China. He has eight principal chiefs, and these forces though they have never fought are demanding pay and arrears of pay on a war schedule. The money comes from the merchants and gentry, who are being forced to find from $1,000,000 to $1,500,000 (gold) per month to run the Canton Republic.

The soldiers have issued an ultimatum to the merchants setting a day for plundering their shops unless money is forthcoming. The chiefs are drawing pay in some instances for three times as many men as they actually have. The City is still trying to prevent additional detachments in the country from marching to the City, and it has in addition its regular soldiers and militia to support.

The powers that be in Canton are known as the "Seventy-two Guilds and the Nine Charitable Institutions." They devised a plan of three measures to throw off the revolutionist army. The most lawless (pirate) soldiers they were trying to ship North to the Yangtse and to Shantung for the "march on Peking." Those that were next most dangerous—the merely hungry class—were detailed to work in removing the City walls so as to make a wide boulevard for the new Capital; and lastly, they actually paid these and also the regular soldiers who must be the stand-bys. By this means the "Seventy-two Guilds and Nine Charitable Institutions" expected to raise the regular soldiery to the point of superiority in numbers and compel the piratical recruits to disperse.

After the first companies had departed for the North, the piratical recruits refused to move. The "hungry brigade" refused to toil. We observed the petty, futile results of the experiment of making them work at a point on the north wall of Canton, where for a few hundred yards they had partly torn away the crenelations. At this time, as we stood upon the scene of their work, only the third of the three provisions named appeared to have any hope of success. The merchants were fearful of the ordeal of being forcibly levied upon by the soldiery, which event was promised in a few days.

The wall littered with the fragments of its crenelations is the first material traces of revolution in Canton that I have seen. But only a little farther on, after we leave the wall, we come to a famous temple to Kwangyin, the Goddess of Mercy, where the iconoclastic revolutionist vandals have destroyed all the shrines. The God of War is substituted for the Goddess of Mercy, but whether done by the priests on their own account or to placate the vandals I do not know.

The incident was made the occasion of a strong appeal for religious toleration by a native scholar, who pointed out that this was one of the reforms which a New China must adopt, and protested against the desecration of any shrine held sacred by men, no matter what it was, as something that could do no good.

We passed the Viceroy's yamen, famous in history, where occurred the attack of April 27, 1911, already mentioned. We approached along the west side under its walls by a narrow passage. The maze of houses, elevations, and angles seemed a suitable environment for the labyrinthine plots perpetrated here in ages gone by, and for the attack of April 27 for the purpose of assassinating the Viceroy Chang Ming-chi. Then 200 or 300 revolutionaries armed with bombs and revolvers rushed the Viceroy's yamen and burned his house within.

The Viceroy was probably saved by being in his office in another building, but the revolutionaries were beaten off by troops under the personal command of Admiral Li Chun, commander of the naval forces of the provinces of Kuangtung and Kuanghsi. This officer hunted them down and had a large number beheaded, and later buried them outside the East Gate of Canton. He found that the instigators of the attack were revolutionists from the Straits Settlements, and Hongkong.

Following this attack the Viceroy made a house-to-house search, incurring the hostility of the people, who in the general revolutionary excitement began an exodus to Macao and Hongkong, which during the summer numbered from 100,000 to 150,000 people. It was not until August 13 that the revolutionaries made reprisals upon Admiral Li Chun, in which he was injured in the side by the explosion of a bomb intended to kill him, and many of his guard and chair-coolies were killed and wounded. In turn the assassin was arrested and executed. In October, when Wuchang revolted, Canton bred rumours of her own rebellion. Then came the assassination of General Feng Shan, October 25, a few minutes after he had landed at the Government pier. Thirty of his escort and ten spectators were horribly mangled and burned. Feng Shan's charred remains were recognized by a bit of silk attached to them. His mother in Peking said, "I received only a button."

On the same day the mass meeting conducted by the "Seventy-two Guilds and Nine Charitable Institutions" to form the "Pao An Huei," or Peace Committee, was held. Tung Wah-hei, ex-Governor of Kueichou, a man over eighty years old, presided. This is the real date of the independence of Canton. The "Pao An Huei" passed its resolution to refuse requests from the Central Government or from other provinces for troops and money, and to hold revenue and preserve resources within the province of Kuangtung.

These events introduced exciting days at the Viceroy's yamen. People were fleeing the City. Chang Ming-chi acquiesced in the action of the "Pao An Huei" notwithstanding it meant secession. Kuangtung revolutionaries in Hongkong decided for joining the Republic. The Viceroy decided to flee. In several meetings in Canton following the declarations at Hongkong the Republicans won, and it became impossible for Viceroy Chang Ming-chi to remain longer in the yamen.

On Nov. 8, about midnight, the British Consul, J. W. Jamieson, helped him to escape. Followed by a sedan-chair, Consul Jamieson walked to the Viceroy's yamen, out of the courtyard of which a little later the Viceroy proceeded in the chair to the British Consulate on Shameen, accompanied by the Consul. The next day he went aboard the British torpedo-boat destroyer *Handy* and went to Hongkong to rooms in the Hongkong and Shanghai Bank, after which he went by the steamship *Roon* to Shanghai. Some of his associate officials left about the same time by other means, and on the same day a mass meeting elected Hu Han-wen, a young man about thirty years old, once editor of a Canton paper and later a student in Japan, as "Governor-General of Kuantung under the Military Government of the Chinese Republic." This was the signal for the raising of the revolutionist flag. On Nov. 9 Kuangtung became a part of the Republic of China.

There was a loss of but one Chinese life in the final action that severed it from the Empire—a guard shot dead at the Government Cement Works.

On Nov. 11 the new Governor-General announced to the doyen of the foreign consuls his own election and responsibility for protection of all foreigners and foreign property. He said that all matters would be conducted in the same manner as now transacted between the Military Government and the China Republic in the province of Hupeh and the foreign Powers.

Canton produced no doubt 50,000 " pirates " to respond to the call of the revolutionists, but perhaps not more than 20,000 were enlisted. They came from all parts of the delta, uniformed and ununiformed, and armed with everything resembling a weapon, from rifles and cleavers to automatic revolvers and bombs. Weapons were produced that must have been the first brought from the West and no doubt relics of piratical attacks on foreign vessels in China.

Heads of the pirate clans led their hosts by sign and compact through the fields and suburbs to the City. " Lamp-Chimney " Lay, who governed Honam Island, warned the Viceroy to surrender. The Viceroy did not believe that " Lamp-Chimney " and his superiors and associates had the forces to warrant the demand. " Come and see," said " Lamp-Chimney." The Viceroy waited until the " pirates " entered the City gates and then fled. " Lamp-Chimney " Lay in the twilight of November 8 led 1500 men from Honam Island past the Canton Christian College to the City. Eight or ten other chiefs led in from 1000 to 3000 men each. To add to the *éclat* of the occasion their associates in the delta pirated a British steamship and killed the British chief officer.

Ten days after the election of Governor-General Hu Han-wen, the revolutionaries who had unsuccessfully tried to assassinate his predecessor in April got up a huge parade that marched through the streets and outside the East Gate to decorate the graves of their late fellows. The pirate element was prominent, and the mob, which was dressed in a riotous mixture of Chinese and foreign clothes, carried all kinds of weapons, with large quantities of ammunition slung in duck jackets and bandoliers. Men and boys waved loaded revolvers, rushing here and there. There was obviously some organization of this mob, because it was made the occasion of a demonstration against

Admiral Li Chun, who had defended the late Viceroy. A part of the mob rushed the Admiralty building in the City near the river and disarmed the guards there, and later Admiral Li Chun received an order to leave Canton, and left, after writing a letter to the community to the effect that things were in a bad way and he was unable to do anything.

About Dec. 20 or 21, just a month later, Governor-General Hu Han-wen followed his predecessor to Hongkong ostensibly to meet the future Provisional President, Sun Yat-sen. But he did not come back. There was no money. The troops from the country had not yet been stopped from coming in. There was a conflict of authority, he feared the reckoning when the clamour should begin and was afraid to face it. The Chinese in America had sent $250,000 (gold) through the British colony at Hongkong to support the Republic at Canton, after first assuring themselves that it would not be held up in Hongkong for reasons of neutrality. There had been no funds left by the departing Imperialist officials, and there was now nothing left of this contribution. A capable official who had been Judge-Advocate of the Army under the late Viceroy Chan Kwing-ming, then took hold.

Among the various military organizations that sprung up at the time of the revolt at Canton was a company of bomb-throwers called the "Bomb Pioneers." Their uniform was a light blue foreign knitted underwear that fitted them like their own skins. They wore brown knitted socks supported by American garters. Over the underwear they wore shoulder-braces from which were stretched across the breast white bands bearing the name of their organization. Their leaders wore blouses and caps, and carried swords. Their standards were white, and bore the Chinese characters in red and black, giving the name of their organization. In parades they sometimes carried arms full of bombs and were in danger of blowing whole streets to atoms. In public meetings on two occasions there were accidents in which numbers of people were killed and wounded.

The late Judge-Advocate had one of these fearsome "pioneers" at his doorway. This "pioneer" looked exceedingly mild to me. He had laid aside his insignia, and having added Chinese sandals and a foreign "Fedora" hat to his underwear and braces, had folded his arms and was placidly smoking a cigarette. The burnt yamen had been partly restored to form the "White House" of the Canton Republic, the white effect being produced by newly whitewashed walls and white flags, the emblem of the revolution. We next pass the place where the Manchu Tartar General Feng Shan was killed. Three or four shops are in ruins from the explosion and fire that followed, leaving a tell-tale gap in the street.

There are new-idea barber-shops inscribed "Universal," entirely foreign in arrangement, where Western hair-dressing is practised. From a little platform in a recess a lecturer is addressing twenty or thirty men. It is a thumb-box picture of the Republic. The lecturer, half bent, shakes his hand over the heads of the group as he drives his points home.

"They are explaining the principles of the Republic," said Mr. Burkwall. "There is a lecture system in vogue here which employs men qualified by foreign education, travel, and observation to lecture to all the people. The people seem to be reading everything they can get. Any kind of book can now be sold in Canton, anything that has covers—one might say, anything that has paper that is printed on, so eager are the people for information."

Already the spell-binder has reached China, and in the future elective system these will be the political orators and politicians.

At the "Temple of Horrors," a famous place in Canton representing the sufferings in Gehenna, pointed out to tourists, a great holiday crowd is being entertained at the food-stalls by fortune-tellers, money-changers, medicine-sellers, and various others. All the "Horrors" in clay, paper, mortar, and paint are destroyed, the work of the mob, and instead of the usual deities, the sculptured representations of the Cycle and other things, the shrine of the God of War is substituted, and incense tapers and oil lamps are burning before it. In front of a wing of the main temple there is a "shooting gallery." Men take turns shooting Manchus,—the Manchus being represented by a picture on wood of a seated mandarin in full official dress. The weapon used is a vacuum gun that shoots a miniature lance with great inaccuracy a distance of six or eight feet. The man behind the gun when I was looking on, punctured the Manchu image with such success as to show unmistakable signs according to his own reckoning of having got his money's worth. This was a favourite pastime in the Republican provinces during the rebellion.

THE BOMB-PIONEERS OF KUANGTUNG.

To face p. 236.

On our way back to Shameen we are passed by armed escorts, of which I had heard a great deal, flourishing weapons as they brush people aside. They accompany somebody in a chair and disappear almost as we turn to look at them, and are swallowed up in the human mazes we are leaving, a striking illustration of the whole drama acted in the Republic of Canton—the disappearance of the dignitary and the individual.

I was impressed at Canton with the fact that there was no single name upon which to pin history or prophecy. Canton was anonymous. Peking, Yuan Shih-k'ai; Wuchang, Li Yuan-hung; Shanghai, Wu Ting-fang; Nanking, Sun Yat-sen; Canton, no one. She is the gipsy who has no master. Her Tartar generals are dead, her viceroys and military governors have fled to foreign soil. Hongkong boasts four ex-rulers of provinces. There is not a vacant tenement in the Portuguese colony of Macao, which for years has been almost abandoned, and Canton is again the Canton of "factories" and the "Hoppo." There is nothing of the Republic about it except that it is in the hands of the many, and a Provincial Assembly is meeting in a foreign-style building, adopting measures whose validity is in the keeping of the future.

Had I walked these streets in 1840 under the muzzle of the British guns, as now, I would have seen what I see now. Its water traffic, floating population and floating wealth, industrial and mercantile activity, and geographical situation still make it the lodestone of foreign commerce. It is still a city of almost inhuman hovels, and unearthly streets and highways, and of gruesome shambles, human filth, avid vanity, immeasurable disdain, and exquisite bigotry. At the commencement of a great revolution of which I was witnessing only the infant efforts it is still to the West an unwon battlefield. It has proved itself worthy of the sharpest wit of the foreign trader, the best steel of the Christian missionary, the envoy's finest invectives. Although raked by foreign lead and ball, cowed by foreign blades and muzzles, its pride is still invincible. Canton, the mother of the unchanging Chinese peasantry of America and other Pacific lands, remains the capital of the dominant spirit in the Chinese. And it is under foreign guns.

The British are being laughed at here in Canton and at Hongkong by outsiders. The question is: Are they right or are they wrong in their past-century attitude to Canton? The long contempt of the people of Canton for merely presumptuous authority such as their officials appointed from Peking have often admitted, and their ignoring of law other than themselves, is shown in the vicissitudes as well as confessions of these officials, including viceroys whose yamens have been periodically assaulted, whose lives have been periodically attempted. The turbulent pride and wrath of the Cantonese have always fretted against the yamen walls. In this and in the risings against the rule claimed over them and against the temples, the spirit of the law that is themselves appears. They seem to say, "The viceroys, the rule, the temples—they are our own; we make them and we destroy them."

In all China this feeling has not existed as at Canton. It may exist in all branches and divisions of the race, and in that possibility no doubt lies the mystery of its political future. In China Canton is the throne of the law that is the people themselves. So secure is the seat of the people's rule in China that usually foreigners acquainted with the Chinese often feel as confident of order and rule when the Chinese are without a viceroy or governor as when with one.

In Canton, when the people rise up *en masse*, or when the rulers are at variance with the people, there is a neutral power that equalizes all forces. It is the people harnessed, and is known as the "Seventy-two Guilds and Nine Charitable Institutions." This is the force that now makes Canton leaderless and anonymous. It is now in fact *the Republic* so far as Canton is concerned.

But Canton is a menace to the reform movement. It has allowed its anonymous piratical hosts to unite in a revolutionary army that is usurping the Government and is only held in control of the "Seventy-two Guilds and Nine Charitable Institutions" by a leash of money. It is this situation over which the British hold their guns, the mob of 1830 and 1840 armed and enthroned. Here is the first struggle of the whole Chinese Republic with lawlessness and anarchy. This situation is keeping the telegraphs between London, Hongkong, Canton, Nanking, and Peking busy. Outsiders laugh, but those having in their hands the fate of this people and of the Revolution and Republic are troubled. They are troubled over Canton the gipsy queen and the mother of revolution.

CHAPTER XXIV

ALONG THE COAST WITH A REBEL GENERAL

CANTON is the Capital of, and dominates, both the province of Kuangtung in which it is situated and the province of Kuanghsi joining it on the west. The eight principal piratical leaders control the whole delta of the West and Pearl rivers, and a region extending fifty miles inland behind Canton. They are administering the region with considerable success. "Lamp-Chimney" Lay is running Honam Island and actually cutting off some heads in suppressing piracy. In Canton perhaps 70 per cent. of the Republican leaders and office-holders in the new organization are Christian-educated, and except for the piratical army this element is on top here and therefore throughout the provinces.

The opposite element is on top in the province of Kuanghsi, where the type of leader that has sprung up is represented to be that of a Triad chief, or arch blackmailer and robber. What the class that governs there is like is shown in one leader who enticed a community of lepers into his power, and under pretence of feeding cut off their heads to be rid of them. In some places this controlling class is opposed by the established militia, and in others by revolutionist bands, each domineering its selected region, holding towns and cities, possessing itself of tax stations and levying on all traffic.

On the east of Canton the piratical party is trying to extend its power by getting control of the forts toward the sea. If it attains this, it will further intimidate the Republic in Kuangtung and will be able to menace the Provisional Government at Nanking.

Before leaving Canton I was rowed up the Pearl River by a boat-woman with a baby on her back, against the tide, and to the sound of vespers on the salt junks—vespers of tom-toms beat to the water spirits. In passing this fleet lying at anchor we were crossed by other boats rowed by mischievous boat-girls. We passed where the junks were thickest, under gay boat-sterns, through villages of boats laughing in storms of gay, fluttering streamers and floating bits of red tissue paper. Canton was ready for its own New Year's merrymaking.

The next day I made my exit from Canton amid the New Year's explosions of untold thousands of fireworks, for me, an American, turning Canton into a city of a hundred Fourths of July. It is a gay and airy rebuke to the pall of heavy tragedy which the British lay upon Shameen, and in which the serious and conservative British Consul, Mr. Jamieson, withstands the gentle banterings of his international colleagues. They are prepared to see him lose face when the British bulldog is obliged to let go at Shameen and the soldiers and guns move out to the sound of the Cantonese republican titter. But the game is not yet finished. "The Seventy-two Guilds and Nine Charitable Institutions" and the "pirates" are just beginning to try conclusions with each other. The old Consul is waiting to see the last cards. From every dooryard on the river front, and every deck above the water, firecrackers are swelling, bursting, spitting, as though each and every deck and door has had an importation of Kilkenny cats. The celebration seems great enough to make it appropriate both for the New Year and the inauguration of the whole Republic of China.

We put to sea—the Republican sea. The baby "Flowery Republic" has not taken possession of its sea; not even a junk is visible. As I looked shoreward I thought to myself: "I am sailing abreast a land having no less than 300,000,000 people—300,000,000 newborn as Republicans." Canton had but 1,250,000 of them. *En route* North I was passing in review scores of millions more aspiring to a heritage such as has been mine from birth.

Imagination tells me these millions are there in the sunshine and the mist, in the night and in the day. But not all of them. Both imagination and actuality show me that one of the 300,000,000 or more is aboard ship—a slight, near-sighted Chinese, like a Cantonese, in the guise of foreign clothes, with an English travelling-cap and spectacles. I must say something of him, for he is the link in the story of the "gipsy queen." He is a general under the Republican Provisional Government at Nanking, and has just come from a serio-comic adventure with the piratical chiefs of the region between Hongkong and

Canton. He is carrying to Nanking recommendations for putting down the pirates that are strangling the Canton Republic. He has been a student at the Military Institute of Virginia, the West Point of the South where Stonewall Jackson was trained, and an alumnus of the real West Point. Thus the spirit of Commodore Kearny and of the first American India Squadron that joined Britons to fight the Canton pirates, is come back from Kearny's own land to fight for him and the British tars whose deeds are written on the same monument in Happy Valley, Hongkong. Favoured by the opportunities offered trained soldiers under the Chinese Republic, he has risen to be a general in Kuangtung, and is in command of the Tiger Hill fort in the direction of Kowloon—an important strategical position. He has been approached by the pirates and asked to turn over his fort and command to them, and the relations between the regular military and the piratical forces have reached a point of rupture.

General Ping, as I will call him, said that Wang Ho-tsun—General Wang—was the principal pirate leader. It was he who led 3000 men to Canton from Waichou, at the time of the revolt.

"But the worst of all the robber chiefs," said he, "is Yang Man-fu, with whom Wang is associated. The former came to me and demanded to have command of the Tiger Hill fort. I was not ready to fight him, so I parleyed, telling him that I could not turn over the command without orders from my superiors, and that I would have to consult with them. He contented himself with taking four of my mountain-guns, together with about 100 shrapnel shells, an act that I could not prevent. My men are new-style troops and can fight three times their numbers of robbers. But to fight now would mean the destruction of the fort.

"The pirates or robber troops number altogether 50,000," said he. "Their leaders in some cases draw pay from the province for full battalions of 600 when they have actually only about 100 men in each battalion. In this way one leader will squeeze $3000 (gold value) per month. They will have to be punished and their men disarmed. This can be done if the Provisional Government will accept my plans. General Ling in charge of the new-style troops in Canton, 3000 or 4000, and myself, could assemble a round 10,000 reliable troops. My plan is this: the Tu Tu, or Governor-General, Chen, at Canton is afraid to take hold of the situation, and it would be best to supersede him. I am going to recommend that a new man be appointed at Canton, which will make it necessary for the piratical leaders to call on him to pay their respects. When they come to make their calls they can be arrested and punished for extortion, coercion of the people and officials, and other crimes, by our troops. Our troops will be strong enough then to execute the worst leaders and disarm their men."

"That is an old game in China," said I, "the superseding of one official by another in order to force enemies to come forward and show their loyalty, and after thus inveigling them into the trap, to seize, condemn, and kill them. These pirate chiefs must be aware of your intentions, as they have played at that game before, and would not overlook so simple a trick."

"That's true; they are suspicious of me and are watching me, but what can they do?"

The plan was invulnerable. As a trick in the official cardbox of Eastern Asia its antiquity has proved it so. A Chinese traitor may decline to pay his respects to his newly appointed superior, but not without confessing his disloyalty. As the years go on, there will be much discussion as to what the Chinese Republic is. It seemed to be prophetic that in Canton New China started with the same old trick, and the Republic worked out its problem on the same old lines as in the piratical past.

In my observation in China few large national or international questions come up that are not in some way connected with or influenced by the old and chronic situation respecting the Cantonese populace—China's first Republicans. In this situation, involving foreigners and Chinese alike, there is a picture of what is to be the future of the Republic. I had my first impressions of this region of political and social romance from books. The magic names of Boca Tigris, Whampoa, the Bogue, and Barrier forts, and Shameen, were now real.

The battle-ground of the independent Chinese spirit delineated in these names had in time brought forth the now typical far-eastern political situation, involving races and nations in all the national jealousies and conflicts that are the principal features of the life of Eastern Asia.

Having seen and heard at Canton the foreign side of this crisis in the Canton Republic and the situation of the British Consul and his critics, so intimately a part of the

Republic of all China, and having heard direct the inside story of the Chinese, I had now a personal interest in the way it worked itself out. General Ping presented his recommendations to President Sun Yat-sen at Nanking. The Provisional Government at Nanking was unwilling at the moment to attempt coercion of the piratical forces, which forces claimed to be the representatives of the Republic. General Ping's plan was disapproved by President Sun Yat-sen, and he returned to Kuangtung to witness worse happenings.

The piratical leaders were aware of conspiracies to disarm them, and they organized a revolt. Governor-General Chen Chun-ming called them together and proposed a gradual reduction of their forces. He told them that the Republic was established, the people had returned to civil pursuits, and that the next thing was the disbanding of the troops. He asked the commanders one by one to state how many they could disband. Several agreed to reduce their forces, 300 and 500, and so on, as the case might be, in a certain proportion to the total unit each commanded. In authority outside the East Gate of Canton was the pirate chief, General Wang, called by General Ping the worst of the lot. When asked how many men he could disband, he replied, "Five hundred."

"But you have five thousand men, can you not disband more than five hundred?" he was asked.

What General Ping expected took place. The proposal was repulsed by General Wang, who retorted, "Yes, I'll disband all of them," and left the Governor-General's yamen in a rage, before he could be intercepted.

The fat is in the fire.

By March 8, 1912, leading Republicans are discouraged by the difficulties confronting the regime at the Governor-General's yamen and its inability to cope with the situation. On March 9, when General Wang walks out of the Governor-General's yamen, all the shops in Canton are reported closed. Next day the Governor-General sends his own soldiers to replace the troops to be disbanded. Civilians are fleeing from the City. When Governor-General Chen's men sent to replace the pirate soldiers which it was expected General Wang might disband, reach the Canton East Gate, they are not allowed to pass. They are told that "here General Wang is in command," that "other troops will not be allowed here," and that "any who attempt to come will be killed."

Eight thousand piratical troops and mutineers are in revolt, and the entire piratical army of 20,000 is unreliable. Four days of disorders and guerilla-fighting ensue, throwing the region into a theatre of war and bringing about martial law. Canton Republic is now having its real baptism of blood, and seems to deserve just as good blood and as much of it as the Viceroyalty has had in ages past. The foreign gunboats, especially the British and French, " clear for action,"—a British gunboat taking position nearest the foreign electric-light plant after a stray bullet has struck the British camp on Shameen. Barricades are erected between the regular or loyalist troops and the piratical army. The latter comes under the domination of the leading pirate chief Luk Lam-ching, who is reinforcing. The pirates have pushed disorder to the neighbourhood of the Admiralty, and on March 12 Luk Lam-ching's men capture the Bogue forts surrendered to them by other mutineers. Then arming themselves from the Arsenal, they take the Admiralty building.

On March 10, when Governor-General Chen Chun-ming's men march out of the East Gate, three of them are killed. By March 13, after three days' attack by the Governor-General's troops along the line of barricades, there are hundreds of casualties.

In the excitement the foreign partisans in the defence controversy at Shameen and in the districts sheltering foreigners have forgotten their differences. On March 12, sixty-three native girls from the Wesleyan Mission escape by British gunboat to the steamer *Fatshan* and go to Hongkong. The British Consul reports to Hongkong the capture of the Bogue forts and takes measures to safeguard all British subjects. Missionaries are ordered to quit Canton. The steamers *Honam* and *Fatshan* carry 3000 passengers of all nationalities to Hongkong, and several steamships are prepared to leave on instant notice. All the foreign gunboats are prepared for action, their men armed in a way strikingly like that of the palmy days of universal piracy a century before, when hand-to-hand fighting was the practice.

At evening the British Consul recommended the British vessels to put out all lights on recommencement of firing from the Bogue forts.

By March 13 there are 400 Indian infantry and Yorkshire Tommies and 100 French sailors encamped on Shameen, with perhaps 1000 bluejackets afloat on twelve international gunboats. There is one additional German gunboat coming up from Hongkong. The British gunboat *Kinsha* damaged by shot shifts her anchorage, and the *Moorhen* has her awning and a spar bullet-torn at her post commanding the electric-light station. Several missionaries narrowly escape bullets. On March 14 shots reach Shameen. Mission houses in outlying regions are hit, and two American ladies make an unsuccessful attempt to leave Canton in a motor-boat. A launch from the U.S. gunboat *Wilmington* tries to rescue them, but is unable to proceed on account of a hail of bullets. Three American gentlemen, including the Vice-Consul, Mr. Hamilton Butler, join the two ladies, and all reach safety.

Five pirate leaders are reported combined to resist disarmament, and their forces are estimated at 28,000. Luk Lam-ching directly controls 10,000 and commands the situation by holding the east end of the City, the Bogue forts, and also Honam Island, staunchly defended by "Lamp-Chimney" Lay. With these forces and advantages Luk challenges the Governor-General to fight him in the open. The Governor-General, with perhaps 20,000 foreign-drilled Cantonese troops under General Ling and aided by a fleet of gunboats, drives Luk's lines back in the vicinity of the Canton-Kowloon railway station, when General Wang for mysterious reasons flees to Hongkong, but nothing decisive is gained by the Governor-General.

March 15 is devoted to the execution of 200 of the piratical element by the Governor-General's troops, near Shameen. Next day, when the two parties are facing each other, the Governor-General insists upon resigning. Luk Lam-ching on his side addresses the merchants and says that if the "People's Army" fails to obtain a victory over the Government in power in Canton he will shell Shameen and precipitate foreign intervention. This is the true character and disposition of the Canton and Kuangtung revolutionists. On March 17 and 18 a few shots are fired, and on the 19th the Governor-General's forces attack Luk Lam-ching, who replies vigorously. They take all the forts at three points on the river—Yuhu, Whampoa, and Fumun—after a long cannonade, principally by the Chinese gunboats. The Governor-General's troops under General Ling are now in control of Canton.

On March 26 the British withdraw their reinforcements, including the artillery, leaving only the original

100 Baluchistan infantrymen on Shameen. The Republic at Canton has proved itself only the Empire.

The staid British Consul was right.

Peace was restored for the time being by paying off the soldiers of General Wang who had precipitated the outbreak and giving them ten dollars (gold value) each for their rifles. The sequel to General Ping's recommendations came a month later, April 25, 1912, when Sun Yat-sen arrived in Canton with the object of reconciling its warring elements. Governor-General Chen Chun-ming fled secretly by night to Hongkong, leaving letters of resignation addressed to the heads of the army and navy, and to the President of the Provincial Assembly. He pointed out that he had not sought the office of Governor-General and felt himself unequal to the task. He could not undertake to return, unless in a smaller capacity in the army. He saw an opportunity to shift the office back upon the shoulders of his predecessor Hu Han-wen, now Sun Yat-sen's secretary, and escape the network of Canton plot and conspiracy.

Hu Han-wen was appointed Governor-General by the City fathers, about 160 of them representing the "Seventy-two Guilds and Nine Charitable Institutions," and Chen Chun-ming was appointed chief of the military forces. This was the belated opportunity for executing the plan of General Ping, and at least two leaders of the revolt were seized and beheaded.

Following his reception in Canton the Cantonese gave Sun Yat-sen a feast at which any toast to President Yuan Shih-k'ai was omitted. Sun Yat-sen pointed out to the proud Southerners that if the disorders were not arranged in Kuangtung the Northerners would assume the aggressive against them and would march upon Canton.

All this illustrates my point that hardly any important questions are raised in China that are not affected by Canton. Canton, by refusing to recognize President Yuan Shih-k'ai and defying the authorities of Nanking, was interfering with the amalgamation of the North and South. By its local warfare it threatened to precipitate the foreign intervention at the very start-off of the United Republic. But most important of all it emphasized this fact, namely, that the obstacle to change and reform in China is a Chinese one. The delusion that the obstacle was Manchu is already forgotten.

CHAPTER XXV

WHEN NANKING FELL

HAD I been a revolutionist marching on Nanking I would have taken the same route that I now took as a war correspondent. It was the highway of the Shanghai revolutionists. After the revolt of Nov. 3, 1911, and the turning over of the troops to the revolutionists next day, those troops stationed at the Wusung forts and other places along the river Huangpu formulated an expedition against Nanking. They proceeded by the Yangtse River, the Shanghai-Nanking Railway, and the Grand Canal to Chingkiang. They had three lines of communication and supply, and gathered up reinforcements at Suchow and elsewhere as they proceeded. I took the middle line in now tracing the scene of the events leading to the establishment of the Republican capital at Nanking.

From Chingkiang, the revolutionist base at the meeting-place of the Yangtse River and the Grand Canal with the Shanghai-Nanking Railway, there are straggling lines of hills that lead thirty-five miles to Purple Hill, newly made famous by the establishment of the "Flowery Republic."

The stage is being set for scenes that make Nanking the wonder of the world—scenes which conclude the capture of the greatest of the world's empires by the Republican idea. It is the greatest city of the Yangtse, and spectacular events have for weeks been dinning in the ears of the world its strategical and political importance. It is the real revolutionary crucible. This was the last viceregal post of Tuan Fang, whose head at the time to which I now refer is still on his shoulders, but cut from his shoulders will soon be on its way to Wuchang, for presentation to President General Li Yuan-hung. The famous ex-Minister of War, Tieh Liang, is Tartar General here. The refugee Viceroy of Wuchang, Jui Cheng, who slipped in the night from the grasp of the Wuchang revolutionists, has stopped here for a few hours in his flight. Tsen Chun-hsuan, appointed to co-operate with Tuan Fang in Szechuan, also stopped here in his flight and made up his mind that he was a revolutionist. Admiral Sah Chen-ping, after leaving Hankow with his mutinous fleet, withdrawing down stream, has been reported by the forts here, and on the eve of the revolutionists' capture of Nanking his late squadron has been threatened in its passage by the loyalist troops.

Foreign warships are gathering. Having heard that the revolutionist movement from the Huangpu is under way, the British Vice-Admiral Winsloe aboard the *Alacrity* and the German Vice-Admiral von Krosig on his ship *Leipsig* leave Hankow during one of the heaviest bombardments there, for Nanking. During Nov. 4, Rear-Admiral Murdock, American, has landed 200 marines at Shanghai and is soon at Nanking aboard the flagship *Rainbow*. The Japanese and other foreign naval forces are present.

Following the Wusung, Shanghai, and Chingkiang troops come the foreign correspondents from Shanghai, with their field dress, pencils and cameras. They seek horses and other means of getting to the "front," and are forming communications with the telegraphs over the immense distances around the city of Nanking. These distances include the foreign warships in the river, the foreign consulates, missions and viceroyal offices within the walls of Nanking, and the hills outside the City where Imperialist and revolutionist troops are taking up their positions. A little later on they promise the world a Waterloo which never comes off, but which promise nevertheless informs the world that the correspondents are present and the carnage may begin.

On Nov. 6 the Throne at Peking instructs Viceroy Chang Jen-chun not to oppose the revolutionaries, and Chang Chien, the President of the Provincial Assembly, consults General Chang Hsun, commander of the Imperialist troops, as to a compromise in order to avert battle. He fails. The Manchu Tartar General, Tieh Liang, also refuses to accept the Throne's instructions to Viceroy Chang Jen-chun, and the Viceroy is in a delicate position. He is in so delicate a position that the war correspondents publish throughout the world that he has "died by his own hand," an event which does not transpire but which they never deny.

Internal Nanking is revolutionary and the loyalty of the Imperialist troops is problematical. On Nov. 8 at

8 p.m. revolutionists estimated at 100 invade the Chinese City in Nanking and attack Viceroy Chang Jen-chun's yamen, where most of them are killed or wounded, and the rest disperse. Next day at 6 a.m. about 200 prisoners quartered near the yamen revolt and make a second attack. They too are suppressed, losing a fourth of their number killed, and their quarters are burned. As if by concerted plot there is an attack by revolutionaries under General Hsu Shao-cheng at Wulingkuan, outside the South Gate of Nanking, and an attempt is made by them to capture ammunition and enter the City. It is frustrated.

Nanking is now ready for revolution. The Provincial Assembly commands the Viceroy to act upon the Throne's edict and prevent the suppression of revolt and the passing of the City to the Republic. It has been a long time since Nanking has witnessed such scenes as now occur. Not since the T'aiping Rebellion, a half-century before, has this City had such excitement. It is the time of gloom, panic, and flight at Peking, and Nanking follows its example. Both Chinese and Manchus are fleeing. The City's gates are closed, but the people make their way over the walls and join those from the suburbs. The City learns of the revolutionary attack at Wulingkuan.

The foreign residents are leaving the City or gathering at their consulates. During Nov. 9 the German warship *Tiger* lands ten marines to bring the German Consul and German subjects out of Nanking, an example followed by the other Powers, Great Britain, Japan, and the United States.

After the morning hours of November 9 no fighting occurs in or around Nanking, but early in the day General Chang Hsun's soldiers dismantle the military wireless station and warn the operators to leave or be killed, and the latter disperse in disguise.

By November 10 something approaching a state of terror exists. The situation is that the City gates are closed upon an internal revolutionary storm. The Imperialist troops have suppressed two revolts and one attack, and their General, Chang Hsun, surrounded by his old-style troops, has risen to supremacy over the mild scholar-Viceroy Chang Jen-chun, and the half-hearted Manchu General Tieh Liang, whose discretion, since he has seen the fate of Jui Cheng and other Manchus, has got the better of his valour. "If the revolutionaries wish my life they can take it," says the old Viceroy. "I cannot comply with their wish that I should hand over the City, but I am willing to obey the Throne's edict. I cannot even send out my few valuables and my wife to Shanghai, Chang Hsun refuses a pass."

The Manchu garrison of approximately 10,000, together with General Chang Hsun's troops, dominate the City's population, approximating 150,000. Every available Manchu from the age of fifteen years to sixty years is drafted into service, and General Chang Hsun commandeers all available supplies to withstand siege. By midday his soldiers are looting Government schools and searching for and executing queueless men from the South Gate to Hsiakuan on the Yangtse. Students who have long doffed their queues are hiding in terror. It is estimated that half the population of the City and outlying suburbs has decamped and is making its way into the country, for the most part in a long procession down the Shanghai-Nanking Railway, toward Chingkiang.

Within a small area inside the walls of Nanking 150 dead bodies, among which are those of women and children, are counted. General Chang Hsun has placed guards along the entire Great Street through Nanking and Hsiakuan to the Yangtse River, and on Pei-chi-ko—a solitary high hill near the middle of the vast walled enclosure of Nanking—is guarding Viceroy Chang Jen-chun and Tartar General Tieh Liang. To this strategic place, surrounded by fields and affording a view of the outlying country, they have retired for safety. The hillside is dotted with Imperialist patrols.

By Nov. 11 General Chang Hsun is master of Nanking, and Viceroy Chang Jen-chun and Tartar General Tieh Liang are virtually prisoners.

Next day the revolutionists in military council at Suchow admit defeat in the attempt to capture Nanking by strategy. They testify to the heavy hand laid upon them by General Chang Hsun by offering $200,000 for his head, or $500,000 to induce his officers not to resist as commanded by the Throne at Peking.

On Nov. 13 the American, British, and German naval commanders pronounce Nanking untenable for foreigners and withdraw their guards from their consulates, which are closed. On Nov. 14 General Chang Hsun summarizes his achievements. He has beheaded 400 men connected with the revolutionist outbreak of November 8 and 9, established military law and a new government, making himself Military Director. As to his plans, he says: "I must be loyal to my Emperor. In suppressing the rebels I will not only resist them if they attack Nanking, but will lead my troops to Chingkiang, Suchow, and Shanghai. It is my intention to win back these places for the Emperor and wipe out all enemies. I have 20,000 soldiers of one mind. I have all the power in Nanking in my hands."

This is the rise of the only star of Manchu hope in all the width and breadth of revolutionary China. Chang Hsun the fire-eater and braggart is the only general of the Empire who has successfully stood his ground in the presence of revolt. He appears for the time being like a Gibraltar in the midst of forces that are breaking up the Empire.

The plans for the movement against Nanking crystallize (November 12) when General Hsu Shao-cheng, newly elected Military Governor of Nanking, and General Commander of the United Forces of the Republic, leaves Shanghai for Chingkiang to prepare the advance. The severity of General Chang Hsun in suppressing the revolutionists within Nanking results in meetings in the Arsenal at Shanghai to form plans to assassinate him. On the night of Nov. 13 three revolutionists from Wuchang address one of these meetings. Nine women with foreign-style coiffure attend, of whom four deliver addresses. A score of "Dare to Die" recruits volunteer for the task of entering the city of Nanking.

Early on November 13, thirteen war-craft, lately the squadron of Admiral Sah Chen-ping, assume the revolutionist flag at Chingkiang and place themselves under revolutionist orders. The Military Governor of Chingkiang reported to the Shanghai Military Government that the said Governor "led a guard of honour with a musical band to welcome them in person; all the naval forces have been paid double wages as an encouragement to the men. Their coal supply has been replenished in preparation for a united assault to be directed against Nanking, for the punishment of Chang Hsun and his rebellious troops."

Eighteen guns are sent from Shanghai by the Yangtse to Chingkiang, and troops arrive from Hangchow in Chekiang. On Nov. 14 these begin leaving by rail and by boat vía the Yangtse and the Grand Canal for Chingkiang. Chingkiang is a scene of marvellous military confusion as the recruits pour in among the old regiments *en route* westward. Suchow troops towed by steam launches pass out of the Grand Canal at Chingkiang and up the Yangtse toward Nanking. In addition the Governor of Suchow sends 400 " Dare to Dies " and a battery of artillery. Nanking has become a theatre of war by this time, and the British staff of the Shanghai-Nanking Railway removes from Nanking to Chingkiang.

The last troops for the expedition against Nanking leave Shanghai during Nov. 17, when 1500 depart amid scenes of enthusiasm at the railway station. In two days nearly 3000 have departed. General Hsu Shao-cheng continues from Chingkiang the advance by three lines, which order he has observed from Shanghai. He sends the main column of 5000 by the centre along the railway squarely upon Nanking. Two thousand move by the south, and the hills, against Purple Hill, and a similar force goes by the Yangtse towed by launches and convoyed by two gunboats which cover its landing and advance.

On Nov. 14 inside Nanking, Viceroy Chang Jen-chun, Tieh Liang, and Chang Hsun issue a joint proclamation saying that the leaders and banditti have been suppressed and that those fooled into believing in the rebels can clear themselves of guilt by destroying their rebel flags, otherwise they will be punished. The Viceroy issues another proclamation ordering the merchants to open their shops and the City gates to open at the ordinary hours, while General Chang Hsun issues a proclamation establishing the old order of things, such as would set Nanking back into the ante-reform era. He sent 1000 men to oppose the revolutionists on the railway between Lungtan and Kaotse, 25 miles away, but his men retired after a repulse. At night the revolutionists ordered up five war-vessels from Chingkiang to hold in check any possible movement by General Chang Hsun.

General Chang Hsun's scouts fall back on their hill position, around Purple Hill, and the wicked old fellow begins to rise to the best that is in him. He has been accused of " tall talk " in his boast of marching on Chingkiang, Suchow, and Shanghai, and recovering them for his Emperor. Report says he cannot read and he cannot write, that he cannot make a diagram or use a map. But he can understand a country when he sees it, and if he can himself scout the Yangtse Valley to Shanghai he might lead an army there. He is a good leader, all that is in him shows, but he cannot do everything himself. Among his troops he has not a single officer who knows the country. He is training his officers to scout when his antagonists move up from Chingkiang and occupy the country. He finds that instead of an advance he is to withstand a siege.

It takes the revolutionists a week to cover 35 miles from Chingkiang to General Chang Hsun's outposts around Purple Hill. On Nov. 23 a letter comes to Viceroy Chang Jen-chun and Tartar General Tieh Liang from the Governor of Suchow, Chang Teh-shan, in command of the secondary revolutionist base, asking them to ensure General Chang Hsun's non-resistance.

Wu Ting-fang gives official warning to the foreign consuls at Shanghai of the early bombardment of Nanking.

On Nov. 24 the advance is announced, and two days later battle begins. This the "Waterloo" of correspondents. The revolutionists have perhaps 13,000 troops. General Chang Hsun the Imperialist in a City wholly revolutionist has perhaps 5000 of his own men, of whom 600 have deserted in a body. He is obliged to hold Purple Hill because it commands the City.

Foreign spectators are sprinkled in a semicircle from the West City in Nanking around to Hsiakuan on the north, and eastward all the way to Chingkiang. Missionaries are watching their homes and schools, foreign marines are watching the consulates, the foreign warships are observing the nature of the military contest, the foreign correspondents are watching everything. "Waterloo" is to take six days. The watchers peer as it were into the pit where the Chinese "Napoleon" with really less than 5000 soldiers keeps down 50,000 revolutionist sympathizers, protects foreign life and property, guards 23 miles of City walls, and holds positions three miles into the hills to the East for his Emperor.

In the excitement of the revolutionist attack an engineer of the Shanghai-Nanking Railway, a foreign military attaché, and a war correspondent take a locomotive from Chingkiang and run up the railway toward Nanking, carried away with the excitement incident to the fighting. Thinking they ought to take someone along, they load ten revolutionist soldiers on the tender. They thus inadvertently make themselves violators of the neutrality of the railway, for they take the revolutionist soldiers into the Imperialist lines. They get in, and get out again, and the next morning realize what they have done.

"Winkleson," says the war correspondent, "do you realize that we might all have been captured yesterday by the Imperialists that were just north of the railway line, our ten soldiers taken and executed by General Chang Hsun, and yourself made captive on the charge of being a combatant, and that you would have lost your job?"

"For Heaven's sake don't mention it," said the attaché. "I didn't think of it until last night, and I couldn't sleep."

During Nov. 27 revolutionists are bombarding General Chang Hsun's position, after which they temporize over the necessity of assaulting Purple Hill, and after five hours' deliberation are persuaded to make attacks from two directions. Much powder is being burned and much shot wasted without any great damage. Chang Hsun's General, Feng, commanding between the South Gate and Purple Hill, has been trying to enlist recruits, but has lost many who have gone over to the revolutionists. General Chao, upon whom General Chang Hsun relies, with two fingers wounded, is operated on by the American missionary Dr. Macklin. He tells Dr. Macklin that he and his men are anxious to surrender but are afraid of the revolutionists, and he cannot leave his men in the lurch.

"You had better get together some leading men here at my house and have a conference about that," said Dr. Macklin—a plan that was soon followed.

On Nov. 30 General Chang Hsun goes himself to Purple Hill with reinforcements of 600 men. He wishes to hold the place against assault, but only a little while after his arrival the revolutionists attacking from two directions move successfully up the southern slope, driving back the Imperialists into the City. General Chang Hsun, when his troops are driven out, is forced back by his own men and leaves the position, it is said, in tears over his disappointment.

By next day General Li's artillerymen on Tiger Hill on the northern limits of Nanking have made an arrangement with the revolutionist artillery on Purple Hill by which they are to fire so as not to strike each other. General Chang Hsun sees that the fire is ineffective, and posts a detachment of Hunan infantry over his artillerymen to force them to score. They do so, and the revolutionists are taken by surprise and send a messenger in great alarm to ask what is the matter. But before their messenger returns a messenger from General Li's artillerymen brings word that it cannot be helped. They have to fire accurately on Purple Hill, where their shells will hit, because they are watched. At the same time the artillery-men propose that the two sides should fire at intervals of not less than three minutes, in turn, to allow each to take cover. This shows the whole nature of the " battle."

It is December 1, 1911, last day of " Waterloo." The revolutionists, foreign correspondents, and curious idlers wander singly and in groups among the debris of the Imperialist camp and trenches on Purple Hill. The revolutionist artillery—here and there a solitary Krupp gun—fires intermittently into Nanking, two shells at intervals striking Pei-chi-ko, where are Viceroy Chang Jen-chun and Tartar General Tieh Liang.

Nightfall comes, and the conference in Dr. Macklin's house has decided on surrender. Darkness finds Dr. Macklin and Chinese assistants alternately scraping the loose rubble with which the T'aiping Gate is barricaded, and peering over the parapet of the walls with the object of communicating with the revolutionists, and by the lanterns drawing fire from both sides in the effort to bring " Wellington " and " Napoleon " together — the age-old comedy of the peacemaker.

General Chang Hsun now has probably 2000 or 3000 soldiers that are still loyal to him—but a tenth of those which he claimed at the beginning when he defied the Throne's edict to the Viceroy ordering non-resistance. General Feng, General Chao, General Li, and all the other commanders have deserted him and are conniving with foreigners for the turning over of the City to his antagonists.

Striking the colours is an unknown thing to General Chang Hsun, likewise going over to the enemy, and plotting with missionaries and consuls for surrender. He leaves the City before dawn by the Hsiakuan Gate, his men finding their way across the river, at various points between Hsiakuan and places as far up as 30 miles.

Viceroy Chang Jen-chun finds refuge on a Japanese man-of-war. Tieh Liang accompanies him, and the two find their way to Japan. All that exists of the Chinese " Waterloo " is written in the Western Press. On Dec. 2 Dr. Macklin, Rev. Mr. Garritt, American missionaries, with Mr. Gilbert, American Vice-Consul, carrying the American flag, arrange between the willing forces of both sides for the transfer of Nanking from the hands of General

Chao, late Imperialist, to General Liang, revolutionist. The latter occupies Nanking, and immediately after, an accident occurs in the Tartar City, the domicile of the Manchu garrison, where a mine unexpectedly explodes, killing and wounding about 40 men. The revolutionists assume that it is the signal for attack upon them and begin killing and burning. When it is over, and the City has resumed its normal life, a Roman Catholic father knowing all the battleground says he has not seen more than 240 bodies. Mr. Stuart, the American missionary, a good observer, told me he thought there could not have been more than 300 people killed at the taking of Nanking.

Thus the last of the great cities in the Yangtse Valley to fall to the revolutionists inaugurates the capture finally by the Republican idea of the greatest of the world's empires.

Leaving the mean task of surrendering the City to his disloyal generals, who fall heir to a battery of six of his 3-centimetre Krupp mountain guns, among other things, General Chang Hsun moves northward to more friendly territory. He commandeers the rolling stock of the Tientsin-Pukow Railway, upon which he loads his men at Pukow. One hundred and fifty thousand dollars (silver) in bullion he dumps down in the train-yard at Pukow, under guard of 200 men, and instructs the Railway to forward it. Another body of soldiers comes along, claims it as arrears of pay, attacks the guard under sanction of the law that the man behind the gun does not have to wait for his pay, and helps itself. The troops move off, and the remainder disappears among camp followers and common coolies.

General Chang Hsun has before him the desolate famine region of North-eastern Anhuei, and must travel a road nearly 200 miles before he can find a suitable base. Revolutionaries with two guns are awaiting him at a point 30 miles up the railway at Pengpu, but warned by telegraph he stops the train, flanks the obstructing force and moves on, leaving 60 bodies around the station. When next heard of he is on the Anhuei-Shantung border with headquarters at Hsuchow-fu in Shantung, where he is undauntedly recruiting. He claims to have 20,000 men, and has about 12,000.

General Chang Hsun does not know what he is going to take or hold " for his Emperor," but he is a " stand-patter." He looms up in the history of Peking in December.

CHAPTER XXVI

SUN YAT-SEN EMERGES FROM OBSCURITY

DECEMBER 2, 1911, found no avowed Imperialists south of the great Yangtse River. By Dec. 5 the Shanghai and Nanking revolutionists, aided by General Huang Hsing, the forerunner of Sun Yat-sen, have selected Nanking to be the Republican capital and are assembling there authorities from the provinces. Tang Shao-yi, the envoy from Peking, has found at Wuchang no one to negotiate with, and on December 11 telegraphs of his departure for Shanghai.

By Dec. 14 the tentative Republican organization at Shanghai has been converted into a wider governmental organization and transferred to Nanking the Capital. Sun Yat-sen is selected as " First " President.

Tang Shao-yi, with suite, assistants, and servants, numbered at no less than 80, passes the Capital on Dec. 16, and next day reaches Shanghai. To safeguard the rights of the conservative Imperialist North he is accompanied by a score of representatives of various provinces, selected by Yuan Shih-k'ai to offset the revolutionist Assembly gathered at Nanking under which the peace negotiations are to be directed. In the Republican atmosphere under which the envoy Tang Shao-yi capitulates, they disappear.

Sun Yat-sen has left Singapore for Hongkong waters, and is in fact on the last lap of the last of his tours of the world. The dispatches say he is accompanied by " General Homer Lea " and is closely guarded. He is a mystery. He is vaguely known as a human shuttle that has moved for some years from colony to colony among those Western nations who have sheltered and encouraged their borrowed Chinese citizens and subjects. Shunning publicity, he has been at intervals since the Szechuan outbreak of September 1911 reported at Chicago, Paris, and Penang. He approaches the region where in his native land the aims of his life are to be realized. Not until December 25 does he come up the Huangpu from Wusung and disembark at the jetty in the foreign settlement of Shanghai. He is met by delegates representing the provinces.

The coming of the future President is very simple. He goes by motor car of a friend to the latter's residence in Bubbling Well Road.

Wu Ting-fang is naturally the first to call on Sun Yat-sen and offers him the Presidency of all China, nothing less, from Wu. Sun Yat-sen returns Wu Ting-fang's visit of state during the day. The plan is that Yuan Shih-k'ai shall be final President, and Wu Ting-fang has in mind the amalgamation of the southern independencies under the Provisional Presidency of Sun Yat-sen.

After the visit Sun Yat-sen establishes his residence in a foreign house, No. 408 Avenue Paul Brunat, closely patrolled night and day. The attention and respect which he commands greatly impress foreigners. Among his first callers are General Li Yuan-hung's delegates from the Wuchang Republic. His simplicity and confidence make him the centre of the republicans and revolutionists. There is nothing spectacular about him, unless it is his mysterious following. It was a fact noted by every interested person in Shanghai that in addition to the deputations of revolutionists and others who were present to greet him on his arrival there were a number of Japanese who became his secretaries and advisers. But the star in the galaxy of his satellites was "General Homer Lea." He had been repeatedly announced by the foreign dispatches as an adviser, in others as the designated chief of staff of the new Republic. He remained an unnecessary enigma to many foreigners and Chinese. Throughout Sun Yat-sen's term of office he was in close connection with him, disappearing from the stage of the Republic with the passing of Nanking as the Capital.

During Dec. 27 the provincial delegates at Nanking attending the revolutionist Assembly visit Sun Yat-sen in a body at Shanghai.

Two days later the revolutionist Assembly at Nanking formally elects Sun Yat-sen President of the Republic of China by 17 votes to one, and elects First Provisional Republican President Li Yuan-hung to be Vice-President.

The peace conference holds a meeting that forms the agreement for determining the future form of government by national conference.

A great banquet attended by 100 leaders of the re-

Sun Yat-sen

Nanking, February 1912.

To face p. 258.

volutionary movement in honour of Sun Yat-sen is held in the evening at the Palace Hotel.

Wu Ting-fang, the peace delegate who has forced the peace negotiations from the beginning, states " fourteen provinces have absolutely declared for the Republic. We control twelve divisions of the army ; two more are coming. We hold the entire navy. Two provinces remain Imperial and two are neutral. There is no Government in Peking. Yuan Shih-k'ai is the only representative of government there except the infant Emperor.

" The sooner the Powers recognize the real situation instead of clinging to harmful and intangible sentiment, the sooner will order be restored in China. Hesitation to recognize the Republican cause will certainly prolong the stagnation of trade and will be responsible for much bloodshed should fighting begin again." Wu Ting-fang at this time was still fighting for recognition by the Powers.

Sun Yat-sen states that the entire movement is united and that there are no serious differences. He looks upon the Revolution as the outcome of his plans and of more than fifteen years of his own revolutionary work.

" I consider it my duty," says he in a communication to his friends in the United States following his election, " to accept the Presidency. My policy will be to secure peace and a stable government by the promptest methods possible. My single aim is to ensure the peace and contentment of the millions of my fellow-countrymen."

The peace conference is disappearing, overshadowed by the " President." Its work is carried on, but it is henceforth directed from Nanking, and it is easy to see that it is not taken seriously by the Republican Government, and that the latter fully expects the Throne at Peking and Yuan Shih-k'ai to obey its demands.

About 2000 soldiers proceed from Shanghai to Nanking on the day of Sun Yat-sen's election, and military concentration at Nanking is an adopted policy, being carried out under General Huang Hsing.

CHAPTER XXVII

INAUGURATING A CHINESE PRESIDENT

EVENTS that are to sweep away the Manchu Throne finally and that make Nanking the centre of the world are now enacted. The revolutionist Assembly at Nanking overrides Wu Ting-fang, making more onerous the so-called peace conditions offered by him, and making all the more appropriate the coincidental action of Yuan Shih-k'ai in cancelling the authority of his envoy Tang Shao-yi as Peace Commissioner. The thing that is most necessary in all the world to be done is begun, when Sun Yat-sen goes to Nanking.

On Jan. 1, 1912, 5.30 p.m. he arrives at the Hsiakuan station at Nanking in a special train from Shanghai. Accompanying him are innumerable delegates, military officers, and last, the Press chorus, native and foreign. The Lion Hill forts nearest the station fire a salute. Revolutionist soldiery guards all the surroundings and extends over the whole route to the Viceroy's yamen, which last has been guarded by Imperialists under General Chang Hsun. This route has been the line of escape of Viceroy Chang Jen-chun and Tartar General Tieh Liang. Ten thousand soldiers are in line, and the route is packed in many places with the populace. It is silent—it does not know a Republic when it sees it. The crowds have never thought for themselves, so they do not know how to give outward expression on this occasion, nor do they know just why there should be any expression. When the inaugural party and the President-elect change their route, nothing happens—the crowds are lost in the night, no one mentions them.

At 6.15 p.m. Sun Yat-sen and the train and its people reach the Viceroy's yamen station, where are the burned buildings connected with the incident of the *émeute* of the prisoners (November 9, 1911). Sun Yat-sen's carriage stops between lines of guards, and in a few minutes there is a furore aboard, and a man hysterically protesting, screaming, weeping and struggling, is brought out and thrown into the station waiting-room and searched. It is the Chinese offering to the democracy of cranks. That fraternity has already had its Republican inauguration, when Sun Yat-sen, closely surrounded by guards, descends from the train and walks silently with bared head to a carriage waiting for him. It is growing dark. It is cold and wet, and there is a drizzling rain. A mounted escort led by trumpeters blowing a fanfare precedes and follows the carriage. The bodyguard, members of the inaugural party, and soldiers follow on foot the short distance to the yamen entrance.

The trumpeters lead the wonderful and glorious little inaugural procession through the throng held back by lines of soldiers, to the spacious and fantastically enclosed court before the Viceroy's yamen. It passes slowly under a quaint wooden p'ailow, or honorary arch, into the almost sacred enclosure from which the last representatives of the Manchus have fled, and from which, next to the last, Tuan Fang, departed by the long road of misadventure upon which he has now lost his head. This quaint p'ailow is an arch of triumph to the simple man of the people whom the people are about to hail as President. No gem-studded cloth of gold and martial banners such as hung from the arches of European conquerors hang from this graceful, quaint, and airy p'ailow of racing dragons, mazy eaves, and floating roofs. It is decorated with the emblem of the peaceable conquest of the Empire by the Republic—the white ensign—and with evergreens from the temples. The rainbow flag is also here, and the naval colours.

It is the evening of the first day of the new year 1912. Sun Yat-sen steps from his carriage and walks the long approach to the yamen leading under a succession of p'ailows and low gate-houses decorated in red paint and lacquer, but for the most part painted white and trimmed with evergreens illuminated by multicoloured electric lights. It is a union of Chinese phantasmagoria and Saxon New Year rite and ceremony. There is a dull glitter on the bayonets of the revolutionist soldiery as the President-elect passes, dressed in a plain khaki military suit with military cape, followed by his entourage.

The fanfare dies away and the horsemen dismount. The guards and the crowd disperse. Leaving the yamen entrance, there are two large courts, divided by gate-houses, and a third leads to a large reception- or audience-room newly papered and whitewashed and furnished with foreign stoves, into which room the party enters. Sun Yat-sen withdraws into a conference with General Huang Hsing, his military chief, and General Hsu Shao-cheng, commander of the expedition that took Nanking, and the leaders of the provincial delegates. Three hours' preliminaries succeed, pending the conclusion of which dignitaries and witnesses arrive in the old audience-chamber to be present at the inauguration.

Before about 100 spectators the inauguration begins. Sun Yat-sen takes oath as President of China. With great dignity and showing something of the strain which the responsibilities of the occasion have placed upon him, he pledges the restoration of peace, the establishment of government founded on the will of the people, and the dethronement of the Manchu rulers, in conclusion swearing to resign office when these are accomplished, in order that the people may elect a President of United China.

Mr. Ching, chairman of the Shansi provincial delegation, hands President Sun Yat-sen the Seal of the Provisional Military Government of the United Provinces of China. President Sun Yat-sen then reads his inaugural address, or proclamation, and the inauguration is concluded half an hour before midnight. This fact serves to date the Republic of China from the first day of the year 1912 and to mark the adoption by China of the Western calendar.

China's first presidential salute, "twenty-one guns," from Lion Hill, nearly five miles away, reaches the midnight listeners. A new Republic is written in the list of nations.

I have related the exciting events of the first month of Sun Yat-sen's Presidency as they affect Peking. The whirl and stir caused in Peking in January was worthy of the energy and vigour with which the new Government was inaugurated at Nanking.

There is now no armistice, it having expired 8 a.m. December 31, 1911, and fighting is going on before Hankow—a consideration that has to do with the promptness with which Sun Yat-sen has taken the oath of office near midnight instead of on the following day as originally intended. The governmental machine which gave the Republic the dynamic power that hustled the Imperialists at Peking was promptly set up.

President Sun Yat-sen made his military chief, General

Huang Hsing, of Hanyang and Wuchang fame, his Minister of War. Wu Ting-fang received the post of Minister of Justice combined with his duties as peace negotiator, while an entirely new man of European education, Wang Chung-huei, was made Minister of Foreign Affairs. Chen Chin-tao of the University of California, late Director of the Government Bank at Peking, late Vice-Minister in the trial Cabinet of Yuan Shih-k'ai, as Premier, is made Minister of Finance. All the important ministries are filled by the President with men of about his own age—most of them younger.

The oath taken by President Sun Yat-sen to dethrone the Manchu ruler is the ring of the lance upon Yuan Shih-k'ai's armour that causes the Lung Yu Empress Dowager to open her purse-strings in an attempt to replenish the Imperial war-chest ; also that causes Yuan Shih-k'ai to take that belligerent attitude on behalf of a monarchy, boasting that he believes he can hold the North until the South disintegrates. It is under these circumstances that Yuan Shih-k'ai declines Sun Yat-sen's offer of the Presidency, which offer is in effect a peremptory notification from the Republic to throw over the Manchus at once.

On January 5, President Sun Yat-sen and his Minister of Foreign Affairs, Wang Chung-huei, issue a manifesto to the Powers, the substance of which the President has read in his inaugural address. It is an indictment of the Manchus for responsibility for all the evils of the country, and a plea for recognition by the Powers and for admission into the family of nations.

Simultaneously with the manifesto of the Republican Government asking for recognition from the Powers is Yuan Shih-k'ai's action in laying before the representatives of the Powers in Peking the peace conference correspondence, in which he scores a point against the Republic—the foreign diplomats taking his view that the Republicans are in error.

The President Sun Yat-sen and Premier Yuan Shih-k'ai are now in communication respecting but one thing, namely armistice.

The effect of the pressure of the new machine of state on Peking is felt on Jan. 10, when the Republican Government offers in terms its demands for abdication. It is insistent, and forces a readjustment in relations with Peking. As a result of Yuan Shih-k'ai's reiterated repudiations by telegraph of the terms of the peace convention agreed to by his envoy, Tang Shao-yi, Wu Ting-fang at Shanghai announces that the Republican armies are prepared to march upon Peking, and President Sun Yat-sen announces that if the negotiations for peace fail he will take the field in person in the advance upon Peking. The renewal of the armistice Yuan Shih-k'ai secures through assurances that the Court accepts the principles of abdication.

The Republic at Nanking is going off with a hurrah. It has given official notification to the Powers of its organization and is extremely active and optimistic. The busiest department is the War Office. Minister of War Huang Hsing is organizing the reinforcement of Wuchang with General Li Tien-tai in command. Twelve Republican war-vessels are lying in the river off Hsiakuan, which the President in the ex-Viceroy's yacht reviews on Jan. 19. Canton troops are arriving at Shanghai, where some are held for the expedition to the North by sea, and others brought to Nanking for the advance up the Tientsin-Pukow Railway. On this latter line the Republican Army has crossed the Huai River and is only about 40 miles from General Chang Hsun's base at Hsuchow-fu.

A continued armistice is made impossible by Yuan Shih-k'ai's repeated repudiation of the so-called peace agreement, and in the deadlock President Sun Yat-sen reinforces the Republican foothold in Shantung. He sends to Chefoo two transports loaded with Cantonese troops and convoyed by a cruiser. The Republic is massing its military and has formulated magnificent plans to force the Manchus out of Peking, obtain recognition from the Powers, and borrow money.

On Jan. 22, a week after his first expedition to Chefoo and Tengchou, and when his second is about to land, President Sun Yat-sen gives out that he is absolutely convinced, as he has always been, of the success and righteousness of the revolt. "If we fail to secure peace and a stable government now," says he, "the responsibility must rest on Peking."

President Sun Yat-sen understands that the Manchus accepted his terms for abdication, and that after assuring him of this fact Yuan Shih-k'ai makes it a condition of abdication that the Republican Government shall dissolve two days after the abdication edict. The Republic is more stirred by this than it has ever been. It perceives the intention of the Throne to delegate its powers, and that it has in view abdicating, as it were, in favour of Yuan

Shih-k'ai. President Sun Yat-sen is convinced that the Imperial Clan and Yuan Shih-k'ai have in this plan the support of " outside influences." In fear of Japan the Republic sends its ultimatum to Peking, demanding full and complete surrender and abdication by the Emperor and the elimination of Yuan Shih-k'ai from participation in the Republican Provisional Government until after recognition of the Republic is obtained from foreign Powers. It is here that the threat to open fighting on Jan. 29, 8 a.m., on expiration of the armistice, is made.

CHAPTER XXVIII

FINANCING A "FLOWERY REPUBLIC"

WITH this magnificent plan of confederation and war it is a mystery where the Republican funds are coming from, and the Government in Nanking is obliged to solve the problem of a system of finance. Money has been contributed from Chinese revolutionary centres in foreign countries for revolt, but for governmental purposes larger sums are required. The Republic has not the legitimate sources of revenue of a State in rebellion, such as have the countries of Central and South America, for example. Her maritime customs are in the hands of the foreign Powers, and their revenues are all appropriated for the payment of China's foreign debts. Part of the native customs revenues are under the control of foreign creditors, as well as the revenues of railways and some industries. The provinces which followed President General Li Yuan-hung's appeal and revolted on their own responsibility with the view of confederation later are still in possession of all their sources of revenue, which in some cases is not sufficient for provincial requirements.

Revolutionary script has been printed at Wuchang from the first, and was begun at Shanghai (November 1911), where notes were issued payable on demand and signed by " M. Y. Sung, Manager of the China Bank, Agents for the Military Government." One side was in English and the other in Chinese. Another note put out at the same time promised to pay three months from date. These notes were widely accepted, but became so plentiful during the period of mobilization and nationalization of government at Nanking that the soldiers who received their pay in them had to dispose of them by force.

President Sun Yat-sen is determined not to embark on the dangerous policy of disposing of natural resources to foreign money-lenders, and to concessionnaires besieging his yamen, and the only visible source of revenue for the Central Republican Government appears to be the Chinese industrial companies. The Minister of War, General Huang Hsing, acting for all the military forces, now calls upon industrial companies to contribute to the Republican treasury. The China Merchants' Steam Navigation Company, one of the largest Chinese industrial concerns, is asked for $7,000,000. Fear of the Japanese, who assume premier place in the offer of a loan secured by it, prevents the hypothecation of this Company. The Hanyang Iron Works at Hanyang and the iron mines in the vicinity are next levied upon. Ironically enough, it is the Japanese who come forward to aid, and it is Japanese money loaned on these Iron Works and mines that the Republic accepts finally.

Finance is to the fore and is in advance of all other interests. Chen Chin-tao nominated Minister of Finance is only a nominal minister, and lives at the Astor House in Shanghai. He was to become later Yuan Shih-k'ai's Minister of Finance, and is the most wanted of all the ministers, unless it is War Minister General Huang Hsing. He is the most pulled and hauled and bandied about of these reformers whose ability is an acknowledged asset to New China. Chen Chin-tao had declined the post of Vice-Minister of Finance in the trial Cabinet of Premier Yuan Shih-k'ai. He was in Peking when first appointed by the revolutionists, and received anonymous warning to accept. He left his home, as previously mentioned, thinking himself unobserved, reached the Peking railway station, entered a coupé, locked himself in, and closed the curtains. When he arrived at Tientsin a card was thrust into his coupé with the written warning that his movements were watched, and again warning him to accept his appointment. Finding himself the object of equal attention from both parties in the Revolution, he turned round and went back to Peking by the next train.

The task of reorganizing China's finance is not an enviable one. The Chinese people have never recognized a national Government. There never has been in China a national domestic bond. There is no such thing within the Empire as national credit. More than this, the Republic has abrogated many taxes, and it is one of the principles of the Republic that the people have long been overtaxed. Valuable as are his talents and future services, Chen Chin-tao can do little.

The various departments of the Republican Government are finding their own funds, and they rely upon Sun Yat-sen, under whose leadership contributions from societies and individuals at home and abroad come in. He is the late financial agent of the Chinese Revolution, having started abroad in 1910 to collect funds for the revolt, which was then planned for April 1912. At Christmas 1911, when he landed at Shanghai he was received by the members of the Shanghai Republic as a valuable financial asset. It was believed that he actually had money or that he held in his grasp the reins of financial connections to vitalize the Revolution. As a matter of fact he did not bring with him the promise of any foreign loan, and upon his inauguration as President he has the same financial question that faces Yuan Shih-k'ai. He must get money from the Great Powers, and before this can be done the Republic must be recognized by them.

The fact that Yuan Shih-k'ai is unable to get a foreign loan encourages the leaders of the Republic to believe that once recognized, the bankers of the Great Powers will loan to the Republic. The whole question of finance is the life of the Republic. The vehemence with which it insists upon recognition is merely the gauge of its financial distress. Recognition to the Republican Government at Nanking means credit.

An illustration of the distress due to the pressure for money is the growing burden of mobilizing at Nanking for the advance on Peking. The budget at Nanking is approaching $1,000,000 daily. President Sun Yat-sen issues an appeal to the generals of the Imperialist Army calling upon them not to resist the Republican advance, which may be said to have resulted in the revolt of almost the whole Imperialist Army, since forty-six "generals" united in acceding to his prayer and gave their ultimatum to the Throne. This is a master-stroke of finance that immediately checks the rise of the war budget.

I was brought in contact with this financial question immediately I reached the Yangtse Valley. Wherever I went I met old friends of the revolutionary party whom I had known in North China. One of them, who had for some years made his home, for safety, in the Shanghai settlements, where he had been an official agent for progressive governors and viceroys of the provinces, came to my rooms in Shanghai to see if he could get a loan of $2,000,000 on the Kiangnan Arsenal at Shanghai. I had not seen him for about six years and my last recollection of him in Peking, where he wore the native dress of cap, queue, and gown, was as a rabid reformer expostulating against ancestor-worship, to the great distress of his venerable Confucianist father. He was now dressed entirely in foreign clothes, and with a thin pompadour looked like a German socialist.

"I represent General Li Ping-shu," said he, after brief salutations, "and I want to get $2,000,000."

"How are you going to get it?"

"I want to get it on the Arsenal," said he. "The Arsenal is worth a great deal of money, and that is a small loan for such a large asset. General Li Ping-shu can get money from the Japanese, but he would rather have it from the Americans and is willing to pay them more for it."

"But I am not a financier," said I, "how can I help you?"

"You can give me references."

"But we have no American bankers here."

"But you have financial agents here and an American bank."

"I can give you their names, but am not sufficiently acquainted with your affairs to give you recommendations."

With these names he went hopefully away. The fact was the Nanking and Shanghai Administrations were buttonholing every promising foreigner, they were catching at every financial straw. The only existing plan of financing the Republic was that of each province being responsible for all expenditures required or made within its limits. Kiangsu, the province in which Shanghai is situated, was responsible for the fleet. The Arsenal was its base. It was not strange that the Chinese did not want to mortgage it to the Japanese. Japan was acquiring a derisive international fame, such as England so long enjoyed in the rôle of the "honest broker." It was for the same reason that the China Merchants' Steam Navigation Company, which furnished the fleet with an auxiliary and was the Republic's *Merchant Marine*, was never finally mortgaged.

There are two views held in China: one that China is in dire need of money, the other that she is rich in her poverty for the reason that a country that believes that it does not need to borrow is invincible in its strength. Such might be the case with a foeless land, but not with China, surrounded as she is by alien, aggressive civilizations. The revolutionary revolt had now brought to an acute stage her foreign questions, of which the main question centred about money. The Republic was now fighting the same foreign questions as was the Empire. The Republican leaders were trying to minimize the importance of China's foreign questions, but these were her whole existence—a fact that was now about to be realized.

The state of China has hardly been realized even in the West. With its economic system on a plane so low that its masses are only a little above the level of actual subsistence, China is obliged to enact her part in the world upon the terms and with the pace set for her by the nations of the West whose prosperity and wealth have reached the zenith of national and human achievement. As the forces of the revolutionary Rebellion were gathering, the staying power of certain principles that had protected Chinese integrity and sovereignty by equalizing the interests of foreign Powers within her borders, was disintegrating. Equality of rights, the "Open Door," and the integrity of China's sovereignty and territory were being defeated in this by the special interests of two Powers, Japan and Russia. The United States of America, which had waged a battle on behalf of peace among the nations and freedom for reorganization and development for China, was defeated in Manchuria and Mongolia. The disintegration of the doctrines to which she secured the adherence of the Great Powers began in 1903 with the signing of offensive and defensive alliances between Japan and Great Britain and between Russia and France. The ultimate purpose of these doctrines was politically defeated by the results of the Russo-Japanese War and the renewal of the offensive and defensive alliances in 1905. America then sought to attain the ends still outwardly championed by the Powers, by means of financial alliances of those Powers and the industrial development of China for the advantage of all, and this was defeated by conventional terms signed between Japan and Russia, making paramount their political and special rights over their equal industrial and commercial rights.

The plan championed by the United States placed the weight of influence and control in the hands of the capitalistic nations of Great Britain, France, Germany, and the United States, leaving the non-capitalistic but military Powers, Russia and Japan, at what the latter took to be a political disadvantage. Although Russia and Japan had the two greatest capitalistic Powers, France and Great Britain, as their allies, they nevertheless dissented from the American plan, which had now been carried so far that a programme for financing China and bringing about her industrial regeneration by successive loans to her in large sums was adopted by the capitalistic Powers. Seeing that the success of this scheme would be a disadvantage to them on account of their inability to participate in it financially in such a way as to have a controlling interest, and that it would defeat their special and political rights, Russia and Japan dissented, and held their allies to their support to defeat the loan programme.

This was the political situation of China at the beginning of the revolutionary revolt. Loans to China approximating £60,000,000 were involved in the plans of the capitalistic Powers. When the revolt came, China could get on account from all sources barely £2,000,000, and soon nothing. The capitalistic Powers having great trade interests in China and holding China's bonds for past loans, would not subsidize war and rapine there.

Japan being the victor in the Russo-Japanese War, now pursuing an aggressive expansion, and being therefore obliged to keep open the way for her advance, was forced to secure an understanding with Russia on the new basis demanded by the policy of the capitalistic Powers. Since she was not a capitalistic Power and was without great moneyed influence, this was the only way in which she could arrive at equality of political influence. Having reached an understanding with Russia and secured agreement to a mutual line of action, arresting the loan project, and uniting the four Powers connected by offensive and defensive alliances, namely Russia and France, Great Britain and herself, Japan held in her hands the key to China's fate.

These facts have placed Japan in the position to play both sides in China's revolutionary Rebellion, where, posing as the "honest broker," she can take the customary commercial profit sanctioned by business morality in peace and war, or, under the sunshine of business bargaining, make political hay. It will be seen how terrible to Chinese reformers and patriots must be this prospect from a powerful and to them aggressive and irresistible nation like Japan.

The terrible leverage of Japan's power, fully appreciated by Japan and all her agents, arises from two causes : first, she has united the four Powers, Russia and France, Great Britain and herself, in the maintenance and extension of her political rights in Northern China and the arresting of the financial projects of the capitalistic Powers in China; and second, Yuan Shih-k'ai cannot borrow money because the capitalistic Powers will not subsidize war on behalf of a doomed Government, and Sun Yat-sen cannot borrow money because the Republic of China is not recognized by the Powers. The bankers will not loan to a Government not recognized by their own. The resulting advantages of her position make Japan the master of a helpless country.

It is necessary to keep in mind these facts in order to understand the tremendous burdens resting in each case with peculiar stress and travail upon the shoulders of President Sun Yat-sen and Premier Yuan Shih-k'ai. The Great Powers do not yet know what the outcome will be of a situation in which they see many tragic possibilities, but they feel, perhaps without exception, that the future is more clearly seen by Japan than by any other Government. One thing is certain, that the leaders on both the Imperialist and Republican sides cannot much longer endure the strain of this ominous fear. This is a confessed fact. President Sun Yat-sen, who was accompanied to Nanking by a group of Japanese secretaries and advisers, has gracefully dismissed them. Though befriended by Japan and the Japanese throughout his career, he is compelled by facts and circumstances to take measures of defence.

. . . .

It is the boast of present-day finance that war and peace are in its hands and that nations now settle their differences in terms of money. This is proving true in the internal differences of China, but only indirectly. Financial considerations are now dissolving into the greater considerations of the safety of the nation. President Sun Yat-sen and the Republican Government fear Japanese influence and assurances of its support at Peking. Premier Yuan Shih-k'ai, whose whole career has been that of an opponent of Japan, fears Japanese power in the Republic.

It is by finance and money interests under the name of trade, that foreign Powers have gained their ineradicable grasp upon China, and the time has now arrived in the affairs of the Empire and of the Republic when the situation is being taken advantage of by outsiders. The two sides are both so identified and opposed that one can be played against the other. Observers of the West who quarrel with the slothful stride which progress takes in

China, and the apparent perversity of nations there, may explain by the formula of this immemorial game in Asia and Eastern Asia the crisis at which the Republic and Empire have now arrived.

As I recapitulate those events at Peking coincident with and immediately preceding what is now going on at Nanking, I recall that an attempt has been made to assassinate Yuan Shih-k'ai, the arch-opponent of Japan and recognized by Japan as such, and also in the minds of many Manchus a doubtful friend of the Dynasty. The origin and motive of the attempted assassination are a secret mystery. Yuan Shih-k'ai and Prince Ching are clear respecting the situation, while the subordinate princes and other dissenters to abdication threaten to seek Japanese aid. The Lung Yu Empress Dowager is partially persuaded in the absence of Prince Ching, head of the Imperial Clan, and Yuan Shih-k'ai, who have withdrawn from the Imperial councils to allow the hysteria of dissension to subside. Following this, the mind of the Lung Yu Empress Dowager becomes more clear, and she signifies her confidence in Yuan Shih-k'ai by giving him the title of Marquis. Nevertheless, it is an act of panic in which she rushes from the shadow of the outsider to her minister for safety, and seeks further to bind the latter to her defence. Under the anarchistic conditions existing, with bombs whose origin no man can determine, all around him, Yuan Shih-k'ai naturally shuns this spot-light attention. He recoils from an honour that is thus so obviously thrust in the face of Japan.

One of the things most emphasized during the revolutionary Rebellion is the benefits obtained by the outsider through China's past internal quarrels, particularly from the hour of the filching of the Throne by the Manchu outsider (1644) down through all her costly foreign intercourse. Passions of nations are like the passions of individuals. International quarrels work themselves out along the same lines as the quarrels of individuals, and in the quarrels of individuals the outsider profits. Thus all these acts at Peking are so human in their motives of pride, cupidity, possession and fear as to escape foreign observers there, who are too close to events to realize their significance, and here is the complex situation which they have said is impossible of elucidation. They are still asking whether or not Yuan Shih-k'ai is a friend or traitor to the Dynasty, whether he is a patriot or a conspirator, seeking the Throne for himself. Coincidentally they suspect Sun Yat-sen of being a political mountebank and adventurer. But under all that now harasses them from within and without, the Premier at Peking and the President at Nanking, are the wheels and cranks of perfectly simple forces working out the question of the unification of the country which both reiterate to be their aim. China's old enemy the outsider, whose shadow had crossed Peking, has now come to Nanking. That enemy is about to furnish a spectacular solution of China's difficulty, which from this moment further mystifies the Powers and the world, and again shows the position of Japan.

CHAPTER XXIX

OLD REVOLUTIONARY FRIENDS

FINANCE is but one of the many questions of the Republic now embraced in the one word "Nanking" questions arising from the aim of the President, "to secure peace, stable government, and contentment for the millions of his fellow-countrymen."

Nanking witnessed here the declarations of other new Governments that had come and gone. The "Illustrious" or Ming Dynasty had its birth here, 1368 A.D., fulfilled the promise of its name, and met a wretched and inglorious end. Here was the Capital of the "Heavenly King" and the T'aiping crusader-Empire (1853–1865). And linked with these events for ever was to be the launching of the "Flowery Republic."

All its traditions are literary, and not martial. "The Seven Idlers of the Bamboo Grove" of antiquity, China's most famous literary circle, might here have had their rendezvous in a hundred flowery fields and gardens. Inviting pathways through scintillating bamboo groves entice the wayfarer from a hundred streets, to shadowy lakes flecked with waterfowl.

It has been her Confucian scholars meditating in her groves, and not her soldiers in her barracks, that have formed the traditions of Nanking; her pagoda-crowned hill Pei-chi-ko, and not her Drum Tower. It has been her porcelain sentinel at the South Gate, and not her Lion Hill fort at the North, that has been her landmark and has pointed her out to nations and won the love of alien poets.

> ". . . yonder by Nanking, behold
> The Tower of Porcelain, strange and old,
> Uplifting to the astonished skies
> Its ninefold painted balconies,
> With balustrades of twining leaves,
> And roofs of tile beneath whose eaves
> Hang porcelain bells that all the time
> Ring with a soft melodious chime:

While the whole fabric is ablaze
With varied tints all fused in one
Great mass of colour, like a maze
Of flowers illumined by the sun." [1]

The contrast between gardens and literature, and war and money, came home to me in those surroundings which for ten years I had looked forward to visiting for sentimental reasons. Nanking was the native place of His Excellency Huang Sze-yung, a man whom I have called my Chinese father, who has been my affectionate benefactor. As a boy of about twelve, with his brother, he here hanged himself to escape massacre by the T'aiping rebels. The rebels cut both down, but his brother was dead. Little Sze-yung was revived by kindly soldiers and kept captive. Later as a Confucian student he walked these fields and gardens until called to Peking. There the Emperor in recognition of his scholarship gave him a house and opened the Chien Men to receive and escort the gentle scholar thither.

Huang Sze-yung became a public benefactor and worked for progress. As a member of his household I had often listened to the reminiscences of this marvellous romance. Nanking was its setting. Since the days of his captivity and of the expulsion of the T'aipings, Nanking had been undisturbed by war-drums and bugles. My visit was something of a pilgrimage to His Excellency Huang's early shrines.

Now again the waterfowl lazily paddling under the silky rustle of the bamboo leaves start in fright at the martial call. It is that of the Republic, and the scholar in the garden gives place to the soldier, conspirator, and statesman.

Early in February I reached this Capital at a spot made famous by its surrender to General Hsu Shao-cheng, and the escape of General Chang Hsun. I stepped from the train at Hsiakuan where first stopped President-elect Sun Yat-sen *en route* to his inauguration. It was of additional interest to me to have arrived in company with Dr. Tenney, the envoy of the American State Department, and of the correspondent Mr. Kennedy, who had seen so much of the important events here.

Night falls before we settle in our hotel, Mr. Martin's Bridge House, and the streets and foreshore of the Yangtse are lighted up by hurrying lanterns, while in the river are

[1] Longfellow's *Keramos*.

the lights of merchant steamers and foreign warships. The Bridge House is one of the now historic structures of Nanking, rich with revolutionist associations, the rendezvous of all the conspirators of the Yangtse Valley. We do not stop for dinner, but go to the flagship *Rainbow* to dine with the American Admiral Murdock.

The officers of the flagship tell stories of their experiences on the Yangtse as spectators of revolutionist warfare, and in peaceful intervals, as sportsmen among the waterfowl, furnishing delicious duck for their guests. The foreign naval commanders are observing the baptism of the Republic. They may not pay official calls on the President and ministers because their Governments have not recognized the Republic. They have to devise unofficial meetings by which they keep in touch with all that the Republic is doing and report to their Governments.

Leaving Hsiakuan, the north suburb of Nanking, I follow the one long road or Great Street, leading through the North Gate, nearly five miles to the Viceroy's yamen. All the grist of Nanking's daily mill passes through it. This is the place to see Nanking—the Republic on parade. Here passes every moving thing, from the Republican pack-mule to the Minister of War's carriage and the Provisional President's automobile, from the revolutionary recruit to the foreign envoy. Threading its way among squads of incoming volunteers, native chairs and wheelbarrows, horsemen, infantry, transport trains, carriers and foot-passengers, in this thoroughfare, came that crowd which thronged the courts and the side streets at President Sun Yat-sen's inauguration.

The cutting of the queue has of itself made one of those " New Chinas " common to Western thought. Without queues the coolies in the road look like the Indians of Arizona and New Mexico.

" What a chance for the Japanese haberdasher!" says my Swiss companion. " All these new hats and other Western clothes the new Chinese are wearing come from Japan.'

All now observe the Sabbath Day just as did the " Heavenly King " and his T'aipings half a century before. All use rickshaws and have one or another of foreign handkerchiefs, hats, socks, shoes, shirts, and even complete suits. We meet Chinese officers in open broughams with their luggage piled all about them *en route* to Pukow and the front beyond the famine region in Anhuei. There are some members of a " bomb company," with black trousers and yellow stripes, and with bright red coats. They are as lively as a drum corps and as dashing as zouaves. A flag announces in glaring letters their object and importance.

Soldiers are hauling a Decauville railway truck bound for the barges that connect with the railway to the front. They pull at the ends of long ropes, moving slowly over the metalled road built for them by the Manchu Viceroy Tuan Fang. Others draw artillery trucks and ammunition limbers. The army seems to have no horses except the shaggy ponies which carry the officers and a few orderlies up and down. One wonders where are the guns of these trucks and limbers. The foreign correspondents have now begun to settle in force in Nanking together with concessionnaires and foreign agents of all kinds. They go by in the best hired carriages on the way to the President's house, where I am going.

On this five-mile Great Street are all the foreign consulates, now open. To the right and behind them are barracks and parade-grounds where the recruits are drilling. Recruits appear from the side streets. One whole company, composed apparently of outcasts and beggars, turns in game-leggedly ahead of me. On the left is the house of General Homer Lea, a foreign two-story brick building with wide porticoes. In the next compound is a bungalow which is the meeting-place of the "Republican Senate." Farther east are the Exhibition buildings, also built by Tuan Fang, where the Republican Assembly is sitting, and the dismantled wireless station and the parade-ground where Wilcox the American mechanic has an aeroplane school and where ardent Chinese aeroplanists are going smash. On the right, again, are modern residence buildings that are being prepared for the new Foreign Office of the Republic. The Great Street leaves the fields, hamlets, and villages at the rusty old Drum Tower covered with Japanese advertising, turns to the left, and finally enters the Chinese City proper. The Missions with their modern church and school buildings, in great contrast to all around them, lie on the right.

I am now in the region of the southern wall of this vast 23-mile enclosure known as Nanking. The southern part is nearly all given over to troops who are seen drilling in every stable-yard, and doing practice marches through the streets. I meet a military officer not of high rank in a carriage escorted by twenty-five men. Two of them are on horseback, riding ahead. Two are sitting as footmen behind the carriage, ten follow in rickshaws, and eleven are on foot—thus a rather small-rank military officer of the Republic. Imagine a Western officer of the rank of Captain so escorted!

On the east of this region is the Manchu or Tartar City where occurred the accidental explosion that brought on its destruction. There is positively nothing that cannot be called dust left of it. The revolutionists sacked and burned it. It is the most complete work of looting I have seen in all China—more complete than if the entire Tartar City had passed through a giant crematory. It is indeed dust to dust. It has an apparent antiquity of a thousand years as it lies treeless and shelterless, in the pitiless sun. Faggot-gatherers hacked at first the branches, then hewed down the trunks of its willows to the stumps, chipped the stumps to the earth itself, and then dug up the roots. As I came back I saw at the entrance to the Chinese town the people in their doorways beating the bark from these green roots and branches and toasting the fragments to make them dry for burning.

A little farther on lies the Chinese "White House," the converted Viceroy's yamen, where for a little over five weeks Sun Yat-sen has been President of the "Flowery Republic." The "White House" guard drilling on the parade-ground a few hundred yards distant, marches in through the p'ailow and gateway to its quarters inside the second court. Long lines of flags flutter from the p'ailows. The evergreens and ornamental lights are absent. The guard admits me on a pass through the right of three gate-house doors, and I enter the court of the guard headquarters. All the wooden parts of the yamen ordinarily encrusted with red paint are painted white, the colour of the Republic. Over the main entrance hangs the five-coloured national standard. It is the same in all the gate-houses and buildings; white everywhere, significant of the regeneration. The Republic is making an example and illustration to the people.

I am about to see that Government—characterized in their minds by automobiles and frock-coats—which critics loudly disclaimed as alien to the country, and an extravagance more alien than the extravagances of the French aristocracy. The doorkeepers lead me into an office in the main gate-house where my name, address, and occupation are registered and from which my card is taken to the Minister of Foreign Affairs, after which I am led through two additional courts to the audience or reception hall, where are other callers. I wait several minutes here, sipping tea and mentally taking in the alterations which make it as a Chinese yamen look so strange. There is not enough of colour in the walls and colonnades to leave me an impression of anything but white. The only thing which makes Nanking seem a part of China is the winds, which here still sweep between the lintels and the pavement, and among the old rafters, without knowing their own.

This strange old place, which I have never before seen, holds some surprises for me. When I enter the office of the Minister of Foreign Affairs, I am received by C. C. Wang, who grew up in Peking, under the tutelage of the American Minister, Mr. Conger, and there prepared himself for his college career in America. He is now the Secretary of the Minister of Foreign Affairs in Nanking. I knew him during that period in Peking, and while he was getting his first ideas of my Republic I was getting ideas of his country. He was then a blue-gowned, sandal-footed Chinese clerk, with a queue and cap. Now he is one of the "frock-coated, silk-hatted" young Republicans that make the Government at Nanking the exotic of the critics. He has all the hopefulness and cheer that is known in America as "the college spirit," with an intense admiration for the leaders, and a great confidence in the Revolution. If I were asked for a definition of the Republic of China I do not know that I could do better than instance Mr. Wang, to whom new worlds have been opened by his foreign friends, and whose light and spirit he has brought home.

The Minister of Foreign Affairs, Mr. Wang Chung-huei, is also dressed in a frock-coat. He is a tall and slender man, with a scholarly stoop, and more in harmony with the Nanking type and Nanking's literary traditions. His qualifications for the position he holds come from his knowledge of foreign law. He is the author, among other works, of an authoritative translation of the German Penal Code into English. I was astonished at the man. All foreigners are. It is impossible for the observer to conceive one so ably qualified in languages not his own, and in sciences unknown in China.

Without recognition by the Powers the "Flowery Republic" has no official foreign affairs, and the Foreign Minister is chiefly engaged in advising the leaders of the

Revolution in matters that will avoid foreign complications, making explanations in unofficial conferences with foreign consuls, and in devising means to gain for the Republic the recognition from the Powers which it craves.

"Oh, Mr. McCormick," says a familiar voice. A hand is laid on my shoulder to stop me, and I look into the face of the son of my old benefactor Hwang Sze-yung. Mr. Wang and I are lost in reminiscences of Peking, and in discussions of the Republic, when I am startled by this presence of my old Peking companion, who is just coming from the President's house. Unlike the members of the "White House" Government, he is dressed in the garb of literary Nanking—of his fathers. He is the favourite son, has inherited his father's literary talent, ability, and thought, and it is fitting I should find him coming through the pavilion overlooking the wisteria arbour in the garden—the least changed of all the courts of the viceregal yamen. He is in the home of his ancestors. But notwithstanding his reverential conservatism and dress, he is a reformer and the secretary of one of the principal Republican generals.

We had parted two years before at Peking, after others of a company of young reformers with whom I had lived there had been dispersed, some exiled—forced to seek refuge in foreign settlements because of their liberal views and reform activities—and all launched on the strange pathways that separate men in times such as the reform movement brought upon China.

We had known each other in Peking when the Republic was a beautiful dream—when we sat over their wine-cups in winter and over our tea in the moonlight courts in summer and they had listened to my stories of my Republic. As they plied question upon question in the atmosphere of steaming dishes, lighted candles, and mellow lanterns—a hundred scenes like Doré's etchings—one vague shadowy name recurred that floated like a wraith. It was the name of Sun Yat-sen, revolutionist.

Separated by the gathering reform upheaval at Peking in years past, we were now, as we stood in the Nanking garden, not unlike those characters in Dickens's *Tale of Two Cities*—in that we were "children of the Universal Mother, else so wide apart and differing," meeting leagues upon leagues distant, still held in the web of those dreams of Peking days.

And Sun Yat-sen, President of the Republic, is in the next court and is waiting for me.

CHAPTER XXX

MY INTERVIEW WITH SUN YAT-SEN

THE President's time at this moment is too valuable to talk over future problems, and the question of the hour, foreign affairs, is too serious for delay. The reformers in planning their Republic looked for and expected to receive their recognition and support from America. Finance, recognition of the Republic by the Powers, and the peculiarly menacing position into which Japan has elevated herself, make all questions of the reformation in China begin and end in that word expressive of mastery in reform, "Japan."

"For eleven years now I have been intensely interested in all your problems," said I to President Sun Yat-sen. "You and those who have aided you have accomplished the thing in the world that was the most needful to accomplish — sweep away Manchu rule here. It was the thing in all the world next to be done.

"Now you want to know what is thought of your great problem—that of eliminating the Manchus and establishing yourselves among the nations. The Manchu rulers have no friends abroad, and it is not on their account that the Powers do not recognize the Republic. As for our Government, it may be the last to recognize you. Its policy is to act in such a manner as to exercise the greatest influence with the Powers in China's behalf. In the case of the latest new Republic, Portugal, it was the last to give recognition."

"But it recognized Panama in three days," said President Sun.

"China, however, unlike Panama, is the prey of foreign nations and is shackled with foreign complications. Premature action by the United States is likely to increase your complications. Our Government is proud of its position, but has difficulties. Our people know little of China. They too are proud of our position and doctrine out here, but even so the Government in its position is ahead of the people. It cannot go much farther than it has gone without risking its influence at home, to say nothing of its influence with other nations. All are friendly to you, certainly all the English-speaking peoples, and at the same time, as you know, too, all are anxious for the Republic to prove its stability."

"But we are outlawed. Here are 360,000,000 people. We have authority in 15 provinces—to the frontiers of Burma. We have a Government, but we are outlawed. We cannot continue like this. Already the people are pressing us. They do not understand why the Powers do not recognize us. They do not understand our foreign questions. You know that there is everywhere an anti-foreign feeling. It might rise up. We could not resist it—we cannot answer those Chinese who press us. Everybody is friendly—all Europeans are friends—we have friends everywhere. But we need recognition. You ought to recognize us."

"If China can demonstrate her ability to govern herself," said I, "and protect foreign interests by settling her internal differences, there would be no trouble about recognition. Under present circumstances it would be taking sides to recognize the Republic and loan it money, or to loan money to the Peking Government. On the other hand, if you would divide the country by agreement with the North, each side setting up a separate Government, you would be recognized."

"No, that will not do. The country is united in sentiment. All are against the Manchus and are on our side. There is no Government in Peking."

While we are talking at the President's house the Minister of Foreign Affairs, Wang Chung-huei, and Dr. Tenney, the American envoy, are discussing elsewhere the same questions of the recognition of the Republic and China's international position.

The two things which the President seems most worried about are Japan, and the possibility of the Chinese people withdrawing their support from the Nanking Government. The abdication edict is written, and only the manner in which the two sections of the country, North and South, are to be united, delays its issue. The Republic will miss its aim if it turns itself over to the Yuan Shih-k'ai who favours a monarchy and has pledged himself to the Throne. If it can turn over to a Yuan Shih-k'ai that is the defender of the " Flowery Republic," it can accomplish its object.

" What is your judgment of Yuan Shih-k'ai ? " asks the President. " On what considerations is he acting ? "

" I have known him for some years and my impressions of him have been very favourable, as have been those of many others. He is an able man, and ever since he became Governor of Shantung and Viceroy of Chihli my observation has been that he has acted in the best interests of the country, and it is certainly true that he has been a martyr to his convictions of reform."

" Do you think he is acting now in the interests of reform or the Dynasty ? "

" He is obliged to make the best bargain he can for the Court, but his real interests must be those of the Empire—that is, the country itself, and not of any individuals. I do not believe it possible that he could be acting merely in his own interests."

" If I could be sure of this, I would be relieved of much anxiety."

Secretaries and ministers are pressing upon the President's time, and the interview, which has lasted nearly an hour, is over. The President has to retire to consult with the head of the Republican Assembly.

On going in for my interview I observed that President Sun Yat-sen lived in a separate court from the yamen proper, in a foreign-style house built by Tuan Fang, now the headless, and occupied later by Viceroy Chang Jen-chun, now the refugee. The old Chinese garden by which I approached this court was one of the most beautiful I had seen, with a pavilion set in a tiny lake and reached by corridors like the " stately Pleasure Dome," decreed by Kublai Khan. I was escorted by an unarmed soldier wearing a white badge on his coat. I went into the room to the left of the main entrance hall. There was no one at the portico or hall door to receive me. The soldier knocked on the door to the right before anyone appeared. I was astonished at finding no guards outside, no door-keeper, and no usher.

It was about two minutes before the President came in, attended by a secretary and an A.D.C. We shook hands, he dismissed his attendants, and we sat down alone at the round table before the grate (in which, by the way, the fire had gone out). It was rather cold in the room and I kept my overcoat on. The President was dressed in a military suit of winter khaki such as the Japanese officers of the army wear. It was of military cut, without insignia. He was a little diffident, I thought because of his mixture of native reserve and foreign training. He smiled boyishly and somewhat sadly. He is forty-seven. He looked about that age, and I have been wondering how much or how little he may resemble in appearance, or possess the qualities of, the " Heavenly Prince," or the founder of the Ming Dynasty and whatever other reformers and invaders in Eastern Asia have worked wonders such as he has worked. A half-foolish, half-sad smile played round his mouth—he seemed more like Siamese or Burmese than Chinese—and his small stature added nothing of impressiveness to him. It was somewhat strange—half disappointing, half wonderful. Here was the man who it appeared had done the one thing in all the world most needful. Everything about him was simple, and his manners took me off guard—he was most like a simple boy. He seemed to be dreaming of some yet greater event, perhaps a yet greater fate which he saw dimly and was trying to make out. It was as though he felt a martyrdom, of which he was not fully conscious, to be hanging over him. I did not wish to leave him. There was no doubt of his magnetism, often proved by the fact that when he was farthest away his followers were most loyal to him.

Although he had been thinking of political questions so long, he was not indifferent to other Chinese interests, and we found time to talk of at least one other subject than that of the fate of the Republic. He asked me about China's great monuments and my work of organizing a China Monuments' Society interested in this subject. He asked me how many members the Society had. I told him about two hundred and gave him some of their names, by which to judge. I told him of the interest among scholars respecting China's ancient things, and that a large and influential class of men in the world gained their high feelings of respect and admiration for the Chinese from a knowledge of these things. A continuation of this admiration, I took occasion to say, would depend upon the continued respect which the Chinese people exhibited for their own antiquities. Unfortunately, the Chinese troops had selected monuments in China for their artillery targets, which was as bad as foreign vandalism in China. In 1843 or thereabouts the English had destroyed the Porcelain Pagoda in Nanking, a most inexplicable act, hard to understand. Now the China Monuments' Society had secured the aid of foreign Governments, some of which kept their military departments warned against the recurrence of such acts. At present we were especially interested, owing to the conditions of the times when foreign Powers were landing troops in China, that no acts of foreign vandalism should occur. Such care would be all the more effective if the Chinese manifested a similar spirit.

For interest and importance my visit to Nanking could not have been better timed. The abdication at Peking is about to take place, and this is the crisis in the life and existence of the Republican Government at Nanking and of the aims of the conspirator and reformer Sun Yat-sen. This man is about to surrender the place of Provisional President to Yuan Shih-k'ai, by a course of reasoning which events will show to be of the most trying character to the strongest man, and after a chain of circumstances to be henceforth memorable in the world's history. Those circumstances or events, for this man, began with the opening of the Republic at Wuchang and led up to the Presidency.

I was in the United States coincident with Sun Yat-sen's tour across the American continent and had much interest in his movements because of the rapid development of the reform rebellion. He visited in order the following cities: San Francisco, Seattle, Portland, Spokane, Denver, Kansas City, St. Louis, Chicago, and New York, where he stayed at a hotel near Madison Square. These are all centres of Chinese reform. In the past they had maintained a united military organization with a nominal total of 4000 men under a plan devised and carried out by Sun Yat-sen's foreign helper and adviser, General Homer Lea.

At Chicago, coincident with the declaration of independence at Wuchang, Sun Yat-sen issued a statement for the benefit of Western nations proclaiming the principles upon which the rebellion was being promoted. The American Press entirely failed in locating Sun Yat-sen, although he missed his steamer, the *Mauretania*, at New York and had to wait for a succeeding boat. He preserved incognito in Great Britain and until he had reached Paris, after which, his mission as director of the Revolution being known, he dropped his incognito, and his progress to China by way of India was open to the observation of the world.

In the United States he had talked very quietly with the reform leaders and made final arrangements for their part in the inauguration of the Republic of the confederated provinces of China.

The first ovation which he received from his countrymen was at Singapore, where his departure was distinguished by a tribute of flowers from Chinese girls. At Hongkong he stopped long enough to make a statement for the information of the State Department at Washington. When he reached Shanghai it was as a leader well known abroad and without clique entanglements at home, and whom for these reasons it would be safe to set up as Provisional President. Wu Ting-fang had made up his mind that China would see many vicissitudes before she settled down to orderly government, and believed in an era of assassination of public men continuing perhaps for a generation, such as Japan had had after her revolution. Such a history would provide for successive presidencies likely to satisfy many aspirations. He said that these dangers did not appeal to him, certainly not if the Capital was to be at Peking.

Wu Ting-fang, for one, numbered Sun Yat-sen first for the Presidency, because he deserved to be recognized. Yuan Shih-k'ai he numbered second. The most important thing was to secure the abdication of the Throne and the uniting of the country by the selection of one man agreeable to the largest number, a thing that would require the resignation of Sun Yat-sen. It was an obvious necessity which Sun saw and likewise agreed to. He was duly elected.

The manner of Sun Yat-sen's election is proof of the very conditions apprehended by Wu Ting-fang. A single example giving the status of some " electors " shows the substance of which he built the Provisional Government or Republic. The " electors " in question represented the province of Szechuan. There was a change of the Military Government there, and the last in power authorized two young men, one twenty-six years of age and the other twenty-three, to represent a part of the province at Wuchang, where the first Republic was declared. When the two " electors " arrived at Wuchang the city of Hankow had fallen, and later Hanyang, taken by the Imperialists, and they journeyed on to Shanghai. By the time they arrived at Shanghai they learned that the Military Governor who had appointed them survived their appointment but four days, when his head was taken off and his successor installed. Nevertheless, the two "electors" went to Nanking and as representatives of the whole province of Szechuan, a province with 45,000,000 people, assisted in "electing" Sun Yat-sen as President. Delegates from other provinces participating in the "election" were many of them similarly qualified.

It was under such conditions Sun Yat-sen actually confederated the Southern provinces.

He had now brought the Provisional Republic to its trial, that of its ability to amalgamate with the North. All the international complications that had ever centred about Peking, for this very reason, must show their menace and have their manifestation at Nanking. Their manifestation came through the doyen of the military and diplomatic nations, Japan, a country that very nearly reversed the plans of the Republic and the personal pledges of President Sun Yat-sen made in his inaugural oath.

CHAPTER XXXI

THE REPUBLIC, JAPAN, AND ABDICATION

THE anxiety for recognition on the part of the Republic so that it could borrow money from a neutral country, as well as the conciliatory methods of the Throne and the Premier in dealing with the Republic, made it apparent that there was something about China's situation that President Sun Yat-sen and the Government at Nanking were unwilling to tell. This was the definitely known plans of Japan.

" Japan is not acting with the other Powers," said one of the highest members of the Republican Confederation. As he spoke he stopped between the short sentences to make sure of their effect. " Japan wants every-thing. She wants all China."

" What ? " said I, thinking that he was merely continuing the complaint against a neighbour whose subjects were perhaps making onerous financial or trade exactions and whose consuls might perhaps be worrying the Republic.

" Japan wants China. She will give us something, but she wants something in return. She will recognize us—that is what we need, and that is why she offers it—but we need it from you. We are helpless. We are now at the mercy of those who can take advantage of us."

" The Government in Washington believes that Japan, which you and I know to be your greatest problem, is acting in good faith. It believes that the Japanese Cabinet informs it of all that Japan does respecting China, in return for which the State Department informs Japan of all that the United States does respecting China."

" But the Cabinet does not know," broke in the Republican member. " It is the *genro* [elder statesmen] that make the policy."

" I know what you mean," said I, thinking he was expressing only the trite suspicions which so many heap upon Japan and which have become so repugnant to disinterested correspondents, so I continued : " The State

Department at Washington believes that the present Cabinet in Japan is sincere in its declarations and desires for neutrality, by all outside Powers, including Japan. The reason is that, like China, Japan has no money and cannot take over in China something she cannot swallow. Therefore she can do nothing on a great scale for fear the China Question will disorganize her alliances and conventions and get out of hand altogether. Do you think that the Government in Washington is not likely to get all the facts of Japan's activities from the Tokio Cabinet ? "

" But the Cabinet, or the Minister of the Foreign Office, may not know what the *genro*—what the Government does. Japan wants to make with us an offensive and defensive alliance." I looked at him in amazement as he went on :

" She asks that of us. We have kept this in the background so far ; she urges it, and if we are not recognized by the Powers and do not come under their united protection, I do not see how we can continue to resist. We could *not* continue to resist, and Japan, of course, offers us something. She has something to offer us and something to receive from us."

" You mean she wants Manchuria ? "

" No. She asks for an offensive and defensive alliance and offers her naval and military resources to build up for us an army and a navy."

" Is that so ? "

" Yes."

" You don't want it ? "

" We would be afraid of it."

" Japan with her greater number of trained men would swamp your few students and reformers and the limited number of trained officials at your command, and your Provisional Government would fall into the hands of Japan's trained men : is that what you mean ? "

The Republican member assented.

" I appreciate the nature of the problem. It is a serious situation that you are facing. Are you obliged to give an answer ? "

" We have kept it in the background. But they are delaying the abdication."

" They want to force you."

" We do not know how long we can resist without recognition. We must have recognition from others than Japan before we can answer her."

" Do you fear a surprise ? "

" Japan is mobilizing. Three divisions are represented in Manchuria, and a fourth has just landed at Dalny—Japan's army and navy are mobilized. Manchuria is one of our bases of operation. We are fighting there, in neutral territory, with Japanese consent. We do not know at what moment Japan might make this an excuse for pressing us. She has been our friend, the only friend now when we need money and recognition. We are indebted to her. She has given us money on the Hanyang Iron Works and other things. But we cannot go on like this. If we do, China will be in the hands of the Japanese in two months."

" How much have you accepted from Japan, taking the Iron Works first ? "

" That is 15,000,000 yen, together with the Ta Yeh Mines and the Ping-hsiang Railway; the Chekiang Railway—Kiangsu section—3,000,000 yen, and the China Merchants' Steam Navigation Company."

" Has that last loan been completed ? "

" Not entirely, but will be in a few days."

" Altogether, that represents about 28,000,000 yen in loans, as I understand it. How much are your expenditures ? "

" About 1,000,000 yen per day—that is, just in this part," said the Republican member, making a movement with his hand to illustrate his meaning that this amount was merely the expenditure in the vicinity of Nanking for the Government there, and the expedition to the North up the Tientsin-Pukow Railway.

" You see we cannot indebt ourselves to Japan alone —we need recognition from others to offset the obligations we have already assumed."

" Why not make your situation known ? If this is the crisis, it might be best to explain China's position and say what Japan has done."

" We cannot afford to offend Japan, she has been our friend."

" It is Japan's plans and what she has in mind that is important, and which if known would influence the other Governments."

" The proposal must not be made known. Coming from the *genro*, it can be officially denied by the Japanese Cabinet. If it were made known the Japanese would immediately work against us."

20

The iron heel of China's foreign complications was now grinding the heart out of her reformers, and was proving itself the master of the Revolution, before which both the Republican Government and the Throne were stunned. Count de Gabalis says : " *Learn of the philosophers always to look for natural causes in all extraordinary events ; and when such natural causes are wanting recur to God.*" In China all things are explained by her foreign complications.

The Republican Government had counted out its assets and found that it was barely possible on its working mines, railways, and steamships to realize 28,000,000 yen, and on its Arsenal 3,000,000 or 4,000,000 additional, which altogether would pay the working expenses of the Nanking Government for one month. Contributions and incomes from other sources would carry the Government forward. But toward the end of the second month, unless recognition came from the Powers and the shelter of international neutrality was extended to the Republic, it would be forced by its eminent responsibility to Japan, for her solitary financial aid, to acknowledge their alliance and to depend upon her for military aid in substantiating the Republic.

From the Great Powers—those allied or united by conventions and unity of interests with Japan, namely, Great Britain, Russia, and France—the Republic could expect no recognition except through and after Japan. This left only Germany and the United States from which the Republic could hope for unqualified recognition. With the United States on record as relying upon the Government in Tokio, in whom it had pledged confidence, Germany was alone, and could do nothing. And now the United States through its representatives definitely informed the leaders of the Republic that they could not expect recognition from " the Great White Father " beyond the waters.

" I hope you have power to recognize us ? " said Tang Shao-yi.

" We have nothing of the kind," said the representatives, speaking for the Government. " We are working for the best interests of China and do not know of any better way of injuring her than independently recognizing the Republic. Our power of aiding China is through the influence which we may exert upon the other Powers."

Germany is alone and equally helpless. The United States have to confess their helplessness, and by reliance upon Japan throw down the hopes of the Republic. President Sun Yat-sen has received these facts in unmistakable substance and with unmistakable emphasis from the representatives of the American Government and is obliged to accept them as a crushing ultimatum from the great Republic which was his best hope of aid. He has now to turn to Peking.

With Great Britain, Russia, and France under control of Japan against him, with Germany and the United States helpless, his situation is resolved into the original equation. It is that of man to man. President Sun Yat-sen has only Yuan Shih-k'ai.

For twenty years Sun Yat-sen has pursued his aims for the regeneration of his country and its redemption from foreign conquest. He has received his support and encouragement from foreign countries, and in the hour of his severest struggles he has a right to expect from them that support which is so essential.

His efforts have been largely directed against Yuan Shih-k'ai. When Yuan Shih-k'ai's treason to the cause of reform 1898 resulted in the confinement of the Emperor Kuang Hsu, Sun Yat-sen had organized a military relief corps to rescue him, a plan defeated by the Boxer War and the flight of the Court to Hsian-fu. Reformers and revolutionaries like Dr. Yung Wing, Kang Yu-wei, and Liang Chi-chiao, with whom he had been schooled, warned him to the last against Yuan Shih-k'ai. It was natural, therefore, that he should receive Yuan Shih-k'ai's repudiation of the peace agreement made by his envoy, Tang Shao-yi, with suspicion, and that in the Throne's edict proposing to delegate its power to Yuan Shih-k'ai he should see the structure of a *coup d'état* to defeat the Republic and all that it had achieved.

Under the circumstances it was impossible to carry out his promise to elect Yuan Shih-k'ai as President and resign in his favour. "I thought," said President Sun Yat-sen (January 22, 1912), "that Yuan Shih-k'ai could sever his connections with whatever concerned the Manchu Government, and could become a citizen of the Republic, so I promised forthwith to elect him President. But judging from his telegrams, Yuan Shih-k'ai's idea is not only the removal of the Manchu Government, but the cancelling of the Republican Provisional Government, while he would form another Provisional Government in Peking. But who knows whether such a Provisional Government will be that of a constitutional monarchy or a Republic? Even assuming that he himself calls it a Republican Government, then who guarantees it? My office will be relinquished when all the Powers have recognized us. My sole aim and desire is the consolidation of the Republic, and there is no clashing between my present and former intentions. If Yuan Shih-k'ai can really carry out our clause of severing his connection with what concerns the Manchu Government and become a citizen of the Republic, then I will keep my words."

On Jan. 25 the Republican Assembly at 7.50 p.m., after a special meeting, declared with reference to the peace negotiations and President Sun Yat-sen's voluntary offer to resign the Presidency of the Republic in favour of Yuan Shih-k'ai, that the offer to resign, and to request the people to elect Yuan Shih-k'ai as President of the Republic, came entirely and solely from Sun Yat-sen himself. Not only was it not suggested by any one of the Republican party, but President Sun Yat-sen had to overcome great opposition from members of the Assembly, and it was only after much persuasion and reasoning that his views were accepted so as to bring about a peaceful solution of the national problem and prevent further bloodshed. It was clearly stipulated that Yuan Shih-k'ai should join the Republican party, and it was not possible for the people to elect him President until he had declared for the Republic. The original terms to the Manchus still hold good as well as the offer to Yuan Shih-k'ai, provided he complies with the conditions just mentioned.

I know no more dramatic moment in the career of the Nanking Provisional Government and the Provisional Republic of China than this, nor in the life of the man Sun Yat-sen. These declarations came on the eve of the arrival of the United States Government's envoy, Dr. Tenney, from whom the Republic learned finally not only the exact position of the United States but confirmation of the helplessness of both before the Juggernaut of the Powers.

"Agree with thine adversary quickly," was the message of this situation ringing in the ears of Sun Yat-sen, "lest at any time the adversary deliver thee to the judge, and the judge deliver thee to the officer and thou be cast into prison." "Verily I say unto thee, Thou shalt by no means come out thence, till thou hast paid the uttermost farthing," came this message from that Western Republic which was the model of the Provisional Government, and the inspiration of the Republic of China.

The period of personal negotiations with Yuan Shih-k'ai during which President Sun Yat-sen expresses confidence in Yuan Shih-kai's sincerity and makes an armistice, can be determined to be continuous up to this moment. Sun Yat-sen, acting on the spirit of this clarion message from the skies, to "agree with his adversary quickly," seeks a compromise by which Yuan Shih-k'ai will accept the delegated power of the Presidency instead of that of the Throne. Thus does Sun Yat-sen seek Yuan Shih-k'ai's commitment to the Republic and a guarantee that by resigning he himself puts the whole responsibilities of China, internal and external, upon Yuan Shih-k'ai.

It seems necessary in order to explain the situation of President Sun Yat-sen, and the course of reasoning by which he was forced, unaided and alone, as events will prove, to decide upon the course of action which he took, to review the public history of Yuan Shih-k'ai in relation to Japan and to China's foreign complications. It begins with Yuan Shih-k'ai's tutelage to Li Hung-chang in the days when Li Hung-chang (1882) brought the United States into Treaty relations with Korea, opening that country to foreign intercourse in order to raise a barrier in that kingdom against Japanese aggression upon China.

A little over ten years later (1894) his representative, Yuan Shih-k'ai, an indomitable opponent of the Japanese, precipitated the China-Japan War. This was an affair in which China lost, and by which Yuan Shih-k'ai became a soberer, more subtle, and more formidable opponent than before.

Through the steadily accumulating failures to arrest Japan's aggression Yuan Shih-k'ai rose in power as the successor of Li Hung-chang. After the failure of Li Hung-chang's device of stopping Japan from crossing the Yalu River by admitting Russia to Manchuria, Yuan Shih-k'ai became Grand Councillor and chief adviser of the Empress [Grand] Dowager in the still more formidable foreign questions arising from this failure—the defeat of Russia in the Russo-Japanese War. Called from retirement and the obloquy placed upon him by the Empress Grand Dowager's successors, the first words which he addressed to the revolutionaries and republicans (Nov. 11, 1911)—words carried through his delegates to Li Yuan-hung at Wuchang—was the warning presented to the nation by the menace of Japan and Russia. Because that danger in all its formidableness reached Nanking, President Sun Yat-sen knows that Yuan Shih-k'ai was right in those warnings ridiculed by Li Yuan-hung owing to the feelings existing at Wuchang at the time against the Manchus.

It was apparent that of the two reasons given by Yuan Shih-k'ai for undertaking the Premiership to which he had been appointed by the Manchus, namely, that he could not but lend a helping hand to the Manchus to whom he was indebted, and also, because of the dangers from Japan and Russia, that the latter was the real reason for his resuming the burdens and dangers of office at Peking.

Sun Yat-sen ignored for the time being some of the most important questions in order to reach an understanding with Yuan Shih-k'ai leading to a settlement. These included the important consideration, first, as to whether Yuan Shih-k'ai should be the sole representative to organize a Provisional Republican Government; second, the establishment of the Capital at Nanking; and third, the removal of Yuan Shih-k'ai to Nanking for inauguration, and taking of the oath before the electors.

But the main question was settled, the definite and final surrender of power by the Manchus. On Feb. 1 the Throne authorized the Chinese Foreign Office (Wai-wu-pu) to make peace by concluding the terms affecting the Court and Manchus. On Feb. 6 the 25 members of the Republican Assembly at Nanking, representing 15 provinces, discussed the terms forwarded by Yuan Shih-k'ai, and on February 9 an agreement was reached, and an armistice declared for a week, to give time for ratification by the Throne and promulgation of the abdication edict.

Two days later the Cabinet at Peking received Prince Ching in audience, to commemorate its farewell to the Imperial Clan, and the Chinese Foreign Office announced the Republic's acceptance of Yuan Shih-k'ai's terms.

Simultaneously with the Chinese Foreign Office's announcement the Republican Assembly, and Wu Tingfang as Peace Commissioner, reiterated the Republic's determination that no other consideration would be entertained until the abdication was an accomplished fact.

On February 12 came the long-expected edict from the hand of the Lung Yu Empress Dowager, who said:

"I, hand in hand with the Emperor, hereby transfer the power of sovereignty to be the public property of the whole nation, and decide that the form of government shall be Republican Constitutional, to satisfy the present feeling within the Seas, the detestation of disturbance, and the expectation of peace, as well as to follow the ancient sages in regarding the world as public property.

" Yuan Shih-k'ai, having been formally elected Premier by the National Assembly, stands at this juncture between the New and the Old regimes, and has surely devised a plan for unifying the South and the North. Let Yuan Shih-k'ai organize with full powers a Provisional Republican Government and confer with the People's Army as to the methods of procedure for the union, so that peace may be assured to the people and the nation, but still with the complete integrity of the territories of the five races of Manchus, Chinese, Mongols, Mohammedans, and Tibetans combined, forming a great Republic of China, and I and the Emperor may retire into a leisured life and spend our years pleasantly, enjoying courteous treatment from the citizens, and seeing with our own eyes the completion of an ideal Government. Would this not be a grand feat? Respect this."

Thus with the twenty-fifth day of the twelfth moon of the third year of Hsuan Tung the Manchu Dynasty and the Dynastic calendar ended.

Abdication was an accomplished fact.

CHAPTER XXXII

WORLD INFLUENCE IN THE REPUBLIC

JAPAN exercises the formidable influence upon the affairs of Eastern Asia that has been prophesied. There is therefore nothing surprising respecting her part in the Chinese revolutionary Rebellion, 1911–1912.

As for the other Powers, Great Britain and France may be mentioned first on account of their extensive contact with the Empire of China, and because their influence upon that Empire has passed through such varied stages. The influence of France in the Empire, exercised through the long contact of the Roman Catholic Church, is not apparent in the Republic. Great Britain's educational and enlightening influence in China is great, but in her principal achievement of the development of industry and commerce there the traditional bearing of her influence is to preserve. It is wholly contrary to revolution, and to change of the form of government.

In her industrial interests in China France has united in a mutual policy, by financial and commercial alliances, with Great Britain. Great Britain allied herself with Japan and acquiesced in her policies and patronage. Simultaneously France joined Russia in an alliance, Japan then in war defeated Russia, and with the rise of Japan, Great Britain and France drew more closely together, and the four nations formed a group, pledged to the extension of their own interests and removed from considerations of any special interest in the welfare of China herself.

Germany is a great nation or Empire exerting a powerful influence in the world at large whose traditions render it impossible that she should ever, except inversely and in spite of herself, promote the Republican or representative system of reform in China. Alone and unaided, she forced her way to an equal share with Great Britain and France, backed by their allies Japan and Russia, in China's industrial and commercial development, and she tends to represent only such principles in China as protect and extend her trade and financial interests. Germany stands alone.

The influence of Italy, Austria, and the lesser Powers in China is not sufficiently important to give it definition. Russia's influence is confined solely to the Mongolian and Manchurian frontier, to regions on the outskirts of China proper inhabited by races different from Chinese, and to the affairs of the four allied nations mentioned, which I will call the Quadruple Group. All other considerations of the Quadruple Group in China and Eastern Asia, are buried in its political and commercial interests. In the questions of the Republic of China this Group and the Powers constituting it are dominated by Japan.

There is but one other great Power whose influence in Eastern Asia is of first rank, and that is America. The influence of America in China as well as in Japan has been educational, and America's example as a Republic has been a powerful force of enlightenment in government and human rights. The ideal leader, in the minds of the revolutionaries who established the Republic of China, has been George Washington. According to Bishop Bashford, it was the greatest compliment America ever had paid to her when China with her 300,000,000 or 400,000,000 people entitled to human rights became a Republic.

The Chinese understand American influence, and they know by the American schools and missions scattered throughout China and by the constant policy of protecting, assisting, and encouraging China pursued by the American Government and people that America's influence is to them a helping hand. Japan, jealous of the extension of those benefits to her neighbours which she has herself received from America, is opposed to American influence in Eastern Asia in the present era because it interferes with politics and intrigue, which is the whole political substance of the era there.

It is easy to see that the influences in China's revolutionary Rebellion divide themselves into two kinds, namely, American and anti-American. The Quadruple Group headed by Japan is a unit on the one side, with America on the other, and they stand opposed.

From the close of the Russo-Japanese War to the opening of the revolutionary Rebellion in China the world rang with stories of war between Japan and America. These war rumours and the known diplomatic and political contentions between the two countries showed that antagonism existed in their opposition. The fundamental basis of such a contingency as war between Japan and America could only be that of American influence in China. These circumstances make the influence of Japan and America in the Pacific with respect to the establishment of the "Flowery Republic" paramount to the influences of all other Powers.

The position of America with respect to China was defined in 1843 in one of complete neutrality, friendship, and disinterested aid in the preservation to China of her sovereignty and place among nations. It has never changed, and with the inauguration of the Republic promises to continue. America introduced the Protestant missions into China as well as Protestant and non-sectarian schools for the diffusion of Western knowledge, and has been the pioneer and chief exponent, leading all other nations, in democracy of learning in Eastern Asia. These things and the signal example of the American Republic among free nations as a message to mankind explains her whole influence in Eastern Asia, whose crowning testimony is the conversion of the despotic Empire of China to a Republic.

However, the question of foreign influence upon the Chinese is more easily defined in the case of Japan than in that of any other outside nation. Her definite and forcible impression on China dates only from the Boxer War or later, and at the opening of the revolutionary Rebellion is not ten years old.

In 1900, when I first went to China, I lodged for a time in the Provincial College of Chihli, at Paoting-fu. I was a guest of the Chancellor, who had a desire to know what was the place occupied by the Japanese among the allied Powers in China. He said that the College, several years previous to that time, had a Japanese student who made a very good impression by his work in the Chinese classics. This student had been entrusted with 400 taels from the College with which to buy printing-paper in Japan, had taken the money, departed for his native land to make the purchase, had never returned, and had neither forwarded the paper nor accounted for the money. The Chancellor was under the impression that the Japanese had borrowed their prestige from their Western colleagues and slipped into China under the foreign mantle. Although the China-Japan War had intervened, this was a fair example of the knowledge possessed among Chinese respecting Japanese.

Therefore it may be said that in 1900 Japan, to the Chinese, was merely a country that had taken everything from China, except modern ideas and warfare, and given nothing in return.

As beneficiaries of Chinese civilization the Japanese have an intercourse with China extensive in its history. Japan's travellers, pilgrims, geographers, warriors, and traders, however, appear to have left no great impression upon the Chinese, and in the light of China's revolutionary present may be passed over.

China took too little account of the China-Japan War of 1894–1896, and in fact began to realize Japan's importance only through the reputation which Japan had in the West. Japan's modern appearance on the continent of Asia came first in Korea, where she made a modern Treaty in accordance with Western practice (her first on her own initiative) in the seventies. What are called civilized diplomatic relations between Japan and China, and the establishment of legations by China and Japan in their two capitals, was brought about largely by an American missionary, Dr. Davie Bethune McCartee. Japan was only established on the mainland through events in Fukien, opposite Formosa. This latter she gained from China by the China-Japan War.

It was only after 1900 that the Japanese can be said to have fully established themselves in all the Treaty ports. At the end of the first decade of the century, Japanese were in the majority among foreigners in China at every Treaty port and Treaty mart north of Chefoo. At Tientsin their colony grew at the rate of 200 annually.

An interesting exchange of official inquiry took place between Russia and Japan in 1910, respecting their subjects in Chinese Treaty marts on the Siberian frontier, that shows Japanese colonization in China to have become a political question of considerable acuteness. The complications of the Russo-Japanese questions led Russia to ask Japan why she had sent a consul to Aigun on the Amur River in the zone of Russia's special trade rights. Japan replied that it was because she had 250 subjects there. She retorted by asking Russia why Russia had sent a consul to Chientao on the Korean frontier. Russia could only reply that it was because she had four subjects there (including the consul). All this is a part of the expansion of Japan expressed in various words and phrases, but best comprehended in the term "Greater Japan."

Apprehension by China corresponding to that of Russia was expressed in almost innumerable protests to Japanese expansion in Manchuria after the Russo-Japanese War, as well as to Japanese activity in South-eastern, Central, and Western China. In 1908 China complained of and was alarmed by Japanese military surveys in the region of the Great Wall and in Mongolia. It was at this time that the Government in Peking began to feel the revolutionary force of reform ideas among students returning from foreign lands, and in masses from Japan. The late Empress Grand Dowager, coincident with the question of education of Chinese in America, under the scheme by which America restored her share of the Boxer indemnities, stated that China must send fewer young men to Japan, because those going to Japan largely became revolutionaries.

It will give some idea of Japanese origins in the Chinese revolutionary Rebellion to state that perhaps 20,000 Chinese reformers and students have learned their ideas of revolution in Japan. As revolutionaries in China they have been to the front since 1903, when the Empress [Grand] Dowager had one of them, Shen Chin, beaten to death with a stave in the Imperial prison outside the Palace gates. They grew to be master revolutionists in China, with unsuspected power of organization if not of agitation. Their progress was marked by revolutionary outbreaks, such as the destruction of a railway carriage by a bomb and wounding of several high officials at Peking, 1905; the assassination of the Governor of Anhuei Province, 1907; and conspiracies at Canton, together with several raids and mutinies.

The progressive movement in China is one of Chinese enlightened by all Western countries, but the foremost revolutionaries in the rebellion of September and October 1911, and in instances where force and violence leading up to it have been employed, come from the school of Chinese revolutionary reformers in Japan. I recall a plot by Chinese students returned from Japan to assassinate the Empress [Grand] Dowager. It came intimately before my observation because I had occasion to persuade a student friend who had been educated in another land, to stay out of this particular conspiracy, which ultimately fell through.

Japan's influence over the Chinese student has been inevitable, and it is not derogatory to the Japanese to say that influences developed on their shores manifested themselves in Revolution on the Asian continent, in political conspiracy, arson, assassination, murder, and other crimes. As far as I know, these accompaniments of China's revolutionary Rebellion are assignable to the leaven of Western ideas.

Certain chapters in the history of Japan on the continent, such as that of Korea when the Korean Queen was murdered by Japanese, have inspired Japan's critics to attribute to her responsibilities for the outbreak of the present Rebellion. There is nothing to show that Japanese in China have violated their right of sanctuary as was done in Korea at the time mentioned. The outbreak in China, mainly due to the endeavours of reformers and revolutionaries who had been to Japan and whose organization for Revolution was developed there, furnishes records of events in the inauguration of republicanism in China that are quite clear.

In Szechuan, which began revolt, a large percentage of the members of the Provincial Assembly were students returned from Japan, and one of them, Pu Tien-chun, their leader, was President of the Assembly. Yang Tu, a Japan-schooled Hunanese, from 1907 was leader of the younger or reform party, whose agitation among the Chinese students in Japan (where anarchy had already established itself) caused Yuan Shih-k'ai, while still in power, to offer him office in order to control his agitation. He attached himself to Yuan Shih-k'ai only after the rebellion was successful.

Sun Yat-sen and Huang Hsing received welcome support for years from Japan, and an influential Japanese friend of Huang Hsing, Mr. Inukai, fomented in the Japanese Diet a movement for recognition of the Republic of China, which the Nanking Government promoted along with the loan contracts which it was giving to Japanese.

Hunan and Hupeh provinces furnish almost the whole history of the rise of the Rebellion. The gentry of Hunan, who have always been the most powerful of the gentry class in China, convinced by the foreign or Japanized young men of their province, furnished the support, under Li Yuan-hung's direction, of the most important Rebellion which China has ever had. It is of greater consequence to China than the mere change of Dynasty, and to a degree is a monument to the Chinese revolutionaries schooled in Japan.

Japan's policy toward the revolutionary Rebellion was shaped in the beginning by the conditions in Manchuria and the interests of the Quadruple Group. She supported the Manchu Dynasty of Manchuria and the North, as against the Republic and the South. America, like other outside Powers, had to follow this lead, which was competent, if necessary, to dictate to China the form the future government should take. The Japanese Minister at Peking, Mr. Ijuin, expressed the adherence of Japan to the principle that a constitutional monarchy was the only safe form of government for China.

The place of Japan in China's revolutionary Rebellion and the place which Japan will have on the continent of Asia hereafter, is explained by the history, since the signing of the Portsmouth Treaty, of the question of Manchuria, a word in which all discussion of affairs in Eastern Asia ends.

CHAPTER XXXIII

JAPAN, AMERICA, AND REVOLUTION

I HAVE called attention to the fact that Rebellion broke out in the industrial region that is the centre of European and American loan operations, due to revolutionaries largely of the Japanese school. Japan is not a capitalistic nation but a military one that leans upon opportunity. Her field since the Russo-Japanese War has been that of chance and fortunate opportunity, out of which she has made Empire. Revolt favoured her policy and interests in this particular, that it came in the centre of the interests of the capitalistic Powers, her natural antagonists, disconcerting them and absorbing their attention. It placed her in a position to be of service to them, leaving her free to promote her own interests and policies. I have never seen these explained. They are essential to the elucidation of Japan's diplomacy with respect to the Republic of China and are as follows :

Two great Russian and Japanese railways traverse Manchuria, one the whole distance east and west, the other the whole length north and south. Together they form a system conveying Russian and Japanese sovereignty to all Manchuria's vital parts.

When the Portsmouth Treaty was signed in New Hampshire (September 1905), it became the immediate business of Japan and Russia, between whom these railways were divided, to keep apart. With their usual alertness the Japanese were foremost in this problem. Before Mr. Komura, Japanese Peace Commissioner, left America for Japan, Marquis Ito at Tokio jumped to the solution of this problem by giving Edward H. Harriman, the American financier and promoter, a tentative agreement for lease to American financiers of Japan's railway in Manchuria, taken from Russia. This would have placed America between Russia and Japan. It would have solved, in a manner, the question of non-entanglement with Russia, so far as Japan was concerned. Marquis Ito believed Japan could not hold her Manchurian territories; he thought Japan was moving beyond her depth.

Immediately after the exchange of this tentative agreement, Komura arrived in Tokio. From thence date two Japans, the passing one that of Ito, the oncoming that of Komura. Komura said Japan must expand on the continent in China. This expansion had sufficient political basis only in the rights which Japan had acquired from Russia by coming into possession of a share of her railways in Manchuria. Japan could not turn her railway over to others. She must cling to all she had acquired in order that she might share all the rights, advantages, and opportunities claimed by Russia. Russia must be supported and made to cling to all she held and claimed in Manchuria, and on the whole Chinese frontier, so as to safeguard this basis for Japan's continental expansion.

Japan thereupon abandoned the Ito-Harriman agreement and found in her Manchurian Railway a bond of union and not a breach with Russia. The facts and circumstances are these:

Komura met diplomatic defeat at Portsmouth in failing to secure a war indemnity which the people of Japan demanded as a condition of peace with Russia. But he secured the insertion in the secret minutes of the Portsmouth Treaty, the obligation on the part of Russia (as a part of the transfer of the railway) to communicate to Japan, upon ratification of the Treaty, all agreements which she had with China respecting Manchuria. When the transfer of these agreements took place, it was found that the contract for the construction of the Chinese-Eastern Railway (the east and west line), 1896, contained a clause known as "Article 6" which gave to Russia the "sole and exclusive right of administration in the railway zone."

Komura saw, as well as did a majority of the Emperor's advisers, that if this article could be appropriated for effect on the Japanese railways, and recognized by Russia, it was in effect a division of China's sovereignty among China, Russia, and Japan, in Manchuria. This fact, joined to the fact that Russia's special frontier trade rights were capable of similar extension so as to benefit Japan, gave to Japan her present "plan of state" upon which Greater Japan rests.

Japan now had new statesmen, who saw that Russia and Japan possessed and could maintain a special position in Northern China, doubtless in spite of all opposition.

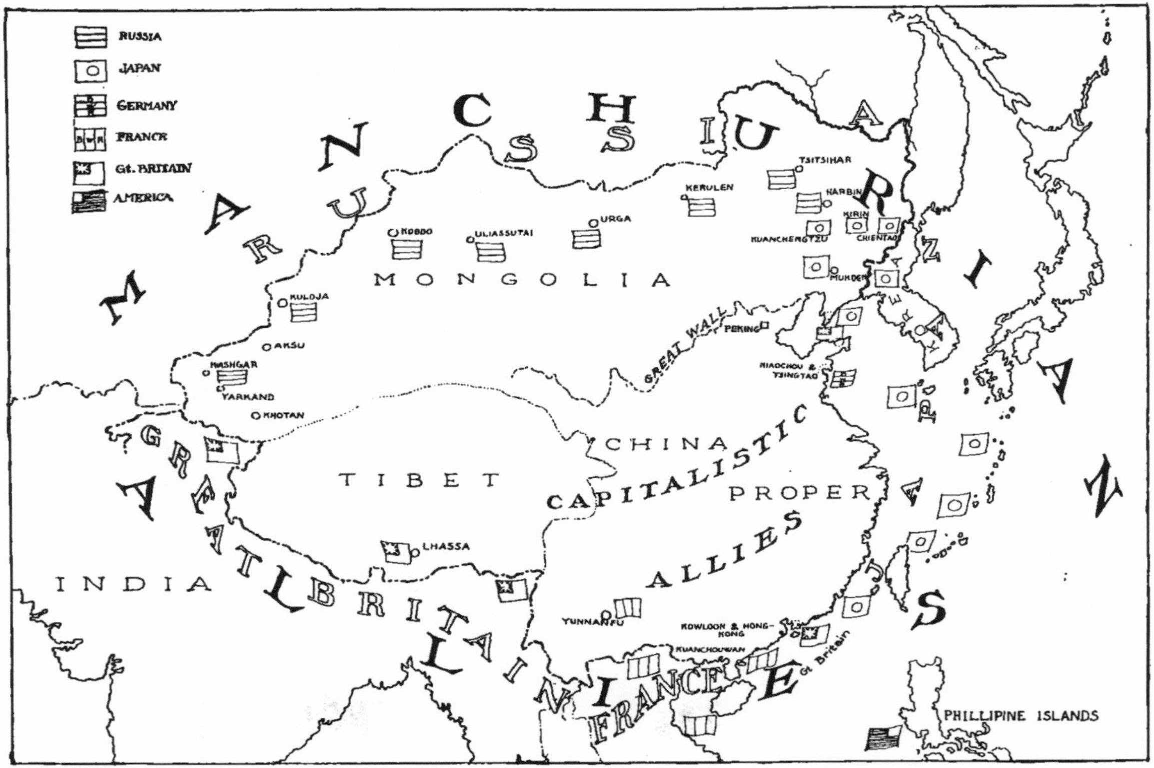

CHINA AND THE POWERS.

To face p. 306.

Japan's problem was to bring about a written tie between Russia and Japan as against a separation, which the ideas and policy of Ito involved. She passed, in her policy, to the Komura, or so-called Katsura, or "war party," which in fact was nothing more than a Greater Japan party, whose programme for some time necessitated peace.

It took four years for Komura to bring about an *entente* and agreement with Russia, which, after many vicissitudes, was fixed on July 4, 1910. Japan's aim was thus attained by a compact to maintain the *status quo* in Manchuria, which no Power has yet essayed directly to disturb, and which compact she has bound three Powers to maintain. The story of these four years for Japan is one of diplomatic pursuit of Russia, and is one of the most curiously interesting in the annals of diplomacy. Suffice to say, Russia evaded Japan's pursuit until forced by circumstances to accept the terms of the situation as viewed by Japan.

During this, in the main subterranean struggle, Russia learned of the Ito-Harriman agreement, and essayed to imitate Ito's success in getting American finance into Manchuria. She offered her own railway in Wall Street in order herself to bring America between Russia and Japan. She failed, with some expense to her pride. Russia's evasion of Japan in this issue was due to fear of the consequences of Japanese invasion of Northern Manchuria, and close contact with Japan, and her actions in the empire-hunt, going on, showed that she was sparring for time.

It was not long before Japan, then, discovered Russia's intentions respecting the Russian railway in Manchuria. These were in effect the annulment of "Article 6" by transfer of her railway to a country, America, that would interpret its provisions in a manner favourable to Chinese sovereignty. This would prevent any wholesale exercise of Japanese sovereignty in Manchuria, and the wholesale extension of Japanese settlement there.

The success of Russia's intention was the greatest blow which Russia could direct at Japan's "plan of state." In consequence Japan did everything to prevent it. In 1908, after repeated failures to open negotiations with Russia on the subject, Japan sent Baron Goto to St. Petersburg, and another officer to Harbin, with a view to opening negotiations. Russia refused to be engaged. Then Japan tried, through her Ambassador, Motono, to bring the matter up again at St. Petersburg and failed

Russia's situation from that point on was one of acute embarrassment. Japan invoked the complicated and almost omniscient weapons of the doctrine of equal rights against Russia, and with China's consent succeeded in pushing Japanese commerce and communications to the Amur River by way of its Manchurian tributaries, invading Russia's exclusive trade zone.

Russia was literally forced along by Japan. At the same time Russia employed every means to dispose of her railway, and what Russia would do in this respect was (1908–1909) a burning question in Tokio. Fearful that Russia would give up the principle of administration in the railway zone, which at that time became an issue with all the Powers, Japan sent Marquis Ito to Russian Manchuria to meet the Russian Minister of Finance, Kokovtseff (later Russian Premier). This is a strange story. Ito was assassinated before he had introduced at Harbin the object of his mission.

Ito was opposed to expansion until Japan could recuperate from the effects of the war with Russia. Almost to the last, as is well known, he denied that Japan would annex Korea, believing that his advice and that of his associates would prevail with the Emperor. He was now a changed statesman. Japan had a new spirit, and he was on an errand for his late opponents. This is the great story of Ito's last days and of his assassination and of Japan's influence and future in China. He became the martyr to the new Japan's ambitions upon the continent of Asia. It was strangely fitting, strange as life itself, that he should, after being defeated in his own plan of state, lend a hand to that of his political adversaries and lose his life in behalf of their policies.

Ito's death saved Russia from one more embarrassment of proffered negotiations, and events followed that further delayed the inevitable *rapprochement* and compact with Japan. America was observing this drama, and, unable to promote singly the policies of these two contending Powers, devised a plan to meet general necessities in Manchuria ; not only of China and Russia, but of what she considered the best interests of Japan. This was the famous " neutralization proposal." The Government at Washington proposed the purchase and neutralization of both the Japanese and Russian railways in Manchuria by the Powers. This proposal forced Russia to face the issue of a division of China's sovereignty in Manchuria, an issue which was so complicated by formal representations and opposition of the United States, Great Britain, France, and Germany, that Russia was isolated, and seeing no friendly hand held out to her but that of Japan, she accepted it. Fearing the consequences from Japan of abandoning "Article 6," and expecting more from its permanency under the Japanese than by any other plan at command for disposing of the question, she signed with Japan, July 4, 1910, as stated, an agreement to maintain it. Japan thus established what she had set out to establish, the corner-stone of her empire in China, that of special right.

Much paper has been written over by Japan and all the great European Powers, and America, setting up the principles of territorial integrity and sovereignty of China and equal rights among the Powers. It is generally believed that these papers are the guarantee of these principles. But one of the great facts brought out by the revolutionary Rebellion is the special position which Japan has made for herself, both territorially and diplomatically, within the borders of China. She now bulks with immense size in the drama being enacted between Nanking and Peking. She has entered the revolutionary era in China, having firmly set up the principle of a division of China's sovereignty. With fine contempt she went to war to demolish it when it was merely a Russian assumption. She then set it up again not as a Japanese assumption, nor as a Japanese-Russian assumption, but by a Japanese-Russian compact contained in a preliminary exchange of notes and in a formal convention.

To anyone acquainted with the nature of the machinery of a nation's expansion, and especially of the nature of the machinery of Japanese expansion, which Japan's statesmen themselves cannot control, there is no obstacle to understanding her anxiety to miss no opportunity for expansion offered by the internal differences in China.

Japan must now be leagues ahead of other nations in appreciation of, and interest in, the Chinese Revolution, and of its responsibilities and opportunities. In her vital position she is obliged to be right respecting all her responsibilities to herself and her opportunities. There is no compact as to policy and action made with any Power, which will ever justify her in missing the main chance and missing enacting the main rôle, such as she had already attained in the Quadruple Group alliance when the revolutionary Rebellion broke. The strengthening and guaranteeing of Japan's special rights in China, to which three other Powers are pledged, depend upon still further special advantages of position.

Special positions and special rights are the outcome of special circumstances. The internal differences in China, such as existed between Republic and Empire, Premier and President, was an opportunity that had not existed in China since 1644, when the Manchus turned it to account. The necessity of being alert to any opportunities that might present themselves at Peking or Nanking was thoroughly understood at Tokio, which had augmented its military in Manchuria, where was centred all the machinery of Japanese expansion working on a problem more complicated than that which Dorgon the Manchu regent solved by merely taking his army to Shan-hai-kuan and on to Peking. That feat could not be repeated.

Japan's declarations to the world at this time are that she is not prepared to recognize the Republic at present, that China's territorial integrity should still be maintained, and that Japan does not contemplate intervention concerning the form that the government in China should take (January 26, 1912).

On Jan. 27 Marquis Saionji the Premier makes the statement that "Japan has followed one and the same policy toward China ever since the outbreak of the Rebellion. It is the observance of strict neutrality. The Cabinet is exerting all its efforts to maintain the territorial integrity of China." In all of these statements there is nothing to complicate or interfere with any designs that may be worked out for acquiring a special position or right with the side that shall come out uppermost in China. Japan's position as an opportunist is now giving anxiety in the Diet, because with all her opportunities Japan threatens to fall between two stools. On Jan. 27 Mr. Oishi, member of the Lower House, expressed these apprehensions in the following criticisms :

"The Japanese policy of administration is shifting. Probably no other question is so vital to Japan as the civil war in China, but our Government has no definite policy to follow. This indecisive attitude of Japan is illustrated by the fact that there are many Japanese in both the revolutionary and Imperial armies. Hence the Chinese people have regarded us with suspicious eyes.

Tokio once lent its countenance to Peking [Ijuin's statements at Peking], but yet claims that it has been strictly neutral. One thing more : What is the cause of the reported dispatch of another army to China ? [referred to by the Nanking Republican member quoted]. Such will only make both Peking and Nanking uneasy and lead them to doubt whether we do not entertain some ulterior motives."

There was little prospect for Japan of obtaining any special position at Peking so long as Yuan Shih-k'ai, Japan's traditional enemy, was Premier and had the Throne in his hands. Although the Japanese Administration at Tokio had supported the Dynasty almost throughout,—pleased to find itself on the same side with Yuan Shih-k'ai,—such a consideration was sufficient, when the fortunes of the Republic rolled higher than ever, to suggest to the Japanese that it would be more profitable to look to Nanking.

When the Throne abdicated and all chances at Peking and Nanking were lost in the unity of the North and South, the Japanese expressed their disappointment, and their realization that the question in China had resolved back into its fundamental elements. At a dinner at Mukden given by Viceroy Chao Er-hsun, a Japanese speaking for the representatives of the Japanese Government said to the Viceroy :

" Is it not a pity that the Dynasty, that is so ancient and has been so great, should be ignominiously discarded in this way ? Events have moved so rapidly that Japan did not know fully just what they meant. Had she another opportunity, she would come to the aid of the Throne for the preservation of the Dynasty."

It is apparent that Japan has little to expect of a voluntary nature from the Republic. With respect to it, as to the Empire, all questions end in Manchuria, the base of operations for Japan, long ago pointed out by the Germans as the base for conquering Asia. Here, too, the situation is fully understood by the Chinese. Viceroy Chao Er-hsun in a speech that may be taken as a reply to his Japanese guests, warned the influential Chinese that if there was trouble at Mukden, " Japan would occupy the City in six hours."

On February 11, the day before the abdication of the Manchus, the revolutionists referred to by the Nanking Republican member as fighting in neutral territory in Manchuria with Japanese consent, were reported by the

Japanese news service as "continuing victorious." It was not until February 14, 1912, that the Japanese Governor-General at Port Arthur ordered two battalions to restore neutrality in Manchuria. Japan then welcomed the Republican leaders to Southern Manchuria and escorted them to take over its various cities.

The Republican Government at Nanking is wise enough to know that there are plenty of interested persons and Powers awaiting an opportunity to take advantage of China in her dissensions, which game has a longer consecutive history in China than any place in the world. Japan being to them the primary enemy, as she is the first and most formidable opponent, the question at Nanking therefore is: Have we done with Japan? Is there any chance for surprise?

CHAPTER XXXIV

UNITING THE REPUBLIC AND EMPIRE

FEBRUARY 12, 1912, brings the vital moment in the question of the future form of China's government and the complete success of the Republic. Simultaneous with the arrival of the abdication edict at Nanking the Republican Government receives a communication from Yuan Shih-k'ai. "That the republican form of government is the best is admitted by all the world," says he. "At one bound, the goal at which you gentlemen have been aiming through years of thoughtful labour, namely, the transformation of the Imperial Government, has now been reached. This augurs blessings and happiness for the people also. Since the *Ta Ching* Emperor has abdicated by the issue of an explicit Decree, which has been published by me, then the day on which it is issued is the end of Imperial Government and the beginning of the foundation of a Republic; and if you gentlemen will make an effort, you should assuredly gain a position of the highest satisfaction, never permitting a monarchical government to regain a foothold in China.

"Now, as the formation of a union is of great consequence, beset with difficulties, I earnestly wish to come Southward, to listen to your advice, to my heart's content, and together with you to plan methods of progress. But the maintenance of order in the North is not easily secured. The divisions of forces here are a forest in numbers, which must be cared and tended; while popular inclinations in the north-east [Mongolia and Manchuria] are not yet unanimous. The least shock may affect the whole. You, gentlemen, being all quite conversant with the present situation, can certainly understand this, my delicate position. As to the more important and weighty questions in connection with the formation of a Republic, you gentlemen have been accustomed to study them, and must have formed your opinion in your mind's eye. It is requested that the proposed methods for the formation of a union should be speedily sent to me."

The caution of the Republican Government due to fear of a surprise is expressed in the reply of President Sun Yat-sen on February 13, 1912.

" After the receipt of your unofficial news of abdication from Tang Shao-yi," says he, " Tang telegraphed to me that the *Ching* Emperor has abdicated and that you will support the Republic. The settlement of this great question is a matter of the utmost joy and congratulation. I will report to the National Assembly that I agree to resign the office of President in your favour. But the Republican Government cannot be organized by any authority conferred by the *Ching* Emperor. The exercise of such pretentious power will surely lead to serious trouble. As you clearly understand the needs of the situation, certainly you will not accept such authority. I cordially invite you to come to Nanking and fulfil the expectations of all. Should you be anxious about the maintenance of order in the North, would you inform the Provisional Government by telegraph whom you could recommend to be appointed with full powers to act in your place as the representative of the Republic ? "

The fact of the abdication is admitted at Nanking and Shanghai to be a great achievement. Wu Ting-fang and Tang Shao-yi proceed to Nanking to participate in the ceremonies preceding the election of the new Provisional President for the unity of the country. Of the heads and ministers of the Provisional Government only Li Yuan-hung, Vice-President and the senior of the great triumvirate, is absent. He continues to bear alone the responsibilities at the territorial and industrial centre of Greater China, at Wuchang.

" To-day," says President Sun Yat-sen in a letter to the Nanking Assembly, " I present to you my resignation and request you to elect a good and competent man as the new President. The election of the President is a right of our citizens, and it is not for me to interfere in any way. But according to the telegram which our delegate Dr. Wu [Wu Ting-fang] was directed to send to Peking, I was to undertake to resign in favour of Mr. Yuan [Yuan Shih-k'ai] when the Emperor had abdicated and Mr. Yuan had declared his political views in support of the Republic. I have already submitted this to your honourable Assembly and obtained your approval. The abdication of the *Ching* Emperor and the union of the North and South are largely due to the great exertions of Mr. Yuan.

Moreover, he has declared his unconditional adhesion to the national cause. Should he be elected to serve the Republic, he would surely prove himself a most loyal servant of the State. Besides, Mr. Yuan is a man of political experience, upon whose constructive ability our united nation looks forward for the consolidation of its interests. Therefore, I venture to express my personal opinion, and to invite your honourable Assembly carefully to consider the future welfare of the State, and not to miss the opportunity of electing one who is worthy of your election. The happiness of our country depends upon your choice. Farewell."

It sounds like Washington.

On Feb. 14, 3 p.m., President Sun Yat-sen and his Cabinet proceed to the Assembly Hall and formally tender their resignations and recommend the election of Yuan Shih-k'ai as President in accordance with the spirit of the President's letter of the day before. The Assembly proceeds formally with the prearranged programme, accepting the resignations, with the provision that the President, Sun Yat-sen, and his Cabinet continue to discharge their functions until the succeeding President and Cabinet assume office, and fixing upon the following day at 2 p.m. for the election of Yuan Shih-k'ai. President Sun Yat-sen's appearance in the Assembly Hall, after his letter, is the signal for eulogy by the Chairman, on the services which he has rendered to the country. As a verbal tribute to the President the Chairman says that his services are such an example of self-sacrifice and purity of purpose as is unparalleled in history, and it is solely due to his magnanimity and modesty that the North has been won.

On Feb. 15 Yuan Shih-k'ai is formally and unanimously elected President of the Republic of China by representatives of seventeen provinces constituting the Nanking Assembly. It is announced that the election is unanimous, which connects it with the election of Washington.

The solemnity of President Sun Yat-sen's farewell is continued in his reverences to the spirits of the last Chinese emperors, carried out amid the ruins of the tomb of Hung Wu, the founder of the last Chinese Dynasty, on the southern slope of Purple Hill. He stands before the large Imperial tablet bearing in letters of gold these words: "The Throne of His Imperial Majesty, Great Founder of the Ming Dynasty." Beyond, to the back of the tablet, is suspended a Chinese water-colour portrait of the founder.

Immediately in front of the tablet, on the sacrificial table supporting it, an incense burner gives forth wreaths of aromatic smoke. A large red candle burns, one on either side.

The master of ceremonies announces that the President of the Chinese Republic has come to present his respects to the great founder of the Chinese destroyed Dynasty. The President, his staff, and all present uncover and make three profound bows before the tablet. A secretary reads the President's announcement to the spirit of the great Chinese hero, the founder of the Ming Dynasty, and to the spirits of the departed ancestors of the Chinese nation, the establishment of a free Republic and the annihilation of the power and prestige of the national enemy.

Turning about and pausing for a moment, President Sun Yat-sen addresses the people and soldiers. He explains briefly how after 260 odd years the nation has again recovered freedom, and now that the curse of a Manchu domination is removed, the free peoples of a united Republic can pursue unhampered their rightful aspirations. He prophesies that a united and free China must enjoy glory and prosperity. Cheers follow, taken up by those outside the enclosures and carried miles away along the road to the City, and finally lost in the sound of distant guns.

Quietly departing, the President returns to the Republican " White House," where he holds a reception for members of the Government and representatives of the army, navy, and people. In response to the ovation from the crowds, Sun Yat-sen says :

" This is the day of joy for all. It is the greatest day in our history. After so many hundred years of struggle against misrule, we are now free to consolidate our nationality by the union of all the peoples into one great Republic. This is a welding of the North and South. The abdication of the *Ching* Emperor means a complete recovery of liberty. Now we can begin the work of national construction and consolidation. The enthusiasm of the South spread rapidly everywhere ; a small section in the North resisted, but in the end completely yielded to the will of the nation.

" Conformably with my oath, I have resigned, and the National Assembly has elected Mr. Yuan Shih-k'ai as the new President, on my recommendation. As Nanking is to be the Capital, we have invited Mr. Yuan to come South and assume his duties. His coming is the embodiment of the union of the North and the South. Although at first the North demanded a dissolution of the Provisional

REPUBLICAN CEREMONY AT THE MING TOMBS, NANKING.

To face p. 316.

Government and the formation of the new Government at Peking, we have firmly pointed out the importance of maintaining the Provisional Government at Nanking.

"Mr. Yuan has given his adhesion to our cause, and is at one with us regarding our aspirations—the development of our resources and the consolidation of our interests. He was our opponent yesterday, but to-day he is our friend. When he comes, he will receive the welcome of the united people. His visit will be a family reunion. On behalf of the Provisional Government, I extend to him an unanimous welcome and voice the feelings of the Provisional Assembly and the people. Through him all conflicting interests will be united. Should he not come or should he be unwilling to come, it might be because he does not rely upon our expressions of sincerity. This would be a disappointment to us. But I think he will come, because he has at heart the desire to bring about peace and concord for our nation.

"I hope that a lasting peace will be established between the South and the North. When I return to private life, I shall be a citizen as one of you and shall try to forward the best interests of the Republic to the utmost of my power. Long live the Republic!"

The Republican Government at Nanking devises a deputation, that shall be headed by Tang Shao-yi, for the purpose of bringing Yuan Shih-k'ai to Nanking. President Sun Yat-sen is determined that Nanking shall be the Capital and with almost a pathetic tenacity adheres to that determination. Yuan Shih-k'ai, who sees the impossibility of a change of the Capital from Peking, relies upon time to modify Sun Yat-sen's views, feeling that the dangers of suspense are more desirable than those of this radical change.

On Feb. 19 Yuan Shih-k'ai proclaims the adoption of the Western calendar and notifies the Powers of his election, requesting recognition for the Republic.

Next day the Republican Government at Nanking elects Li Yuan-hung Vice-President and arranges a Republican Commission of Welcome under Tsai Yuan-pei to go to Peking along with Tang Shao-yi and his suite, in accordance with plans so near to the heart of Sun Yat-sen. Yuan Shih-k'ai then telegraphs Sun Yat-sen that he will not discuss the question of coming to Nanking until the delegates arrive.

All through Sun Yat-sen's speech of the 15th appeared the vision of hope which he entertained with respect to

Yuan Shih-k'ai, now that the great question of the abdication and unity of the country was settled. As the envoy, Tsai Yuan-pei, accompanied by Tang Shao-yi, journeys Northward the military vigilance of the Republic is relaxed and troops are being withdrawn from the North. The expedition to Pi-tze-wo on the border of the neutral territory in Manchuria is completely withdrawn to Chefoo, and the Tientsin-Pukow Railway brings back Chekiang troops from North Anhuei.

On February 27 the Nanking delegates together with Tang Shao-yi reach Peking and are given a great ovation at the railway station and in the streets through which they march. At 3 p.m. President-elect Yuan Shih-k'ai, in uniform similar to that worn by Sun Yat-sen, receives them at his yamen, the Wai-wu-pu building. Representations regarding his journey to Nanking are made by the delegates.

On Feb. 29 about 5 p.m. a meeting of Chinese soldiers occurs on the north-east of the City outside the Ch'i Hua Gate and Tung Chih Gate, and looting begins.

One of these gates then being closed is forced by artillery fire, two shells penetrating a door.

The soldiers outside the Tung Chih Gate begin to exchange their uniforms for ordinary clothes, in the stores and pawn-shops. One soldier tears his shoulder-straps away and drops them in the hollow of a tree, where a week later they are picked up by Captain Reeves, American Military Attaché, and handed to a young lady accompanying him. At 7 a third shell sails away, to drop in the compound of the American Legation Guard, falling through a tent-roof among the tent-mates. One of the Guard officers is with Captain Summerling, the Second Secretary of Legation, in the latter's house.

" Isn't that firing ? " says Summerling, who has been an army officer.

" Only firecrackers," says the officer, thinking of the deceptions into which the men of the Guard are perpetually led by the custom of the Chinese of letting off firecrackers throughout the night.

Pretty soon again :

" I believe that's firing," says Summerling.

" No, that's Chinese firecrackers," says the officer assuringly.

Soon the bugles sound, and Summerling stops, throws down his cards, and says :

" Isn't that the call to arms ? "

The officer cannot ignore this, and gets up. Both go out. The men of the American Guard are in position on the Wall and have taken possession of the tower on Ch'ien Men and of the west end of Legation Street.

William J. Calhoun, the American Minister, sitting in his library, receives a visit from the Commander of the Guard, Major Russell, who stands at attention and says :

" I have the honour to report that a shell has fallen into the Legation Guard compound and bullets are flying overhead."

The Minister telephones to the American Missions. Plans for getting in American residents from the native city are made and relief parties sent out for them. The inmates of the Legation compound find themselves in an atmosphere of mounted orderlies, sentries, and relief parties.

It is now the dinner hour, and foreigners throughout the entire Legation Quarter are gathered in groups discussing the rioting and mutiny. The turmoil is at first mistaken for a great lantern parade which it had been intended to hold in celebration of the arrival of Tang Shao-yi and the Nanking delegates. When their guests from the native city do not come, the groups in the Legation Quarter break up into rescue parties to bring them in. Going out, they find Legation guards at the exits barricading these with sandbags. Squads of infantry, mounted and on foot, pass out *en route* to the Missions and other foreign premises to guard them.

Major Russell informs other Legation guards of the artillery souvenir which he has received. All guards are called out and the entire Legation Quarter placed in a state of defence. The British mounted infantry patrol, with the Japanese, for weeks together, have been visiting outposts all over the City. They now do special outpost service for all Legations. Frederick Moore the correspondent, going out in the evening, sees the Italian Guard drawn up in Canal Street, opposite the Imperial City wall, not knowing what to do and without orders. He sees Colonel Willoughby, British Military Attaché, who has been at Hankow and at the taking of Nanking, come out from the British side of the Canal, and says to him :

" Colonel, can you not give these men some orders ? They ought to man the wall here, open the portholes and be ready for action."

It proved unnecessary.

Captain Holcomb, American language officer, passes the open square in front of Ch'ien Men *en route* to the Imperial Chinese Bureau of Engraving and Printing in the extreme south-west of the Chinese City to bring in Mr. and Mrs. Hatch, and thinks best to leave the Tartar City by the Shun Chih Gate on account of the disorders outside the Ch'ien Men. From inside the Shun Chih Gate Dr. Ferguson's family are brought to the Legation Quarter. By midnight the Quarter is crowded with foreign refugees coming to their Legations.

The track of the Nanking delegates is marked by a lurid line of disorder, flame, and death,—from the railway station, through the Ch'ien Men, to the Nobles' School situated in the heart of the burning section between the East Gate of the Imperial City and the Wai-wu-pu building, yamen of the President-elect, Yuan Shih-k'ai. In this School the Nanking delegates are caught in the night (of February 29) by one of the numerous bands of plunderers roaming the City. It fires one of the buildings in the compound. Tsai Yuan-pei and his companions take refuge in a court adjoining the premises of the Y.M.C.A. They mount to the top of the enclosing wall, pass along the comb of the roof of one of the Y.M.C.A. buildings, creep down the gable and drop into a portico, from which they are rescued by the American Secretary, Robert Gailey. They pass the night on rugs laid on the floor of his drawing-room, and later present him with two scrolls to commemorate his hospitality.

Another band of looters and fire-bugs operates near the house of Dr. Morrison, the *Times* correspondent, who watches them at their work busy as pirates, while smart foreign patrols go by bringing in foreign refugees.

By 10 a.m. March 1 Major Russell has the Legation Street entrance toward the Ch'ien Men barricaded with sandbags, reinforced with wire entanglements, and defended by machine-guns. The American artillery is planted in the Guard compound to command the Chinese City approaches to the Ch'ien Men. The German guards occupy the Hata Gate on the East, constructing similar barricades to those made by the Americans on the West, and preparing a similar artillery defence. The French, Austrians, Italians, and British have that front of the Quarter facing the rioters and are ready for them.

Looting and burning has been carried from the eastern suburbs to the East Gate of the Imperial City, where in an

INTERNATIONAL GUARDS PARADING STREETS OF PEKING.

BARRICADE OF LEGATION STREET.

To face p. 320.

area half a mile square there is a great conflagration. The lawlessness reaches to the yamen of Yuan Shih-k'ai, the Wai-wu-pu building. 1900 lives again. The number of mutinous troops plundering the City and carrying the rabble with them is unknown.

Mutineers fire fusillades to intimidate the inmates of the shops, then burst through the doors. Gathering up blankets and silks, they rush into pawn-shops, art and curio shops, and the shops of the gold and silver workers, and later emerge staggering under their burdens of plunder. Hundreds of houses are plundered, but only articles of greatest value taken. Like in 1900, first levies are cast aside to give place to better values. Several dead and wounded are lying in the streets. Here and there a shop-keeper who hesitates to disgorge is killed.

The Lung Yu Empress Dowager has distributed 300,000 taels to soldiers of the Imperial Guard to keep them loyal. A rich family has paid 16,000 taels to the mutineers for immunity. Another has paid 8000 taels. Soldiers break down the gates and loot the mansion of Kuei Hsiang, brother of the late Empress Grand Dowager. The East Gate of the Imperial City is burned, and the Imperial Guards construct two lines of barricades to protect the East Gate of the Forbidden City. Sixty people loot a Manchu family in the Imperial City. Twenty of them are soldiers, and the others probably neighbours. Some of the latter lead the soldiers to the place, which is plundered and the family driven out. Later, the family regains its premises and fortifies them with a machine-gun.

By evening, fires are started in the Great Street of the Chinese City outside the Ch'ien Men.

"With a mounted detachment of marines we brought in the Hatches from the Southern City to-night," said Captain Holcomb. "As we crossed in front of the Ch'ien Men and looked out through the Middle Gate that had been opened for the Nanking delegates to enter some days before, the flames from some great shops burning outside rolling up and filling it made it look like the gate to hell, giving an impression never to be forgotten." "Went to see Commander Gillis after dinner," he continues, "and later watched the looting from the Shun Chih Gate, and then stood with a companion on the Ch'ien Men semi-lune wall and heard the wild destruction outside. There was in one moment pounding and the fall of crashing glass, a single shot, and all was then still.

Perhaps it was an incident in the Silver Workers' Street to the right, where gates barred each end, and the silver workers had strong guards."

An American soldier for days told a story of his adventures there. He said himself and a companion were outside when the main gates were closed, and couldn't get back to barracks. Himself and companion ran into a side street and were pursued by Chinese guards, who fired in their direction, killing a Chinese. Both Americans finally made a safe return.

Soldiers of the Legation Guards on top of the City wall are silhouetted against the light of the flaming sky of the Chinese City. The light flares over the golden-tiled roofs of the Forbidden City and throws a glare upon thousands of people in the streets, and upon the loot orgy of the mutineers.

On March 2 General Chiang Kuei-ti, with his cheery face and bent shoulders, creeps jauntily into his tight little carriage, and with a very small guard, and a headsman following on behind, goes out into the City. He is showing the nations that they " have him." His orderly carries a list of names in his hand. Here and there the old General stops, and a man is led up to be questioned and to give evidence. From the people in the street someone is then swiftly beheaded, perhaps on general principles, perhaps because he is guilty or has been merely denounced by an enemy. Then come two or three mutineers and looters deserving their fate. Captain Reeves and Captain Holcomb riding through the looted section, see five dead in the streets, and farther on General Chiang Kuei-ti and his beheading party.

Two battalions of the mutineers commandeer a train at the station of the Peking-Hankow Railway and start Southward. Long lines of carts bring refugees and valuables into the Legation Quarter, and fugitives crowd the trains to Tientsin. At evening, fires start on the north side of the City and shooting begins. The destruction of property is estimated at $10,000,000.

The fleeing mutineers are approaching Paoting-fu, the provincial Capital 80 miles to the South, where another mutiny occurs and that city is looted and burned. Communications in that direction are stopped. Mutineers are looting and burning Tientsin. They plunder the Mint and keep up rifle firing to intimidate the people. The British Somerset Regiment sends one company to protect the railway station. A German physician is shot dead.

On March 3, 1 a.m., firing is heard at Fengtai, on the Tientsin Railway, 10 miles distant. The 20th Chinese Division from Manchuria has mutinied, and the loyal 3rd Chinese Division from Liu-kou-ch'iao, a few miles distant, is attacking it. One hundred British troops at Fengtai are obliged to give an ultimatum to the Chinese troops, as they are threatening the railway yards, shops, station, and settlement there. The British Commander gives the Chinese one hour to vacate their positions 100 yards distant. Several hundred of the British Inniskilling Fusiliers arrive in time to take the Chinese positions, and the Chinese, about 1500 in number, move away. Train service is arrested, and the representatives of the Powers meet in the Legations to consider measures for restoring communications with the sea. Peking is in a state of war, and martial law is declared in the North. The Legations summon reinforcements from Tientsin, Port Arthur and Shanghai, and prepare for siege.

An international force of 800 men, representatives of the Legation Guards of all nations, march through the main streets of Peking as a demonstration.

CHAPTER XXXV

THE MIDNIGHT WAR VIGIL AT NANKING

On the morning of March 3, at Nanking, *all that is known* of the disorders at Peking the Manchu Capital, at Paoting-fu the Capital of the metropolitan province, and at Tientsin port of Peking and the metropolis of Northern China, is that the disorders have followed the arrival at Peking of the Nanking delegates.

No word has been received from these delegates. Telegraphic reports received at Shanghai reiterate previous reports that Yuan Shih-k'ai has been assassinated. These are followed by dispatches saying that he has taken refuge in the Foreign Legations. Acting-President Sun Yat-sen can get no word from President-elect Yuan Shih-k'ai, nor from Tang Shao-yi, whom he knows has been separated from the Nanking delegates. But now Sun Yat-sen receives from the Nanking delegates at Peking a cryptic telegram, asking for a Republican army to be dispatched at once to Peking to support Yuan Shih-k'ai.

The question at Nanking therefore is: Why the disorder at Peking? Is it the political surprise from without, which the internal dissensions of China have invited from the first? Has the outsider grasped the fleeting opportunity—its last chance to sunder the country? Has the shadow returned to blot out unity?

I will never forget March 3, 1912, at Nanking. It inspired the Chinese soothsayer with gloomy prophecies, which hang in the mind as the words of the Roman seer: "Beware the Ides of March." It was drizzling rain, there were no carriages, and in order to reach the Acting-President's "White House," I hailed in the street a dilapidated rickshaw, dragged by two ragged, unkempt beggars. I had no lap-robe of any kind. The rickshaw had a leaky top which flapped in my face. I stopped at the buildings newly occupied by the Foreign Office, and found that the Minister of Foreign Affairs, Wang Chung-huei, had gone to the President's yamen.

I started out again. The road was in some places swimming in watery mud, and it was an achey, rheumatic day. The Minister of War, Hwang Hsing, passed me in a carriage, at speed, with his escort, their capes flying in the wind, flourishing their automatic revolvers, and anon sighting at imaginary targets by the roadside.

I too finally arrived, to find that a State council of war had been called. The men of the Minister of War's escort were clanking about with their swords and spurs on the raised pavements in the courts, while their steaming ponies were being led up and down under the gate-houses, where we had to dodge here and there to get through.

My name and address were written down in the inner gate-house, and the gate-keeper took me to the reception-room. Mr. Ma Su, the President's secretary, was reported absent. He could not be found. At last, when he did come, he told me that the Cabinet meeting had begun and might not end until 7 p.m. or 8 p.m. It was then not 5 p.m. The meeting had been called, said Ma Su, on account of the turn of affairs at Peking. It dragged on through the night. A telegram was received from Tang Shao-yi asking for troops, and the Cabinet took up the personal situation of the President-elect Yuan Shih-k'ai and Tang Shao-yi, who were believed to be refugees in the Legation Quarter, and planned for their rescue.

Sun Yat-sen proposed personally to lead 20,000 men to the rescue of Yuan Shih-k'ai. The status of Peking was discussed, and he was persuaded against this resolve. The argument was that Nanking was the Capital and seat of the *de facto* Government. The members of the Government could not move to a local centre. Disorder at Peking was a local and isolated condition not affecting the rest of the nation, for which the nation centred at Nanking assumed full responsibility and would act accordingly. On this hypothesis a plan of relief was agreed upon. The Republican expeditionary force of 3000 centred at Chefoo was to be sent at once to Tientsin. The army on the Tientsin-Pukow Railway was to move across Shantung and Chihli to Peking, and Vice-President General Li Yuan-hung was to send a large force Northward from Wuchang. Orders were immediately dispatched for the force at Chefoo to move to Tientsin, and for the war-vessels in the North to co-operate with it. Vice-President General Li Yuan-hung was asked by telegraph respecting his ability to co-operate.

The meeting did not end until daylight. It was after 5 a.m. March 4. About 11 a.m. Ma Su was up and had just finished dressing. He said that the President was not up yet, because they had all gone to bed so late on account of the Cabinet meeting. However, we could go in. We started toward the court, and were met by another secretary, who stopped to say that the President was not up yet. We went on through the garden by the usual path, passing the guard and reaching the President's door. Ma Su ran up the steps, and I followed him. We went into the west room, as usual. It had been slightly changed. The round table on which we had had coffee when I was last there, was gone. There was a small round stand in its place, and the sides of the room were arranged with small tea-tables—each with two chairs, in Chinese fashion. But the place was strictly foreign in style, Suchow curtains hung at the windows.

Ma Su asked me to sit down, and from one of the small tables took two photographs which the President was going to sign for me. " See," said he, " these have not been touched since yesterday," and went out to the President's room. Sun Yat-sen signed them, one with his English signature, one with his Chinese signature, and the two came back together, an orderly accompanying. Sun Yat-sen shook hands with me, and we sat down. I mention these facts thus minutely because this was the last time I saw Sun Yat-sen as the head of the Republic of China, and as he appeared and lived in the last days of his Presidency.

The orderly stood at attention within three feet of the President's chair. Ma Su waited at the door for a few moments while we were exchanging preliminary remarks, and then went out. Although he had just got up, the President was not more composed than usual. Telegrams were coming in from the North and were brought to him while we were talking. He told me what had happened at Fengtai and at Tientsin and what the condition was believed to be in Peking.

" It is very serious," he continued.

I replied that it seemed to be a local affair, and that from my experience of news reports and of outbreaks in China it was not so extensive or threatening as the telegrams asserted, and that it would undoubtedly die down.

The President shook his head and said that the troops had engaged the British at Fengtai and that these were

Yuan Shih-k'ai's own soldiers. The secretaries came and went, carrying cards of newly arrived visitors and bringing outgoing telegrams for approval. One telegram was brought in that had evidently arrived from the North and was carried out again. I asked if the reports about the killing of foreigners in the North were true. One foreigner, he said, a German, had been killed. I said I thought the danger to foreign life and property on the railway in Chihli, and in Peking and Tientsin, was slight, as there were ample foreign troops there.

"That is just what the telegram was about. The soldiers of Yuan Shih-k'ai have attacked the Austrian Concession at Tientsin."

The President's long distrust through fourteen years of warfare against Yuan Shih-k'ai was evidently forced back into his thoughts, but he did not give expression to it. He knew that the telegrams were in a sense unreliable.

Personally, I could not think it possible that Yuan Shih-k'ai was responsible for the outbreak in Peking or that his party could attempt a political surprise. But there seemed nothing for me to say more on that subject.

"The most important thing now," I said, "appears to be the plans for the inauguration. If this is more than a local trouble, it will be necessary to change your plan of having the inauguration here."

"We have provided against that," he replied.

"Can you send troops to Peking?"

"We have about 30,000 troops we can send there, 3000 at Chefoo, who are going to Tientsin, the rest to the north of here."

"How soon will they arrive?"

"They must cross Shantung; it will take ten days."

"It is a large movement," said I; "I hope it will not be necessary. I have believed from the first that the real Revolution in China would be that of the Chinese people, that the Manchus would go, but that then the Revolution proper would begin. I am not sure that all this is the beginning, as it will be. I would not have prophesied a war at once, but only as the result of changes to come."

"I do not think so," answered the President quickly. "I do not think there will be a Revolution of the Chinese people."

Before leaving, I asked President Sun Yat-sen if

there was anything I could do for him, as I was going to Peking.

"The most important thing is a loan," he replied, "we must have a loan; the financial is the most important."

"Have all the other loans fallen through?"

"Yes, the Japanese one. But we have made a loan."

"How much do you want?"

The President hesitated, and then said: "Fifty millions of dollars, or a hundred million dollars."

"That is the sum of the original four-Power loan," said I. "The money will have to come from the banking groups of the four Powers, I suppose?"

"Yes, or from others. If they don't give it to us, we must get it from others."

"In the end," I explained, "a large loan must necessarily come from the capitalistic nations—that is, France, Great Britain, Germany, and the United States. If I could be of service to you in this matter, I would be glad to help. But I presume the obtaining of a loan by China now depends, as before, on the security, the manner of paying, the use made of the money, and the welfare of foreign trade. But when the Republican Government is recognized there must be no difficulty about the loans; they can be carried out, and in fact money could be advanced to China to relieve immediate embarrassment."

President Sun Yat-sen merely assented to this. I arose—secretaries were still coming and going, and a number of callers were waiting outside. I went over to a sofa on the north side of the room where lay the two photographs that the President had signed. He followed me and stood beside the sofa while I tied the photographs up in an old newspaper that had been around them. Strangely and confusingly enough, he stood diffidently at the end of the sofa with nothing to say, so that I had to make conversation. He was the embodiment of some kind of immense force, not so much of himself as of those who, like myself, felt that he was a mobile, dependable centre for whatever forces require a centre. As I leaned over the photographs I wondered if he knew these things and had learned that in himself a single man is nothing, really nothing, in a great task like a Revolution, unless as a visible point to the mass, or a medium, fluid and impressible, touching all the units.

I commented on the photographs and expressed my admiration of his signature in Chinese, though I suppose

I should have complimented his writing in English, which he perhaps would have appreciated more.

But I tied the parcel with a grass string, said good-bye and departed. The President advanced half-way across the room, and as I went out was scanning a card that had been put into his hand by one of the secretaries—it was possibly that of his next visitor. We had been three-quarters of an hour together. This was the last time I saw him.

CHAPTER XXXVI

THE INAUGURATION AT PEKING

It was drizzling and misty when I went out, making my way hastily across the garden as before, alone. The guards in their ulsters were huddled together at the doors and gates as I passed. The impression I received from my last visit at the "White House" offices was that the Nanking Government could not depend upon the information it was receiving from the North, and this proved to be correct. It sought information of the foreign consuls. The President and the Cabinet showed anxiety regarding the position of Tang Shao-yi and suspected that the telegrams from Peking were being tampered with As the representative of Yuan Shih-k'ai they were more concerned about him, Tang Shao-yi, than about Tsai Yuan-pei and his associates, whose mission was merely that of inviting Yuan Shih-k'ai to come to Nanking. The possible conspiracy which the situation at Peking showed on the night of March 3 and the morning of March 4 from the point of view of Nanking might be thus outlined :

Yuan Shih-k'ai, the opportunist, is known to Chinese revolutionaries as an astute turncoat and political trimmer. Tang Shao-yi, his envoy, has lately turned to the Republican side unreservedly and almost without persuasion. Both are reunited and suddenly involved in a new revolutionary situation. This is the first element. The second element is the foreign danger. At least one Power, Japan, on account of its great grasp of Chinese affairs, its special position and power in Eastern Asia and the world, is in a position to profit by China's internal dissension. The Nanking Government acts on the knowledge that the aid of this Power has been considered in Peking by the Manchu Dynasty and has appeared at Nanking. While the Republic of China in the South is united by race and traditions, Northern China is divided by traditions and separate forms of administration of four different peoples and is the centre of international complications that form the foremost political question in the world, making it in all the world the most inviting sphere for a *coup d'état*. Such a stroke at the Republic, led by Japan, it would be expected would be followed by all her allies.

I could appreciate what I was sure must be the feelings of the President and Cabinet in Nanking on the morning of March 4. Before I left the President's house they telegraphed the Diplomatic Body, representing the Great Powers at Peking, their assumption of governmental rights under the conditions existing throughout China, deploring the events of the past few days and accepting all responsibility, thus shutting out all other authority before the Great Powers. They informed the Powers that measures were being taken to reinforce Yuan Shih-k'ai.

The Minister of War asked Mr. Tuckey, Chief Engineer and Superintendent of the Tientsin-Pukow Railway at Nanking, for four locomotives for use on the Northern Anhuei section of the railway to transport troops. The railway was to be turned over to the Republican military on March 5, a fact that had not a little to do with British action on this occasion, since this was British property.

Upon receipt of the Nanking Government's notification of the military advance upon Peking the Diplomatic Body, which regarded the disorders at Peking and elsewhere in Chihli Province as the acts of the irresponsible soldiery, took alarm. Regarding an advance on Peking as an unnecessary measure and a great mistake in diplomacy on the part of the Nanking Government, one almost certain to create unnecessary hostilities in the metropolitan province, and perhaps further disorders, certain ministers sent unofficial advices through their consuls at Nanking persuading the Nanking Government to abandon these plans.

When the Nanking delegates reunited at the Hotel des Wagons-Lits, Peking, after their escape, they selected four of their number to return to Nanking and persuade the Republican Government against insisting upon the voyage of President-elect Yuan Shih-k'ai to Nanking, but on the contrary proceed with the formation of the Coalition Cabinet. President Sun Yat-sen was already convinced by the disorders in the North that it was sufficient to have Yuan Shih-k'ai's inauguration at Peking.

The abdication, election of Yuan Shih-k'ai, and unity of the country removed the necessity of giving an answer respecting further Japanese loans, which loans collapsed, and with the reassurances of the other Powers sent from Peking the shadow of Japan passed for the time being. Before leaving Nanking for Peking I asked the Republican member already mentioned if there was any embarrassment of that kind remaining, and he said no, that was past now. China again drew a long breath of relief.

My personal situation as a correspondent, when quitting Nanking, was like that of the Nanking Government—one of bridging the gulf between the Empire and the Republic. I was to get to Peking for the inauguration, to see it and the conversion of the old City from a royal to a republican Capital. The war correspondent's situation is often that, in miniature, of those whose great deeds he reports. My course was now as stormy as that of the leaders of the Peking or of the Nanking Government.

The merchant steamer service on the China coast was disorganized by the Rebellion and I was obliged to take passage on a naval auxiliary. It was a soaking day on the Yangtse when with a wet coolie and sampan I got aboard a 4000-ton vessel loaded with nearly 6000 tons of ammunition and other war materials. We put out of the Huangpu and the Yangtse into the China Sea. As the political sky cleared for the President at Nanking the situation for us cleared as we neared the Chihli coast, and when we landed near Taku the sun was shining as though the storm had lifted from the Republic.

When I passed in a special train bearing 200 American troops to Peking the Inniskillings were crouching behind their fortifications at Fengtai. Playing the rôle of the Capital, as through the ages, Peking in her foreign military dress and appearance was more warlike than at any time since the revolutionary Rebellion opened. Now rising as the Capital of the Republic, it is still the Chinese Paris, and has passed into the hands of its "citizens." With its blackened walls, its charred timbers, its ashen fields, it has done its revolutionary best to rival the Capital of the French.

Glorious old Peking has been trailed in the dust. It is like a venerable gentleman appearing in Court with his eyes blackened, face bruised, hat gone, and his clothing soiled and torn, in the hands of those who defame him, for trial, set upon by his own sons, and with none but strangers to speak for him.

Or Peking is like a discredited queen who gathers up

her torn robes to face her accusers. Turning upon them, she says : " Thus far shalt thou come and no farther." She has dismissed Nanking's aspirations to be Capital. However disreputable her present, she will not be robbed entirely of her birthright. With her last contention surrendered and, as it were, with her back against the wall, she claims honour for her Minister, the last official of her Imperial Government; all others she has given up. He must be acclaimed under her roof-tree.

Tried in fire, the old Capital triumphant was lighting the torch of the Government of a United Republic when I arrived. Yuan Shih-k'ai was being inaugurated. The once called traitor is chosen. Out of the hundreds of millions, this one called to save the Dynasty and the Empire is singled out to unite the country in a Republic. " My rheumatism," "my enfeebled health," his mechanical dialogue with the Throne in October in Peking, ends in the Presidential oath. He has passed through many dangers, leading a woman and a little boy and all their tribe and kin whom he has brought to safety, and he now receives that which at various times has been offered him by President General Li Yuan-hung, Wu Ting-fang, Tang Shao-yi, and Sun Yat-sen.

After the Dynastic cataclysm, assassinations and attempted assassinations, the threatened interference of the Powers, Yuan Shih-k'ai is uppermost—he is more than he was in the beginning.

Every step of his pathway since October has been amid turmoil and disorder, in which he has stood firm. On Feb. 29, when the disorders occurred and the shops were burning around him, Yuan Shih-k'ai had been receiving His Excellency Sun Pao-chi, ex-Governor of Shantung, who had come up from the Astor House at Tientsin to see him. Some of those present in the excitement urged Yuan Shih-k'ai to save himself. " The President-elect, however," said Sun Pao-chi, " merely replied, ' I stand firm ! ' "

He had given old General Chiang Kuei-ti command of the City. Few stood with him. Report said he was abandoned by his following, and only Tsai Ting-kan, his faithful secretary, who had been one of the envoys to General Li Yuan-hung at the beginning of November, remained with him. " Tons of valuable loot," says one, " were carried into the premises of his yamen, the Foreign Office, by his own soldiers and by the ragamuffins of

General Chiang Kuei-ti, from whence it was taken in the early morning of March 1 to the railway station and to Paoting-fu."

Tang Shao-yi asked the Ministers of the Powers to take measures to prevent further bloodshed and loss of property in Peking, which was followed by the reinforcement of the Legations.

On March 1 Yuan Shih-k'ai issued a *communiqué* to the foreigners in which he said:

"The unexpected disturbance has filled me with sorrow. One of my chief duties is to preserve order in the Capital. Hitherto I have been uniformly successful. Unto you, strangers in a strange land, I wish particularly to convey my sincere regrets. Every measure of precaution is now taken to prevent recurrence."

General Chiang Kuei-ti's soldiers returned to their allegiance and patrolled the streets, administering justice with the executioner's sword. I looked into the diary of a friend for these exciting days, and read: "Beheading everywhere." J. W. Chambers, another friend, told me he was walking along the street, and with a companion stopped to intercede on behalf of a Chinese boy of twelve or fourteen years who was tied with his hands behind him along with two men. All were kneeling. He asked the soldiers to let the boy off, as he was too young to be killed for anything he had done. The soldiers said they were not going to kill the boy—all three prisoners were to be kept there until four o'clock, when they would be released. The soldiers said this was to scare the prisoners.

The only reason ever given for the disorders was that the ignorant soldiers feared the reduction of their pay and being compelled to cut off their queues. Yuan Shih-k'ai ascribed the disorders to this. On March 7 he issued a communication to the soldiers reminding them —whom he has "always treated as members of his family— of his care and affection." He admonished them to remain mindful of their duties and discipline, and pointed out that otherwise the consequences of their lawless acts might be intervention in China by foreign Powers.

The homeless Chinese are scraping in the ashes of their ruined shops and homes. The beheading of luckless Chinese for natural moral lapses, no different from those exhibited by officials of the Legations and their wives and families in 1900, has nearly ceased. Many photographs of the decapitations and other sensational events and scenes, now called the sack of Peking, are being printed by and sold among foreigners.

Yuan Shih-k'ai is being inaugurated.

President Sun Yat-sen and the Nanking Assembly have approved a plan for the inauguration at Peking and the subsequent sending by Yuan Shih-k'ai of a representative to Nanking to assist in the formation of a Provisional Cabinet, with the approval of the Nanking Assembly, after which the site of the Capital of the Provisional Government shall be decided in accordance with the needs of the situation.

It is Sunday, March 10, 1912. The rainbow flag flies over the gate-house of the modern Foreign Office building, lately the yamen of the Premier and President-elect, built by the American engineer C. D. Jameson under the direction of Tang Shao-yi, and by the support of Yuan Shih-k'ai and the late Empress Grand Dowager.

The Empress Grand Dowager, whose name is even now imperishably linked with the best plans of government progress in China, lives in this scene. The incongruous juggling of the days of autocracy and despotism with the present is further shown in the shrubbery of the garden, which conveys some notion of the bizarre setting in which the Republic comes into being in Peking. It is winter, and on the leafless twigs and branches are fixed bright paper flowers. In this the Republic seems to hark back to the beginning of the seventh century A.D., to the usurper Yang Ti, who squandered large sums of money on his palaces and gardens, decorating the trees of his park in winter with flowers and leaves of silk. From his place among the rabble in the street the Chinese soothsayer looking through the gates and remembering the suspicion of Yuan Shih-k'ai's motives might say, " Beware Yang Ti ! "

Resemblance to the past disappears at the doorway, where one steps through a foreign portal, ascends a foreign stair opening into a foyer, and comes to a grand staircase.

In the reception and banqueting hall on the upper floor gathers the small and remarkable mixed and imposing audience consisting of President-elect Yuan Shih-k'ai, his secretary Tsai Ting-kan, his suite, the Nanking delegates led by Tsai Yuan-pei, Tang Shao-yi the man selected for Premier, the Mongol princes, the high lamas, high civil and military officials, together with a few foreign officials and foreign employés from the Chinese Maritime Customs and Postal Bureau, a dozen foreign correspondents, and other foreign spectators from the Missions and hotels.

Yuan Shih-k'ai is dressed in the uniform of military cut in which he first received the Nanking delegates. In stature he is shorter than anyone present except a few of these delegates. He holds his head back in an expectant, strained attitude which, with the incongruity of his foreign clothes, suggests to one who has known Yuan Shih-k'ai the wrench in the Chinese order marked by this epochal event. There is undeniable dignity and breadth in the man who has been successively beaten in his defence of the Throne, as he reads in a solemn silence, from a prepared oath, these declarations :

" Since the Republic has been established many works have to be performed. I shall endeavour faithfully to develop the Republic, to sweep away the disadvantages of absolute monarchism, to observe the constitutional laws, to increase the welfare of the country, and to cement together a strong nation embracing all the five races. When the National Assembly appoints a permanent President I shall retire. This I swear before the Chinese Republic."

He hands the written oath to the senior Nanking delegate, Tsai Yuan-pei, in accordance with the procedure agreed upon.

Yuan Shih-k'ai is Provisional President.

Standing listening was this strange agglomeration of participants and spectators. The Mongol princes, wards of the nation, in Mongol dress, stand in wonder before this strange " kurultai," the strangest in all the gatherings of the Clans to them since Genghis was made the Great Khan and Kublai ruled all China. The Mongol and Tibetan lamas ; they are the Church ; most dignified of all in their rusty gold and wine-coloured robes ; they too stand for what was the Throne, and come from the Yellow Temple under its patronage since the lamaist Church was established at the Capital in Peking by the Emperor Chien Lung. Around these two groups from the dependencies are the civil and military officials of Peking in a strange mixture of mandarin and Western cosume. The Chinese Press, too, is there.

Shoulder to shoulder with the " five races " are the actual representatives of the Western world whose civilization has brought this strange event to pass. Sir Robert Bredon, late Acting Inspector-General of Customs, a noted foreign figure in the drama of China's change, is there. Mr.

T. Piry, Postal Secretary for the Chinese Government, is there. Not far from Yuan Shih-k'ai stands Dr. Morrison, the *Times* correspondent; General Munthe, long the aide of Yuan Shih-k'ai; and Major Menzies, a faithful English partisan and attaché.

Edward T. Williams, First Secretary of the American Legation; Dr. Tenney, Chinese Secretary of the American Legation; and Captain Reeves, American Military Attaché, in his uniform of the General Staff of the United States Army, are officials of the American Legation "unofficially present." "Your Legation," said General Munthe to me, "is the only one officially represented at the inauguration." The foreign correspondents are in their big clothes, some of them carrying silk hats,—attired in their "glad rags," as the American journalist expresses it, to greet the President and the rainbow flag.

"Near me," said a distinguished foreigner, "stood Wang Chao-ming. He is the man who attempted to assassinate the Prince Regent by placing an explosive in the roadway, or under a bridge, where the Prince was to pass." "I believe he is regarded as one of the heroes of the Republic," said he in a manner expressive of the strange associations brought about by the inauguration. Wang Chao-ming had been the representative at Peking of the revolutionary Rebellion, and was now one of the Nanking delegates and a distinguished figure among Republican leaders.

Through all this moves General Yin Chang, ex-Minister to Germany, ex-Minister of War, ex-Commander of the Imperial Army and victor in the capture of Hankow, a Manchu, in his official uniform but humbly picking his way around the Republican delegates, the lamas, the Mongol princes, the foreigners and the rest, to some place where he will be unobserved. Republicans have demanded that he should be made answerable for the deeds of the Imperial Army. To them he is the shade of unnumbered thousands massacred at Hankow, not to say the shade of the Dynasty itself. He is the ghost at the feast, and cannot be hid. Nevertheless, he has been a man, one who has done his duty. He is one with the woman and the little boy, and is under the shelter of the great President.

Where are the others? Poor Prince Ching, last of the great Manchus of the old school, is in refuge, sick at St. Michael's, the French Hospital in the Legation Quarter opposite the American Guard barracks. Prince Su, the genial mediator between the Manchus and revolutionaries, is in Port Arthur or Dalny, a refugee from revolution and debt. Yu Lang, a worthy and modest Prince, is lost altogether. Na Tung, late Minister of Foreign Affairs, is—where? at Tsingtao or Tientsin. The belligerent Prince Tsai Tao, the brother of the Regent, so it is said, is in the German Legation. Prince Tsai Hsun, the fat Prince, ex-Minister of the Navy, brother of the Prince Regent and Prince Tsai Tao, the nabob, the leader of Manchu fashion, the nobody—of him none has thought to inquire. Pu Lun the pleasant is remembered. Hsi Liang, the great ex-Viceroy, ex-Tartar General in charge of Jehol the Court's contemplated refuge, is as though he never existed. Tieh Liang, ex-Minister of War, ex-Tartar General of Nanking, alone is saved from being forgotten by a mean rumour to the effect that in Dalny he is plotting against the President-elect.

The great names are those of the Cantonese and Hunanese revolutionists: Li Yuan-hung the Republican Nestor, Wu Ting-fang the advocate, Tang Shao-yi the mediator, Huang Hsing the soldier, Wang Chao-ming the would-be assassin of the Prince Regent. Oh yes, the Prince Regent, where is he? There is the Emperor also, and the Lung Yu Empress Dowager. All the mighty are scattered and fallen. Long live the mighty!

The written oath having been handed to Tsai Yuan-pei, a band plays the National Anthem, approved by the Throne in 1911, after the fall of Szechuan. It is the last word and comes as it were from the Empress Grand Dowager. All acknowledge Yuan Shih-k'ai President, and disperse. The inauguration is over. Eight thousand armed men revolt at Canton. Fighting begins. The pirate hellions of the delta rally around the flags of their chiefs Wang and Luk at the East Gate. These mosquito and bull-frog junk fleets, scoundrels from the bayous, the firecracker rascals of the sampans, blaze away over barricades and housetops until they score 1500 death casualties in all, and stop blood-drinking on March 14 with a battle. Next day they look indifferently upon the beheading of 200 of their own men, and after four days put up their arms again. It is Canton's contribution to the inauguration of Yuan Shih-k'ai. It is the Canton initiation of the "Flowery Republic." There is nothing tame about it.

On March 12, in answer to an invitation from the lama

temple inside the An Ting Gate, the Nanking delegation visits the lama priests there—those representatives of the ancient ecclesiastical rule of so much of China. Here the extremes of social and political notions of the Republic and of the Empire meet. The Church is here making its bow to the new Power in China. And in response the senior delegate, Tsai Yuan-pei, standing with his associates around him, addresses the head lama, a young man, and says :

"You must not think that the overthrow of the Dynasty and the establishment of the Republic has been the work of a clique made up of a few men and of a few conspirators. It has been accomplished by the rising of the whole people. Under the Republic all have their responsibilities, and each one must do his best."

Thus the welding of Republic and Empire. It is evening, and in the Legation Quarter all sorts of Chinese and Manchu officers are dodging, incognito, in and out of the narrow passages. While ruminating over the probable effects of the last two or three days' work, I see a mysterious native in a long buttoned coat and a military cap pulled down over his eyes, come out of the lane beside the Hongkong and Shanghai Bank, evidently from the house of the comprador. General Yin Chang slips from the Hotel des Wagons-Lits and goes to the German Legation, to dine, it is said, with Prince Tsai Tao and the Kaiser's officers.

The work is done : who knows what will come of it ?

CHAPTER XXXVII

SUN YAT-SEN'S FAREWELL

YUAN SHIH-K'AI signalized the inauguration of his administration and the beginning of the Republic by remitting all delinquent land taxes and pardoning prisoners, excluding only murderers and robbers.

On March 11 the Provisional Constitution of the Republic was adopted.

Before I left Nanking the Republic had turned with great relief from the Japanese, and fear of Japanese control, to the Belgians and to combined Russian and Belgian loans and counter-influence. The Nanking Assembly in the paramount question of finance agreed with the President-elect, at the earliest moment to form connections with neutral sources for financial aid. The loan which President Sun Yat-sen told me had been made was the preliminary loan agreement with Belgium, succeeding complications of which were promptly to throw the Republic into the financial relation with the Powers that existed under the Empire.

It is at least a relief that the danger from Japan either at Peking or Nanking, apparently, has not created any innovation in China's foreign relations. On March 12 Tang Shao-yi is formally named Premier and proceeds with the attempt to complete the Belgian loan. On March 19 Tang Shao-yi leaves Peking to go to Nanking for the formation of Yuan Shih-k'ai's Cabinet. On March 29 the Cabinet is fixed, and on April 1 President Sun Yat-sen and the members of his Cabinet, at a meeting of the Nanking Assembly, formally lay down their offices and give over the Seal of the Republic to the President of the Assembly and to Tang Shao-yi, the Premier and representative of President Yuan Shih-k'ai.

In this, President Sun Yat-sen fulfils the oath of his inauguration. A military band plays a German march as the President and his Cabinet take their places in the Assembly room. Thirty-five members are present, together with half a dozen foreign spectators and a "handful" of young reformers. Nine Chinese suffragettes occupy a conspicuous position in the gallery and observe a noteworthy propriety. Mr. Chao S. Bok, President of the Assembly, states that the President will address the Assembly in a farewell message. Walking to the rostrum, President Sun Yat-sen says:

"I came to Nanking on January 1 to be inaugurated President of the Provisional Government of the Republic of China, and to-day, April 1, is just three months from my induction to office. During this interval we have accomplished what we aimed at, namely, the establishment of a Republic. Now that the union of North and South is perfected, and a Coalition Government formed, I come here to resign my office.

"On taking leave of you, I feel that I would like to say a few words. The Republic of China should always aim at the promotion of the world's peace, for only by so doing can the welfare of mankind be advanced. Before this can be done we must firmly lay the foundations of the Republic. This is the duty of all of us. If we are faithful to this duty, our object can be attained quickly. Though most of our people are ignorant of the meaning of the word and of Republicanism, yet for centuries they have enjoyed peace and have been lovers of peace. To instruct them in the principles of Republicanism and world peace should not be a hard task. And if the mission should be successfully accomplished, what an effect will it not have upon the world, when 400,000,000 people, a quarter of mankind, champion the cause?

"This is our duty, and we must try to do it. I have resigned my office, but my resignation does not mean that I have done, and am done, with my duty. Far from it. Only hereafter I am going to discharge my duty in the capacity of a private citizen. It will be my object to help my 400,000,000 countrymen, and endeavour to make the blessings of the Republic a reality."

He is applauded, and bows in acknowledgment as well as farewell. A single appreciative Assemblyman rises and returns the retiring President's bow.

Sun Yat-sen takes the red bag containing the seal of office and solemnly places it before the head of the Assembly.

One of the members of the Assembly then reads from a yellow scroll a eulogy on the services which Sun Yat-sen has rendered to China. Before the band finishes another tune the ex-President and ex-Cabinet have withdrawn. Sun Yat-sen has put into effect the full letter of his presidential oath and of his provisional resignation.

On April 2 the Nanking Assembly by a vote of 20 to 6 authorized the transfer of the Provisional Government from Nanking to Peking, and on April 3, accompanied by Tang Shao-yi, the citizen revolutionist Sun Yat-sen left Nanking, retracing the route to Shanghai by which he had come to be President. This man, unschooled in statecraft and having given his life to agitation, conspiracy, and organization of rebellion, showed conspicuous gifts as the head of the Republic of China. Under the eyes of all mankind he was calm, self-sacrificing, and hopeful. He was an extremist among revolutionaries. According to his own words, he would not hesitate to invoke the aid of every engine of warfare to attain the revolutionary aim of freeing his countrymen from the bondage of the past represented by Manchu rule. Yet his ideal was the attainment of this end without bloodshed. He was not alone in his aim, but in a country of such large and diverse forces working for Revolution he attained to the most conspicuous position in the triumvirate with Li Yuan-hung and Yuan Shih-k'ai. He has the best power of the agitator, and he is notably honest, making the kind of impression most likely to remain, that of sincerity and high purpose. He made himself known to all reformers inside his country, as well as to all the Chinese outside his country—and these are all reformers. He pursued his aim for twenty years undaunted, and then realized it, and his great services were recognized, almost unanimously, in his election to be first Republican President of the federated provinces. He is a prophet honoured in his own country.

Sun Yat-sen had no large organization in China, but he united the reformers on the one side and the conspirators on the other. He realized his hopes by seizing and making the psychological hour of revolt in Szechuan and at Wuchang his own. He saved himself from the fate suffered by Kang Yu-wei and Liang Chi-chiao, who allowed reform and revolution to get past them. When the time came for him to give way, to resign the Presidency and secure the selection of Yuan Shih-k'ai, the reform party standing behind him that may be called his own, was against him in this. Eminent Chinese abroad, like Dr. Yung Wing of Hartford, warned him never to trust Yuan

T'sai Yuan P'ei, Minister of Education. — Huang Hsing, Minister of War. — Sun Yat-sen (Signed Sun Wen). — Wei-Chen Tso, Vice-Minister, Foreign Affairs. — Hu Han-ming.

THE NANKING ASSEMBLY, FEBRUARY 1912.

To face p. 342.

Shih-k'ai. Competent and influential foreigners shared these views. But in the end Sun Yat-sen trusted Yuan Shih-k'ai in the interests of the nation, secured his election to the Presidency, and returned to the people no longer an outlaw but—Citizen Sun Yat-sen. As the "stone which the builders refused" he gave himself a country and his country a government.

CHAPTER XXXVIII

YUAN SHIH-K'AI

REPUBLIC and Empire are formally welded in the President, Yuan Shih-k'ai. " The whole people," whose rising, Tsai Yuan-pei says, has accomplished the establishment of the Republic, are now represented in one man. How does such a man, yesterday the hope of the Empire, with such a varied career as Imperialist, represent the people ?

A man has arisen in the wilderness of men where the West has said no man existed. At the same time—that is, since 1900—Yuan Shih-k'ai has been hailed as " the one man." There was one Manchu, the Empress [Grand] Dowager ; there was one Chinese, Yuan Shih-k'ai. For him the times called and he came. Now he is President of the " Flowery Republic," the finished man of fifty-four, of pure Chinese lineage, the product of the revolutionary era in Eastern Asia.

In 1858 Yuan Shih-k'ai was born, as it were, under Mars, in the midst of the period (1857–1861) when the Allies were forcing their way by war and negotiations into China's capital, Peking, and establishing themselves there. I remember him first as the Governor of Shantung, when I arrived in China in 1900. He was then executing Boxers who claimed to be invulnerable to bullets. A Boxer delegation visited him at his yamen in Tsinan-fu. It was received with great politeness, and Governor Yuan Shih-k'ai listened to all it had to say. At the conclusion he told the members of the delegation that he would test their claims at having achieved invulnerability by Boxer rites, had them stood up against a wall before his soldiers, and shot.

I then saw him on the occasion of his arrival from Shantung at the end of 1901, when he came to succeed his late " teacher " and patron, Li Hung-chang, as Viceroy of Chihli. He was a handsome man of forty-three, with mobile, swarthy face and typical Chinese drooping moustache. He came by train, surrounded by the bodyguard essential to the dignity of a high Chinese official and necessary for his protection. He got off the train at the Peking-Hankow railway station, outside the Ch'ien Men, in his big mandarin clothes such as all officials wear. His outer long coat was of plum colour, with the insignia of official rank on the breast and back such as all officials wear—embroidered animals for the military, birds for the civil officials—and the official round turban mounted by a button indicating degree of rank. Preceded by mounted infantrymen and guarded on each side by rows of foot-soldiers, he was carried away in his chair to the temporary quarters from which he afterwards went to attend audience and to thank the Throne for his appointment.

Following these ceremonies and his calls on the foreign ministers at the Legations, I accompanied the party to witness the entrance of the new Viceroy into his vice-regal Capital. Representatives of the administration of the metropolitan province and of the foreign Powers thronged the railway station at Tientsin. It is a side-light on Chinese character, and upon the idiosyncrasies of Yuan Shih-k'ai, that during the period of his rise to power he kept four soldiers of uncommon stature as his personal bodyguard to impress the populace. He passed in his chair, borne by four chair-bearers, with two of these giants in their plum-coloured Chinese uniforms with black trimmings and velvet boots, turbans, and with swords on each side. The foreign civil and military representatives, British, Japanese, French, Italian, and others, in the uniforms of their different services, saluted, and he returned their courtesies by bowing his head and occasionally saluting with his hand in the Western fashion.

Yuan Shih-k'ai's administration at Tientsin was a very distinguished one. He gave a comprehensive municipal government to the native city, and a common school system to the entire province. In the latter work he selected the American educator Dr. Tenney to organize the system. He also began the formation of the Metropolitan Army—afterward numbered at 80,000 men. The exercise of his authority over the masses at the time is illustrated by the following:

In 1902 a foreign traveller had trouble with one of the soldiers of this Army. Complications resulted which embarrassed Yuan Shih-k'ai, and he had the soldier beheaded. The luckless soldier, however, was a man connected with an influential family, and in order to hush the matter up, the Viceroy paid for his rashness by giving 30,000 or 40,000 taels to the injured family. The same year Yuan Shih-k'ai sent troops and surrounded the town of Kuang Tsun, in Southern Chihli, whose people had been rioting, and executed, as he said, about 1000 people. In explaining this act, at Paoting-fu, he said:

"Foreigners may not think well of me for doing this, nor of this method, but it is my way."

His army became more or less completely foreign-drilled, and by the time he was called to Peking in 1902 was a reckonable quantity in China's foreign affairs. These achievements mark the zenith of his power and fame under the Empire. He was fifty years of age. On Sept. 15, his birthday, the Empress [Grand] Dowager sent him gifts whose value was estimated at a fabulous sum, unprecedented in the annals of Her Majesty's long reign in connection with Imperial favours. This fact inspired expressions of wonder in the Legation Quarter at so pronounced a partisan being shown so great a mark of Imperial favour.

Yuan Shih-k'ai's official career was twenty-four years old. It was in 1884 that he received his first important appointment, that of Director-General of Trade and International Relations in Korea, and took up his post at Seoul. He succeeded the Manchu Tartar General in charge of Chinese troops there after international troubles in 1882, the year Korea was opened by the American Treaty to international trade. Complications with the Japanese (1884) enabled him to get their troops out of Korea and force them into the background, after which he consulted with his patron Li Hung-chang at Tientsin as to the future policy for excluding Japan from interference in Korea's internal affairs, with the result that he was promoted to a higher rank. In October 1885 he returned to Seoul as Imperial Chinese "Resident," a term conforming with that applied to the Imperial representatives at Lhassa in Tibet and at Urga in Mongolia.

From that day until he went to Hsiao-kan and Niekou to negotiate a compromise with General Li Yuan-hung in Nov. 1911, the man now President of China was never farther from the scene of his official triumphs—Chihli Province—than when at Seoul. He never went abroad, knew no foreign language, and was without any special literary attainments such as generally distinguish the mandarins of China. An American diplomat at Seoul who knew Yuan Shih-k'ai during the period of his official service there, 1884–1894, in words which deserve to be invested with permanency, as expressing a foreigner's observations, says :

"Nobody understands the meaning of the term arrogance who didn't know Yuan in those years. He was arrogance personified. He would not meet or associate with the Ministers of other Powers unless he was allowed to occupy a sort of throne and 'receive' them as though they were vassal envoys. At a Korean state dinner he always occupied the foot [one end] of the table, which then became the head. He rode the half-mile through the Palace from the gates to the audience hall in his chair, and had his interview first, while the rest of us waited outside, after walking all that distance through the mud.

"He was in my time just a big, brutal, sensual, rollicking Chinaman. Having vast powers, he frequently cut off the heads of Chinese gamblers and others, and I was an unwilling witness of some of these street-side pastimes of his. He would imprison Korean gentlemen who objected to parting with their ancestral estates in order that they might be used to enlarge Yuan's palatial Legation. He would not let a physician save the life of one of his soldiers in the *émeute* [1884] by amputating his arm, saying, 'Of what good would a one-armed soldier be?' Yet he kept as a pensioner another soldier whose life was saved but who was useless as a trooper. He was extremely quick, quite fearless, very rash, yet given to consultation with Tang Shao-yi and others, and therefore inclined to be reasonable. He was altogether unscrupulous, but absolutely faithful and devoted to his patron and largely to his friends. He would sacrifice an enemy or one who stood in his way, but would at the same time sacrifice himself readily for his patron."

These are the spirited words of an opponent and experienced observer about which there need be no question unless with respect to those internal details of which it is always hopeless in the Orient to get complete information and evidence.

When Yuan Shih-k'ai went to Seoul he was a young man of twenty-six. As the keeper of the door of the continent through which China's great antagonist was to enter, he possessed some of the best qualities of youth—vigour, daring, and self-sacrifice, but he had more the qualities of a soldier than those of a civil mandarin or statesman, and as he could not draw upon the resources of experience all that could have served him was the essential resources of an occult sense, an intuition. This he did not have.

From the moment he showed his high-handedness in the *émeute* of 1884, Japan began preparing for war. Knowing full well from experience that China would violate her pledges, Japan arranged a convention the following year by which the two Powers agreed not to land troops in Korea without first informing each other. It is charged against Yuan Shih-k'ai that when an opportunity came in 1894, he broke the convention by calling for Chinese troops to suppress a Korean uprising, and thus he fell into a Japanese trap, bringing about a *casus belli*.

Yuan Shih-k'ai was giving an official dinner when he learned of the starting of the troops for Korea. The information came in telegrams received by him and his Japanese official guests as well. The news broke up the dinner. The actions of the self-satisfied Japanese were so suspicious that Yuan Shih-k'ai took alarm and immediately fled from Seoul, without waiting to remove his mother and concubines, who were left in the care of some of his associates.

Li Hung-chang, who was directing from Tientsin these state affairs against Japan and had succeeded in drawing America into the complications, was evidently relying upon success in war with Japan. War came in ten years, and its outbreak has always been attributed to the arrogance at Seoul of Yuan Shih-k'ai. As Japan came off an easy victor, Yuan proved to have been the wrong man at the door. But these ten years of crass error and its consequences were the making of him.

Yuan Shih-k'ai was thirty-six when he got back to Tientsin, and he was thirty-seven when the treaty of Shimonoseki was signed ending the war with Japan. For three years he is not mentioned in the official lists of the Empire, but in July 1897 the fact that he becomes Judicial Commissioner for Chihli indicates that he is an older and much wiser man. At the same time it shows the interesting fact that he has not lost prestige with his patron Li Hung-chang and is making friends and alliances.

During Sept. 1898 Yuan Shih-k'ai was given the rank of Vice-President of a Board (one of the departments of the Central Government) and the control of an army corps.

YUAN SHIH-K'AI

Peking, 1911–1912.

To face p. 343.

That he had made good use of his experiences in Korea was shown by the fact that he turned his attention with great energy to building up an army on foreign military lines. In June 1899 he received an actual appointment as Vice-President in the Board of Works. In Dec. 1899 he became Acting-Governor of Shantung, and in March 1900 Governor.

In September 1908, the time of which I am speaking, when his services and abilities are recognized by the Empress [Grand] Dowager, foreign observers and students of Chinese history and character speak of him as the only Chinese or Manchu visible who can be called a statesman and placed in that rank among the men of nations.

In twenty-four years he has been hammered from a rash young soldier into a statesman. He started with the metal of strong character, intelligence, and amenability to persuasion, and developed a judicial mind and power of decision. The latter quality is that which impresses foreigners most, for the reason that that quality is almost lacking in Chinese diplomacy and is undoubtedly the one which more than anything else draws from them the tribute of " statesman."

At the time of his birthday celebration, September 1908, he occupied the very pinnacle of his fame under the Empire. He was the acknowledged mentor of the Dynasty. He was living, for the summer, at Hai Tien, a village near the Summer Palace, where he had taken a villa in order to be near the Court. It was here that I called to felicitate him upon his fiftieth birthday and talk about China, the last time I saw him under the Empire. On Sept. 14 he sent me word that he would like to see me at the " Kua Chia T'un "—his villa—on Friday, September 18, at 2 p.m. But on account of the festivities connected with his birthday and the unexpected attention, from the nobility and officialdom generally, excited by the honour shown him by the Empress [Grand] Dowager, the date had to be postponed. For several days he was involved in audiences at Court and journeys back and forth between his villa and the City to attend the trying affairs of Manchuria, active at the time, and his social duties to the princes and others who were calling on him and following up the example set by the Empress [Grand] Dowager. He was the man of the hour. Even foreigners hastened to recognize the Empress [Grand] Dowager's stamp of importance given him. His whole life was brought under inspection to see wherein this greatness lay.

Personally, I was disappointed. He did not look the part. He was somewhat corpulent. He sat in his chair like one reared in the saddle, with his knees wide apart like a Mongol. He was like a small-rank military official in aspect. He had bright, penetrating eyes which he flashed on the Chinese secretary present with a message that unmistakably said : " Get that exactly right. Be careful what you say." These eyes were rather prominent and began to show a bulging effect that was already increased by years. He did not look fifty, was very active considering his weight, but he had undoubtedly lost the good looks of his middle age. Pushed back on his head was his little round Chinese mao-tzu, or hat. His black, drooping moustache was marked a little with grey and had already commenced to straggle. His clear and swarthy skin was clouded and somewhat more than suggested the high living with which he was charged.

Twenty-four years after his youthful mistakes at Seoul he showed traces of character that made the foreign diplomat's observations of him when he first arrived there appear so fair. But all was toned down into an agreeable maturity.

The embers of his youthful arrogance showed in the way in which he still clasped his hands to his knees and threw up his shoulders and head. It gave him the air of the sultans of Central Asia.

Among those characteristics which years had matured and tempered was that of seeking information wherever he could find it. The first and last impressions that one received was his intentness in getting at the speaker's viewpoint and the things the speaker understands and knows about. I had brought him copies of my books on the Russo-Japanese War. At the time of that war he was Viceroy at Tientsin and was consulted by the Peking Government on all important matters, such as neutrality and other foreign questions, in which he was virtually the head of the Government. He was naturally very much interested, and the first question he asked was about the real difference between the Japanese and Russian soldier. It may be said that in a sense that is the first question of China. It is this quality of getting at the vital point, of being able to think in a direct line, that has given him his standing in the estimation of foreigners.

The presentation of the books was the opportunity for the servants to bring in the tea which we drank to each other, always the signal in Chinese life that the call is ended. I bowed and went out, escorted to the courtyard by the great Councillor.

It was a perfect autumn day, the courts of the villa were flooded with sunshine in which the leaves of the aspen glistened. Outside the villa entrance, waters from springs that feed the lakes in the Summer Palace flowed through a bed of watercress where chattering ducklings splashed in the water. The branches of old willows swayed blithely above a little pool where happy Chinese-doll girls were washing their garments.

As I thought afterwards of this scene, Yuan Shih-k'ai seemed lifted to this pinnacle of glory for this brief autumn day, held high in the matchless sunlight of North China that all the world might see how far he could fall. Yuan Shih-k'ai was on the political brink.

The moment that marked the heyday of his favour was at the same time the beginning of his decline.

He had not been at Court a year before the metropolitan glare that dims the brightest star from the provinces had made him but a common luminary. In the fierce light radiating from Peking official strife the weaknesses in his armour and the tarnishable qualities that exist in every reputation were exposed to common view. The heaping of gifts upon him by the Empress [Grand] Dowager was the signal for attack by his enemies. Those gifts were something like a millstone about his neck.

Coincident with the lavishing of Imperial approval upon him, a censor named Chiang Ch'un-lin brought impeachment charges against him, and was joined in the indictment by Liang Ting-fen, Provincial Judge in Hupeh. The latter disclosed what Yuan Shih-k'ai's detractors thought of him. "His favourite pastimes," says Liang Ting-fen, "in his youth were horse-riding and fencing, and he was not a man of education." The accuser then proceeds to explain how Yuan Shih-k'ai has risen to power through the patronage of Jung Lu, a favourite of the Empress [Grand] Dowager, and by bribing Prince Ching, whom he says at first on three different occasions refused to receive Yuan Shih-k'ai. Prince Ching being a weak man naturally, and his expenses being very heavy, Yuan Shih-k'ai took advantage of him. Yuan Shih-k'ai, after ingratiating himself at Court, then secured high positions for his henchmen. These henchmen are all enumerated by the accuser, who warns the Court that it ought to be alarmed at the great military authority exercised by Yuan and his protégés in Chihli and Manchuria. Finally, Yuan Shih-k'ai is compared with Ts'ao Ts'ao the arch-traitor of the Han Dynasty and one of the three most execrated characters in Chinese history.

What was not expressed in impeachments came out in the Chinese Press. Here he is made responsible for all of China's misfortunes, which he germinated in the China-Japan War and caused to blossom in the *coup d'état* of 1898. It was because of him that China's existence was well-nigh terminated in 1900 by the Boxer rising, when he drove the Boxers out of Shantung into Chihli, thus forcing them on to Peking. And it was through the Russo-Japanese War, to which Boxerism led, that Manchuria practically passed into the hands of aliens.

But for the China-Japan War China's weaknesses would not have been immediately discovered ; but for the *coup d'état*, reforms would have succeeded and in ten years China might have taken rank with first-class Powers. With the Japan-China War thousands perished and China's national prestige of thousands of years. For this would not the people have liked to taste his flesh? However, the Emperor whom he traduced showed him unprecedented favour which could not be repaid had he died on horseback on the battlefield. But he sold his master for glory and did not play his part.

The clamour of Yuan Shih-k'ai's detractors induced the Empress [Grand] Dowager to command him to clear himself of the charges lodged against him, and the Throne issued an edict appointing Prince Pu Lun and Grand Secretary Sun Chia-nai to investigate, principally, the indictment made by Censor Chiang Ch'un-lin to the effect that Yuan usurped all governmental power and was ruling like an absolute despot against whom nobody could achieve his purpose. Yuan Shih-k'ai was forced to excuse himself from Court by asking two weeks' sick leave.

The charges against Yuan Shih-k'ai were just such as could be brought against any Chinese or Manchu official, and he would have survived them with an undiminished influence and power had the Empress [Grand] Dowager lived. China needed him, and the Empress [Grand] Dowager needed him, for she was growing old. The impeachments were preceded by scandal. He was charged

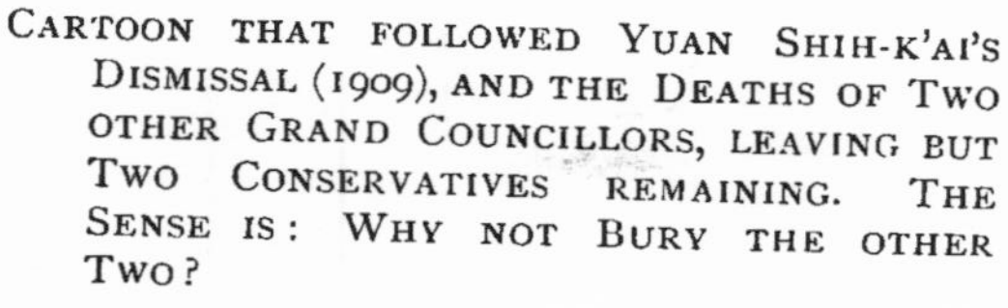

Cartoon that followed Yuan Shih-k'ai's Dismissal (1909), and the Deaths of Two other Grand Councillors, leaving but Two Conservatives remaining. The Sense is: Why not Bury the other Two?

The Powerlessness of the President: While in North China (Compartment) trying to send the Arrow (Ancient Emblem of Authority) into South China (Compartment).

To face p. 352.

with having too large a household—rumour said more than a score of concubines. This was not considered an immorality in itself, and would not have been thought worth mentioning in connection with an official of less importance. His opponents considered that there had not been anyone equal to him in power during the whole Manchu era, not excepting his patron, Li Hung-chang.

The three most exciting months of Yuan Shih-k'ai's life so far had their beginning in these September birthday festivities in his villa at Hai Tien. For six weeks he withstood the attack of his political opponents. At the end of this time the Emperor and his Imperial protector the august Empress [Grand] Dowager suddenly died. In another six weeks he was a fallen idol. He disappeared in three days and his place knew him no more. In a week he had been lost completely in the maelstrom of the new reign.

The event of Yuan Shih-k'ai's fall was not uncommon to China, which passed serenely on to the next event. Only foreign observers paused to examine the merits and demerits of the fallen. It was remarked by many that he had missed the opportunity to seize the State and save it. Although he was a self-made man, he was charged with lack of determination and energy such as would have enabled him to overcome his enemies and prove himself a leader. Though he had good sense and political ability, it was said that he had not the strength to resist the enervating pleasures of life. He had not followed the self-denial of his teacher Li Hung-chang, but early in life had capitulated to the seductions of the harem system. On the other hand, ability, administrative capacity, and understanding of constitutional government and of foreign affairs, together with energy, will-power, and decision, were merits attributed to him.

It was a fact that he was the prop of China's credit abroad and the creator of the only policy toward the Powers that China ever possessed. He rescued the Foreign Office from ridicule and made it a workable body. The successful management of the succession to the Throne upon the demise of the Emperor and that of his august patron the Empress [Grand] Dowager, was attributed to him by the best-informed foreigners. " He was the first to show China the practical way to reform."

As he was leaving Peking the bitterness in his heart was expressed in these words to those around him :

" Now we shall see how they manage. Even if they send for me to put things right for them I shall not come out again."

Following this all that is heard of Yuan Shih-k'ai is anecdotes of his life in his retirement at Weihui-fu in Honan, where he is reported as saying :

" I am quite able to confront my heart with Heaven above ; posterity will decide upon the justness of my cause."

He has a little estate the improvement of which together with the interests of his family occupies his time. His diversion is fishing. He sits in a boat at the edge of the rushes in the most approved style of the ancients, with a common reed, peaked hat of the people on his head and a mantle of rush leaves to shield him from the sun and rain. Compared with the fustian and consequence of official life it is a life of solitude, almost melancholy. He shuns publicity and receives few visitors—only family friends. He is content with the simple life of a country gentleman, without the mass of servants his household so long required. He is a great man and his regret is not personal so much as on account of the State. He is aware of the impossibilities connected with statesmanship in Peking under the Regent, and appreciates the opportunities of his new life. Much of his thought and anxiety are for an invalid brother for whom he seeks medical aid. He brings foreign physicians who come with electrical batteries and other treatments, from Tientsin. He gives similar care to the rest of his household. He feels the deprivation of his old associates and assistants, especially of Tang Shao-yi, who was with him in Korea and whom foreigners as well as Chinese have said made Yuan what he is.

" In a certain sense this is true," one who knows him writes me," for in the early days in Korea when Yuan was new to everything, Tang certainly informed him and enlightened him on many of the things that belong to the Western world, and Yuan conceived a very warm affection for Tang ; I would go so far as to say the only real affection the man ever knew, for there was no one of his family or harem who occupied the place Tang occupied. His influence was so great that we were wont to say it amounted to a sort of hypnotism. It was good for Yuan to have a soft spot in his heart, which is necessarily taken up with matters of state and diplomacy—not the best atmosphere for growing the finer graces."

CHAPTER XXXIX

THE PRESIDENT, THE NATION, AND THE WORLD

During his retirement Yuan Shih-k'ai has been compared with Achilles sulking in his tent, and Bismarck glowering in his library. Naturally his mind reverts to old battle-fields, for they are his life and character, and the whole substance of his relation to the world, to the nation, the presidency, and all his future.

The great events of Yuan Shih-k'ai's life have been the clash with Japan (1894), the *coup d'état* (1898), and his dismissal (1909). They are all living issues. In his responsibilities as President they meet him wherever he may turn. What he is in the " Flowery Republic " and in the world is comprehensively shown in these events and their effects. The last goes back to the first. His dismissal by the Throne takes us in an instant to Seoul and the now quarter-of-a-century-old and still unforgotten warfare between the two nationalities, Chinese and Japanese, and to what the American diplomat calls the arrogance which Yuan Shih-k'ai exercised over the Ministers of the Powers there. This was something which that diplomat says Yuan " knew quite well to be as distasteful to the King of Korea [who was forced by Yuan] . . . as it was to us, particularly to the Japanese Minister, whom Yuan treated with marked contempt. . . . As late as October 6, 1893, the Japanese Minister was afraid to join us in refusing to attend an audience with the King unless allowed to ride into the Palace as did Yuan Shih-k'ai—an action which he so heartily approved." The sequel to these initial relations between Yuan Shih-k'ai and the Japanese was Yuan Shih-k'ai's flight from Seoul, the Japanese Minister's entry to audience with the King thereafter in a horse-drawn carriage, on equality with the highest, and the final annexation of Korea by Japan.

The last antagonist Yuan Shih-k'ai saw as he left the stage of Peking at the time of his dismissal, January 2, 1909, was Japan, who rose up on that occasion of China's wretched weakness to deal both another blow. At that time Tang Shao-yi as special financial envoy was about to arrive in Washington, sent by Yuan Shih-k'ai to secure $50,000,000 American capital with which to establish uniform currency in China and strengthen the country. His mission was regarded by Japan as inimical to her interests in China and she was opposed to it. She therefore took advantage of the opportunity to promote at Washington an exchange of notes between the two Governments expressing mutual confidence. This was telegraphed in advance by Japan to Peking in such a manner as to embarrass China's envoy to Washington, and discredit Yuan Shih-k'ai, his patron and sponsor for the mission.

Japanese action in using the exchange of notes between the United States and Japan to forestall Tang Shao-yi and discredit Yuan Shih-k'ai was a weight thrown in the balance against Yuan. Japan's notification to China of Japan's understanding arrived at with America reached Peking two days before Yuan's dismissal. It is likely that only Japan was aware of the impending bolt. All the other Powers were surprised and alarmed when it came. The edict read: " Yuan Shih-k'ai, Grand Councillor of State and Senior Vice-President of the [Chinese] Foreign Office, has received rapid promotion during the reign of their late August Majesties the Empress [Grand] Dowager and the Emperor, and after Our Accession to the Throne We were supported by his inestimable assistance, for he really has remarkable talent.

" Unfortunately, now he is suffering from rheumatism of the leg. He walks with difficulty and We believe it is impossible that he can carry out his functions; therefore We place him on the unattached list and authorize him to return to his native place so that he may nurse himself to health. Thus We manifest to him Our clemency."

Yuan Shih-k'ai's position in Peking was this: After the China-Japan War, when Li Hung-chang left Tientsin, Yuan Shih-k'ai ingratiated himself with Li Hung-chang's successor, Jung Lu, under whom he held command of, and developed, Chihli's modern-drilled army corps. Jung Lu died in 1903, and Yuan Shih-k'ai pushed his own interests with Prince Ching, as a compensating support to that of the Empress [Grand] Dowager. He now had the Manchus, except the Empress [Grand] Dowager and Prince Ching, against him, as well as those Chinese partisan sympathizers with the late Emperor Kuang Hsu, one of whom was the Censor Chiang Ch'un-lin. Of his own party none were nearer to Peking than his successor at Tientsin, the Viceroy Yang Hsi-hsiang. His great opponents in power were the Prince Regent, Na Tung his associate Vice-President of the Foreign Office, and Tieh Liang, Minister of War. Grand Councillor Chang Chih-tung, China's foremost Confucian scholar, was not unfavourable to him but was helpless, and was as much surprised at his dismissal as anyone.

On December 31, 1908, the Throne granted a princely title to Prince Ching as a bribe to quiet the old Minister. The Prince Regent received in audience the Censor who had impeached Yuan Shih-k'ai. On the next day the Prince submitted an edict to the Grand Council for approval, reported to be a cancellation of the offences of the reformer Kang Yu-wei in connection with the reform movement of 1898. It was disapproved by Prince Ching and Yuan Shih-k'ai, and was withdrawn. Both Councillors knew what they might expect from this attempt to rehabilitate the fame of the late Emperor's reform party, against which Yuan Shih-k'ai was held to be an enemy. Prince Ching was not deceived by the Prince Regent's gift to him, but on the other hand alarmed. To protest against the honour, he called on the Prince Regent, who assumed a lofty attitude, said it was his plan, and the Prince should accept what he had received and be satisfied. The old Prince retired to his home ill and remained there. On Jan. 2, when Yuan Shih-k'ai was at the Foreign Office (Wai-wu-pu), he received a circular summoning the Grand Councillors to audience. He went to the council hall. As he was about to enter he was informed that his presence was not required. He immediately hurried home and sent the women of his family by evening train to Tientsin. The Prince Regent at the council hall laid, signed and sealed, before the astonished Councillors, the edict of dismissal, forbade discussion, and asked the Councillors to sign it. Not all of them were present, and Prince Ching's name was attached to it with the check opposite denoting his absence.

Later, at ten minutes to three o'clock in the afternoon, the foreign Ministers became aware of the edict of dismissal, and in two hours the British, German, and American Ministers were in conference at the British Legation, and held another conclave in the evening with representatives of other Powers included. It was apparent that Japan was aware of the Prince Regent's programme and that she was the doubtful element in the situation.

The British and American Ministers agreed that the dismissal of Yuan Shih-k'ai should not pass unnoticed by the Powers. On Jan. 3 they met with the German and Japanese Ministers and submitted an outline of representations to be made to the Chinese Foreign Office. All agreed that peace and international interests were in danger, but Japan dissented from any action on the ground that foreign interests were not technically involved, and that therefore foreign action would not be justified. In this she was joined by Germany.

Yuan Shih-k ai fled to Tientsin and took refuge in the British settlement, at the Astor House Hotel. The Court and Grand Council took alarm at Yuan Shih-k'ai's flight and the activity of the foreign Ministers, and a messenger, Yuan Shih-k'ai's own son, was sent after him with assurances that the Grand Council would guarantee his safety if he would return. The Grand Councillors who framed this message pointed out that they had been ordered to comply with the edict of dismissal, and explained that China would be in danger from the Powers if Yuan Shih-k'ai by remaining away confirmed erroneous impressions of the real situation.

Prince Ching's signature to this appeal gave confidence to Yuan Shih-k'ai and he returned at once to Peking. His family followed on Monday, and on Tuesday Jan. 5 he left by special train for Weihui-fu, Honan.

The Chinese Press was almost unanimous in stating that the dismissal of Yuan Shih-k'ai was due to his part in the *coup d'état*, 1898, by which the Emperor's reform party and its programme was defeated through what the reformers called Yuan Shih-k'ai's treachery. This reason was so given out to all the newspapers in Peking. His impeachment, which according to reports embraced 12 to 32 counts, was understood to have been framed on charges referring to this event. The Prince Regent had accepted these charges, and he let it be known that he was determined not to continue to take part in the government of China with Yuan Shih-k'ai. It was true that the late Emperor Kuang Hsu until his death nursed against Yuan Shih-k'ai a resentment. A persistent circumstantial story declares this was embodied in a valedictory command written on his death-bed by Kuang Hsu holding Yuan Shih-k'ai responsible for the failure of the reform movement and leaving it as a duty upon his survivors to see that Yuan Shih-k'ai's offences should not go unpunished. A more important fact was that Yuan Shih-k'ai was an obstacle to the reapportionment of Imperial patronage for the benefit of the numerous impecunious members of the Prince Regent's family and that of the new Lung Yu Empress Dowager. He was an obstacle to the monopolizing by the original reform party of what its successor, the general reform movement, held to be its rightful inheritance under Kuang Hsu. The charges brought to accomplish Yuan Shih-k'ai's elimination were dictated not by patriotism but by jealousy and greed, and the weak Prince Regent and hysterical Lung Yu Empress Dowager (who was daily wailing at her Emperor's bier) were not strong enough to withstand the temptation for vengeance.

The wretched imbecility of their act was not strong enough to provoke Yuan Shih-k'ai to his own defence.

Thirteen years he kept silence—until November 1911. Coincident with his return to office in Peking, in response to appeals from the Throne to save the State, he gave to the world the first explanation of the 1898 episode, showing that the ostensible charges on which his dismissal was accomplished were without an essential basis. To set posterity right, as the last survivor on the Imperial side, he said in substance, as given to Dr. Morrison :

" On the night of September 18, 1898, the reformer Tan Tzu-tung, one of the Kang Yu-wei party, and secretary of the Grand Council, called on me. The main facts of the plot on which he was bent are well known, but the statements published in the public Press purporting to describe my participation in it are largely misrepresentations of facts. The reform party led by Kang Yu-wei, considering that the Empress [Grand] Dowager and the Viceroy of Chihli, Jung Lu, blocked the way of their reforms, conspired for their removal. Jung Lu was to be put to death in his yamen at Tientsin, and the Empress [Grand] Dowager was to be interned as a State prisoner. My progressive views being well known, I was to execute these plans. I was to go to Tientsin, put Jung Lu, my patron and benefactor, to death, and then immediately return to Peking with my corps of foreign-drilled troops, and there seize and imprison the Empress [Grand] Dowager.

" After ordering all the servants out of the room, and after a few words of introduction, Tan Tzu-tung denounced Jung Lu in scathing terms, and laid this plan before me, saying that it had the Emperor's consent and approval. He produced a rough draft of the plot, written in ordinary black ink, and invited my co-operation.

" I replied that there was no Imperial Order for me to undertake the task.

" Tan Tzu-tung said that on the 20th a secret Order from the Emperor would surely be given. On my further objecting that such a plan could not be executed suddenly but needed mature deliberation and a ' Vermilion Decree,' Tan said :

" ' I have the Imperial Order with me,' and forthwith handed me a document in black ink, neatly written, in a style couched in the tone of the Emperor. It stated that His Majesty was bent on reform, but since conservative opposition was met everywhere, Yang Jui, Liu Kuang-ti, Lin Hsu, and Tan Tzu-tung [four of the most active members of the reform party] were to devise some ' sound plan of action.'

" I once more objected that the document was not an Imperial Order, since it was not written in vermilion ink, nor did it mention the execution of Jung Lu and the confining of the Empress [Grand] Dowager in the Summer Palace. Tan said the Vermilion Order was in Lin Hsu's hands and that what was produced was only a copy, and added that in truth an Imperial Order had been issued three days before. He assured me that the phrase ' sound plan of action ' referred to the disposal of Jung Lu and the imprisonment of the Empress [Grand] Dowager.

" As I insisted on the Vermilion Order from the Emperor and Tan could not show one, there was nothing definite arranged between us. On taking leave, Tan said :

" ' We depend on you.'

" I decided that at my audience on the 20th I would sound the Emperor on the subject by referring to the reform movement. Accordingly, when I was summoned for audience, I spoke of the new reform and its difficulties, and the late Emperor was much affected by my words, but made no reference to the ' sound plan of action.'

" The Conservatives were also active. Huai Ta-pu, Li Shan, and Yang Chung-yi [whose son married the daughter of Lord Li Ching-fang] went off to Tientsin and deliberated in secret with Jung Lu, who was well informed of what was going on through them and communications with the reactionaries.

" When I retired from audience with the Emperor

I joined a friend at the railway station and proceeded to Tientsin. On my arrival at Tientsin in the evening I called on Jung Lu, who said to me :

" ' You have come for my head. You had better confess all, because a man [Yang Chung-yi] who was here just now, before you came, has told me everything.'

" ' What you have heard is but the plot of a few political schemers,' said I. ' His Majesty the Emperor said nothing to me about such a plan, and he is innocent of such a measure.'

" At this juncture in the conversation the late Admiral Yeh was announced, and later on Ta Yu-yen arrived. They stayed until 11 p.m., and seeing no chance of renewing the conversation I returned to my lodging. Next morning, September 21, Jung Lu called on me and said :

" ' Lately, friends from Peking have repeatedly informed me of the reformers' minutest movements. Their daring is astounding. We must rescue the Emperor from their clutches.'

" When Jung Lu returned to his yamen he summoned Ta Yu-yen for consultation, and sent for me in the evening. Yang Chung-yi was present, and produced an edict sent by wire, informing Jung Lu that the reformers' plot had been exposed in Peking, that the Emperor was in durance, and that the Empress [Grand] Dowager had resumed the Regency. On dismissing me from his presence Jung Lu pointed to the tea-cup and said : ' You can drink—there is no poison in your tea.'

" Four days afterwards, September 25, Jung Lu was called to Peking, and on Sept. 28 was transferred to the Grand Council and given the rank and power of Generalissimo."

This narrative shows that the reformers of 1898, the Chinese and foreign Press, and Yuan Shih-k'ai's enemies and opponents greatly exaggerated Yuan Shih-k'ai's responsibility in the failure of the reform movement of 1898 and his importance in the *coup d'état*. It shows much more. It shows the value as a weapon at the end of 1908, on the eve of Yuan Shih-k'ai's fall, of the prevailing beliefs respecting this part of Yuan Shih-k'ai's record, in serving the interests of his opponents. These opponents were, the original reform movement of Kang Yu-wei, and the outsider. The outsider whose interests are most vital in China's affairs, and to whom every advantage is vital, is Japan. Upon Yuan Shih-k'ai's dismissal it was instinctively recognized by the European and American Ministers, as well as by Yuan Shih-k'ai's own party, that Japan was an opponent. Her nominee Na Tung, whose interests she backed against her opponent Yuan Shih-k'ai, was immediately appointed Yuan Shih-k'ai's successor. He had been on several missions to Japan, beginning with the expiatory mission of 1901 to apologize for the murder of the Japanese Secretary of Legation at Peking by Boxers in 1900, and from that time he was recognized without contradiction as a Japanese partisan.

When Japan now refused to join Great Britain and America in representations to China on the dangers involved in her unconscionable dismissal of Yuan Shih-k'ai, she was accused of infidelity to her ally Great Britain, and to the principle of a community of interests of the nations in China.

Japan's defence must be recorded. She represented that she would have sided with the majority of Ministers, but as the majority—she counted, of course, the nations having no power of initiative in China—were not going to act, she would remain neutral. The situation so far as the action of the Ministers was concerned no longer had any bearing on the merits of the question, when Japan announced her position. It had arranged itself for Japan with strict reference to the diplomacy of Eastern Asia that adjusts itself to the *fait accompli*. But Japan's position and course in this was diplomatically incontrovertible.

On Jan. 15, 1909, Sir John Jordan, British Minister, and W. W. Rockhill, American Minister, visited Prince Ching, head of the Chinese Foreign Office and of the Imperial Clan, and surviving patron of Yuan Shih-k'ai, in accordance with instructions from their respective Governments and expressed the anxiety of these Governments over Yuan Shih-k'ai's dismissal and China's policy. This act necessitated a formal expression by China of her policy. It formally placed her on record as committed to a continuation of her traditional relation to the Powers without change, and, by establishing and emphasizing in the understanding of the Throne and the Dynasty the importance to China's welfare of the safety of Yuan Shih-k'ai, it set before all the nations of the earth the paramount question of Eastern Asia : China against Japan, Japan against China.

This is the measure at this moment of Yuan Shih-k'ai

and his importance in China's future. I give these details because of the great importance to men and nations of a full knowledge of the events that have brought on the struggle of China—the most stupendous struggle man has ever known.

It was precisely three and one-half years since Yuan Shih-k'ai had set the date for my last interview and I had last seen him. When I next saw him he had been President for a week. My mission was a personal one. I called at 10 a.m. Tsai Ting-kan, his secretary, took me in. The President was busy, there were many demands upon his time. My visit was prearranged ; Tsai had spoken to the President about it, reminding him that I had visited him at his villa at Hai Tien in 1908, when I had presented some books.

We went across the garden of the Foreign Office building that Jameson had made—Tsai and I. Pink paper roses in full bloom still were tied to the wintry shrubbery in front of the *porte cochère*, giving the garden a gay but chilly appearance even in the brilliant winter sunshine.

Guards at porch and door, threshold and stair and landing, salute us.

" Sit down in here," says Tsai, showing me into a reception-room.

" Now come," says he, when he reappears a little later.

Yuan has seen many foreigners. He has become used to it long ago, as Li Hung-chang did, shows his feelings when he is busy or worried, and thinks of when they are going to leave. Foreigners say Yuan is thinking of bombs. There is no Government, but he has much to do in negotiations with foreigners on international questions and in trying to use these questions to get money out of the rich foreign nations to pour into China's poverty-stricken treasury.

He is brown, very dark brown, but not so white-haired and old as his photographs have lately made him look. And he has shaved away the whiskers worn in his retirement and exile, leaving only his moustache which I remembered as black, but which is now grey. His eyes somewhat start from their sockets, and he is a little short of breath, like a reasonably corpulent man should be. He is standing, and shakes hands. And in answer to my inquiry as to how he has been these past years, he says he is well. He offers me a chair, and we sit down at a table immediately in front of the door. The room is furnished in foreign style though with some Chinese comforts. Next to our personal relations I have but one thing to mention—the question of his own people, especially their relations to their own affairs. I had been to Canton and this fact was the first to arouse him.

" What is it like there ? " he asked instantly.

I told him the story of how they had soon forgotten the war-cry of the revolutionary Rebellion and raised the great question of the future of the Republic. He listened intently. I got my first vivid impression of "The President" at this moment. He impressed me as does a man who is powerless and who has been thrust into a strange position. Of course he could not seem to me to be a President He asked questions, and when I had finished he expressed no views but was revolving something in his mind. I told him that I had talked with many persons interested in China and that those most prominent held views respecting the revolutionary movement which tallied with the original view of His Excellency, namely, that China ought not to move too fast and that a centralized government like a monarchy seemed most desirable at first. Yuan then said what was in his mind :

" The condition of China is such that it is not longer in the power of a few men to decide. They can do nothing, and the matter of China's future is in the hands of all the people. The responsibility is now upon all, and each one must do everything he can."

I think it was this confession of his helplessness that led me to say that I was about to leave for Western countries. Naturally many would ask me what I thought, and I would give them an account of my observations. I was interested in promoting the best interests of China, and I told him I would be glad to do anything I could for the Chinese people. If His Excellency knew of any such offices, which he could suggest, and which were in my power to perform, I would be glad to perform them.

" Your country and mine now have the same kind of government," said he, " and you can do a great deal for China. Our relations have always been of a close nature and America has always been a good friend of China. You can speak well for us. I hope you will do so when you return."

No one knew better than Yuan Shih-k'ai the value of help for China. He saw China as she was. The Dynasty was a small thing—it could be dismissed. The Republic though a great aim was a name—it could be dismissed. The people knew little of the Dynasty or what the Empire meant, and no less of the meaning of the Republic. He had had in his hands a woman and a little boy at bay against the revolutionists. He now led a woman, a little boy, and unnumbered millions, guarding them against themselves and standing against the world.

CHAPTER XL

QUEUE-CUTTING PARTIES

LI YUAN-HUNG, Sun Yat-sen, and Yuan Shih-k'ai the triumvirate are three men. To stop with them would be to leave out China and all that must be the Republic if it is to exist hereafter. What exists is the people, and they are the whole answer. Their first universal move was with respect to the queue, which outside Peking was nearly all that existed in China of the Manchu.

"I will part with my head but not my queue," said a venerable Chinese member of the National Assembly at Peking in Dec. 1911, in a speech opposing legislation directed at the abolition of the queue. The queue measure before the Assembly was immediately passed without other opposition. An examination showed that its provisions made the wearing of the queue optional; it did not abolish it or penalize the wearing of it. An examination of the head of the old gentleman showed that the queue which he had defended so passionately was a mere wisp attached by only a few desperate hairs.

He was the expression of conservative China regarding all her established customs. But his attitude on the queue question was more Northern than Southern. I noticed in passing through Northern China, where the queue custom originated, there was no noticeable cutting of queues. In Manchuria, where the fashion was begun in 1618, there had been no real change in the government nor in the attitude of the people toward Peking. There had been a showy declaration of independence, but there was no reality of it. Going thence into the metropolitan province of Chihli, I saw queues everywhere. I saw them everywhere in Shantung, where the custom was unchanged except at Chefoo, a Republican port in possession of Republican troops. The Manchu rulers themselves had no objection to China's abandoning the queue, but people hesitated to change, first because of habit, and second because whatever they did might be made a pretext by their enemies in the approaching Rebellion. Yuan Shih-k'ai cut his queue to show that the Government he served did not impose the fashion upon him.

All this region was conservative China—the Past. But the iconoclastic Present of the Republic, which went so far as to appropriate ancient monuments as targets for the practice of its artillery, struck first at the queue. The immemorial temperamental and social division of the Empire at the Yangtse River was emphasized by the uprising and attitude of the two sections, North and South, respecting all fashions. The North, conservative, retained its established dress. The South grasped for whatever was new, especially in appearance. In the South the hair-dressing infection of *Ch'ang mao* (T'aiping) days survived. One of the first popular demonstrations there was the sacrifice of the queue amid scenes of good-natured delight. It was a kind of " March through Georgia," at which the sweet potatoes might well have " started from the ground."

To me the first signs of real queue-cutting came at Tientsin. It reached the college-prank state at Shanghai—which had been the centre of the anti-opium-pipe crusade —and became a popular diversion at Canton. It was of the nature of a City festival, lasting several days. I am sure that more queues fell in this campaign of shears than did opium pipes in the opium crusade. There was a flash in the sunlight, a snip, and gone was the glistening braid.

In a City of two and a quarter millions not a queue was visible in the streets after three days. Citizens who were determined to hold on to their ancient and honourable appendages remained in seclusion and fear. It was a gala day for all those Republicans who could arm themselves with shears. They paraded the streets ready to sunder every queue. Shopkeepers joined the groups and mobs of queue-cutting outlaws, all good-natured, awaiting the unsuspecting victims—carriers, chair-bearers, teachers, salesmen, farmers. Clip, and off came the victim's queue —his mortification greeted with howls of delight from the crowd. It was a kind of daylight " Boston Tea Party," in the Canton style.

Visitors who wished to go by chair through the City were annoyed to see their chair-bearers take a new and circuitous route.

" Where are you going? Why do you not take the main route?" they asked.

Down comes the chair—the chair-bearers look at each other in perplexity, and one of them timidly replies :

"If we go that way we will meet the queue-cutters and lose our queues."

The wayfarer could not long escape. If he took alarm and dodged into a near-by shop for refuge, he was not pursued. But he could not escape eventually. He had to go home some time, and when he did emerge, he found the enemy livelier than at first and increased in numbers. So the citizen would go away, in the end losing his queue gracefully with a smile, as the Chinese do their heads when necessary. "Saving of face" was the compensation for the loss of queue, as for every disaster.

The queue-cutting mania spread. In this the Chinese agent of a foreign sewing-machine company quickly seized the opportunity to advertise. He opened a barber-shop in his premises and announced queues cut free. Embryo Republicans nearly overran his shop. A restaurant-keeper who had just bought a fine pair of shears, joined in the popular sport. It was his boast afterward that he had cut off at least three hundred queues. When the sport began to lag in the streets, the cutters went to the river front and awaited there the arrival of travellers, shearing amazed and helpless strangers as the latter came ashore. The people were making China into a "Republic."

"Republicanized" by these processes, the Chinese took on airs often somewhat startling to us foreigners. For example, when a friend of mine handed his "boy" the customary half-month's pay at the New Year—the usual "cumshaw" or tip—the boy said politely, "No thank you," and declined it. The Republican idea, citizens all.

There was no becoming accustomed to this "new" China. There was no time. Discarding queues only gave it a taste : it began changing its dress, and here the women joined in—foreign headgear, walking-sticks, umbrellas, and if you please, foreign clothes. The demand for foreign-cut clothes was so great that a large fan-shop slack of work at that season—late autumn—opened a cap factory and did a thriving business. The foreign-style tailors, who had been obliged heretofore to subsist on a meagre trade with the foreigner, were so beset by native customers that foreign residents of Canton could get nothing. All the sewing-machines in South China were sold out to stock the tailoring shops.

To one like myself, a student spectator, the Cantonese race appeared to be changing outwardly into something between a Boxer indemnity student of 1905 and a Japanese reformer of 1870. Many of the Cantonese closely resemble the Japanese in appearance (some of the coast tribes of South China being allied to the Japanese by blood). Hats appeared everywhere in Canton, just as they had done in Japan in the seventies. During the Chinese New Year, celebrated for the last time it was said in February 1912, nearly all the men wore foreign trousers. Many had coats of foreign cut, some had foreign-style shoes. Not a few startled us by appearing in foreign underwear worn as outer adornment, ornamented with braces to support the drawers, accompanied with socks supported by a popular brand of American garters proudly displayed. The "hobble skirt" among Western women was not more loved than were these visible garters, braces, and suits of underwear by Chinese Republicans.

As an accompaniment of these foreign fineries, smokers in their haste to adopt things foreign, smoked Manila and Dutch cigars in their tinfoil wrappers. This converted the burning things into little, puffing, smoking engines giving out continuous streams of smoke. The smokers did not mind a little thing like that. The Canton heart beat strong with republicanism and all it meant in the way of new fashions and customs.

On the Yangtse River queue-cutting was practised or ignored as the temperament on the boundary of China's historical differences dictated. But in the places where the traveller looks, between Shanghai and Hankow, hardly a queue remained. Strange to say, in Shanghai, the upper classes cut off their braids, responding readily to the innovation. It was the lower classes, coolies and workmen, especially along the river, who were the conservatives. They refused to part with their queues. In the disputed territory lying north of the Yangtse River, where Republican and Imperial armies faced each other, the people grown cunning through ages of ravages by famine and war and exploiting by officials, sought safety in a middle course. At Nan Hsu Chou, headquarters of the Imperialist General, Chang Hsun, later occupied by the Republicans, the people compromised by cutting their queues far down the neck. Thus the cut end could be braided in again, "when General Chang Hsun came back."

The Rebellion did not abolish the queue by any means.

Six months after the Republic was declared, people in the Republican regions were wearing their queues concealed beneath their new foreign hats. The former usage of wearing false queues attached to the inner crown of hats was observed in the North, where queues were the prevailing custom. An old Cantonese gentleman who visited foreign friends at Shameen, was unable to reconcile the prevailing craze with self-respect and dignity. He could not change his lifelong fashion. He was willing, however, to adopt a foreign hat, under which he wore his queue concealed. This he would not take off, even at dinner in a foreign house, fearing that the Republican servants of the place could not resist the temptation surreptitiously to clip him.

Regions of Honan and Anhuei, between Peking and the Yangtse River, especially in the famine parts, became a kind of no-man's land, looted by Republican troops and by Imperialists, and scourged by robbers. Here a few Chinese—servants of foreigners—saved their queues when all strategy failed, by keeping close to their foreign masters. The American Red Cross Engineer Jameson, who was exploring the famine district during the winter of 1911-1912, gave his servants orders to take the baggage to the railway station at Nan Hsu Chou and await his arrival there to take the train. The " boys " (as upper servants are called in China) hedged and debated so much that it was apparent they were afraid to go.

" Isn't master going that way ? " they asked.

" What's the matter ? " asked Jameson. " Are you afraid you will get your queues cut off ? "

" Yes," said the boys ; " men stand at the gates of the City to cut off the queues of all farmers as they come in to market and they will want to cut ours."

China is a land of barbers, and they hold a peculiar place in the social system. They are an itinerant class, and one of the places where they are most frequently seen is in the open spaces before the yamens or official residences. It has been a law that they could not aspire to advancement and could not hold office. On the other hand, it is said that the sign of the barber—a low staff on his tonsorial cupboard—is a miniature of the great poles that stand before every yamen, and indicates that barbers had authority, in the early days, to behead anyone refusing to conform to the queue fashion ; probably only authority to have them punished. That is a singular compensation for being condemned to what has been a hereditary vocation, namely, the power to force the people to support their trade.

A war correspondent, like other people, has to change and readjust many of his preconceived ideas concerning a country and the customs of its people. I found when I looked into it that I could not retain the common view held in the world respecting the Chinese queue and its symbolism. That view is that it is worn by the Chinese under protest and that it is odious because it symbolizes Chinese subjection to the Manchu ruling race. But this, if once true, is no longer true. The queue in China at the time of the overthrow of the Manchus was a fixed fashion.

For many years Chinese abroad had cut their queues for fashion's sake, and some in the foreign settlements on Chinese soil had also done so. When the reform movement began, a decade before the Rebellion, reformers offended custom and the conservative ideas of the people as well as the ideas of the State, by cutting their queues. This was done in contempt of the prevailing system of government. It was an excess, foolhardy and often hazardous, indulged in by Radicals. They gambled with their queued or queueless heads as Garibaldi did with his fez-crowned head. They idolized men like Garibaldi. They threw their hats into the air as the French revolutionists did. They learned to stamp upon and revile the queue as the effigy of their complaints and grievances against the authors of China's condition, and to sacrifice it as their countrymen sacrificed the opium-pipe.

The ridicule given the queue by foreigners in the term " pig-tail " nettled many Chinese students who visited Europe and America. The European and American arriving in China, greeted the " pig-tail " with laughter. This was curious, since the queue was quite the fashion in Europe and in America only a hundred years ago, and the wearing of this quite elegant and dignified head-dress still prevails among jurists in the courts of Great Britain. Foreign soldiers cut off Chinese and Manchu queues as trophies at the relief of the foreign Legations at Peking in 1900, a kind of scalping act. An American soldier who wished to do me a great kindness presented me with one of these treasures from the head of a Manchu soldier killed in the quadrangle in front of the Ch'ien Men. He took it from its place in his locker, carefully wrapped in paper, showing how much he had prized it. It was something he had succeeded in preserving when silks, porcelains, ivory, cloisonné, lacquer, looted from the abandoned shops and mansions of Peking by foreign soldiers, had been lost.

So far as I know, history has not slighted the queue in China. Wan Li, the Emperor of China, allowing himself to become involved in border politics, mistakenly championed the cause of a chief who was an enemy of Nurhachu the rising Manchu. Nurhachu retaliated by invading China, marching on Liaotung in 1618. The army sent by Wan Li to oppose the invasion was defeated in detail and Nurhachu annexed Liaotung. The people of Liaoyang, Capital of the region, according to Chinese annals, acknowledged their "allegiance to their new masters by shaving the front part of their heads." Pott, who refers to this, observes that "this is the first mention of a custom that has since become universal in China." As a matter of fact the Manchus became more enslaved to the Chinese by the shackle of the queue than did the Chinese to the Manchus. In that rather elegant fashion conferred upon the Chinese—which is certainly half the dignity upon which the Chinese gentleman prides himself and his race in the matter of dress—the Manchu found a fetter which in the end finished him.

The queue has always played a picturesque part in Chinese rebellion. And Chinese rebellion since 1644, regardless of its original aim, has always ended by being anti-Manchu. If it did not start out that way, its conflict sooner or later with Manchu authority made it so. With the Chinese "ruling themselves," this latter authority was the only force to cope with brigandage or any form of outlawry above that of individual crime like common burglary or murder. In the course of time all movements in China were suspected and regarded as anti-Manchu. The T'aiping Rebellion—the greatest rebellion with which the Manchus have had to contend in their history of 268 years—was a religious movement whose name means "Great Peace." When it became necessary to the Throne to suppress this movement, its adherents turned upon the Government and abandoned the custom of shaving the front part of the head. They adopted the war-cry, "Down with the Manchus!" The people gave them the name of "the long-haired ones," "Ch'ang Mao." In China the rebels are everywhere known by this name. With the disappearance of the movement the queue again became universal in the Empire and is likely to be retained for some time as a fashion. The conservatism of the people may be relied upon to cling to many established usages.

There has been a fight among the Chinese and the Manchus and in the ranks of the Chinese themselves since at least 1898, for the abolition of the queue. In that year the Emperor Kuang Hsu and his reform associates decreed its abolition. This was one of the innovations that brought on the *coup d'état* of that year. The result of this and other actions of the Emperor was his deposition and practical confinement for the balance of his life. He died in Nov. 1908. The queue was a fashion to which the Chinese scholars and statesmen as well as the Manchus ardently clung. The Manchus feared the innovation merely as an expression and inspiration of rebellion and the coming deluge—something thoroughly understood by them. It was then only a custom. It was a custom merely twenty years before, when foreign historians were already writing of the decline of the Manchus.

In 1907 incendiarism broke out in Peking, and there was an epidemic of queue-cutting in North China. This greatly alarmed the Manchus. The Empress [Grand] Dowager at that time reorganized the police and had tubs of water placed at close intervals in all streets, as security against fires. Peking acquired an unusual and decidedly revolutionary appearance.

Before the precipitation of the Rebellion of 1911, the Throne by decree abolished all political significance that had existed in the queue. There was no longer any reason on the part of the reformers for queue-cutting as a mark of defiance of the State. Such a form of defiance was without effect. The Empress [Grand] Dowager had anticipated them, and rebellion in China.

In Jan. 1911 progressive Chinese, as well as Manchus, met together in parties to discuss the queue and mutually agreed on doffing it, celebrating the event with fire-cracker conflagrations as a mere prank. It led to a certain amount of excitement, however, which alarmed the Lung Yu Empress Dowager and the Court. The Lung Yu Empress Dowager asked the viceroys and governors of the provinces for advice in the matter, because it was important that it should not become dangerous. It was one of the methods of the reformers to poke ridicule at the queue, and they adopted the foreign nickname "pig-tail" because it conveyed a sense of odium. They added to this : the reform Press compared Chinese men with tailed animals, and printed cartoons of the tailed group, notably Chinese, dogs, and pigs. The queue was called the emblem of mundane backwardness, which placed China behind all other nations and made her the tail of mankind.

But as a matter of fact the reformers almost missed the chance of using the queue fashion as revolutionary capital. General Yin Chang, one of the foremost Manchus and the Minister of War, with all his staff, had abolished the queue. A newspaper at Peking, that represented the Lung Yu Empress Dowager as opposed to the anti-queue movement, was suspended by the Imperial police. The only discouragement of the movement came from the literati in places like the Imperial University—a school ranking lower than a Western high school—where the pupils were always delighted with opportunities to shock and affront their conservative, old-fashioned elders.

In October 1911 queue-cutting received Republican sanction at Wuchang, when General Li Yuan-hung authorized it and doffed his own queue. This made short hair the sign of loyalty to the Revolution. Other cities and provinces as they joined the Republican revolt proclaimed the abolition of the queue. On Nov. 15 the revolutionary commander at Hangchow, in Chekiang, proclaimed that queues had been the special sign of the Chinese ever since the Tartars entered within the Great Wall and that the Chinese were laughed at because they had this useless thing hanging from their heads nearly to their heels. Therefore they ought to doff the queue—the sign of submission to the Tartars—within one month. All who refused could not enjoy the privileges of law-abiding subjects.

Six days after this proclamation the revolutionary commanders, guard, and police at the City gates were cutting the queues of the people by force.

The National Assembly now took the matter up, and the Throne was obliged to take notice of what it would gladly have ignored, and issued a brief and interesting edict, one of its last and best. It said : " With reference to a memorial from the National Assembly earnestly requesting the issue of a Decree for the immediate doffing of the hair to demonstrate a universal assimilation : All Our servants and subjects are hereby permitted to doff their hair at their own free will. Signed with the Imperial Seal and by all the Ministers of State."

The reformers and revolutionaries now did precisely what the Manchus had done, they made the matter a test of loyalty. Scenes resulted not unlike those which attended the introduction of the queue. At Kashing, in Chekiang, the Republican proclamation abolishing the queue and the appearance of queue-hunters surreptitiously cutting off queues in the streets caused the merchants to close their shops in protest. Volunteers had to come out and keep order, after which another proclamation reassured the people by telling them that the queue-cutters were self-appointed, but defending their action as a good thing. The people had no prejudice against doffing their queues and soon doffed them willingly.

The queue has not been a badge of heartfelt loyalty. That it had become merely a fashion was shown at Changsha, Hunan, one of the most anti-Manchu centres. The people were much offended by the anti-queue movement, and when the queue-hunters appeared the revolutionary commander issued a proclamation against them. In Kueiyang, province of Kueichou, most of the soldiers refused to obey the queue-doffing proclamation.

During July 1912, when the agitation had subsided generally, a revival of queue-hunting occurred at Chefoo and elsewhere in Shantung. A revulsion of feeling resulted and three ringleaders of a queue-cutting riot at Chang-yi were executed. In the revolted provinces south of the Yangtse River the queue was generally abolished, but the people accepted the change in the spirit of the Throne's edict, and not that of the Republican proclamations, and wore it or not at their option.

Having served its purpose of arousing controversy and antagonism leading to the revolutionary revolt, queue-doffing changed as a question. While it may still play a spectacular part in the question of a revival of the Throne, or loyalty to the prevailing oligarchy, it long ago ceased to have any important connection with China's revolutionary problem—that of being Chinese.

CHAPTER XLI

THE CHINESE PRESS

THE Germans say that in an autocratic country (as in Germany, Austria, or Russia) the Press is not of so great consequence, but in a country like China its influence is everything. In the revolutionary movement the Press was the only means of universal communication carrying individual opinion, uniting group to group and section to section.

The Chinese students—the term used to designate Chinese young men who have had a Western education—first learned the influence of the Press when abroad and quickly demonstrated its influence in China. There were hardly more than a half-dozen established newspapers in China before the year 1900, which marks the rise of the Revolution, so its Press may be said to be that Revolution.

When the Germans awoke to the need of guarding against the criticism of the Chinese Press, Japan and Russia had their own Chinese newspapers in the Capital, and foreigners observed that altogether there were twenty-six newspapers and periodicals published in Peking when the revolutionary Rebellion broke. The total number of newspapers in the Empire was estimated at nearly two hundred.

Peking is the newspaper centre. Newspapers sprang up in all the large cities, and the South furnished the revolt, but it was from Peking that the national Press was created, and in five years all stages of the newspaper drama that in the West covered decades was worked out.

After the Boxer War in 1900, the Chinese took up journalism. Among the first reform periodicals in Peking was *The Child's Educator*, started in 1902. It contained little stories in geography, natural history, physics, and extracts from Æsop's Fables. Under its innocent title much wisdom was pushed out to the masses. Its principal aim was to correct the countless fallacies among the people respecting foreign countries. Its proprietor, Huang Sze-yung, was an old man, famous as a writer, philanthropist, and reformer. I lived in his family, and his personal history, strange as any Oriental tale, was very well known to me. At the end of a long train of incredible experiences and adventures, he was imprisoned by the Boxer leaders in 1900, his family was lost and his house destroyed. In *The Child's Educator* was recited in detail, humiliating to every self-respecting Chinese, all the disgraceful acts of his Boxer countrymen.

By 1903 the young reformers had gained a secure hold on the Press. They were utilizing the Japanese to teach them the uses of foreign printing machinery and the arts of process-engraving. They were making use of metal type from Japan. We had Japanese associated with the Press enterprises of our household, and though they were hard for the Chinese to get on with, they were tolerated for what they could teach. The editors of the Press coterie to which I was admitted in Liu Li Ch'ang Street—then the haunt of Chinese newspaper men—were feeling their way in the direction of all that the Japanese and Western peoples possess and in their newspapers were continually speculating on China's power in this, that, and the other.

In our discussions which we had around the guest-table in the new-fangled half-Chinese, half-foreign restaurants of the Chinese City of Peking, where the expensive food was neither one thing nor the other, and in our own house—where we had only simple and substantial Chinese food—the budding journalists asked many questions about the relations of the people and officials of the West, and especially about the relation between the officials and citizens in a Republic. To one of these questions, I remember once to have replied that the difference between China and my country in this respect was very marked.

" More often," said I, " the people look down on the office-holders, especially the place-seekers, and hold themselves above that ilk."

Not long afterward a cartoon appeared in the paper to which my listener was attached expressive of this idea.

The influence of the Western Press at this time is shown in the newspaper titles. Taking Chinese newspapers from various parts of the Empire, they are as follows: *Illustrated News*, *Universal Gazette*, *Northern Official Gazette*, *Woman's Journal*, *Public Opinion*, *Daily News*, *Black and White*, *People's Voice*, *Politics*.

The acquisition of courage is marked by the change in these titles. The new spirit struck boldly out with the ringing banner of *China.* Another paper was *The New Loyalist,* and other titles were *The True Loyalist* and *Eastern Morning Herald. The Wisdom Opener* was an organ of the revolt in Szechuan. *The Risen Hans* [nation] *Press* (*Hsin Han Pao*) was one of the Republican papers at Wuchang. *The Great Hans* [nation] *Press* was another. *Liberty* was a paper published in Honolulu whose circulation in China was forbidden by the Board of Interior at Peking. *The People's Wail* of Shanghai suffered a similar ban. The *Hsin Ming Tsung Pao* and the magazine *Kuo-feng-pao,* organs of the original of the modern reform parties, that of Kang Yu-wei, were published in Japan and edited by Liang Chi-ch'ao and circulated widely in China.

The power of the Press in China was something truly startling in the end, the most comprehensive demonstration of that power which the Press has ever had. In the West the Press has been of slow growth, but in China it may be said to have arisen in a day, equipped like a giant. It brought on the greatest experiment in constitutional government ever attempted, and in five years it aroused and overturned an Empire and subverted a Dynasty. " The loyalty of the army, upon which the Prince Regent relied, and on which one-third of the revenue of the Empire was spent, was sapped by the propaganda of hundreds of journalists," said a Chinese public man. Overturning the Manchu Dynasty would not have been possible without the men of the Press and those whom the Press prepared.

But the beginnings of the Press were humble. Its editors were drawn oftentimes from nobody knew where. There appeared to be considerable truth in the indictment made by an old conservative memorialist in Peking that they were recruited from the " dregs of literature." Witness the following comment of a Peking newspaper on a non-sectarian lecture under the auspices of foreign missionary women. The lecture was a popular one, entertaining to everybody, with all references to religion omitted. It was a modern educational lecture. It proved a neighbourhood event. But " damned with faint praise " perhaps never had a sturdier illustration than in the criticism by the newspaper mentioned. It said: " These are not the demi-mondaine ; these people are not the low-class ladies of the street."

In respect to the attitude of the Chinese toward foreigners, it was not one of anti-foreignism, but rather of "China for the Chinese." One Chinese editor who in his paper made use of derogatory epithets with respect to foreigners, willingly accepted an invitation from a foreign Mission to lecture before it. When asked for an explanation of what he had said in his paper, he replied that he was constantly accused by his enemies of being in foreign pay, and he used the derogatory articles merely to be able to controvert his accusers. While such ethics are not up to the Confucian standard boasted of by the memorialist referred to, they cannot be said to be different from the official ethics that has produced the memorials and edicts in *The Peking Gazette*, the organ of the Throne, that has been called China's first enigma. Dr. Arthur Smith has said that if one could hope to understand its contradictions and absurdities, that one would have a clue to China herself.

These illustrations show the obliquity of Chinese views concerning the relations of Chinese to foreigners and of the whole subject of the outside world. China has always looked down on foreigners, an attitude that has prevented her understanding them. Ignorant of their needs and real motives, and suspicious always, her Press has almost invariably gone astray on foreign questions. Its interpretation of foreign news was characterized by an inventiveness that flabbergasted foreigners. Grotesque and preposterous motives such as we could not even imagine were assigned to us.

But, without understanding the meaning of foreign matters, their editors occasionally stumbled upon international news items that would have been invaluable to correspondents like myself had we known their connection at the time. For instance, in 1905 a Chinese newspaper made a statement to the effect that Americans intended to purchase the Shenking coal mines (in Manchuria) and that a representative was negotiating for them with the Government of Japan. This was the only thing published in any newspaper respecting important international negotiations for the transfer of Japan's railways in South Manchuria to the American financier Edward H. Harriman—an incident that later had the most important political effects. It escaped the eagle eyes of the Western Press for six years and until explained by the author in the *Century Magazine* in 1911.

The *North China Daily News*, an English newspaper published in Shanghai, claims that a native paper, before the end of 1899, "published its sixty-third notice of the [approaching] Boxer movement" of 1900. Considering that the foreign Press never discovered it, and neither did the representatives of foreign Governments at Peking, this may be taken as at least a straw showing that at the beginning of the revolutionary movement the Press of China had developed the news-gathering sense. After twelve centuries there was developed such a journalistic being as a Chinese reporter and such a thing as a Chinese "nose for news."

Although it was in China that movable type was invented, that type in all these centuries has been used only for books. The medium of conveying news, for the masses, was the tea-house and the guild-houses. The mandarins had *The Peking Gazette*, the oldest newspaper in the world. It was an official newspaper founded by the Emperor Ming Ti (712–756 A.D.) and began by foretelling the disruption of the Empire. It was a true prophet. Officials of the reform Government of the Manchus (1909) tried to supersede or kill it by creating the *Government Official Paper*, but did not succeed. It has therefore a close connection with revolution in China and may outlive a disruption of the Empire as it did in the eighth century.

It was before China "officially executed" *The Peking Gazette* that I visited it in its ancient habitation near my Chinese home. It was not easy to find. Strange to say, *Peking Gazette* is not the name of it. Its most general and respectable name is one most execrated in the Press of the West—the *Yellow Paper*. It is a hydra-headed thing and it is easy to understand why it could not die. In another form it is called the *White Paper*. The "Yellow" one is printed, the "White" one is written. *White Paper* (*Pai Pao*), however, is not inscribed on that particular *Peking Gazette*—it is only *called* that. *Pai Pao* (White Paper) is only its verbal name. What is written on its title-page is *Shang Yi* (Edicts). "Edicts" is its name in this form.

In my work in Peking I have had to do with three *Peking Gazettes*, and in 1903 I started out to find "it" in all its numerical and alphabetical forms. The learning of my Chinese official, and literary, friends and associates did not embrace any knowledge of this one great newspaper of their country—a fact which showed the state of the public newspaper taste—and I had to inquire elsewhere as to where it was located, and send a servant to find the way. Although I was known as a journalist, my quest was regarded as an idiosyncrasy. The servant came back and explained that it was in our own locality, just beyond Liu-li-ch'ang (our street).

One of the Chinese gentlemen accompanied me. Led by our guide, we went on our search like ferrets. Passing through streets where we had to stand in the doorways to let the water-carriers pass—something unusual in Peking—and turning a sufficient number of corners to get completely lost right in our own neighbourhood, we arrived at a little alley door which the guide said was the place. The street had gradually risen until it was several feet above the floor of the house, so that entering the building before us was like descending into a pit. I recollect it as having the air of a foundry pre-empted for living purposes. Between the beds, bureaus, and tables was the engraving and printing apparatus. Here was produced daily by a letter-cutter, an engraved block of wood about 3 by 7 inches, from which was casually printed by an apprentice, a little filmy page, dirty and frail as the gossamer from the reed pond where the paper material in China is gathered. This done, behold *The Peking Gazette*, price approximately a fifth of a cent; the circulation from this office probably two or three hundred copies daily.

The day's voluminous edition had apparently been run off. The workmen and editors were evidently resting from their labours. Whether because of exhaustion or other reasons, they did not appear on the scene to receive us. The engravers' bench, a low table under a window half of whose light had been cut off by the rise of the street level, was deserted. I examined the engravers' tools with which the letters for the *Gazette* were cut, and a denizen of the cave who looked as if he might be the apprentice mentioned, showed us the engraved block form from which the last issue had been printed. From such a block each day, this boy, with a roller saturated with fluid ink, prints, as his convenience allows, these 200 or 300 copies "hot from the steaming press" for the "eager eye" of the Chinese "Constant Reader" trained through centuries and with traditions fresh from 712 A.D.

The Peking Gazette was never interfered with by the police. When I visited it, it had an unbroken record of tranquillity of nearly twelve centuries. It was police immune. It had prophesied but never propagated revolution or disruption of empire. Its dignity had never permitted it to "throw its hat in the ring." It had never "espoused." It had never had a Latin motto. It had never seen a Sunday, and consequently it had never had a Sunday edition. But it was exclusive. It had had twelve centuries of "scoops" and "beats," and that without any special correspondents, any extras, or any fuss. It never voluntarily enlarged its edition, and the nature of its contents never changed. Never written but always understood, these were: Edicts, Rescripts, Memorials. If on occasion there were no edicts, their place was taken by a statement to that effect conveyed by two characters. It was delivered to subscribers only in fair weather.

The *Cheng Chih Kuan Pao*, or "Government Official Paper," established to supersede *The Peking Gazette*, consisted of eight to twelve pages. A specimen of its contents is as follows: Edicts, Rescripts, Extracts from foreign news telegrams, Memorials of high officials, Editorial discussion of the Constitutional system and means of amalgamating Manchus and Chinese, Extracts from other Chinese newspapers. This was all dry bones from even the Chinese journalists' standpoint. There was not even an advertisement to relieve the dull monotony to the reformer, to say nothing of the revolutionist. Both these papers were above soliciting advertisements. They were immensely alone in their grandeur, however. Their reform and revolutionary contemporaries numbered by scores, without exception solicited advertisements with the avidity of the modern Western Press, and there was perhaps not one with that kind of Western scruples that prevented it accepting, without discriminating, whatever came to the mill.

In contrast with the contents of the official and time-honoured Press of the Capital are the contents of an illustrated paper of Peking—*The Capital News Picture Paper*—in the height of the Rebellion. In its six pages it showed in one issue: "Revolutionists presenting the head of the Manchu Viceroy Tuan Fang to the Republican leader Li Yuan-hung; Amazon Corps of the Revolutionists at Chingkiang; Fight in the First Division at Kalgan; Dispatching troops to defend Kai-ping; Revolutionists taking Hwai-hsien City; Revolutionists discussing the landing of troops at the German port of Kiao-chau to attack Tientsin; and, Audience by the Lung Yu Empress Dowager to the Mongol Princes. The contents of most of these reform journals showed that though they might lack the advantages of having plenty of capital and struggled along with the smallest circulations and incomes, they did not lack in journalistic imagination and did not want for an editorial or pictorial theme.

A Chinese inquiry into the essential circumstances of the five leading Chinese newspapers of Peking just before the revolutionary revolt showed the following: *Peking Daily News*, circulation 3500, the most influential paper of the Capital, owned by Chu Ch'i and edited by himself, assisted by two subordinates, organ of no class or party; *The China Newspaper*, a party organ, circulation 1500, chiefly among scholars, owned by shareholders; *The Prefectural News*, circulation 1500, a Japanese controlled organ with Japanese editors assisted by one or two Chinese writers, read by the Chinese for news but without special influence among them; *Kung Yen Pao*, circulation 800, reported to be the Russian organ and receiving subsidies from the Russian Legation, influence less than that of those mentioned; *The Empire News*, circulation 2500, a paper promoted by students who had studied in Japan. It appealed to all interested in the Constitution. The two Viceroys at Tientsin and at Canton each took 1000 subscriptions, giving the paper an income from this source of $600 monthly.

The prevailing idea among Chinese officials was that the Imperialist, or national, organ should be printed in a foreign language, preferably English, in order to exercise the widest influence in foreign countries. Peking officialdom long felt the need of a newspaper to represent its views and safeguard China's welfare in her foreign relations. The professed object was to combat the foreign Press issued from foreign colonies, cities, and settlements in Eastern Asia, and gain access to the largest number of editorial offices in Europe and America—the latter an impossibility, from their standpoint, with a paper printed in Chinese.

In a conference with the young Prince Tsai Tao I held the opposite view, on the ground that an Imperial organ in English would only be another "foreign newspaper" to the foreign Press, suspected of being an expression of foreign opinions, whereas a newspaper wholly

Chinese, conducted by a few able native writers, would constitute something which the Press of the world had, until now, looked for in vain. It would be the expression of Chinese thought and ideas which would ensure the universal circulation and influence of its opinions. The foreign Press in Eastern Asia would be certain to translate all its important news and opinions, and China could thus make this Press do her work for her.

Although the plan was never realized, it brought out the whole story of the revolutionary character of the Chinese Press, the nature of the breach between the Chinese students and other reformers and the Manchus, and the efforts of the Manchus at the last to heal the breach, centralize the Government, and make China strong and independent.

Liang Chi-ch'ao was the hero and idol of Chinese reformers and regarded by them the greatest of the Chinese exiles. Next to Dr. Young J. Allen, an American missionary who was a Press pioneer for China, he has done most for Chinese journalism and is the father of the revolutionary Press. His comparisons of China with the West, and his revelations of the outside world to China's progressive and unprogressive classes, made his writings of the past decade almost classical in Eastern Asia. In the judgment of the reform leaders at Peking, including many Manchus, he deserved a higher place in the Revolution than any other man. In 1898 he was the adviser and reliance of Kang Yu-wei, in the world at large the best known of China's reformers. On account of the conspiracy of these two men with others in the cabal with the Emperor to revolutionize China and to segregate the Empress [Grand] Dowager, he was sentenced to death by that resolute maker of emperors (she had made two of them) along with Kang Yu-wei and others.

Six years later, 1904, on her seventieth birthday, the Empress [Grand] Dowager issued a decree granting amnesty to most of the reformers of 1898, excepting only Kang Yu-wei, Liang Chi-ch'ao, and Sun Yat-sen. Now Prince Tsai Tao, who was looking for means of being useful to the reign, adopted the idea which I had recommended to him and invited Liang Chi-ch'ao to come to Peking and conduct a national newspaper. When he received the offer Liang Chi-ch'ao was editing, at Kobe in Japan, a newspaper and a magazine which easily held first place among Chinese newspapers and periodicals.

But although he was one of the monarchist party, the revolutionary movement had gone so far that he could not bind himself to the support of a purely Manchu Imperialist organ, and in a little while events showed the wisdom of his judgment. When the revolutionary Rebellion broke out in September and October 1911, the Prince Regent issued a decree of pardon for both Liang Chi-ch'ao and Kang Yu-wei, who were known to be opposed to the Republican principles of Sun Yat-sen. This divided the revolutionary reformers, but as a measure of staying the Revolution it was too late, and even Sun Yat-sen was beyond the need of any concessions from the Throne of China, and the native Press had come into its own.

Note: It is interesting to observe that the Government of the English colony of Hongkong was maintaining upon its statutes a ban against the Republican revolutionist Sun Yat-sen, and his brother, Sun Mow, long after the inauguration of the "Flowery Republic," in curious accord with the statutes of the late Manchu Dynasty.

CHAPTER XLII

THE CARTOON WARFARE

FEARING the Peking Government, the newspapers of the students and reformers at first operated from the foreign settlements. It was four years before the Government awoke to the fact that China had a Press situation and began the devising of a Press Law. By this time student journalism, made bold by its freedom in the settlements, had invaded Peking. Here there was an ancient department of the Government called the Board of Censors, made up of scholars invested by the Emperor with the highest of political offices—that of criticizing everything in the Middle Kingdom, including all that pertains to the Emperor.

Pei Shou, a Manchu member of this Board, conservatively epitomized the power of the Press in a memorial to the Throne, asking for regulations "to prevent the Press libelling the Throne, maliciously attacking the Central Government, fanning the flames of revolution among anti-monarchists, making reckless comments on the assassination of high ministers of the Throne, thereby encouraging revolutionaries in the provinces." This statement by Pei Shou was said by a Chinese official to reflect the apprehension of the Government. He stated that the members of the Imperial Family and the high ministers, as well as the viceroys and officials in the provinces, were fearful of newspaper attack and exposure and were trying to buy up the newspapers.

At this time the Government and all its institutions were gradually changing. Among the first of these institutions to change—in fact it disappeared—was the Board of Censors, whose name leads to a confusion in the mind with that of the Press Censorate. They represented opposite principles. Whereas the Censors had no public and were an exclusive body who could only appeal to the Government, the Press was universal. One of its most significant achievements was the dissolution of the Board of Censors by rendering it obsolete.

The Censors began to join the Press, from the first dissenting from the conservative view taken by Pei Shou, and supporting the ideas of a man named Shan Hsi-hung, who in an audience with the Empress [Grand] Dowager told her that most Western countries trusted the Press and utilized it for maintaining a mutual understanding between the Government and people. " This policy," said he, " would make a country powerful and China should imitate it. She should not suppress the newspapers but should favour them." Chinese report stated that, at this speech, the Empress [Grand] Dowager's face flushed with astonishment. On Sept. 1, 1906, she had announced in an edict the decision of the Throne to grant constitutional government : the Revolution was moving so rapidly the Throne was already catching its breath. The Throne was all too slowly in the minds of the student journalists making up its mind for a Press Magna Charta.

The first official attention with which the Press in China was honoured after the founding of *The Peking Gazette* (712–756 A.D.) came on October 8, 1898, in the form of an edict. " As newspapers serve only to excite the masses," it said, " to subvert the present order of things, and the editors are composed of the dregs of the literary classes, no good can be served by the continuation of such instruments, and we hereby command the entire suppression and sealing up of all newspapers published within the Empire, while all the editors connected with them are to be arrested and punished with the utmost severity of the law."

The newspapers at that time were as nothing in comparison with what the students, as their ranks swelled, and the reformers, true and false, soon made of them. Newspapers sprang up like mushrooms, had no traditions to hamper them, were on new turf and pitched into everything and everybody, carrying the Board of Interior which had charge of the Press problem with them. They secured a " Press rate " for telegrams over the Imperial telegraph lines, and in September 1907 the Press of the Capital petitioned the Government for railway passes ; for access to the courts of justice in order to report law cases ; and for the right, in case of a newspaper office being closed by the police, of having the real cause of closure posted on the office door, so that the public could understand.

Before the Press Law was issued, when a paper was

suppressed by an arbitrary official, only an explanation like the following respecting a paper suppressed in Manchuria would be given: "Suppressed on account of reckless and libellous attacks on the Administration, thereby endangering the public peace."

Showing further what they were fighting for, the reform Press tried to get advance copies of the edicts, rescripts, and memorials from the Board of Interior, such as were given to *The Peking Gazette*, but failed. The old *Gazette* still stood secure on its traditions and privileges.

Late in 1907, a Press Law of thirty-six articles was framed, so that a censorship could be exercised by the Board of Interior, which in Feb. 1908 promulgated the law. It was immediately objected to by the Press, and modifications demanded that would "prevent officials from attempts to muzzle such of the Press as are respectable and conducted on honest and clean-handed lines."

The Empress [Grand] Dowager could no longer stay the reform movement. On Aug. 27, 1908—two years lacking four days after she had given her promise—she granted a Constitution, to be realized, however, only after a probationary period of nine years. Many of the student journalists and reformers hailed this concession with acclaim, but they wished the Constitution, especially a Parliament, at once.

The Press wanted the Parliament so keenly that it trampled the whole Press Law under foot, and a new law of forty-two articles was devised and sanctioned by the Throne. In this the censorship passed from the hands of the officials to those of the police.

The Throne showed the process by which it had been making up its mind—and by which the editors were now out of the frying-pan into the fire—by an edict, contrasting the wise and conservative plans of the Manchu Government for converting China into a constitutional monarchy with the clamorous demands of student journalists. It also showed what the revolutionary character of the Press was, as it appeared to the Government, and the consequent problem with which the Government had to contend. The edict stated that the time of preparation for the Constitution had not elapsed and it could not be carried into execution at once. Laws had to be drawn up by the superiors, and then the people had to learn how to obey them and be taught their duties under them.

When this was accomplished a date could be fixed for receiving all constitutional rights, which would come sooner or later, depending on the speed or delay with which the country had prepared itself.

"Under a constitutional monarchy," it said, "the central authority exercises the power and takes into consideration public opinion, deciding whether it will act or not act upon it. Popular meetings in their speeches and arguments must be governed by laws. There is not one nation that allows its representatives to give out arguments incompatible with the law and against the prestige of the nation. How much more should China be proud of and cherish her etiquette [complete subservience of the "low" to the "high"], which has always been very exacting.

"In selecting from the laws of other nations we must keep our own ceremonies and civilizations. In the provinces are many ignorant and unprincipled men, and now when the Government wishes to introduce a new regime, these people seize the opportunity to make remarks. For example, 'One man sings and a hundred answer.' They gab. What is false is transmitted false for a long time. The lower classes insult the upper classes and the fundamental code is violated. The first step to a constitutional government is thereby hampered and the main business of ruling is turned into disorder. There is therefore no date possible for establishing the Constitution and no hope for making the country powerful. Public opinion ought to be met, but the people's voice [expressed in the newspapers] must by no means become higher respecting the establishing of a Constitution. All must honour the Sovereign so as to maintain order. There are explicit regulations for discussing affairs. There is also clear limitation. It is certain that not everyone can talk of affairs, and furthermore not all affairs are included in the things that may be discussed. At present Peking has the Imperial Assembly and the provinces have the legislative councils [provincial assemblies]. This is the first step toward a Parliament. Hereafter affairs of the people are to be discussed in the legislative council and may afterward be referred to the Imperial Assembly. This matter is to be done in parliamentary order and not otherwise in useless talk."

With instinctive editorial perspicacity the Press took refuge in cartoons. The pictorial art is more universally understood in China perhaps than in the West. A cartoon labelled "The Modern Editor" represented the Chinese Press at the top of a treacherous, complicated stilt, like the uppermost and most insecure object in a juggler's hand. The protest of one paper was expressed by the picture of a cock with the inscription, "A cock must crow when the time comes." One newspaper commented on its fellows with a cartoon labelled "The eyes of the newspapers see much, but the mouth is closed."

The fabric of Chinese paper is filled with fibre hairs and sometimes chaff and straw. One paper characterized the pettiness of the police censorship by an official blowing up the hairs of the paper to see if he could find a thorn. A paper somewhat more bold, *Black and White*, represented the Press Law as the sealing up of the captive editor's mouth. As the fight between the Government and the Press grew hotter, the cartoons increased in force. From a state wherein the mouth of the editor was imprisoned in the official tongs he passed to a pictorial state where he was being boiled in oil or water. This is one of China's most horrible punishments which history says was practised by Genghis Khan. The cartoon is intended to represent the editor in Hell, "orienting" himself in view of his permanent residence—Hell being all that a Chinese editor can expect of fate.

Aside from cartoons, the editors had at their command a language which in its written form is itself pictorial, and under the tradition of Chinese literary style and the cleverness of literary execution which the Press abundantly possessed was capable of every trick of suggestion, impression, and thought. The papers satirized, derided, goaded, scorned, ignored, in a character. An art that had belonged exclusively to the literati, among whom it was a polite accomplishment, became a weapon in the hands of the Chinese student journalist.

Under "Article 7," the most offensive in the Press Law, the police would have been virtually the editors of the newspapers. They tried to enforce "Article 7," thus driving the editors into a position where they were at bay. Chinese editorial resource became something to marvel at. From this being the period of the real birth of the Chinese newspaper cartoon, it became the period which will be recognized as that in which Chinese newspaper expression rose to the plane of art, and China had journalism.

The journalists soon showed the officials that they were not entirely recruited from the "literary dregs."

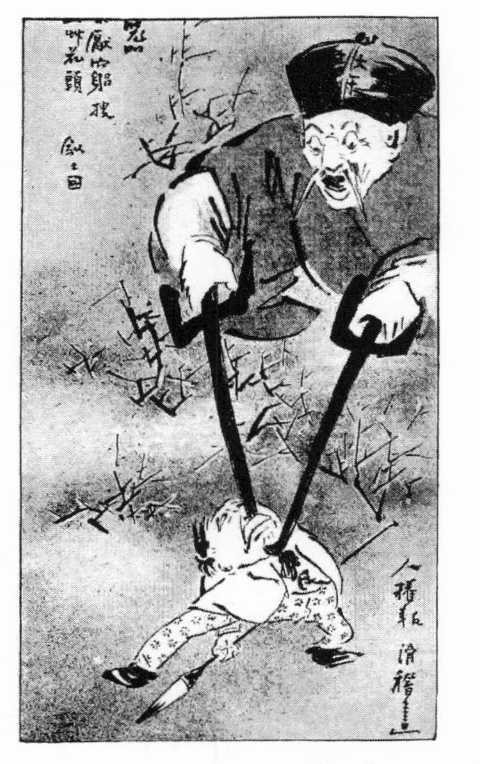

THE CENSORSHIP.

THE EDITOR'S FINAL HOME—HELL.

To face p.

Finding they had to be discreet, they took refuge in over-discretion—a medium for telling everything.

This was an ingenious literary usage which had its parallel in the West in the age of Johnson. Boswell was a perfect Chinese in being so discreet in his celebrated biography as to have packed every page with not only every indiscretion about Johnson but about everyone of his whole age, as well as a masterful dissection of Boswell more acute than any mere critic could have made. Boswell would have loved the editors of Peking. The art of indirect expression was practised by the reform Chinese newspapers in the foreign settlements in order to push their circulation into the country at large. Here is a Boswellian discretion from Shanghai : " A friend of ours has spent some time up the Yangtse River, where, in many cities, even the word ' Revolution ' is still unknown. But we may teach them its meaning in a decade or so."

In the present situation, when the Press had for some time freed itself from the bonds of exile in the foreign settlements, it doubled the exasperation of the police and Government officials by its editorial subterfuges and its covert threats to return to those refuges. One paper wrote : " There is no country without newspapers, but there may be newspapers without a country." Elsewhere the Censorate was represented by the funereal figure of a magpie beneath which was the inscription : " You like to talk and I like to listen, but if you propose to say that I have no good in me, I will drive you away."

Pictures of all China's tyrants, royal profligates, traitors and other enemies of the State, and people, were printed in contrast with China's famous heroes and heroines—the " deadly parallel " of Western journalism and caricature. Beside a cartoon of a worthless minister of state at a vital period in China's past, was printed a cartoon showing " an ancient heroine who destroyed all her father's useless books,"—a hit at the Conservatives with their tenacity for the classics.

Occasionally the Press fell into a trap carefully laid by the police to discover its underground sources of news. On one occasion its confederates in the telegraphs were seized and convicted. Before the Press Law was enacted one editor had been sentenced to imprisonment for ten years for indiscretions. Not long afterward, along with a Press correspondent, two clerks in the Grand Secretariat were found acting as Press informers and imprisoned for two years, for making known prematurely the fact that the Throne intended to give posthumous titles to five patriots who met death at the hands of the Boxer Government in 1900.

The Press was continually in hot water from publishing Government secrets, against which the Government kept issuing repeated orders which it could not enforce. In the beginning each paper fought its own battles, but a national Press Law and the effects of trying to enforce it, drove them to unite. Then the embarrassment of the Government from this position caused the Regent in 1909 to propose a revision of the Press laws. The newspapers had become objects of dread. They published statements in regard to gambling and opium-smoking in the palaces. Time-servers of the Court and all official delinquents were startled and wondered what was coming next. The newspapers were referred to with fear as the "paper Censors" (a reference to the all-powerful Board of Censors of the past, which the newspapers had superseded). They not only attacked the governmental system and affairs, the highest officials and personages, but they made themselves the voice of China respecting international affairs and men of other countries.

The Foreign Office (Wai-wu-pu) could not control a semi-official newspaper which it had promoted, and was obliged to oppose it. At the time of Prince Ito's assassination (1908) there was an almost unanimous approval of the deed among Chinese. When a Peking newspaper published gratification over Ito's death, the ministers of the Foreign Office feared that this would affect the relations of China and Japan, and a joint meeting was held with the Grand Council to discuss it and to determine how to punish the offending journalists. They could not agree. The Foreign Office, the Grand Council, the Grand Secretariat, and the Board of the Interior held conflicting views, and the Press went merrily on under the cover of divided opinions. From what might be called its outpost in Peking, it worked with the Press under foreign protection in the settlements where was reflected in violent agitation and propaganda the supervision and coercion of the Peking police.

The Board of Interior tried to devise a plan to get hold of the Press in the foreign settlements, and having no jurisdiction there, thought to do this by pressure on the Peking Press contingent. The Peking papers were so hard pressed that they threatened to suspend unless freed from police supervision. One of their number was singled out by the police to be made an example. The editor was called in and scolded for inaccurate statements. Seeing what was coming, the others banded together and gave fight. They notified the Press of the country of this attempt to make one of their number a scapegoat. The Prince Regent stepped in and instructed the officials in the provinces not to be too strict with the editors, for fear the Press would bodily take refuge in the foreign settlements. He contrasted newspapers with the memorials of his ministers and officials, and said that he read the newspapers because the memorials did not contain the news.

The Press now had defenders among the highest ministers. The Manchu Viceroy, Tuan Fang, and the Manchu head of the Board of Finance, Duke Tsai Tseh, advocated liberality and progression in Press matters. One of the late Censors espoused the cause of the scapegoat newspaper that had been closed and of two others that were suspended. The newspapers then petitioned the Prince Regent to decree freedom of speech. The police recognized their inability to enforce police censorship. The Press Law was declared a failure, and the solution of the problem was taken out of the hands of the unregenerate Board of Interior by the Prince Regent and placed in the hands of a Bureau that had been created for solving new questions arising from the introduction of the constitutional system.

What had now happened was in part the fulfilment of the New Year's birthday hope of one of the reform newspapers, *The Eastern Times* :

" Our wish is that this year [1909, the first year of Hsuan Tung, the last Emperor] the Press laws shall be revised, and control of the newspapers vested in the hands of the local executive and police, modified." " Otherwise," it said, " there can be no freedom of speech, popular opinion cannot be expressed, and it will be vain to expect progress in the country. The year is a momentous one on account of the measures to be carried out for bringing about the constitutional system, including as they do, the opening of the provincial assemblies, the establishment of local governments for cities and villages, the taking of China's first census, and the investigation of China's wealth, resources, and financial needs."

It hoped that all these reforms pledged by the Throne for the second year of the nine years set for realizing a constitutional government would be sincerely and energetically carried out. It concluded with the admonitory hope that the Chinese people would make the best use of the year, each acting up to his responsibility as an integral part of the nation, to assist in its progress along the road of rejuvenation, and by so doing escape further regrets for the loss of time and opportunity.

CHAPTER XLIII

THE REVOLUTIONISTS

In 1909 a progressive Chinese at Vancouver said that the leavening process going on in China due to foreign influences would result in a Revolution within thirty-five years. A foreigner acquainted with China replied that twenty or twenty-five years would be sufficient to bring that about. Within two years the most important Rebellion China ever had was an accomplished success and the Revolution was on.

It may be possible from a consideration of the elements of the Revolution in China to determine what its duration may be. The first successful Rebellion recorded in Chinese history was that which gave the throne to Prince Tang, 1766 B.C. China has never had any revolution in the present sense, but her history from that time onward is marked by one Rebellion after another, and at different times she has been under military despotism. This was the case after the fall of the Tang Dynasty (907 A.D.), when the Chinese had become military by long practice of civil war and combating the raids of the Tartars.

In the working out of her political and military history the great Yangtse River early became a dividing line between separate kingdoms, and has always remained a rebellious border region. Into this region in modern times has spread the mania of "secret societies" that in China has mystified Western students of the Chinese and has furnished the curious and enigmatical expression of the inscrutable nature of the race. Among the first of the secret societies mentioned by historians is the "Red Eyebrows" (they dyed their eyebrows) of Shantung—the home of secret societies. They are spoken of in the year 9 A.D., and appear to have disappeared in 58 A.D. The "White Lily Society" and other secret societies originated between 1260–1368 A.D. (Yuan Dynasty). In 1796 the "White Lily Society," or "Water Lily" (Pi-lien-chiao), later merged into the "Celestial Reason Society" (Tien-ti-huei). Taking as a signal the appearance of a comet in that year, it raised the standard of revolt in Hupeh, where the present Republican Government was first set up, and was supported in Honan, Shensi, Kansu, and Szechuan, all but one of which also joined the present Republican revolutionary Rebellion.

The object of the " White Lily Society " was the extermination of the Manchu Dynasty and the restoration of the Hans. The conspirators nearly succeeded in assassinating the Emperor ; one attempt occurred in the streets of Peking, and another in his private apartments in the Palace, something more daring and sensational than anything that has taken place in Peking during the setting up of the Republic. This event marked the zenith of the influence, power, and daring of secret societies in China which threatened the existence of the Empire.

The last great movement for putting down the Manchus and elevating the Hans was the T'aiping Society or organization. In 1852, when it crossed the Yangtse with its soldiers, it found the Imperial troops " utterly demoralized and unable to offer any vigorous resistance," exactly as has been the case in the initial conquest of the Yangtse Valley by the Republican soldiers. The Triads, still the leading secret society of Southern China, joined the T'aipings, and when the latter were driven out by foreign aid the disbanded soldiers for self-protection formed the " Elder Brother Society " (Kao-lao-huei), a secret society that has played a prominent part in the present Rebellion. Starting in Hunan—the province which furnished the agitators for the Republican revolt at Wuchang—this Society (1891) rioted along the Yangtse River from Wuhu to Kiangyin. It was a Chinese protest against reform in educational matters combined with a desire to plunder—the latter a survival from the T'aiping Rebellion. It made victims of the foreign missionaries, whose houses were plundered and wrecked.

The importance of secret societies in the revolutionary Rebellion is epitomized in the history of the Boxers, or " Righteous Harmony Fists Society," the most famous to foreigners of the secret societies, especially those claiming an anti-foreign reason for existence. It originated in Shantung with the old purpose of driving out the Manchu Dynasty and restoring the Hans. Its importance has been very great in the initiation of China's Revolution, and to explain it would require the whole history of China's international relations since 1900 and of the constitutional movement. The consequences to the Society, due to its purpose and activities, were so serious and dangerous as to be self-destructive. The Government, the people, and foreign Powers united to exterminate it, so that within a few years it was difficult to find a man who would own connection with the Boxers.

The better classes in China regard the secret societies merely as blackmailing and robbing organizations. Such are the " Red Beards " (Hung-hu-tzu) of Manchuria, and the " Red Lantern Society " (Hung-tien-chiao), the robber society of Szechuan. There is no doubt about the power and influence exercised by secret societies when we realize that the Boxer movement was at first anti-Manchu and was found worthy by the Throne's deputy, Kang Yi, to be turned to Imperial advantage by an artful contribution of money by the Empress [Grand] Dowager. The knowledge of this fact explains several things which many foreigners have never been able to clear up with satisfaction, notably, why the Legations were not destroyed; why the Manchu Government and Throne were so irresolute in the siege of the Legations. The immemorial division among those in authority respecting the merits of secret societies prevented the success of the aim of the Boxers and the Boxer party at Court in exterminating foreigners—the third party in China's situation.

The rites of the Boxers were similar to those of other Chinese secret societies that have survived it, and one of these, the "Elder Brother Society," will serve as an illustration of what the doings and the place of secret societies of China are in China's social system. Allied to it is the " Younger Brother Society " (Ti-lao-huei), and below these was the P'ao-ko-huei, composed of riff-raff who were used by the higher orders as instruments. These affiliated divisions of the brotherhood societies had a nocturnal oath of brotherhood, sworn to with the kotow, before a Buddhist idol in the temple. The initiate dipped his finger in chicken's blood, spilled, and running warm on the shrine, and then sealed his oath by a blood-written cross.

From an investigation made in Szechuan, where this organization figured in winning over the Imperial troops to the revolutionists, I learned that within the ranks of these societies those of the P'ao-ko-huei are known as " Turbid Water." Those of the two higher branch societies are known as " Clear Water," and a general term of the members for their fellows is " Long-gowned Brethren." Lodges, called Ma-ti'ao (or Teo), are numerous. The officers are " Great Brethren." The chiefs of the military arm are two, " Black Flag " and " Red Flag," and they punish obstreperous members, sometimes forcing them to suicide, and executing plans of murder and assassination. All classes are found in the " Elder Brother Society " and its branches, joining from motives of fear or hope of profit. These societies do not even exclude officials between whom and themselves exists a deadly feud. In Szechuan an official on taking office usually recognizes the Society locally and disclaims it in Peking.

The " Elder Brother Society " and its branches were so strong at the time of the September 1911 anti-foreign loan outbreak at Cheng-tu that it was commonly remarked that the militia was all " Long-gowned Brethren." When the rising began outside the walls of Cheng-tu it was the " Elder Brother Society " lodges who claimed control of it and were called upon for assistance by the lodges within Cheng-tu to help them put down the regular soldiers, whom they said were so numerous as to be " like vermin in the streets."

When General Lan Tien-wei, in South Manchuria, dispatched his expedition of 200 men to Teng-chou on the coast of Shantung to make a demonstration there, these men were " Red Beards " (Hung-hu-tzu) from Manchuria. General Lan's subordinates paid the Japanese captain 300 taels to transport these men to Teng-chou, and as it turned out a friendly act toward the Republic, the Japanese captain's story that his entry into the closed port of Teng-chou was by *force majeure* was accepted by the Chinese Customs, and the boat—otherwise subject to confiscation—was released. " Those ' Red Beards ' were nearly all killed," said General Lan Tien-wei, " at Huang-hsien. Only about thirty escaped death; they were uncontrollable fighters."

It was with the two " Red Beard " generals, Feng Liang-ko and Chang, that the Viceroy of Manchuria, Chao Er-hsun, kept Manchuria quiet and prevented a Republican movement that would have precipitated Japanese and Russian intervention. A large part of the so-called Republican land forces consisted of the rabble of the sworn brotherhood societies of the Yangtse Valley, the pirate clans of Kuangtung, and even of "the Triads," the lowest and most disreputable of all blackmailing, murderous, secret organizations.

The main fact respecting secret societies in China is that they are not progressive in spirit, and up to the present time have existed for the furthering of self-interest. In the revolutionary Rebellion the existing societies, especially all the older ones, merely took advantage of conditions to pay off old scores and better their own material state. They profess and have the highest moral and patriotic tenets, but unless they can be converted to better uses in the future they will be a source of danger to the reform State.

The connection between the subject of the secret societies and the influence of Western Christian missions is made more intimate by the Chinese habit of mind in reducing everything to terms of its own system, thus making the Missions another form of their "huei," or societies.

Since all China's change and reform is due to the West, everything relating to the history of foreigners in China is important. In 1275 fifteen years after Peking was made the seat of government, Marco Polo, the Italian traveller, arrived there. His influence as an intelligence officer official, and envoy under the reigning Emperor was erased by the time the Jesuit missionaries, led by Matheus Ricci, January 24, 1601, entered Peking and began their work. The influence of these missionaries was slight. They were not successful as propagators of religion. They attained office at Peking, but the influences of their learning were nearly wiped out under the regency of the second Manchu Emperor soon after 1661, when the bigoted courtiers of the literati had them condemned to death. The Roman Catholics began to acquire small congregations in the eighteenth century, but it was in the beginning of the nineteenth century when Protestants reached China, that the learning of the West took its first effect.

The fundamental elements of the Revolution in China were established by the arrival of the Protestant missionaries, sent out from New York. When the British East India Company interposed in opposition to missionary work in China, Olyphant and Company of New York sent the first Protestant missionary, Dr Morrison, a British subject, to Canton and assisted in establishing his work. He was joined by American missionaries and it was from one of the latter that the T'aiping leader about 1851 acquired the smattering of Christian doctrine and American ideas on which he formed and conducted the greatest rebellion China has had in the modern centuries. It was at Hongkong that American missionaries established the first school of foreign learning for Chinese.

From this first school established by American missionaries went Yung Wing, to study in America and become the first of China's foreign-educated reformers. He lived to see the successful revolutionary Rebellion and the inauguration of a new Government such as he had worked for.

From this time the extension of schools of foreign learning was continued in China, especially by America, with ever widening influence. Beginning with India, where American philanthropy at the commencement of the revolutionary Rebellion in China expended per annum three times as much money on education of Orientals as did the Indian Government in Japan, it led and was pushing the extension of Western learning with all the force of its philanthropic resources.

The revolutionary spirit of the people working through the secret societies led them to make use of the Missions from the first. An incident which shows the connection between the different elements of the officials or Government, the secret societies, and the foreign Missions, occurred at Kia-ting, in Szechuan. In 1895, because of the complications in these relations, the officials instigated an anti-foreign movement which made it necessary for all foreigners to leave the province, and their premises were destroyed. When they wanted to return they found they could not easily get new premises. One mission sought accommodation immediately adjoining the mission ruins and secured them from a member of the "Elder Brother Society." The member obviously regarded the missionaries from a common fraternal standpoint, and in order thus to give the mission a home he took his life in his hands. A little later the Kia-ting official sent him a message saying he wanted to see him. Knowing well the intention of the official to decapitate him, he took opium and died.

So close and subtle was the relation between the secret societies and the native Christian Church that during the propagation of the present revolutionary Rebellion it was impossible in some places for the foreign missionaries to know when their chapels and congregations were being used for revolutionary purposes. Szechuan

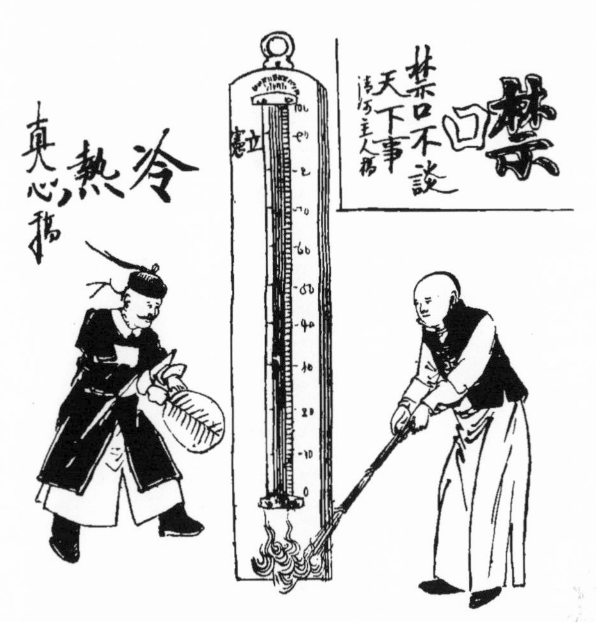

THE PEOPLE ARE WARMING UP CONSTITUTIONAL AFFAIRS, THE OFFICIALS ARE TRYING TO COOL THEM.

THE RETURN OF THE FOREIGN EDUCATED STUDENT.

THE JAPANESE EDUCATIONAL MACHINE—
"IT WORKS QUICKLY."

To face p. 400.

for example, like the other Yangtse provinces, was in a revolutionary state for at least five years preceding its revolt. Revolutionaries joined native Christian congregations as " inquirers," by which they became users of the chapel. In the absence of the foreign missionary, sermons and addresses were often made the vehicles of revolutionary doctrines to an extent that will perhaps never be known. The springing up and existence all over China of foreign-protected mission chapels and churches of various kinds holding up the light of Western knowledge was an engine whose disintegrating and crushing power was something which the defences of no Oriental system of society and government could withstand. By its dissemination of its knowledge of Western sciences it directly and indirectly supplied a large part of the sinews of the revolutionary Rebellion.

Beginning with the earliest of the Chinese students sent abroad, such as Yung Wing, the seekers for Western knowledge who acquired their desire through the teachings of the Missions increased in unnumbered thousands. I refer to Szechuan because it furnished the initial outbreak of the revolutionary Rebellion. In 1895, when the officials and literati instigated the anti-foreign outbreak, a Chinese member of the American Mission Church at Kia-ting began reading the *Scientific Magazine*, edited and published by Dr. Young J. Allen, the American missionary and pioneer in Chinese journalism. As a result he sent four sons to Japan to be educated. They became revolutionaries, and in Sept. 1911, after the Szechuan revolt, their father was elected Mayor of Kia-ting.

All the forces for revolution supplied by the Missions were supported by those whom commerce had carried abroad, and as a result the revolutionary Rebellion and the establishment of the " Flowery Republic " is generally attributed to a small body of foreign-schooled Chinese students. The number of Chinese young-men leaders in the Revolution now going on who have acquired Western ideas from foreign schools abroad and in China, I have numbered as being under 50,000. From this body emanated the revolutionary party—sometimes called a secret society—the Keh-ming-tang, simply translated as " Against Orders Party." It was a rival of the party of Kang Yu-wei, the Pao-huang-huei, and had as its idols the reform martyrs of twenty years past, including the " Five Patriots " who met death at the hands of the Boxer leaders in 1900 in Peking: Lien Yuan, Li Shan, Yuan Chang, Hsu Ching-cheng, and Hsu Yung-yi.

Due to its connection with the Throne, the Pao-huang-huei suggests a varied and distinguished company of reformers:

Weng T'ung-ho, the Imperial tutor to the Emperor Kuang Hsu, recommended the reformer Kang Yu-wei to the Emperor and was subsequently deprived of his rank for doing so. There is no more pathetic figure among the ranks of reformers in China than the Emperor Kuang Hsu himself, who was removed from the throne and was imprisoned on "Ocean Terrace," in the Western Park, Peking, where life left him. Kang Yu-wei, Liang Chi-ch'ao, Yung Wing, and Sun Yat-sen were the notable reform exiles. Sung Po-lu was cashiered because he recommended the very moderate reformer Liang Chi-ch'ao to Emperor Kuang Hsu. Chang Yin-huan, one-time Minister to Washington, was banished to Turkestan and there put to death (1900) by the order of the Empress [Grand] Dowager. Hsu Ching-cheng was condemned to imprisonment for life. Among the last to lose his life in the cause of reform was Shen Chin, killed in the Board of Punishments prison at Peking. He wrote the following appeal just before his execution:

> "With clanking chains I leave my prison pen
> Alone, to die beside the Shun Chih Men,
> Where, in the market-place, their life's blood runs,
> Five loyal and six learned Hukuang sons:
> I too shall lie there with you. I have won
> But little, and my day is done.
>
> Japan and Russia striving for the East,
> China her second capital hath lost;
> Partition comes apace, O bitter thought!
> Rulers, look ye on the Allies' maps for nought?
> My countrymen and foreign journalists!
> O publish forth in the Five Continents
> My buried wrongs!
> The secret treaty I have dared to tell—
> For this 'twas Ch'ing and Chung Lang used me ill.
> The little reputation I have won,
> How worthless; this year I am but thirty-one!
> Henceforth come weal, come woe, I shall not heed,
> Amidst the choirs of Heaven shall my spirit feed."

The death of Shen Chin was one of the events that marked the beginning of the decline of the Throne, which never after had the hardihood to persecute the reformers.

Of the innumerable conspirators and revolutionaries

whose names were not celebrated by being incorporated in the famous Imperial edicts of banishment and death, the most distinguished is no doubt Huang Hsing, Sun Yat-sen's confederate. In the making of the Republic the names of many men properly arise because of their place in the events immediately connected with the revolt. But the long line of liberal, broad-minded men of China connected with all the various phases of foreign influence on China must not be forgotten. Kublai Khan keenly appreciated the merits and value of Western ideas as he saw them exhibited in Marco Polo. So Ni, one of the Manchu regents, was a man of enlightened and noble mind, who saved the Roman Catholic fathers from being executed in Peking by the advisers of the Emperor Kang Hsi. The nobility and broad-mindedness of the Imperial Commissioner Ki Ying, who negotiated with England, France, and America the treaties of trade and commerce in 1843 and 1844, had he lived in a happier Chinese era would have exercised a greater enlightening influence upon the race over which his Manchu brethren ruled.

Among those Chinese reformers whose minds have been opened by an insight into Western things, and who deserves most to be remembered because of his temerity in advocating the introduction of Western ideas, was the Governor of Chekiang, who in the sixties eulogized Washington. He was degraded and removed from office for doing so—afterward, however, being restored to a post in Peking. Li Hung-chang, Chang Chih-tung, Sheng Hsuan-hwai, and even the Empress Grand Dowager herself, must not be forgotten as reformers, not to mention the very men against whom the revolutionary Rebellion was directed, Jung Lu, Tuan Fang, Jui Cheng, and some of the Manchu princes.

The causes of civil war as it manifested itself in September and October 1911 were stated by a conservative Chinese observer at Peking to be due to four things: first, the wretched incapability of the Prince Regent and his ministers; second, the prejudicing and misleading of the Chinese public mind by the reiterations of discontented journalists; third, the incubation of secret parties and rebellious students in Japan; fourth, repeated famine in the Yangtse Valley, and commercial panic and contraction of credit during late years. These conditions were only the immediate cause of the outbreak. A sense of them had been brought on by reform progress.

It was after twenty years of what may be truly said,

for China, to have been years of seething, boiling revolution, thought and feeling in the Chinese Empire became so turbid that the merits of the reformers of no class or cast of opinion could be appreciated. In this situation civil war was a question of but a short time, and when disorder came it was due to conditions far removed from the original starting-point of reform.

The methods of the reformers in the efforts which resulted in the Republic changed with years and the experiences gained through failures. After the failure of the conspiracy of 1898, by which the reformers were about to take possession of the Government at Peking, and hold it with the modern army corps of Yuan Shih-k'ai, the aim of the chief conspirators to overthrow the Manchus, and the establishment of a new State, was still that of a surprise with arms. Sun Yat-sen proceeded for several years on the line that a possession of the Viceroy's yamen at Canton would give him revenues and the control of troops that would enable him to overthrow the Empire. He failed repeatedly to get possession of this yamen, and together with Huang Hsing passed through romantic and picturesque adventures in attempts to invade Kuangtung, capturing and holding for a time border fortresses, but failing and meeting disappointment in his hopes of being met by a general uprising of the people.

During 1905 the revolutionaries commenced utilizing foreign questions in China to stir up the people, creating China's first boycott, that against America. At that time leaders told the American officials that they had nothing against America especially, but that they would use every pretext that could possibly aid them in revolution, and that the treatment of Chinese by America under the Exclusion Act was an asset against the Manchu Central Government which would not be overlooked. This boycott was followed by opposition to English loans for railways in Chekiang, and its coming was apprehended by Sir Ernest Satow, the British Minister, who warned his colleagues in Peking what the effects of the American boycott would be. Then came the agitation over the Shanghai-Nanking Railway, and the reform agitation was proceeding up the Yangtse Valley. It showed its military and rebel character in the mutiny of a battalion of soldiers at Anking (1908), and by this time it was a well-known fact that the Imperial Army was honeycombed with reformers and revolutionaries. Those who wanted to inaugurate a forcible Revolution were distinguished by their anarchistic views. One pamphlet, in 1908, advocated the killing off of all Manchus, all officials, all landlords and men of wealth, the abolition of marriage, and the extermination of the literati.

But by this time the Revolution was in the hands of students, teachers, and reformers everywhere, and was no longer a movement of the conspirator. It had virtually dispensed with the idea that the Revolution was to be brought about by equipping large numbers of men and raising enormous sums of money, and was working to win over the Government and its agents as they existed. It was in this way that the military, upon which the Throne had expended one-third of the Imperial revenue, and which the Prince Regent blindly imagined he had placed in his own hands by conferring upon himself the title of Generalissimo, and by putting his brothers at the head of the land and naval forces, was won over, and within four months turned the Empire's military over to the Republicans. The movement by this time had vaulted over the heads of its promoters and was no longer under control of any man or set of men. The Imperial Army corps at Wuchang when it joined the revolutionists said: "We fight not the people of our own race." The movement had the universal slogan of the Chinese, expressed in the words—the ancient cry against the Tartars—"We are of one mother."

CHAPTER XLIV

SUFFRAGETTES AND THE FRANCHISE

WHEN Dorgon the Manchu regent took possession of the vacant throne at Peking in 1644, he called the advisers of the late Chinese Emperor and discussed with them the subject of what form the pledge of Chinese allegiance in the Empire should take. The principal adviser approved the introduction of the queue fashion, which had become the vogue in Manchuria beyond the Great Wall. This, he said, would be readily accepted by the Chinese men.

With respect to women and the prevailing Manchu head-dress, the old adviser cautioned against the imposing of it or of any other fashion in hair and dress upon Chinese women. The reason for this, he said, was that if there was any attempt to coerce women, whatever they were obliged to wear would be held up to their children as objects to be abhorred.

"Chinese mothers," said the old adviser, "will point out to the children at their breasts the abhorred fashions you have imposed upon them. They will say, 'The Manchus made me do this.' In a generation you will have a nation of enemies."

Dorgon saw the wisdom of this and made no requirements of women. The Chinese man, however, received the queue which, considering he has been the ruler of China, has not been a fashion abhorrent to him. Chinese women, therefore, like the Mongols, can claim themselves unconquered, and as a matter of fact they taunt their men with the fact that the Manchus subdued the men but never subdued Chinese women. This perhaps is the greatest cause for the revolutionary aversion to the queue fashion.

The influence of women has always been recognized in China. "Woman is more powerful than the sword" was the inscription accompanying a cartoon showing the ideal feminine in China during the reform agitation. *The Woman's Paper* was an influential Chinese newspaper published in Peking at this time by Madam Chang. The influence of Chinese women in the reform movement was apparent in all the newspapers. And among the numerous means devised for promoting the revolutionary idea was that of printing portraits of all China's heroines of the past. Mu Yo was the celebrated mother of a famous general in Chinese history. The teachings of Mencius were those among the Chinese classics that most nearly conformed to the spirit of revolution, since they set the seal of sanctity on the will of the people ; so that Mencius's mother—she who " cut the threads of her loom and moved to a worthier neighbourhood "—may be said to deserve first place among women of the past, celebrated by the Republic. Chao Chun was a famous heroine " who went outside the Great Wall," that is, abroad and into the " wild and untamed regions."

The virtues celebrated in China's feminine idols are shown by the inscriptions beneath their Press portraits : " Hsieh Tao-yun was a faithful wife and poetess of the Chun Dynasty who committed suicide when her husband died." "Madam Li Yi Chiu Miang wrote poems urging her husband not to squander the golden days of his youth." In order to incite both men and women to higher ideals, cartoons were printed with such suitable legends as the following : " This man continues to smoke opium—his wife [sitting beside him] is more and more qualifying herself in reading the newspapers." " Chinese women are increasingly indulging in reading ; We hope one day they can be the same as the women of Western countries."

China had many enlightened women when the revolutionary Rebellion came on, and some of them played important if spectacular parts. Several female conspirators lost their lives. The most notable feminine martyr enmeshed in the revolutionary movement was Madam Ch'iu Chin, a school-teacher in Central China. She was a bright, progressive, but somewhat eccentric woman who lived in Peking for a time, and later went to Japan to study. Returning to China, she started a girls' school, and shortly after the revolutionary assassination of the Governor of Anhuei, in the summer of 1907, she was arrested on the charge of complicity in the assassination, and executed.

Madam Ch'iu Chin's name deserves to be mentioned with those of the reform martyrs of 1898, 1900, and 1903.

Madam Lien—a lady who might be called the Elizabeth

Barrett Browning or Felicia Hemans of China—became the best known of women patriots through her efforts to rehabilitate the reputation of Madam Ch'iu Chin. The charges against Madam Ch'iu Chin were everywhere believed to be false, and two under officials connected with the action of the Government against her were driven out of office. Madam Lien erected a tomb over the remains of Madam Ch'iu Chin, placed a tablet and shrine before it, and announced her intention to dwell there so that she might take care of it. Following this, in 1908, she was arrested by the Governor of Chekiang and commanded to be tried. Before the order could be carried out, her Chinese friends came to her defence. Her foreign friends joined in, publishing throughout the world the facts concerning her situation, and altogether they brought about her release and the dismissal of the charges. To a foreign friend she wrote on the occasion of her arrest: "Because of the burial of Ch'iu Chin, your sister's arrest and trial have been commanded. I feel no reproofs of conscience, and what regrets can death cause me? To bid my sister an eternal farewell, I send this message."

The Chinese women of the revolutionary Rebellion were the successors of numerous military and other heroines of Chinese history celebrated in Chinese poetry, story, and the drama, and to be seen impersonated on every Chinese stage. Their appearance at Wuchang, Shanghai, and Nanking was as Amazons, the immemorial type of Chinese heroine. They came equipped in foreign fashions, a testimony that though they were unconquered by the Manchus they had surrendered to the West. Small companies dressed in male military attire were formed at Shanghai and appeared at Nanking, where one of them—a mounted company—insisted on sharing especially the hardships of war. Its members went so far as to declare they would not accept railway accommodation on trains because of depriving the regular soldiers of that convenience, but would march overland to the front in Shantung. One of their leaders, Miss Chang Chun-yin, joined with several other "Amazons" to demand a commitment by the Nanking Republican Assembly on the subject of woman suffrage. Nothing came of it, the majority of the members abstaining from the discussion. The last time I was in Nanking I found representatives of these women of the Revolution in President Sun Yat-sen's official reception-room, and they made a striking impression, just as the suffragists of the West have made in such places, because such things were hitherto unknown.

Owing to the popularity of the subject of woman suffrage in English-speaking countries, and the fact that Chinese women appeared in foreign styles of head-dress and delivered addresses at revolutionary meetings, those women who participated in China's rebellion received abroad the designation " Chinese Suffragettes." A statement to the effect that Chinese women had the suffrage became a suffragist war-cry in America. "Why not suffrage for American women?" asked the American suffragists. Onlookers and listeners were not critical of this war-cry simply because it was an untruth. The cry "Down with the Manchus!" was based on assumptions nearly wholly untrue, but nevertheless it assisted in accomplishing perhaps the most important thing necessary to accomplish in the world at the time. If, therefore, the cry that woman suffrage existed in China could do any good, all might close their ears to the facts.

Suffrage in China is only a name, a part of the great problem of the limited right to vote to be first worked out in the course of future years. " Only in the guilds and self-governing institutions of individuals in China is there a form of voting," says Yuan Shih-k'ai. " Suffrage is unknown among the people, and it will be years before it can be applied in China. It must be arrived at gradually and put into practice by the slow process of education and the fixing of qualifications for voting. Even in local affairs the people have no convictions, and do not express themselves respecting their preferences. If asked to vote this way or that, they would be confused and alarmed and would run away in fear. No, they must first be taught by schools for the teaching of self-government."

No doubt the closest and best friends at large of Chinese womankind are the foreign missionary, and other women workers in China. During the revolutionary changes in government at Peking, when the subject of woman suffrage came up among Chinese women reformers, one of the foremost foreign women educators, the head of a girls' school, told her Chinese friends that her support of their reforms would vanish at this point of suffrage for Chinese women. China, in the Western sense, was without suffrage for anybody, man or woman. Not until the Chinese system—the only one in existence in China—is changed could there be anything resembling general suffrage. It must be apparent to everybody, therefore, how far-fetched is any comparison of political and social conditions in China with those in a Republic like the United States, and what a violence the foreign imagination must undergo in order to picture the Chinese woman as being now in the situation which the American or British woman suffragist considers ideal for herself.

The question of who is the Martha Washington of China as a Republic will come up as time goes on and the ideals of the reformers become more fixed. The honour will lie between Madam Sun Yat-sen, wife and mother of revolutionaries and reformers, and Madam Li Yuan-hung, wife of the man who has been called the Chinese Washington, and a lady known as the Minister to the Wounded at Hankow. It is likely that the greatest Chinese heroine of the future will be the ministering angel who can bring humanity into the treatment of the starving in China, alleviate generally the suffering connected with Chinese life, and raise the value of the individual being through educating and enlightening the Chinese mothers.

CHAPTER XLV

PART OF THE PEOPLE

FAMINE had prepared the country for rebellion. On Sept. 1, 1911, the budget of the Board of Finance showed a decrease of over 50,000,000 taels due to this one cause. In Hunan and Hupeh, the two provinces where the Republic was declared, three millions to four millions of people were suffering from flood and famine, and over 100,000 persons had lost their lives by the time of the outbreak. In the third of the famine provinces, Anhuei, there were estimated to be 1,000,000 sufferers in a single district in the North, a description of whom will give an idea of a section of the millions who are charges of the "Flowery Republic."

The principal facts are from the observations of the American Red Cross Engineer, C. D. Jameson, and his assistant, Rev. Mr. Beaman. At Hwai-yuan, seven out of ten families have no seed grain for 1912, and there are six other similar centres of famine. By the time the Rebellion is on, all trees and land have been sold, and the last stage preceding starvation is indicated by the sale of the roofs of houses. No pigs or fowls are to be seen; all is bare, with the mud plains beneath and the beautiful blue sky overhead. Parents beg food on behalf of sometimes only a single son, willing to sacrifice other children in hope of saving the family line. The story becomes more sickening as the Red Cross agents go from centre to centre. General Chang Hsun's Imperialist troops bind to small trees near the station at Ling-hwai-kuan 200 or more looting soldiers, shoot them to death and leave them to be mutilated with sword and bayonet. The Republican soldiers alternately commandeer supplies and punish looting, executing on the spot those found with the smallest articles of loot.

"These people fell between the devil and the deep sea—famine and robbers," says a Roman Catholic priest. "The strong became robbers, the weak went to the wall. The streets were filled with pools of blood which the starving relatives of the victims—wives, mothers, and sisters—kissed or licked with their tongues as they knelt before the authorities pleading for mercy for their kindred." Four consecutive years of flood and famine prepared the horrors of the first winter of the Republic here.

Father de Glois saw a mother and two children dead from starvation in the snow by the roadside. Again, a mother and son, the mother dead, the son some distance away in the last stages of starvation but not quite dead. " I took him up," said the priest, " and tried to place him in my saddle. He vomited, and with a few gasps died, before his body reached the saddle. I administered the last rites and laid the body beside the mother, and went on. Every night scores of helpless families lie at the door of my Mission calling for help."

Amid these scenes, on Chinese New Year's Day, the abdication proclamation was posted. " It made the simple statement," said Mr. Beaman, " that the Throne had been given back to the people and that they were to be united under one People's Government. Few took trouble to read it, and it seemed to make very little impression. Worship went on in the usual way, except that the name of the Emperor was erased from the household tablet and in its place ' People's Kingdom ' was inscribed."

Farther on the country is infested with robber bands, and many families straggle Southward in search of food, after being overtaken by starvation at home. Their path is along a roadway where those who have preceded them have added exhaustion to starvation and become food for scavenger dogs. One body is seen in a field, half eaten. Here and there is a new-made grave strewn with tattered rags dug up by the dogs ; the stronger men pushing wheelbarrows bring the last scraps of household furnishings. Children too small to walk peep from wooden pails here and there tied to the wheelbarrow frames. Others are falling behind, as they become more and more weak, perhaps as night comes on to fight helplessly a moment with the dogs. They look old and pinched and hungry. There is one old woman, " clad in tatters, bent and unsteady, with a stick across her shoulders holding a small basket of weeds—her food. She has a fixed gaze in her eyes, is shrunken and hungry, with strength enough for one step at a time. Perhaps soon after nightfall she falls by the wayside to die alone in the cold."

As the road leads westward—crossing the famine region from east to west—some of the villages and hamlets have a few stacks of straw, and occasionally a few animals. Again

FIGHTING BANDITS IN HONAN.

TRAVELS OF A PEASANT—AT THE WINDLASS.

A CHINESE NOW HAS HEAVY RESPONSIBILITIES AND SMALL PRIVILEGES.

To face p. 412.

no straw, animals, or fowls are to be seen, and many houses are roofless and empty. People wander aimlessly about with vacant, staring eyes, and women and children kneel down begging for food. Homes have practically nothing in them. Reports from larger cities show ragged and hungry filling the streets. In the smaller district cities, many houses are deserted after the doors have been sealed with blocks of mud and plastered over. Where roofs have been sold and removed the walls are crumbling. There are no markets and no food-stuffs to purchase. Children are offered as gifts to passers-by. Mud fortifications are thrown up about the more important villages with drawbridges so guarded as to be taken up at a moment's notice and the bridges removed altogether. These are the wealthier villages or the strongholds of robber bands. Those who are strongest plunder, destroying whole cities. Chang-tang-tao is an example of this. It contained about 1000 families. One afternoon a band of 300 robbers came and demanded food. Having eaten, they began killing, looting, and burning. "When the robbers began," said the son of one family, "they rushed into our house and with swords and bayonets slew my father, mother, brother, sisters, and a young cousin, looted the house and set it on fire. The front entrance alone remained." Nearly 100 innocent people were slaughtered, and women of the better families carried away captive.

Fifteen villages and hamlets, burned and desolated, line the roadway along the north of this famine region. Sometimes all the surviving inhabitants of a village or hamlet are found huddled together under one remaining roof, eating thin gruel mixed with dry weeds. One such company is made up of helpless women and children, with a few maimed, aged, and decrepit men. "We can hold out only a little longer," they say.

The region of the Tientsin-Pukow Railway has been swept by two armies, the Imperialists and the Republicans. What they left, robbers inherit. No authority exists and no security, and an occasional official having to cross the region leaves marks of his passing by the wayside where are bodies of robbers shot by his militia guard.

At Chi-chia-tien, a noted robber village, all the blacksmiths are busy making firearms. These native weapons are worth one dollar and fifteen cents—four shillings and sixpence—each. An armed rabble is the village guard which meets all visitors outside the town. It is part of an organized robber band preparing to plunder a neighbouring town. Before the traveller go robber bands, inaccurately estimated by the dying people and vaguely reported. From the west comes a Roman Catholic priest, arriving after a week's wheelbarrow journey. He could not ride a horse or other animal, because it would have been taken from him. He passed an encampment of 2000 robbers at the large and important city of Ying-chou-fu. His compound was looted four times. A brother-priest near by was twice looted ; even his eyeglasses were taken from his nose.

Nan Hsu Chou is the borderland of the Imperialist and revolutionary armies and is the Republican outpost. In the environs people are digging roots and weeds in the fields for food. An occasional donkey or cow is seen, the two sometimes hitched together and drawing wood taken from the houses to market. Everywhere is anarchy. The bodies of soldiers killed at the occupation of the City by the Republicans remain unburied. The skeletons are still intact, the skulls not yet bleached white, and tufts of long hair strewn about by the dogs. Within the year 1911 200,000 people have died of starvation in this region alone ; 400,000 still suffer after four years of flood and famine.

All the horses which the region possessed after the raids of the robbers are picketed at the Republican camp, gathered in by the soldiers who have scoured the country. Outside are the deserted villages of the great monotonous plain, like the broken hamlets of Manchuria during the Russo-Japanese War, and occasionally robber towns where in rude forges native blacksmiths make gun-barrels. They beat iron around a core, and removing the core drill a touch-hole at the breech end. Between are the wolf-like dogs, following the robber, the soldier, and following all come the European and American priest, pastor, and the succouring Red Cross. Red, raw skulls grin in the fallow or gnaw dirt among thin and chaff-like stubble. Skeletons lie about with only the arms and feet gone, and the dogs hide behind a line of graves away from the passer-by. This is a picture of China in rebellion. Even the gentry, China's immemorial bulwark, are here turning bandit in obedience to the first law of nature.

Amid all this, the Chinese officials temporize with the Red Cross over famine relief expenditures with the view of getting control of the funds for themselves. Who would not say that China's disease and problem is that of being Chinese ?

CHAPTER XLVI

LAST COURT OF THE MANCHUS

THE Chinese are hungry for food, for enlightenment, and for relief from themselves, their system, customs, and self-bondage. But all these ills they have laid at the door of the Manchu, who, judging by the Republican cry, is their one grievance. The Manchus did not take care to place themselves above blame. While they conferred a monarchical system of government with a Constitution upon China and promoted reforms beyond the capacity of Chinese to reform, the Dynastic system and the Court were not altered in any important particular.

A picture of the Palace under the Lung Yu Empress Dowager half a year before the outbreak of the revolutionary Rebellion was furnished me by one of the reformers who was sent into the Forbidden City bearing certain presents from a foreign Court for the little Emperor Pu Yi. The occasion was that of the birthday anniversary of the foreign monarch, and the reformer entered the Palace on the eve of the birthday anniversary of George Washington. The mission took seven hours to perform, although the time required to enter the Palace was but a few moments. The gift-bearer had arrived inside the eastern gate of the Palace by 2 a.m., the usual hour for reception of official visitors. He thus describes his feelings and experiences :

" I have been up all night without sleep, and am tired out with the effects of my visit, especially the strain of being so discreet. You see, I was selected to explain these royal presents, which I did not very well understand, not having seen them before. I went in in the night. It was very dark and of course I could not see much. I could not wear my glasses [it is impolite in China to wear glasses in company], and so I could not even read the characters over the gateways between the courts as I went along. As I knew not what the inscriptions were, I learned very little about the inside of the Palace.

" I was taken into a room where the presents had been laid down and were opened. The directions were written in a foreign language, so that I could not read them, but nevertheless I was obliged to explain. Some of the objects I had never seen the like of before. Among other things there was an aeroplane. When it came to this, I said that I would demonstrate what it was but that I was afraid something might be broken before it reached His Majesty. Besides, it was dangerous to try it on account of there being so much glass about.

" I was talking to the principal servants of Her Majesty the Lung Yu Empress Dowager, and I said that they need but give the word. They, of course, said with one voice, 'Oh no,' because, naturally, they could not risk having an accident. Regarding a battery of some kind which the boxes contained, I said that as it was electrical, and as the Palace was fitted with an electrical plant, it was only proper to turn it over to the care of the engineers there, as they would understand how to operate it. One of the eunuchs spoke up quickly and said, ' Why, of course; we will have the engineer brought in at once, so that you can explain it to him.'

" I was embarrassed and asked my companion from the Chinese Foreign Office what I should do. Then I observed that the battery was very nicely packed in its case and that some knowledge and care were necessary in order to take it out, so I suggested that inasmuch as it was so carefully put up it might be best before proceeding further to let the Emperor examine it. This I recommended as apparently the safest way to proceed. The eunuch seemed taken with this idea and consented at once, so I saved myself again. I was astonished at my success and how well my answers worked. My companion remarked how clever I was in dealing with the eunuchs.

" There were other things, including a wagon about two feet long, with a ladder which when extended was several feet high. There were many mechanical toys, and I think these pleased the Palace attendants more than anything else. There were several musical toys, including a musical chair which would play a tune whenever sat upon. As I left the place I saw it carried out in the direction of other buildings, while the remaining presents were left in charge of servants-in-waiting.

" When the exhibition was over, the ladies of the Court, who all the time had been looking on by peeping in at the windows, came in. I had noticed them, but could not look up—that was impossible, according to our ideas. When they began to come in, of course I had to make my escape, and I did this just in time by slipping down a side passage.

"During the explanations messages were carried in to Her Majesty the Lung Yu Empress Dowager. At the end I had to express my thanks to Her Majesty and this message was likewise taken in. Word came back that Her Majesty would excuse me from this formality. I then had to go to the head eunuch and make my manners. I was shown into his room, and found him sitting at a table eating. He rose in a most peculiar way, and according to his own ideas must have shown me considerable deference. So I thought. When he was up, he was standing on his right foot, with his left in the chair in which he had been sitting. His arms were akimbo and he looked boorish and overbearing. In this position he turned at first a haughty look upon me. It was as much as to say, 'What are you here for?' I told him I had come to ask that my thanks be given to Her Majesty.

"'Won't you have something to eat with me?' said he.

"This was the proper thing for him to say.

"'I dare not,' I replied, this being the polite address to a superior under such circumstances.

"'Well, won't you be seated and rest yourself?'

"To this I again replied:

"'I dare not.'

"'Well, then, please drink, at your pleasure, some tea.'

"This being the essential termination of my interview, I thanked him, and asked him to convey my thanks to Her Majesty.

"The head eunuch to whom I had spoken was such a handsome person that if I had been asked I would have said he was a woman. His name was Sung. He was strikingly handsome, in fact beautiful. When he spoke so cordially to me, the other eunuchs took their tip from him and treated me accordingly. They asked my full name, my personal name, and then called me by the latter.

"But it was quite different when I first went in and we opened the presents. The eunuchs were lofty and overbearing. They looked at me as though I was a housebreaker, and then scowled and asked me what I wanted and what I was doing in there. Having told them, I got on very well, for they saw that as the messenger of a rich and powerful country I was a fat prospect for 'squeeze.' They saw they could get money out of me, and told me I should get the finest presents from the Palace.

"But let me tell you," he went on, "I have received a present from the Emperor ; yes, I have received a present from the Throne, from my Emperor. When I had finished showing our presents, one of the high eunuchs said of me that I had done well and should have some of the best presents from them. As a matter of fact, when the presents came, they were only fruit—not good fruit, either.

"I have not told you all. It was very funny, after I told the eunuchs my errand. All asked in one voice :

"Who is the tribute from ?"

"The 'tribute' (*chin-kung*), they said, with a clatter of voices. 'What country does the *chin-kung* come from ?' And then came the answer from several. I couldn't report this to the Minister of that proud foreign Power. But what do you think he would have said had I told him that in the Palace we were 'tribute-bearers' ? Oh, I was disheartened by going in there. There is no hope of changing the Palace and stopping the abuses and 'squeezes.' I am ashamed that they know nothing. They do not know that the presents were not tribute. It cost me ten dollars [silver value—an outrageous imposition] to have the presents which I received carried to the Palace outer gate. When I got home, I found them to be nothing more than four baskets of fruit. For curiosity's sake I reckoned the cost to me, and found it to be about twice the market price in the street. There were about 150 pieces. The baskets were not even of different assorted fruits, such as a proper present of this kind must be, but just what happened to be lying about. One was of oranges, one of pears, and the other two were only of apples. This is the method of 'squeezing' by the eunuchs. It is necessary to pay everyone in each court through which one passes. It is necessary to give money to everyone visible, because they make themselves noticed.

"You know that the Foreign Office [Wai-wu-pu] is in charge of all such gifts to the Emperor. It is bled atrociously for these formalities. If the Foreign Office does not pay properly, the things they send in are damaged in some way, or arrive late, or something else to cause inconvenience happens to them by design, and the Throne then punishes the Foreign Office. That is the reason the Foreign Office sent one of its representatives with me, so that the blame would not be put upon it. And this made it necessary for me to pay the costs. Everybody complains, and the Foreign Office more than anyone. The eunuchs cannot all read. I have been told that the Emperor's head eunuch Chang cannot read."

The personnel of the Palace at this time, besides the child Emperor Pu Yi, may be enumerated thus :

The Emperor Kuang Hsu and his predecessor Tung Chih were heirless. Kuang Hsu had but two consorts besides his wife, the Lung Yu Empress Dowager. One of these consorts, Chen, committed suicide the day the Court fled from Peking in 1900. The surviving one was Chin. Tung Chih left consorts Yu, Ch'in, and Hsun, of which the first is the most alert. A consort of the Emperor Hsien Feng, known as Chi, was reported to me as a still active member of the Imperial Family at the beginning of 1910. The Empress [Grand] Dowager had an adopted daughter, and the Court personnel was then followed by the eunuchs Sung and Chang (An Teh's, or guardians), belonging to the Lung Yu Empress Dowager, and the eunuchs Chang, Sun, and Lin, all belonging to the consort Yu. The inferior eunuchs were estimated to number between 2000 and 4000, the census never having been published. Needless to say, the Lung Yu Empress Dowager was the important member of the Court. The Chinese attributed to her the sincere desire to reform Palace abuses. Her predecessor's chief eunuch, Li Lien-ying—the most notorious corruptionist in the Palace—retired at the beginning of the new reign and had two successors. Sung (An Teh), the first, was degraded and was succeeded by Chang (An Teh).

All these and no more were permitted to reside in the Forbidden City, and from these no more than the Throne selected might accompany the Court to reside in the Western Park adjoining the Forbidden City, the Summer Palace in the Western Hills, the Southern Hunting Park outside the South Wall of Peking, and to the Eastern Tombs and Western Tombs, to which the last Court journeyed. There was an interesting exception in 1908, when Prince Chun, father of the Emperor Pu Yi, had a palace in the Imperial premises set aside for his use where he might spend the night, but he was ousted soon after.

The Palace attendants managing all Court affairs and the relation of the government of the Empire with the Imperial Family and Throne, are, in 1910, shown to have remained unenlightened since the first embassies to Peking, when the Ministers of foreign Powers were asked to kotow before the Emperor of China, and the procession of boats bearing their belongings up the Pei-ho were labelled with flags marked "Tribute Bearers." And in 1911, when rebellion came, the Court and Palace and the laws of the Imperial Household, Imperial Clan, and internal government of the Manchus were not essentially different from what they had been for 100 years and more. There were no modern schools within the Forbidden City, no enlightenment was provided for the Palace servants and Palace officials, no audit system was in existence, the child Emperor Pu Yi was entrusted solely to the care of Palace women and eunuchs, the latter pronounced by enlightened men as being among the most degraded menials and hangers-on in the world.

It was one of the plans of Yuan Shih-k'ai to avert such a fate for the child Emperor Pu Yi as that of being brought up under petticoat rule by degraded eunuchs, and to sweep away the abuses of "squeeze" of which the Foreign Office complained, and which it said cost high officials such as viceroys 30,000 to 50,000 taels (in gold dollar value approximately two-thirds this amount) at each audience.

One of the ways devised by Yuan Shih-k'ai for accomplishing these objects shows what was the magnitude of the task he had set for himself. He thought it of such magnitude as to require the assistance of the foreign Powers, and he therefore devised a plan by which the foreign Powers should replace their Ministers at Peking with Ambassadors. These, by having the right to demand audience of the Emperor, could overrule Palace practices and abuses.

The historian will find on examination of the reform programme of the Empress [Grand] Dowager that while ample provisions were made for the evolution of the Chinese themselves, social and governmental, the Manchus in their own internal affairs made no important changes. On Jan. 31, 1910, the Manchus nominally abolished the ancient institution of slavery among the Chinese. Their slaves were first to be set free without exception. But the slaves of the Manchus (and Mongols, a yet more primitive people) were only changed in status. The constitutional plan of the Manchus had not gone so far that any change in the Imperial house law reforming Court practices and Imperial Family government had been adopted. In fact, the only visible changes in Imperial customs was a temporary effort at social intercourse with foreign ladies during the last few years in the life of the Empress [Grand] Dowager, and a few banquets to foreign officials given by the Prince Regent.

In some respects the Manchu Court had at the same time deteriorated. Previous rulers had rid the Court of the numerous actors and mountebanks which in the Chinese system are classed together and reckoned with the lowest class of menials. They had flourished in the previous Dynasty (the Chinese Ming), and they appeared in the Forbidden City in the reign of Chia Ch'ing, which ended in 1820. There is no other mention of them in connection with the Palace during the Ching Dynasty, but they flourished under the late Empress Grand Dowager.

It was not until the outbreak in Szechuan became uncontrollable that the subject of the Imperial house law and the internal government of the Manchus was taken up. And it was significant of their self-conscious guilt and knowledge of the great weakness of their position that the Imperial Clan took action. An edict was issued by the Prince Regent, "in obedience," it said, "to a desire verbally expressed to him by the Lung Yu Empress Dowager," to decrease the total Palace expenses 20,000 taels per year and make other reforms. Prince Pu Lun of the Constitutional Bureau and Duke Tsai Tse, Minister of Finance, in conjunction with the High Chamberlain, and the Elders of the Four Clans, were appointed to devise new rules for assigning duties to officials of the Board of the Imperial Household and to those of the Palace.

Prince Pu Lun and Duke Tsai Tse were ordered to adopt a course of rigid economy in expenditures of the Imperial Household and of the Board of Clansmen, acting in concert with the Presidents of these two departments. The latter officers gave out that as an initial step toward retrenchment it was decided to dismiss two-fifths of their staffs. Upon examination it was found that the budget for the Imperial Household, instead of a decrease, provided for an increase of 380,000 taels, making the total estimate 8,385,057 taels.

It was interesting to note the progress of this belated effort at self-regeneration coincident with the progress of events in the setting up of the Republic. The last heard of it was in the beginning of October, when Prince Pu Lun memorialized the Throne that he dared not adjust the wide difference between the expenditures of the

Imperial Household and the revenue available for it, since it affected the economy of Their Majesties the Lung Yu Empress Dowager and Emperor. Thereupon the Lung Yu Empress Dowager issued a rescript to the effect that the matter must be decided by herself.

This action of the Lung Yu Empress Dowager respecting the affairs of the Palace, which have always been of a nature personal to it, and therefore sacred in the minds of Chinese officialdom, threw them back to their original status, wherein the Palace was politely ignored as nobody's business.

The habitation of the Court was a sovereignty in itself; the most striking thing about it, its being called the "Forbidden City," was a correct characterization. Its affairs were still a monopoly of the eunuchs, notwithstanding these creatures were known to be an abuse as well as a danger to the Empire. It was a never-to-be-forgotten example connected with the fall of the Mings that the corruption of the Palace brought about the situation which gave China to the Manchus. But the Imperial Family remained in the hands of the eunuchs, through whom all transactions with the outside world always had been conducted.

Officials could never obtain access to the Throne except through them; all communications passed through their hands; they were the depositary of the Throne's information respecting the entire mandarinate; their recommendations carried weight with the Throne and were obtainable by bribery; they controlled the expenses of the Palace and made up the budget; no business could be transacted with the Court without greasing their palms. The stories of the lives of the eunuchs is a sealed chapter to the world at large. The only instance I can recall in the modern history of the Forbidden City wherein they are not execrated by the Chinese is that of a faithful eunuch of the suicide Emperor Hsien Feng, who voluntarily died with his Imperial master—a Chinese custom adopted by the Japanese.

This, together with the mixed element of dignitaries from without the Palace, is the physical aspect of the Court's make-up, and its domestic life. Its official functions were occupied with Dynastic or Court politics, which consisted of at least three interesting propositions in the Dynasty's internal diplomacy. The first was the maintenance of balance between the Manchu Clan party of the Yellow Girdles, who traced their descent from the founder of the Dynasty, Hsien Tzu, and called themselves the Aisin Gioros, and the party of the Red Girdles—Yehonala Clan—who are collateral relations of the Imperial house. The Throne in the period of China's Revolution has been in the possession of the latter.

The second proposition was the maintenance of balance between the great political parties (existing since 1860), that of Tseng Kuo-fan of Hunan, and that of Li Hung-chang and his brother, Li Han-chang, of Anhuei. The third was the maintenance of the official balance between China and the Manchus. The latter was the easiest, since the Manchus had no party to serve and distributed themselves on the sides of both, using the Chinese parties as a balance to support the Dynasty in power.

All this was no mean task, and it was complicated by the inclinations and proclivities of foreign nations, as their interests dictated, to exalt one official and disparage others, as, for example, the support of Na Tung by the Japanese against Yuan Shih-k'ai, or Great Britain, United States, and others supporting Yuan Shih-k'ai. There was a wide crevice between these opposing forces for the Dynasty to fall into and find destruction, which it did in the revolutionary Rebellion, when the Canton party arose and was joined by the reformers.

In addition to all this there was the "petticoat rule" within the Court, divided at the last between the Lung Yu Empress Dowager and Princess Ch'un, the wife of the Prince Regent. The dismissal of Yuan Shih-k'ai from the Government when the last Court came into power, commencing the downward path of the Dynasty, was an affair of the men of the Court. The Lung Yu Empress Dowager was not a sympathetic mate for the late Emperor and did not side with him against Yuan Shih-k'ai at the time of the *coup d'état* of 1898. On the contrary, she sided with her aunt, the Empress [Grand] Dowager. Princess Ch'un was the daughter of Yuan Shih-k'ai's patron Jung Lu, and had no cause of her own for intriguing against Yuan Shih-k'ai. But she set up a rivalry with the Lung Yu Empress Dowager, who was the Imperial mother of her own son. In this she was joined by her husband's mother, and it has been said in derision that these two were the Regency. They set out to monopolize the cream of the metropolitan offices in Peking. There were three princes in the family, the Prince Regent, Prince Hsun, and Prince Tao, all poor and in need of money to rehabilitate their estates and family reputation. The Navy Bureau was given to Prince Hsun, the Army Bureau to Prince Tao (along with a senior Prince, Yu Lang), and the Prince Regent himself assumed the position of Generalissimo or Commander-in-Chief. After the dismissal of Yuan Shih-k'ai this was the next and greatest step in the Dynasty's descent.

Outside of the Palace and the Imperial Family, forming the natural bulwark of the Throne, was the Imperial Clan, consisting of the eight iron-capped, or helmeted, princely families, and other nobility, headed by Prince Ching. They included the princes just mentioned, as well as Prince Kung and Prince Pu Lun (who were both candidates for the throne when the Emperor Kuang Hsu died), Prince Tuan of Boxer notoriety, and many others. Among them no voice was raised and no hand lifted to rescue or battle for the Throne and Dynasty. All responsibility rested upon Prince Ching, an able minister but a very old man. In all the Imperial Clan he could discover no leader, and confessed that the only successor for himself which he might point out to guide the Dynasty was the Chinese, Yuan Shih-k'ai. The Manchu Dynasty seemed then to need nothing more than the ceremony performed by Sun Yat-sen at Hung Wu's tomb to dispose of it for ever.

Not a single member of the nobility possessed the least foreign training or modern education. The Throne was a polluted fountain-head, and while giving more to the Chinese of reform than it gave to itself it could not govern.

Except for the assault of the mob on Feb. 29, 1912, upon the mansion of Duke Kuei Hsiang, brother of the late Empress Grand Dowager, the awakened Chinese gave no attention to the Imperial Clan and Court. Those Clansmen outside the Palace made personal dispositions of their affairs without reference to united defence, relying only upon the protection of foreigners.

While they were dispersing to foreign colonies and settlements the Throne in its solicitous care for a few loyal soldiers who had regained the military spirit of the past and died at their posts rather than surrender them to the mob, was rewarding their spirits with posthumous honours. Then those within the Palace remained quiet, and the Manchus were thus engulfed in the great rise to consciousness of the Chinese race—only the second rise in a thousand years.

There were many able men deserving of the rank to be called statesmen in China during the period of the influence of the late Empress Grand Dowager in the Palace, but in the last reign none who deserved to be remembered. If they had but cleaned out the Palace and educated some of their princes, thus sweeping their own doorstep, they would at least have placed themselves above blame. But they did nothing. The Court occupied itself with Palace intrigue, formed no connection with the world, and its life seemed to show that the Manchu Dynasty was above all aid and the Manchus the only human beings who did not need friends.

What the Dynasty lacked to meet the fate confronting it is shown by contrast with Japan, which has solved a similar problem. The Japanese say that China as she confronted the Revolution lacked all the essential elements that existed in Japan in the same emergency. Her Throne was not a rallying-point upon which was centred reverent affection, and there was no large party of progressive leaders who, to hereditary prestige, added high intellect, profound foresight, and invincible courage. And it did not have behind it a nation swayed by patriotic sentiment, and not by selfish individualism. To this indictment has been added another, which while it reflects upon the Chinese seems to be the last syllable of damnation for the Manchus. The Manchu Dynasty had furnished China with perhaps, from all standpoints, her greatest emperors. Under it China had reached her greatest prosperity, prestige, wealth, and dimensions. "Multitudes of Chinese," observed the Japanese, "must have received from them benefits deserving eternal gratitude. Yet among all these beneficiaries not one was found to lay down his life for his Sovereign at the supreme moment."

There was not a prince of the blood or blood-relative of any kind, there was no minister of state, there was no censor, to sacrifice his life in accordance with immemorial custom born into them; there was not even the lowliest eunuch to signalize, by offering his own life, the drawing of the curtain over the Manchus, such an act as accompanied the lowering of night upon the Mings.

CHAPTER XLVII

REPUBLICAN STATE PAPERS

THE revolutionary Rebellion was one without marked warfare. It was a campaign of peace propaganda, Press enlightenment and anathema, aided by conspiracy. It succeeded on principles of conservation rather than destruction, while the nation, as was observed by the Japanese, showed unwonted moderation and restraint—some might say indifference—when the object of the revolt was achieved. Unregarded by, and unknown to the unlettered hordes, the Manchu Dynasty passed, execrated by the revolutionary reformers and by specific indictments of the Republican leaders and Government in their State papers. Among all the phenomena of China's revolutionary Rebellion nothing struck me more forcibly than the revolutionary documents.

Chinese "Independence" began during Sept. 1911 with Pu Tien-chun, in the province of Szechuan. "The Chinese Republic and Presidency" began in October with Li Yuan-hung, at Wuchang. Provincial "Federation" began in November with Wu Ting-fang, at Shanghai, and "The Provisional Republican Government" began in December with Sun Yat-sen, in Nanking. January 1912 opened a first-class Revolution in the Chinese Empire.

The declarations in Szechuan were simple conservative declarations, respecting only the nationalization of railways. Popular support of these declarations embraced worship of the spirit of the late Emperor Kuang Hsu. Those from Wuchang, in which Li Yuan-hung said, "I, the General of the Hupeh Army, am to overthrow the Manchus and elevate the Hans," first defined the lines of the revolutionary Rebellion. At Peking the "Nineteen Articles," promulgated on Nov. 3, 1911, by the National Assembly and sanctioned by the Throne, intended to define and fix the form of government. They are the best part of the revolutionary papers, and though monarchical, were made in the interests of those who declared Republican independence. They were based upon the wisdom which the Constitution-makers of Peking had acquired during seven years of labour upon the constitutional government, devised and published in 1907 by the Empress [Grand] Dowager. They were a revolutionary advance over that constitutional scheme which was modelled after the Constitution of Japan, and was itself thought by conservative foreign friends of China to be an acceptable one.

The "Nineteen Articles" were a drastic curb to the powers of the Manchu Throne. They were entirely directed at the Manchu sceptre. They were in fact a Constitution of parliamentary rule and placed no definite restrictions upon Parliament itself at all. They served to unseat the Dynasty from the constitutional refuge which since 1907 it had been providing for itself. Nearly all the inhabitants of the late Chinese Empire, if reformers at all, are conservative reformers. Some idea of where their representatives, the conservative revolutionists at Peking, stood with respect to constitutionalism, may be seen from a comparison of the "Nineteen Articles" with the Japanese Constitution.

The first four articles conform to those of the Japanese Constitution.

In another—the 10th Article—the Emperor of China was granted the direction, but not the supreme command of the army and navy, which the Japanese Emperor enjoys. Whereas in Japan the Emperor makes treaties, the Parliament in China was to assume this power; whereas in Japan the Government or Ministers of the Emperor, in consultation with the Emperor, framed the Imperial house laws, the National Assembly intended that the Parliament should make these laws.

Article 14 was an emergency measure to cover the financial affairs of China that were the stated cause of the outbreak of revolutionary Rebellion. It placed control of the budget, antedated one year, with Parliament, and prevented the Government taking extraordinary financial measures. This was for the purpose of blocking foreign loans then pending. To me these "Nineteen Articles" appear to exhibit the calmest and best thought of which the Revolution showed itself capable. They show a knowledge of the American Constitution, and their clearness and sanity had the effect for the time, in the outside world, of ennobling the National Assembly that endorsed and passed them.

The " Nineteen Articles " appeared in advance of the curious documents which friendly nations were asked to receive as the voice of the new Chinese people, addressed to the world from Shanghai. In the latter the Sargossa Sea of mixed Chinese and alien thought and revolutionary banality engulfed the schooled, honest, and thoughtful patriots. One of these emanations was that in which George Washington, Thomas Jefferson, and Wu Ting-fang were rolled into one, November 7, 1911. It might be called the first official appeal to the world put out from China by the Republicans, and reads :

" The Chinese nation, born anew, in the travail of revolution, extends friendly greetings and felicitations to the world.

" As the Republic of China it now asks that recognition by the civilized Powers which will enable it, with the assistance of their kindly offices, to erect upon the foundations of honest government and friendly trade and intercourse with all peoples, a peaceful and happy future.

" The Chinese people are not untried in self-government. For countless ages they ruled themselves : they developed observance of law to a degree not known among other races ; they developed arts and industries and agriculture, and knew a peace and contentment surpassingly sweet.

" Down upon them swept the savage hordes of an alien warlike race. The Chinese people were conquered and enslaved. For 270 years the bondage existed. Then the Chinese people rose and struck a blow for freedom. Out of the chaos and dust of a falling Throne emerges a free and enlightened people—a great natural democracy of 400,000,000 human beings.

" They have chosen to set up a Republic, and their choice we believe is a wise one. There is no class nobility among the Chinese, and they have no recognized royal family to set up in place of the Manchu royal house. This is a great democracy. The officials spring from the people and to the people they return. There are no princes, lords, dukes, among the Chinese. With the Manchu Throne removed there is left a made-to-order Republic. Already we have provincial assemblies and our National Assembly. Already we have a Republic with a full set of competent officials.

" Within a very few days our constitutional convention will meet : arrangements for it were made long ago.

At this convention there will be fully authorized delegates from every province in China. A Constitution of the most enlightened character will be adopted, and new officers of the Provisional Government elected. Following this will come, under the provisions of the Constitution, the provincial and national elections.

"It is imperative for our Government to be recognized at this time, in order that business may not be subjected to prolonged stagnation. There is peace everywhere save at Hankow, but business cannot proceed until the new Republic shall be welcomed among the nations of the world.

"We ask recognition in order that we may enter upon our new life and our new relationships with the Great Powers.

"We ask recognition of the Republic because the Republic is a fact.

"Fourteen of the eighteen provinces have declared their independence of the Manchu Government, and have proclaimed their allegiance to the Republic. The remaining provinces will, it is expected, soon take the same course.

"The Manchu Dynasty finds its power fallen away and its glitter of yesterday become a puppet show. Before going it has stripped itself of authority by consenting to the terms of the proposed Constitution which already have been made public.

"The most glorious page in Chinese history has been written with a bloodless pen.

Wu Ting-fang,
Director of Foreign Affairs."

This document has been attributed to an American newspaper man. It was telegraphed to an American editor, who was reported to have replied that he was rushing off to the President of the United States with it at once.

On Dec. 5, 1911, the Republic at Wuchang adopted interesting "Articles of Confederation," but they are without originality or striking revolutionary character. Following the inauguration of Sun Yat-sen as Provisional President, several historical documents appeared, none of of them more memorable than the appeal to the Imperialist military commanders, which was followed by the disaffection of the 46 officers who turned the Imperialist Army over to the Republic. But the most interesting to the world at large was the proclamation to the friendly Powers, promulgated on January 9, 1912, at Nanking, and signed by President Sun Yat-sen and his Minister of Foreign Affairs, Wang Ch'ung-huei.

In 24 paragraphs the " Republic of China " charges the Manchus with thirty-four crimes and abuses against the Chinese race and Empire, among them: the usurpation of the Throne; the suppression of individual qualities and national aspirations of the people; misrule; oppression beyond endurance; slavery and bondage; unequivocal seclusion and unyielding tyranny; ignorance and selfishness; exclusion of the outer world; plunging the Chinese into a state of benighted mentality; arresting the intellectual, moral, and material development of China, thus committing a crime against humanity and civilized nations; desire for perpetual subjection of the Chinese; a vicious craving for aggrandizement and wealth; governing to the lasting injury and detriment of the Chinese; creating privileges and monopolies and erecting about themselves barriers of exclusion; levying irregular and unwholesome taxes without consent of the people; restrictions of foreign trade to Treaty ports; placing likin embargoes upon merchandise in transit; obstruction of internal commerce; retarding the creation of industrial enterprises; rendering impossible the development of natural resources; wilfully neglecting to safeguard vested interests; denying a regular system of impartial administration of justice; inflicting unusual and cruel punishments; and nine other charges.

These crimes are the mangle upon which the people of China are represented to be stretched, mauled, and torn by the Manchus. It is the most complete expression of the " grievances " that are the defence of the revolutionary reformers. What strikes me so forcibly about these " grievances " is that they constitute a catalogue of Chinese customs, crimes, and abuses of immemorial antiquity, and which have engulfed not only Chinese aspirations and development but Manchu as well. In the first place, they are at variance with the utterances and position of the gentry, scholars, and student reformers of Szechuan, Hunan, Hupeh, and even of Kiangsu and Chekiang, who made the Revolution possible.

Taken on its face, this document suggests that it would be difficult to assemble another company of enlightened and unenlightened Chinese such as wrote this document, and such as combined so much ignorance of Chinese history, life, and character, and of the world and its Governments. Put out from Nanking, my first impressions gained on reading it was that it was just such a State paper as might have been put forth by the truant Mings (1644 to 1662) in the same region—that triangular section between Shanghai and Wuchang on the North and Canton on the South, identical with the region that asserted its independence in the first war to down the Manchus. It has all the provincial narrowness of view and all the provincial limitations in its reading of the history of all China. It indicates a clouded vision filled with vast, imaginary wrongs such as the Chinese accused foreign nations of visiting upon them —a decided prejudice in favour of their own infirmities.

I will place Chinese and Manchus in the " deadly parallel " comparison to show what lies back of the Republican arraignment:

The Manifesto of the Provisional Republican Government to the friendly Powers is therefore the most important document of the revolutionary Rebellion. It begins with a profound and illimitable untruth. It says that the primary cause of the suppression of the individual qualities and aspirations of the people is due to Manchu sway. The actual cause of the arrested development of the people of China has been known to foreigners and to some Chinese for ages to be the petrifying Chinese educational system of China, and has no possible connection with the Manchus, except that they abolished it (1905).

The second paragraph of the Manifesto, to the effect that the Revolution was a national aspiration, is not so important, but it appears equally untrue. The leaders and Sun Yat-sen himself claimed that the Revolution was a conspiracy, and Sun Yat-sen's friends claim for him the credit for its success. It cannot be said to have been at that time the aspiration of the people of China. The rest of the Manifesto may be similarly disposed of.

It is difficult for Occidentals to comprehend the degree of official baseness reached in China by the Asiatic Court system, or the popular and immemorial customs, but it is impossible for the most indifferently informed observer to attribute the evils of China to the Manchus. The evils of which Wu Ting-fang and Sun Yat-sen complain in behalf of all Chinese are those attributed to the Manchu Court. The corruption of the Government in China is always charged by Chinese history to the eunuchs (all Chinese) in the Palace and the office-holders (nearly all Chinese).

Chinese history, by Chinese, is complete up to 1644

on all bookshelves in China—that is, until the Manchu Dynasty began. Therein is the story of the Chinese Court rule and misrule which, as given by the Chinese, is corrupt, cruel, and base beyond all present-day Western understanding. The eunuchs from the Han Dynasty downward were the curse of China. In the Tang Dynasty they were a national danger threatening the unity of the Empire, and the Chinese, perpetuating them and their malign influence, had brought themselves in their latest Dynasty, the Ming, to such a state of rottenness that when the Manchu Dynasty held its initial Imperial audience, the eunuchs rushed in before the highest ministers and claimed first recognition from the Emperor.

The Ming Dynasty of the Chinese vanished because of the extinction of all moral qualities at a time when the absence of these, according to modern history, had enthroned pandemonium in the Palace. But then and there the Manchus deprived the eunuchs for ever of their office-holding power and reduced them to their places as menials. Though the Manchus continued the system, they improved it, and executed eunuchs for exceeding their powers.

The charges of Wu Ting-fang and Sun Yat-sen cannot be reconciled with the history provided us by their countrymen nor that of Western historians. The history of the last Chinese or Ming Dynasty is that written by the Chinese (not the Manchus). That of the Manchu Dynasty, though written, is not yet available owing to the Chinese law of the Empire which forbade anyone, even the Emperor, seeing what is written, and releases that history for the inspection only of posterity. Allowing for Manchu bias, no doubt that history when written will be a very favourable one to the Manchus.

I have tried to find in the Manchu Government parallels for the maximum baseness and corruption of the Ming Dynasty, but without success. China at the precise time of the Manchu conquest was anything but a peaceful land of content that is carelessly and ignorantly described as receiving the onslaught of an " alien horde sweeping down upon it." Such charges sound as though China was starting her Republic on the basis of China's situation as it was at the end of the Ming Dynasty, and with similar devices. The methods of warfare carried out by the Chinese people, as well as the famine horrors, are certainly those of the Dark Ages.

CHAPTER XLVIII

THE MANCHU DYNASTY

THE Manifesto or Proclamation to the friendly Powers, promulgated in January 1912 at Nanking, is directed solely to foreigners, ostensibly in their interests, as it is addressed to their cupidity. China's foreign relations in their Chinese and Manchu aspects will show the truth or falsity of the charges that the Manchus have been anti-foreign and guilty of bringing about all the evils of China's foreign complications. They will show also the pro-foreign or anti-foreign possibilities of a Republic under these declarations or those of any other Chinese leaders in other future forms of government in China.

I have referred to the Ming, or Chinese, historians. Since the commencement of the modern or Manchu Dynasty the foreign affairs of China and the West have their own clear Western history to rely on. This shows that the Chinese mandarins opposed trade with foreigners for two centuries. The widowed family of the last Ming Emperor, in pitiable extremity, turned Roman Catholic and took Latin names in order to bring about foreign intervention through the Pope at Rome to expel the Manchus. This was done in the same spirit in which their Chinese subjects had let the Manchus into China. Thus again the Chinese.

Respecting the anti-foreign record of the Manchus, history shows that they erred in delegating foreign affairs to their Chinese agents. The Roman Catholics, who created for themselves their troubles in China, were opposed by the second Manchu Emperor, Kang Hsi (1716). But foreign historians have absolved the Manchus from blame in anti-Roman Catholic measures. Yung Ching, the next Emperor, deported the Roman Catholics from Central China on recommendation of the literati (Chinese) and the Governor of Chekiang. His reason was that the Roman Catholic Church appeared to him to set up an authority that rivalled his own in dealings with the people. He was the first Emperor of China to receive the credentials of foreign envoys directly in his own hands—a credit which thus is due to the Manchus. In 1833 Emperor Tao Kuang opposed the British upon representations of the Portuguese—not due to the existence of any policy of his own, and more in the spirit of opposition to foreign trade at Canton, opposition that had been established long before the Manchus came.

Under Tao Kuang, however, the Chinese anti-foreign policy culminated, and the essential differences in the characters of Chinese and Manchus in this respect is clearly shown. The point of contact was still Canton. Of the most famous men of China in that period was the notorious Commissioner Yeh, a Chinese; the other the Manchu, Ki Ying. The contrast of these two men is striking. Yeh died in enforced exile in Calcutta, in expiation of his anti-foreign crimes, execrated by all honest men. Of Ki Ying, the Manchu, foreigners vie in their laudations. Sir John Davis, Governor of Hongkong, described him as the best type of official of the Empire of China that foreigners had yet seen, and paid just tribute to his statesmanship, scrupulous honesty, and high principles of honour. Ki Ying the Manchu came as a great light and blessing to foreign intercourse after two centuries of benighted Chinese opposition.

The Chinese notion of international relations was one which the Manchus had great difficulty in altering. It was the Chinese who scouted the idea that the Queen of England was equal with the Emperor of China. The Manchus, the rising of whose sun had been described to them by men whose fathers remembered it, had no such notions—these were notions resulting from the "Son of Heaven" traditions of China.

The Manchu Throne rarely took decided attitudes on the questions of foreign intercourse, and was obliged to yield to the temper of the Chinese people. It interposed the Manchu ministers between the Chinese and foreigners often with success, but as often with fatal failure. The Manchu Viceroy of Chihli, Kwei Liang, was unable to avert the disaster of the British and French march on Peking in 1860, when the Chinese committed such barbarities upon their English and French captives. But of the officials of the Empire of that time, the Manchus Prince Kung, Wen Hsiang, and Kwei Liang are the only ones spoken of by Western historians as "wise and liberal statesmen." There was an anti-foreign Manchu conspiracy at this time that had arisen under the Manchu Emperor Hsien Feng, who was an irresponsible weakling; but Prince Kung, who was his brother, together with Wen Hsiang and Kwei Liang, as well as the widow of the Emperor, the late Empress Grand Dowager, put them to death (including two Manchu princes, Chai and Tsin).

On recommendations of the Emperor's Manchu advisers, Anson Burlingame was sent as universal Envoy to the nations. It was one of the criticisms made of his Mission that unintentionally it "gave a wrong impression as to the desire of the Chinese people to adopt progressive measures." The Chinese were then incapable of the reform expected, and in 1870, before the Burlingame Mission returned, tracts were circulated calling for the extermination of Christianity, and causing the Tientsin massacre of twenty helpless foreigners, as though to repudiate the Throne's act of greatness before Wen Hsiang's eyes. In 1873 Tung Chih, the Emperor himself, gave audience to foreign ministers against all teachings of his Chinese subjects.

Three Chinese names of distinction follow the names of these Manchus to show that Chinese were not dead to enlightenment: Tseng Kuo-fang and Li Hung-chang, and with them Chang Chih-tung. The two first gained fame in the suppression of China's great civil war the T'aiping Rebellion, and then by their attempts to introduce foreign learning into China. Their efforts were almost counteracted by Chang Chih-tung, whose place in history as one of the last statesmen of the Manchu Dynasty appears to be that of the last great Imperialist demagogue. His attitude on public issues of reform was built upon a colossal ignorance such as Chinese possessed only in the first years of China's international relations. No good and great act is recorded of him. He wrote a book in which he showed that foreign enlightenment was "China's Only Hope," and executed numbers of reformers, most of them men in his own service.

Wen Hsiang the Manchu outstripped every Chinese of his time by devising the Burlingame Mission to bring China into intimate contact with all the Powers of the globe. In the most savage manner the Chinese people, in whom an inherent dislike of foreigners seemed to exist, visited upon foreigners a retaliation that had the consequences of Manchu liberality and statesmanship as much as any other thing for its origin. This is the repeated testimony of history in Chinese-Manchu foreign intercourse.

The Manchu chief and regent, Dorgon, who placed the Manchus on the throne, was a statesman of the first order, who brought a relatively civilized army which without bloodshed delivered the land from civil war. It buried at Peking with civilized honours the abandoned body of the suicide Ming Emperor, and instead of sweeping down upon the Chinese with an alien horde to enslave them, with one proclamation established complete peace throughout one-half of China.

In the other half the Manchus dethroned cut-throat kings, as in Szechuan, and consolidated the Empire. Though their reprisals were brutal and awful in the extreme, in accordance with the practices of the age, yet for those whom they displaced history can find no words that are too severe. The Manchus were conciliatory in their treatment of the Chinese, and counteracted the hatred with which they were received at first in China by giving Chinese equal representation with the Manchus in all the official appointments. They at first treated foreign embassies with haughtiness, in accordance with the universal Chinese attitude. But it is evident they learned better long before the Chinese did. It was the Manchu Emperor Kang Hsi's mother and one of the Manchu regents, So Ni, who secured the cancellation of the sentence of death obtained by the Chinese literati against the Roman Catholic priest, Abbé Schaal.

The Manchus consolidated and made the Chinese Empire out of bloodshed among Chinese by Chinese. It is the only Dynasty that respected the graves and homes of its predecessors, refraining from desecrating and obliterating them. It gave the country back to the people. From that moment China developed under the Manchus, until she is larger, richer, and greater, and therefore has more happiness within, notwithstanding her foreign evils, famine, and other internal ills, than ever before in her history. She has been steadied and held together by the Manchus, whose place has now been taken by the Powers.

In the region to which Wu Ting-fang and Sun Yat-sen and other Republican leaders belong, and which to this day has retained its separate individuality and identity, opposition to Manchu rule, law, order, and progress (the only modern progress China has had) was carried on. A little string of emperors (Ming so-called) kept up a losing fight for ten years there, after 1644, during which time they moved back and forth between Kiangsu and Kuanghsi, the precise region of the Republican revolutionary "Federation." For three years thereafter they had a stronghold in Kueichou, from which they were driven to Yunnan, and finally to Burmah, where their last independency was run to earth. The boundaries of the first "Republic of China" were practically the same as this recalcitrant region of the middle of the seventeenth century. Szechuan in which political chaos sprang up, Yunnan where feudalism was revived, and Kueichou where feudal independence recrudesced, when the Republican revolutionary revolt came, all reverted to the same state of independence as when the Manchus came to China.

The Tartars, who have ruled China except for the Ming period for a thousand years, were at first "rude and barbarous people." But they accepted the civilization of the Chinese whom they conquered, became acquainted with their learning and adopted their customs and manners, assimilating all this readily. At the same time, removed from the rigorous North, where they were unaccustomed to luxury, they became enervated and effeminate and lost their spirit and virility as conquerors, and were absorbed into the Chinese nation.

Kublai Khan, whose followers suffered this fate, was more enlightened than the Chinese. He maintained religious freedom except with respect to the lowest form of worship in China, Taoism, whose books he had burned, except one. He established the postal system, reconstructed the Grand Canal, and sent out peaceful missions to various foreign countries, including India, and it is said Madagascar.

The great Manchu emperors of China were Kang Hsi and Chien Lung, to name them in order of their reigns. One of the very greatest Manchus was Tze Hsi An, the Empress Grand Dowager. At the beginning of the tenth century—the early part of the Ming Dynasty—China's population was estimated to have risen to 60,000,000 in numbers. Kang Hsi's reign was one of the most brilliant in China's whole history. He was a great warrior, a great scholar, and a great ruler. Pott says: "In his treatment of foreigners he was more liberal than those who surrounded him." He completed the Manchu conquest of the Empire. Chien Lung reigned sixty years, and brought the Manchu Dynasty and China to the summit of Chinese glory, and the Empire numbered "upwards of 400,000,000."

The Empress Grand Dowager had yet more to contend

with, and in her old age was besieged by an anti-Manchu movement, the Boxers, which she was obliged to turn against others in order to protect the Throne. She had tried to turn over the affairs of state to the incompetent Emperor two years before, but was obliged to resume control. The Manchu Dynasty needed leaders, and she surrendered to the young Manchu princes the control of the Government. This, notwithstanding the fact that the Manchus were now utterly decadent and laid themselves open to charges which made the Boxer movement a sufficient grievance for the overthrow of the Dynasty, and notwithstanding she committed the worst political errors possible, yet when the Empress Grand Dowager again resumed control of the Throne she placed herself at the head of the reform movement, became a convert to it, opened the Court, put forth reform edicts and propaganda, and made herself the greatest of China's Imperial reformers.

In the case of the Boxer movement the foremost Chinese officials were against the Throne and Court. Chang Chih-tung, Viceroy at Wuchang; Liu K'un-yi, Viceroy at Nanking; Li Hung-chang, Viceroy at Canton; and Yuan Shih-k'ai, Governor in Shantung, entered into a compact with the consuls of foreign Powers to resist the Boxer movement. They were supported by enlightened Chinese in the Central Government at Peking, who lost their lives for their trouble. But they were not alone. Within the Court circle the Manchu Jung Lu, protected by the Empress Grand Dowager, fought the anti-foreign princes and the bloodthirsty Chinese generals and ignorant people; while Kuang Hsu, the Manchu Emperor and weakling, stood profoundly out from the "four hundred millions," was indeed a pitiable giant, a martyr to reform, but amid what seas of pygmies without.

The Empress Grand Dowager established four great reforms: the Constitutional System; Opium Suppression; Military Reform; and Industrial Development. She abolished slavery. This and opium suppression were accomplished, and were two of the greatest achievements of the rulers in China.

It has been charged against the Manchus that the fact that they were so ready to give up and quit was evidence that they had a lot of money and wanted to get away with it. One of the charges against them made by the reformers and revolutionaries was that they had enriched themselves at the expense of the Chinese nation. I myself have never

CH'IEN LUNG.

From a scroll belonging to the Imperial Archives.

To face p. 438.

looked upon the Manchus as an enviable family. Anyone who has seen the decimated and impoverished Manchu communities hiding within the ancient walled and now utterly wretched strongholds lining the highway by which they entered China from Manchuria, would never envy them. The annual budget vouchsafed them by the Chinese for maintaining the Central Government was assuredly not more than that of some of the smallest independent states of Europe. The parsimony with which the Court and Central Government was treated by the Chinese was such that during the most of her life the Empress Grand Dowager was obliged, as it were, to hold the knife to the throats of the Chinese mandarinate to get together the sums required to conduct the Imperial establishment and administration. She had to appropriate sums under the disguise of other names in order to rebuild the summer home of the Court at the Western Hills. Besides, no one who knows the Chinese can by any stretch of imagination conceive of their being got the better of by a Manchu or suffering in the minutest from the craft of the Manchu. What the Manchu got from the Chinese, he deserved and earned. It is an immemorial maxim in China that the Tartar is an " easy mark." The great corruptionists of the last four reigns in China were the Chinese, Li Hung-chang, Li Han-chang, and the Chinese reformers notably of the Cantonese party, whose foreign training should have made them ashamed of the processes they adopted, and lifted them above their less fortunate Manchu fellows. That some of them were the first to fly from the cataclysm was incontrovertible proof of their guilt in corruption, for they paraded their wealth abroad. If there was rejoicing among officials at the final release from the exactions of the Dynastic system in order to repair to safety with stolen riches, the chorus of the Chinese mandarinate must certainly have drowned any cry that may have escaped the Manchus.

Corruption in the directions charged by the Chinese reformers had its origin, according to tradition, in the reign of the Emperor Mu, one thousand and one years before the Christian era, and never was modified by the Chinese. My observation of the lives of the Manchu princes at Peking was that outside a few families the princes were quite poor. Prince Su, one of the foremost and most influential, was a bankrupt when the downfall of the Dynasty came, and fled to escape his creditors. The great estates appropriated by the Manchus and Mongols at the time of the conquest were some of them only nominally rich. When Prince Chun became Regent and found it necessary to put his brothers Hsun and Tao into office in order that this, one of the foremost Manchu princely families, might make a respectable appearance in keeping with its standing in the State, it was penniless.

Prince Pu Lun was among those who had nothing but a bare living. Princess Pu Lun, in December 1911, expressed the sense of relief among Manchus at the prospect of future escape from Court etiquette and the exactions of the Throne. She said she hoped when these troubles were over she would be unimportant enough to take a walk on the City Wall. "The things the foreign and other women did must be perfectly grand," she said. She had never been to the Yellow Temple or to the Temple of Heaven (the places all tourists and foreign residents in Peking visit), or any place but in her own house and at a foreign home.

In the final trial the Manchu Court and Clan acted with moderation and discretion. In all the complications that mystified foreigners at Peking, Nanking, and Shanghai, it seems to me that the Court and Imperial Family acted up to the revolutionary side, on a high plane of conduct. I find little relatively to blame in the Manchus. Their genius conferred upon China as beneficent rule as she had ever had, and it was through the period of her greatest difficulties, when such tigers of outside enemies as China never had seen, were upon her back. It terminated with a dignity that must always command respect, sustained for nearly forty years by the miraculous strength of but one old Minister pecked at by the critics of the whole world. And what a contrast in its demise to the preceding Chinese Dynasty, whose last Emperor first cursed the San Kuan Temple because the joss of the oracle there was bad, and went to Coal Hill and hanged himself.

With their backs against the wall, the last representatives of the matchless line of Manchu Emperors, the weakling Lung Yu Empress Dowager with the little Emperor, refused to make of themselves poltroons and surrender unconditionally to the hot-headed revolutionaries.

CHAPTER XLIX

THE "FLOWERY REPUBLIC"

By the testimony of the Chinese themselves the opening (September 20, 1909) of the Chinese-built Kalgan Railway, and the death (October 4, 1909) of Chang Chih-tung, properly mark the passing of Old China. The last of the great triumvirate of the Empire—Li Hung-chang, the Empress Grand Dowager, and Chang Chih-tung—was dead. "The triumvirate is dead," we said, "and China still lives."

In two years China has another triumvirate, that of Yuan Shih-k'ai, Sun Yat-sen, and Li Yuan-hung. The Dynasty is gone, and there remains a more complicated, wonderful, and incalculable China than before, because of the spirit of the West that has now fully permeated it.

As I left Peking, following the inauguration of Yuan Shih-k'ai, China was an oligarchy under its new triumvirate according to which it was more Chinese if possible than ever before. What it is at the beginning of its new life is described well by the conditions at its three Capitals—for it has in effect three Capitals : Nanking (or Canton), Wuchang, and Peking.

At the dissolution of the Government at Nanking Sun Yat-sen and the Assembly there are sitting alone in the shelter of the Imperial structures erected by the Manchu Tuan Fang. Half a hundred officials and reformers are present, and all but two or three are foreign to the province. At Sun Yat-sen's farewell, the City, the province, and their people are not represented, and the wind in the bamboo is calling Nanking to her old life.

Deputies are sent from Nanking to reconcile the now warring, incorrigible elements at Wuchang that gave the Republic to China. Li Yuan-hung writes to Yuan Shih-k'ai crying out against the lust for gain on the part of the military commanders suddenly raised to power in the provinces and the terrible plight of the people under themselves. He finds the revolutionists plunderers, and not patriots, marauding through the land.

In despair, Li Yuan-hung writes: "The patriots are not deterred by any fear of execution, . . . the final catastrophe cannot be long delayed. One dictator after another tries to have his way, and the law is swept into oblivion. If this continues, China must perish, not by the hands of the princes of the Manchu Dynasty but by the hands of the heroes of the Republic; not because of a corrupt despotism but because of the new-born government. I choke in speaking of these things, but silence is impossible. From dawn to dark I am as one sitting on a carpet of needles, while a fishbone sticks fast in my throat; I rise from my bed at night in perturbation, and my dress is bathed in perspiration."

President Yuan Shih-k'ai replies to Li Yuan-hung from Peking, confirming what he says.

"If our China is to be preserved by Providence," says he, "it will be due to your warning message emphasizing the ten evils [in China the maximum] under which we labour, and the three qualities [the essentials] which we lack. Little did I dream that I would ever witness in our beloved country what the European sage calls mob tyranny. Poland and other nations did not perish at the hands of others; none but themselves were responsible for their ruin. The present anarchy brings our State near to that of Poland. As I sit alone and ponder these things I can only find relief in the welling tears."

Sun Yat-sen leaves Nanking for the rebellious centre Canton and the south-east—his territorial responsibility in the triumvirate. The press is printing cartoons, one of which shows China to be like the reeds and the waterfowl—stirred by the least sound or zephyr. Another, called "The Situation," shows the province as eggs precariously balanced above the hand of the foreigner. Chinese officials and citizens attacking each other with swords have the inscription "Guess the meaning."

A cartoon showing Chinese dressed like the freemen of enlightened Western countries has the inscription "The appearance is correct, but the spirit is far off." A cartoon labelled "A hero's appearance" shows a two-faced being, all smiles in front, and fierceness and brutality behind. With their foreign clothes the men of the Revolution are represented with their eyes fixed upon gain and influence, and not upon virtue.

China is so big, uncouth, and unwieldy that the triumvirate is hopeless of getting hold of her. The superficial

1. PORTRAIT OF A "HERO."

2 REVOLUTIONISTS HAVE THEIR EYES ON THE MOTTO, "GAIN AND INFLUENCE," AND NOT ON THAT OF "VIRTUE."

3. CHINA—ROUSED AT THE LEAST DISTURBANCE.

4. THE REPUBLIC—THE APPEARANCE IS CORRECT, BUT THE SPIRIT IS FAR OFF.

To face p. 442.

nature of the anti-Manchu sentiment, which was only the chronic sign of unrest, was proven, and as a war-cry had been greatly abused. It was seen that the people themselves were not intelligent respecting the object of overthrowing the Manchu Dynasty, but were plundering each other.

At the time of the abdication a foreigner crossed the country afoot from Shan-hai-kuan to Peking and inquired everywhere about the Revolution, but found that no one had heard of it as such. The number of Chinese who were in connection with the revolutionary Rebellion or of the reform movement, or knew of it, were estimated by the Japanese Intelligence Service—presumed to be, among foreign nations, the best with respect to Chinese affairs—to be not more than two-fifths of the whole people.

Yuan Shih-k'ai, from close studies of China made especially during his retirement covered by the last three years, said that not more than three-tenths of the whole people belonged to the advanced party. As for the remaining seven-tenths, they were still conservative and satisfied with the regime of the Empire. If the revolutionists should succeed in overthrowing the Dynasty, he thought another revolution might take place headed by the conservatives and having for its object the restoration to a monarchy. According to his mind, this would mean chaos for several decades. Wu Ting-fang anticipated a generation of assassination of political leaders.

The condition of China and the capabilities of the Chinese for a long time past are well known. They have been presented to me from every viewpoint during my twelve years in China, labouring upon it all. To me as to all men of the West, China must always mean not the few enlightened leaders, the Republicans, but the masses scourged by contagion, famine, burdened with a new poverty due to the higher plane of living of the nations who surround and antagonize her, hitherto badly governed, and now as in the past without any government at all. At the start off of her "Flowery Republic" China is without efficient labour, is cursed by ignorance, has no common language or means of inter-state, or even, in many places, inter-neighbourhood communication, no systematic currency or taxation, no internal national credit, no adequate communications, no money capital with which to elevate her economical plane so as not to be ground between those of rich opposing nations. Her forests are impoverished and her rivers uncontrolled. Furthermore, she is encompassed without by strong nations before which her frontiers are crumbling.

Had China entered the school of nations a century ago, or even a half-century ago, when Japan came into the international arena, she could have worked out her problems in detail—and the "Chinese Question" would not have existed. But as she is the last, she stands alone against the world. Civilization is her opponent, and even the massive oligarchy of the "Flowery Republic" may well be staggered at such a situation. Its dangers are to be read in the opinions held in the chancelleries of the Great Powers. The plans laid for China by the nations along her frontiers are such as she cannot fully realize. The Great Powers have already taken her foreign Customs. She has yet to work out her emancipation from foreign finance, and her foreign relations are more complicated and formidable than ever before because of the very events that have brought her to consciousness. Some of her leaders now profess indifference to these foreign questions—they are the whole substance of her political existence. It is the Powers who have succeeded the Manchus, at least for the time being. As an entity and a nation her fate is in the hands of four Powers whose territories completely surround her—Japan, Russia, Great Britain, and France. Powers like the United States, Germany, and the lesser European countries can exercise little influence over the Chinese policies of these four Powers. Near or far, there is no border or outside nation to come to China's aid as in the past. There are no virile Manchu tribesmen now to assume the leadership, as was the case in 1644. Those stronger outside peoples have worked out their own salvation, and China can no longer expect anything from them. And, moreover, the "Flowery Republic" has taken China's fate in its own hands.

As I retrace my steps across Manchuria the problem of the "Flowery Republic" impresses me as one which its leaders and its people have yet to grasp. China has completely digested and assimilated the Manchus, and is now supremely the undisguised and ungoverned "Chinese Question." Any revolution for her regeneration must henceforth be a revolution of the Chinese people. They have been steadied within and held together by the Manchus, whose place has been taken by the Powers who now hold China together from without.

The unrest of China's population is the greatest proof of China's growth and prosperity. At the zenith of her power she confronts those who have replaced the Manchus. It is obvious that the national antagonism must now be concentrated upon the outsider, whether that outsider is personified in one nation or in all the Great Powers together. And what must be the consequences in such a case when, guided by her own self-selected helmsman, she meets some such immovable obstacle ?

The authors of the Republican documents and State papers have shown that even a plausible cause on paper is not necessary to a Revolution in China. If the Republican State papers correctly express the feelings of Republicans, it is to be wondered what a united Republican nation of so many millions, in such a mood, has in store for those who have taken the place of the Manchus. When other rebellions come, they must now necessarily be anti-foreign, at least in inspiration, war-cry, and sentiment, because of the immovable and gnawing reefs of the Powers around that form the international ocean in which the ark of China floats. The Revolution has but begun. China is careering onward in her fate, subject perhaps alone to that Providence which "clears the grounding berg and steers the grinding floe"—images so befitting China.

As I leave the "Flowery Republic" my absorbing thought is : What will China do when she looks in the glass ? When she discovers that the thing ailing her is that she is not Manchu, but Chinese ; when she has nowhere to look but to herself ; with no longer a scapegoat upon which to visit her own sins ; and when her antagonist, Civilization and the world, is not one she can accuse and banish. She must sooner or later see her unchanged spots, her coat close as the skin. And what will she do ?

China has shown that she is no longer a dead whale on the ocean of international affairs. She is a civilization and Nation in which race persistence, and the persistence of social problems, are the greatest force. But, as has been said, "the Revolution has been like a gale of wind—it lashed the surface of the water into angry white caps, but did not reach or disturb the deeper currents of the great sea of Chinese life." Will time ring her political changes through the various chords named despotism, republicanism, democracy, monarchy, and despotism again, until all the gamut of revolution and the travail of slow regeneration is run? The people have never taken part in government, and taxation "seems the only sensitive nerve in the body politic." Through revolutionary eruption, until the people find their places as sovereigns indeed, will the ashes and the lava of Chinese life and existence settle back again—China still, as Vesuvius still—the phases differing but slightly to prove that there is progress; nothing changed much but geography, and that change brought about by her neighbours, sometimes friends and sometimes enemies? At present she stands her ground only because of diplomatic balance. Her civilization, without power of resisting outside political forces, and without staying power, is pre-eminently "Chinese," and "being Chinese" is the only possession of which she cannot be robbed. This has been adjudged sufficient to reunite eventually all the territorial members of China, now or later disunited, but what will be her fate under foreign pressure through the metamorphosis of the secret societies within, the breaking up of the trade guilds in the formation of commercial companies, the overthrow of existing society by the development of the natural resources of the country, laying down of communications and taking up of foreign knowledge? These are the real revolution of China, the revolution that is alone in the lives and possibilities of the unnumbered millions. It is locked up in the Chinese whom Yuan Shih-k'ai leads and whose path of salvation is along the stubborn road of eternal vigilance, willingness to learn, adaptability, and unceasing toil. Mankind has at least come to the real "Chinese Question": Chinese must at last save China, if not Eastern Asia.

China's struggle is the greatest man has ever known. She is the last link in civilization encircling the earth on which we dwell. She may disrupt the work of solution of the mystery of races and of political existence so far developed by mankind. But 400,000,000 of sober, brainy, industrious, imaginative people, whose desires are peace, I believe to be capable of adding the greatest of all contributions to civilization.

APPENDICES

I. THE MANCHU DYNASTY

AND ORDER OF THE IMPERIAL LINE FROM CH'IEN LUNG TO PU YI, WITH THE PRINCIPAL NAMES HEARD DURING THE REBELLION

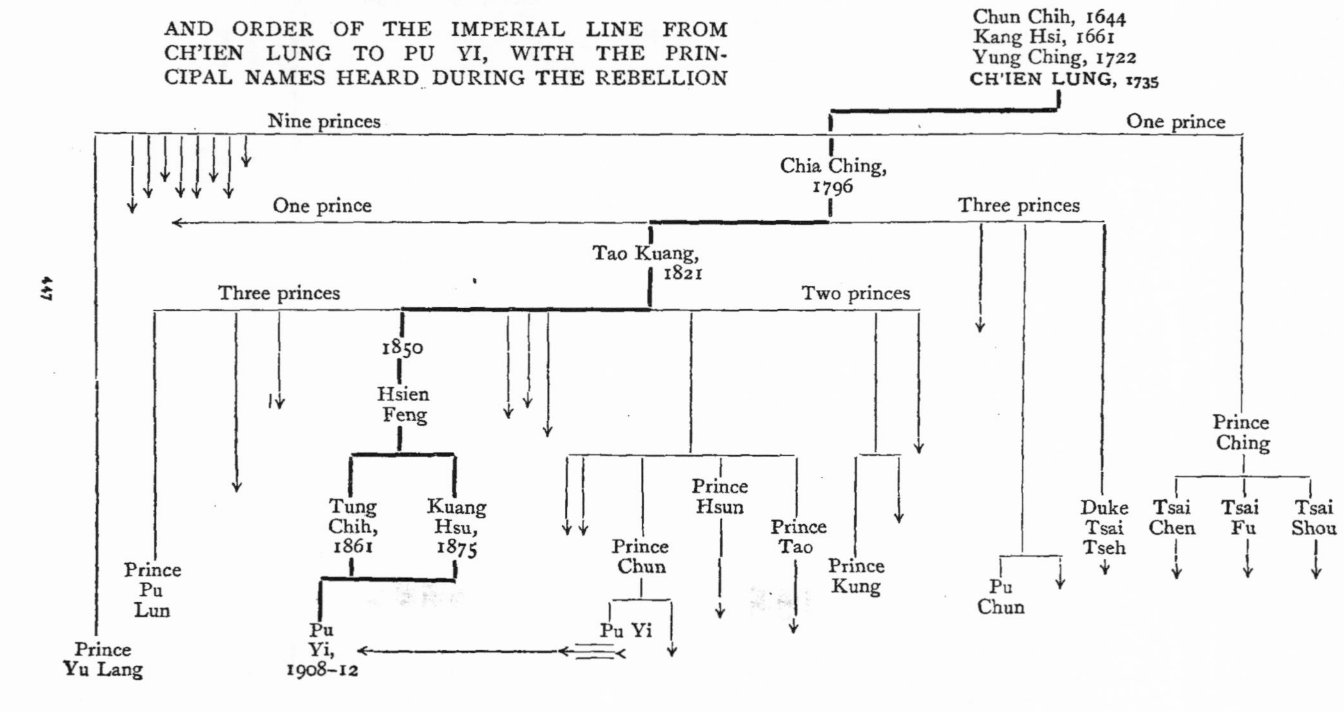

II. BIOGRAPHIES

HSUAN TUNG (PU YI)

PU YI; last Manchu Emperor; son of Prince Chun; born 1905. An edict of November 13, 1908, said:

"It is the excellent will of Tzu Hsi, etc., the Empress [Grand] Dowager, that Pu Yi, son of Tsai Feng, Prince of Chun, be taught and reared in the Palace, and that he study in the 'Upper' (Imperial) Schoolroom."

November 14, 1908, the Empress [Grand] Dowager issued the following edict:

"Inasmuch as the Emperor Tung Chih had no issue, on the fifth day of the twelfth moon of the thirteenth year of that reign (January 12, 1875), an Edict was promulgated to the effect that if the late Emperor (Kuang Hsu) should have a son the said prince should carry on the succession as the heir of T'ung Chih. But now the late Emperor has ascended on the Dragon to be a guest on High, leaving no son, and there is no course open but to appoint Pu Yi, the son of Tsai Feng (Prince Chun), the Prince Regent, as successor to the Emperor Tung Chih and also heir to the Emperor Kuang Hsu."

In acknowledgment of this the Emperor Pu Yi (in an Edict) is made to say:

"We received in Our early childhood the care and love of Tsu Hsi, etc., the Great Empress Dowager. Our gratitude is boundless. We have received the command to succeed to the Throne and We fully expected that the gentle Empress Dowager would be vigorous and reach a hundred years, so that We might be cherished and made glad, and reverently receive her instruction so that Our government might be established, and the State made firm. But Her toil by day and night gradually weakened Her. Medicine was constantly administered in the hope that She might recover. Contrary to Our hopes, on the 21st day of the moon (November 15, 1908), at the 'Wai-K'o' (1–3 p.m.) she 'took the fairy ride and ascended to the far country.' We cried out and mourned how frantically. We learn from her testamentary statement that the period of full mourning is to be limited to twenty-seven days. We certainly cannot be satisfied with this. Full mourning must be worn for one hundred days and half mourning for twenty-seven months, by which Our grief may be partly expressed. The order to restrain grief so that the affairs of the Empire may be of first importance We dare not disregard, as it is Her parting command. We will strive to be temperate so as to comfort the spirit of the late Empress Dowager in Heaven."

After February 1912, the date of abdication, Pu Yi continued, with the Lung Yu Empress Dowager and late Court, to reside in the Forbidden City and adjoining State premises.

PRINCE CHING

CHING, PRINCE (Yi Kuang); Manchu; head of the Imperial Clan. Investiture of the title occurred in the beginning of the reign of Tao Kuang (1821–1850). 1884, appears in the official lists promoted to be Prince of the Second Order and President of the Foreign Office (Tsung-li Yamen). Regularly promoted to offices in Imperial Clan Court; Board of Admiralty, and other offices; made Grand Chamberlain; Lieutenant-General of Troops, Director of Imperial Equipage Department, and Superintendent of Imperial Armoury. 1894, made a Prince of the First Order. 1901, President of Government Council. 1903, Grand Councillor, and following this numerous posts connected with evolution of the constitutional system granted by the Empress [Grand] Dowager. 1901, he was the Court's emissary to meet representatives of foreign Powers who had taken possession of Peking. Thereafter he carried the whole weight of the Imperial Clan and Central Government affairs.

PRINCE CHUN

CHUN, PRINCE (Tsai Feng); regent; Manchu; father of Pu Yi (Emperor); son of Prince Chun and brother of Emperor Kuang Hsu. January 1891, succeeded to his father's title. 1901, made Lieutenant-General and sent on embassy to Germany in expiation of murder of German Minister at Peking, 1900. Made Regent, November 13, 1908, by the following edict:

"An edict reverently received by Us (the Emperor). It is the excellent will of Tzu-hsi, etc., the Empress [Grand] Dowager, that Tsai Feng, Prince of Chun, be appointed Prince Regent (She Cheng Wang)."

December 6, 1911, an edict reciting a request of Prince Chun to abdicate his regentship and resume his title of Prince Chun was issued by the Lung Yu Empress Dowager.

PRINCE HSUN; PRINCE TAO

HSUN, PRINCE; TAO, PRINCE; brothers of Prince Chun and the late Emperor Kuang Hsu. Held titles of Dukes until 1909, promoted Princes of the Third Class. Prince Hsun first appointed head of the Naval Organization Bureau, and, 1910, visited Europe. 1910, visited United States. 1909, Prince Tao appointed to organize

Peking gendarmerie; later Special Commissioner with Prince Yu Lang to organize Imperial Guard, and made a tour of Europe and America. Much disliked by reformers on account of their lack of education, lack of experience, and because of the partiality shown them by their brother the Prince Regent in giving them high offices.

JUI CHENG

JUI CHENG; Manchu. 1901, first mentioned in official lists. His promotion was slow. Suddenly attracted attention by receiving appointment of Viceroy at Wuchang, a post that had been held by the most eminent officials, among them Chang Chih-tung. 1911, was a little past fifty years old when driven from Wuchang by the revolutionary outbreak. July 18, 1912, died in a house in Ferry Road, Shanghai, where he had taken final refuge. Was a cousin of Duke Tsai Tseh, and related to Tuan Fang. In Shanghai was threatened by revolutionist blackmailers, and his experiences hastened his death. Had many friends. His remains closely guarded at the funeral to prevent revolutionist outrage.

NA TUNG

NA TUNG; Manchu. 1899, first mentioned in official lists as Director of Court of State Ceremonials. Promoted to subordinate position in Grand Secretariat, and during Boxer uprising made Minister of Foreign Office, then called the *Tsung-li Yamen*. Proceeded in rapid promotions: 1902, became Acting-Minister of Foreign Affairs (Wai-wu-pu); 1903, President, Board of Revenue; President, Board Foreign Affairs and member Finance Committee. 1904, head of the gendarmerie. 1905, Assistant Grand Secretary. 1906, Grand Secretary, and with other appointments, 1907, became a member of the Government Council. On account of his intimate association with Prince Tuan and his appointment as Minister to the *Tsung-li Yamen*, June 1900, has been regarded as one of the foremost Boxers, and the inner history of the Court during 1900 convicts him of complicity to exterminate the foreign Legations in Peking, and foreigners generally throughout China. On occasion of the Court's return to Peking after its flight of 1900, Na Tung feared that he had been blacklisted by the Powers and would have to retire from public life. On account of his abilities and happy faculty of adjusting himself to conditions his anti-foreign past was forgotten. 1901, conducted an embassy to Japan to expiate the murder of Japanese Secretary of Legation in Peking, 1900.

SAH CHEN-PING

SAH CHEN-PING, of Fukien; Chinese. 1902, was Brigade-General in Kuangtung. 1903, was Admiral in command of the

Northern Squadron. 1905, was Admiral of the Southern Squadron, and Commander-in-chief of the land and sea for Kuangtung, 1906. When the Navy Bureau was established, 1908, was made head of the Naval Staff, a post which he held when the revolutionary outbreak occurred. Trained in the Naval Academy at Fuchow under French instructors. Progressive and of high character.

SHENG HSUAN-HUAI

SHENG HSUAN-HUAI, of Kiangsu; Chinese. 1886, was Taotai at Chefoo and interested himself in all kinds of reforms. Promoted the extension of telegraphs and organized and controlled China's largest steamship enterprise, the China Merchants' Steam Navigation Company. Appointed Administrator-General of Railways in Central and South China, and held several honorary appointments in Peking, including that of Junior Guardian of the Heir Apparent. Assisted in the revision of Commercial Treaties after the Boxer War; especially encouraged education, helping to establish the Tientsin University under Dr. Tenney, and the Nanyang University at Shanghai under Dr. Ferguson; conducted China's negotiations with respect to the Hankow-Canton, Peking-Hankow railways, and the Shanghai-Hangchow-Nanking railways. His response to the Throne's call to conclude vast loans for the rehabilitation of China's finances and the industrial development of the Empire was consistent with his convictions as to China's needs and necessities, in order to save the country. His dismissal, October 1911, was recognized by the Powers as the beginning of a series of blunders and disasters.

TANG SHAO-YI

TANG SHAO-YI, of Kuangtung; Chinese. Studied in America during several years, finishing at Columbia University. 1882, returned to China. Became secretary to Yuan Shih-k'ai at Seoul, and Yuan's protégé, on his return. Entered Northern Railway's Administration and was regularly promoted coincidental with the rise of Yuan Shih-k'ai. 1904, Special Commissioner to Tibet and Special Envoy to negotiate the Tibet convention with the Government of India. 1905, appointed Minister to England but did not serve. Became Vice-president of the Foreign Office; Director-General of railways; Controller-General of the Revenue Council; created the Board of Communications; was Governor of Fengtien, Manchuria; 1908, Special Commissioner to foreign countries to negotiate financial matters, making a tour of the world. Retired from office on occasion, Yuan Shih-k'ai's dismissal, and resumed as President of the Board of Communications upon Yuan Shih-k'ai's recall. Resigned to conduct peace negotiations, became China's first Republican Premier.

PRINCE TAO

TAO, PRINCE. (*See* under HSUN, PRINCE.)

TIEH LIANG

TIEH LIANG; Manchu. 1901, first mentioned in the official lists. Followed the usual promotions in regular succession common to favoured Manchu officials. Was connected with the Grand Secretariat, Board of Revenue, Army Re-organization Council, Board of War, Grand Council, Revenue Council, Army Board, Government Council, and 1908 became Minister of War. 1910, superseded by General Yin Chang and transferred to the post of Tartar General at Nanking. His demotion after 1908 was on account of changes due to the Regency of Prince Chun.

TSAI TSEH

TSAI TSEH, Duke; Manchu and Imperial Clansman. 1901, first mentioned in the official lists as Deputy-Lieutenant-General of Troops. 1905, Chief of the Imperial Mission to foreign countries. September 24, slightly wounded by a bomb explosion as the Mission was leaving Peking. On his return he collaborated with Tuan Fang, who was associated with him in the Mission in a book: "Diaries of a Journey Abroad." 1906, became Acting Minister of the Presence; Controller of the Imperial Armoury, and was employed on the "Reform Commission" or Department of Constitutional Affairs. 1907, became President of the Board of Finance, and, 1911, was fifty-six years old when with Sheng Hsuan-huai he attempted to carry through the Throne's programme of loans for the rehabilitation of the Empire. His wife is the sister of the Lung Yu Empress Dowager and niece of the late Empress Grand Dowager.

TUAN FANG

TUAN FANG; Manchu. 1898, first mentioned in the official lists, Secretary to the Board of Works; served as a judicial commissioner in the provinces of Shensi, and, 1900, Acting Governor when by his proclamations to the people he protected foreign missionaries in Shensi from the Boxers; was Judicial Commissioner in Honan; rose to be Governor of Hupeh, and afterwards of Kiangsu and of Honan; was Governor-General of Fukien and Chekiang; 1905, member of the mission to foreign countries to investigate governmental systems; 1906, became Viceroy at Fuchow, then at Nanking. 1908, Viceroy of Chihli. 1909, dismissed by Prince Regent on pretext of violating ceremonial requirements in connection with the funeral of the Empress Grand Dowager. He was a progressive without the advantages of Western education, but was adaptable, and educated his sons abroad. He profited by his travels abroad. 1905, published his diary of the journey (together with that of Tsai Tseh), and applied his ideas in the promotion of the Nanking Industrial Expedition 1908, at Nanking, and other improvements that were among the reforms that hastened the overthrow of the Dynasty. 1911, appointed to pacify Szechuan, and murdered there. An ardent antiquarian, connoisseur and collector.

WU TING-FANG

Wu Ting-fang, of Kuangtung; Chinese. An enlightened, progressive Chinese schooled in Hongkong. First mentioned in the official lists as Minister to the United States, Spain and Peru, 1896–1903. 1903–1906, served in appointments in Board of Commerce, Foreign Office, Board of Punishments, and also acted on the Commission to revise laws. 1905, slightly wounded by a bomb explosion at Peking. Retired 1906. Returned to office 1907, and re-appointed Minister to the United States but did not serve, and permanently resigned from service of the Imperial Government 1909, retiring to Shanghai. November 3, 1911, joined the cause of the Rebellion.

YIN CHANG

Yin Chang; Manchu. First appearance in official lists, 1901, as Deputy Lieutenant-General. 1901, was attached to Prince Chun's embassy to Germany to expiate the Boxer murder, 1900, of the German Minister at Peking. Minister to Germany 1901–1910. Held several subordinate appointments and, 1910, became Minister of War. October 1911, mobilized the Imperial Army and, November, re-captured Hankow and Hanyang. December, returned to Peking.

III. IMPERIAL AND REPUBLICAN STATE PAPERS

"THE NINETEEN ARTICLES"

Passed by the National Assembly at Peking

November 3, 1911

1. The Emperor shall reign for ever.

2. A person of the Ta Ching Dynasty (the great pure, or Manchu, Dynasty) shall be Emperor inviolable.

3. The power of the Emperor shall be limited by the Constitution.

4. The order of succession to the Throne shall be prescribed by the Constitution.

5. The Constitution shall be drawn up and adopted by the National Assembly and promulgated by the Emperor.

6. The power of amending the Constitution shall belong to Parliament.

7. The members of the upper house shall be elected by the people from among those particularly eligible.

8. Parliament shall elect and the Emperor shall appoint the Premier, who will recommend the other members of the Cabinet, who shall be appointed by the Emperor. The Imperial Princes will be ineligible for the office of Premier or members of the Cabinet or administrative heads of the provinces.

9. If the Premier, when impeached by Parliament, does not dissolve Parliament he must resign. One Cabinet shall not be allowed to dissolve Parliament more than once.

10. The Emperor shall assume direct control of the army and navy, but when this power is used in connection with internal affairs the Emperor must observe special conditions to be decided by Parliament.

11. Imperial decrees cannot be issued to replace the law except in the event of urgent necessity, in which case they may be issued in accordance with special conditions.

12. International treaties shall not be concluded without the consent of Parliament, but a treaty for the conclusion of peace or a declaration of war may be made by the Emperor if Parliament is not sitting, the approval of Parliament to be obtained afterward.

13. Ordinances in connection with the administration shall be settled by Acts of Parliament.

14. In case the financial budget fails to receive the approval of Parliament the Government may not act upon the budget of the previous year, nor may items of expenditure, not provided for in the budget, be appended thereto. The Government shall not adopt extraordinary financial measures outside the budget.

15. Parliament shall fix the expenses of the Imperial household, and any increase or decrease therein.

16. Regulations in connection with the Imperial Family must not conflict with the Constitution.

17. The two houses shall establish the machinery for the administration of the Court.

18. The Emperor shall promulgate the decisions of Parliament.

19. The National Assembly shall act upon Articles 8, 9, 10, 12, 13, 14, 15 and 18 until the opening of Parliament.

EDICT AND OATH OF THE EMPEROR HSUAN TUNG

Recited by the Prince Regent in the T'ai Miao (Ancestral Temple of the Manchu House)

November 26, 1912

After formally eulogizing the virtues and achievements of the departed Emperors and Empresses, the oath says:

" Since the accession of Our grand ancestor, Emperor Kao, the wise plans of Our ancestors have passed down for three hundred years. Since We reverently entered upon the great heritage We have in trembling and fear followed out the outlines of Our predecessors' constitutional policy, and strenuously have We sought to advance in improvement. Morning and night did we devise means to attain this end.

We proved, however, unequal to the burden, and in the employment of men and exercise of the administration We failed to carry them out satisfactorily, resulting in a barrier between the high and low and causing disagreement in feelings.

Since a month ago disturbances have been rife in the Empire, and We fear lest that heritage bequeathed by Our sacred ancestors should fall to the ground, and thus it would bring overwhelming guilt upon ourselves.

The Ministers of the Senate [National Assembly] have made a selection of the best Constitution rules from other countries, and in accordance with the precept that the nobles should not meddle in administrative affairs, the Senate has drawn up 19 important articles of Constitution. All other matters not touched upon therein will be included in the Constitution, which shall be immediately drawn up. Parliament should be immediately opened in accordance with constitutional systems.

"We have studied the situation and emergencies and have agreed to carry them out, and we now vow before Our ancestors that henceforth our insignificant person and numerous clansmen will abide by the articles with Our Ministers, in and out of the capital, and soldiers and people. Our descendants for a myriad generations shall not transgress them. This is in order to alleviate the anxiety of Our wise ancestors' departed spirits and to satisfy the hopes of the people in the land. We pray that Our ancestors will mark this."

MANIFESTO FROM THE REPUBLIC OF CHINA TO ALL FRIENDLY NATIONS

January 5, 1912

(PROMULGATED JANUARY 9, 1912, AT NANKING)

GREETING—The hitherto irremediable suppression of the individual qualities and national aspirations of the people having arrested the intellectual, the moral, and the material development of China, the aid of revolution has been invoked to extirpate the primary cause, and we now proclaim the resultant overthrow of the despotic sway wielded by the Manchu Dynasty and the establishment of a Republic.

The substitution of a Republic for a monarchical form of government is not the fruit of a transient passion. It is the natural outcome of a long-cherished desire for broad-based freedom making for permanent contentment and uninterrupted advancement. It is the formal declaration of the will of the Chinese nation.

We, the Chinese people, are peaceful and law-abiding. We have waged no war except in self-defence. We have borne our grievances during 267 years of Manchu misrule with patience and forbearance. We have by peaceful means endeavoured to redress our wrongs, secure our liberty, and ensure our progress, but we have failed. Oppressed beyond human endurance, we deemed it our inalienable right as our sacred duty to appeal to arms to deliver ourselves and our posterity from the yoke to which we have so long been subject, and for the first time in our history inglorious bondage has been transformed to an inspiring freedom splendid with the lustrous light of opportunity.

The policy of the Manchu dynasty has been one of unequivocal seclusion and unyielding tyranny. Beneath it we have bitterly suffered, and we now submit to the free peoples of the world the reasons justifying the revolution and the inauguration of our present government.

FROM LIGHT TO DARKNESS

Prior to the usurpation of the Throne by the Manchus the land was open to foreign intercourse and religious tolerance existed, as is evidenced by the writings of Marco Polo and the inscription on the Nestorian tablet of Sianfu.

Dominated by ignorance and selfishness, the Manchus closed the land to the outer world and plunged the Chinese people into a state of benighted mentality calculated to operate inversely their natural talents and capabilities, thus committing a crime against humanity and the civilized nations almost impossible of expiation.

Actuated by a desire for the perpetual subjugation of the Chinese, by a vicious craving for aggrandizement and wealth, the Manchus governed the country to the lasting injury and detriment of our people, creating privileges and monopolies and erecting about themselves barriers of exclusion in national custom and personal conduct which have been rigorously maintained throughout the centuries.

They have levied irregular and unwholesome taxes upon us without our consent, have restricted foreign trade to Treaty ports, placed likin embargoes upon merchandise in transit, and obstructed internal commerce.

They have retarded the creation of industrial enterprise, rendered impossible the development of natural resources, and wilfully neglected to safeguard vested interests.

They have denied us a regular system and imperial administration of justice ; inflicted unusual and cruel punishments upon all persons charged with offences, whether innocent or guilty ; and frequently encroached upon sacred rights without due process of law.

They have connived at official corruption ; sold offices to the highest bidder, and subordinated merit to influence.

They have repeatedly rejected our most reasonable demands for better government, and have reluctantly conceded pseudo-reforms under most urgent pressure, making promises without intention of fulfilling them ; and obstructing efforts towards national elevation.

They have failed to appreciate the anguishing lessons taught by the foreign Powers in the process of years, and have brought themselves and our people beneath the contempt of the world.

NEW PLEDGES

To remedy these evils and render possible the entrance of China to the family of nations, we have fought and formed our government, and lest our good intentions should be misunderstood we now publicly and unreservedly declare the following to be our promises :

All treaties entered into by the Manchu Government before the date of the Revolution will be continually effective up to the time of their termination; but any and all entered into after the commencement of the Revolution will be repudiated.

All foreign loans or indemnities incurred by the Manchu Government before the Revolution will be acknowledged without any alteration of terms; but all payments made to, and loans incurred by, the Manchu Government after the commencement of the Revolution will be repudiated.

All concessions granted to foreign nations or their nationals by the Manchu Government before the Revolution will be respected; but any and all granted after the commencement of the Revolution will be repudiated.

All persons and property of any foreign nation within the jurisdiction of the Republic of China will be respected and protected.

It will be our constant aim and firm endeavour to build upon a stable and enduring foundation a national structure compatible with the potentialities of our long-neglected country.

We will strive to elevate our people, secure them in peace, and legislate for their prosperity.

To those Manchus who abide peacefully within the limits of our jurisdiction we will accord equality and give protection.

We will remodel our laws; revise our civil, criminal, commercial and mining codes; reform our finances; abolish restrictions to trade and commerce, and ensure religious toleration.

The cultivation of better relations with foreign peoples and governments will ever be before us. It is our earnest hope that the foreign nations who have been steadfast in sympathy will bind more firmly the bonds of friendship, that they will bear in patience with us the period of trial confronting us in our reconstructive work, and that they will aid us in the consummation of the far-reaching plans which we are now about to undertake, and which they have so long and so vainly been urging upon the people of this our country.

With this message of peace and goodwill the Republic of China cherishes the hope of being admitted into the family of nations, not merely to share their rights and privileges, but also to co-operate with them in the great and noble task called for in the upbuilding of the civilization of the world.

(Signed) SUN YAT-SEN, President.
(Countersigned) Minister for Foreign Affairs.

Dated at Nanking, fifth day of the first month of the first year of the Republic of China (January 5, 1912).

IV. PERSONNEL OF THE PROVISIONAL GOVERNMENTS

SHANGHAI REPUBLICAN GOVERNMENT

November 3, 1911

OFFICIALS APPOINTED BY THE SHANGHAI COMMITTEE OF THE REVOLUTIONARY GOVERNMENT:

Director of Foreign Affairs—WU TING-FANG
Assistant Director of Foreign Affairs—YU YA-CHING.
Director of Commercial Affairs—WANG YI-TING.
Director of Financial Affairs—SHEN WAN-YUNG.
Director of the Civil Administration—LI PING-HSU.
Commander of the Military Forces—LI HSIEH-HO.
Vice-Commander of the Military Forces—CHENG HAN-CHING.

FIRST CABINET AT PEKING UNDER THE PREMIERSHIP (OF YUAN SHIH-K'AI)

November 16, 1911

Premier—YUAN SHIH-K'AI.
Ministry of Foreign Affairs—LIANG TUN-YEN.
  Vice—HU WEI-TEH.
Ministry of Finance—YEN HSIU.
  Vice—CHEN CHIN-TAO.
Ministry of Communications—YANG SHIH-CHI.
  Vice—LIANG JU-HAO.
Minister of War—WANG SHIH-CHENG.
  Vice—TIEN WEN-LIAO.
Justice—SHEN CHIA-PEN.
  Vice—LIANG CHI-CH'AO.
Ministry of Agriculture and Commerce—CHANG CHIEN.
  Vice—HSI YEN.
Ministry of Navy—(ADMIRAL) SAH CHEN-PING.
  Vice—TAN HSIAO-HENG.
Ministry of Education—TANG CHING-CHUNG.
  Vice—YANG TU.

Ministry of Colonies—TA SHOU.
Vice—JUNG HSUN.
Ministry of Interior—CHAO PING-CHUN.
Vice—WU CHEN.

NANKING PROVISIONAL GOVERNMENT

January 1, 1912

President—SUN YAT-SEN.
Vice—LI YUAN-HUNG.
Minister of War—HUANG HSING.
Vice—CHIANG TSO-PING.
Minister of Marine—HUANG CHUNG-YIN.
Vice—TANG HSIANG-MING.
Minister of Justice—WU TING-FANG.
Vice—L'IU CHI-YI.
Minister of Finance—CHEN CHIN-TAO.
Vice—WANG HUNG-YU.
Minister of Foreign Affairs—WANG CH'UNG-HUEI.
Vice—WEI CHUNG-TSU.
Minister of Home Affairs—CHEN TEH-CHUAN.
Vice—CHEN CHENG.
Minister of Education—TSAI YUAN-PEI.
Vice—CHIN YAO-YUEH.
Minister of Industry—CHANG CH'IEN.
Vice—MA CHUEN-WU.
Minister of Communications—TANG SHOU-CHIEN.
Vice—YU YU-JEN.

PEKING PROVISIONAL GOVERNMENT

March 29, 1912

President—YUAN SHIH-K'AI.
Vice—LI YUAN-HUNG.
Premier—TANG SHAO-YI.
Minister of Foreign Affairs—LU CHENG-HSIANG.
Minister of Interior—CHAO PING-CHUN.
Minister of Finance—HSUNG HSI-LING.
Minister of Education—TSAI YUAN-PEI.
Minister of Justice—WANG CHUNG-HUEI.
Minister of Agriculture—SUNG CHIAO-JEN.
Minister of Commerce—CHEN CHIAO-WEI.
Minister of Communications—LIANG JU-HAO.
Minister of War—TUAN CHI-JUI.
Minister of Navy—LIU KUAN-HSU.

THE PROVISIONAL CONSTITUTION

THE REPUBLIC OF CHINA

CHAPTER I. GENERAL PROVISIONS

ARTICLE 1. The Republic of China is composed of the Chinese people.

ARTICLE 2. The sovereignty of the Chinese Republic is vested in the people.

ARTICLE 3. The territory of the Chinese Republic consists of the 18 provinces, Inner and Outer Mongolia, Tibet and Chinghai.

ARTICLE 4. The sovereignty of the Chinese Republic is exercised by the Advisory Council, the Provisional President, the Cabinet and the Judiciary.

CHAPTER II. CITIZENS

ARTICLE 5. Citizens of the Chinese Republic are all equal, and there shall be no racial, class or religious distinctions.

ARTICLE 6. Citizens shall enjoy the following rights :—

(*a*) The person of the citizens shall not be arrested, imprisoned, tried or punished except in accordance with law.

(*b*) The habitations of citizens shall not be entered or searched except in accordance with law.

(*c*) Citizens shall enjoy the right of the security of their property and the freedom of trade.

(*d*) Citizens shall have the freedom of speech, of composition, of publication, of assembly and of association.

(*e*) Citizens shall have the right of the secrecy of their letters.

(*f*) Citizens shall have the liberty of residence and removal.

(*g*) Citizens shall have the freedom of religion.

ARTICLE 7. Citizens shall have the right to petition the Parliament.

ARTICLE 8. Citizens shall have the right of petitioning the executive officials.

ARTICLE 9. Citizens shall have the right to institute proceedings before the Judiciary, and to receive its trial and judgment.

ARTICLE 10. Citizens shall have the right of suing officials in the Administrative Courts for violation of law or against their rights.

ARTICLE 11. Citizens shall have the right of participating in civil examinations.

ARTICLE 12. Citizens shall have the right to vote and to be voted.

ARTICLE 13. Citizens shall have the duty to pay taxes according to law.

ARTICLE 14. Citizens shall have the duty to enlist as soldiers according to law.

ARTICLE 15. The rights of citizens as provided in the present Chapter shall be limited or modified by laws, provided such limitation or modification shall be deemed necessary for the promotion of public welfare, for the maintenance of public order, or on account of extraordinary exigency.

CHAPTER III. THE ADVISORY COUNCIL

ARTICLE 16. The legislative power of the Chinese Republic is exercised by the Advisory Council.

ARTICLE 17. The Advisory Council shall be composed of members elected by the several districts as provided in Article 18.

ARTICLE 18. The Provinces, Inner and Outer Mongolia, and Tibet shall each elect and depute five members to the Advisory Council, and Chinghai shall elect one member.

The election districts and methods of elections shall be decided by the localities concerned.

During the meeting of the Advisory Council each member shall have one vote.

ARTICLE 19. The Advisory Council shall have the following powers:

(*a*) To pass all Bills.

(*b*) To pass the budgets of the Provisional Government.

(*c*) To pass laws of taxation, of currency, and weights and measures for the whole country.

(*d*) To pass measures for the calling of public loans and to conclude contracts affecting the National Treasury.

(*e*) To give consent to matters provided in Articles 34, 35, and 40.

(*f*) To reply to inquiries from the Provisional Government.

(*g*) To receive and consider petitions of citizens.

(*h*) To make suggestions to the Government on legal or other matters.

(*i*) To introduce interpellations to members of the Cabinet, and to insist on their being present in the Council in making replies thereto.

(*j*) To insist on the Government investigating into any alleged bribery and infringement of laws by officials.

(*k*) To impeach the Provisional President for high treason by a majority vote of three-fourths of the quorum consisting of more than four-fifths of the total number of the members.

(*l*) To impeach members of the Cabinet for failure to perform their official duties or for violation of the law by majority votes of two-thirds of the quorum consisting of over three-fourths of the total number of the members.

ARTICLE 20. The Advisory Council shall itself convoke, conduct and adjourn its own meetings.

ARTICLE 21. The meetings of the Advisory Council shall be conducted publicly, but secret meetings may be held at the instigation of members of the Cabinet or by the majority vote of its quorum.

ARTICLE 22. Matters passed by the Advisory Council shall be communicated to the Provisional President for promulgation and execution.

ARTICLE 23. If the Provisional President should veto matters passed by the Advisory Council he shall, within ten days after he has received such resolutions, return the same with stated reasons to the Council for reconsideration. If by a two-thirds vote of the quorum of the Council, it shall be dealt with in accordance with Article 22.

ARTICLE 24. The President of the Advisory Council shall be elected by ballots signed by the voting members, and the one who receives more than one-half of the total number of the votes cast shall be elected.

ARTICLE 25. Members of the Advisory Council shall not, outside the Council, be responsible for their opinions expressed and votes cast in the Council.

ARTICLE 26. Members of the Council shall not be arrested without the permission of the President and of the Council, except for crimes committed at the time of arrest or for crimes pertaining to civil and international warfare.

ARTICLE 27. Procedures of the Advisory Council shall be decided by its own members.

ARTICLE 28. The Advisory Council shall be dissolved on the day of the convocation of the National Assembly, and its powers shall be exercised by the latter.

CHAPTER IV. THE PROVISIONAL PRESIDENT AND VICE-PRESIDENT

ARTICLE 29. The Provisional President and Vice-President shall be elected by the Advisory Council, and he who receives two-thirds of the total number of votes cast by a sitting of the Council consisting of over three-fourths of the total number of members shall be elected.

ARTICLE 30. The Provisional President represents the Provisional Government as the fountain of all executive powers and for promulgating all laws.

ARTICLE 31. The Provisional President may issue or cause to be issued orders for the execution of laws and of powers delegated to him by the law.

ARTICLE 32. The Provisional President shall be the Commander-in-chief of the army and navy of the whole of China.

ARTICLE 33. The Provisional President shall ordain and establish the administrative system and official regulations, but he must first submit them to the Advisory Council for its approval.

ARTICLE 34. The Provisional President shall appoint and remove civil and military officials, but in the appointment of Members of the Cabinet, Ambassadors and Ministers he must have the concurrence of the Advisory Council.

ARTICLE 35. The Provisional President shall have power, with the concurrence of the Advisory Council, to declare war and conclude treaties.

ARTICLE 36. The Provisional President may, in accordance with law, declare a state of siege.

ARTICLE 37. The Provisional President shall, representing the whole country, receive Ambassadors and Ministers of foreign countries.

ARTICLE 38. The Provisional President may introduce Bills into the Advisory Council.

ARTICLE 39. The Provisional President may confer decorations and other insignia of honour.

ARTICLE 40. The Provisional President may declare general amnesty, grant special pardon, commute punishment, and restore rights, but in the case of a general amnesty he must have the concurrence of the Advisory Council.

ARTICLE 41. In case the Provisional President is impeached by the Advisory Council he shall be tried by a special Court consisting of nine judges elected among the justices of the Supreme Court of the realm.

ARTICLE 42. In case the Provisional President vacates his office for various reasons, or is unable to discharge the powers and duties of the said office, the Provisional Vice-President shall take his place.

CHAPTER V. MEMBERS OF THE CABINET

ARTICLE 43. The Premier and the Chiefs of the Government Departments shall be called Members of the Cabinet (literally, Secretaries of State Affairs).

ARTICLE 44. Members of the Cabinet shall assist the Provisional President in assuming responsibilities.

ARTICLE 45. Members of the Cabinet shall countersign all Bills introduced by the Provisional President, and all laws and orders issued by him.

ARTICLE 46. Members of the Cabinet and their deputies may be present and speak in the Advisory Council.

ARTICLE 47. After members of the Cabinet have been impeached by the Advisory Council, the Provisional President may remove them from office, but such removal shall be subject to the reconsideration of the Advisory Council.

CHAPTER VI. THE JUDICIARY

ARTICLE 48. The Judiciary shall be composed of those judges appointed by the Provisional President and the Chief of the Department of Justice.

The organization of the Courts and the qualifications of judges shall be determined by law.

ARTICLE 49. The Judiciary shall try civil and criminal cases, but cases involving administrative affairs or arising from other particular causes shall be dealt with according to special laws.

ARTICLE 50. The trial of cases in the law Courts shall be conducted publicly, but those affecting public safety and order may be *in camera*.

ARTICLE 51. Judges shall be independent, and shall not be subject to the interference of higher officials.

ARTICLE 52. Judges during their continuance in office shall not have their emoluments decreased and shall not be transferred to other offices, nor shall they be removed from office except when they are convicted of crimes, or of offences punishable according to law by removal from office.

Regulations for the punishment of judges shall be determined by law.

CHAPTER VII. SUPPLEMENTARY ARTICLES

ARTICLE 53. Within ten months after the promulgation of this Provisional Constitution the Provisional President shall convene a National Assembly, the organization of which and the laws for the election of whose members shall be decided by the Advisory Council.

ARTICLE 54. The Constitution of the Republic of China shall be adopted by the National Assembly, but before the promulgation of the Constitution, the Provisional Constitution shall be as effective as the Constitution itself.

ARTICLE 55. The Provisional Constitution may be amended by the assent of two-thirds of the members of the Advisory Council or upon the application of the Provisional President and being passed by over three-fourths of the quorum of the Council consisting of over four-fifths of the total number of its members.

ARTICLE 56. The present Provisional Constitution shall take effect on the date of its promulgation, and the fundamental articles for the organization of the Provisional Government shall cease to be effective on the same date

Sealed by
THE ADVISORY COUNCIL.

V. DIARY OF THE REVOLUTIONARY REBELLION

SZECHUAN INDEPENDENCY

1911

August	24 .	General strike at Chengtu against the Imperial railway policy.
September	7 .	Viceroy Chao Er-feng surprises and arrests strike leaders and revolutionaries.
,,	8 .	Martial law at Chengtu.
,,	12 .	Throne orders Chao Er-feng immediately to suppress disorder.
,,	14 .	British and American Consuls order their Szechuan missionaries to places of safety.
		Throne appoints Tsen Chun-hsuan head of the Szechuan military forces, and Tuan Fang commissioner to arrange the railway difficulties.
		Throne confers the Yellow Jacket on Princes Tsai T'ao and Tsai Fu.
,,	16 .	The Regent Prince Chun reviews the Imperial Body Guard at Peking, presenting it with his own colours.
		Army manœuvres on an unprecedented scale arranged to take place near Ka'i-ping, Chihli.
,,	29 .	Throne refuses Prince Ching permission to resign.
October	4 .	National patriotic anthem and music adopted.

WUCHANG REPUBLIC

October	9 .	Revolutionist bomb explosion at Hankow.
		Viceroy Jui Cheng raids revolutionary resorts at Wuchang; twenty-eight revolutionaries arrested.
,,	10 .	Revolutionist revolt in Wuchang.
		Throne commends Jui Cheng and others.
,,	11 .	Revolutionists subdue Wuchang and proclaim war upon the Manchu Government.
		Throne commends Jui Cheng.
		Jui Cheng flees.
,,	12 .	Revolutionists take Hanyang.

October 12 . . Throne cashiers Jui Cheng.
,, 13 . . Revolutionists occupy Hankow.
,, 14 . . Yuan Shih-k'ai appointed Viceroy at Wuchang.
Tsen Chun-hsuan appointed Viceroy of Szechuan.
Revolutionist newspaper *Ta Han Pao* appears at Wuchang.
,, 15 . . Informal exchange of views among the great Powers.
,, 16 . . Imperialist Admiral Sah Chen-ping arrives at Hankow.
Foreign bankers at Peking refuse a war loan to the Imperial Government.
,, 17 . . Li Yuan-hung revolutionist leader notifies foreign Consuls of intention to attack the Imperialists.
Admiral Sah Chen-ping assembles eight war vessels.
,, 18 . . "Battle of Kilometre 10."
,, 19 . . Throne orders Yin Chang, Minister of War, Yuan Shih-k'ai, Tsen Chun-hsuan and Tuan Fang to administer rewards and punishments to stop rebellion.
Ichang passes over to revolutionists.
,, 20 . . Imperialists retreat from "Kilometre 10."
Throne orders memorials submitted to the Cabinet instead of to the Throne.
General Yin Chang mobilizing Imperialist Army at Sin-yang-chow.
,, 22 . . Hsian-fu, Shensi, revolts and sets up an independency.
,, 25 . . Feng Shan assassinated at Canton.
Changsha passes over to the revolutionists.
Imperial Assembly impeaches Sheng Hsuan-huai.
,, 26 . . Throne dismisses Sheng Hsuan-huai.
Tang Shao-yi appointed Minister of Communications.
,, 27 . . Li Yuan-hung proclaimed "President of the Republic of China."
Lung Yu Empress Dowager contributes 1,000,000 taels for military expenses in Hupeh.
Yuan Shih-k'ai appointed High Commissioner of all naval and military forces.
Admiral Sah notifies the foreign Consuls he will bombard Wuchang.
Casualties for the day before Hankow estimated at 2000.
,, 28 . . Imperialists retake "Kilometre 10."
Imperial Assembly and Army League demand political freedom for the people.

October 29 . Throne orders the arrest of Jui Cheng.
Imperialists capture and begin burning Hankow.

„ 30 . Throne issues a decree of penitence, and grants the Imperial Assembly's demands.
Throne grants general amnesty.
Throne orders General Yin Chang and Admiral Sah Chen-ping to recapture Hankow and Wuchang.

November 1 . Conflagration of Hankow reaches climax.
Yuan Shih-k'ai near Hankow opens negotiations with revolutionists; General Yin Chang returns to Peking.
Prince Ching, Na Tung, and Hsu Chih-chang resign.
Yuan Shih-k'ai appointed Premier and ordered to form a Cabinet.
General Yin Chang appointed Chief of General Staff.
Nanchang passes to the revolutionists.

„ 2 . Tai-yuan-fu passes to revolutionists.
Throne transfers the framing of the Constitution from the care of the Nobles to the Imperial Assembly.
Throne orders Yuan Shih-k'ai to return with haste to Peking.
Imperial Assembly and Army League frame the "Nineteen Articles"—demands upon the Throne.

SHANGHAI INDEPENDENCY

November 3 . Shanghai passes to the revolutionists and forms the following Government:
Director of Foreign Affairs—Wu Ting-fang.
Vice-Director of Foreign Affairs—Yu Ya-ching.
Director of Commercial Affairs—Wang Yi-ting.
Director of Financial Affairs—Shen Wan-yung.
Director of Civil Administration—Li Ping-hsu.
Commander of Military Forces—Li Hsieh-ho.
Vice-Commander of Military Forces—Cheng Han-ching.
Throne accepts the "Nineteen Articles."
Powers land troops at Shanghai.

„ 4 . Soochow passes to the revolutionists.
Admiral Murdock lands 200 marines at Shanghai.
Germany adds 50 marines to her garrison at Tientsin.

November 5 . Throne recognizes the revolutionists in an edict giving them the status of a political party.

Mass meeting at Tsinan-fu, Shantung, declares independence, elects Sun Pao-chi President and demands:

1. That no foreign loans be raised to suppress the revolt;
2. Hostilities cease and Imperial Government yield to the demands of the southern army;
3. That soldiers be not required to leave their own provinces;
4. That taxes be retained within the province;
5. The establishment of a Republic;
6. Complete provincial autonomy, including things military.

Wholesale resignations of officials at Peking.

Yuan Shih-k'ai declines Premiership.

Huang Hsing reaches Wuchang and becomes Commanding General under Li Yuan-hung.

Revolutionists protest against the activities of the Imperial Assembly.

" 6 . Throne seeks a foreign loan, urges Yuan Shih-k'ai to hasten to Peking, appoints General Chang Shao-tseng envoy to conciliate the people.

Amoy, Ningpo, Shaohsing, Chingkiang, Changchow, Quinsan, and Sungkiang fall to the revolutionists.

Throne instructs Viceroy Chang Jen-chun at Nanking not to oppose the revolutionists.

Throne releases imprisoned revolutionists at Peking.

" 7 . Foreign Powers take measures for protecting their citizens and subjects in China.

General Wu Lu-cheng murdered at Shih-chia-chuang.

Imperial Assembly formally appoints Yuan Shih-k'ai Premier and adjourns.

CANTON INDEPENDENCE

November 8 . Foreign Legations at Peking put on a defence footing.

Li Yuan-hung and his five Generals agree to ask Yuan Shih-k'ai to become President.

Uprisings around Canton; British Consul protects Viceroy.

Panic in Peking and flight of many people.

November 8 . General Chang Shao-tseng resigns and takes refuge in Tientsin.
One hundred revolutionists attack Viceroy's yamen in Nanking.

„ 9 . Canton proclaims a "Republic of Kuangtung" and elects a Governor-General; Viceroy flees to Hongkong.
Foochow, Swatow, Anking, Yunnan-fu, and the provinces of Yunnan and Kueichou pass to the revolutionists.
Yuan Shih-k'ai promises to start for Peking, having failed to reach any understanding with Li Yuan-hung.
About 200 revolutionaries unsuccessfully attack the Viceroy's yamen, Nanking.
German, British, Japanese, and American naval vessels land marines at Nanking to bring off their nationals and consulates.

NANKING—REPUBLIC OF CHINA

November 10 . Slaughter of revolutionary suspects by Imperialists at Nanking.

„ 11 . Wu Ting-fang publishes appeal to Prince Chun to abdicate.
Two delegates from Yuan Shih-k'ai fail to secure an understanding with Li Yuan-hung.
Shanghai Government urges organization and unity of provinces.

„ 12 . Admiral Sah Chen-ping's fleet begins turning over to revolutionists.
Revolutionist council of war at Suchow.
Chefoo passes to the revolutionists.
Panic and flight at Peking.
America unofficially gives out her policy.

„ 13 . Yuan Shih-k'ai reaches Peking.
Throne appoints Yuan Shih-k'ai commander of all troops in the region of Peking.
Revolutionists at Hankow reject Yuan Shih-k'ai's terms.
Manchurian revolutionists at Mukden declare autonomy and elect Chao Er-hsun President; they declare all revenues shall be retained by the province, whose connection with Peking is severed; that Manchuria would aid neither revolutionists nor Imperialists and would afford the fullest protection to foreigners.

„ 14 . Yuan Shih-k'ai confers with Prince Ching.

November 14 . Revolutionists mobilizing at Chingkiang.
General Chang Hsun Imperial Commander declares defiance.

" 15 . Yuan Shih-k'ai accepts Premiership.
Throne consents to Sun Pao-chi's presidency in Shantung.
Chihli Provincial Assembly recommends a Republic.
Reign of terror at Nanking.

" 16 . Yuan Shih-k'ai names his first Cabinet.
Li Yuan-hung through foreign Consuls asks recognition of the federated provinces.

" 17 . Revolutionists advance on Nanking.
Increased fighting at Hankow.

" 18 . Yuan Shih-k'ai's Cabinet resigning.
Foreign Ministers instruct missionaries to leave interior.

" 19 . Admiral Sah's ships bombard Imperialists at Hankow.
Three-fourths of Hankow destroyed.

" 20 . Sun Yat-sen leaves London.

" 21 . General Chang Hsun prepares to withstand siege.
So-called " National Convention " at Shanghai.

" 23 . Wu Ting-fang notifies foreign Consuls of impending attack upon Nanking.

" 24 . Revolutionists under General Hsu Shou-cheng advance on Nanking.
Battle of Hanyang begins.

" 25 . Shantung forswears independence.
Manchurian troops respond to Throne's orders.

" 26 . Attack upon Nanking.
Diplomatic body represents to Yuan Shih-k'ai the necessity of no disorders in Peking.
Throne swears allegiance to the "Nineteen Articles."
Szechuan revolutionists announce a Republic.

" 27 . Imperialists take Hanyang.
Tuan Fang murdered.
Republic declared in Szechuan.

" 28 . Kuangtung preparing to send 10,000 troops north.

" 29 . Revolutionists repulsed before Nanking.

" 30 . Revolutionists take Purple Hill, Nanking.
Three days' truce and an armistice arranged at Hankow.

Nov.–Dec. . Outer Mongolia and Tibet revolt.

December 1 . General Chang Hsun abandons Nanking.

" 2 . Occupation of Nanking by the revolutionists.

" 5 . Nanking selected to be the Republican capital,

December 5 . Dismissal of the Prince Regent arranged.
" 6 . Throne decrees Prince Chun's abdication.
" 7 . Armistice extended to December 21.
" 8 . Republican Assembly at Wuchang makes known its constitution, providing for the election of a Provisional President and National Assembly.
The Provisional President must call an election within six months to confirm the Constitution.
" 9 . Tang Shao-yi leaves Peking for Wüchang and Shanghai.
" 11 . Tang Shao-yi reaches Wuchang.
" 14 . Nanking made capital and Sun Yat-sen selected to be the first President.
Huang Hsing appointed to act as President pending Sun Yat-sen's arrival.
A Constitution modelled on that of the United States adopted by the Republican delegates at Nanking; with provision for calling a convention of the people within six months:

ARTICLE 1.—THE PROVISIONAL PRESIDENT

SECTION 1.—The Provisional President shall be elected by the delegates appointed by the Governor-Generals of those Provinces which have declared their independence. A two-thirds vote shall be necessary for his election. Each Province shall be entitled to one vote.

SECTION 2.—The Provisional President shall be vested with full power to administer the affairs of the Republic of China.

SECTION 3.—The Provisional President shall be Commander-in-Chief of the Army and Navy of the Republic of China.

SECTION 4.—The Provisional President shall have power, with the concurrence of the Assembly, to declare war and peace and make treaties.

SECTION 5.—The Provisional President shall have power, with the concurrence of the Assembly, to appoint the Ministers of the Executive Boards of the Provisional Government and special Diplomatic officials.

SECTION 6.—The Provisional President shall have power, with the concurrence of the

Assembly, to establish a system of National Courts of Justice.

ARTICLE 2.—THE ASSEMBLY

SECTION 1.—The Assembly shall be composed of representatives appointed by the Provisional Government.

SECTION 2.—Each Province shall be limited to three representatives in the Assembly, the method of appointing such representatives to be determined by the Government of the Province from which they come.

SECTION 3.—Each representative shall be entitled to one vote in the Assembly.

SECTION 4.—The duties and powers of the Assembly shall be as follows :—

(*a*) To determine the matters referred to in Article 1, sections 4 and 6.

(*b*) To approve the action of the Provisional President in matters referred to in Article 1, section 5.

(*c*) To determine the Budget of the Provisional Government.

(*d*) To supervise the accounts of the Provisional Government.

(*e*) To determine all matters concerning the taxation, currency, and public debt of the Republic.

(*f*) To make laws for the Republic during Provisional Government.

(*g*) To determine all matters referred to the Assembly by the Provisional President.

(*h*) To answer questions put to the Assembly by the Provisional President.

SECTION 5.—No matter shall be passed without the concurrence of a majority of the representatives present in the Assembly. Matters referred to in Article 1, section 4, must have the concurrence of two-thirds of the representatives present in the Assembly.

SECTION 6.—Every measure which shall have passed the Assembly shall, before it becomes law, be presented by the Speaker of the Assembly to the Provisional President for confirmation. If he approves he shall sign and seal it, and instruct the executive officers concerned to act accordingly.

SECTION 7.—If the Provisional President disapproves any measure, he shall return it to the Assembly with his objections for reconsideration by them within ten days from the time it was first presented to him. If the Assembly after reconsideration shall, by a two-thirds vote, agree to pass the measure, it shall become law and be put in force according to the preceding section.

SECTION 8.—The Assembly shall elect its Speaker from among its own members by ballot, and a majority of votes shall determine the election.

SECTION 9.—The Assembly shall determine its own rule of procedure.

SECTION 10.—Before the Assembly is organized the delegates appointed by various Provisional Governments shall temporarily perform the duties of the Assembly, but the delegates from each Province shall cast only one vote for that Province.

ARTICLE 3.—THE EXECUTIVE BOARDS

SECTION 1.—The Executive Board shall be as follows :—

(*a*) Board of Foreign Affairs.
(*b*) Board of Civil Affairs.
(*c*) Board of Finance.
(*d*) Board of War.
(*e*) Board of Communication.

SECTION 2.—There shall be a Minister for each Board, who shall have charge of the affairs of that Board.

SECTION 3.—Rules governing and defining the powers and duties of the officers of each Board shall be approved by the Provisional President before being put in force.

ARTICLE 4.—BYE-LAWS

SECTION 1.—Within six months after the establishment of the Provisional Government the Provisional President shall call a convention of the people. The Assembly shall draw up rules to govern the calling of this convention.

SECTION 2.—The articles of Confederation for the Provisional Government of the Republic of China shall become void from the day when the Constitution of the Republic of China comes into full force.

December 16 . Sun Yat-sen leaves Singapore.

Nanking Republican Assembly adopts minimum conditions for peace.

" 17 . Tang Shao-yi reaches Shanghai.

" 18 . Yuan Shih-k'ai moves into the Foreign Office, Peking.

General Lan Tien-wei telegraphs Yuan Shih-k'ai to be quick in making his choice as to whether he will be a Tsao Tsao, a Wang Mang, or a Washington—the first two famous Han traitors.

Peace Conference opens at Shanghai.

United States, Great Britain, France, Russia, Japan make representations to the Peace Commissioners counselling conciliation. State Department gives out the following:

"The identic note is to the effect that these Governments consider that the present struggle in China seriously affects not only China herself, but also the material interests and the security of foreigners in that country. The note continues with a statement that the Governments, while maintaining an attitude of strict neutrality, deem it worth while to point out to the two delegations the necessity of bringing the present disturbances to an end. The Governments express the belief that this attitude responds to the desires of both factions."

" 20 . Armistice extended seven days.

" 21 . Yuan Shih-k'ai refuses to accept a Republic.

" 25 . Sun Yat-sen arrives in Shanghai.

Conference of Japanese Cabinet with Elder Statesman agree that in case the Chinese revolutionists insist on a Republic for China, Japan will place no obstacles in their way.

Peace conference agrees to a national convention to decide the future form of government.

December 25 . Republicans declare the Revolution completely successful.

" 26 . Yuan Shih-k'ai accepts plan of deciding future form of government.

" 27 . Court signifies willingness to agree to abdication.

" 28 . Emperor " ceases His studies."

Court and Imperial Clan accept the Republican proposals for determining the future form of government.

" 29 . Sun Yat-sen elected Provisional President at Nanking.

Yuan Shih-k'ai repudiates his acquiescence in the Republican proposal to decide the future form of government on account of the circumstances attending the election of Sun Yat-sen.

Tang Shao-yi resigns.

" 30 . Imperial Assembly resumed and votes against the Republic.

1912

January 1 . . Sun Yat-sen inaugurated.

Yuan Shih-k'ai accepts Tang Shao-yi's resignation.

Eight hundred troops at Lanchow, Chihli, mutiny.

Yuan Shih-k'ai declares he will fight for a monarchy.

" 2 . . Nanking Government notifies the Powers of its formation.

" 3 . . Nanking Government invites Yuan Shih-k'ai to Shanghai to negotiate.

Sun Yat-sen offers Yuan Shih-k'ai the Presidency.

" 4 . . Yuan Shih-k'ai invites Wu Ting-fang to Peking.

American Minister Calhoun telegraphs for troops, so that the United States will not default in its obligations to assist in guarding the international line of communications to Peking.

Lung Yu Empress Dowager orders the Princes to disgorge in order to meet military expenses.

Fighting at Huang-pei, north of Hankow.

Lanchow mutineers subdued.

Recriminations between Yuan Shih-k'ai and Wu Ting-fang.

Wu Ting-fang declines Yuan Shih-k'ai's invitation to Peking, and his counter proposals.

Foreign troops garrison the line of communications from Peking to Shan-hai-kuan,—Americans lacking.

" 6 . . Yuan Shih-k'ai declares Sun Yat-sen's oath to be in violation of the terms of peace.

January 8 . . Russia presses China on frontier questions.

,, 10 . . Nanking Government offers terms to the Manchus to abdicate, namely:

"Provisional Government to Yuan Shih-k'ai:

1. The Emperor shall be treated with all the dignity attaching to the Sovereign of a foreign nation on Chinese soil.
2. The Court shall reside at the Summer Palace.
3. His Majesty shall receive a liberal allowance, the amount to be settled by the National Assembly.
4. All their ancestral mausoleums and temples shall be secured to them.
5. The person of the Imperial Family shall be fully protected, and their property and wealth retained by the Manchus.
6. Manchus, Mohammedans, Turkestanese, and Tibetans will be treated as Chinese citizens, and their private property protected.
7. The Eight Banners shall continue to draw the same pensions as heretofore, until further means can be devised of enabling them to find a comfortable living. The former restrictions put upon the bannermen's right to trade and to reside outside fixed localities are removed.
8. The Imperial Princes shall retain their titles and property under the protection of the Chinese Government.

PEKING—THE FLOWERY REPUBLIC

January 15 . . Revolutionists land at Tengchow, Shantung.

Imperial Clan and Yuan Shih-k'ai arrange plan of abdication.

Revolutionist expedition leaves Shanghai for Chefoo.

Attempt to assassinate Yuan Shih-k'ai with a bomb.

,, 17 . . Imperial Court selling the Palace treasures of Mukden.

,, 18 . . Seven Mongol Princes in Peking oppose abdication, and the Republic, in concert with several Manchu Princes.

January 19 . . Detachment American 15th Infantry to guard line of communications to Peking arrives at Ching-wan-tao.

" 22 . . Lung Yu Empress Dowager favours hostilities.

" 23 . . Yuan Shih-k'ai urges Manchus to stand together, pay the troops and resist.

" 25 . . Yuan Shih-k'ai orders Imperialist Generals to await the revolutionist advance before fighting.

" 26 . . Throne confers title of Marquis upon Yuan Shih-k'ai.

General Liang Pi wounded by a bomb thrown by an assassin.

" 27 . . General Tuan Chi-jui devises a combined refusal of forty-six generals and lower officers to fight the revolutionists, and telegraphs it to Yuan Shih-k'ai.

Attempt to kill General Chang Huai-chih with a bomb at Tientsin.

" 28 . . Assembly of representatives of the revolutionist provinces inaugurated in Nanking.

Yuan Shih-k'ai brings 3000 of his own troops to Peking.

" 29 . . Armistice expires.

" 30 . . General Liang Pi dies.

Lung Yu Empress Dowager finally agrees to abdication in accordance with the Republican conditions, and summonses a Cabinet meeting.

" 31 . . Cabinet receives the Lung Yu Empress Dowager's notification of intention to abdicate.

February 1 . . Throne instructs the Foreign Office to consummate peace.

" 9 . . A week's armistice arranged.

Terms of abdication ratified at Nanking and Peking.

" 11 . . Yuan Shih-k'ai's Cabinet receives Prince Ching.

" 12 . . Throne abdicates.

" 13 . . Yuan Shih-k'ai assumes position of organizer of the Republic.

" 14 . . Sun Yat-sen resigns to take effect upon the election of a new President.

Nanking Government objects to Yuan Shih-k'ai's assumption as organizer of the Republic

" 15 . . Nanking Assembly elects Yuan Shih-k'ai President.

" 19 . . Yuan Shih-k'ai adopts the Western calendar and notifies the Powers of his election.

" 20 . . Li Yuan-hung elected Vice-President.

" 23 . . Nanking Government sends deputation to Peking.

February 27 . . Deputation from Nanking and Tang Shao-yi reach Peking.
„ 29 . . Soldiers mutiny at Peking and begin burning and sacking.
March 1 . . Mutineers continue looting and burning.
„ 2 . . Order restored in Peking.
„ 3 . . Demonstration of international troops at Peking.
Inniskilling Fusileers drive Imperial troops out of Fengtai.
„ 3–4 . . Council of War at Nanking.
„ 10 . . Yuan Shih-k'ai inaugurated.
Eight thousand armed men revolt at Canton. Fighting begins.
„ 11 . . Provisional Constitution adopted at Peking.
„ 12 . . Tang Shao-yi designated Premier.
„ 13 . . Casualties at Canton, estimated 1000 killed.
British and French garrison Shameen.
„ 14 . . Battle at Canton.
„ 15 . . Two hundred mutineers executed at Canton. Casualties aggregate 1500.
„ 16 . . Fighting at Swatow.
„ 18 . . Heavy fighting at Swatow.
„ 19 . . *Emeute* at Canton ended.
„ 29 . . Yuan Shih-k'ai's Cabinet formed.
April 1 . . Sun Yat-sen lays down office.
„ 3 . . Nanking Assembly transfers the seat of government to Peking.
„ 3 . . Sun Yat-sen leaves Nanking.

INDEX

Printed by
MORRISON & GIBB LIMITED
Edinburgh

T.N. HIBBEN & CO.
ESTABLISHED 1858
VICTORIA, B.C.